Geography of Israel

Geography of Israel

Efraim Orni and Elisha Efrat

Third Revised Edition

THE JEWISH PUBLICATION SOCIETY OF AMERICA

Published by
THE JEWISH PUBLICATION SOCIETY OF AMERICA
1528 Walnut Street, Philadelphia, Pa. 19102

First published in Israel by Israel Universities Press, a publishing division of
ISRAEL PROGRAM FOR SCIENTIFIC TRANSLATIONS LTD.

Library of Congress Catalogue Card Number 71-178048

Rewritten by Efraim Orni from the Hebrew Edition, Achiasaf Publishing House Ltd., Jerusalem, 1963

First Edition 1964
Second (Revised) Edition 1966
Third (Revised) Edition 1973, Second Printing, 1976
Third (Revised) Edition 1973, Third Printing, 1977

ISBN 0-8276-0006-2

This book has been composed, printed and bound by Keterpress Enterprises
Jerusalem, Israel 1977

Printed in Israel

Contents

Foreword

Over the centuries, the geography of the Holy Land has been the most amply documented in the world. Travelers and pilgrims—pagan, Christian, Jewish and Moslem—have reported their impressions for over two thousand years, some with painstaking exactitude, others with an imagination fired by religious enthusiasm. In the Middle Ages, Palestine was the principal subject of map-makers. The development of the scientific approach to Bible research has, since the end of the 18th century, brought to the country theologians, historians and archeologists, geographers and naturalists, many of whom published their findings. With the Zionist Movement's unique work of construction, and the founding of the State of Israel, literature on the country gained further scope, and included politics, sociology, economics, etc.

The very wealth of the material available may, in part, explain the limited number of modern, comprehensive and yet concise geographies on the Land of Israel, particularly in languages other than Hebrew. This book, first published in Hebrew in 1960, is an attempt to present the geology, morphology, climate, population, history, and economy of the country and its regions, with special emphasis on the interrelationships between these fields.

In preparing the English, German and French versions, the authors have aimed to adapt the book to the background and needs of the non-Israeli reader. The rapid developments occurring in all spheres of life in the country necessitate a complete rewriting of considerable parts of the book in preparing each new edition. Not only are there constant changes in the country's political and economic situation, demographic structure, etc., but also novel approaches to planning evolve and even new ideas on the scientific interpretation of its natural phenomena are developed.

The present, third English edition called for even more fundamental revision than its predecessors, as the Six Day War of 1967 caused the former, provisional armistice lines to disappear, made new regions accessible to the Israeli, and created novel economic and cultural opportunities not only for the State, but also for the population which came under Israel's administration. A need was thus felt to add to those parts of the book dealing with physical geography a detailed description of the Sinai Peninsula, and also to include chapters covering the human geography of Sinai and the Gaza Strip, Judea-Samaria and the Golan. All these tasks were facilitated by the fact that one of the authors himself not only carried out the first English translation but also wrote the additional English material subsequently required. In the present volume, great care has also been taken to enrich the cartographic and illustrational material.

The correct transliteration of Hebrew and Arabic place names and geographical terms had to be determined. This book generally keeps to the rules laid down for the Israel Place Names Committee by the Hebrew Language Academy, and to the rules for transliterating Arabic names adopted by modern maps; in the case of famous Biblical or otherwise well-known names, the customary English spelling has been used (e.g. Beersheba, Eilat, Hebron, Nazareth, Tiberias, Safed, etc.). It should be kept in mind that 'a' is pronounced as in 'but' or 'far,' 'e' as in 'pen' or 'ale,' 'i' as in 'inn' or 'eat,' 'o' as in 'hot' or 'role,' and 'u' as in 'butcher' or 'root'; 'y' is always a consonant; 'h' is always clearly audible; 'ḥ' and 'kh' are gutturals, the former pronounced somewhat softer, the latter somewhat sharper than in the Scottish 'loch' (this differentiation is clear in Arabic, less so in Hebrew); 'g' is always as in 'goal,' 'k' and 'q' are in Hebrew both identical with the English 'k' (the Arabic 'q' is more guttural); 's' is sharp as in 'sing'; 'z' is soft as in 'zeal,' while the Hebrew 'ẓ' is pronounced like 'z' in German (or 'ts'); 'sh' does not differ from the English (like 'share'); 'j,' existing in Arabic only, is identical with the English letter (like 'joy'). The majority of Hebrew words are accented on the last syllable; as there is no such rule in Arabic, the accented syllable in Arabic words is indicated by the sign (ā) (which does not necessarily indicate a long vowel). An apostrophe signifies that the slight clicking sound, heard when an English word begins with a vowel (as in 'at'), should be pronounced in the middle of a Hebrew or Arabic word (e.g. 'biq'at'). The same transliteration also applies to titles of Hebrew books in the bibliography.

The number of Hebrew terms in the book has been kept to a minimum. 'Naḥal' (abbreviated: N.) means a small stream, similar to the Arabic 'wadi' which in general is a dry watercourse carrying only occasional floods. 'Har' is mountain, 'giv'a'—hill, 'Emeq' and 'Biq'a'—valley, 'Yam'—sea or lake; 'Kefar' means a village, 'Kibbutz' is a collective settlement, 'Moshav' a cooperative smallholders' village, and 'Moshav shittufi'—a settlement form intermediate between the former two.

The authors wish to express their thanks to the geologists Mr. Ya'akov Nir, for his comments on geological problems, and Dr. Uri Wuerzburger and Mr. Michael

Beith, for data on Sinai geology and minerals; to Mr. Yoav Zur of the Tahal Company for his advice on matters relating to water and water planning; to Mrs. Ruth Wolff and Mr. David Catarivas of the Israel Ministry for Foreign Affairs for their advice on various problems relating to the country's recent history and politics; to Dr. Shaul Colbi and Dr. Yona Malachi of the Israel Ministry of Religious Affairs for details on minority communities, their rights and institutions; to the Achiasaf Publishing House Ltd. for making available graphic material from the book's Hebrew edition; to the Jewish National Fund Head Office and the Government Press Office for the numerous photographs from their archives; to Mrs. Rita Orni for her extensive aid in preparing the English edition; to Messrs. Sh. Barlev, B. Shelkovitz and D. Oren for their work on maps and graphics; to Mr. R. Amoils for editorial assistance; and to the staff of Keter Publishing House for their kind and efficient cooperation.

Introduction

This book seeks to draw a comprehensive picture of the Land of Israel—its landscape and geological past, its climate, its population and history, its economic resources, and the great development projects being carried out today. Such a wide scope makes it necessary to determine the country's area and to define its borders.

The term 'border' is one of the fundamental concepts of geography. A distinction is drawn between physical borders, based on topography, or on factors such as climate, vegetation, etc., and historical and political borders. Among the former there is, in effect, only one boundary which is sharp and indisputable—the shorelines separating land and sea. Between hills and plains, valleys and plateaus, there are generally only gradual transitions and no definite frontiers. The borders of climatic and vegetation regions are even less clearly defined. Moreover, all these limits are liable to change over short or long periods.

This is even more marked in the case of historical and political frontiers; whole geographical-political units may cease to exist and be supplanted by others. Only rarely will a political border coincide with a physical one; in fact, political changes may, to a degree, even entail transformations of the landscape.

The terms 'State of Israel,' 'Land of Israel,' 'Palestine,' etc., all roughly referring to the same area, furnish a striking example of this phenomenon. The events of June 1967 illustrate how a new situation necessitates a rethinking of accepted notions. The Six Day War brought the Sinai Peninsula, the Gaza Strip, Judea-Samaria (known as the 'West Bank' under the former Jordanian regime) and the Golan Heights under Israel administration—an area more than three times as large as that of the State of Israel prior to 5 June, 1967. According to both geographical and historical criteria, however, these regions form part of the Land of Israel in its natural boundaries.

At the time these lines go to print, no decision has yet been reached concerning Israel's definitive peacetime frontiers, as this depends on various factors, primarily on the acceptance, by Israel's Arab neighbors, of her existence and their preparedness for normal, friendly and stable relations with her. However this problem may finally be solved, it may be expected that the future frontiers will coincide with the country's physical features to a larger degree than did the purely accidental demarcation lines of the 1949 armistice agreements.

The State of Israel's pre-1967 borders were the outcome of an intricate historical development. Taking into consideration events of the present century only, the following details should be mentioned: the frontier between Israel and the Sinai Peninsula, which was held by the Egyptians, originated in an agreement, arrived at by Turkey and Great Britain after protracted bickering; it demarcated the area under the jurisdiction of the British Governor of Egypt who, formally at least, was but a subordinate of the Turkish Sultan. The northern frontiers, between Israel and Syria and between Israel and Lebanon, were the outcome of a prolonged silent struggle between Britain and France during and after World War I over the delimitation of their respective mandated areas. The borders along the Jordan River and the Arava Valley stemmed from the British Government's decision, in 1922–23, to separate Transjordan from Western Palestine and remove it from the area validated by the Balfour Declaration for the establishment of a Jewish National Home. They hoped by this step to conciliate the Arab nationalists and make amends to the Hashemite family, one of whose members they named 'Emir' of Transjordan. The other frontiers, separating Israel from the Jordanian Kingdom and the Gaza Strip, mostly reflected the position of the front lines in the 1948 War of Independence on the dates of the cease-fire orders.

These accidental frontiers had roots neither in physical geography nor in the existing realities of demography, economy, etc. It is true that developments on both sides of those borders gave them a tangible content when new, sharply contrasting political, economic, cultural and demographic units came into being. During the three and a half years since the Six Day War, these differences have already become blurred, with the multiplication of various economic and human contacts between the inhabitants on both sides of the former demarcation.

'Ereẓ Israel' (Land of Israel), also the 'Holy Land,' Biblical and traditional terms, came into use after the Children of Israel had entered the 'Land of Canaan'; these names have been preserved not only by the Jewish people, but by all those who cherish the Bible as the 'Book of Books.' Additional names, however, have been introduced, including 'Palestine.' The area referred to by the term 'Ereẓ Israel' has undergone radical changes with time, in accordance with changing realities, needs and concepts. The greatest area was that of the

Land promised to Abraham (Genesis XV, 18–21) and of the kingdom ruled by David and Solomon, extending 'from the great river, the Euphrates, unto the River of Egypt.' The smallest area was that delimited by the Jewish sages under Roman and Byzantine rule, who attempted, by defining its borders as narrowly as possible, to free many of the poor, persecuted Jewish communities from the 'precepts which are dependent on the land.'*

Faced with so many contradictions, this book has to adapt each of its chapters to the subject matter dealt with therein. The parts devoted to physical geography are therefore based on the country's physical features, describing organic units within their natural borders.

With the inclusion of descriptions of the Sinai Peninsula, the physical region covered by the present edition is bounded in the west by the Mediterranean Sea, the Suez Canal and the Suez Gulf, in the east by the Great Syrian Desert and the Eilat Gulf, in the south by the Red Sea, and in the north by the lower section of the Litani River (between its sharp bend and its mouth), the northeastern slopes of Mt. Ḥermon and the hill chains separating the Basan from the Damascus Depression.

The historical chapters, on the other hand, must clearly deal with the area which, at one time or another, was populated by the Jewish people or by the other groups predominant in the country at the time. In the chapters dealing with the State of Israel, its projects, economy and population, the 1949 frontiers and Jerusalem's municipal boundary (the latter redefined in 1967) in general constitute the framework, while new chapters have been added in this edition describing the population, economics, major centers, etc., of Sinai, the Gaza Strip, Judea-Samaria and the Golan.

Three geographical factors determine the character of this country: its position within the Mediterranean zone, on the crossroads of three continents and two oceans, and on the boundary of the desert and the sown.

In common with other Mediterranean lands, this country has a predominantly hilly topography, rock foundations in which limestones and chalks prevail, a sunny climate characterized by a sharp seasonal division between a rainy winter and a totally dry summer, and the resultant soil and vegetation types.

In this context the history and mode of life of man can be understood. Man appeared in this country very early; indeed, his traces here are among the earliest found anywhere. At first he was a gleaner and hunter living in the open;

* The scriptures made the performance of particular precepts conditional on entering Palestine, for example Leviticus XIX, 23; Exodus, XIII.

subsequently, when the climate became more inclement, he took refuge in caves and subterranean shelters. He began to domesticate animals, became a herdsman and, finally, a tiller of the soil. Later he learned to build houses, towns, and fortifications of the stones excellently suited for these purposes, which abound in the country.

The farming that developed under Mediterranean conditions united the three fundamental branches of grain cultivation, fruit orchards, and cattle. The hill regions may have seen the invention of the art of terracing, aided as it was by the natural structure of the steplike slopes. The hilly topography of the country and the profound differences in landscape, often over very short distances, explain the tendency to tribal separation and isolation into small units such as the Biblical city and its 'daughter towns,' which were ruled either by a local king or by an aristocratic or democratic 'council of elders.' These political forms contrast sharply with those of the great river valleys in Mesopotamia and Egypt where mighty empires and autocratic regimes rose, based on feudal land holdings, slavery, and oppression of the inhabitants.

The country's position at the crossroads between Asia, Africa and Europe, and between the Mediterranean Sea (communication with the Atlantic) and the Red Sea, a part of the Indian Ocean, led to wide cultural and trading contacts. It made easier both the absorption of foreign influences and the spreading of cultural and spiritual values which had developed in the country, in some cases over an area much larger than its own. The same position, however, drew the country into the whirlpool of armed clashes between great powers. Campaigns of foreign armies competing for control over this invaluable strategic area wrought havoc and utter destruction. Palestine thus passed from one empire to another, to Egypt, the Mesopotamian empires of Babylonia and Assyria, Persia, Greece, Rome, Byzantium, the great Moslem caliphates, the Ottoman-Turk and the British empires.

It would be a mistake, however, to assume that the lines of communication in this country have always been particularly easy. Travel in the hills of both Cisjordan and Transjordan is difficult. The Coastal Plain with its dunes and, until the recent past, swamps and brush presented in most periods an obstacle to contacts between the coast and the inland region, or between neighboring countries. In addition, the unbroken Palestinian shoreline was unsuitable for both shipping and fishing. Only people possessing great technical talent were able to overcome all these difficulties. Under the rule of overseas people who came from the west, the political center of the country usually moved to the Coastal Plain and returned inland after they had left.

In most of the border regions of Palestine, there are abrupt transitions from areas of permanent settlement to empty desert. The Judean Desert, for example, reaches the very gates of Jerusalem, and in Transjordan and the Northern Negev well-cultivated fields border on arid spaces which, at best, serve as grazing grounds for the nomads' flocks. Although this border is always sharply delineated, it is mobile, moving one way or another. In rainy years the border farmers may cultivate land which normally belongs to the desert and, in drought periods, abandon fields regarded as lying well within the settled area. In addition to these short-term alterations, there are also more profound changes over broader zones and more extended periods. Such phenomena led scholars to assume that as late as in the historic past Palestine's climate underwent considerable changes which caused the cultivated land to retreat and the desert to invade large portions of the country. These hypotheses, however, have proved erroneous. Today, scholars believe that the shifting of the border line is due exclusively to man's behavior, a reflection of the eternal conflict between the herdsman and the peasant. The former needs a zone of comparatively great rainfall to graze his sheep and camels in summer when all the desert plants wither. Naturally, he tries to widen the marginal zone by molesting the peasants settled there, by destroying their property and by felling all fruit and forest trees he finds. An industrious and intelligent farmer, on the other hand, learns to extend his cultivation to marginal lands by using crop rotation and correct agrotechnical methods. The desert, therefore, retreats when an energetic regime in the cultivated land can restrain the unruly nomads, but makes new inroads as soon as that regime shows signs of weakness and decline.

The preceding paragraphs indicate that the Land of Israel cannot be included among the countries most favored by nature for human settlement. This is particularly significant in the modern world, when resources of minerals, fuel and water determine the density and wealth of a country's population even more than do its climate and soils.

The State of Israel was created in this country, which less than two generations ago was counted among the poorest and most backward in the world. It came into existence out of a historical necessity, born from the Jewish people's distress and from their ever-present attachment to this land. As a result of this necessity, the builders of the Jewish community and the State were spurred to full utilization of the country's sparse resources to ensure decent conditions for the life of a large, well-established population.

Today, Israel endeavors to broaden its agricultural basis by land reclamation and soil amelioration, terracing and drainage, and introduces scientific methods to aid intensive cropping and to obtain record harvests. Water resources, both surface and underground, are utilized here more fully than anywhere else in the world; Israeli scientists were among the first in the world to experiment in the desalination of sea water and in the production of artificial rain. All potential mineral resources are being investigated intensively; the recent development of the chemical industry, which relies largely on nonmetallic minerals such as potash and phosphates, found here in substantial quantities, has aided Israel somewhat in this respect. Finally, initiative and technological knowledge help to create many new branches in agriculture, industry, communications, and commerce, and to develop productive services such as tourism and recreation.

Along with the strengthening of the State's economic foundations its cultural and spiritual life intensifies and broadens. This culture, shaped by the landscape and nature of the country, is now flourishing thanks to the renewed contact with the ancient soil of the Land of Israel.

Part I
The Country and Its Regions

The Country, Its Structure and Geological History

Regions*

Although small in area, the Land of Israel contains a large number of regions and subregions. These differ from one another so sharply that there is no real need to discuss their identification and delineation. The Biblical definitions are still valid today, and the old terms and names can be used unchanged in modern geographical analysis.

The deep rift of the Jordan Valley, the Dead Sea, and the Arava Valley divides the country into western and eastern parts, Cisjordan and Transjordan. In most cases the regions of Transjordan have much in common with their western counterparts. In Cisjordan the climate and its results—landscape features, vegetation, and settling conditions—clearly differentiate the south, the arid Negev, from the central and northern sections which are typically Mediterranean in character.

The map clearly shows a subdivision of Cisjordan into three lengthwise strips running south (or southwest) to north: the Coastal Plain, the Hill Regions, and the Rift.

The Coastal Plain is divided into southern, central and northern sections. Only its southwest tip belongs to the Negev; beginning at Gaza, where it is broadest, the Plain gradually narrows through 'the South' (the Philistian and Judean Plain) to the Sharon. The very narrow Carmel Coast strip is a separate region. In the north the Coastal Plain is interrupted twice by hills jutting into the sea—the Carmel Cape and the Cape of Rosh ha-Niqra. The Haifa Bay, interrupting an otherwise almost unbroken shoreline, and the adjoining Zebulon Valley differ from the rest of the Coastal Plain in possessing features of a subsiding graben.

* The Sinai Peninsula, forming a large geographic unit on its own, is not included in this chapter; it is treated separately on pp. 123–132.

En Avdat Spring, in the Avdat Canyon of the Central Negev

The Hill Regions of the Negev differ from the northern ones in their climate and desert topography and in the orientation of the axes of their ridges and valleys in a southwest-northeast direction and not south-north as is the case in the central section. The flat Beersheba Depression, between the Negev Hills and the Judean Hills, accentuates this division more sharply. Three subregions can again be discerned in the Negev Hills—the Eilat Hills in the far south, the Paran Plateau and the Central Negev Hills.

The central section of the Hill Regions includes Judea and Samaria. While the structure of the Judean Hills is simple and compact, that of Samaria is more complicated with internal basins and valleys isolating mountain blocks and ridges. In Judea, the western Foothills differ in altitude, rock, soil, and climate from the Hills; these, in turn, only slightly resemble their eastern slopes, the Judean Desert. Samaria has three parallel upfolds—Eastern Samaria, the Irron Hills, and Mount Carmel. The Nablus Syncline and the Menashe Region lie between them.

Galilee is separated from Samaria by the valleys of Zebulon, Jezreel and Ḥarod. These, in many periods of history, served as a road between the coast and the interior. Galilee itself includes Lower and Upper Galilee; the latter attains twice the altitude of the former.

In the Great Rift, the Arava Valley in the south is part of the Negev, owing to its climate and to communication lines. The Dead Sea and its shores are unique in many respects; although the hottest and most arid of all the country's regions, the area is historically and economically linked with the central parts, particularly with Judea, rather than with the Negev Desert.

The lower section of the Jordan Valley is still largely desert-like, with the exception of a few oases. The character of the Central Jordan Valley is largely determined by the presence of the Sea of Galilee (Lake Kinneret). The Ḥula Valley in the north is an almost closed basin which has many geographical peculiarities.

Transjordan can also be divided into three main sections: in the south, Edom with its ancient rocks, Moab, Ammon and Gilead in the center, and the Basan and Golan in the north; the last region is differentiated by its thick cover of basaltic rock and soil and by its moister climate, the result of this plateau's slope westward which thus opens it to the influence of the Mediterranean Sea.

Rocks and Landscape Forms

The majority of the country's surface rocks are marine sediments. These were largely deposited in the ocean, which covered the country over long geological periods, as well as in lagoons; to these have to be added lacustrine sediments which have their origin in fresh or brackish lakes. Most of the Central Negev Hills and the Judean Hills, large portions of Samaria, the core of the Galilean Hills, and the higher reaches of the Gilead Plateau have hard limestone and dolomite. Softer rocks, particularly chalk, prevail on the outskirts and in the lower parts of the hills, e.g., on the Paran Plateau of the Southern Negev, in the Northeastern Negev, in the Judean Foothills and Desert, in the Nablus Syncline and Menashe Region of Samaria, in the perimeter of the Galilean Hills and on large portions of the Transjordan Plateau. Lacustrine sediments, chiefly 'lissan marl,' and also gypsum and rock salt, characterize sections of the Rift Valley.

Nubian sandstone, mostly of terrestrial origin, is exposed in the Southern Negev and Edom; it is outstanding in its vivid colors and curious landscape forms. The 'kurkar' sandstone of the Coastal Plain also belongs to this group; it contains sand thrown up by the sea, but has been consolidated in general on the land. Finally, the rock meal and soils in all parts of the country must be mentioned here.

Volcanic rocks, particularly basalts, cover most of the Golan and Basan and smaller portions of Eastern Lower and Upper Galilee and patches appear in Moab and Edom. Small patches of older volcanic rocks, also basalt and tuffs, are found on the three anticlines of Samaria and in the Ramon Cirque of the Negev.

Plutonic and metamorphic rocks are relatively rare in this country. In Cisjordan, they form a small area in the Eilat Hills at the southern tip of Israel, and are more prominent along the edge of the Edom Plateau, east of the Rift Valley. On both sides of the valley they are remnants of the northern outskirts of the ancient continent which comprised large parts of Southern Egypt, the Sudan, and the Arabian Peninsula.

With the exception of the extreme south, the forming of the country's present landscape features began at the end of the Mesozoic with a gradual uplift from the sea accompanied by folding movements which are better traced west of the Rift. In the north and center, the fold axes are generally north-south; in the Negev they turn southwest, and, near the Sinai border, west. In Judea, Samaria and Galilee one to three folds are discernible; in the Negev there are five.

Uplift and folding movements intensified the strain of the rock crust, which ultimately led to faulting. The faults separated blocks, some of which subsided as rifts or grabens, while others were tilted, or uplifted as horsts. One of the largest fissures on the earth's crust, the Syrian-East African Rift, runs the entire length of the country. The Dead Sea is the lowest continental section of this rift, as well as the lowest spot of any continent. Branch valleys of the Rift exist on both its sides. There are also, particularly in Samaria and Galilee, a number of graben valleys which are not directly connected with the Rift. Mount Hermon is by far the

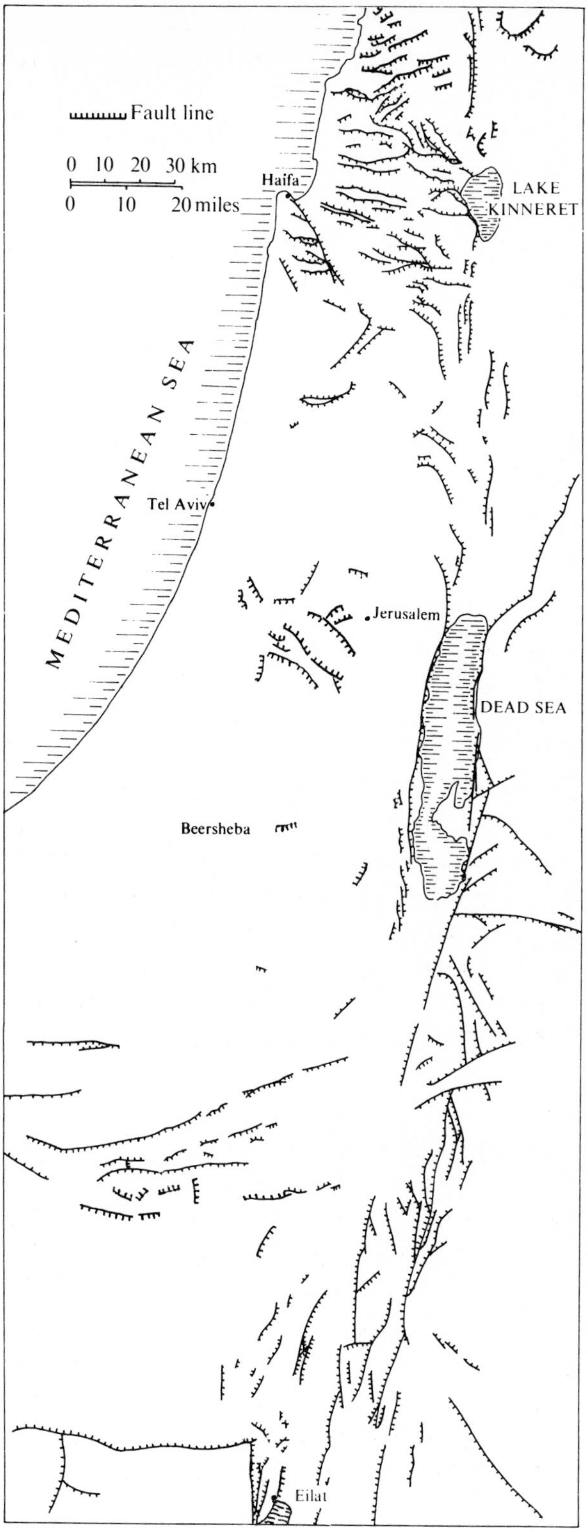

Main fault lines in the country

highest and most spectacular of the blocks; Mount Carmel is marked by its steep slope and proximity to the sea. Other blocks, shoved sideward, formed two tilted block series in Western and Eastern Galilee. Faulting features become more prominent from south to north, until they constitute the dominant landscape element in Galilee.

Exogenic forces have imposed the definite morphological features on these tectonic foundations. In this respect the north and south differ sharply as the climate of the south is in the present—if not in the geologic past—pronouncedly arid. The Negev, therefore, displays typical desert features (e.g., canyons, table mounts, desert pavement or 'ḥammada', talus mounds, etc.), while the morphology of Galilee is that of a semihumid region. These differences are further emphasized by the vegetation which, in parts of the Galilean Hills, forms a dense brush while large areas in the Negev remain bare.

Erosion and degradation gradually transform the landscape relief created by tectonic forces, causing it to 'mature' and, later, to 'grow old.' In this respect, most of our landscapes can be classed as 'young.' The anticlines of the Negev still appear as ridges; the synclines as valleys. The Negev 'craters' or 'cirques' are the very beginning of relief inversion. Further along in this process, although far from completion, is Samaria, where parts of the Nablus Sycline are higher today than adjacent anticlines. However, even in Galilee with its comparatively wet climate, the present morphology recalls the original tilted blocks, valleys, gorges, etc., created by folding, uplift, fracture and subsidence.

One of the reasons for the straightness of the country's shoreline may be its nature as an emergent shore. The continental shelf of the Mediterranean shore is not particularly broad; from a width of 25 km (15 miles) or more opposite Rafa (Rafiaḥ) in the south it narrows to an average of 6–10 km (4–6 miles) in the central and northern sections of the coast. The Eilat Gulf, which subsided as part of the great Rift and was flooded by the sea, has a very narrow shelf.

Geological History

Precambrian. Our knowledge of the geological events in the region during this earliest and most extended age of the earth's crust is limited. The rock of the Precambrian apparently underwent intensive, and perhaps repeated, folding processes which erected very high mountains in the southern part of the country as well as in the southern Sinai Peninsula, Arabia, Egypt, and the Sudan. This was the 'Arab-Nubian Massif,' later a part of the ancient Gondwana Continent. Crystalline rocks were uplifted, kneaded by folding, hardened, and split by faulting. Fissures and veins were filled intrusively with newer rock, and volcanic eruptions added extrusive rock types. The straining and the pressure, the heat generated at depth or by the contact of the lava or magma with solid rock, and gases emanating from intrusions and extrusions transformed some of the existing stone into metamorphic rock.

Over millions of years, toward the end of the Precambrian, the mountains were ground down by erosion and almost flattened out. Much of the detritus seems to have been carried off into an ancient ocean in the north, approximately in the direction of the present Mediterranean. In some periods this ocean may have invaded and flooded parts of the Arab-Nubian Massif.

Paleozoic and Mesozoic. The ocean which geologists call 'Tethys' and which almost circled the earth in these latitudes, spread to the north and west of Palestine, at least since the early Paleozoic. The Arab-Nubian continental mass lay to the south and east. This continent alternately rose and subsided over hundreds of millions of years; in each case this caused a regression or transgression of the sea. This explains the marine Paleozoic strata appearing between terrestrial rocks; the marine strata are comparatively thin as they probably underwent erosion in the subsequent regressional and continental stage.

It may be assumed that the climate in our region during most of the geologic past was a desert or near-desert one. This is indicated by the colored Nubian sandstone, created from the detritus of the crystalline rocks in its vicinity. On the bottom of the Tethys Sea limestone, chalk, marl and, less frequently, dolomite and flint, were deposited. Many of the limestones can be termed as organogenic as they are composed mainly of mollusk shells, corals, and other sea fossils. In contrast to these limestones, dolomite is poor in fossil traces.

In every transgressional stage the northern and western parts of the country were the first to be inundated and the last to be vacated by the sea, while in the south and east the sea lingered for comparatively shorter periods. Hence, marine strata thicken as we proceed north and west while in the south and east terrestrial rocks or shore deposits (marl, etc.) predominate. It is also assumed that a geosyncline of the Tethys, where deposition of marine strata was most intensive, lay toward the northwest.

A diagram prepared by L. Picard traces the assumed vacillations of the coast line between the Tethys Sea and the Arab-Nubian land mass. It depicts five major Paleozoic transgressions. The Permian at the end of that era brought a sustained regression with desert conditions on the continent. Three Mesozoic transgressions can be noted, each successive one penetrating deeper into the massif: in the Middle Triassic the sea covered most of Cisjordan and parts of Transjordan; in the Upper Triassic and Lower Jurassic, Nubian sandstones point to a terrestrial regime; in the Middle and Upper Jurassic the sea returned and flooded most of

Duration of time (million years)	Million years before today	Age	Period	Cisjordan	Transjordan	Arabian Peninsula
6	6	Cenozoic	Quaternary			
17	23	Cenozoic	Pliocene, Miocene,			
43	66	Cenozoic	Oligocene, Eocene			
55	121	Mesozoic	Senonian, Turonian, Cenomanian, Lower Cretaceous			
40	161	Mesozoic	Jurassic			
35	196	Mesozoic	Triassic			
30	226	Paleo-zoic	Permian			
70	296	Paleo-zoic	Carboniferous	SEA		LAND
40	336	Paleo-zoic	Devonian			
30	366	Paleo-zoic	Silurian			
70	436	Paleo-zoic	Ordovician			
60	496	Paleo-zoic	Cambrian			
~2,000	~3,000	Precambrian (Archaic)	Precambrian			

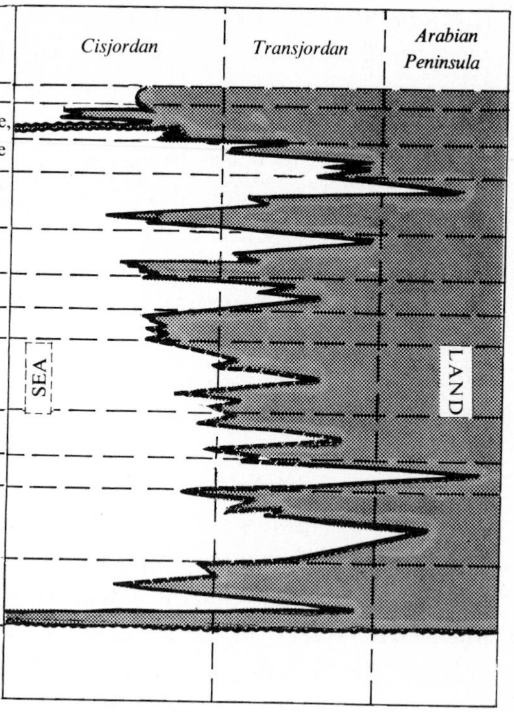

Transgressions and regressions in the Middle East (after L. Picard, 1943)

the land on both sides of the present Jordan, excluding only the Southern Negev. The Lower Cretaceous brought another regression, with Nubian sandstones deposited in the Negev, and marls or chalks further north. The largest transgression both in duration and area was in the Middle and Upper Cretaceous. Most of the rocks exposed on the hills of Palestine and Lebanon came into being then, and the impact of that period is recognizable even in the heart of the Arabian Peninsula. In the Cenomanian and Turonian, thick strata of limestone and dolomite are dominant, the former rich in fossils such as ammonites and other cephalopods, rudists (thick-shelled, asymmetric mussels), etc.; thin layers of marl are intercalated in these massive strata. In the Cenomanian, volcanoes were active in different parts of the country, some of them possibly erupting at the sea bottom.

Toward the end of the Cretaceous (Senonian) and in the early Tertiary (Eocene), the Tethys Sea lingered in many parts of the country but was much shallower than in preceding periods. Soft chalks were deposited, sometimes with banks of dark, hard flint set between. Flints are most prominent in the south, where they often appear in thick strata. The important phosphate deposits in the Negev and Transjordan belong to the Senonian.

Cenozoic. The Eocene of Southern and Central Palestine is characterized by chalks and limestones rich in nummulites (coin-shaped fossils of the Foraminifera class). In the north, where the sea seems to have temporarily deepened, coral limestone is found.

It is difficult to determine the Eocene coast line as rocks of that period may have been destroyed by erosion, in certain parts of the country without a trace. The Oligocene, in any case, brought a strong uplift and regression which continued into the Lower Miocene and were renewed at the end of that period.

The Lower Miocene is regarded as the principal stage of mountain-building in the country. These movements were part of the Alpine-Himalayan revolution (which is still taking place, although less vehemently at present). Here, however, the folding did not reach the intensity in the Taurus, Pontus, Zagros chains, etc., further north. Simple folds were created. Along with the folding and uplift, faults began to appear and the Jordan Depression outlined itself as a series of isolated shallow basins at first, rather than as a continuous rift. Some of these basins may have been covered by inland lakes or flooded by the sea when, in the new cycle of transgression, the water penetrated into the synclines between the newly risen hill ridges. A deep bay, for instance, extended over today's Beersheba Depression; its northern end was in the Tel Aviv vicinity, and it had soft marls deposited at its bottom.

In the Lower Pliocene the sea reinundated the Beersheba Region, the lowlands between Samaria and Galilee, etc. The subsequent uplift of the Upper Pliocene, however, placed the Mediterranean shore not far from its present location. Pliocene rocks (chalks, sandy marls, conglomerates, kurkar sandstones, gypsum) characterized very shallow seas, inland lakes, or a transition to continental conditions.

This last great uplift of the Upper Pliocene landscaped most of the country's regions. Faulting intensified, particularly in the north. The Rift deepened, creating its branch valleys. The basalt covering the Golan, Basan and Eastern Galilee dates from volcanic outbursts at the time.

Geological events of the Quaternary influenced the country's topography to a degree. It is assumed that a slight uplift in the Lower Pleistocene was followed by limited subsidence and then by another inconspicuous rise in the Upper Pleistocene. In our own period, the Holocene, certain sections of the Mediterranean shore are beginning to disappear under water; this, it seems, must be ascribed to the worldwide rise in sea level following the melting of the last ice age's continental glaciers, rather than to local tectonic movements.

In the Pleistocene most of the present mantlerock and soils were formed: the loess of the Northern Negev, the red sands of the Coastal Plain, the sand dunes of the shore, the terra rossa of the Hills, etc. 'Lissan marls' were deposited in the

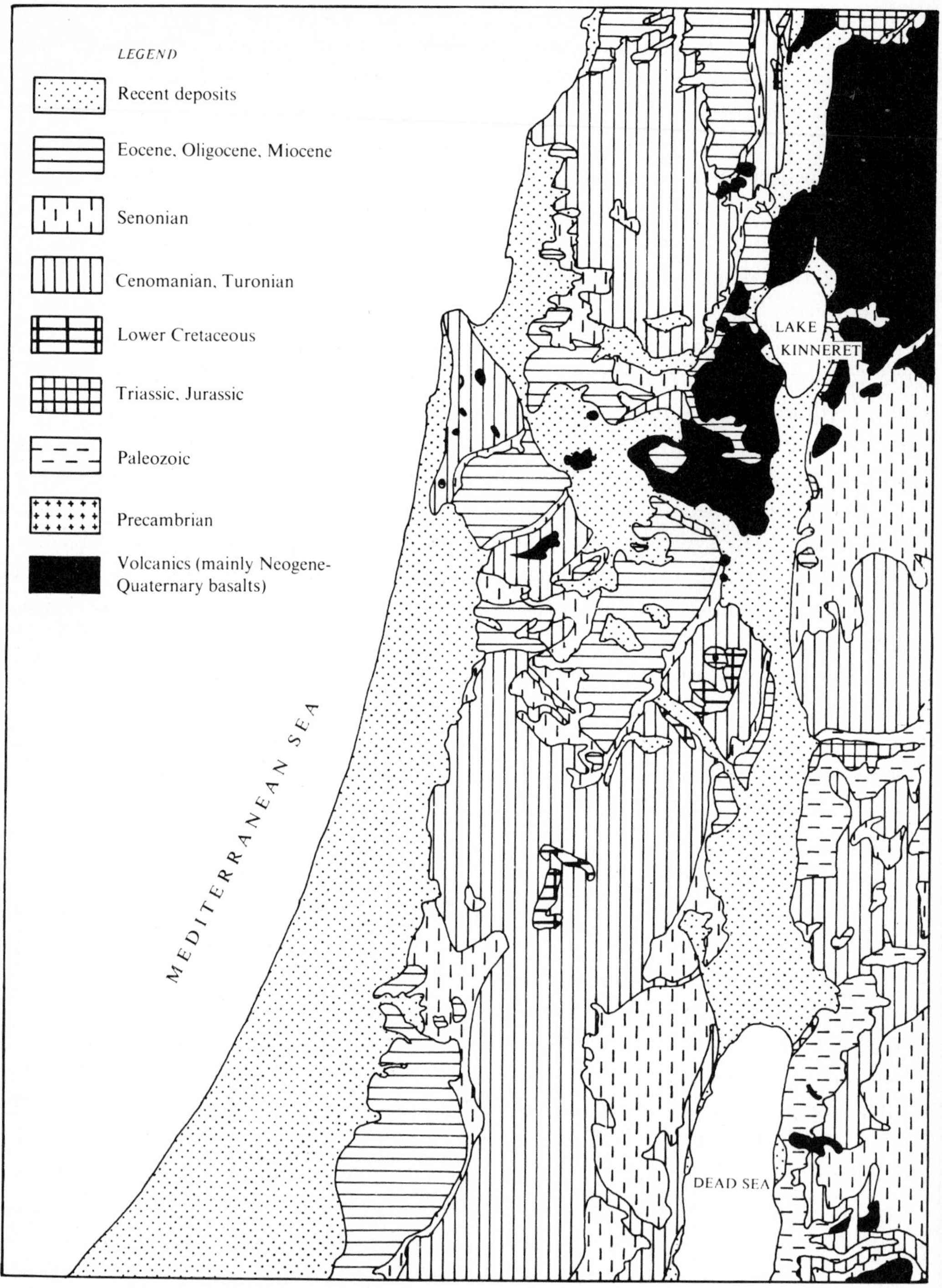

Generalized geological map of the country (north)

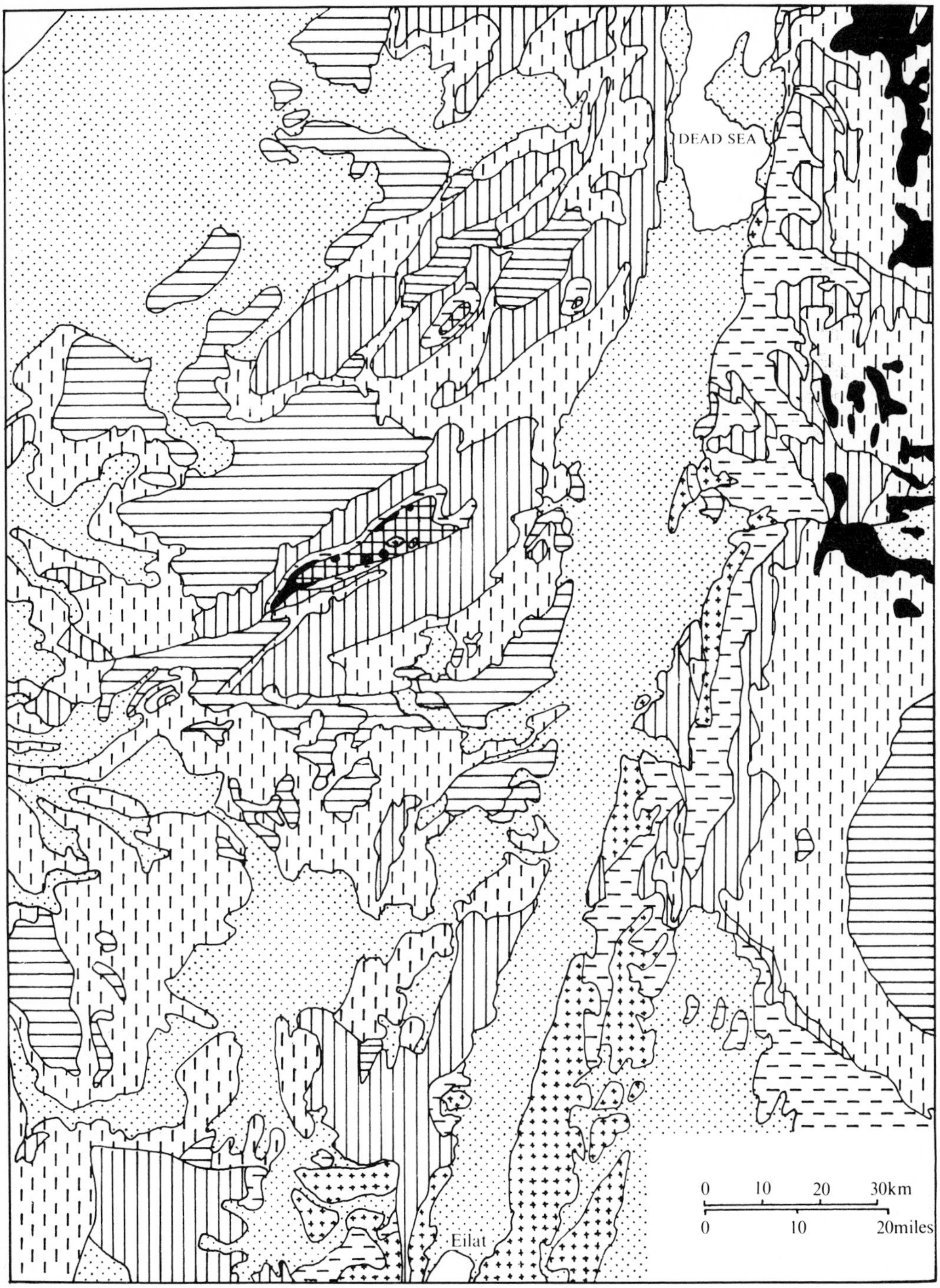

Generalized geological map of the country (south)

Jordan Valley, and the chalks of the Foothills received their crust of hard 'nari.'

The Middle Pleistocene was the last volcanic phase, during which more basalts and tuffs were added in the Golan, Basan and Eastern Galilee.

Climatic changes during the Quaternary affected rocks, soils and, to some extent, topography. The more northerly ice ages were paralleled in this country by pluvials, i.e., periods of increased rainfall; the interglacials—by hotter and drier interpluvials. Inland lakes and swamps spread in the Coastal Plain and particularly in the Jordan Rift and its branch valleys but shrunk again in the interpluvials. Certain sedimentary deposits, e.g., the 'lissan series,' mirror these changes. Streams, rich in water during the rainy intervals, carved spectacular gorges and filled their beds with coarse, clastic debris. The pluvials of this country are tentatively dated in the Lower Pleistocene (600,000 years ago), Middle Pleistocene (300,000 years ago), and Upper Pleistocene (50,000–30,000 years ago), the last being the weakest.

The Negev

Area and Borders

The Negev occupies approx. 12,000 sq km (over 4,600 sq miles) within the pre-1967 frontiers of Israel, then about 60% of the State. This fact, among others, clarifies its importance to Israel as the greatest challenge to constructive efforts. The vast, as yet empty expanses, the mineral wealth unequaled in the northern half of the country, the Negev's position as a communication link with the Red Sea and the countries beyond the Indian Ocean all invite this effort.

On the map the Negev forms a triangle with its base in the north, on the outskirts of Judea, and its apex in the south at Eilat. Its borders, for the most part, adhere to topographic features, excluding those in the northwest which touch upon the Coastal Plain and are determined by climatic factors. The lower course of Wadi el-'Arīsh and, further south, the watershed between this stream and Naḥal Paran may be regarded as the natural border between the Negev and the Sinai Peninsula. The former political frontier between Israel and Egypt ran further east, from Kerem Shalom (south of Rafiaḥ = Rafa) in an almost straight line to Taba on the shore of the Eilat Gulf. In the east, the foot of the Edom Mountain escarpment, rising above the detritus which fills the Arava Valley, forms a sharp border line. However, as the political border was marked there along the lowest level of the Arava Valley, it runs closer to its western rim; Israel holds approximately one-third of the valley and Jordan, two-thirds.

In the northwest the Negev reaches the Mediterranean Sea. From the mouth of Naḥal Besor the border runs to Lahav (historical Ẓiqlag) at the southwest corner of the Judean Hills, in general following the line of 350 mm (14 in) average annual rainfall. This line roughly limits those areas where wheat growing becomes a risk without auxiliary irrigation. Further east, the border runs along the southern extremity of the Judean ridges of Adorayim and Qiryatayim (Yuta). The high ridge of Rosh Zohar is the meeting point, at a 120° angle, of the north-south directed anticlines of Judea and those of the Negev which run southwest. The border then descends to the Dead Sea.

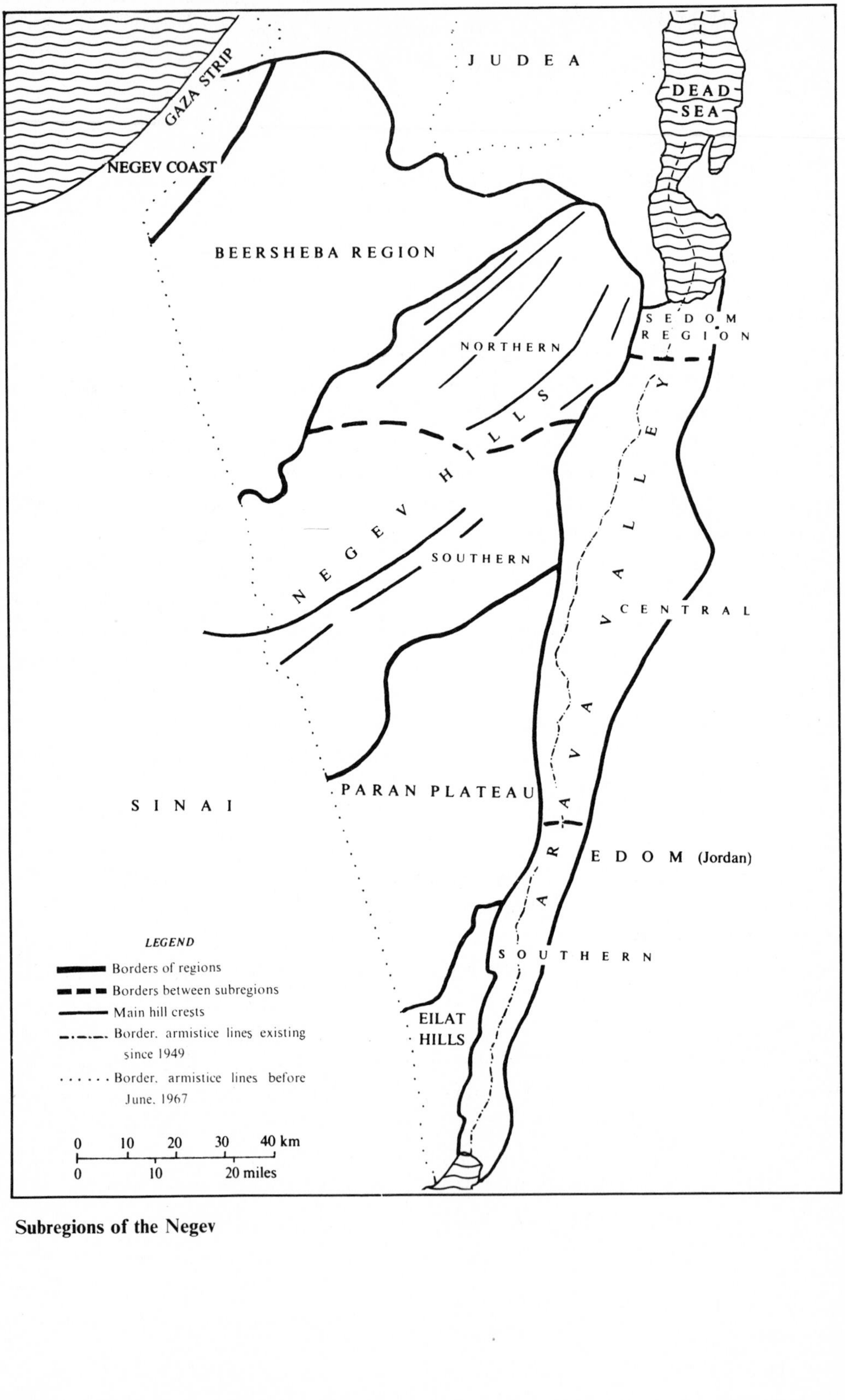

Subregions of the Negev

The Negev may be subdivided into six regions: the Eilat Hills in the south, the Paran Plateau, the Central Negev Hills, the Beersheba Region, the Arava Valley, and the Negev Coastal Plain.

The Eilat Hills

The Eilat Hills, like the adjacent southern half of the Sinai Peninsula, eastern Egypt and Western Arabia, expose the Precambrian fundament of plutonic and metamorphic rocks. The region thus lies on the fringe of the ancient Arab-Nubian Massif of the Gondwana continent identifiable on both sides of the Red Sea.

The Arab-Nubian Massif appears to have been covered by the sea through relatively short periods of its geologic history; the marine sediments deposited were mostly destroyed in the long intervals of a continental regime. The ancient rocks were bared even more when the region was uplifted and the Great Rift subsided at its side. Degradation of the steep fault scarps on the sides of the Arava Valley completed the exposure of igneous rocks.

Within the Negev, crystalline rocks appear on the surface up to 34 km (21 miles) north of Eilat, but at a width nowhere exceeding 3–5 km (2–3 miles). The detritus of these rocks, spread thickly around them, fills the gorges between the steep hills. The mountain bases are buried deeply, often with only their peaks emerging, comparable to arid islands in a frozen sea.

The rock debris of former geologic strata has been cemented into the multicolored Nubian sandstones which form an outer ring around the Precambrian nucleus. Hills of Nubian sandstones differ from those of crystalline rocks by their flat tops and smooth, often vertical slopes.

The plutonic and metamorphic rocks of the Eilat Hills show great variety. Light-colored granites and darker diorites, fine-grained quartz-porphyry of pale violet or reddish hue, greenish diabase, dark gray dolerite, banded gneiss, hard quartzite, etc. are intermingled.

The sharp temperature changes in the desert climate wear down crystalline rocks on the surface, i.e., the heated crystals expand and are loosened from the cooler internal rock. Cleavages are often vertical, resulting in steep slopes and scarps, crenelated mountain-tops, and finely chiseled surfaces. The coarse rock debris fills the gorges and covers the surrounding areas, and only little of it is carried to the sea, since gravity is a principal transporting agent; small ledges jutting from rock walls are thickly covered with detritus which will fall with the ledge itself.

Every rock is affected differently by erosion. Imposing mounts with sharply indented crests are typical of granites and diorites; conical hills signify the

Crystalline rocks and Nubian sandstones at the entrance of the Amram Canyon; the view is toward the Arava Valley and the mountains of Edom

presence of quartz-porphyry; gentle forms indicate soft rocks. The crystalline rocks of the Eilat Hills contain such minerals as quartz, orthoclase, mica, etc., none of which, however, have hitherto proven exploitable commercially. The same is true of most minerals of the Nubian sandstone series, where in the Eilat Hills at present only copper is mined at Timna (see pp. 474–477).

The only settlement in the region is the town of Eilat, Israel's Red Sea port (the kibbutzim Elot, Yotvata and Gerofit, and the Be'er Ora farm are at the foot of the Eilat Hills in the Arava; the Timna Copper Works are not permanently inhabited).

Three subareas can be distinguished in the Eilat Hills—the Eilat Block in the south, the Sheḥoret Block in the center, and the Timna Block in the north. Some mountain peaks, e.g., Mt. Uzziyahu, Mt. Shelomo, Mt. Seguv, etc., rise to 800–900 m (approx. 3,000 ft) and are awe-inspiring with their abrupt walls and the abyssal gorges surrounding them.

Many gorges, some only a few feet in width, are hemmed in by rock walls over a thousand feet high and cut through the Eilat Hills in various directions. Some of them run along fault lines which delineate different rocks; others were created by differences in rock resistance to erosion—for example, softer rocks filling vertical or diagonal dykes were washed out while the harder igneous rock remained as a compact wall. Spectacular among these gorges are those of Naḥal Shelomo, Naḥal Sheḥoret, Naḥal Amram (leading up to the Amram Columns, sculptured by erosion in violet and flaming red sandstone) or Timna (the site of the copper mines and of the magnificent Solomon's Pillars in yellowish brown sandstone).

Dark crystalline rocks in the Reḥav'am Gorge near Eilat face folded Cenomanian limestone. The ground is thickly covered by fluviatile gravel

The Amram Columns near Eilat

Solomon's Pillars in the Timna Gorge

The Paran Plateau

This fairly large region is named for the stream (wadi) which runs through it lengthwise from southwest to northeast. The Plateau, inclined in the same direction, descends from 600 m (almost 2,000 ft) above sea level at the Sinai border to only 100 m (330 ft) where Naḥal Paran enters the Arava Valley.

Naḥal Paran originates in Sinai territory, southwest of Eilat. Its lower section, called Naḥal ha-Arava, reaches the Sedom salt swamps south of the Dead Sea. It has a large drainage basin with numerous tributaries from the south, west, and north. The Paran is the largest stream in the country, surpassing the Jordan in the length of its course (240 km—140 miles) and in the width of its bed (up to 3 km), although it is dry most of the year. An occasional rainstorm may flood its bed partly, or, on rare occasions, entirely. As it thunders through the bed its carries a great load of silt, cobbles and even large boulders. In some sections of its middle course, Naḥal Paran has carved its bed far below the level of the Plateau, and bold scarps and rock pillars tower on both sides.

A 'mushroom' of Nubian sandstone at the entrance of Timna Gorge, created by wind and water erosion

Parallel to Naḥal Paran, in the south, runs Naḥal Ḥiyon. One of its tributaries forms the curious Uvda Valley, which is actually a broadened section of the wadi bed, over 6 km ($3\frac{3}{4}$ miles) wide and 13 km (8 miles) long, filled with light-colored fine-grained sand.

Most of the Paran Plateau is flat or slightly undulating. Its bedrock is formed by limestones, chalks, and marls of the Turonian and, predominantly, the Senonian. The flint intercalated in the Senonian chalk accumulates on the surface when the soft chalk is eroded away. This is termed 'reg,' 'serir' or 'ḥammada' according to its being angular, rounded, loose or firmly rooted in the ground.

The small, closely grouped hill tops of Mt. Ẓenifim are a remarkable element of the Paran Plateau. They extend in a straight line from southwest to northeast, forming the watershed between the wadis of Paran and Ḥiyon. Mt. Ẓenifim may be regarded as the edge of the Plateau, which rose slightly while pressed against the unyielding Arab-Nubian Massif. Desert erosion covered the surroundings with a thick mantle of detritus from which only the highest points of the raised edge stand out today.

Near the northern outskirts of the Paran Plateau lies the round area of Meshar, hemmed in by hills on practically all sides. As flood waters run toward its flat center, fine material appears in the center, and coarse matter on the outskirts. Phosphate deposits have been located in the Meshar area, and a search for oil was started there in 1965.

The Central Negev Hills

Structure and Rocks. This region occupies more than half the area of the Negev. Some hills exceed 1,000 m (3,280 ft) above sea level (Har Ramon, 1,035 m—3,396 ft, Har Saggi, 1,006 m—3,290 ft, etc.). The deep canyon of Naḥal Ẓin divides the region into a higher southern and a lower northern half.

The Negev Hills, created in the Miocene folding, were later comparatively little affected by faulting. Erosion, too, changed but little of the fundamental landscape traits. The geologic structure and topography are, therefore, substantially identical; most anticlines are still present as hill ridges, and synclines as valleys.

The resistance of hard flint strata covering soft chalk results in 'table mounts' characteristic for the central Negev Hills. Angular flint covers the ground as 'ḥammada' or 'serir'

Anticline and syncline axes strike northeast-southwest. Near the Sinai border they turn west and some of them, beyond the border, even northwest. Many folds are asymmetric, their northwestern flanks (facing the direction of the pressure which elevated them) gently inclined; their other side, which is turned toward the resistant Arab-Nubian Massif, is much steeper.

The large Ramon Anticline dominates the southern portion of the Negev Hills. Beyond its high southwestern end no parallel ridges are discerned, as stream erosion has isolated solitary hills and scarps. Many hills here register over 900 m (3,000 ft); in addition to those cited, Har Loẓ (957 m—3,135 ft) and Har 'Arif (957 m—3,135 ft) are also worth mentioning.

The deep and broad Zin Canyon was formed almost exclusively by erosional processes; tectonic factors played only a small part in its creation.

North of the Ẓin Canyon at least four anticlines run parallel, all northwest of the Ramon Anticline.

The distribution of rock species in the Negev Hills is basically simple: in the synclines, Senonian and Eocene chalks have been preserved while harder limestones of the Cenomanian and Turonian are exposed in the anticlines.

Scenery of the eastern Negev Hills, sloping down to the Arava Valley. Identity of strata and landscape relief is clearly shown

The Cirques (Craters): Variety is added to this simple pattern by the 'Makhteshim,' the erosional cirques which present a magnificent panorama and a fascinating story of geomorphologic evolution. There are three craters of different sizes; each represents a stage in cirque development: Makhtesh Qatan ('the Small Cirque') lies on the Ḥaẓera Ridge, Makhtesh Gadol ('the Large Cirque') on the Ḥatira Ridge, and the giant Makhtesh Ramon—on the Ramon Ridge. There are also two embryonic cirques on the top of Har 'Arif. The craters serve, in a sense, as 'geological windows,' exposing ancient strata which are elsewhere deeply concealed.

It is generally accepted that these cirques were formed mainly by exogenic forces. An exception is the south side of the Ramon Cirque, along which runs a long fault. The cause for this particular form of erosion, however, lies in both the tectonic structure and the desert climate. Anticlinal crests inherently subjected to tectonic strain are always liable to be affected most strongly by erosion. Short, violent rains create cracks which later deepen and widen to form a round cavity with perpendicular walls. Rainwater filling this cavity seeks an outlet toward the erosional base level which, for all three cirques, is the Dead Sea in the northeast; the water flowing in this direction cuts out a narrow defile which opens in all three cases to the northeast.

The rounded Small Cirque can be regarded as the first stage in this erosional process. When the cirque expands along the line of least resistance, i.e., along the anticlinal crest, it becomes elongated. This stage, the second, is represented by the Large Cirque, which is twice as long as it is wide; and the third—by the Ramon Cirque, which is three times as long as it is wide.

Erosional cirques are typical of desert conditions, where the erosional power of stagnant and flowing water by far exceeds that of the occasional rain hitting the sharp edges of the cirques; the cirque bottom thus deepens quickly while the walls retain their vertical angle and gradually increase in height. In a dry climate a single, narrow outlet suffices to drain off the water collecting on the crater bottom, so that the east and north rock walls exist indefinitely, breached only by the defile.

As the cirque deepens, lower and more ancient rock strata are exposed. In the area surrounding the Small Cirque (its upper rims attain 550 m—1,940 ft above sea level, and its bottom 50 m, or 160 ft, below sea level) Eocene rocks have been preserved; on the wall crest proper Senonian chalk appears, while at the Makhtesh base Nubian sandstones, marls and gypsum of the Lower Cretaceous, and even a small patch from the Jurassic are exposed. Hard rock strata exposed in the cirque walls have a perpendicular face, whereas that of softer beds is steeply inclined.

The highest point of the wall around Makhtesh Gadol is 650 m (2,350 ft) above

Section of the Ramon Cirque. Note vertical walls of the cirque rim indicating hard rocks, and inclined walls of softer rocks. On the cirque bottom, bushes line watercourses; dark spots are basalt outcrops

sea level; the bottom is 300 m (less than 1,000 ft). Senonian rock appears on the wall top, and at the bottom are Jurassic rocks containing kaolin, glass sand, and hematite deposits.

The Ramon Cirque is the most spectacular of the three and the most complicated structurally. At its western end Har Ramon is 1,035 m (3,390 ft) above sea level. The crater's bottom at this point is 670 m (2,200 ft), and it descends northeastward to 470 m (1,540 ft) and less above sea level. On the wall rims Cenomanian and Turonian limestones are exposed, and on the bottom—Jurassic and Triassic rocks. Besides the limestone, dolomite, chalk and gypsum found here (as in the other cirques), patches of basalt appear between the Lower Cretaceous rocks, and a batholith, sills and dykes of crystalline rocks between the Triassic. Mineral deposits, such as gypsum, kaolin, and quartz sands, are present on the cirque bottom in substantial quantities. The scarp in the south-southeast is broken by a broad opening which permits drainage into the Arava Valley. Har Ardon, which juts into the cirque at its northeastern end, with its rock walls steeply descending north, west, and south, permits the assumption that Makhtesh Ramon in its development to the northeast followed the line of the anticlinal axis which here splits in two. The tectonic fault to the south of the Ramon Cirque resulted in the subsidence of the southern wall; its rock strata, thus, appear at a lower level than the corresponding ones north of the cirque.

Water Courses: The desert climate, naturally, allows no perennial streams in the Negev. Dry wadis carry water a few times each year and then only for a few hours. The width and depth of their courses bear out the assumption that they were carved in the pluvial geological periods. To a large extent the drainage patterns of the streams mirror the morphology and rock species of the region: a coarse stream network typifies hard limestones and dolomites, a finely meshed one—areas of chalk and marl. Inside the Large and Ramon cirques, and in areas where ridges are close, a 'trellis pattern' develops (with tributaries meeting the main stream at right angles); elsewhere, the usual 'dendritic pattern' prevails (on the map resembling a denuded tree crown).

Naḥal Paran, Naḥal Ẓin, and other wadis descending to the Northern Arava Valley and the Dead Sea, a base level which is closer to the Hill tops and 398 m (1,200 ft) lower than the Mediterranean Sea, possess greater erosional power and therefore capture tributaries of the western wadis (e.g., Naḥal Niẓẓana, which reaches Wadi el-'Arīsh, and Naḥal Besor). The watershed is thus gradually pushed westward. Rectangular 'capture elbows' in the central part of the Negev Hills bear witness to this process, demonstrated (among others) by the tributaries of Naḥal Ẓin (Naḥal Aqev, Naḥal Avdat and others) whose upper courses descend northwest (in the past linking up with Naḥal Niẓẓana), then turn at 90° to the northeast, and finally turn to the southeast.

Northeast outlet of the Large Cirque. Erosion has created 'flatirons' in the steeply dipping strata of the outer crater rim

Settlement: The Central Negev Hills, where, until a few years ago, only bedouin roamed, are today the object of a great development effort. Foremost among the new centers is the town of Dimona, with approximately 20,000 inhabitants who are employed in the Dead Sea Works and in the Oron and Ẓefa' phosphate mines, as well as in the textile industry and other branches. Miẓpe Ramon and Yeroḥam are nuclei of towns to be based on mining and industry. The kibbutz Sede Boqer is a solitary desert outpost experimenting in a number of farm branches.

The Beersheba Region

The Beersheba Region is a depression forming a triangle on the map, its base paralleling the Mediterranean shore in the west and its apex in the east wedged in between the Negev Hills and the Hills of Judea. It rises nearly imperceptibly from 50–100 m (150–350 ft) above sea level in the west to approx. 250 m (800 ft) around Beersheba and attains 500 m (1,650 ft) at its eastern extremity.

The Beersheba Region subsided with the opening of the Jordan and Dead Sea Rift, which began in the Miocene and continued, at an accelerated rate, in the Pliocene. In the latter period the sea penetrated the region deeply and deposited chalk in many of its parts.

Since the sea's final recession toward the end of the Pliocene, the region became thickly covered with loess soil which, in many parts of the world, is characteristic of the fringes of large deserts. This soil is mainly of eolian origin, i.e., it was transported by the winds. The streams descending from the Negev Hills are also considered by scholars to have participated in carrying the loess to the Beersheba Region.

The yellowish brown loess is fine-grained; only thus can it be lifted and transported by winds over large distances from the desert to less arid regions where it adheres to the ground. Loess soil, potentially fertile, contains many substances necessary to plant life, e.g., silica, calcium, alumina, iron, etc. In the Beersheba Region it is frequently 30 m (100 ft) thick or more. Some mechanical properties of this soil, however, contribute to sheet erosion and badland formation and pose serious problems to the farmer. In the first winter rain the surface grains swell and coalesce into a hard crust which is impenetrable to seepage of additional rainwater into the subsoil. Rainwater then collects on the surface, and wild flash floods tear open deep, zigzagging gullies. The soil crumbling into the bed in summer from the vertical gully banks obstructs the floodwaters in the winter. This causes them to break out of the wadi bed and to open additional gullies. Near the course of Naḥal Besor, in the vicinity of Be'eri near the Gaza Strip border, in the area of Dorot and Ruḥama further north and

After a rainstorm floodwaters have torn open a wide new gully in the loess soil near Naḥal Besor in the northwestern Negev, completely destroying the highway as well

at other sites gullying has created a typical badland, i.e., a torn relic level of the original surface, mostly narrow strips rising 10–20 m (30–60 ft) above the gully beds.

The gullies unite in a number of main wadis which are usually very broad and deep, filled with cobbles and boulders transported from the hills. In its final stage gullying restores a rolling topography of low, rounded hillocks typical of large parts of the Beersheba Region.

The loess surface soil crumbles in summer, and the fine particles are transported again in dust storms. Plant roots are alternately exposed to the searing sun, or their leaves are choked by the dust settling on them.

Sand dunes cover large areas totaling approx. 500 sq km (200 square miles) in the western and southwestern section of the Beersheba Region, one-third of its entire surface. These dunes are but the eastern tip of vast sands occupying the northern half of the Sinai Peninsula. In the Beersheba Region strips of loess separate the dunes into smaller units, e.g., the Ḥaluẓa, Shunra and 'Agur dunes. Although the quick seepage of water into the porous sand, as well as the dry climate, are aridity factors, vegetation on the dunes may be richer than on adjacent loess. This is explained by the thinness of the sand layer covering the loess soil beneath; rainwater filters swiftly through the sand and reaches the loess, where it is blocked, protected from evaporation, yet available to most plant roots. The irregular distribution of sand and loess areas in the Beersheba Region is hard to explain; the sand is not found much nearer to the hills where seemingly both sand and loess originate, as should be the case since sand is heavier.

Almost the entire Beersheba Region is in the drainage basin of a single stream, Naḥal Besor, which runs down from Har Ḥaluqim in the Negev Hills. This wadi takes up important tributaries—Naḥal Beersheba which runs due west from Rosh Zohar and unites in the Beersheba precincts with Naḥal Ḥevron (the latter drains the southern part of the Hebron Hills), and Naḥal Gerar, running from the southwestern flank of the Judean Hills (the Adorayim Ridge).

Settlement: Since 1943, intensive settling has been under way in the Beersheba Region. Beersheba itself, evacuated by its Arab inhabitants in the 1948 war, numbers 75,000 inhabitants and is a first-rate industrial center, as well as the home of important institutions of science and culture (notably, the Negev Research Institute). In addition to about 60 farming villages there are two semiurban centers, Ofaqim and Netivot. In 1963, construction of the town of Arad, which is based on a large chemical and petrochemical complex, was begun at the region's eastern extremity. Another project is that of dense settlement of the Eshkol Region, in the west.*

The Arava Valley

The southernmost section of the Great Rift in Israel, between the Dead Sea and the Red Sea, is called the Arava Valley, or, in short, the Arava. Thickly covered with alluvial sand and gravel, and hemmed in by rock walls on both its sides, it bears typical graben features. With a length of 165 km (103 miles), the Arava falls into three parts; the Southern Arava, 77 km (48 miles) long and 5–15 km (3–9½ miles) wide, extending from the Eilat shore to the low hill ridge of Sheluḥat Noẓa which projects into the valley from the west; the Central Arava, 74 km (46 miles) long and up to 32 km (20 miles) wide; and the Northern Arava or Sedom salt swamps, an almost rectangular area not over 14 km (9 miles) in length.

The Negev Hills in the west do not form a continuous or particularly high rock wall; scarps rise only at a few points to 300 m (985 ft) above the valley's bottom. In the southern section, from the Gulf shore to about 32 km (20 miles) north of

*The Negev Coast is described in the chapter dealing with the Coastal Plain.

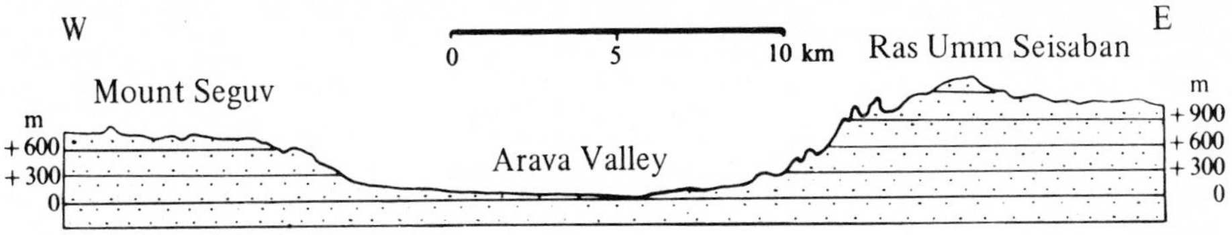

East-west section of the Arava Valley

Eilat, crystalline rocks and Nubian sandstones are exposed on the western side of the Arava, interrupted by stretches of marine sediments; from there northward appear exclusively marine strata—Cenomanian and Turonian limestones and dolomites, and Senonian and Eocene chalks.

A very different picture is presented on the eastern side. Precipitous rock walls, continuing for 120 km (75 miles), may attain 1,000 m (3,280 ft), exposing crystalline rocks and Nubian sandstones whose reddish hue, it seems, gave Edom its name (Hebrew 'adom' = 'red').

The flash floods descending into the Arava Valley, although rare, carry vast amounts of detritus and build up alluvial fans at the foot of the mountains on both sides. As the streams from Edom carry more water (owing to the wetter climate) and have greater erosive power (because of the height and steepness of the slopes), their alluvial fans are much larger and thicker than those of the opposite side. As a result, the base level of the Arava, marked in its middle and northern sections by Naḥal ha-Arava, has gradually been pushed westward to approach the foot of the Negev Hills. The rainfall differences between the Negev and Edom also explain the relatively strong and sweet springs on the eastern rim of the Arava, while the western ones are weak and mostly brackish.

The Southern Arava rises gradually from the Eilat shore to 230 m (755 ft) above sea level near Sheluḥat Noẓa; this ridge forms the watershed between the Dead Sea and the Red Sea. The term watershed, however, is somewhat misleading here since the short streams of the south do not form a continuous drainage pattern; most of them do not reach the sea since they are barred by alluvial fans. The water thus seeps into the subsoil and it is drawn up again by capillary action during the hot, dry summer. Playas or salt flats are formed on the surface and are often covered with a thriving halophytic vegetation. Among others, tamarisks, rushes, 'doom' palms in the southernmost section and, under relatively favorable conditions, date palms are to be found.

The Southern Arava contains four playas: the Eilat Playa, today partly reclaimed for date palm plantations and other crops grown by kibbutz Elot; the Avrona Playa near Be'er Ora; the large Yotvata Playa, parts of which are now cultivated by the kibbutzim Yotvata and Gerofit; and, mostly on the Jordanian side of the border, the a-Sa'idiyīn Playa, the soil of which, with good spring

Be'er Ora in the Eilat Region. Nubian sandstone hills in the middle ground separate the side valley from the Arava Rift; an alluvial fan spreads in front of the high crystalline rock walls of Edom

water and better drainage, is less salty and resembles the Beersheba Region loess. The Yotvata Playa and the a-Sa'idiyīn Playa are separated by an area of fine sand dunes differing greatly from the coarse gravel cover of other parts of the Arava.

The Central Arava opens out north of Sheluḥat Noẓa. Here, Naḥal ha-Arava is formed by the confluence of Naḥal Paran, Naḥal Ḥiyon, and several other wadis coming from the Negev in the southwest and Edom in the southeast. The Central Arava slopes toward the Dead Sea; its southern 40 km (25 miles) are still above sea level, but the northern section gradually descends to 210 m (690 ft) below sea level. The southern section is covered with coarse gravel and sand; from the Ḥaẓeva oasis (and spring) northward whitish or yellowish lissan marl appears in addition to the rocks of the 'Ḥaẓeva series' as a deposit of an inland lake, a predecessor of the Dead Sea. Wadis, such as Naḥal ha-Arava, Naḥal Amaẓyahu, and others, have carved wide, deep courses in the soft, friable sediment; erosion has sculptured fantastic shapes along the vertical rims of these wadi courses.

The largest spring of the Central Arava is Ḥaẓeva, where fresh water has given rise to an oasis. Smaller oases spread round other springs, e.g., Be'er Menuḥa, En Yahav, Enot Raḥel on the Israeli side, and others in Jordanian territory.

The transition from the Central Arava to the northern part, the Sedom Region, is quite sudden; in less than two miles, the valley bottom drops 140 m (460 ft). The ground of the Sedom Region, in contrast, is almost flat and is only slightly above the level of the Dead Sea. The Sedom Flats are, therefore, frequently flooded by waters rushing down Naḥal ha-Arava, which takes up more tributaries here from the Edom Mountains, as well as by Naḥal Amaẓyahu, Naḥal Ẓin in the west, and Wadi Ḥasi (Naḥal Zered) in the east. There are also

Scene in the Arava Valley. The ground is alternatingly covered with sands, brackish soil and ḥammada gravel. The bushes belong to the Saharo-Arabian vegetation zone

Brackish pond at the southern end of the Sedom Swamps, near Neot ha-Kikkar, lined with reeds. Bare marl hills of the Lissan series rise above the flats covered with halophytic vegetation

several strong springs; those on the eastern side, in the Ẕo'ar Valley, are fresher and more abundant (e.g., 'Ein Khaukhān, 'Ein a-Dīsa, etc.), while the western ones (En ha-Kikkar, En Tamar, etc.) are strongly brackish. Rainy winters may raise the water level of the Dead Sea, which then penetrates the Sedom swamps, and adds its highly saline water to the swamps. The perennial or seasonal flooding of partly saline water has its impact on the Sedom Region landscape. The ground next to the Dead Sea shore is impassable mud, interspersed with water puddles and salt patches. Further south there is dark loam, usually wet, which cracks into uprolled scales when drying. Most of the swamp region, particularly the spring areas, has a thick cover of vegetation, partly halophytic and partly (notably in the Ẕo'ar Valley, in Jordanian territory) belonging to the Sudanese (wet-tropical) plant region. Settlement in the Arava is restricted to these playas; the outpost villages on the Israel side of the border (Ne'ot ha-Kikkar, En Yahav, Yotvata, etc.) form small desert oases. The Arava has no permanent settlement in Jordanian territory.

The Coastal Plain

The Coastal Plain of the country, along the eastern shore of the Mediterranean, is interrupted at only two points, at the capes of Mount Carmel and Rosh ha-Niqra. Its length from north to south, within the country's natural limits (from Wadi el-'Arīsh to the mouth of the Litani River) is 340 km (210 miles); 188 km (117 miles) of these are within the pre-1967 boundaries of Israel as measured from the northern end of the Gaza Strip to Rosh ha-Niqra. The plain gradually narrows from south to north. At the latitude of Gaza it is 40 km (25 miles) wide, as opposed to 4–5 km (2.5–3 miles) near Rosh ha-Niqra.

The long plain is conveniently divided from south to north into smaller geographical and administrative units. These regions differ to a certain extent in climate, vegetation, land use and population and, to a lesser degree, in their geological features and the quality of their soils. The following are the main units, from south to north: the *Negev Coast,* between Wadi el-'Arīsh and the mouth of Naḥal Besor; the *Southern (Philistian) Plain* stretching to the mouth of Naḥal Lakhish; the *Judean Plain,* separated from the *Sharon* by the Yarqon River; the narrow *Carmel Coast,* between the sea and Mount Carmel; the *Zebulon Valley,* hugging Haifa Bay; and the *Acre Plain* and *Tyre Valley,* south and north of Cape Rosh ha-Niqra, respectively.

A more striking distinction than that between these regions can be drawn between the three narrow strips running the entire length of the Coastal Plain:

(a) the sea shore and belt of arid sand dunes;
(b) the western plain;
(c) the inner or eastern plain.

Each of these is a topographical unit with its own geological history, its characteristic soils and vegetation; hence, each also differs from its neighbors in its conditions for human settlement.

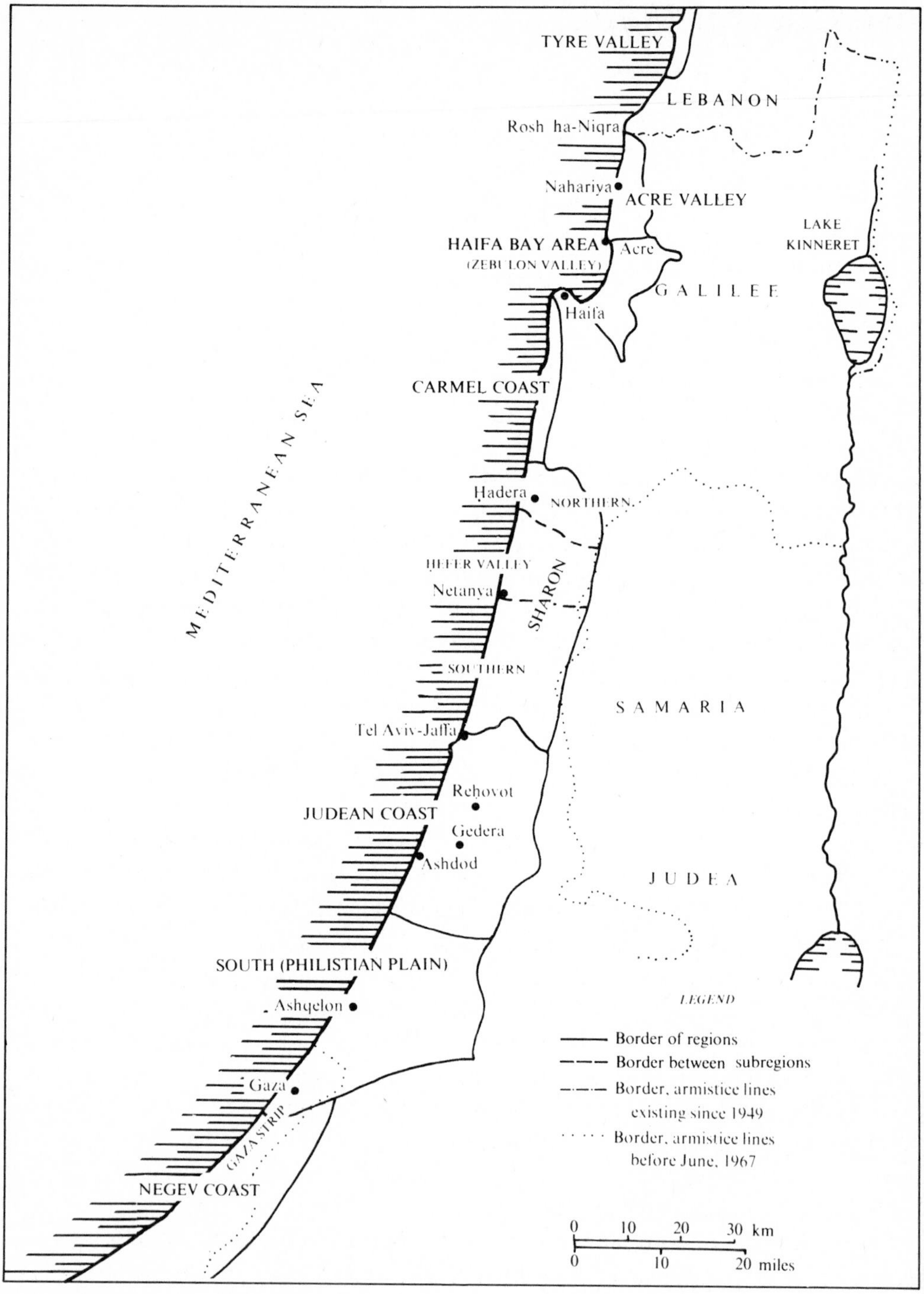

Subregions of the Coastal Plain

The Shore

The Mediterranean shore of the country forms an almost straight line in most of its sections. Such a coastline, poor in promontories and deep embayments, is often found when the shore is parallel to the principal mountain ridges inland. It is a 'concordant' shore, as compared with a 'discordant' coast line running at right angles to the ridges. A straight coast is often regarded as a sign that the land is in the process of uplifting. On the sea bottom new layers of rock, generally horizontal, gradually build up; these bear no relationship to the profile prevailing before the invasion of the sea. The sea's regression, thus, leaves an almost flat surface, and the new, 'regressional' shore forms an almost straight line.

The uplift of the land and the sea's regression continued in our region, with temporary interruptions, through most of the Tertiary and Quaternary periods. Geologists are, however, not sure whether this uplift movement is still in progress. On the other hand, a slight, steady rise in sea level is noticeable on the Levant Coast, as on most other sea and ocean shores of the world. This is ascribed to the gradual warming up of the world climate since the end of the last ice age. This warming causes more and more continental glaciers to melt and to thus increase the volume of the oceans. In Israel this new cycle of transgression is not yet strongly pronounced and is recognizable only at certain spots in the northern part of the coast.

Those few headlands and indentations still existing are slowly disappearing. The headlands are ceaselessly attacked and eroded by strong waves and breakers; the sand and gravel resulting from the destruction of the promontories are deposited, together with silt, sand, and pebbles brought down by rivers and streams, in the quiet water of the bays. On the Israel coast this process of sedimentation is aided by the Mediterranean Longshore Current, which flows counterclockwise from Gibraltar eastward along North Africa, then northward along the Levant Coast and, finally, back to the west, skirting Southern Europe. This current carries vast amounts of sand which fill up the embayments along our coast and aid in a further straightening of the shore line.

Different opinions are held regarding the origin of these sands. Most regard the Nile River as their principal source; during the pluvial periods of the subtropical areas (parallel to the ice ages of North America and Europe), the Nile brought down to the sea not only fine alluvium as in our days, but also coarse sand from the Abyssinian highlands; the hardest components, quartz sands, were transported through the sea and cast up on the Palestinian shore. Others hold that the sand was carried by Wadi el-'Arīsh from the lofty mountains in the south of the Sinai Peninsula. At all events, the quantity of sand on the coast decreases, proceeding from south to north. The siliceous sands south of Dor (on the Carmel

The port installations of Caesarea, built 2,000 years ago, now partly flooded by the sea

Coast) are clearly derived from external sources. From this point northward the sand is composed essentially of calcium carbonate; in other words, it originates in the limestones, dolomites and chalks of Mount Carmel and Galilee, and is brought to the sea by local streams. Fine grains of quartz sand, however, are carried northward, past Dor and the Carmel Cape, and deposited at protected sites, e.g., on the Haifa Bay shore. Parts of the calcareous sands are organogenic material, made up of the finely ground shells and bones of sea animals.

The shore itself has two different types: either precipitous cliffs, attaining 10–40 m (30–120 ft) and more in height, with a platform of very shallow water in front of them, or a rather gently inclined shore, usually covered with sand dunes.

The high cliffs and flat platforms were created by wave abrasion. The beach may be assumed to have begun as the inclined type and was frequently transformed by wave action. Waves tend to describe full vertical circles, providing the sea is over 2–3 m (6–8 ft) deep. Where the sea is too shallow for the waves to move full circle, however, their lower part skirts the bottom and is forced back along it while the upper part drops vertically with its full weight. At the bottom the breakers hollow out a cavity running parallel to the shore. High waves in stormy weather deepen the notch line and push it inland. If this process continues long enough, a vertical cliff begins to emerge and grow higher as it recedes landward. The breakers smash against its base and hollow out caves; the projecting rims and ledges, loosened by gravity and by the shattering of the waves, fall, are drawn into the sea by the undercurrent and are deposited at the outer fringe of the shallows. The level of the flat platform is determined by the diameter of storm waves. Rock surfaces are flattened and hollows filled with sand. The platform is thus constantly widened on both the land and the sea side, and a relationship is noticeable between the height of the cliffs and the width of the platform.

Such cliffs develop mainly where the original beach is reinforced by a continuous sandstone ridge emerging at a comparatively steep angle as on the Sharon shore. The cliffs rose rapidly and today reach the crest of the ridge.

Although the process of wave abrasion takes place all along the coast, the cliffs are absent from many of its sections although hard sandstone ridges may run near the beach. Closer inspection shows that a breach in the cliff wall occurs where streams, which tend to lower their beds to the erosional base level of the sea, reach the cliff edge and destroy the wall from the land side. The continuous cliff wall is thus first torn open by the rainwater running down its side. Where a crevice is opened to a swamp or stream dammed up behind the cliff wall, it is rapidly deepened and widened into a broad rift. Small tributaries of the stream lower the sides of the rift, and a wide and gentle valley, sometimes creating a mile or two mile long break in the cliff wall, is formed (see sketch, page 40).

Dunes and Swamps

Vertical cliffs effectively protect the land from the ingress of sands cast up by the sea. With the cliffs' removal and the creation of broad openings, the sands are deposited in the stream's mouth and are driven eastward up the valley by the sea wind. When a stream mouth is choked by sand, the weak flow of its waters forms a swamp behind the obstacle. An abundant swamp vegetation, enriching and darkening the soil, soon takes root. The stream constantly adds fine alluvium.

The interplay of these factors explains the characteristic configuration of stream mouths on our Mediterranean coast—an absence of cliffs and two sand dune tongues which penetrate inland and encircle a swamp. In the Sharon, a second ridge of sandstone hills, parallel and half to one mile east of that along the shore, often blocks further inland penetration of both sand and swamps; these must then spread along it in a southward and northward direction.

As is the case in regions of a prevalent wind direction, the western, seaward slopes of the coastal dunes are gentle, in contrast to their steep eastern sides facing the land. The dune axes lie at right angles to the dominating western winds. Most of the dunes are crescent-shaped since their lighter ends are driven forward more quickly than their heavy centers. The dunes are covered with ripple marks, each a miniature replica of the dune.

The size of the sand grains reflects the length of their exposure to the grinding and milling waves. The siliceous sand of the south, carried by the sea over a long distance, tends to be finer than the calcareous sand originating locally in the north. Sands on a sloped shore are likely to be driven inland soon after they have

Destruction of shore cliff, inland penetration of sand and forming of swamp

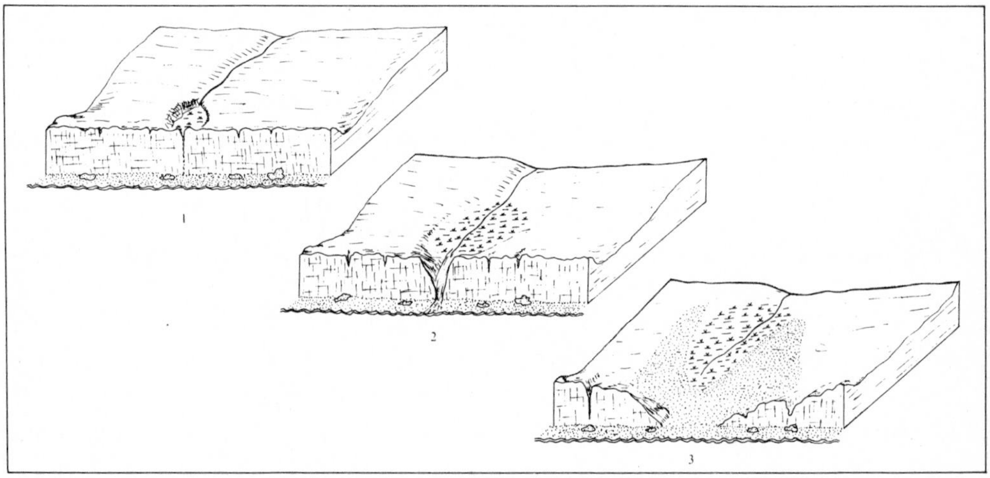

been cast up by the waves and are therefore often coarser than those which are obstructed by the cliffs and swept back seaward by high water, again to be ground by waves. The finest-grained sand in Israel is that south of Acre in Haifa Bay, used for glassmaking in Roman days. The coarsest is found on the inclined Nahariya beach, made up almost entirely of crushed animal matter.

South of the Yarqon mouth the coast configuration is somewhat different from the above-described. Sand accumulation on the beach and the absence of sandstone ridges near the shore frequently prevent formation of abrasion cliffs and platforms. The belt of dunes is broader and more continuous owing to the more abundant supply of sand. Swamps are very rare, probably because of the drier climate.

The Sandstone Ridges

Three continuous ridges (beside the shorter ridges and isolated hills), low and composed of coarse sandstone, stretch from south to north along the entire Coastal Plain. The ridges lie closer to each other as one proceeds northward. These sandstones, locally called 'kurkar,' originate in dunes of the Pleistocene era cemented together by calcareous solutions. Although this stone as a whole crumbles easily, the sand particles composing it are often extremely hard and as sharp as glass splinters. Kurkar stone hardens under water; it was therefore chosen for the construction of breakwaters and jetties in the port of Haifa.

The Streams

The streams from the Hills, seeking to reach the Mediterranean by the shortest possible route, tend to cross the Coastal Plain from east to west. They are, however, barred by the sandstone ridges which deflect them sideways until they find a breach with enables them to continue westward. The map shows that nearly all stream courses in the Coastal Plain form at least two wide loops, which in most cases are directed toward the north (see sketch map, page 42).

The Soils

The Western Plain and the Eastern Plain differ from each other principally in the quality of their soils. The Western Plain has 'red sands' (also called ḥamra soils), distinctive for their vivid, orange-red color. They occur in their most character-

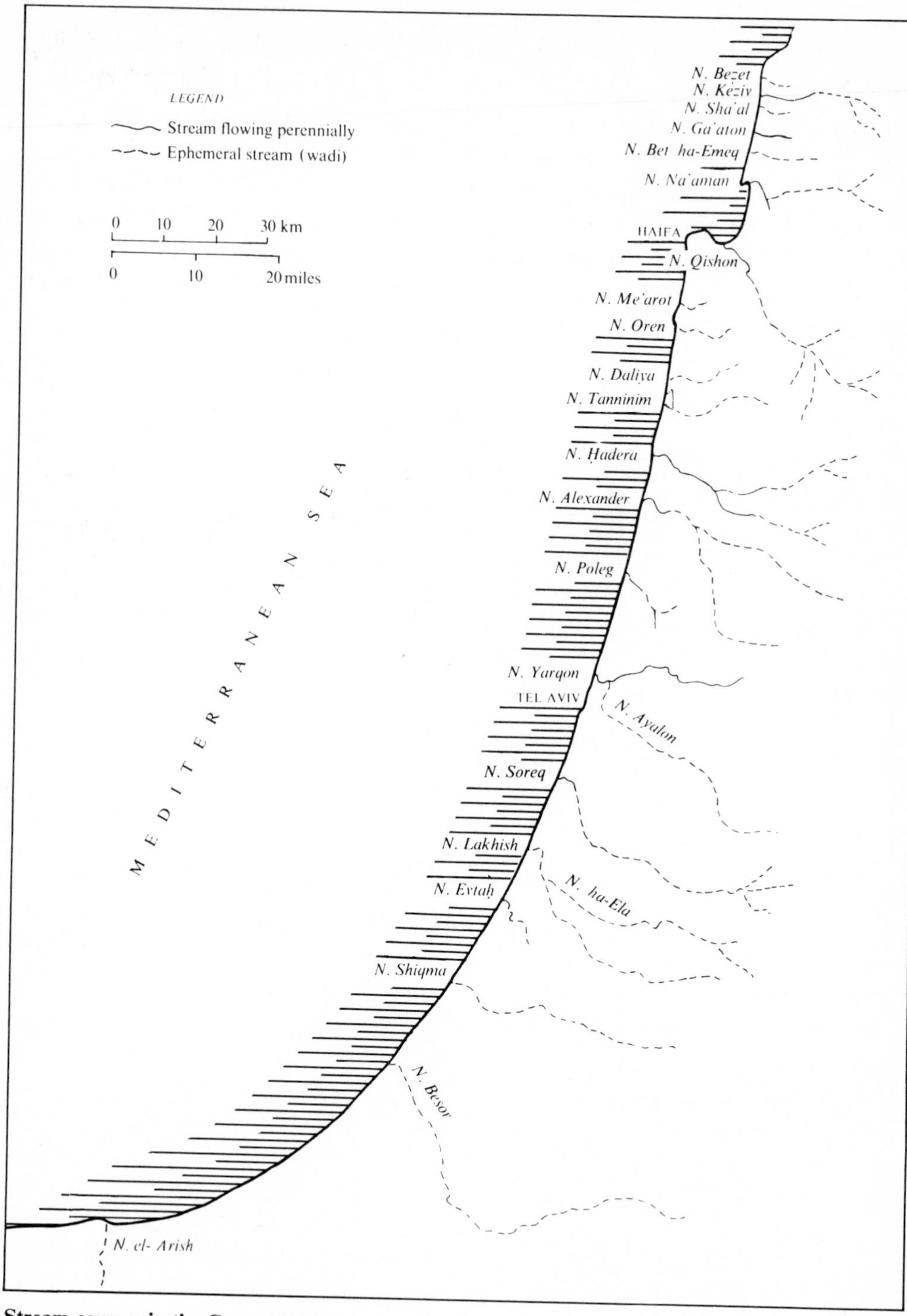

Stream courses in the Coastal Plain

istic form on the Judean Coast and in the Sharon. Every sandy grain has a clayey cover of ferrous, aluminous, and other components. While the coarse-grained texture allows permeability and aeration of the soil, the covers contribute materials essential for plant growth. This is the ideal soil for citrus cultivation, especially for the 'Jaffa' type of oranges. In contrast the Eastern Plain soils are of a heavier, alluvial type (grumusols), formed by deposits of terra rossa transported down by the streams from the Hills in the east. They have been partly darkened by swamps which may have spread during the Pleistocene period in circumstances resembling those which created the recent coastal swamps. The heavy soils are suitable for vegetables, fodder, grain, cotton, sugar beets and other plants; certain summer crops can here be cultivated without irrigation.

Toward the south the swamp soils diminish, but instead there is an increasing admixture of heavy loess characteristic of the Northern Negev. The mixture of red sand and loess produces soil of an intermediate type, considered very good for agriculture but frequently endangered by sheet erosion.

Groundwater and Springs

The Coastal Plain is rich in water, either stored in different groundwater horizons or appearing in springs (the latter mainly on the region's eastern border). Almost all this water has been tapped and is being used for irrigation, industry, and home consumption.

The uppermost horizon is in many places only a few yards below the surface of the red sands. Strong winter floods and heavy rains may tear the clayey cover from the red sand grains and carry it down where it forms a hard, impervious crust, locally called 'nazaz.' The nazaz crust is the shallowest horizon for water, which is available there in limited quantities. Where the impervious nazaz lies near the surface, it aids the spreading of swamps in the Western Plain of the Sharon; some even consider it to be the main factor of their formation at low-lying sites.

The horizon supplying most of the water for the Coastal Plain settlements is 20–120 m (60–400 ft) deep, upon a layer of impermeable Pliocene loam termed 'saqiye.'

The rains in the hill regions east of the Coastal Plain are readily absorbed by the permeable limestones and dolomites on the surface. As those rock layers dip west the waters seep toward the plain. Due to fault lines on the fringe of the plain these waters partly rise to the surface and appear as springs. The most productive springs in the country—Rosh ha-Ayin, En Na'aman, En Kabri, etc.—are all on these fault lines.

General Cross Section of the Coastal Plain

The following generalized west-east cross section may serve as a summation of the Coastal Plain: The seashore lies in the west, including an intermittent belt of moving sand dunes. These are broad in the south, narrow in the center, and nonexistent in the north. The westernmost kurkar ridges are either concealed by the sands, emerge as high cliffs or, further north, appear as small headlands, reefs or islets. Beyond these is the central sandstone chain, also lower in the south than in the Sharon, but in general definitely limiting the eastward spread of sand dunes. Further inland the Western Plain is covered mostly by red sands. The eastern kurkar ridges separate it from the Eastern Plain, which stretches up to the hill slopes and which, mainly in the Sharon and the Zebulon Valley, has dark, heavy and fertile soils.

The Negev Coast

The greater part of this region remained, until 1967, outside the borders of Israel, being included in the Sinai Peninsula and Gaza Strip.*

A wide belt of loose sands is found along the shore; it also covers most of the kurkar ridges on its eastern limits. In sections of the Negev Coastal Plain two parallel chains of low sandstone hills are recognizable, with a fertile area up to two miles wide in between. Some of the ridge crests served as ancient city sites, while others still retain their strategic importance. Loess soil, frequently covered with a thin layer of sand, is found in the inner part of the region. This configuration is conducive to agriculture: the upper sand facilitates ready absorption of the rainwater and minimum loss through evaporation, and the impermeable loess below enables most plant roots to reach the water.

Due to this absorbent sand cover, the subsoil is often richer in water than might be expected from the annual precipitation averages. Wells become more frequent near the shore, appearing at shallower depths with less saline water. These waters irrigate orange groves, fruit orchards, and vegetable gardens in the Gaza area as well as extensive date palm plantations at Deir al-Balaḥ (the Arabic name means 'Date Palm Convent').

The region also has a heavy dewfall, an additional blessing to agriculture. Experts ascribe to the dew the outstanding success of watermelons, obtained despite the low rainfall (150–350 mm—6–14 in—per annum).

* The Sinai Coast is described in detail on pp. 131–132. Population and settlements of the Gaza Strip are dealt with on pp. 388–397.

There is only one stream in the entire region, Naḥal Besor, flowing down from the Negev Hills and sometimes carrying strong, dangerous floods. The sand spread over the region apparently causes the rainwater to seep into the ground quickly, and thus obviates the need for an extensive network of surface runoff.

Naḥal Besor, with its wide catchment area and devastating winter floods, has created a very large bed 100–150 meters wide, not only in the Beersheba Region (see pp. 28–29), but also in the region of the Negev Coast. In the stream bed gullying has created a spectacular 'badland' topography; parts of the bed have been proclaimed a nature reserve. In the lower section of Naḥal Besor, near the Gaza Strip border, construction of a large reservoir is planned to cover an area of about 4,000 acres. It is hoped that a considerable part of the floodwater (estimated at 20–30 million m^3 annually) will thus become available for farming.

Outside the Gaza Strip which in the Six Day War came under Israel administration, exist the development town Netivot and over 20 kibbutzim and smallholders' villages; the population is expected to increase further with the progress of the Eshkol regional settlement project.

The Philistian Plain

In several respects the Philistian Plain presents a transition zone. The sloped beach found on the Negev shore continues while the first cliffs begin to appear. The soil changes gradually from loess sands or sandy loess to the terra rossa and red sands of the Center and the North. The dune belt, although still broad and almost continuous, is no longer the dominant feature of the landscape.

The streams crossing the region carry water only after strong winter rains. Naḥal Shiqma, which runs through broad dunes, has been chosen for an important pilot project: the floodwaters are directed to the sand flats to seep underground quickly. Protected from evaporation losses, they are stored and may be pumped for irrigation in summer. Naḥal Lakhish is the largest stream and with its tributary, Naḥal ha-Ela, is among the most important in the entire Coastal Plain. At the mouth of Naḥal Lakhish the port of Ashdod has been built.

Good farmland, suitable in the western part for citrus (groves have quickly expanded here in recent years) and in the eastern part for field and garden crops, and a mild climate with annual precipitation averaging 350–500 mm (14–20 in) make the South one of the most important economic regions of Israel, with a rapidly increasing population. In addition, it is rich in groundwater. The porous Cenomanian rock layers, fed by the rain falling in the Hebron Hills, form a wide subterranean anticline in this region which can be tapped with relative ease in the Gevar'am-Nir Am wells. Lower strata of this anticlinorium (of the Lower

Cretaceous) hold the oil of the Ḥeleẓ, Beror and Kokhav fields. At present additional water is brought to the South from the Rosh ha-Ayin springs by the national irrigation network, and more has become available with the completion of the National Water Carrier.

The region forms a network of rural and urban agglomerations. The West has the coastal cities of Ashqelon and Ashdod as well as semiurban centers—Sederot (on the Negev border) and Qiryat Mal'akhi—and many villages. The eastern part, the Lakhish Region, is the first in the country to have been settled in the framework of comprehensive regional planning (see p. 305); Qiryat Gat serves as its urban center.

The Judean Coast

In this region three bands of soil are clearly distinguishable: drifting dunes in the west, red sand in the center, and heavier terra rossa in the east and northeast with small stretches of dark swamp soil near the banks of Naḥal Ayalon.

South and north of Naḥal Soreq's mouth the dunes widen to nearly five miles. As late as 2,000 years ago the dunes covered a smaller area; while excavating foundations for new buildings in the town of Ḥolon, vestiges of Roman structures standing on fertile soil overlain with arid sand over 3–5 ft thick, were discovered. The moving dunes endanger the fields and gardens at their edge. At Rishon le-Ẓion they are checked by high eucalyptus and sycamore trees whose trunks are almost buried in the sand.

Citrus groves cover a large part of the region's middle section. These orchards, mainly on the red sands of the area, can be irrigated with groundwater. The abundant Rosh ha-Ayin springs at the northeastern margin of the region yield up to 14,000 m^3 per hour. A subterranean fault running diagonally through the region in the southeast-northwest direction is assumed to have created the hill of Jaffa; slightly jutting into the sea, the hill constitutes the only break in an otherwise entirely straight coast. The fault also apparently adds to the groundwater reserves of the area.

The streams crossing the region are Naḥal Soreq and Naḥal Ayalon, the latter a tributary of the Yarqon. Both display the two wide northward bends characteristic of most streams in the Coastal Plain. Naḥal Soreq becomes a stream only in the last few miles of its course; the same is true, to a certain extent, of Naḥal Ayalon, where at least isolated puddles of water remain in the dry summer. In contrast to these, the Yarqon, reaching the sea in the northern part of the Tel Aviv municipal area, is fed by the Rosh ha-Ayin springs; it had a strong and constant perennial flow until most of the spring water was diverted southward as part of the national water planning program. The lower section of its bed has been mostly filled since then with sea water or with sewage from the adjacent industrial and residential areas. The absence of wide bends in its course may be ascribed to the powerful flow which overcame rather than avoided the obstacles rising in the river's course. The Yarqon, until very recently, seasonally flooded areas on both banks, thus creating the Petaḥ Tiqwa swamps; these have now been entirely drained by Jewish settlers.

Occupied in its central and northern part by the Tel Aviv-Jaffa 'conurbation' (see p. 336ff.), the Judean Coast is today, with approx. 1 million inhabitants, the most densely populated region in Israel.

The Sharon

The Sharon measures 54 km (34 miles) from south to north and is about 16 km (10 miles) wide from west to east. A number of phenomena mark the transition from the Judean Plain to the Sharon. The cliff wall on the shore grows higher and becomes nearly continuous while the dune belt narrows and is interrupted over long stretches. The sandstone ridges become prominent features and form clear divides between the three lengthwise strips of the region. A narrow dune zone lies between the shore and the central ridge. The next ridge defines the western limit of the red sands while the easternmost kurkar chain, although concealed by red sands, separates these from the darker, heavier soils of the east.

The Sharon streams have a perennial water flow in their lowermost parts; until drained by settlers during the last sixty years, swamps existed in their neighborhood.

The streams of the Sharon, from south to north, are: Poleg, Alexander, Ḥadera, Ada and Tanninim. The smallest of them, Naḥal Poleg, follows an almost straight course and is assumed to be a drainage channel dug by the Romans rather than a genuine stream. A breach hewn in the kurkar ridge near the former swamps has, however, been identified as the moat of an Iron Age fortress. Naḥal Alexander flows in the Eastern Sharon, crosses its center (the Ḥefer Valley) and reaches the sea accompanied by a band of dunes, mainly on its northern side. The wide lowest part of its course contains salt water which seeps in from the sea. Naḥal Ḥadera, receiving many tributaries from the Samarian Hills, flows northwest to the town of Ḥadera, then turns west to the sea. Naḥal Ada leaves the Menashe Plateau to unite with Naḥal Tanninim (meaning 'Crocodile stream'—these animals were reportedly there in the recent past); it circles the southern 'nose' of Mount Carmel, then divides and reaches the sea in two arms which are three miles apart.

Young orange groves in the northern Sharon, near Binyamina

In the past the Sharon was among the most backward and neglected regions of the country owing to its malaria swamps, the red sands' unsuitability for crops other than irrigated, and the cover the brush afforded to robbers of caravans. Today it is Israel's best-developed farming region and the center of its citrus industry. The red sands and dark soils afford a great variety in the Sharon's agricultural products. Further assets are its mild climate, where frost is practically unknown and precipitation averages 500–600 mm (20–24 in) annually and abundant groundwater furthers highly intensive farming, while its position in the center of Israel and astride the most important communication lines is an asset to its industrial development. Herzliya, Ra'ananna and Kefar Sava are the principal urban and semiurban centers of the Southern Sharon, Netanya of the center and Ḥadera of the north. The eastern rim of the Sharon, on both sides of the former 'armistice border' of 1949, has a predominantly Arab population.

The Carmel Coast

The Carmel Coast, 32 km (20 miles) long, narrows from 2½ km (1½ miles) at its southern extremity to a few scores of meters near the Carmel Cape in the north.

The shore is divided into two widely differing sections. Between Dor and Atlit the westernmost kurkar ridge, lower than in the Sharon, has been partly flooded by the sea and forms many diminutive bays and headlands; a second, often interrupted kurkar ridge runs somewhat further east in the narrow space between the shore and the third main ridge. North of Atlit the first sandstone chain has entirely disappeared beneath the waves, consequently straightening the shore which retreats slightly east.

The soil in the narrow strip between the eastern sandstone ridge and the steep rise of Mount Carmel is deep, dark and heavy. Red sand may be absent owing to the proximity of Mount Carmel, from which pure terra rossa is swept down, and to the continuity of the kurkar chain in the west; all invading sands are held back and the streams, which cannot flow freely to the sea, sometimes inundate the surrounding land and give it swamp soil characteristics.

A fault line 200–1,000 meters west of the Carmel slope, which serves as an effective trap for groundwater, thus creates a surplus available for neighboring areas.

Many small streams emerge from the Carmel but do not unite to form major streams because the area is so narrow. Some of them, unable to overcome the sandstone barrier, seep into the ground and disappear.

The fertility of the soil, the comparatively high precipitation (600–700 mm—24–28 in per annum), and the rich groundwater produce a thriving agriculture. The steep wall of Mount Carmel rising against the sea constitutes an effective windbreak for plants especially sensitive to winds, such as bananas.

Settlements on the Carmel Coast, most of them rural in character, fall into three groups: villages of the shore, some of them fishing villages; those on the flat ground, all based on intensive farming; and those on the Mount Carmel slope, where some have specialized in additional occupations (recreation, educational centers, the Artists' Village of En Hod). The oldest is Atlit, where salt is won from the sea. Tirat Karmel is practically a suburb of Haifa.

The Zebulon Valley (Haifa Bay Area)

The region differs essentially from other parts of the Coastal Plain in its being a rift valley which sank when the Carmel block rose as a horst. The sea, being pushed back from the Carmel Head, invaded the area further north and created the wide crescent of the bay. The subsidence of the Zebulon Valley appears to be connected with the creation of the great Jordan Rift. It is the westernmost link in the chain of valleys separating Galilee from Samaria, although itself separated from the neighboring Jezreel Valley by the low Shefar'am Hills.

The waters of Haifa Bay are deepest in the southwest, along the fault running at the foot of Mt. Carmel. This fact explains the choice of Haifa as the country's first deep-sea port. Most of the Zebulon Valley's soils are dark and heavy since they were frequently flooded by streams barred by sands from reaching the Bay. The two streams in the region, Qishon and Na'aman, have a perennial flow. The Qishon enters from the Jezreel Valley through a narrow gap between Mount Carmel and the lower Shefar'am Hills. The Na'aman is fed by a strong, slightly brackish spring in the valley itself. Normally, since the streams in the flat valley flow sluggishly and are unable to overcome the sand bars at their mouths, they thus cause the water to spread over the surrounding low-lying fields. At times of high water and westerly storms, sea water may be driven into the shallow stream course to mingle with the swamp waters and to make them brackish. Natural halophytic vegetation (blue tamarisk, etc.) and salt-tolerant date palms planted by man characterize the Qishon and Na'aman stream vicinity.

The white expanse of fine sand dunes contrasts strongly with the black swamp soils and dark terra rossa alluvium inland. Grains, fodder, cotton, and vegetables

Diagrammatic sketch of rising block of Mt. Carmel and subsiding Haifa Bay

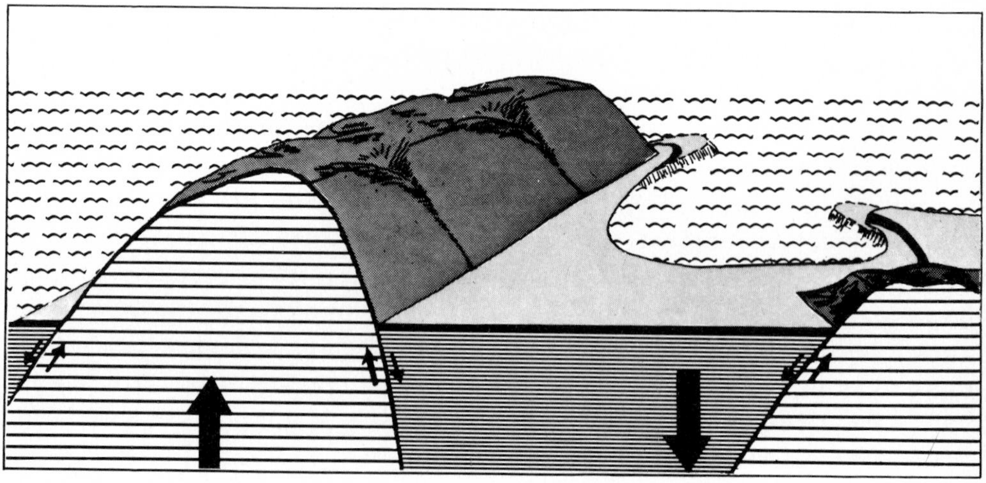

are the dominant crops. Citrus groves are totally absent; other fruits are grown mainly on the eastern outskirts of the valley.

The landscape of the Zebulon Valley has been thoroughly changed by man, especially over the past few decades. Haifa Port, with its long quays and breakwaters, has been built, its bottom deepened, and the dredged rock and sand used to add a strip of new land to the shore; on it, large warehouses and other port installations have been constructed. The lowest section of the Qishon has been greatly widened and deepened to become part of the newest port in the Bay. Like its veteran neighbor, it has also been protected by two breakwater jetties reaching far into the sea. The Qishon and Na'aman swamps have been drained, and the stream courses straightened and deepened.

Hardly any sandstone ridges are found in the Zebulon Valley. Some of the mounds in its center and on its eastern outskirts are, at least in their upper parts, artificial, bearing ancient foundations of settlements and fortifications.

The Acre Plain and Tyre Valley

The Acre Plain shore is mostly straight, but some small embayments are found, mainly near Shavey Ẓion and Akhziv. The shore belongs to the inclined type, with no cliffs. The westernmost kurkar chain has been flooded, and its tops form reefs. Some of these, less than half a mile from the coast, opposite Nahariya and south of Rosh ha-Niqra, are permanent small islets or break the surface at low water. Other kurkar rocks, about to disappear beneath the waves, lie on the beach. The belt of coarse sand dunes is very narrow, never wider than a few score meters. The innermost kurkar ridge is parallel to the coast at a distance of about one mile. Many settlements, both ancient and new, have been built upon this ridge.

The soils of Acre Plain are mostly of the heavier terra rossa type, with only a small admixture of sand. Their excellent quality, good amounts of precipitation (700 mm—28 in and over) and abundant springs and groundwater allow for a rich and variegated agriculture. Acre and Nahariya are the urban centers; the latter is based on industry and tourism.

The streams, of which Naḥal Keziv is the largest, cross the plain and run almost straight east-west courses. Some streams flow perennially, but their water is increasingly being used for summer irrigation.

The Tyre Valley, entirely in Lebanon, lacks unity more than does any other part of the Coastal Plain. Apart from the Tyrian Ladder, which separates this valley from the Acre Plain and meets the sea in the high Rosh ha-Niqra Cape with its impressive glaring-white limestone cliffs, there are mountain ridges which

The Rosh ha-Niqra Cape, at the northern end of Acre Valley. Oncoming waves ceaselessly pound its white limestone cliffs

approach or reach down to the shore. The shore is no longer a straight line. This is not, therefore, a coastal plain originating in a continental uplift, but rather a series of 'pocket beaches' filled by the deposition of sand and silt transported by streams from the mountains. The town of Tyre is built on a sandstone hillock at the end of a narrow land tongue projecting into the sea. The hillock is connected to the mainland by a narrow strip of sand, thought by some to be deposited by the waves (a landscape feature termed 'tombolo'), while by others—to be built by man, or at least artificially reinforced by the inhabitants of the island town.

Many small ephemeral streams from Northern Galilee flow northwest, down to the Tyre Valley; the most important of these is known as Wadi 'Azziye. The soils of the valley, heavy terra rossa, resemble those of the Acre Plain. All the level land is intensively farmed by a large peasant population.

The Hill Regions

Hills occupy most of the country west of the Jordan, in the Negev and in the northern half of the country. In the latter they comprise three main regions—Judea in the south, Samaria in the center, and Galilee in the north.

Geology and Morphology. All parts of the hills were formed during the last great mountain-building phase of the earth, the Alpine-Himalayan revolution. In this country folding movements were strongest in the Miocene, although still far from the violence which created the mountain chains further north, e.g., the Taurus and Antitaurus of Turkey or the Zagros of Iraq and Iran. In the subsequent geologic periods faulting, volcanic activity, and erosion imprinted upon the various parts of the hills their individual characteristics.

Northward, a gradual change becomes noticeable in the hill landscape. The Judean Hills present a compact upfold or dome, little disturbed by faults. The strong impact of erosional forces here has not yet obliterated the essential features of tectonic origin created in the landscape.

In Samaria, three folds run parallel, directed south-southwest–north-northeast, the eastern one being the highest of the three. Faults become more numerous; Northern Samaria particularly is rich in small tectonic basins and rift valleys; many lie between fault lines at right angles to the fold axes. In certain parts of Samaria erosion, together with upfaulting, has inverted the landscape relief; the highest mountains happen to be situated in the 'Nablus Downfold' or Syncline.

In Galilee we find a main fold running north-south, with secondary folds parallelling it on both flanks. The landscape features of this northern region, however, were finally determined by taphrogenic (faulting) movements, presumably strongest in the Pliocene. Fault lines cross the folds, in most cases at right angles. Pressures from different directions created two series of tilted blocks.

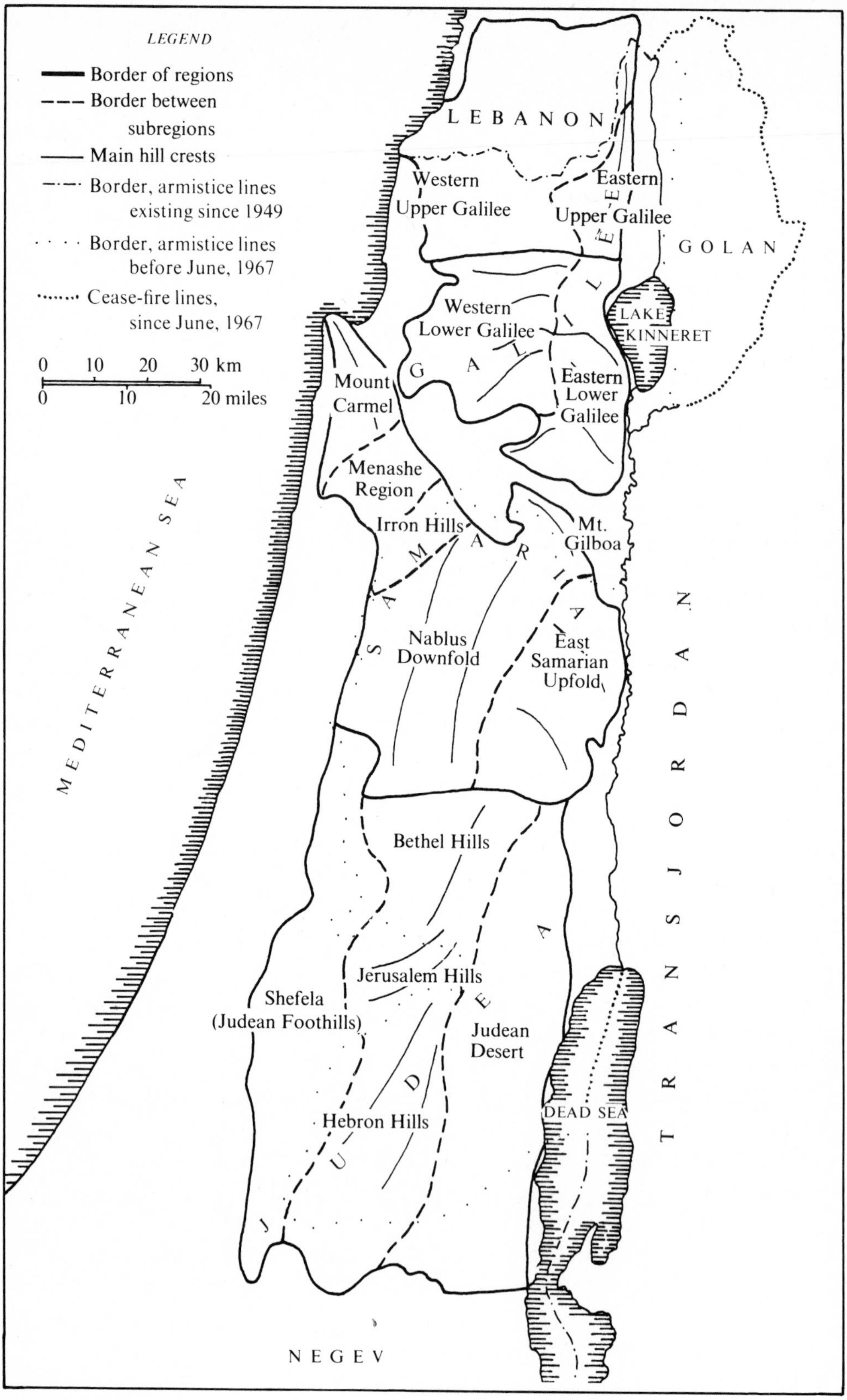
LEGEND
Border of regions
Border between subregions
Main hill crests
Border, armistice lines existing since 1949
Border, armistice lines before June, 1967
Cease-fire lines, since June, 1967
0 10 20 30 km
0 10 20 miles
LEBANON
Western Upper Galilee
Eastern Upper Galilee
GOLAN
LAKE KINNERET
Western Lower Galilee
GALILEE
Mount Carmel
Eastern Lower Galilee
Menashe Region
Irron Hills
Mt. Gilboa
SAMARIA
Nablus Downfold
East Samarian Upfold
MEDITERRANEAN SEA
TRANSJORDAN
Bethel Hills
Jerusalem Hills
Shefela (Judean Foothills)
Judean Desert
JUDEA
Hebron Hills
DEAD SEA
NEGEV

Subregions of the Hills

Additional elements were introduced into Upper Galilee by cross-faulting and into the east of both Lower and Upper Galilee by volcanic activity. The Galilean landscape, therefore, presents a complicated picture of isolated mountains, narrow ridges and elevated plateaus, of valleys, gorges, and small basins.

Geologists try to explain the strong faulting in the north, as opposed to its small extent in the south, as reflecting the distance between the Mediterranean Sea and the Jordan Rift, which narrows from south to north; some authorities maintain that the sea in the west and the rift in the east pressed upon the rock crust which was uplifted between them; the nearer these two pressures to each other, the stronger the strain in the upfold, until its rock crust was broken and faulted. Others say that movements were mostly horizontal, going in either a north-south or south-north direction; the dual strain on the rock crust was particularly heavy in Galilee, where areas very close to each other were pushed either from the north or from the southwest.

Rocks. Limestone and dolomite of the Cenomanian and Turonian (Upper Cretaceous age) prevail in the higher parts of Judea, Samaria, and Galilee. These rocks are hard, relatively resistant to surface erosion, but strongly affected by chemical destruction processes termed 'karst.' These processes depend on water and carbon dioxide, the latter provided mainly by vegetation. The cracks in the rock caused by seepage are deepened by plant roots, until parts of the rock split off vertically. Escarpments, steep slopes and gorges result in the course of time and typify the limestone areas of the hills.

Thin layers of chalky marl are usually interposed between the limestone or dolomite hill strata. As the marl does not suffer from karstic dissolution, most hill slopes in the country have a steplike appearance. These natural steps prompted man's first impulse, thousands of years ago, toward completion of the work of nature by terracing, i.e., reinforcing the outer edge of each step with a stone wall in order to protect the loose surface soil from being washed down by the rains.

As might be expected, karst processes become more intensive toward Galilee with its rainier climate. The karst appears in 'lapies formations' (surface rocks riddled by holes and split by deep vertical cracks) as well as in caves, some of which have stalactites and stalagmites. In Galilee, sinkholes, ponds (several holding water the year round) and small 'dolines' filled with alluvial soil are also found.

In the lower parts of the hill regions (Judean Foothills, synclines of Samaria, western reaches of Galilee), as well as in the Judean Desert, somewhat younger rocks have been preserved. These are mostly soft, light-colored chalks of the Senonian, Eocene, in some instances also Oligocene and Miocene periods. In the Senonian chalk, intercalations and concretions of brown or dark flint frequently

Stalactites and stalagmites in a karstic limestone cave of the hill country appear. In some Eocene sediments of the north (Mt. Gilboa, Metulla Hills, etc.), coral limestone replaces the chalk.

Chalk rocks, particularly in Judea, are often covered by a thin, hard crust locally termed 'nari.' Rainwater which seeps into the rock in winter is drawn up to the surface during the hot, dry summer and evaporates. The calcium dissolved in the water is thereby deposited on the surface as 'nari.' This crust sometimes hampers the development of natural vegetation and of farm crops.

Volcanic rocks, predominantly black basalts, thinly cover soft chalks in Lower Galilee. Basalts appear equally on the Dalton and Alma plateaus north of Safad and on the outskirts of the Jordan Rift in Galilee. Outcrops of basalts and tuffs of Cretaceous age are found in Samaria on Mt. Carmel, in the Irron Hills, and on the East Samarian Fold.

Soils. The famous Mediterranean terra rossa, conditioned by a regime of winter rains and summer drought, is typical of all the regions where limestones appear on the surface. Terra rossa is totally different from its gray-white parent rock in its deep, red-brown color as well as in its chemical composition. Limestone is essentially calcium carbonate; in dolomite, magnesium is also present. Terra rossa, in contrast, contains up to 50% silica and 10 to 15% each of aluminum and iron (the latter lending the soil its reddish hue) while only five percent or less of this soil is calcium. The reason for this curious incongruity lies in the differing solubility of the various components: the easily soluble calcium is readily absorbed by rainwater and washed off the surface, or it seeps to depth where it is again precipitated in crevices, cavities or caves. The less soluble siliceous, ferrous, or aluminous matter, however, mostly remains in its place, ground into rock meal and later transformed into living soil. It is estimated that in this country an average of one centimeter of surface rock is weathered into terra rossa in the course of 1,000 years.

In its texture and composition terra rossa is well suited for farming. Where the topsoil is quickly eroded, new, deeper soil layers are constantly bared, consequently forming 'young' soil. In the hills the forming of new soil often cannot keep pace with runoff; costly soil-conservation measures such as construction of elaborate terraces must be applied to secure a minimum of cultivable soil on the slopes. In Israel's hills, perennial crops, such as deciduous fruit trees and vines, which hold the soil in place with their deep roots, are given preference over grain crops. Wheat cultivation often hastened erosion in the past, and the rock was bared on many slopes; where this has happened, afforestation is effective in retaining the old and in promoting the formation of new soil.

Weathering in soft chalk regions forms a grayish white to yellowish brown 'rendzina' soil which is rich in calcium and differs widely from terra rossa, In intermontane valley grounds it is frequently enriched with organic matter and thus turned into dark, fertile 'grumusols.' Rendzina, though poorer than terra rossa, is friable and easy to till. It forms no hard crust in summer nor does it become viscous mud under the winter rains. On the gentle Foothills slopes it is less affected by runoff and is thus usually deeper than hill soil. Therefore, farmers generally prefer it to terra rossa. Rendzina soils support a wide range of crops, e.g., fruit trees, vines, grains, cotton, tobacco, etc.

Basalt soils, prevalent in Eastern Lower Galilee, resemble terra rossa in color (although some shades darker) as well as in texture and chemical composition. This is surprising, as the parent rocks are totally different. While the terra rossa's composition is far removed from that of limestone, basalt soil is quite similar to the basalt rocks of Lower Galilee which contain about 45% silica and only 0.2% calcium. Basalt soil on mountain slopes is no less endangered by erosion than is terra rossa and therefore requires stringent conservation methods. The almost level basalt plateaus of Lower Galilee, however, have deep soil and thus can easily support grain and other field crops.

The Judean Hills

The Judean Hills are divided into three subregions, distinct from each other in morphology, rocks, soils, and climate: in the west, the Foothills, in the center, the Hills, and in the east, the Judean Desert. The pre-1967 frontiers gave Israel almost all of the Foothills, the 'Jerusalem Corridor' in the Hills leading to the capital, and the southern section of the Judean Desert; the greatest part of the Hills and two thirds of the Desert were left in Jordan. After the Six Day War, these lines still have administrative and demographic significance.

The limits of the three subregions are most sharply marked by rock differences: chalks characterize the Foothills and the Desert, limestones and dolomites—the Hills.

Variety in rainfall, too, is extreme; the Foothills average 400–500 mm (16–22 in) annually, while precipitation on the Hills attains a maximum of 800 mm (32 in); the Judean Desert, however, receives only 300 mm (12 in) annually 6 miles east of the hill tops, and a mere 50–100 mm (2 to 4 in) of rain are measured near the Dead Sea shore escarpment.

Rainfall distribution and rock properties determine the natural drainage system of Judea. Streams have gouged narrow, winding gorges deep into the hard rock on the western slopes of the Hills. The streams generally flow due west toward the sea; only a few of them, like Naḥal En Kerem or Naḥal Adullam, flow in a different direction. The drainage network is rather 'coarse,' with a relatively small number of streams in relation to area. On the map the streams with their small tributaries form an outbranching tree crown ('dendritic system'). In the Foothills these streams unite and flow in a few wider, alluvium-filled valleys. Of note are Naḥal Shiqma which drains the western slopes of the Adorayim Ridge; Naḥal Lakhish and its tributary, Naḥal ha-Ela, which emerge from the Adullam Region; Naḥal Soreq which has cut a spectacular gorge southwest of Jerusalem where the railway runs between the capital and the Coastal Plain; Naḥal Ayalon which joins the Yarqon River inside the municipal boundary of Tel Aviv; and Naḥal Shilloh, the upper section of the Yarqon. Only one stream, Naḥal Ḥevron, drains the Hills toward the southwest, from Hebron to Beersheba, where it enters Naḥal Beersheba. All these streams carry water only intermittently, in the winter. The abundance of coarse gravel and stones in all stream courses points to pluvial periods in the recent geological past when their flow was perennial, much more powerful, and their erosional force much greater than at present.

The drainage system on the eastern flank of the Hills, i.e., in the Judean Desert, is finer than in the west and typical of the prevalent chalk rock. On their relatively short way from the watershed to the Dead Sea the streams do not unite into major courses. In their middle and lower sections, where they cross the high fault escarpments with their limestone outcrops, deep canyons with perpendicular rock walls at some places rising to 200 m (600 ft) or more are cut. Naḥal Qidron, which originates near the Old City of Jerusalem, is the best known of the eastern streams. Naḥal Ḥever, Naḥal Arugot and others have recently received publicity thanks to the archeological discoveries in the caves high on the canyon sides.

The Hills of Judea (in the narrow sense): The Judean upfold exceeds 1,000 m (3,200 ft) above sea level. The axis of the dome is directed south-southwest–north-northeast. The watershed is much closer to the Jordan River and the Dead Sea than to the Coastal Plain and the Mediterranean Sea: from Tell 'Asūr (Mt. Baal Ḥaẓor) in the north, 1,016 m (3,333 ft) high, the distance is only 15 km (9 miles) to the Jordan Valley cross-country, but 37 km (23 miles) to the Coastal Plain (near Lod Airport) and 57 km (33 miles) to the coast itself. Mt. Ḥalḥul near Hebron in the south is 25 km (15½ miles) away from the Dead Sea, and over 60 km (39 miles) from the Mediterranean Sea. The eastern flanks of the upfold are consequently much shorter and steeper than those of the west.

The crest of the upfold is compact and broad. It is somewhat higher in the south ('Hebron Hills') and in the north ('Bethel Hills') than in the center ('Jerusalem Hills'). The narrow Hebron Dome slopes steeply both west and east. South of Hebron, Naḥal Ḥevron runs along the upfold crest through a broad valley which separates the Adorayim Ridge in the west from the higher Yuta (Yatta), or Qiryatayim, Ridge in the east.

Scene of the Judean Hills southwest of Jerusalem. Interchange of hard and soft rock strata creates step-like slopes. Some alluvial soil is retained on the gorge bottom. Afforestation has been begun on the higher reaches of the hills

The central section of the Jerusalem Hills, which is 100–200 m (300–700 ft) lower than the southern and northern extremities, forms a saddle between them. It broadens to the east, and even more so to the west. This fact explains the development of important towns (Gibeon, and later Jerusalem) in this section in antiquity; the north-south highway (the 'Hill Road' of the Bible), which used the flat upfold crest, at this point crossed the vital west-east road which took the least difficult path, i.e., the one where the hills are less steep, and the Dead Sea does not bar the way to Transjordan (as it does further south). Another relatively easy entry to the heart of the Judean Hills is through Naḥal Ela Valley; at its upper end lies Bethlehem.

In the Bethel Hills of the north, the upfold again narrows and grows higher. It attains its maximum elevation in Mt. Baal Ḥaẓor on the Samarian border. The area between al-Jib (Gibeon) and Mukhmās (Mikhmash) is rather flat and little-eroded, and has therefore been used for farming and settlement since ancient times. The town of Ramallah takes, in our days, the place of ancient Bethel whose site lies further to the northeast.

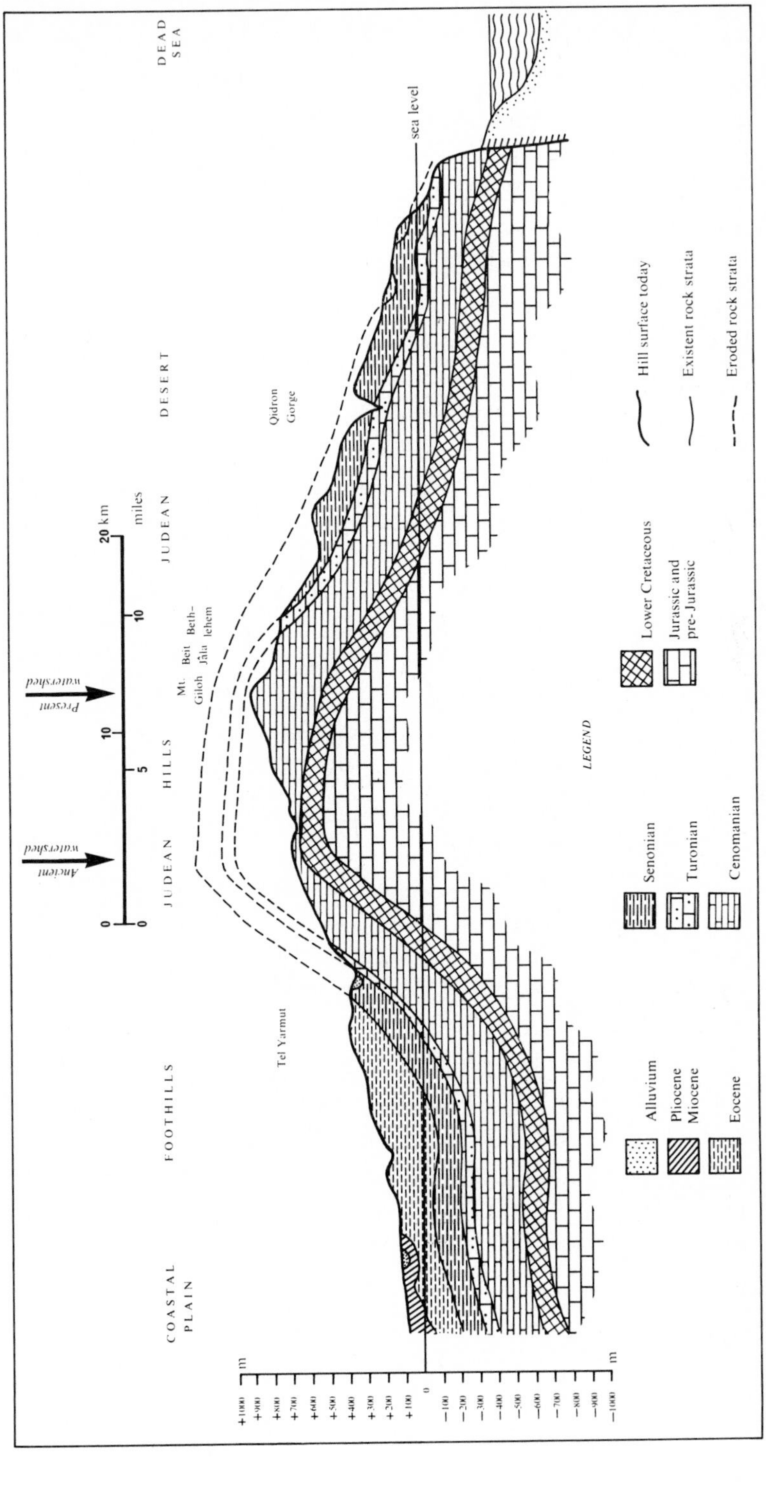

Eastward displacement of surface watershed in the Judean Hills (diagrammatic sketch)

It may be assumed that the original anticline of Judea was almost symmetrically built; perhaps it sloped slightly more sharply in the west. The fold axis was some 10–12 km (6–7 miles) west of the present watershed. Through geologic ages erosion changed the picture. Rains, incomparably more intensive on the western slopes than in the east, washed off the top layers and bared the Turonian and Cenomanian rocks which had lain concealed. On the eastern slopes, far less exposed to destruction, the Senonian surface chalks were preserved. The watershed was thus gradually displaced eastward, in its first stages perhaps at a swifter pace than today, as then the western slope was very steep and runoff proportionately strong. As a consequence, the oldest surface rocks (Lower Cenomanian and, west of the town of Ramallah, also Lower Cretaceous) are found along the line of the original fold crest. This crest still forms the underground watershed for rainwater which seeps into the porous rock and flows, with the dip of the strata, west and east respectively. Therefore, from the strip between the ancient and the modern watershed (which, incidentally, receives the largest amounts of precipitation in Judea), surface waters are drained to the west, groundwaters to the east. This explains the strange phenomenon of the appearance of the strongest springs of the region in the Judean Desert ('Ein al-Qelt, 'Ein Farī'a, 'Ein Fashkha, En Gedi, etc.).

The fold crest of Judea, like all anticlines, is subjected to tectonic strain and is therefore most sensitive to erosion. Although the region is too young geologically for a complete relief inversion (i.e., for original upfolds to become valleys, and synclines to appear as hills), signs of incipient opening of trough valleys along the original crests are discernible.

In the last 3,000 years, Jerusalem has constituted the dominating center of the Judean Hills. Recent developments point to its linking up, in the future, with the towns of Bethlehem in the south and Ramallah in the north, thus creating the country's third conurbation which also expands westward to Mevasseret Ẓion. In the south, Hebron serves as an urban center. The 1948 War of Independence carved out Israel's 'Jerusalem Corridor,' occupying ca. one tenth of the total Judean Hills, which was covered, in the ensuing years, with a network of Jewish settlements. After 1967 the settlement of the Eẓyon Bloc north of Hebron was renewed. Arab agglomerations are spread over the rest of the Judean Hills. They form a dense network of relatively small villages in the western and central parts, while the eastern reaches, confronting the Judean Desert, have fewer but larger villages.

The Foothills. This is a strip approximately 65 km (40 miles) long from south to north and up to 12 km (8 miles) wide between the Coastal Plain in the west and the Judean Hills in the east. It is a transitional zone, beginning at less than 100 m

View over kibbutz Ma'ale ha-Ḥamisha toward the west. Planted forests have thoroughly transformed the landscape

The Ela Valley in the Judean Foothills. The mound in the center is that of Azeqa, one of King Rehoboam's fortresses

Partial view of the new town of Bet Shemesh, on the border of the Judean Hills and Foothills. The cement factory uses the heavy soil of the valley and the limestone of the hills as raw materials

(300 ft) above sea level in the west and rising to a height of over 400 m (1,300 ft) on its eastern rim. A Lower and an Upper Foothills Region may therefore be distinguished, but the transition is too gradual for a clear partition line to be drawn.

A sharp fault north of the Ayalon Valley outlines the limit of the northern Foothills. Some small faults also exist along the eastern border of the region, near the upfold of the Hills. Flat troughs mark portions of the border line; a stretch of the Jerusalem-Tel Aviv highway runs through one, between Sha'ar ha-Gay and Bet Shemesh, and further to Bet Guvrin.

In geological cross section the Foothills Region appears as a synclinal structure; the youngest rocks, of Eocene age, are in the center, flanked by Senonian chalks in the east and west.

Several wider valleys lie between the gentle, rounded hills of the region. Outstanding are the valleys of Ayalon, Soreq, and Ela. Because of their fertile alluvial soil, important population centers were founded in antiquity. These towns also served as fortresses guarding the valleys, which were natural military thoroughfares between the Coastal Plain and the Hills. These valleys thus witnessed decisive battles (Joshua against the Canaanites in the Ayalon Valley, or the Philistines with Goliath against the Israelites in the Ela Valley).

Urban centers exist mainly on the western rim of the Foothills (Qiryat Gat, Ramla); in the region itself the new town of Bet Shemesh bases its economy chiefly on industry (metals, textiles and other branches).

The Judean Desert. The dry east slopes of the Judean dome are a classic example of 'lee side' effects. This meteorologic result of the topographic relief is augmented by the impermeable quality of the chalk rocks and by the steepness of the slopes. Little of the scarce rainwater is absorbed by the top rock layers; surface runoff, hence, forms sudden floods which are quickly drained off the steep slope.

The flank of the upfold which descends to the Jordan and Dead Sea Rift is broken by a number of high steps or escarpments along the parallel fault lines accompanying the Rift Valley. The most imposing of these rock walls is the lowest, nearest to the Dead Sea, which is uninterrupted for a length of 65 km (40 miles) and attains 100–400 m (300–1,200 ft) in height. It is along such fault scarps that the Cenomanian limestones and dolomites are bared beneath the younger chalk, and it is there that very spectacular canyons are gouged by

The Massada Rock in the Judean Desert, seen from the east. The three steps of the Herodian palace are clearly visible at the north (right) end. In front of the mountain—phantastic shapes created by erosion in lissan marl

View of the Zohar Gorge in the southern Judean Desert, descending to the Dead Sea floodwaters rushing toward the Dead Sea. Two canyons at a small distance from each other with a tributary entering one of them at a right angle isolate one part of the high step as a 'relic mountain,' which slopes down almost vertically on all sides. The most famous of these, made particularly impregnable by being uplifted as a horst, is the Massada Rock fortress, scene of the last, desperate resistance of Jewish freedom fighters against the Roman legions in 73 C.E.; it is only 49 m (150 ft) above the Mediterranean sea level but rises over 300 m (1,000 ft) above its immediate surroundings.

The Samarian Hills

The hills of Samaria are morphologically variegated. Three parallel folds form the skeleton of their structure—Mount Carmel in the northwest, the Irron Hills in the center, and the East Samarian Fold (Teveẓ Hills) in the southeast, with two synclinal areas in between, the Menashe and Nablus regions.

The small intermontane rift valleys, often bordering on uplifted blocks or horsts, lend a pronouncedly mountainous character to many parts of Samaria, although the elevations do not equal those of Judea. A comparatively dense rural population lives on the hills around the valley grounds because of the good farming conditions provided by the more ample rains and fertile alluvial soil. Valleys opening west, north and south give easy access to the center of Samaria; perhaps this explains why Samaria was, historically, more receptive to foreign influence in politics, culture and religion than was the 'closed' hill region of Judea.

The East Samarian Fold. The highest of the three folds of Samaria touches Mt. Baal Ḥaẓor in the southwest on the Judean border, and in the northeast, the Bet She'an Valley. As a result of the fold's strong elevation at the beginning of the erosional cycle, the particularly active erosion has bared ancient strata: not only Cenomanian limestone but also Lower Cretaceous sediments in the center (Ras Jedira = Mt. Teveẓ, 712 m [2,279 ft] above sea level), as well as basalt and tuff patches, which signify volcanic activity during that age.

The proximity of the Rift influences the morphology of the eastern upfold; the eastern slopes follow fault lines and drop abruptly. From the Rift, northwest-directed branch valleys penetrate the fold and divide its northern part into separate sections. Most typical of these are the broad and rather shallow Wadi Buqei'a, and Wadi Farī'a; the latter is narrow and very deep, its bottom largely below sea level. At its side Jebel Kabīr (792 m—2,598 ft) rises in the south, and Jebel Tammūn (647 m—2,123 ft) in the north. The difference in level therefore exceeds

800 m (2,600 ft) over a distance of only 2 km. The immense, bare slopes on both sides of the valley, contrasting with the strip of green orchards and vegetable gardens of the valley bottom, create an atmosphere of grandeur.

At the southeastern end of Jebel Kabīr rises Mt. Sartaba, 377 m (1,237 ft) above sea level, which juts into the Jordan Valley and dominates large stretches of it in the north, east and south. The strategic importance of this spot was recognized by the Hasmonean kings of antiquity, who erected the fortress of Alexandrion; the sages of the Mishna chose the mountain as a beacon station, one of a chain which signaled the sighting of the new moon in Jerusalem to the Mesopotamian diaspora, to indicate the beginning of a new month in the Jewish calendar.

Since the valleys of Samaria opening out to the west allow the moisture-bearing sea winds to reach even the eastern folds, the 'rain shadow' area is at most 10 km (6 miles) wide. Even there, with an annual rainfall exceeding 250 mm (10 in), it is not pronouncedly arid.

The Nablus Syncline. The topography of this fairly large region has become varied, owing to both tectonic movements and erosional activity. The southern extremity of the syncline touches the southern Sharon Plain and the Bethel Hills of Judea; its northern end is formed by Mt. Gilboa, which drops abruptly to the Ḥarod Valley.*

In the central parts of the Nablus Syncline, Eocene chalk is the top layer; the flanks show older, Senonian strata. The highest elevations of Samaria, Mt. Ebal 940 m (3,084 ft) above sea level and Mt. Gerizim 881 m (2,890 ft), lie precisely in the center of the syncline. Erosion has certainly contributed to this 'inversion of relief' by attacking the strata of the anticlines more strongly than the downfold, which has better resistance; it must be assumed, however, that the decisive processes for the present topography were the simultaneous tectonic uplift of two mountain blocks, separated by the narrow Nablus Valley opening out in the east to the larger Sokher Valley.

The larger tectonic valleys of Samaria lie in the northern part of this downfold. Of note among them are the Sahl Arraba (Dotan Vale, mentioned in the Bible as the site where Joseph was sold by his brothers to the Midianites) and Marj Sanūr. A small valley, very deep and steep-sided, is that of Marj Lubbān (Levona) near the southern border of Samaria. The only interior rift valley paralleling the fold axis is that of Sahl Mūkhna (Mikhmetat), where the highway from Ramallah to Nablus runs.

* Mt. Gilboa belongs, structurally, to the tilted blocks of Galilee; it is therefore described in connection with these on p. 75.

The Levona Valley is a tectonic depression in southern Samaria

The fertile soil (terra rossa or rendzina) covering the valley grounds and many slopes of Samaria supports well-established farms based on traditional Mediterranean agriculture, e.g., wheat, olives, fruit, vines, and tending of sheep and goats. Villages are numerous, some of them quite large. Nablus (the Biblical Sichem) is the only urban center; the towns of Tul Karm and Jennīn lie on the outskirts of the region, in the Sharon and the Jezreel Valley, respectively.

View of the town of Nablus, with Mount Gerizim in the background

The Irron Hills. This rectangular upfold region, lying between the Nablus and Menashe synclines, borders on the Sharon Plain in the southwest and the Jezreel Valley in the northeast. It resembles Mount Carmel in origin, as both are uplifted as horsts to a present post-erosive 500 m (1,640 ft), both have limestones and dolomites along with patches of Cretaceous basalts and tuffs, and both mostly dark terra rossa soil. About half of the Irron Hills is drained toward the Coastal Plain, and the rest, by streams joining Naḥal Qishon in the Jezreel Valley. The pre-1967 border crossed these hills from southwest to northeast.

The Irron Vale, through which runs a vital section of the age-old thoroughfare known as 'Via Maris,' marks the limit between the Irron Hills and the Menashe Region. To the traveller the terrain affords a living lesson in geology; the little brook on the valley ground sharply defines the lines between the southeast limestones and lighter-colored chalk of the northwest. Tiny tributaries,

At Yoqne'am, the Menashe Hills border on the Jezreel Valley (right) and Mount Carmel (left). The peak on the upper left is Qeren ha-Karmel; in the upper right, the narrow Qishon outlet toward the Zebulon Valley is visible between Mt. Carmel and the Tiv'on Hills

descending from both sides, have built small alluvial fans around which Naḥal Irron curves; these are composed of terra rossa on one bank, and of light gray rendzina on the other.

The Menashe Region. This area extends from the Irron Vale in the southeast to the Naḥal Yoqne'am Valley in the northwest, where, bordering on Mount Carmel, it forms, like the Irron Hills, a quadrangle on the map. Lower than the neighboring upfolds, with an average altitude of 200 m (650 ft), and only a few points 300 m (1,000 ft) high, it presents an elevated plateau between the Coastal Plain and the Jezreel Valley. Most of it is nearly flat, except its eastern corner, which passes into rolling hills. The distribution of rock strata on the surface confirms the synclinal structure of the region: most of them are Eocene, with Senonian on the outskirts and a small patch of younger Oligocene in the center. Rendzina soil, blackened by organic matter in low-lying parts, covers most of the plateau.

The 'corridor' of the Menashe Region, between Mount Carmel and the Irron Hills, is open to the sea winds and produces a draft effect. Precipitation therefore attains higher values (600–700 mm, or 24–28 in) than might be expected of its low altitude.

Mount Carmel. This is an uplifted block forming a triangle whose base line, 32 km (20 miles) long, borders on the Carmel Coast in the west; its apex, Qeren ha-Karmel, protrudes into the Jezreel Valley in the southeast; its greatest width amounts to 14 km (9 miles). The southern 'nose' of the Carmel is wedged in between the Carmel Coast and the northeastern corner of the Sharon Plain; on it is the large village and summer resort of Zikhron Ya'aqov. The highest elevations of Mount Carmel are those nearest to the fault escarpment which dominates the Jezreel and Zebulon valleys; these are Rom ha-Karmel, 546 m (1,792 ft) above sea level, Har Allon, 515 m (1,690 ft), and Qeren ha-Karmel, 482 m (1,581 ft), traditionally held to be the site of the Prophet Elijah's contest with the priests of Baal.

Mount Carmel, originally a simple upfold, rose later as a horst between fault lines. The northeastern fault escarpment is the most spectacular; the western one is now covered by the alluvium of the Carmel Coast. The rock wall on this side has receded a few hundred yards by degradation, yet maintains its near-vertical slope. Least visible is the southeastern fault which runs along the Naḥal Yoqne'am Valley and the rim of the Menashe Plateau.

It is not known whether Mount Carmel was covered by younger strata at any time in the geologic past. All present surface rocks are Cenomanian, most of them limestones and dolomites strongly affected by karst weathering, with a few patches of basalts and tuffs which some geologists believe erupted from submarine volcanoes.

Two shallow depressions on the hill crest, both running obverse to the fold axis and parallel to the northeastern fault, are filled with terra rossa and are the main farming area of the two Druze villages 'Isfiya and Daliyat al-Karmil.

Water courses have created picturesque narrow gorges on Mount Carmel. The longest wadis run from the edge of the northeast escarpment to the west, e.g., Naḥal Daliya, Naḥal Me'arot, Naḥal Oren, etc. Naḥal Gibborim, its bed overshadowed by precipitous rock walls, is the only stream to run from the hilltop directly into Haifa Bay. This canyonlike gorge, like others cut into the northeast escarpment by tributaries of Naḥal Qishon, is filled with boulders which have been carried down by floods with devastating force and deposited at the foot of the mountain in the Zebulon Valley.

The numerous karstic caves of Mount Carmel have repeatedly played an important role in human prehistory and history. Some of them (in the Me'arot and Oren gorges) sheltered man in the Paleolithic and Neolithic eras; others, like the Prophet Elijah's Cave near Haifa, have become part of Jewish, Christian and Arab folklore.

Since ancient times, Mount Carmel has also been famous for its verdant plant cover; the fairly abundant precipitation aids the preservation of the natural Mediterranean hill-type vegetation, which is better developed here than in most other parts of the country. Large parts of wood-covered Mount Carmel have been declared a nature reserve.

Besides the city of Haifa in the northwestern corner of Mount Carmel, there are two large villages inhabited by members of the Druze community and several Jewish settlements.

Galilee

All borders of the hill regions of Galilee are clearly outlined. In the west, Galilee meets the northern portion of the Coastal Plain (Zebulon, Acre, Tyre valleys); the large outbranching of the Rift (Ḥarod, Jezreel valleys) marks the southern border of Galilee; in the north it is delimited by the gorge of the Litani River; and in the east, by the Rift.

There is a traditional distinction between Lower and Upper Galilee. Differences of altitude, climate and vegetation justify this division. No height in Lower Galilee exceeds 600 m (2,000 ft)—greatest elevations are Mount Kamon, 598 m (1,962 ft); Mount Ḥazon, 584 m (1,916 ft); Mt. Tabor, 588 m (1,929 ft); Mt. Aẓmon, 548 m (1,798 ft); and Giv'at ha-More, 515 m (1,690 ft)—while in Upper

Galilee mountain tops attain double the height: Mt. Meron, the highest elevation inside Israel's former borders, rises to 1,208 m (3,963 ft); it is surrounded by Mt. Shammay, 1,071 m (3,514 ft); Mt. ha-Ari, 1047 m (3,453 ft); Mt. Addir, 1,006 m (3,301 ft), and others.

Upper and Lower Galilee are clearly divided by the almost straight Bet ha-Kerem Valley, and the deep gorge of the Ammud Stream.

As mentioned above, Galilee's present-day topography has been decisively determined by faulting and uplifting of tilted blocks in the Pliocene and Pleistocene. Prior to this development, and later along with it, came the gradual subsidence of the great Rift. In this latitude it is supposed to have begun as a broad and shallow basin filled with water, dubbed by geologists 'the Eastern Galilee Lake'; it covered not only the area of the present Lake Kinneret, but also large portions of Eastern Lower Galilee and Western Golan. Fossil evidence in the soft chalk deposits led to the assumption that this lake held alternately sweet and brackish water; for a short interval it may even have had direct connection with the ocean.

When Galilee was uplifted during the Miocene and Pliocene, the Eastern Galilee Lake contracted, retreating into the deepening Rift. A further stage in tectonic movements caused strong faulting and the tilting of two block series. In Western Galilee, pressure came from the north; therefore, the abrupt fault scarps face south, while mostly gentler slopes descend north.

The opposite is true of Eastern Galilee: there, pressure was exerted from the southwest, the fault scarps turned northeast and the blocks dipped south-southwest at a small angle. Between these two block series a spinelike, narrow strip relatively little affected by faulting runs from Mount Tabor northward through Eilabūn and Parod. An additional element of difference between the two series is the result of strong volcanic activity in the east. Lava which issued from fissures and craters covered most of Eastern Lower Galilee and smaller portions of Eastern Upper Galilee with a layer of tuffs and hard basalts, the latter protecting the soft Neogene chalk underneath from erosion.

Both volcanic and Neogene lacustrine and marine rocks are absent in Western Galilee, where Cenomanian and Turonian limestones and dolomites prevail. As blocks in Western Galilee not only tilt north, but also dip west, younger rocks, Senonian and Eocene, have been preserved at their least-exposed western extremities. At the foot of the fault scarps, rocks of the Lower Cenomanian and, at some sites, also of the Lower Cretaceous appear. The latter are composed predominantly of chalk and contain low-grade iron ores.

In Western Galilee the tilted block formations show clearly on the map. The southernmost scarp is that of the Nazareth Ridge, which dominates the Jezreel Valley and confronts Mount Carmel and the Menashe Region in the south.

The Bet Netofa Valley in Lower Galilee, an alluvium-covered graben, is often flooded after the winter rains

Erosion, by cutting gorges into this scarp, has isolated some sections of it, such as Har Qedumim near Nazareth (Mount of the Ancients, as skeletons of prehistoric man have been found in a cave; Christian tradition calls it 'Mount of the Leap' and views it as the site where Jesus escaped his persecutors). The Nazareth Ridge descends northward to the small Tir'an Vale. Beyond it rises Mount Tir'an, a horst rather than a tilted block. A fault runs at its south side as well as north of it, where the Bet Netofa Valley is sunken as an alluvium-covered graben between Mount Tir'an and the scarp of the next ridge, the Yodfat Hill Chain. The Yodfat Hills dip north to the Sakhnin Valley which, in turn, is separated from the Bet ha-Kerem Valley and Upper Galilee by the narrow Shezor Ridge.

The eastern series of Lower Galilee commences, in effect, in the south with Mount Gilboa, which attains 500 m (1,640 ft) above sea level, i.e., 600–800 m (2,000–2,500 ft) above the deeply-embedded rifts of the Ḥarod and Bet She'an valleys at its sides. North of the Ḥarod Valley rise Giv'at ha-More and the low Ẓeva'im Ridge, which is delimited further north by Naḥal Yisakhar. Ramat Kokhav and Ramat Tavor stretch north-northeast, two basalt-covered plateaus separated from each other by the Naḥal Tavor gorge. The next fault scarp drops to the Yavne'el Valley, which is an outbranching of the Jordan Rift lying partly below sea level. The Poriya Ridge, separating the Yavne'el Valley from the Sea of Galilee, rises in the east. Since the blocks situated north and northeast of the Yavne'el Valley (Ḥittim Ridge and Vale, Arbel, etc.) grow smaller and more steeply tilted, this part of Galilee has a more mountainous character than the southeast portion. Above the Ḥittim Vale rise Qarne Ḥittim, 'the Horns of Ḥittim,' one of the few identifiable extinct volcanic craters west of the Jordan. In the crater depression lie the ruins of an ancient synagogue; near the hill is Nebi

Scene of the Bet ha-Kerem Valley, between Lower and Upper Galilee. Mount Ḥaluẓ, whose ridge appears in the background, is a huge tilted block

Shu'eib, the shrine of the Druze faith in this country. Qarne Ḥittim was the site of the battle between Saladdin and the Crusaders in 1187. Northeast of the Ammud Gorge further small blocks may be hidden beneath a thick Pleistocene basalt cover.

Upper Galilee. Faulting and tilting have thrown Upper Galilee into stronger relief than Lower Galilee. The landscape picture is complicated even more by the fact that the east-west faults are crossed by others which run southeast-northwest, or in other directions. Since some small blocks have been uplifted and others have subsided between these fractures, a maze of valleys, gorges, basins, ridges, and isolated peaks has been created.

Mount Ḥaluẓ with its imposing scarp face rises 1,000 m (3,280 ft) high north of the Bet ha-Kerem Valley (along which runs the Acre-Safed highway). At its eastern end it joins the massif of Mount Meron and the surrounding hill tops. The beautiful, rounded Mt. Addir, north of this block, is isolated.

North of the precipitous Ḥaluẓ escarpment we find narrow ridges and small peaks, gorges, and basins, thrown further into relief by stream erosion. The dramatic gorge of Naḥal Keziv, its slopes covered with dense brush, with the famous Crusader fortress ruin of Montfort standing guard, cuts in its middle section diagonally through the west-east ridges. Most of the surface rock in this part of Galilee is hard Cenomanian limestone. The karst topography results from the fairly humid climate. Soft Senonian chalk has been preserved in small basins like that of Meona; some flat-topped table mounts of this rock form a curious contrast to the surrounding landscape.

The Israel-Lebanon border is drawn, in its westernmost section, along the crest of the Ḥanita Ridge which protrudes into the sea with the white rocks of Cape Rosh ha-Niqra (the 'Tyrian Ladder') and broadens further east into the small Adamit Plateau. This ridge drops southward steeply, and descends gently to the north and northwest. In that part of the Western Galilee which is included within the borders of Lebanon, the ridges and stream-cut gorges and valleys are mostly directed southeast-northwest (a recent theory assumes this direction to be due to pressure exerted by the rising anticline of Mount Ḥermon further east). Since antiquity, many hills, isolated by surrounding vales, have borne villages on their tops, the location chosen for security reasons.

The picture in Eastern Upper Galilee is even more complex. The Safed Block is separated from Mount Meron by the deep gorge of Naḥal Meron, which runs south. The Safed Block seems to have been less uplifted, and therefore less eroded, than its neighbor; its surface rocks are Eocene and Senonian limestones and not the harder Cenomanian rocks. Still the Safed Block rises to a considerable height; Mount Canaan at its eastern rim attains 955 m (3,133 ft) above sea level.

North of the Safed Block lie, steplike, the two small basaltic plateaus of Dalton (elevation 800–900 m or 2,700–2,950 ft) and Alma (about 700 m or 2,300 ft). The deep Dishon Gorge circles the Alma Plateau in the north and northeast. Naḥal Dishon is fed by springs rising in its bed, and it thus flows during most of the year; the verdant vegetation along the stream lends the wild landscape additional charm.

Beyond the Dishon Gorge to the northeast lies the small, round basin of Qedesh Naftali, surrounded by hills and ridges. It has a thick cover of black, alluvial soil. Its lowest point is 380 m (1,250 ft) above sea level. In some winters, rainwater that has been incompletely drained off by streams remains standing for months in puddles and small lakes over parts of the basin.

View from Safed northwestward to Mt. Meron. Behind it rises rounded Mt. Addir

The Naftali Ridge runs from the Qedesh Naftali Basin northward. Its strong uplift is related to the subsidence of the Ḥula Valley at its side, and reaches 880 m (2,887 ft) in Mount Pe'er near Kibbutz Menara. The scarp confronting the Ḥula Valley is a sheer wall up to 800 m (2,600 ft) high, although geologically it is a series of faults; ancient chalks of the Lower Cretaceous, containing the iron ore of Menara, thus confront the Eocene coral limestones quarried under the name 'Metulla marble.'

The Naftali Ridge descends in the west (in Lebanese territory) to Wadi Dubbe which flows due north to join the Litani River.

Settlement: Nazareth is the principal center of Lower Galilee; Safed—of Upper Galilee. Karmiel and Ma'alot are new towns being built under the integrated development plan for the Hills of Galilee.

The economy of the villages is based on tobacco, olives, vines, deciduous fruits, etc., adapted to the hilly terrain and to local climate. Grain is grown on the plateaus of Eastern Galilee. Israel's minority groups (Arab Moslems, Druzes,

Christians of various denominations, Circassians) live principally in parts of this region. In Galilee, Jews are to be found in Safed, Upper Nazareth, in the new development towns and in many villages.

Mount Meron

The Jordan Rift and Its Branches

The great Rift of the Jordan, the Dead Sea and the Arava Valley, which runs the length of the country from north to south and divides it into Cisjordan and Transjordan, is a relatively small section of the giant Syrian-East African Rift. This Rift, one of the longest and deepest scars in the earth's rock crust, reaches the Turkish province of Hatay (Antiochia) in the north, where it touches on Mount Amanos. It runs between the Ansarīya (Alaoui) Mountains and the Zaouie Hills of Syria and, further south, separates the Lebanon Mountains from the Anti-Lebanon Block. In Israel it is divided into five sections: the Upper Jordan (Ḥula Valley), the Middle Jordan (Lake Kinneret, the valleys surrounding it, and the Bet She'an Valley), the Lower Jordan, the Dead Sea, and the Arava Valley.

The Eilat Gulf and the Red Sea continue the Rift southward. Near the southern outlet of the Red Sea, at the Bab al Mandeb Straits, the Rift splits; its eastern branch separates the Arabian Peninsula from the 'Horn' of Africa, and its western branch enters Africa. The latter forks again and contains most of the elongated East African lakes (Tanganyika, Rudolf, Albert, Nyasa, etc.). The overall length of the Rift exceeds 6,500 km (4,000 miles).

The Rift is not a true 'graben' in all of its section, i.e., not accompanied by fault lines on both its sides. In Western Syria, for example, a fault can be traced only west of the Rift. In other sections not only one but several faults parallel the Rift on each side. There are also stretches where the Rift's continuity is hardly recognizable, as in the Jebel Dhahr of Lebanon which, at Baalbek, forms the watershed between the Orontes and Leontes rivers; or in the Metulla Hills which separate the Iyyon Valley in Lebanon from the Ḥula Valley in Israel. The Rift also sends out branch valleys to both sides. Some of them, such as the Ḥarod and Jezreel valleys, are directly connected with it, and others, such as the Zebulon Valley, are separated from it by hill ridges. In our country most western Rift

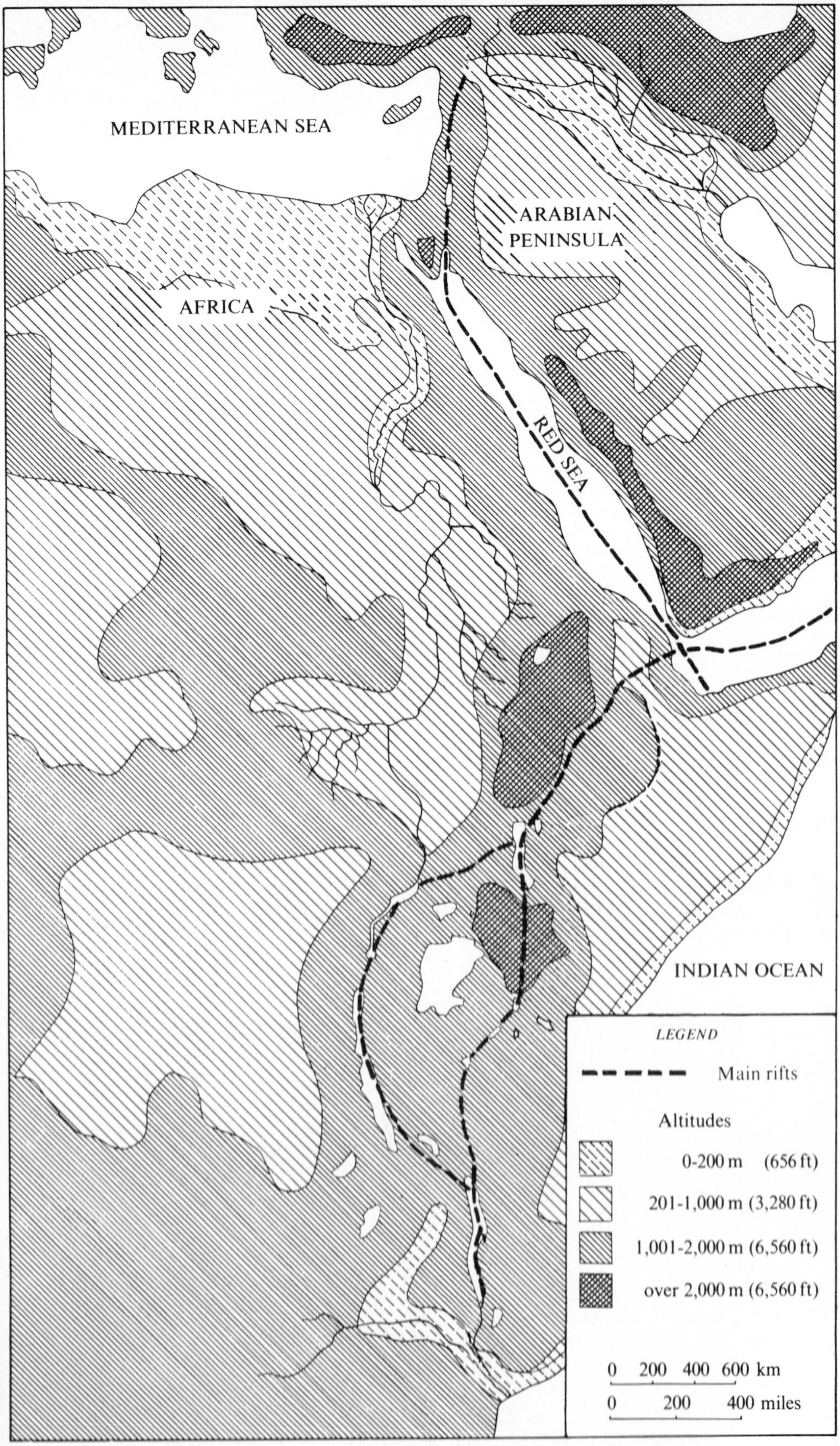

The Syrian–East African Rift

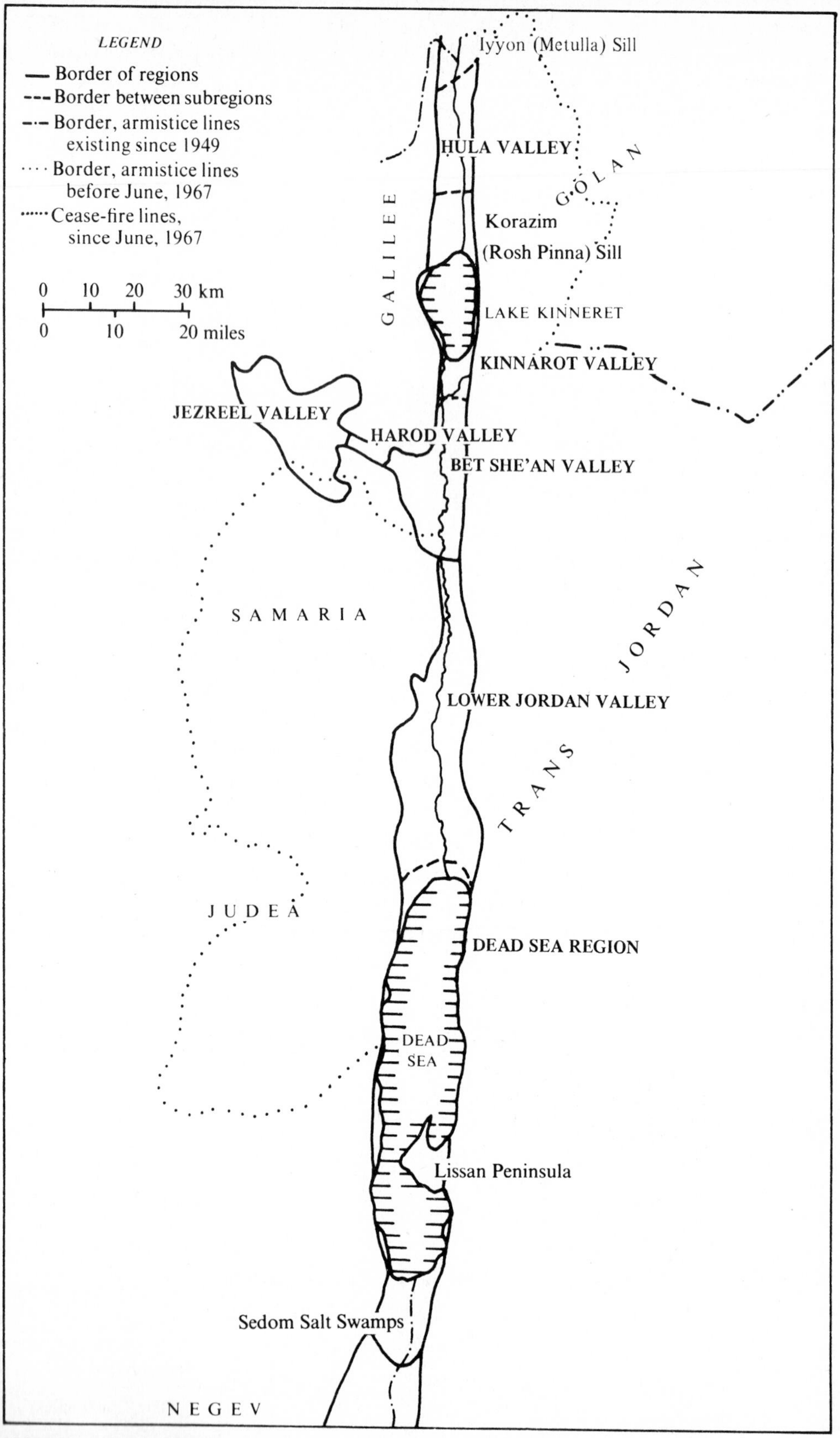

Subregions of the Rift in Israel, from the Ḥula to the northern Arava Valley

branches are directed northwest, the eastern ones, northeast. Not all sections of the Rift bottom subsided to equal depth, so that lakes and swamps were formed in some portions and further differences resulted in local topographic and climatic features, and, therewith, in conditions for settlement.

Geologists assume that the first signs of subsidence in the Rift area appeared in the Cretaceous. In its first stages the Rift seems to have been a very shallow basin. With the subsequent uplift, folding, and horizontal displacement movements of the Miocene, tension became stronger until the crust began to break and an actual rift to be outlined, although at that time it was a series of broad, not very deep, and perhaps often disconnected basins. In the late Miocene and early Pliocene, a lake spread in what is now the Middle Jordan Valley; it covered parts of Lower Galilee and the Lower Golan. At its bottom, lacustrine chalks and marls were deposited.

Only when faulting was intensified, toward the end of the Pliocene and in the Pleistocene, did the Rift approach its present morphology as the valley's bottom continued to subside while its rims were further uplifted. The sinking of the bottom was accelerated by the weight of the alluvium deposited by the streams; horst mountains rose at the sides, some, like Mount Ḥermon, to a great height. On the basis of geophysical tests in the Dead Sea region, unconsolidated alluvium over the bedrock is estimated to be—at some spots—a minimum of 7,000 m (23,000 ft) thick. Recently, geologists have come to the conclusion that horizontal movements may have been decisive in the creation of the Rift when Transjordan was shoved northward, probably over a distance of 40 km (25 miles).

The 'younger' faulting movements were accompanied by earthquakes and volcanic eruptions on both sides of the Rift. The seismic character of the Rift and the adjacent area is corroborated, especially in and around Lake Kinneret and the Dead Sea, by numerous hot mineral springs. These rise through rock crevices from a great depth, and become enriched on their way with dissolved sulfur, magnesia, bromine, iodine, radioactive and other salts. Although no volcanic activity occurs now, earthquakes (more common in the hills and plateaus at both sides than in the Rift itself) still testify to continued tectonic activity.

The Upper Jordan Valley

The Upper Jordan Valley has three subregions: the Ḥula Basin, the Rosh Pinna Sill, and the narrow Jordan Gorge east of it.

The Ḥula Basin is almost completely hemmed in by hills and mountains. The Naftali Chain of Upper Galilee in the west rises to a height of 800 m (2,600 ft) and more above the valley's bottom; at a small distance eastward the Upper Golan

Plateau attains more than 1,000 m (3,300 ft); the mighty massif of Mount Ḥermon, towering in the north (up to 2,814 m or 9,232 ft above sea level) is connected with the Basin's western rim by the Metulla Hills (about 500 m or 1,650 ft high); in the south, finally, the Rosh Pinna Sill, 100–200 m (320–650 ft) higher than the Basin, separates it from the southern continuation of the Rift.

On the western fault escarpment relatively ancient rocks are exposed—Cenomanian limestones and Lower Cretaceous limestones and chalks; near Kefar Gil'adi, in a secondary depression, conglomerates and coral limestones of the Eocene, as well as Neogene sediments, are preserved. Mount Ḥermon has Jurassic limestone. On the rim of the Golan Plateau, all older rocks are hidden by a thick basalt cover. In the valley, in the municipal area of Qiryat Shemona, lava has welled up through one or more crevices and consolidated into a chain of low, narrow, steep-sided basalt hills.

The Ḥula Valley measures 25 km (15½ miles) from north to south and 6–8 km (4–6 miles) from west to east. Its area amounts to 177 sq.km (68 sq. miles). The surface of the former Lake Ḥula lay 71 m (220 ft) above sea level. The valley bottom rises imperceptibly from south to north, with large, almost flat portions. The angle only steepens near the northern rim, where the villages of Dan and Dafna lie at 170 m (525 ft) above sea level.

Findings in a well bored in the area of the former Ḥula Swamps prove that the southern outlet of the valley, toward Lake Kinneret, must have been blocked at least twice in the geologic past. The valley thus twice became a closed basin containing a lake. The uppermost layer in the well hole, about 10 m (33 ft) thick, is peat; below it appears a stratum of lacustrine chalk, about 30 m (100 ft) thick; beneath that, to a depth of 100 m (330 ft) is a second peat layer, again resting on chalk. Geologic history can hence be reconstructed as follows: in the Pliocene, lava flows in the south, consolidating into basalt, created the Rosh Pinna Sill and dammed up the water in the valley. A lake spread over large parts of the valley ground, depositing the lower chalk layer at its bottom. The lake's water level rose until it reached the lowest point in the basalt barrier. A new outlet for the lake water was thus created, gradually eroded, broadened and deepened by the water flow. This caused the water level in the lake to drop again. The lake contracted and became shallower. Where its maximum depth was 2 m (6½ ft), swamp vegetation—papyrus and other reeds, nenuphars, water lilies, etc.—could take root. These annual plants, each autumn sinking into the lake water and rotting, formed peat. This continued until the Pleistocene, when the southern outlet was again sealed by a lava flow; the process was thus repeated and two more layers, of chalk and peat respectively, were deposited. This theory is also borne out by two lake terraces near the northern rim of the valley which indicate the largest extent of the two former water bodies.

Naḥal Senir is one of the main headstreams of the Jordan. In rainy winters, it carries huge amounts of water

Ample precipitation in the regions surrounding the Ḥula Basin to the north, west, and east (900 mm or 36 in annually on the Naftali Ridge, 1,000 mm or 40 in on the Golan Plateau, and up to 1,500 mm or 60 in on Mount Ḥermon) provides an abundant flow of water into the Basin, partly in the form of surface runoff to the streams and rivers, most of which carry water the year round, and partly in the form of strong springs, fed by rainwater seepage into porous rocks, which rise at the valley's rim. Besides the Jordan's headsprings, the strongest group is that of Enot Enan, yielding between 1,800 and 2,700 m^3 per hour. Total inflow into the Ḥula Basin is estimated at 740 million m^3 annually.

The three headstreams coming from the north and uniting into the Jordan are Naḥal Ḥermon (Wadi Banias), Naḥal Dan, and Naḥal Senir (Wadi Ḥasbani).

Naḥal Ḥermon, which rises at the northeast corner of the valley, near the village of Banias where it flows forth from a high rock wall, was dedicated, together with the surrounding grove of tall trees, as a Hellenistic sanctuary to the god Pan and thus called Panaeas. At the former frontier there is a beautiful waterfall divided by an ancient oak tree growing in its midst. Naḥal Ḥermon rushes southwest where it unites first with the Dan and later with the Senir, near Kibbutz Sede Neḥemya. The Dan Spring emerges on the northern frontier at the foot of Mount Ḥermon, where it forms a crystal-clear pond; its waters, fed by melting mountain snow, are ice-cold even in midsummer. Naḥal Dan flows south in a series of small waterfalls. A part of the stream has been diverted into the ponds and swimming pools of Ḥurshat Tal Park. Naḥal Senir is the longest of the three headstreams. Its spring rises on the northwest slope of Mount Ḥermon in Lebanon, 52 km (32 miles) northeast of Metulla. It enters the Ḥula Valley proper near the frontier of Israel with Lebanon. Inside the valley, Naḥal Senir flows another 6.5 km (4 miles) to the point where the Jordan itself is formed. In contrast to the Dan and Ḥermon streams, most of the Senir water is surface runoff; its flow therefore vacillates: it is strongly reduced in summer, but floods in winter. There are also large differences between dry and wet years: while its average annual flow amounts to 117 million m^3, a maximum of 235 million m^3 was measured in 1948/49. The average flow of Naḥal Dan is given as 252 million m^3, and that of Naḥal Ḥermon—as 122 m^3.*

A fourth stream is Naḥal Iyyon which, before the Ḥula Drainage Scheme was effected, did not unite with the other water courses and reached the Ḥula Swamps on its own. This stream drains the 'Ayūn (Iyyon) Valley in Lebanon and descends into the Ḥula Valley in a high waterfall called 'Tannur.' In winter Naḥal Iyyon carries much water and causes floods; in summer, diverted for irrigation by the peasants of the Iyyon Valley, it frequently dries up in the Ḥula Valley.

Naḥal Qallil, which collects the waters of several short streams descending from the Golan Plateau, runs in the eastern part of the Ḥula Valley; part of its course has disappeared with the Ḥula Drainage Scheme.

The surface streams rushing down the steep sides of the valley carry great amounts of erosional material. Upon reaching the flat valley ground their tractive force diminishes at once and the alluvium is deposited. The extent of this process may be gauged from the remains of a settlement of the late Byzantine and early Arab eras (i.e., 7th–8th cent. C.E.) found buried under an alluvial soil cover 4 m (13 ft) thick. Most of the alluvium is deposited in and near the stream courses; these are thus elevated above the surrounding terrain instead of flowing naturally at the lowest level of the valley. This raises the groundwater horizon in the

*Figures by D. Ashbel.

The Ḥula swamps and lake, before their drainage, covered with yellow nenuphars and other aquatic vegetation

In the Ḥula Valley today. Carp ponds, fruit orchards and other intensive crops have taken the place of the former swamps

adjoining fields close to the surface, creating problems in the growing of deep-rooted fruit trees and other perennial plants; the roots would rot in the water. When the streams overflowed after winter rains, they immediately flooded large expanses and caused extensive damage.

Alluvium also settled near where the Jordan leaves the Ḥula Basin in the south. The alluvial deposits obstructed the outlet and slowed the natural process of deepening the watercourse and emptying the Ḥula Lake and swamps.

The necessity for the two major stages in the Ḥula Drainage Scheme (carried out between 1951 and 1958) can thus be easily understood: deepening, widening, and straightening of the Jordan's course south of the Ḥula Valley to lower the water level of the lake and swamps, and the construction of artificial new watercourses—along the lowest levels inside the valley to lower the groundwater horizon and prevent disastrous floods. The 'Northern Canal,' by connecting the other two, regulates the water flow. The Northern Canal also isolates the peat south of it. An underground conflagration in the peat is liable to spread there in the dry summer and burn for months; to prevent this danger, the canal can be opened to flood the peat. A network of secondary drainage canals and irrigation installations also belong to the scheme. A total of about 15,000 acres* of excellent soil has been won from the former lake and swamps, and another 15,000 acres have been ameliorated through lowering of the groundwater horizon. At the southwestern corner of the former swamps, a 700-acre nature reserve has been marked off as an example of the former colorful, near-tropical flora and fauna.

The alluvial soil of the Ḥula Valley is dark, heavy, deep, and rich in organic matter. Even richer is the peat soil of the former swamps.

Four miles south of the Jordan's outlet from former Lake Ḥula, the watercourse deepens and thus forms a narrow gorge; basalt escarpments on both sides attain a height of 100 m (300 ft). Here, the Jordan drops 270 m (850 ft) over a distance of only 14.5 km (9 miles); its erosional power is therefore considerable, even in rocks as hard as basalt.

The urban center of the Ḥula Valley is Qiryat Shemona, many of whose citizens are employed in the fields and the factories of the numerous collective and smallholders' settlements in the valley and on its outskirts.

The Central Jordan Valley

Lake Kinneret and Surroundings. This valley must again be subdivided into four—Lake Kinneret (the Sea of Galilee, also Lake Tiberias), the Bethsaida

* One acre = 0.45 hectares.

(Buteḥa) Valley at its northeast corner, the Ginnesar Valley in the northwest, and the Jordan-Yarmuk Plain in the south. South of the Ginnesar Valley the hills of Lower Galilee are separated from the lake by a level strip which at some places where it is only a few meters wide barely permits the passage of the highway. Similarly, the Golan slopes south of Bethsaida Valley in the east jut into the Lake, forming high cliffs of which the 'Kursi' ('Chair') is best known; from this point southward, a coastal strip between 100 meters and 1.6 km (1 mile) wide runs through En Gev and Ha-On to the southern end of the lake.

The Central Jordan Valley is widest (16 km—10 miles) in the north, between the Ginnesar and Bethsaida valleys; it gradually narrows southward until it is 7 km (4 miles) wide near Naḥal Tavor's inflow into the Jordan.

Lake Kinneret covers 165 sq. km (63.7 sq. miles). Its water surface varies, according to season and amounts of rainfall, between 209 and 214 m (684 and

View over the old part of Tiberias southward to Lake Kinneret. On the horizon—the rim of the Lower Golan Plateau

710 ft) below Mediterranean sea level. The deepest point of the lake bottom lies 254 m (833 ft) below the Mediterranean Sea.

Although the waters of the Jordan and of other streams emptying into it are fresh, the lake water is comparatively saline. The chlorine content vacillates between 250 and 400 milligrams per liter; it rises in drought years and decreases after rainy winters. Mineral springs rising near the lake shore as well as on its bottom contribute to the salt content of the water. An additional factor is the strong evaporation from the surface, due to the warm and sunny climate. Since Lake Kinneret serves as the central storage body for the National Water Carrier, efforts are being made to divert the salt springs at the lake's bottom, thus to reduce the salinity of irrigation waters carried from here to the center and south of the country.

A number of streams draining Eastern Galilee enter the Sea of Galilee from the northwest, in the Ginnesar Valley; two, Naḥal Ammud and Naḥal Ẓalmon, carry water all year round, while Naḥal Arbel is an ephemeral stream. From the Golan to the Buteḥa Valley, four water-rich streams and some smaller wadis descend into the lake. Of the western tributaries of the Jordan after its outflow from the Sea of Galilee, Naḥal Yavne'el and Naḥal Tavor are important; their annual total water flow, however, is small. From the east comes the Yarmuk River which (until the diversion of practically all its waters to the Syrian and Jordanian irrigation schemes) almost equaled the Jordan in the amount of water it carried to the meeting point of the two.

It may be assumed that the Lake Kinneret Region was situated, in the Miocene and Pliocene, at the center of the ancient Eastern Galilee Lake, where chalks and soft limestones were deposited. A deepening of the Rift and contracting of the lake at the end of the Pliocene may have blocked the lake outlet and caused its waters to become saline. The sediments deposited changed in character; friable lissan marl and gypsum replaced the chalk.

In the recent geologic past the continued subsidence of the Rift seems to have been uneven. Whereas the bottom of present-day Lake Kinneret continued to sink, perhaps even at an accelerated rate, the area south of it remained stable or was even somewhat uplifted. The Jordan water flowing from the north was held up by the sill thus created, and only when the lake filled to overflowing did a new outlet open to the south and the lake waters freshen again.

The lake is thought to have begun as more or less a rectangle. The north shore was rounded off by the streams coming in from the northwest and northeast. These streams, which brought with them great quantities of alluvium, created the Ginnesar and Buteḥa valleys. The lake water pressing toward the outlet in the south, on the other hand, cut back the protruding edges of the shore, and thereby extended the lake southward. Thus, the lake received its characteristic pear-like

The Jordan-Yarmuk Plain south of Lake Kinneret, with the kibbutz Deganiya in the middle ground. In the background is the Transjordanian Plateau, where the Yarmuk Gorge divides between the Lower Golan (left) and the Gilead (right)

shape. Ancient commentators tried to explain the Hebrew name, 'Lake Kinneret,' as derived from 'kinnor,' a stringed instrument mentioned in the Bible. The process of shore erosion and lake extension continues in the south. This is made clear by the ruins of the ancient town of Bet Yeraḥ, which was situated on the high escarpment at the lake's southwestern corner. The buildings and fortifications of this Canaanite town which existed since the second millennium B.C.E. could be identified, but the section of its wall running along the lake shore is missing; the streets leading to the shore break off abruptly at the escarpment edge, and even house foundations have been cut in half there. The erosion of the outflowing water must have undercut the walls, and caused them to tumble down into the lake.

The soil map of the Sea of Galilee Region shows considerable variety. The Ginnesar and Buteḥa valleys have heavy alluvial soils, derived from limestone, chalks and basalts, and enriched with organic matter. In the south, between the Jordan and Yarmuk beds, lissan marl soil prevails, typical of the Jordan Valley between the Sea of Galilee and the Dead Sea, as well as of parts of the Arava Valley. Its name derived from the Lissan Peninsula of the Dead Sea, it originates in the chalky marl deposits on the bottom of the ancient 'Lissan Lake' of the recent geologic past. This soil is in general light-colored, gray to yellowish brown. It is crumbly and easy to till and, of all soils in the country, the richest in calcium (over 30%) and the poorest in silica. It is not very fertile inherently, but can easily be improved with organic and chemical fertilizers. The gypsum of Gesher and Menaḥemya west of the Jordan belongs to the same group of deposits.

The seismic character of this part of the Rift is borne out by numerous mineral and hot springs, among them those of Tiberias, Ḥammat Gader (al-Ḥamma) and Tabgha.* These springs have been famous since antiquity for their curative properties, and they give Tiberias its importance as a health resort today.

The town of Tiberias has, besides its recreation facilities, only small industries. Several of the rural communities of the region (such as Deganiya and Kinneret) play an outstanding role in the collective settlement movement. All engage in highly intensive farming that emphasizes out-of-season crops and tropical varieties like bananas and dates. En Gev, Ginnosar, etc., also work at lake fishing. Some villages, such as Afiqim and Ashdot Ya'aqov, have large factories of plywood, food preserves, etc.

The Bet She'an Valley. Its situation at the point of the Rift's largest ramification inside the country explains its special morphological features and its function in human history and settlement. In the north along Naḥal Tavor, it borders on the Kinneret Region; its southern limit is drawn where the Rift narrows to less than three miles in width between Samaria and the Gilead; the border between the Bet She'an Valley and the Ḥarod Valley in the west is not easy to define, while in the east, between Wadi 'Arab and Wadi Kafrīnje, the steep slopes of the Gilead Plateau form a sharp boundary.

In the Bet She'an Valley the Jordan receives many tributaries both from west and east; the most important on the western side is Naḥal Ḥarod, which, flowing the year round, draws most of its water from the strong Ḥarod Spring (owing to increased use of its waters for irrigation, the flow has in recent years been greatly reduced, particularly during the summer months). Flowing over the river terraces in the Bet She'an Valley, this stream bed is cut deeply into the soil and creates small waterfalls. Other streams on the west bank (Naḥal Tavor, Naḥal Yisakhar, Naḥal Bezeq, Wadi Māleḥ) flow ephemerally or, at best, have a trickle of water in summer. Several small streams fed by springs rising at the foot of Mount Gilboa do not reach the Jordan; in the recent past, their water was lost in the swamps, while today it is being used for irrigation and fish ponds.

From the Gilead Plateau in the east, important tributaries descend toward the Jordan, some of which carry water the year round along most of their length. The

* This Arabic name originates in the Greek 'Heptapegon' = 'Seven Springs.'

largest of them are Wadi 'Arab, Wadi Tāyyibe, Wadi Yābis (Naḥal Yavesh Gilead), and Wadi Kafrīnje.

As in the Jordan-Yarmuk Plain, the subsoil of the Bet She'an Valley is formed of friable, light-colored lissan marl. With the disappeareance of the ancient Jordan Lake, at whose bottom the marl was deposited, alluvium came to rest upon it but was later again partly eroded by the Jordan River. Two river terraces were thus created along the Central and Lower Jordan Valley; in the Bet She'an Valley, even a third, higher terrace becomes noticeable.

Terraces are typical of rivers whose flow velocity was subject to changes in the course of time. In periods of the recent geologic past, when the water level of the Dead Sea was higher than it is today, the Jordan had a smaller gradient. Because its flow must then have been sluggish, the river meandered over the entire width of the Rift Valley, where it deposited its surplus load and built a thick alluvial cover. When the erosional base level of the Dead Sea was lowered, the Jordan flow velocity increased. This straightened the river's course and cut a lower terrace into the alluvium previously laid down. This lower terrace was widened again as new meanders began to form and the river bends gnawed at the upper terrace rim. Geomorphologists are intrigued by the cause of meander formations by the Jordan in the past and present, as its gradient must always have been steeper than that of most meandering rivers: over a distance of 105 km (65 miles)—as the crow flies—it drops approximately 200 m (650 ft).

From the Bet She'an Valley southward, the lower Jordan River meanders on the lowest flood terrace which is frequently flooded and therefore covered with vegetation. The bare marl hills of the higher terrace appear in the background

The lowest terrace, where the Jordan bed meanders today, is frequently flooded by its water in winter and spring. This terrace therefore has enough moisture to permit the growth of a dense tropical and subtropical brush which sharply contrasts with the parched higher terrace. True, the arid character of the latter is obscured in the Bet She'an Valley by the waters of the many springs flowing over it from sources at the foot of Mount Gilboa. This valley clearly shows the influence, positive or negative, exerted by man throughout history upon its landscape; while a civilized population lived there, the waters were used to irrigate fields, orchards and gardens; when the population lacked technical knowledge or when, as in the Byzantine defense against the Moslem onslaught in the 7th century C.E., the canals were wilfully destroyed, the water became stagnant and formed malaria swamps.

Most of the Bet She'an Valley is today under cultivation, and malaria has disappeared.

The highest terrace of the Bet She'an Valley, forming the transition zone to the Ḥarod Valley, is thought to have originated in the springs rising in it. These waters are saturated with calcareous matter; when they reach the surface and partly evaporate, the material is deposited as soft travertine. The kidney-shaped travertine sediments are visible at the Gan ha-Shelosha (Sakhna) Pool, which today is a nature reserve. In addition, marls have remained from lakes which spread in the past, and alluvial fans can be found at the foot of Mount Gilboa.

The Jordan bed is 260 m (850 ft) below Mediterranean sea level in the north of the Bet She'an Valley, and descends to 300 m (985 ft) in the south. The second terrace rises 10–40 m (30–120 ft) above the Jordan, while the travertine terrace reaches 40 m (120 ft) higher than the second. The town of Bet She'an, with its center 160 m (525 ft) below sea level, lies near the scarp between these two terraces.

The town of Bet She'an has in recent years been industrialized. The rural settlements, mostly collective, engage in highly intensive farming (cotton, grain, fodder, date palms, pomegranates, fishponds, etc.), and in industrial enterprises.

The Valleys of Ḥarod and Jezreel

In contrast to other western branches of the Rift, which should be regarded as parts of the hill regions where they lie (e.g., the Yavne'el Valley and Naḥal Tavor Gorge in Lower Galilee, or the Buqei'a and Farī'a valleys of Samaria), the valleys of Ḥarod and Jezreel form a separate geographical unit.

The Ḥarod Valley. This valley belongs, morphologically, to two different regions. It is part of the tilted block series of Eastern Galilee (see p. 75) and, at the same

Mount Gilboa, rising with a sharp fault scarp over the Ḥarod Valley, bears the typical features of an uplifted block

time, separates Samaria from Galilee and links the Rift and the Jezreel Valley. It is a transition zone between the two in soils, climate, and settlement conditions.

On the map the Ḥarod Valley is a corridor, 18 km (11 miles) long and not more than 5 km (3 miles) wide, between Mount Gilboa in the south and the low Ẓeva'im Ridge in the north. It descends from about 40 m (120 ft) above sea level in the northwest to 115 m (380 ft) below sea level in the southeast. It is not altogether clear whether the Ḥarod Valley is a true graben, or only the sunken part of a tilted block covered with alluvium. The former would be definite if a fault, paralleling the southern one at the foot of Mount Gilboa, were identified on the north side of the valley; the cover of alluvium and Pleistocene basalt makes that identification difficult.

The erosional material carried down from the basalt and chalk rocks in the north and the limestones and chalks in the south has built up a layer of good soil, enriched by the organic swamp matter which spread here up to a generation ago. The valley is also blessed with water from the strong Ḥarod Spring which flows through Naḥal Ḥarod to the Jordan, as well as from an ample groundwater horizon whence it is pumped up in wells.

The former Ḥarod Valley swamps are thought by some to have been formed by alluvium deposited by small tributaries in the middle course of Naḥal Ḥarod. The alluvium impeded the water flow down the Bet She'an river terraces; the Ḥarod Spring water could not overcome this obstacle, and this caused the swamps to spread.

Today, the landscape of the Ḥarod Valley has been thoroughly transformed, with villages perched on its north and south sides, and the valley ground a mosaic of fields, gardens, orchards, of water storage and fish ponds.

The Jezreel Valley. The Jezreel Valley is triangular, with its base in the north at the foot of the Nazareth Ridge and its apex near the town of Jennīn (in Judea-Samaria) in the south. In the west the low Shefar'am Hills separate it from the Zebulon Valley. In the southwest the Jezreel Valley borders on Mount Carmel, the Menashe Region, and the Irron Hills of Samaria, and in the east it borders on the western edge of the Gilboa Block, the Ḥarod Valley, Giv'at ha-More, and Mount Tabor; two tongues of the valley thrust northeast, the Davrat Vale south of Mount Tabor and the Kesullot Vale on its north side. The slightly undulating ground of the Jezreel Valley lies 20–50 m (60–160 ft) above sea level.

The subsidence of the Jezreel Valley apparently took place in stages more or less parallel to those of the opening of the Jordan Rift. As a result of this subsidence, upfolds created earlier seem to have been broken apart. It is assumed, for instance, that Mount Tabor represents the northeastern extremity of the Irron Anticline, was isolated from it when the Jezreel Valley sank down between faults, and only later was eroded to its characteristic, rounded form. In the geologic past, portions of the valley may have been covered temporarily by the waters of the ancient Eastern Galilee Lake. For a shorter interval the Rift lakes possibly had access to the sea through the Jezreel Valley.

The faulting on the valley rims was accompanied by minor volcanic eruptions which left small patches of basalt (e.g., near Mishmar ha-Emeq, Ginnegar, Sarid, etc.).

The center of the Jezreel Valley subsided to a considerable depth and is thickly covered by alluvium. Hence, there is little chance to reach the groundwater horizon in the center while at the outskirts (Tel Adashim, Yoqne'am, Ginnegar, etc.) the water is trapped where the porous rocks of the surrounding hills meet the impermeable alluvial soil, and wells there have an abundant yield.

The soil of the Jezreel Valley is throughout dark, heavy, and rich in organic matter, due to the swamps which existed until recently. This soil is fertile and holds water well, but with the winter rains is liable to turn into deep mud, while deep cracks open with the advent of the dry summer.

The Qishon Stream runs through the valley diagonally from its source on Mount Gilboa in the southeast to the gap in the northwest between Mount Carmel and the Shefar'am Hills. From there it passes into the Zebulon Valley and its mouth in Haifa Bay. The Qishon's gradient is very small, and the outlet into the Zebulon Valley easily blocked; swamps thus spread here and disappeared only thanks to the drainage work carried out by Jewish settlers in the 1920's. Even later, the upper groundwater horizon often lay too high, rotting plant roots, and had to be lowered by 'agricultural drainage,' i.e., narrow ditches and subterranean pipes. The soil's imperviousness, on the other hand, facilitated the construction of the Qishon Storage Lake as part of the National Water Scheme. In its first stage it holds the winter floodwaters of the Qishon and its tributaries, while in the second, surplus waters from Western Galilee are adducted.

Afula is the urban center of the Jezreel Valley, but the character of its settlement is decisively determined by the pioneer villages founded here in the 1920's and 1930's (Nahalal, Mishmar ha-Emeq, Sede Ya'aqov, etc.).

The Lower Jordan Valley and the Dead Sea

The Lower Jordan Valley. This section of the Rift stretches from the narrow passage between Gilead and Samaria (at the border of the Bet She'an Valley) southward to the shore of the Dead Sea.

Nineteen kilometers (12 miles) south of the Bet She'an Valley, the Rift broadens into the Sukkot Valley, where the Farī'a Valley branches to the northwest and the Yabboq River Valley to the east. South of Mount Sartaba, the Rift widens even more into the Peẓa'el Valley, and finally attains a width of 32 km (15 miles) in the Jericho latitude. The Rift's bottom drops, from 270 m (885 ft) below the Mediterranean sea level in the north to approximately 390 m (1,310 ft) at the Dead Sea shore. Toward the south the mountains walling the Rift grow higher—the crests of the Judean Hills in the west rise 1,400 m (4,300 ft) above the Dead Sea level, and those of Moab in the east even more. The contrast between the lower floodplain terrace of the Jordan and the higher arid terrace sharpens as the annual average of rain diminishes from 200–250 mm (8–10 in) at the region's northern extremity to only 100 m (4 in) near the Dead Sea.

Most of the valley bottom is covered with lissan marl, deposited in the ancient Jordan Lake which spread in the region until the last pluvial of the Upper Pleistocene. In the marl near the Dead Sea shore, laminated deposits are discernible, with alternating thin layers of coarse, mostly chalky marl, and fine-grained gypsum and other sediments.

When the Dead Sea gradually contracted at the end of the pluvial, three lake-shore marl terraces were left, the highest almost 200 m (650 ft) above the present water level. Deep crevices and canyons have been carved in the soft marl by ephemeral wadis which repeatedly changed their course. This results in a broken badland topography, criss-crossed with stream beds and relics of the former marl level shaped like towers, castles, mushrooms, statues, etc.

To the south soil salinity gradually increases, so that the higher terraces near the Dead Sea can hardly support any vegetation, while the dense brush on the Jordan floodplain terrace includes many halophytic species. The highly interesting experiments carried out by the kibbutz Bet ha-Arava north of the Dead Sea (the site had to be abandoned, in the War of Independence, in the summer of 1948) have shown that even this extremely saline soil can be won for farming: large quantities of fresh Jordan water were led into shallow basins to seep into the soil and carry the salt down. The 'washed' soil was then extremely fertile and gave record yields of early vegetables, grain, fruit, etc.

In its lower course the Jordan receives important tributaries from the west, and still larger ones from the east. Wadi Farī'a comes from Samaria, paralleled in the south by Wadi 'Auja which marks the northern border of Judea. Wadi Qelt descends through the Judean Desert to the vicinity of Jericho. Among the eastern tributaries the Yabboq River is longest and has the deepest gorge and the most water; also important are Wadi Nimrīn and Wadi Ḥisbān (Naḥal Ḥeshbon). Some of the streams receive additional water from springs rising along the fault lines in the east and west. Several springs have fostered a tropical, Sudanese vegetation.

The only urban settlement in this part of the Jordan Valley is Jericho, probably the oldest city in the world.

The Dead Sea and Its Surroundings. The Dead Sea covers the deepest continental depression in the world. Its water level in 1963 was 398.5 meters (1,308 ft) below the level of the Mediterranean Sea. This figure, however, is subject to frequent change; after a series of drought years it may drop by 5 m (16 ft) or more and may rise again after prolonged rains. During the beginning of the 19th century, it rose by 12.4 m (37 ft), and fell by at least 5 m (16 ft) since the beginning of our century; in 1935 it was over 4 m (13 ft), and in 1960 65 cm (2 ft) higher than in 1963. It is assumed that tectonic movements at the bottom of this sea also influence the water level. Meteorological and tectonic factors equally cause changes in the area of this large inland lake which alternately expands and contracts, particularly at its north and south ends.

The Dead Sea from north to south measures 80 km (50 miles); its greatest width, north of En Gedi, is 18 km (11 miles). The Lissan Peninsula (Hebrew: 'Lashon' = 'Tongue') divides the Dead Sea into a larger northern and smaller southern basin, 761 and 254 sq km (294 and 99 sq. miles), respectively. The northern basin at some spots is 400 m (over 1,250 ft) deep, i.e., 800 m (2,625 ft) below Mediterranean sea level, while the water depth south of the Lissan Peninsula averages only 6 m (20 ft). (These figures, too, vary with the vacillations in water level.)

Air view of the southwestern shore of the Dead Sea. Note sharp fault scarps on the right, torn by deep canyons, and alluvial fans built by wadi mouths and protruding into the sea. At upper left Mount Sedom appears. On the lower slopes, ancient shore lines are recognizable

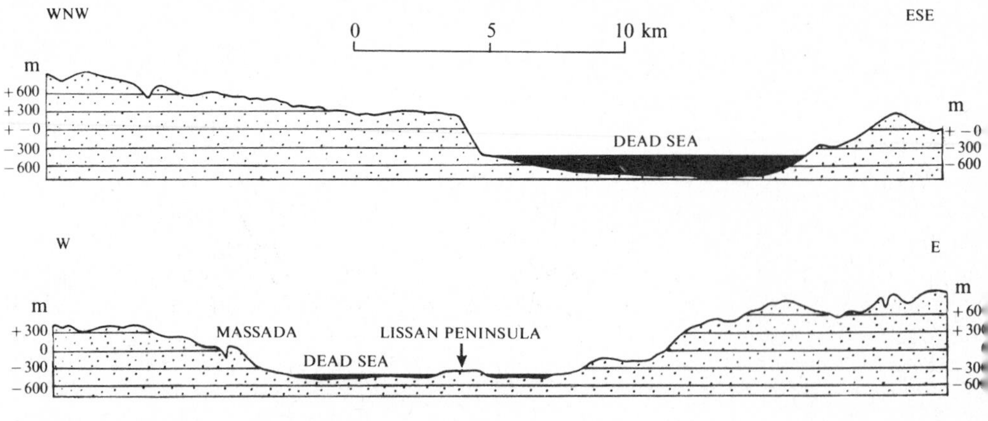

Sections through the northern basin of the Dead Sea (above) and at the latitude of the Lissan Peninsula (below)

In its elongated form the Dead Sea is a characteristic graben lake. It flat northern and southern shores contrast sharply with those of the west anc particularly of the east, where vertical rock walls plunge into the water. Ancien rock strata are exposed in these walls—Turonian and Cenomanian dolomite beneath Senonian chalk in the west; red-brown to orange Nubian sandstone supposedly belonging to the Lower Cretaceous and the Jurassic, in the east. A Saramūj, at the eastern rim of the Dead Sea, even Paleozoic shales appear, as wel as Carboniferous and Cambrian sandstones and limestones which are exposec hardly anywhere else in this country. Finally, streams descending from the Edon Mountains have brought gravels of crystalline rocks to the Dead Sea shore.

All streams descending to the Dead Sea from the west carry only rare anc short-lived floods in winter. Nevertheless, these have carved magnificent canyons in the rock walls which mark the fault scarps, and some have built deltas on the lake shore and alluvial fans at the foot of the fault scarp. The streams descending from the Moab Plateau in the east are richer in water; four of them flow all yea round. Of, these, the Arnon and Zered streams are among the most important ir the country. The wildest and most spectacular gorge near the Dead Sea is that o the Arnon, its width hardly exceeding 30 m (100 ft) with perpendicular rock walls rising on both sides to 500 m (1,600 ft) and more; palm trees and bushes grow from the rock walls above the riverbed.

By far the greatest amount of water is brought to the Dead Sea from the nort by the Jordan River. Four desert wadis enter into the Sedom salt swamp at the south: Naḥal ha-Arava (the lower section of Naḥal Paran coming from the Southern Negev), which also receives tributaries from the Edom Mountains Naḥal Iddan; Naḥal Amaẓyahu; Naḥal Ẓin.

Erosion and changes in the Dead Sea's water level have created bizarre shapes in the saline lissan marl near the northern shore

Inland lakes have, at least since the Miocene, covered this section of the Rift repeatedly. The present-day Dead Sea, however, is certainly one of the youngest important water bodies in the world. Recent investigations estimate its age as 12,000 years. Alluvial deposits beneath it reach a great depth; on the basis of geophysical probes, the compact bedrock is assumed to lie at least 7,000 m (23,000 ft) deep; 4,000 m (13,000 ft) of alluvial strata have been ascertained and found to be composed of coarse clastic material at the outskirts, and of almost pure halite in the center; they are mostly Pleistocene and, to a very small degree, Upper Pliocene. Since that period, subsidence is supposed to have deepened this section of the Rift by more than 1,000 m (3,000 ft). Still younger is the southern basin of the Dead Sea, which may have been created as late as in the historic past. Since the sill at the northern end of that basin seems to have subsided or been broken by tectonic movements, the water could spread southward. The soft, friable marls of the Lissan Peninsula were simultaneously uplifted. Today, watercourses open deep cracks in the peninsula, and the waves beating against the soft rock walls unceasingly alter its shoreline.

The water of the Dead Sea, like that of all inland lakes with no outlet, has become increasingly saline in its relatively short existence; today it registers the hightest salt content in the world—over 30% near the surface of the southern basin, and 33% at depth. This rate of salt accumulation is ascribed to the hot and arid climate which speeds up surface evaporation, to the many mineral springs rising at the bottom and on the shores of the Dead Sea itself, and to others in the Rift to the north and south whose waters are drained toward the Dead Sea. These springs provide salts, e.g., bromide and sulfur, which are relatively rare in the oceans and in other continental lakes.

At different stages the dissolved minerals in the Dead Sea reach the saturation point, i.e., where the crystallizing energy inherent in the minerals prevails over the solving energy of the water. Most of the gypsum of the Dead Sea has thus reconsolidated and sunk to the bottom. Next to recrystallize is sodium chloride, or common salt. Other chemicals, e.g., magnesium bromide, potassium chloride, etc., are even more removed from the saturation point. The extraction of minerals from Dead Sea waters, described in greater detail on p. 479ff., is based on this process, aided by evaporation pans.

Near the southwest corner of the Dead Sea rises Mount Sedom, 11 km (6.8 miles) long and 1.5–3 km (1.2–1.8 miles) wide. It rises 245m (755 ft) above the Dead Sea level. This mount is complicated in structure. Its geological history does not seem to be identical with that of the salt domes or plugs known in Louisiana, Texas, Persia, etc. In any case, Mount Sedom is to be regarded as a remnant of an earlier Dead Sea. That ancient lake, too, becoming increasingly saline, deposited salt on its bottom. Later, hard rock overlaid the salt and exerted pressure

Precipitous rock walls of Nubian sandstone tower over the mouth of River Arnon on the eastern shore of the Dead Sea

Evaporation pans of the Dead Sea Works south of the Dead Sea. In foreground small experimental pans and meteorological station

upon it. Those upper strata must have been fractured by young faulting movements, so that the 'plastic' salt yielded to the pressure, welled up through rock fissures, and created the block of Mount Sedom on the surface. Only small portions of the mountain top, however, are salt, most being cap rock (marls, etc.) lifted by the pressure from beneath. In the center of the mount, shales and sands form vertical layers up to the top.

Rain dissolves away salt and other soft, soluble matter from the top and slopes of Mount Sedom; the salt reserve in the depths seems unexhausted and replaces the washed-out minerals, so that the height of the mount remains more or less constant. Harder portions, more resistant to solution, stand out from the steep slope in shapes resembling towers, statues, etc., until they break and tumble to the foot of Mount Sedom; the Biblical tale of Lot's wife, who was transformed into a salt pillar, seems to originate in this phenomenon.

Rainwater standing in small puddles on the top of Mount Sedom penetrates the vertical fissures between the salt and the other rock layers in the course of time. Vertical funnels going down to the bottom of the mountain where they meet insoluble rock are thus created. The water there, seeping out laterally, opens narrow caves and tunnels which afford ingress to the funnel bottoms. An eerie atmosphere created by the reflection of the weak sunlight off the sheer, blueish salt walls prevails in the caves.

Apart from the kibbutz En Gedi and the nuclei of bathing resorts at Meẓad Zohar and En Boqeq, there are no permanent settlements on the Israel shore of the Dead Sea; workers of the huge Dead Sea Works reside in Dimona, Arad, and elsewhere.

Transjordan

The term 'Transjordan' includes all the regions between the Rift of the Arava, the Dead Sea and the Jordan, and the great Syrian Desert. Geologically as well as climatically, these regions are in most cases the continuation of their counterparts west of the Rift, separated from them only by the Rift's subsidence in the relatively recent geologic past. Whereas the western boundary of Transjordan is sharply delineated by the Rift faults, the east has a gradual transition zone, which also fluctuates under the influence of man in the unending struggle between the desert and the sown.

Four main regions can be discerned in Transjordan: Edom, from the Gulf of Eilat northward for over 170 km (100 miles) to the gorge of Wadi Ḥasi (Naḥal Zered); Moab and Ammon, between the river gorges of the Zered and Wadi Zerqa (the Yabboq River), with a south-north length of about 130 km (80 miles); the Gilead, between the Yabboq and Yarmuk rivers, with a south-north length of 55 km (35 miles); and the Basan (or Bashan, in the wider sense of the term), north of the Yarmuk to the Ḥermon Massif and the northern slopes of the Hauran Mountains, measuring 55 km (35 miles) from south to north at its western, and 80 km (50 miles) at its eastern border.

Almost all parts of Transjordan were uplifted after the Mesozoic. This movement, which later coincided with the Rift's subsidence, was strongest at the western rim. The plateau therefore slants gently eastward. The rising of the western Edom horsts and of Mount Ḥermon further emphasizes this structural picture. Ancient rocks were exposed at the Rift escarpment in the west, and were later bared even more by erosive action on the steep scarps and slopes. As the plateau descends eastward the rock strata are successively younger.

The topographic incline results in a sharp decrease in rainfall from the plateau's edge to the east. The only exception to this rule is the Basan, where the terrain rises from west to east, up to the Hauran Mountains, and with it the rainfall increases in that direction.

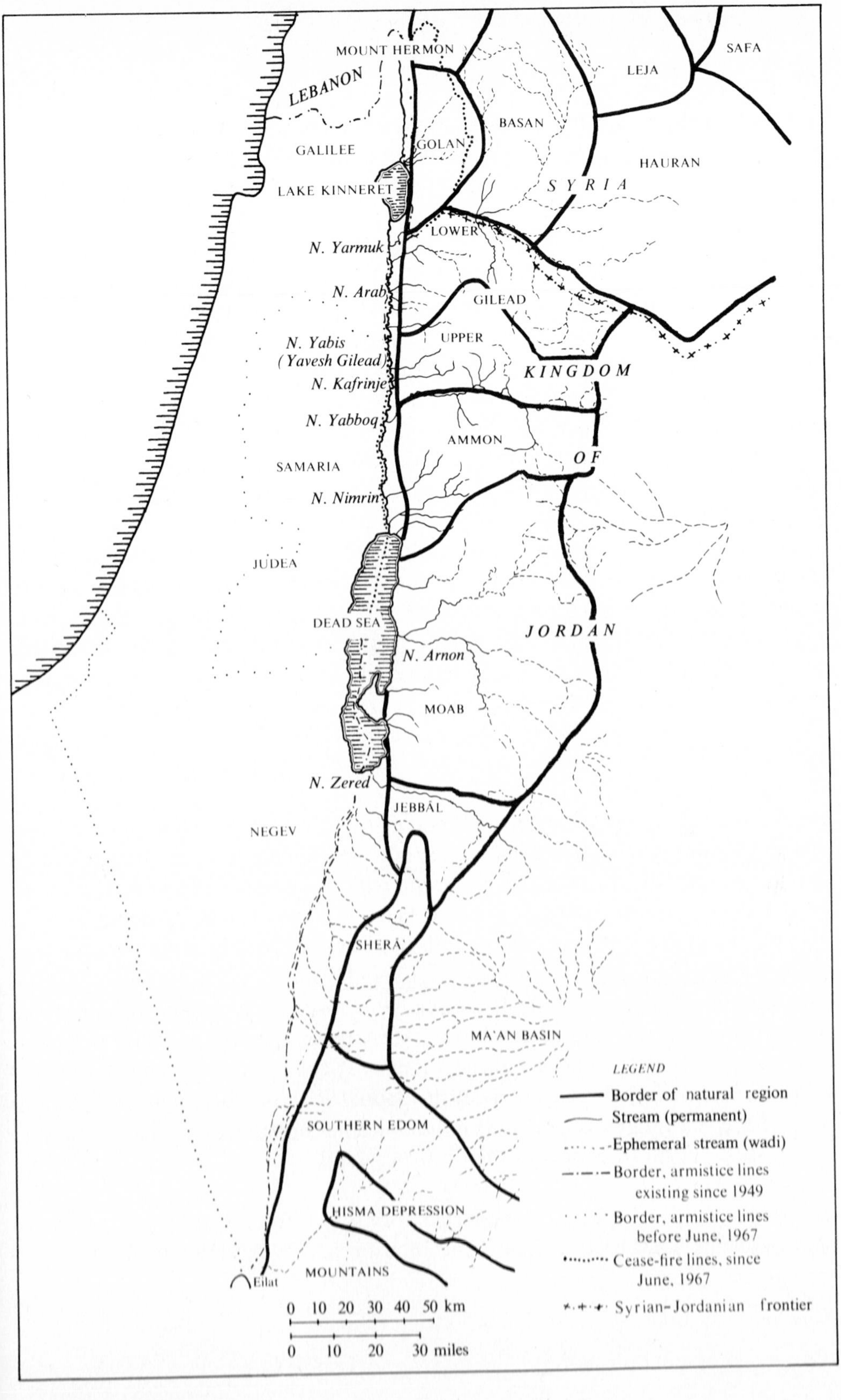

Subregions of Transjordan

Edom

This large region falls into three sections—the Southern Edom Mountains, the Sherā' Mountains, and the Jebbāl (Biblical Geval) Region. To these sections the Ḥisma Depression and the Basin of Ma'an (Maon) in the east are to be added.

The Southern Edom Mountains reach to over 1,500 m (5,000 ft) above sea level; Jebel Bāqir, 1,592 m (5,225 ft), is the highest peak. The western section, uplifted as a horst between fault lines, has crystalline rocks, predominantly granites, often reddish, which may be the source of the Biblical name ('adom' = 'red'). These rocks, chiseled by degradation into infinitely varied forms on the abrupt slopes and crenelated crests, contrast sharply with the orange, red, yellow, and violet Nubian sandstones further east which form bulky table mounts, pyramids, cones, or huge rock towers, all deeply buried in detritus.

Most of the numerous gorges cutting through the crystalline mountains terminate abruptly in front of insuperable rock walls. Wadi Yitm, however, leads from the Aqaba (ancient Eẓyon Gever) shore up to the plateau in the northeast. The King's Way of antiquity ascended through this gorge from Egypt to Transjordan, Damascus and Mesopotamia; today, the highway through Wadi Yitm links the Jordanian Kingdom with its only sea outlet at Aqaba; the branch line of the Hedjaz Railway, today ending at the upper outlet of the gorge, is planned to continue through to Aqaba.

The Southern Edom Mountains receive minimal rainfall and are practically devoid of vegetation.

The Sherā' Mountains are, in structure and rock variety, more complicated than those of Southern Edom. Faults multiply and create a rock mosaic where limestones, dolomites and chalks are found with crystalline rocks and sandstones. To the latter belongs the small basin of Petra, the famous capital of the antique Nabatean Kingdom. Ancient artists hollowed out artificial caves in the imposing brown sandstone walls as royal sanctuaries and ornamented them with engraved and sculptured columns, portals, statues and inscriptions, many of enormous size. At the northern end of the Sherā' Mountains, the Arava Valley broadens toward the east and the Ma'an Basin widens toward the west, so that the mountains are narrowest where they meet the Jebbāl Region. Although the southern part of the mountains is arid and uninhabitable, permanent villages (Tāyyiba, Wadi Mūsa) begin to appear at their northern end.

The Ḥisma Depression is, at its western extremity, 800 m (2,600 ft) above sea level and descends southeastward into the interior of the Arabian Peninsula. It is

The 'treasury'—one of the imposing tombs carved by the Nabateans into the sandstone of Petra, Edom hemmed in by the sharp ridges of the Southern Edom Mountains and the Sherā Mountains which tower 700–800 m (2,200–2,600 ft) above the valley bottom. The fantastic rock towers, columns, needles and castles of multicolored sandstone create a landscape of sublime magnificence which has always deeply impressed nomads and pilgrims using this gateway to Arabia.

The Jebbāl Mountains are even more varied than those of Southern Edom. Faults separate the region from the deeply embedded Northern Arava and cut through it in different directions, isolating rather flat areas, each one with a large village (Shaūbak, Dhāna, Tāfila). Crystalline rocks and Nubian sandstones occupy parts of western Jebbāl; further east appear first limestones and dolomites, then chalks. Large patches of volcanic rocks (basalts) are found; at the sides of the Dhāna Gorge, Paleozoic sediments are exposed. The highest of the Jebbāl blocks is that of Dhāna village, where one peak attains 1,600 m (5,181 ft).

Conditions are more favorable for human settlement and farming in the Jebbāl Region than elsewhere in Edom. Annual precipitation averages 400–500 mm (16–20 in), and relatively frequent snowfall upon the hill crests benefits the water balance of the region. These conditions promoted the growth of natural forest and brush which provided the wood for the antique copper smelters of Punnon, Timna, and Eẓyon Gever. The vegetation was, however, finally destroyed in World War I when the Turks used wood instead of coal for the engines of the Hedjaz Railway. The Biblical name 'Har Se'ir,' used for Edom, may derive from the forest which gave a hairy aspect to the skyline of these mountains when viewed from the west (Hebrew 'sa'ir'—'hairy'); the Biblical legend of the Edomites' ancestor Esau, whose body was covered with a thick pelt of hair, may have originated here.

Moab and Ammon

The Moab Plateau is east of the Dead Sea and the Lower Jordan. From the Dead Sea to about 30–40 km (20–30 miles) to the east, it descends gently to a shallow depression, along which stream courses run north or south. The ridge beyond is only slightly elevated above the plateau and forms the watershed between the Dead Sea and the streams directed into Arabia. The Moab Plateau is highest at its southwest corner, above the Zered Gorge, where Jebel Khinzīra is 1,234 m (4,056 ft) above sea level, or 1,626 m (5,340 ft) above the Dead Sea, only 8 km (5 miles) away.

The bedrock of most of the Moab Plateau is Senonian chalk and flint; in the south, patches of basalt, the extinguished crater of Jebel Sheiḥān, and warm springs bear witness to volcanic activity. Ancient rocks, particularly sandstones, are exposed on the western escarpments and on the sides of the deep gorges, while crystalline rocks and Paleozoic sediments appear at Saramūj near the Dead Sea.

Streams thrusting through the high western edge of the plateau carve abysmal canyons, the wildest of which are those of Wadi Mūjib (Naḥal Arnon), Wadi Heidān which, cutting diagonally through central Moab, joins the Arnon near its mouth, Wadi Kerak in the south, and Wadi Zerqa Ma'īn in the north. The gorge scarps are often impassable.

The Moab Plateau, higher than the Judean Hills in the west, receives a more or less reliable winter rainfall which makes grain farming possible. The Book of Ruth relates the migration of Bethlehemites to Moab, which had not suffered from the drought as much as Judea.

The canyons cut Southern Moab into easily defensible blocks which served as important links in the Roman 'limes arabicus' as well as in the Transjordanian chain of Crusader fortresses; notable among the latter is Crac du Désert (Kerak), whose ruins are impressive to this day.

The mountainous topography of southwestern Moab grows flatter north of Wadi Zerqa Ma'īn, from which roads radiate in all directions. Medba is famous for the mosaic floor found in the ruins of its Byzantine church. The mosaic contains the oldest original map known, a pictorial map of the Holy Land and the surrounding countries. Measuring 20 m × 8 m ($65\frac{1}{2} \times 26\frac{1}{4}$ ft), it is an amazingly exact and impressive rendering of landscape features (hills, rocks, watercourses, flora, fauna, etc.) and of villages, towns, and cities. Based on the 'Onomastikon'— the list of place-names compiled earlier by Eusebius— it is an invaluable treasure for the geographic and historical research of the country. Large parts of the mosaic, unfortunately, were destroyed at the end of the last century, when the construction of a church was begun on the site with the immense value of the mosaic unrecognized. With its renewed growth in our century, Medba has replaced Ḥisbān (Biblical Ḥeshbon), which remained a small village.

Northwest of Medba, Mount Nebo, 795 m (2,631 ft) above sea level, jutting westward from the Moab Plateau, commands a wide view of the Lower Jordan Valley, the Dead Sea, and the Judean Hills; this site, with the nearby spring called in Arabic 'Ein Mūsa ('Moses' Spring') forms a most credible background to the Biblical tale of Moses, to whom God showed the Promised Land from Mount Nebo and did not allow entry (Deuteronomy, XXXIV, 1).

Wadi Ḥisbān and other streams of Northern Moab do not form canyons. The plateau, almost flat, gradually rises to the north and attains altitudes of 890–1,070 m (2,900–3,300 ft). No clear boundary is perceptible between Moab and Ammon; the two regions should be regarded as one geographic unit;

therefore, it seems preferable not to link Ammon with Gilead further north, as has been done by some.

The city of 'Amman (Biblical Rabbat 'Ammon, Hellenistic Philadelphia) lies in the wide, shallow basin of the upper Nahr Zerqa (Yabboq River), which flows eastward, and later arches widely north and west. 'Amman, in 1948 little more than a large village of mud brick houses, has, as the capital of the Jordanian Kingdom, become a modern city with over 450,000 inhabitants.

Northeast of 'Amman, a road and a railway lead along the Yabboq River to Zerqa, an important airfield, army camp, and outpost on the desert border, situated on the Hedjaz Railway. Near it lie the Jordanian phosphate mines of a-Rusāyfa and al-Khāsa. Another road leads from 'Amman northwest to the junction of a-Salt; there it splits into a northwest arm over the Jordan bridge at Dāmiya leading to Nablus, and a southwest arm over Allenby Bridge leading to Jericho and Jerusalem.

The Yabboq River, its course changing direction from southeast to northeast (between 'Amman and Zerqa), northwest, west and, finally, southwest, is one of the largest in the country. Its tributaries come from 100 km (60 miles) east of the Jordan. The bottom of its profound gorge lies below sea level up to 11 km (7 miles) east of the Rift, while the Ammon Plateau to the south and the Gilead to the north exceed 600 m (2,000 ft) above sea level in its immediate neighborhood. Degradation by the river has been extreme; it has removed Eocene and Senonian

The new city of 'Amman covers the hilly terrain on the banks of the upper Yabboq River

chalk of the plateau 20–30 km (12–20 miles) north and south of its course and revealed, in approximately concentric circles, Turonian, Cenomanian, Lower Cretaceous, Jurassic and, at the center, Triassic rocks.

Gilead

In landscape, climate, vegetation, and settlement conditions, Gilead resembles the hill and foothill regions of Western Palestine more than any other part of Transjordan. The belt of permanent settlement here attains a width of 45–70 km (30–40 miles) compared to 32 km (20 miles) in Moab. Gilead's southern part is higher, with mountainous topography, while in the north the plateau flattens out, sloping rather gently toward the impressive escarpments which dominate the deep Jordan and Yarmuk river valleys. In Southern Gilead, stream erosion has accentuated the relief and exposed Cenomanian and Turonian limestones and dolomites. Terra rossa soil characterizes this region. The highest elevation, 1,247 m (4,092 ft) above sea level, is Umm al-Dāraj. Central and Northern Gilead, on the other hand, have Senonian and Eocene chalks, and rendzina soils. Two large patches of Neogene basalt appear there, one in the northwest corner of Gilead, near the Yarmuk mouth in the Jordan, and the second northeast of Irbid.

Annual rainfall attains 700–800 mm (28–32 in) in Southern Gilead, but much less in the north. The many perennial streams, which descend from Gilead to the Jordan, e.g., Wadi Rājeb, Wadi Kafrīnje, and Wadi Yābis (Biblical Yavesh Gilead) which drain the southern section, and Wadi Ziqlāb, Wadi Tāyyibe, and Wadi 'Arab which flow further north. Some important tributaries of the Yarmuk also come from Gilead, among them Wadi Shalāla and Wadi Shūmer.

Important centers of settlement in Upper Gilead are 'Ajlūn which has given the region its Arabic name, and Jērash, the Hellenistic Gerasa where magnificent ruins have been admirably preserved. In Lower Gilead, Irbid (ancient Arbela) is the principal town, followed by Umm Qays, the Hellenistic Gadara which dominates the confluence of the Yarmuk with the Jordan. In the Hellenistic and Roman eras Gerasa, Gadara, and Philadelphia ('Amman) formed, with Bet She'an and six other cities in the Gilead and the Golan, the 'Dekapolis,' the Ten Cities' association cherishing Greek civilization.

Basan and Mount Ḥermon

In two respects the region of Basan is fundamentally different from the rest of Transjordan—in its surface gently sloping from east to west which, by opening it

The antiquities of Roman Gerasa (Jērash, Geresh), one of the cities of the 'Dekapolis,' are among the best preserved in the Levant

to the rain-bearing sea winds, pushes the desert back 120 km (70 miles) east of the Rift and 200 km (125 miles) of the Mediterranean Sea, and in its thick, continuous cover of basalt rock and fertile basalt soil. Both factors made the Basan the granary of the Levant in ancient times.

Three subregions compose the Basan from west to east: the Golan* from the Jordan Valley to the Ruqqād Stream; the Basan Plateau, between the Ruqqād and the foot of the Hauran Mountains; and the Hauran, which includes Jebel Druz and the rugged areas of solidified lava called Lēja and Sāfa.

The Lower Golan is nearly flat tableland sloping toward the Yarmuk in the south and, less so, toward the Jordan and the Sea of Galilee in the west, although towering above both rivers with abrupt scarps. Between 200 and 600 m (650 and 1,950 ft) above sea level, it bears a thick cover of fertile basalt soil which adds to the flatness of its topography. The region has both ephemeral and year-round streams. Most flow too weakly to erode the hard basalt rock underlying the soil,

* For details on the recent history, population and development blueprints of the Golan, which came under Israel administration in the Six Day War, see pp. 420–430.

The lower Yarmuk Gorge is of tectonic origin. Black Pleistocene basalt covers chalk of Neogene age

Stream gorges cut through the basalt plateau of the central Golan, revealing chalk and limestone strata at several spots

but two, the Yarmuk and the Ruqqād, having succeeded in cutting through this resistant stratum, have quickly dropped their courses through the soft chalk underneath. Thereby, the difference in level between them and their small tributaries increases, with resultant waterfalls at the latters' mouths. In the lower Yarmuk Gorge, black basalt ledges, jutting out above glaring white chalk, overshadow the railway running along the river.

Neogene and Eocene chalks have been exposed by erosion along the western plateau rim rising above Lake Kinneret, above the southern rim dominating the Yarmuk River gorge from the north, and both sides of the Ruqqād and Sāmak stream gorges (the latter falls into Lake Kinneret south of the Bethsaida Valley).

The hills rising above the Wadi Sāmak gorge, east of Lake Kinneret. Bulldozers reclaim land for future plantations of tropical fruit and other intensive crops

Since antiquity, the Lower Golan has been famous as grain-farming country. The region attained its greatest prosperity in the period between the Hellenistic era and the end of Byzantine rule. While Hippos (Susita, on the mountain above Kibbutz En Gev), Dion and other centers were affiliated with the Greek 'Dekapolis,' Jews were sent by Herod the Great to settle in the Golan, where they remained the dominant element until the Moslem conquest in the 7th century C.E.

The Upper Golan differs from the Golan in its pronounced relief, volcanic cones forming the most prominent features. The highest elevation is Tell a-Shaīkha,

The northern Golan, with volcanic cones and the Berekhat Ram pond, as seen from the southeastern slope of Mt. Ḥermon

1,280 m (over 4,250 ft), lying near the northern plateau rim and close to Mount Ḥermon. Vulcanism was active until the Pleistocene period. The Golan shows a great variety of volcanic material and surface forms (massive basalt boulders, tuffs, basaltic-lacustrine deposits, etc.; explosion craters, stratified cones, ropy lava flows, etc.). Volcanic cones are arranged in more or less recognizable lines, mostly running from north-northeast to south-southwest. Gaping craters of extinct volcanoes are found in many of the hills. More recent lava flows have contributed to flattening the relief, filling out cavities and vales which had previously been created by erosive processes.

The largest extinct volcano is Tel Avital (Abu Nīda—Father of Dew) near Qunaītira; its wide rim has been breached by erosion in several places; a secondary cone rises within its crater whose fertile bottom soil is under cultivation.

Berekhat Ram, a beautiful small water body of elliptic shape, lies near the northern plateau border. Called 'Phiale' by the Greeks of antiquity, it is held to be a typical crater lake. One opinion explaining it as having its origin in karstic dissolution of a nearby limestone stratum, thus being a doline, has now been discounted. The lake has no outlet. If it is a crater lake, it must be fed mainly by rains, a theory corroborated by the extremely low salt content of its water.

The ample rainfall of the Upper Golan, attaining annual averages of 1,000 mm (40 in) and more, has washed out the loose soil from many fields and laid bare the basalt boulders. These impede plowing and frequently make it more rewarding to use the land for grazing than for grain cultivation. Many stretches appear, in the past, to have borne forests or brush, of which, however, only little has been preserved. Biblical expressions like 'the cows of Basan' and the 'oaks of Basan' seem therefore to allude to the Upper Golan.

The Basan Plateau, a-Nūqra in Arabic, rises gradually from 200–500 m (700–1,600 ft) above sea level in the west and to 920 m (3,000 ft) in the east. In the north it is separated from the Ghuta Depression of Damascus by a rugged hill chain of solidified lava. Like the Lower Golan, this region bears a thick cover of fertile soil; hillocks of bare rock, however, jut out at many spots. The highest elevation is 1,100 m (3,590 ft). The streams flow southwest to the Yarmuk; among them Wadi 'Allān and Wadi Ḥarīr are important. Annual precipitation, amounting to 300–600 mm (12–24 in), is generally sufficient for grain farming. Rainfall, however, is irregular, so that bumper crops are often followed by years of severe drought.

The center of the region and of the entire Basan is Dar'a, the Biblical Edrei, which is a road and rail junction. Moslems from Syria, Iraq, etc., assemble there each year to make the pilgrimage to Mecca.

The Hauran is a region of volcanic peaks which rise steeply above the surrounding areas, and especially over the Damascus Depression in the north. The highest mountain, Tell al-Jēnnah, is 1,820 m (5,900 ft) above sea level. The intensive volcanic activity which began in the Pliocene lasted longest here, until the Upper Pleistocene. Lava constantly issuing in new spots created a wild, irregular landscape. On the other hand, abundant precipitation promoted the weathering of the basalt into the soil which is preserved in intermontane valleys. The western slopes of the Hauran Mountains receive heavy winter rains as well as snow which, sometimes remaining on the ground for months on end, increases mositure for the crops and particularly favors the growth of deciduous fruit trees.

Since the 17th century, Druzes from Lebanon have settled in the region; they arrived in increasing numbers after the bloody clashes between Druzes and

Christians in Lebanon in 1860. These settlers established villages, planted fruit orchards, and developed vegetable and grain farming. Poplars and forest trees, planted for construction wood, lend a gay character to the landscape.

The region which has since been dubbed 'Jebel Druz,' 'the Druze Mountain,' was given autonomy in 1860 which was endorsed and amplified under the French Mandate of Syria. However, during Syria's temporary merger with the United Arab Republic in 1958, Jebel Druz lost its political status, and retained a very limited autonomy in religious matters only. The Syrian authorities, in an attempt at obscuring this religion's individual character, even resorted to renaming it 'Jebel al-'Arab.'

The Lēja and Sāfa, northwest and northeast of the Hauran Mountains, are practically uninhabited. Low, steep-sided ridges of angular basalt rock, formed by ropy lava welling up from long, crisscrossing fissures, partition them into isolated 'cells.' There is little arable soil, and the climate is too dry for farming. The two regions, somber in coloring and landscape, have since antiquity served mostly as a hiding place for robbers and desperadoes, as the Arabic name 'Lēja' = 'Refuge' indicates. The Greeks called the region 'Trachonitis' = 'Torn Land.'

Mount Ḥermon (Jebel a-Shaikh in Arabic) is a huge massif whose uplift was accompanied by the subsidence of the Litani (Leontes) Valley in the northwest,

The snow cover of Mt. Ḥermon, remaining on the ground for several months, is the principal factor in the development of a rough karst topography

The snow-clad Ḥermon Shoulder, from the southeast

the 'Ayūn (Iyyon) Valley in the southwest, the Ḥula Valley in the south, and the Damascus Depression in the northeast. This process of uplifting is impressively demonstrated by a narrow ridge near the Druze village Mājdal Shams in the southeast; strata of Jurassic and Lower Cretaceous age were forcefully drawn upward and tilted together with the rising anticline of the Ḥermon Shoulder. The only connecting link is in the north formed by Jebel Dhahr, to the Anti-lebanon chain. At a height of 2,814 m (9,232 ft), Mount Ḥermon towers above its surroundings and deeply influences their climate and water economy, as its top enjoys an annual precipitation averaging 1,500 mm (60 in). Most of this falls in the form of snow, which stays on the peak until midsummer. It seems, however, that even the peak of Mount Ḥermon never bore glaciers, as no typical features of mountain glaciation (U-valleys, arêtes, needles, cirques, etc.) are found. On the other hand, karst processes, which have been most active on the Jurassic limestone, make the rock highly porous and promote the seepage of water, which reappears in strong springs on all sides of the mountain. These feed the head-streams of the Jordan as well as tributaries of the Litani River and streams flowing to the Damascus oasis.

Mount Ḥermon is mostly uninhabited, but villages, peopled mainly by minority groups such as Druzes, Alaouites, etc., nestle in protected sites on its lower slopes. Since June 1967, the southeast ridge of the mountain massif (Ketef ha-Ḥermon—'The Ḥermon Shoulder'), whose highest point lies 2,200 m (7,220 ft) above sea level, is under Israel administration.

Mount Ḥermon seen from the south. A fault running through the massif separates the huge anticline of the 'Ḥermon Shoulder' from the western and northwestern parts

The Sinai Peninsula

The Sinai Peninsula stands out from the other regions of the Levant by virtue of its size, being three times that of the State of Israel prior to the Six Day War. However, it constitutes a well-defined geographical unit and contains readily identifiable topographic regions, these features being the outcome of its geological history. Meteorological data, too, are easy to trace, as all of Sinai falls within the subtropical desert zone. The lack of water is the reason for the sparse vegetation cover and the strict limitations of farming, and these, in turn, explain the extremely low population density of this vast area at all times. The lines of communication crossing the peninsula have always been of prime importance, in times of peace, and even more so, of war. As far as is known, Sinai contains a number of valuable minerals deposits, only a part of which has been exploited up to the present.

Extent, Structure, Geological History and Landscape Forms

Area and Distances. The Sinai Peninsula covers ca. 60,000 square kilometers. Triangular in shape, it is wedged between the continents of Asia and Africa, forming the transition between the two, although most geographers include it in the former. The Mediterranean coast in the north constitutes the base line of the triangle, while its apex points to the Red Sea in the south. On the side facing southwest and west, the peninsula borders on the Suez Gulf and Suez Canal, and on the southeast and east side—on the Eilat Gulf and the Negev.

Distances (all indicated here as the crow flies) are considerable. Sinai measures 400 km from Rafiaḥ on the Mediterranean coast to the cape Ras Muḥammad in the south. West-east distances are 190 km between Rafiaḥ and both al-Qantāra and Port Sa'īd, 200 km between Niẓẓana and Isma'īliya, 210 km between

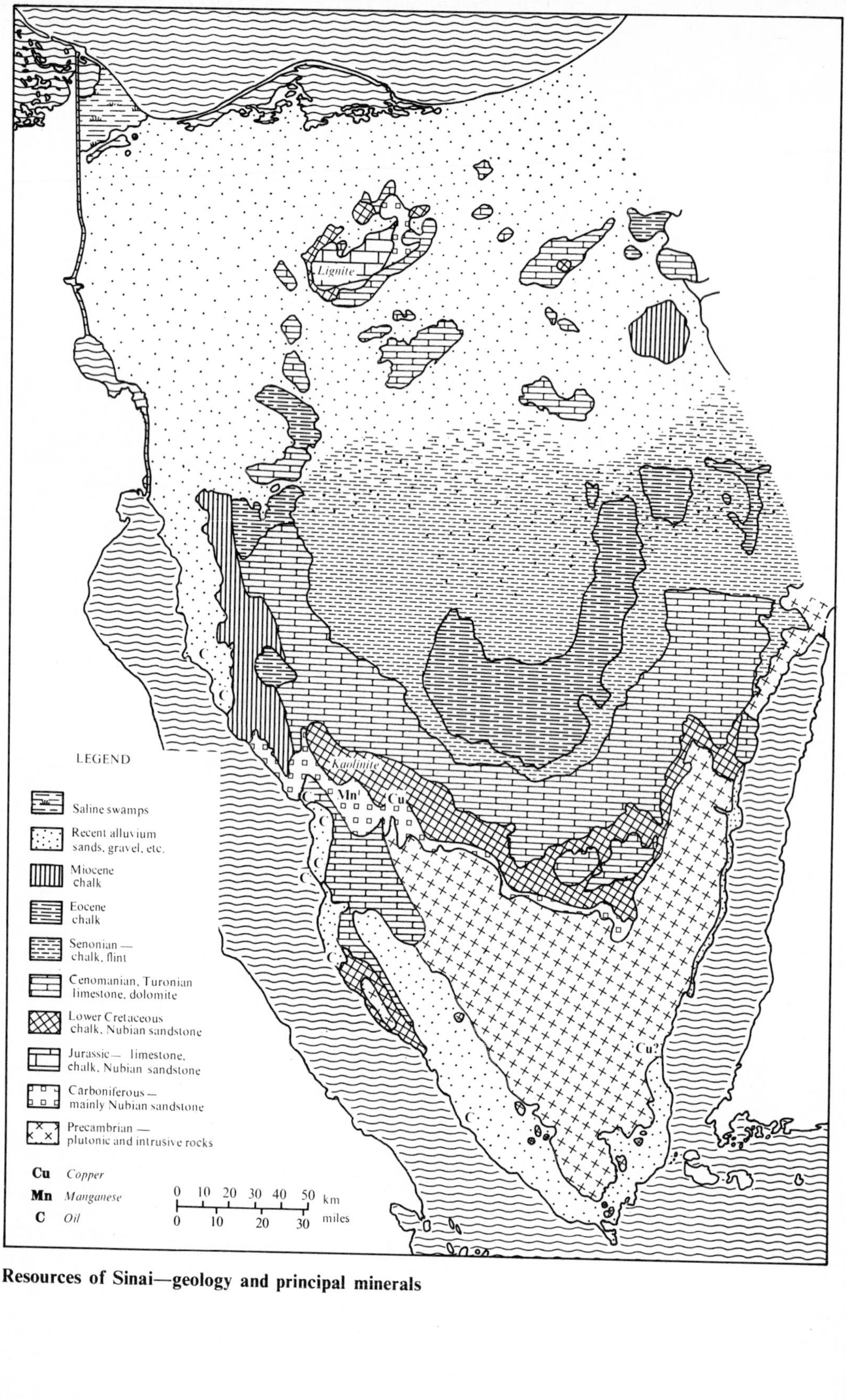

Resources of Sinai—geology and principal minerals

Kuntīlla and Suez, and again 210 km between Eilat and Ras Matarma. South of this last line distances become progressively shorter. The Eilat Gulf has a length of 205 km, and the Suez Gulf—over 300 km. The direct line Suez-Port Sa'īd measures 153 km (the Canal itself is somewhat longer, see p. 372).

Principal Regions. From its highly elevated southern tip, the Sinai Peninsula dips northwards. Sinai falls into the following three main parts: (a) the high mountains of the south, composed of crystalline rocks, with a narrow northern strip of Nubian sandstone and a low hill chain, in part igneous rocks and in part marine strata of Paleozoic age, rising on the Suez Gulf shore in the west, beyond a valley covered by recent, unconsolidated deposits; (b) the a-Tih Plateau (in its southern part called Jebel 'Iqma), with marine sedimentary strata of late Mesozoic and early Cenozoic age; (c) the northern plain, mostly bearing a cover of gravel or wandering sand dunes, but also having steep ridges and individual hills rising abruptly from its flat expanses.

This distribution of rock measures and topographic features is the outcome of tectonic and erosional forces active in the geologic past. Sinai is located between two branches of the giant Syrian-East African Rift, the gulfs of Suez and Eilat. As a typical feature of rift faulting, the flanks of these branches were uplifted while their floors subsided. The pressure elevating the crust seems to have been particularly strong in the south, where the main rift bifurcates. Of the two gulfs, that of Eilat is the narrower but also by far the deeper one, reaching depths of 2,000 m and more, as against an average of 50 m in the Suez Gulf. The former's strong subsidence entailed a correspondingly high uplift of its flanks; therefore, the southeast rim of the peninsula bordering on it was raised higher than the southwest side near the shallower Gulf of Suez. The interior of the peninsula has remained somewhat lower, a feature that is most clearly pronounced on the a-Tih Plateau.

The Drainage Network. These main structural elements have determined the peculiar drainage network of the Sinai Peninsula. Most water flows inward from the elevated rims, to collect in Wadi el-'Arīsh. Its main course, tracing as it were a spinal cord on the Sinai map, follows the peninsula's general inclination from south to north, and reaches the Mediterranean Sea at the town of el-'Arīsh. Over a third of the total area of Sinai, and within it most of the a-Tih Plateau, lies within this drainage basin.

Wadi el-'Arīsh measures about 250 km in length from the point of confluence of its main tributaries, among them Wadi Burūk, Wadi 'Āqaba and Wadi Qurāyya, to its mouth on the Mediterranean coast. These, together with their own small affluents, form a radial network, featuring as spokes of a wheel on the map. In certain sections, some of the wadi courses broaden their beds to a width of 8–10 km and are often filled with fine or coarse sand.

The great granite block of the south is situated outside the Wadi el-'Arīsh drainage system. It has precipitous, narrow gorges, some of which extend west or east to the gulfs while others have no contact with the sea. An area situated west of Eilat drains, via upper Naḥal Paran, toward the Arava Valley and the Dead Sea. Most of the territory of the northern plain lacks a continuous drainage network. Its absence stems from the moving sand dunes which block or fill the few existing stream beds, and from the coarseness of the sands which readily absorb the rainwater, permitting it to percolate to depth instead of flowing on the surface to the sea.

Rocks. The more pronounced the uplift of Sinai's regions, the greater was their exposure to denudation and erosion. The younger strata which once might have been present in the more elevated regions have been removed, and older and deeper rocks are now exposed there. Thus, the crystalline core is today encountered as surface exposures in the south, while toward the north ever younger strata have been preserved, and the rocks of the outskirts of the a-Tih Plateau are older than those at its center. The stronger uplifting of the western and, particularly, eastern rims explains why border lines between rock formations trace a semi-circular course, from northwest through south to northeast.

The Southern Block. The mountain block of the south and the coast of the Eilat Gulf constitute a part of the vast ancient Arab-Nubian Massif. Granites, diorites, porphyries, schists, gneisses, etc. have a far wider distribution here than in the Eilat Hills, which form but the northeastern tip of this large block.

Several mountain peaks of the crystalline region rise 2,000 m and more above sea level, the highest being Mt. Catherine (2,637 m). Jebel Lū'ra and Jebel Umm Shōmar, 7 and 15 km further south, respectively, also attain altitudes exceeding 2,500 m. The peak nearest Mt. Catherine on the north side is Jebel Mūsa, 'Moses' Mount' (2,285 m), by tradition regarded as Mount Sinai where Moses received the Tablets of the Law.

In the southwest, not far from the shore of the Suez Gulf, runs a secondary rift, in part called al-Qā' ('the Depression'). Weathering products of the nearby crystalline rocks—sand, gravel, etc.—form a thick cover in this valley, concealing compact igneous rocks beneath.

The crystalline rocks, mostly of reddish and dark hues, create a dramatic landscape of precipices and peaks which often rise 1,000 m and more above their bases. The mountain tops either have the form of tightly vaulted domes or jagged peaks. Veins of intrusive or extrusive rocks run through the mountainous area,

Scene near the peak of Jebel Mūsa. Mt. Catherine is in the middle background

frequently stretching for several kilometers and differing from their surroundings in both color and hardness. Where the vein is harder than the country rock, it forms a protruding sill, and where softer and more easily weathered—a deep cleft or furrow. In addition to narrow gorges cutting through the crystalline massif, there are also broader valleys, the largest of which is Wadi Feirān; its upper portion, called Wadi a-Sheikh, leads to St. Catherine's Monastery which nestles at the foot of Jebel Mūsa.

The hill chain (consisting of crystalline rocks in the northwest and Paleozoic strata in its other parts) which separates al-Qā' from the shore averages only 300 m in height, and only two hill tops attain 600 m.

The narrow shore lines of the two gulfs have stretches of sand dunes. In the saline, tropical waters, coral banks are abundant. They are close to the shore in the Eilat Gulf, and somewhat further offshore in the shallower Suez Gulf, where they seal off numerous small lagoons.

As the Red Sea tides are far more pronounced than those in the Mediterranean, reefs emerge at low water, and certain lagoons are emptied at ebb tide, strips exceeding 200 m in width becoming dry land. Stretches of the southernmost shores are fringed by tangled mangrove brush, rooted on the shallow sea bottom.

Desert erosion in the crystalline rocks of Southern Sinai creates tightly vaulted domes. This scene is near Jebel Mūsa

The crescent-shaped band of Nubian sandstones north of the crystalline block has a landscape of its own—conical hills, steep, smooth slopes, broad-set table mounts, rock pillars, 'mushrooms,' etc. Here, as in the southern Negev, the mineral content determines the variety of brilliant hues in sandstones—ocher, flaming orange and red generally indicating the presence of iron, black—manganese (as at Umm Būghma where this ore has been mined), blueish-green—copper, etc. These sandstones are considered to range in age from the Carboniferous to the Lower Cretaceous.

The a-Tih Plateau. Cenomanian-Turonian limestones and dolomites constitute a third series and are characteristic of Jebel 'Iqma, the southern rim of this vast plateau. As these rocks are more resistant to weathering than the soft sandstones

A hidden gorge between crystalline rock walls of Southern Sinai

bordering on it in the southwest, south and southeast, they have been preserved as a ridge reaching 1,000 m above sea level and dominating the surroundings with imposing, precipitous walls. A number of faults running to the west and east of the plateau may have contributed to the differences in level between its rim and the surrounding country.

At the southernmost point of Jebel 'Iqma lies its highest peak, Ras al-Ganeīna (1,626 m). Several other mountains top 1,000 m.

The drop of the plateau surface from the sides toward the center and from south to north is barely perceptible but continuous; the lowest parts are no more than 400 m above sea level. In the same directions, the limestone is found to be overlain by Senonian chalk which here, as in other parts of the Levant, has intercalations of flint banks. In the center of the plateau, Eocene chalk forms the top of the sedimentary series.

The plateau occupies no less than 60% of the peninsula's total area. The topography is not uniformly that of an elevated plain. Water courses have incised canyon-like gorges and narrow clefts, particularly in the harder limestone. But also the chalk areas have numerous broad table mounts, pointed 'relic mountains' and other forms which introduce variety into the plateau scenery. The hard flint layers capping these hills have helped to preserve their upper levels. Desert conditions and the absence of a plant cover contribute here, as in the central Negev, to the sharpness and angularity of landscape forms.

The elevated circumference of the a-Tih Plateau, seen from the outside in the west

The Northern Plain. In the north the a-Tih Plateau merges imperceptibly with the Northern Plain. From this flat region, however, rise individual steeply sloping hills and longer ridges which should be regarded as the western continuation of the Negev folds. The general direction of the fold strike in Sinai is likewise northeast-southwest, although some of the folds change to an east-west trend. Similar to the higher parts of the Central Negev, Cenomanian and Turonian limestones and dolomites are predominant in these hills. One of the western hill groups, Jebel Mughāra, has older Jurassic rocks.

The higher of the two chains (which are interrupted over long stretches) is that of the south. In its eastern part, Jebel Hallāl rises suddenly, from entirely flat surroundings, to a height of 892 m above sea level. On all sides, its almost perpendicular slopes are visible from afar. On clear spring mornings, white clouds may cling to its top. It is therefore quite understandable why certain historians and travellers, among them C. S. Jarvis, the British governor of Egypt, have proposed identifying Jebel Hallāl with the Biblical Mount Sinai, offering as further evidence the flat surrounding terrain where the Children of Israel could have camped and grazed their flocks while Moses received the Tablets of the Law. This view, however, has recently been challenged by the Israel geographer M. Harel, who points to the great distance between the mountain and Goshen province of Egypt, a feature which does not tie in with the description of the route given in the Book of Exodus; instead, he sees as the probable site Jebel Sinn Bishr (the Arabic name of the hill is translated by him as 'Heralding the Doctrine'), which lies not far to the southeast of the town of Suez.

The largest hill block in the southern chain is Jebel Yi'āllaq in the west, which attains a height of 1,094 m. The faults surrounding it permit the assumption that taphrogenic processes participated, together with upfolding, in its creation.

In the northern chain, the flat expanses between the hills occupy most of the area. Jebel Lībni (463 m) and its surroundings were of strategic importance both in the Six Day War of 1967 and in the Sinai Campaign of 1956. Further to the west lies the larger Jebel Maghāra whose highest points are at elevations of 776 and 735 m. In its center is located an erosional cirque similar to but less developed than those of the Negev Hills.

The northernmost hills, e.g., Jebel Aḥmar and Risān 'Anīza, rise at a distance of no more than 20–30 km from the Mediterranean shore and are of moderate height. Their white rocks stand out sharply against the background of moving sand dunes.

The dunes have quartz sand as their predominant component. In Sinai, these sands cover a manifold larger area and are considerably thicker (individual dunes piling up to a height of several score meters) than those in the Beersheba Depression, where the Ḥaluẓa and Shunra dunes represent their easternmost extremity. Many dunes are crescent-shaped and bear ripple marks on their surface. Over large areas, the dunes stretch in parallel chains. There are, however, also localities where the arrangement of the dunes is less uniform, apparently as the outcome of lesser regularity in wind directions and velocities. Towards the south, gravel flats frequently take the place of dunes. At certain sites, especially in the vicinity of the lower course of Wadi el-'Arīsh, loess, and loess-sand soils are to be found, but their impact upon the scenery is slight.

The Mediterranean Shore. The Mediterranean shore line of the Sinai Peninsula measures 230 km. In general, the beach has a gentle slope and the coast line is straight or slightly curved. The entire western section of the shore, however, is but a narrow sand spit closing off the large shallow lagoon Sābkhat el-Bardawīl (its name recalls the Crusader King Baldwin I who won a victory here over the Saracens in 1118 but soon after died nearby of an illness). The inner, southern bank of the lagoon is rich in bays and headlands, with diminutive islets or submerged sand reefs offshore. A narrow inlet in the northeast connects the lagoon with the sea; sand blocks this opening from time to time, and the local fishermen clear it anew to provide passage for fish from the open sea. In 1955, the Egyptian Government undertook the broadening of this inlet and of a second one further to the southeast. The width was increased to 7–8 m and the banks were reinforced with concrete. Because of inadequate maintenance, this inlet was soon obstructed again. It is possible that in the historic past the main inlet lay further to the west.

The shore of the Nile delta has four more lagoons—Mariut, Idku, Burullus and Manzala. Their formation is attributed to the Mediterranean coastal current which sweeps the river-borne alluvium in an easterly direction and deposits it on its landward side, thus building up the spits sealing off the lagoons. Some hold that even in the recent past another arm of the Nile was in existence ('the Pelusian Arm'), reaching the sea on the Sinai coast and giving birth to the Bardawīl lagoon. Its existence is difficult to ascertain, although Wadi Thumeilāt is considered by some scholars to show traces of such a Nile branch. The western part of the spit and the continuation of the coast swinging to the north form a rounded bav. 'the Pelusian Bight' (at present called a-Tīna Bay). The northwestern corner of the Sinai Peninsula forms a totally impassable salt swamp which is a refuge to a unique flora, and a rich fauna of fish and water fowl.

Part II

Climate, Vegetation and Wildlife

The Climate

Climatically, almost all regions of the Land of Israel form a part of the Mediterranean Zone, with the outstanding characteristics of winter rains and summer drought. The Mediterranean climate is typical of countries on or near the west coasts of continents and approximately between the latitudes 25° and 35° in the northern and southern hemispheres; among these are Israel, most countries adjoining the Mediterranean Sea, part of California in North America and of Central Chile in South America, and small areas on the southern and southwestern coasts of South Africa and of Australia.

Israel belongs to the countries near the equatorward border of the Mediterranean Zone. Its conditions can therefore be described as 'extreme Mediterranean,' with a comparatively short rainy season and 3–4 completely rainless summer months.

Length of Days, Insolation and Temperature

Israel's position on the earth grid, between 29° 30′ and 33° 15′ northern latitude,* results in moderate seasonal variations in length of day and night, and in high values of insolation, or sunlight intensity. While on the equator day and night the year round are exactly 12 hours long, and the poles have only one day and one night per year, each 6 months long, in this country the longest day, June 21, is sunlit for 14 hours, and the shortest, December 22, for 10 hours (as compared with 18 and 6 hours, respectively, in London).

The angle formed between the sun's rays and the ground decides the amount of insolation, i.e., sunlight and warmth received on the surface and near it. On the

* Referring to the pre-1967 borders. Details of the climate of Sinai are given on pp. 160–163.

days of the equinoxes (March 21 and September 23) at noon the sun stands vertically above the equator, and insolation rates in this country are 60° 30' at Eilat in the south, and 56°45′ at Metulla in the north. Israel's maximum insolation is on the day of the summer solstice (June 21), when the Tropic of Cancer (23½°N), has vertical sunlight: 84° at Eilat and 80°15′ at Metulla . The minimum occurs on December 22, the winter solstice, when the Tropic of Capricorn (23½°S) receives maximum possible insolation, with 37° at Eilat and 34°15′ at Metulla (for comparison: values for London, 51°30′ northern latitude, are 38° for March 21 and September 23; 62° for June 22; 15° for December 22).

In addition to these rates (only slightly inferior to those of the tropics), insolation is strengthened in the summer by the almost completely clear skies. Even in winter the cloud cover and consequent reduction of insolation in this country are less than in Western Europe or Eastern North America.

Temperatures are comparatively high in this country, as a result of strong insolation. They vary considerably, however, from place to place, not only according to geographical position but also to differences in altitude, exposure to marine influence, predominant wind directions, etc. On the world map, Israel lies astride the 20°C (68°F) isotherm of annual temperature. Practically speaking, this figure is true of the Coastal Plain only; the Hills register an annual average of 17°C (63°F), and the Jordan Valley an average of 25°C (77°F).

January is normally Israel's coldest month, and August the warmest. January temperature averages amount in the Hills to 8–10°C (46.5–50°F), in the Coastal Plain to 12°C (53.5°F) and in the Jordan Valley to 12–13°C (53.5–55°F). The August figures are, in the Hills, between 22–26°C (71.5–79°F), in the Coastal Plain between 24–26°C (75–79°F) and in the Jordan Valley between 28 and 34°C (82–93°F).

As a rule temperatures drop abruptly in November, and the coolest days of the year come in January or February. At winter's end temperatures begin to rise again, but warming of the atmosphere in April and May is normally slower than the November cooling. Throughout the country the hottest days of the year occur in August. Although no place has monthly averages below 0°C (32°F), days with temperatures below the freezing point are registered nearly every winter in the Hills and, not infrequently, also in the interior and intermontane valley (e.g., Ḥula Valley, Bet Netofa Valley, etc.), where an inversion of temperature occurs on windless nights. In the Coastal Plain, on the other hand, freezing temperatures are rare.

In summer, peak temperatures hover around 40°C (104°F); they are most frequent on sharav days (see p. 141). The highest values ever measured were those of Tirat Ẓevi in June, 1941, where the thermometer indicated 54°C (129.2°F); Tel Aviv registered in that month a maximum of 46°C (114.6°F), and Jerusalem

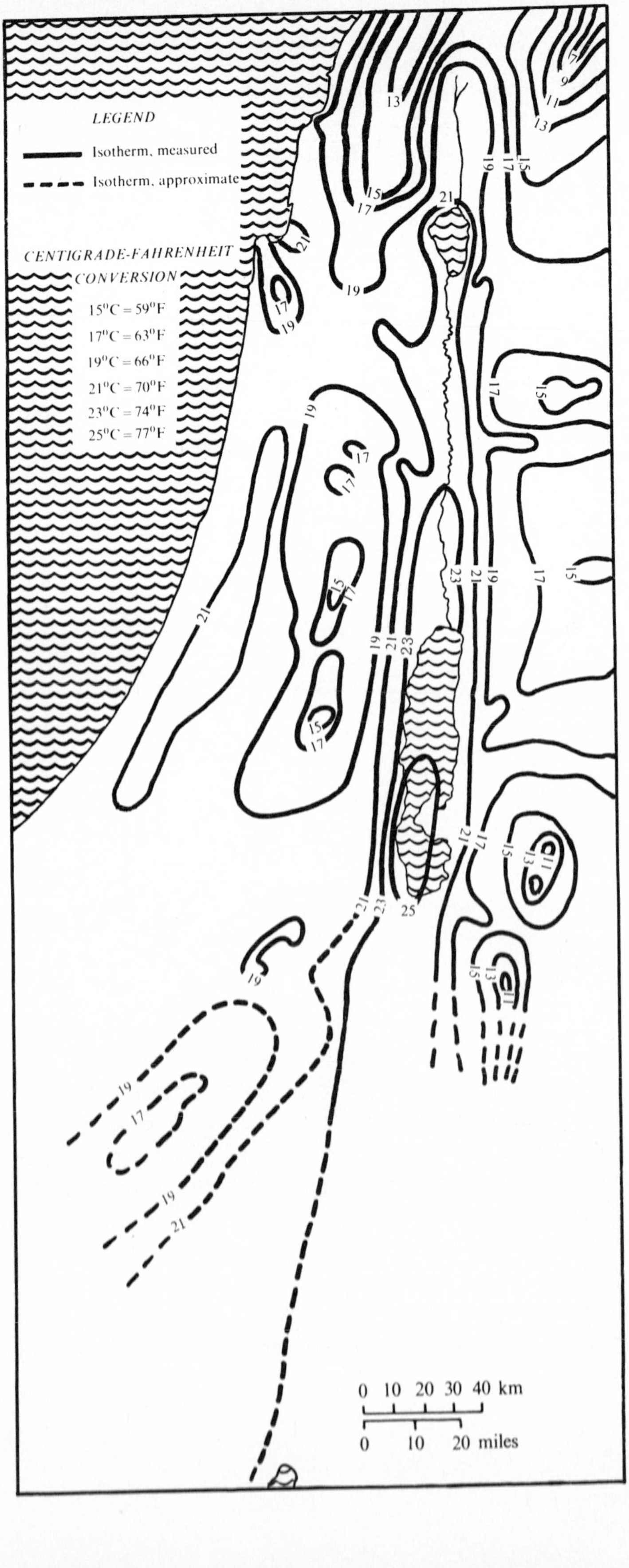

Annual temperature isotherms in the country

44°C (111°F). Winter cold was particularly severe, during the last quarter century, on February 5 and 7, 1950, when Tel Aviv registered 1°C (34°F), Jerusalem −4.4°C (24°F), and the lowest absolute temperature was measured in the Bet Netofa Valley of Lower Galilee: −13°C (8.6°F).

The daily temperature range, as is to be expected, is smallest in the Coastal Plain, where the sea's proximity exerts a mitigating influence, and largest in the Central and Southern Negev, which have a pronouncedly continental climatic regime. Surprisingly enough, the daily march of temperature in the Hills shows few extremes and hardly differs from that of the Coastal Plain. Eilat, on the other hand, although lying on the Red Sea shore, has sharp differences between day and night temperatures; winds blowing the year round from the north, i.e., from the interior of the land, bar marine influence from this shore.

MONTHLY MEAN TEMPERATURES IN TEL AVIV AND JERUSALEM

	Tel Aviv		*Jerusalem*	
	°Centigrade	*°Fahrenheit*	*°Centigrade*	*°Fahrenheit*
January	13.7	56.7	9.7	49.5
February	14.3	57.7	11.6	52.9
March	17.2	63.0	13.8	56.8
April	19.1	66.4	17.7	63.9
May	21.3	70.3	21.3	71.0
June	22.5	72.5	23.7	74.7
July	24.1	75.4	24.4	75.9
August	24.8	76.6	25.0	77.0
September	23.6	74.5	23.9	75.0
October	22.3	72.1	21.8	71.2
November	18.7	65.7	17.2	63.0
December	15.2	59.4	12.3	54.1

In general, temperatures in the country can be regarded as propitious for farming. In the Coastal Plain, citrus fruit and other crops sensitive to cold are very rarely endangered by frost, while deciduous fruit and vines on the Hills receive in most winters the moderate 'cold ration' needed to enter dormancy. The sharav heat waves in May and June adversely affect humans and animals and damage pastures, which wither quickly. On the whole, however, they benefit farming, as they hasten the ripening of grain and fruit, and are thus comparable to the 'killing frost' of colder regions in aiding the farmer to combat weeds and pests. The variety in temperatures registered in different parts of the country enables planners and farmers to stagger harvesting dates and avoid market gluts. As a result of these circumstances, for all practical purposes agriculture in Israel has no 'dead season.'

Atmospheric Pressure and Winds

In the system of global atmospheric pressure belts and planetary winds, Israel in summer lies in the subtropical zone of the northern hemisphere. When the entire system is displaced southward during the northern winter, the country moves into the middle-latitudes belt of 'westerlies' or cyclone winds.

The subtropical zone, or 'horse latitudes,' roughly covers the latitudes 25 to 35°. From this zone air diverges and strikes, near the earth's surface, southwest as 'trade winds,' toward the equator and northeast, as 'westerlies,' in the direction of the North Pole. This divergence creates a vertical downward movement of air in the subtropical zone itself. Subsiding or settling air is therefore characteristic of the 'horse latitudes' belt. As vertical air movements do not create the sensation of blowing winds, this zone is also described as 'high pressure calms.' The descending air is compressed and heated and is thereby desiccated.

All these phenomena are most pronounced in those subtropical countries which, like Israel, lie near the western margins of large continents.

In the virtual absence of other strong winds, horizontal air movements in Israel are in summer restricted to breezes, i.e., local or, at most, regional winds. The breeze is caused by the differences in the diurnal march of temperature over the land and the adjacent sea. The land warms quickly during the day and cools quickly at night; the land is therefore cooler than the sea and has stronger atmospheric pressure late at night, with opposing conditions during the day. Thus, winds are likely to blow from the land to the sea at night and reverse their direction during the day. The incoming sea breeze usually begins to be felt on Israel's Mediterranean shore between 7 and 8 o'clock in the morning, reaches the hilltops toward noon, and arrives in the Jordan Valley at about 2 o'clock in the afternoon. While the breeze ascends the western slopes of the Hills, the expanding air is cool and refreshing, but on its steep way down to the Jordan Rift, it is quickly heated and becomes sultry and oppressive. Rising to the Transjordan Plateau during the afternoon hours, the breeze is cooled and regains its pleasantness.

The summer day sea breeze is incomparably stronger and more persistent than that blowing from the land at night. This is caused by the barometric low which develops in summer over the Persian Gulf. It sucks in air from the west, and thus reinforces the sea breezes and weakens land breezes in the Levant countries.

An essential change in conditions occurs with the advent of winter, when the country enters the zone of the westerlies. Typical of this zone are cyclones, units of low and high barometric pressure which move in a general west-east direction and alternately reach the eastern Mediterranean basin. The higher the pressure gradients, the stronger the winds emerging from anticyclones and circling around cyclone centers, counterclockwise, as everywhere in the northern hemisphere. In midwinter the Polar Front stretches from west to east above the Mediterranean Sea; there air masses from the polar regions converge with tropical air and generate many cyclone cells. In addition, cyclones moving over the Atlantic Ocean from America to Western and Northwestern Europe during most of the year are deflected south in winter, since the powerful anticyclone hovering over the 'cold pole' of Siberia and Inner Asia bars their way northeast. The Mediterranean Sea, therefore, is the only open track for cyclones between the Inner Asian high pressure center in the northeast and the subtropical high pressure belt which, in that season, is over the Sahara in the southwest and south.

The onmoving cyclones and anticyclones of the winter cause an approximately regular change of wind directions in this country. As long as a cyclone is over the

Cyclones (L) and anticyclones (H) moving over the eastern basin of the Mediterranean Sea and the Levant countries (arrows indicate wind directions over Israel)

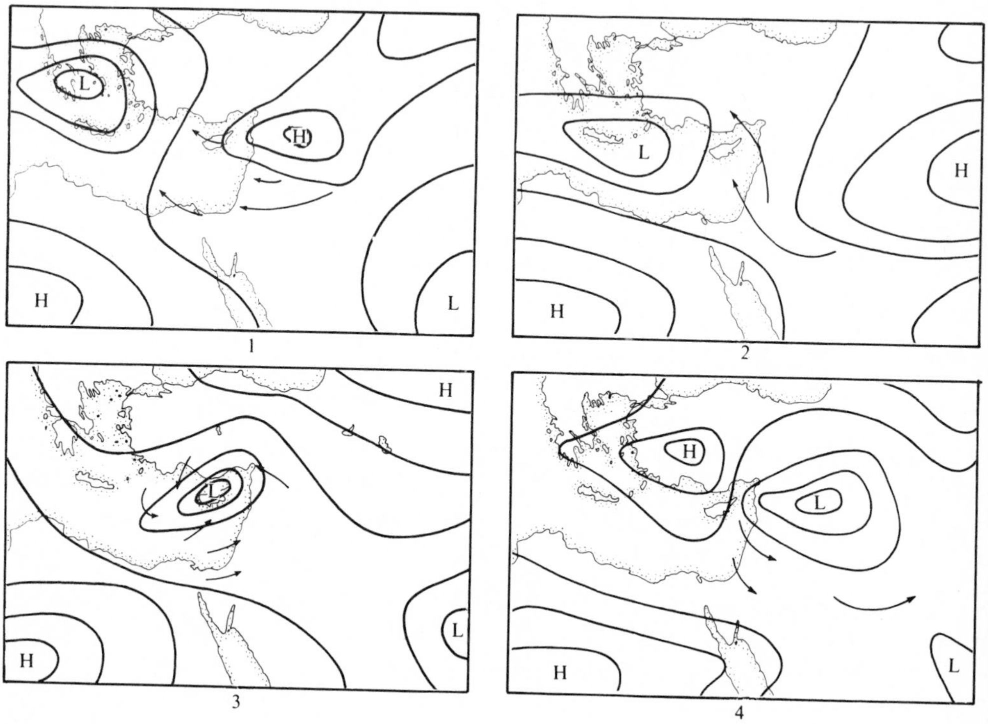

Central Mediterranean Sea and Greece, and an anticyclone over the Levant, winds in the country blow at first from the northeast and east, and later from the southeast; they issue counterclockwise from the anticyclone and strive toward the cyclone. After a day or more, the cyclone reaches the eastern basin of the Mediterranean, and often stays for a while over Cyprus ('the Cyprus Low'). Winds over Israel then change their direction and come from the sea in the southwest. As the cyclone moves eastward, winds veer to the west and northwest and, finally, again to the northeast.

Air masses of different qualities are sucked into the cyclone. With the eastward displacement of the cyclone center, they meet and create 'fronts.' Winds blowing from the southwest into the southeast quadrant of the cyclone strike the colder air of the area. Thus, a 'warm front' is formed where the buoyant warm air rises diagonally over the heavy, cold air and in turn cools down in the process. The opposite occurs when the country moves into the southwest quadrant of the cyclone. There, cold air from the north or northwest is the 'aggressor'; because of its greater weight, it flows close to the surface and pushes in beneath the retreating warm air, which is lifted and thus cooled. As cyclone tracks usually run to the north of Israel, with each passing low pressure center the country comes under the successive influences of warm and cold fronts.

Sharav and Similar Winds. Three main synoptic situations are apt to cause eastern and southeastern winds in Israel or a rise in barometric pressure: (a) 'khamsin,' resulting from a barometric low over Libya or Egypt, which attracts winds that blow over Israel from the east; (b) 'sharav,' a barometric high developing over the country itself where the subsiding air is compressed and heated; (c) a barometric low reaching the country from the direction of the Red Sea, bringing with it unseasonally warm air. In midwinter easterly winds cause a relative warming of the pronouncedly cold air. Less frequent are the bitingly cold, dry winter winds blowing out from the high pressure areas of Siberia and Middle Asia, occasionally bearing large amounts of fine dust.

Most of the sharav winds appear in the beginning and at the end of the winter cyclone circulation, i.e., in September-October, and from May to mid-June. The sharav may cause temperatures to soar by 15°C (27°F) and more, and relative humidity to drop by as much as 40%. It may last for two, three, or more days on end. When sharav conditions reach their peak, fine dust impairs visibility, and weak but hot and dry winds blow. A winter sharav may raise the temperature by 10°C (18°F). Most sharav winds, set into motion by a barometric low west of the country, blow from the east or southeast at first, later veer to the south; when the low moves eastward, the incoming air from the west brings coolness and moisture.

The heat and dryness of the sharav cause discomfort to most people, especially when the air temperature exceeds that of the human body; the dust is a further irritation factor. In the Hills, the sharav is usually stronger and less bearable than in the Coastal Plain, where cool, moist air clings to the surface, and the hot desert wind strikes above it. Often, during the descent from the Hills westward in the morning of a spring sharav day, the Plain below is seen shrouded in mists while the sky above is clear and the hill air oppressively hot.

Moisture and Precipitation

Dry Summers and Rainy Winters. In Israel, conditions of rain formation change abruptly with the autumn shift from the subtropical to the cyclone belt, and again in spring when the country returns into the former zone. In subtropical regions, the predominant movement of the air is subsidence. Air thus compressed warms up, its relative humidity decreases, and rain is impossible; the only possible form of precipitation is night dewfall. Similar conditions are found in the trade wind region, south of Israel, where the air moving equatorward is warmed up on its way. In the cyclone regions, on the other hand, the air ascends over the centers of barometric lows, along warm and cold fronts, or along the Polar Front of converging air masses, which is in winter over the Mediterranean Sea. In all these cases, the air cools and gains in relative humidity, and chances of precipitation improve. In Israel, this phenomenon is particularly pronounced, as the onmoving cyclones bring winds from the southwest and west saturated with moisture from their passage over the Mediterranean Sea. When the cyclone proceeds east and an anticyclone follows, winds change their direction, and the air subsides on its way from the east toward the next cyclone approaching from the west. During the Israeli winter, 'rain periods,' each lasting several days, are therefore usually followed by somewhat longer intervals of clear skies, sunshine, and dry air.

Geographical Distribution of Rainfall in Israel. In autumn the northern part of the country moves first from the dry subtropical into the wet cyclone belt, and in spring it shifts last back into the subtropical zone. Consequently, the rainy season is likely to begin in the north a few days earlier than in the south, and to end a few days later. In addition, the north of Israel is nearer to the usual track of cyclones, where pressure gradients become steeper. Hence, air masses move more quickly, rise at a steeper angle, are better cooled, and gain in relative humidity. The larger vapor content reaches the saturation point earlier and contributes to the buoyancy of the air, whose ascent and cooling is thus eased. All these phenomena add up to the 'northern direction factor'—rainfall increase from south to north.

This imposing waterfall, of one of the tributaries of Naḥal Ḥermon, ceases to exist in summer

Precipitation also decreases from west to east, although less than from north to south. While the amount of moisture in the air is depleted when rain falls on the way inland from the shore, only slight prospects exist of new water vapor being absorbed through evaporation from the land surface. Of two places, situated at the same latitude and altitude and under the same exposure conditions (see below), one in Cisjordan and one in Transjordan, the latter is likely to receive a somewhat inferior rainfall. Against the background of these general factors, rainfall distribution over Israel is decisively influenced by landscape relief (the 'orographic factor'). Air rising over a hill slope cools, and its relative humidity increases; conversely, when allowed to flow downhill, the air warms up, and rainfall diminishes or ceases. This is why sites exposed to the sea winds, in this country on hill slopes opening to the west or southwest, receive far more rain than those in the 'rain shadow' or on the 'leeside of rain,' on slopes facing east, southeast, or northeast.

The angle of the slope, too, is important. The steeper the ascent, the smaller the area where the amount of rain yielded by the cooling of the air concentrates. By drawing cross sections through the country we can follow up every one of the factors influencing rainfall distribution. The 'northern direction factor' is illustrated by comparing sites along the Coastal Plain, from north to south: KhanYūnis, in the Gaza Strip, has 263 mm ($10\frac{1}{2}$ in) annually; Negba (in the Southern Plain) 441 mm (about $17\frac{3}{4}$ in); Be'er Tuvya (southern border of Judean Plain) 467 mm ($18\frac{3}{4}$ in); Ramla (Judean Plain) 505 mm (20.2 in), and Tel Aviv 516 mm (20.6 in). The reduction of amounts from the coast inland and, to a certain extent, the leeside effect, become evident along a line running through the Jezreel and Ḥarod valleys from Sha'ar ha-Amaqim with 650 mm (26 in) through Nahalal with 550 mm (22 in) and Merḥavya with 450 mm (18 in) to En Ḥarod with 400 mm (16 in). The differences caused by exposure are strikingly apparent upon a comparison of Sha'ar ha-Gay Gorge, on the western slope of the Judean Hills, to 'Ein Farī'a on the eastern slope, both at the same latitude, and at an altitude of 330 m (1,000 ft): the former receives 516 mm (20.6 in) of annual rainfall, the latter 276 mm (11 in).

The Rainfall Map of the Country. Israel's rainfall map indicates the combined influence of all these factors. In the Southern and Central Negev, isohyets run approximately from southwest to northeast. Eilat, with about 15 mm (0.6 in), is the driest spot in the country. The Ramon Ridge in the Central Negev, because of its height, has over 100 mm (4 in), a somewhat larger precipitation than that of the surrounding areas. In the Northern Negev, isohyets run on the whole from west to east but turn north when approaching the leeside of the Judean Hills which descend to the Dead Sea and the Jordan Rift.

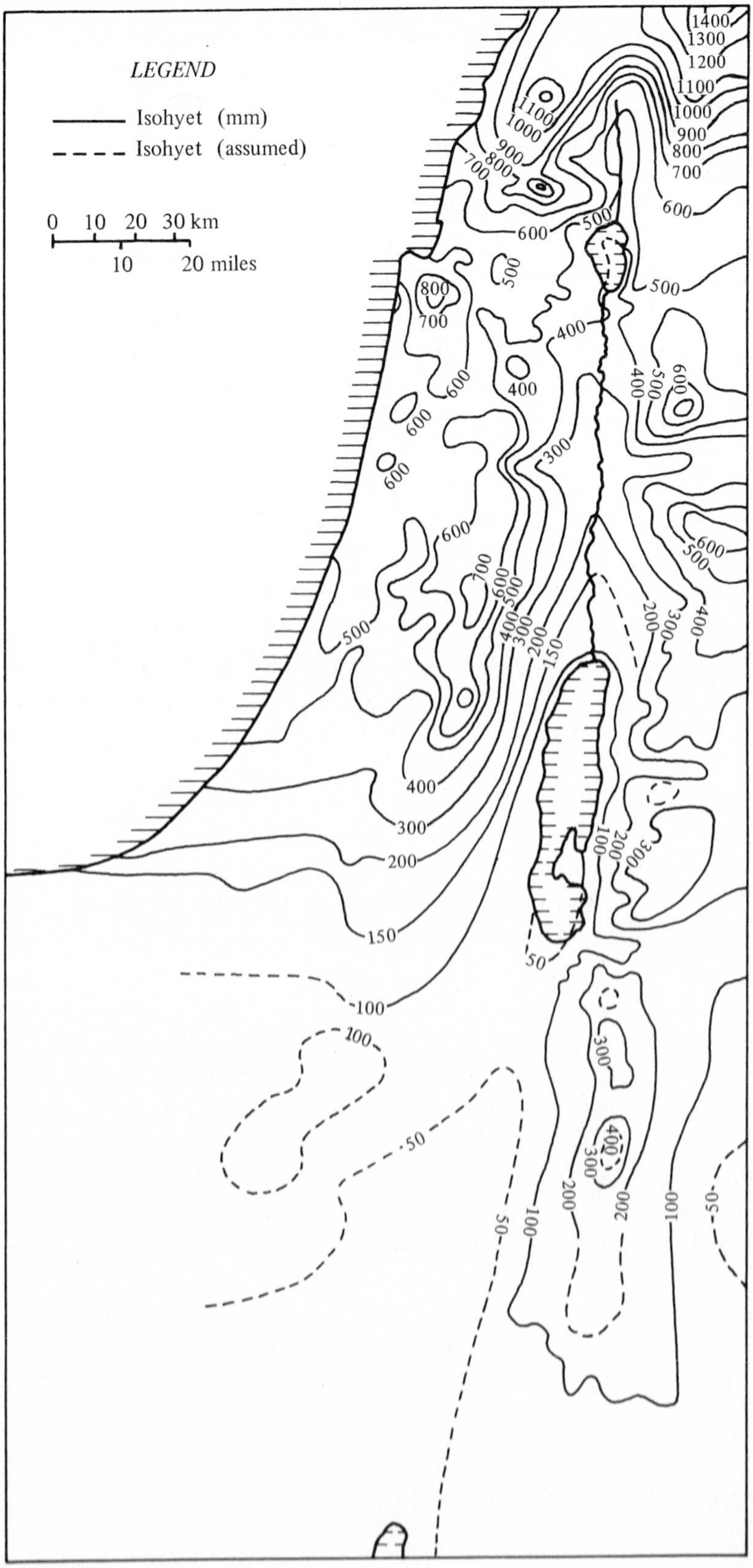

Annual rainfall distribution in the country (isohyets—in mm)

The orographic and exposure effects become clearly evident from the course of isohyets in Judea, where rainfall increases from under 500 mm (20 in) on the coast to over 700 mm (28 in) on the highest reaches of the Hills, and then abruptly drops to 100 mm (4 in) and less on the Dead Sea shore. In Transjordan, on the ascent to the Moab Plateau, there is another rapid rise in rainfall, but, from the uplifted western rim, a quick decrease becomes noticeable toward the desert conditions prevailing 15–30 km (10–20 miles) to the east. The higher southern and northern portions of the Judean Hills—the Hebron and Bethel Hills—receive a somewhat larger rainfall than the lower central 'saddle' of the Jerusalem Hills.

The Samarian Hills, lower in altitude than the Judean Hills, on the average enjoy the same rainfall amounts (northern direction effect). Outstanding is Mount Carmel, whose ridge is only 230–500 m (700–1,600 ft) high, but registers an annual rainfall of 800–900 mm (32–36 in), as a result of its proximity to the sea and its steep slopes. The Jezreel Valley, though surrounded by hills on all sides, is only partly in the rain shadow, since the Menashe Region to the southwest opens a 'corridor' for the rain-bearing winds. In Lower Galilee, the detailed rainfall map (as distinct from the more generalized one in this book) reflects the irregularity of topographical relief. Central Upper Galilee, especially Mount Meron, has, with annual averages of 1,000–1,100 mm (40–44 in), the highest rainfall west of the Jordan. Mount Ḥermon, because of its great altitude and its more northern location, registers annual averages reaching 1,500 mm (60 in).

The Rainy Season. Israel's rainy season is short. Between November and February almost 70% of the annual rainfall occurs. In most parts of the country, January is the rainiest month. In March, precipitation usually decreases sharply, and only small quantities are registered in the first half of April, as in the second half of October. Rain in September and May is rare and comes to negligible amounts, while June, July and August, as a rule, have no rain at all. Although the rainy season in Galilee sets in a few days earlier in autumn, and ends a few days later in spring, the rule is subject to exceptions; some heavy showers, limited in duration and area, may fall somewhere in the Negev in April or even in May, while the sky is clear throughout the rest of the country.

Chronological rainfall distribution over the country is varied: the Coastal Plain receives 50% of its annual total as early as the beginning of January, the Hills attain that percentage toward the end of the month, and Transjordan only in February; this phenomenon is not fully explained as yet.

Rain Days and Rainfall Intensity. Rainfall is, on the whole, more intensive in this country than in temperate or cool climatic regions. This is clear from the relationship between annual rainfall totals and the number of rain days per year (a rain day, in international terminology, must have at least 0.1 mm of diurnal rainfall). Thus, both Jerusalem and London have an annual average of about 550 mm (22 in) of rain, but this quantity is distributed in Jerusalem over an average of 50 days, while in London—over 300 days.

The number of rain days per season increases from south to north, and decreases from west to east. The Southern Coastal Plain registers 30–40 rain days per year, Judea and Samaria about 50, the Jordan Valley about 25, and Upper Galilee between 60 and 80.

Rainfall may be highly concentrated. Thus, 500 mm (20 in) were measured in the Coastal Plain during ten days in December, 1951, and 160 mm (6.4 in) over 5 days in November, 1938. Such violent rains are apt to cause disastrous floods and erosion, particularly at the beginning of the season, when the soil is not yet readily absorbent. Heavy showers are most frequent at the beginning and toward the end of the season, with clashing air masses which differ strongly in temperature and moisture content. The Negev and the Jordan Valley showers are particularly violent and short-lived.

Snow and Hail. A small percentage of the country's precipitation may take the form of hail or snow. Snowfall, normally limited to higher parts of the Hills, is even there rather infrequent. Jerusalem has, on the average, two days of snowfall per year, and Safed five. Snow usually falls in January or February, the coldest months. Outstanding was the snowfall of February 5, 1950, which covered the whole country; Acre then registered 55 cm (21½ in) snow, Jerusalem 70 cm (27½ in), and even Tiberias 15 cm (6 in). Mount Ḥermon receives a considerable portion of its precipitation in the form of snow.

Few data are available on hail in the country. The Coastal Plain has an average of 5–8 days of hail per year, mostly in midwinter. This hail is liable to cause damage principally to vegetables and ripening oranges in the Coastal Plain, while the winter grains, still low, are unharmed. In any case, hail in this country is far less menacing than it is in Western and Central Europe or North America.

Dew. Dewfall provides a limited amount of moisture even during the dry summer, and is important to summer crops such as watermelon. The nearer the area to the sea, the better are its prospects for dewfall on windless nights when the soil grows colder than the air which touches its surface. In general, the Coastal Plain has more dew than inland regions; richest is Mount Carmel, which has an average 250 nights of dew per year.

Evaporation. The moisture available to plant growth, animal life, and man is ultimately determined by the relationship between rainfall and evaporation. This can be expressed by the 'rain factor,' i.e., annual precipitation (in mm) of a place, divided by its mean annual temperature (in centigrade). In the more humid regions of the country, the rain factor attains 50, while over large expanses it sinks below 15, the borderline for absolute desert conditions.

There are, however, several other facts which influence the evaporation rate. Naturally, evaporation is particularly strong in summer, owing to the high temperatures, to intensive insolation under a cloudless sky, and to the low air humidity on sharav days. The Coastal Plain has, because of its year-round high air humidity, a comparatively low evaporation rate (3–4.5 mm = 0.12–0.18 in per day); in the Hills, this rises to 4.5–7 mm (0.18–0.28 in), and during the summer in the Dead Sea Region to a maximum of 13 mm (0.51 in). It must be remembered, however, that only water surfaces, which are in full contact with the air, are fully affected by evaporation, while water that has seeped into the ground is, for the most part, protected. Fortunately for Israel, its rainfall is concentrated in the cool season, so that there is less evaporation upon reaching the ground than would be the case with summer rains. The 'rain factor' can therefore be taken only with reservation as a criterion of the climatic character of regions in this country. It is estimated that in Israel 50–60% of rainwater evaporates immediately (for comparison: countries with tropical summer rains register up to 95% evaporation). Another 10% or more is lost later, and between 5 and 15% returns to the sea in surface runoff. Only 10–25% of the precipitation, therefore, remains for the needs of the country and its inhabitants.

Drought and the Aridity Border. Drought, in Israel, means either a period without precipitation during the rainy season, or an entire rainy season with precipitation markedly below average. Lack of rain, as well as unseasonal heat and the resulting high evaporation rates, are factors of drought conditions. In the north, drought is a comparatively small menace, as a drop of 100 mm (4 in) or more from the annual average cannot seriously affect the water balance of the region. In the Northern Negev, on the other hand, 100 mm (4 in) less of rain is, in effect, a third, or even a half, less than the annual total. Not only are the regions of the 'aridity border' most sensitive to vacillations in rainfall, but precipitation there is most unpredictable. While in Western Europe deviations of more than 10% from the annual mean are exceptional, the Northern Negev or the Bet She'an Valley may receive only one third of their average annual rainfall and, in other years, twice the normal amount. Even if the annual total attains the average, a region may suffer from 'agricultural drought,' when the rains begin too late, are interrupted for several weeks in midwinter, or cease too early in spring, so that the growth of crops is impeded, and they wither before bearing fruit.

Drought years in Israel are frequent, and often affect the entire country. In

1950–51, for example, only 35% of the annual average fell on the northwest shore of the Sea of Galilee, 43% in Jerusalem, 53% in Haifa, and 65% in Tel Aviv. Often there are series of drought years, as in the five winters between autumn 1958 and spring 1963. There is, however, no recognizable regularity in the incidence of ample rainfall periods and of drought years. In Jerusalem, where rainfall has been measured continuously since 1846, the periods 1854–1859, 1880–1898, 1917–1922, 1936–1939 and 1941–1945 had above-average rainfall, while between 1869 and 1873, or between 1924 and 1936, most years were those of drought. A drought in a certain year does not necessarily affect all parts of the country to the same degree; the Negev or the Judean Hills may be severely hit by drought while rainfall in the north is normal, or vice versa.

The lower the annual total of precipitation, the larger the likely deviations from the average, and the greater the danger to crops. An annual rainfall of 250 mm (10 in) suffices, on the heavy loess soil of the Negev, for the success of the winter wheat crop. The 'aridity border,' however, must be drawn further north, along the 350 mm (14 in) isohyet, for beyond it the precipitation for too many years has been considerably below that average and not even attained the necessary minimum of 250 mm (10 in). The 350 mm (14 in) isohyet runs along the northern margin of the Negev, separates the Judean Hills from the Judean Desert, and cuts through the Bet She'an Valley.

Climatic Regions of Israel

The division of Cisjordan into four main geographical regions—the Negev, the Coastal Plain, the Hills, and the Jordan and Dead Sea Rift—is also valid for climatic conditions.*

The Climate of the Negev

The Negev differs vastly in climate from the country's center and north. Two climatic subregions can be discerned—the Northern Negev, which includes only about half of the Beersheba Region and can be described, at best, as semiarid, and all other parts of the Negev which are desert proper. Although the climatic conditions of the Negev are better known today than they were prior to 1948,

* Transjordan south of the Yarmuk River is not included due to lack of data and to the fact that its climate is irrelevant to the economy of the State of Israel.

data are still far from complete, owing to the difficulty in covering a vast, empty area with a dense observation network.

Temperatures. With the exception of the Sedom Region and the Arava Valley, temperatures in the Negev on the whole are hardly more difficult to endure than those in the northern half of the country. On summer days temperatures rise from the Mediterranean Coast inland. In August, Beersheba has 33.7°C (93°F), Oron 35.1°C (95½°F), and Eilat 40°C (104°F) and over. The continentality of the Negev climate is well illustrated by the diurnal span of temperatures, which in Beersheba attains 15–16°C (27–29°F) in May and June.

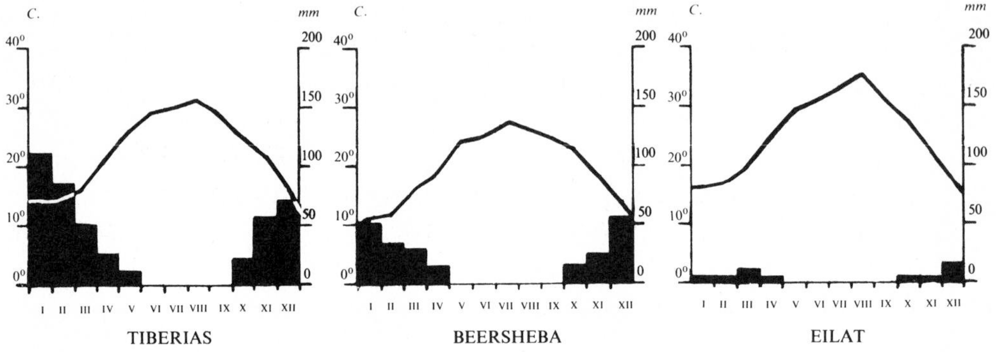

Monthly temperatures and rainfall averages at selected stations in the Negev and the Jordan Rift

Winds. The summer breeze is more marked in the Negev than elsewhere, due to sharper differences between sea and land temperatures. In Beersheba summer winds blow from the southwest or west during the morning, veer to the northwest in the afternoon, and to the southeast during the night. In winter, wind directions are irregular. Strong easterly or southeasterly winds carry great amounts of dust.

The Arava Valley has, throughout the year, constant north or northeast winds, which are responsible for the pronouncedly continental climate of the Eilat shore. Only when a barometric low passes north of Eilat in winter or spring, does a sudden southern storm arise, throwing up high breakers and wreaking havoc on this otherwise perfectly calm shore.

Air Humidity. Relative air humidity decreases in the Negev as one proceeds inland from the Mediterranean. Thus, Nirim, on the Gaza Strip border, has an average relative humidity only slightly inferior to that of Tel Aviv. In the Beersheba Region, the annual average is 58%, but at Oron, to the southeast, only 48%. In the high parts of the Negev Hills, however, air humidity approaches that of similar altitudes in Judea and Galilee. The lowest humidity values of the country are

MONTHLY AVERAGE OF RELATIVE HUMIDITY (IN %)

Place	*Jan.*	*Feb.*	*March*	*April*	*May*	*June*	*July*	*Aug.*	*Sept.*	*Oct.*	*Nov.*	*Dec.*
Haifa	75	65	58	61	53	64	66	67	64	64	54	64
Tel Aviv	66	78	66	71	52	72	72	74	69	68	64	78
Negba (Southern Coastal Plain)	74	74	69	59	56	60	64	68	64	62	57	65
Mount Canaan (near Safed)	76	73	58	57	39	45	47	51	57	52	57	73
Jerusalem	72	58	47	38	54	45	53	49	60	61	42	63
Dafna (Ḥula Valley)	70	70	66	64	40	53	56	59	57	55	61	71
Sedom	54	50	38	49	44	30	33	33	39	43	41	56
Eilat	52	47	32	29	64	26	29	33	37	38	44	45
Beersheba	64	64	42	41	73	46	54	58	60	58	44	60
Miẓpe Ramon (Negev Hills)	65	62	50	48	67	53	59	50	63	60	54	66

measured in the Arava Valley where En Yahav, for example, has an annual mean of 40%.

Precipitation. While rainfall north of Gaza amounts to 400 mm (16 in) and more per year, the 300 mm (12 in) and 200 mm (8 in) isohyets run through the Beersheba Region from west to east, and turn north in the Arad Region. At Niẓẓana on the Sinai border, the annual total remains below 100 mm (4 in). In the Negev Hills precipitation varies, according to local topography, between 100 mm (4 in) and 200 mm (8 in) per year; most of the Arava Valley registers 50 mm (2 in) or less. Rainfall is most capricious in the Negev. The number of rainy days, like the precipitation totals, decreases toward the south and east. Gaza counts an average 45 rain days per year, Beersheba 33, the Negev Hills 15–20, and the Arava Valley 8 or less. Extremely intensive rainstorms are characteristic of the Negev desert. On December 5, 1934, for instance, 64 mm (2.6 in) fell in Beersheba during 24 hours.

The Climate of the Coastal Plain

Temperatures. The inner part of the Coastal Plain has a wider diurnal and annual range of temperatures than that of the shore strip, although the annual mean amounts in both cases to 19°C (66°F). January averages 13°C (55°F) and August 26°C (79°F). Winter frost is extremely rare in the Coastal Plain; the hot sharav is less frequent here than in other parts of the country, and is practically absent from the shore proper. The built-up areas, particularly Tel Aviv, suffer from sultry summer heat, as the houses bar the refreshing breezes, and their whitewashed walls reflect the sun's heat onto the streets.

Air Humidity. During most of the year, relative humidity attains high values in the Coastal Plain with averages of 65–70%; it is highest on the shore and decreases inland. In many places humidity is highest toward evening, but on the seashore there are smaller diurnal oscillations. Summer months are most humid, and October is driest. On sharav days, the air's moisture content may sink below 10% in the inner part of the Coastal Plain. Humidity is greatest in built-up areas like Tel Aviv, where it adds to the discomfort during the hot summer.

Precipitation. Rainfall increases from 250 mm (10 in) annually at the southern extremity of the Coastal Plain to 800 mm (32 in) in its northernmost section. The Carmel Coast also receives nearly 800 mm, since the rock walls of Mount Carmel force the moisture-laden air from the sea to rise and cool. The Haifa Bay Area, on the other hand, which is beyond Mount Carmel on the leeside of the rain, receives only 500–600 mm (20–24 in). Kibbutz Yagur, however, lying at the foot of the high and steep northeast escarpment of Mount Carmel, represents an anomaly there; following the law of inertia, the moist air reaching over the escarpment rim continues to rise for a small distance; it thereby increases its relative humidity, so that the highest amounts of rainfall (800–900 mm—32–36 in) are received, not on the top of Mount Carmel, but at its foot.

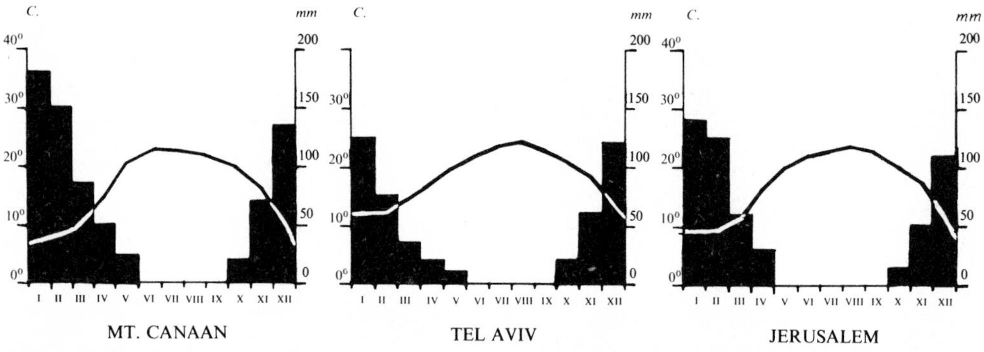

Monthly temperatures and rainfall averages at selected stations in the Coastal Plain and the Hills

As mentioned above, December and January are normally the rainiest months in the Coastal Plain, and 60% of the season's rain falls by the end of January. Although rains are not particularly intensive here, the season may begin with very heavy showers.

Dew. The Coastal Plain is rich in dew, particularly in the south where the sea supplies the moisture and the continental regime of the nearby desert cools the air at night sufficiently to warrant condensation. Dewfall is weaker on the shore and on the eastern margin of the Coastal Plain than in its interior parts. Up to 200–250 nights of the year have dew, with an average of 200. The total of annual dewfall in the region is estimated at 30 mm (1.2 in). The hottest month, August, which also has the highest absolute humidity rates, brings most dew to the central and northern parts of the Coastal Plain; on the Negev Coast, dew is most abundant in May and June.

The Climate of the Hills

Temperatures. Hill temperatures are generally lower than those of the rest of the country, with an annual average of 16–17°C (61–62°F). Between December and March, the daily average does not exceed 11°C (52°F), with minima of 4°C (39°F), and maxima of 15°C (59°F). Absolute minima are lowest not on the hill tops, but in intermontane valleys, where they are caused by temperature inversion on windless nights. While the valley ground remains excessively cold only for a few hours at a time, cold waves may persist on the hill tops for over a day or more. In summer, however, parts of the Hills register slightly higher temperatures than does the Coastal Plain, as shown in the table comparing monthly averages of Jerusalem to those of Tel Aviv (see p. 138).

The Foothills, with an annual average of 20°C (68°F), are much warmer than the Hills, and even warmer, by 1°C (1.8°F), than the Coastal Plain. Winter temperatures resemble those of the Coastal Plain, but heat waves are frequent on sharav days at the beginning and end of summer. The daily temperature range may amount there to 13°C (23°F).

Winds. The Hills, particularly Galilee, sometimes have violent winter storms. Wind velocities of 120 km (75 miles) per hour have been measured at places such as Menara, Mt. Canaan, etc.

Humidity and Evaporation. Relative humidity, with an annual mean of 60%, is lower in the Hills than in the Coastal Plain, except in the winter months, when the rates are about equal. During the sharav periods extremely low humidity may last for days on end in the Hills (in contrast to the Coastal Plain). A sharav which raises temperatures by 10–15°C (18–27°F) may depress relative humidity by as much as 30–40%. Humidity minima are generally registered in May, and maxima in January and February.

The low moisture content of the air entails strong evaporation, and the surface of the soil dries rapidly at the beginning of summer. Local topography exerts a decisive influence on evaporation: slopes opening south and subject to direct insolation during most hours of the day are perceptibly drier (hence much poorer in natural vegetation) than slopes facing north. Heat, evaporation, and desiccation are stronger on bare rock slopes than on those covered with soil. Light-colored limestone and chalk, like the whitewashed walls in the cities, reflect the sun's rays. Black basalts, on the other hand, become very hot from absorbing these rays. To prevent young saplings from being burnt by the heat emanating from the basalt stones it was found advisable to remove stones from around them.

Precipitation. The Hills have the largest rainfall west of the Jordan. The Judean Hills register annual averages of 600–700 mm (24–28 in) and over (with top values in the Hebron and Bethel Hills). Mount Meron, in Upper Galilee, receives as much as 1,100 mm (44 in). The Foothills average, in their southern extremities,

AVERAGE MONTHLY RAINFALL AT SELECTED STATIONS (IN MM)

Station	*Sept.*	*Oct.*	*Nov.*	*Dec.*	*Jan.*	*Feb.*	*March*	*April*	*May*	*Yearly total*
Nahariya	1.2	28.1	98.1	140.5	173.5	119.7	50.3	21.9	5.7	639
Haifa Port	—	19.0	86.8	143.4	181.3	132.2	42.5	21.5	6.3	633
Bet Oren (Mt. Carmel)	0.3	21.4	106.9	177.1	191.4	131.6	50.4	24.6	8.3	712
Ḥadera	0.9	15.3	83.5	165.9	153.0	105.2	37.9	14.1	4.2	580
Tel Aviv	3.3	17.8	83.1	150.4	124.0	89.9	34.4	13.8	2.3	519
Ashqelon	0.2	13.0	68.4	104.8	109.1	76.5	34.8	13.3	1.9	422
Mt. Canaan	2.1	15.5	80.4	139.0	195.3	172.2	72.0	35.6	15.9	728
Nazareth	0.6	11.8	71.9	139.1	172.2	146.2	63.3	27.5	6.4	639
Nahalal (Jezreel Valley)	0.3	12.1	70.6	131.2	142.9	132.6	45.1	18.0	5.2	558
En Ḥarod	0.4	12.7	51.1	81.1	109.9	91.3	35.3	17.9	4.3	404
Jerusalem	0.8	9.2	61.8	89.4	153.0	143.3	68.0	22.8	2.7	551
Bet Shemesh	0.1	9.4	60.1	84.0	124.8	106.6	54.8	18.3	2.9	461
Beersheba	0.3	4.0	25.2	39.6	47.9	40.8	30.5	7.4	4.3	200
Niẓẓana (Sinai border)	0.1	2.1	12.4	19.8	10.9	18.1	15.1	7.7	3.8	90
Dan (Ḥula Valley)	0.7	11.6	69.5	111.3	163.0	142.1	67.8	37.8	11.2	615
Kinneret	—	5.6	46.7	84.8	120.0	86.6	41.2	26.0	5.1	416
Tirat Ẓevi (Bet She'an Valley)	0.5	10.3	37.2	62.5	65.6	61.9	27.5	12.7	9.8	288
Jericho	—	3.0	18.6	27.5	35.5	31.1	17.0	7.1	3.2	143
Sedom	—	5.2	3.6	8.5	11.8	8.2	9.2	2.5	2.0	51
Eilat	—	0.2	1.6	9.1	11.6	6.1	6.2	4.2	1.0	30

only 400 mm (16 in), but up to 700 mm (28 in) in Northern Judea and Western Galilee. Because of the variety of topographical relief, the rainfall map of the Hills lacks homogeneity.

The rainy season sets in later in the Hills than in the Coastal Plain, and rainfall reaches its peak between mid-January and mid-February. The number of rain days per year attains 50–60 in Judea, 70–80 in Galilee. Snow falls in the highest parts of the Hills almost every year; a maximum was recorded in February, 1920, when the snow lay at a depth of 1 m (3 ft) in Jerusalem.

Dewfall in the Hills, averaging between 100 and 180 nights per year, is more restricted than in the Coastal Plain. In addition to Mount Carmel, however, Western Lower Galilee is rich in dew, with 200–250 dew nights annually. Eastern Galilee and Southern Judea, on the other hand, have only sparse dewfall. The geographical distribution of dew, like that of rain, is very irregular, due to differences in topographical relief.

The Climate of the Jordan Rift

Since climatic conditions change considerably between sections of the Jordan Rift, each subregion must be described separately, and the interplay of the diverse factors governing them pointed out.

Ḥula Valley. The climate of the Ḥula Valley is characterized by two topographical features which exert opposing influences. The basin-shaped valley is hemmed in by steep mountain sides; it is thus in the rain shadow and, to a certain extent, is also protected from winds; this entails a continental temperature regime, with heat hovering over the valley ground in summer. On the other hand, Mount Ḥermon, blanketed with snow, creates cold waves in the Ḥula Valley in winter; the steepness of the mountain slopes favors temperature inversion (i.e., cold, therefore heavy, air from the mountains flowing to the valley ground on windless nights and settling there raises the warmer and lighter air). This explains the frost nights in the Ḥula Valley every winter. It also assures the success of the extensive apple orchards, which need winter cold, and prohibits banana cultivation, in spite of the summer heat and the abundant water supply.

Between mean temperatures of January, 11°C (52°F), and August, 27°C (81°F), the range is considerable: 16°C (29°F). The annual mean of relative humidity has decreased surprisingly since the Ḥula Lake and Swamps have been drained; it would be still lower if not for the extensive carp ponds in the valley. Precipitation averages 550 mm (22 in), less in the southern reaches of the Ḥula Valley, and more at Dafna and Dan on its northern rim.

Kinnarot Valley. This region's climate is also controlled by two topographical factors opposed in their effect, although quite different from those of the Ḥula Valley. The valley ground, 200 m (650 ft) and more below sea level, therefore has a high barometric pressure. Temperatures are high during most of the year, because of the steep descent into the valley, where the air is compressed and warmed by friction. Winter temperatures are also mitigated by the water body of Lake Kinneret, which fills a large portion of this section in the Rift. The August mean reads 31°C (88°F), and the January mean does not sink below 14°C (57°F). Thus, bananas, date palms, and other crops sensitive to cold succeed, as do out-of-season vegetables and fruit in the region. The valley, although on the leeside of rain, is open to westerly winds. Lake Kinneret creates a breeze circulation of its own; during the late hours of the night, especially in summer, weak winds blow from the shores of the lake toward its center. In the morning the direction is reversed and the surrounding areas receive a light wind from the lake. In the early afternoon, however, the stronger breeze from the Mediterranean shore overrides this local regime; compressed in its descent into the low-lying valley, it adds to the oppressive heat and dryness. Since it hits the eastern rim more sharply than the western shore of Lake Kinneret, summer afternoons at En Gev are usually hotter than those at Tiberias.

In winter violent winds sometimes enter the narrow valley; unable to continue out through the east side, they whirl over Lake Kinneret, raise high waves in it, and sometimes create thunderstorms accompanied by torrential rain. Averaging 350–500 mm (14–20 in), annual precipitation is not great, but usually comes down in short, concentrated showers. The number of rain days never exceeds 50 per year. The presence of the lake raises relative humidity to an annual mean of 65%.

Bet She'an Valley. The Bet She'an Valley lies even deeper below sea level than does Lake Kinneret and its surroundings. With the absence of a mitigating water body, it has a pronouncedly continental temperature regime. Although the highest temperature ever recorded in the country was measured at Tirat Ẓevi in the Bet She'an Valley, January, averaging 13°C (55°F), is quite cool. Winter cold excludes bananas from this valley, although it permits the cultivation of date palms. Relative humidity is low, and dewfall sparse, but both have recently increased somewhat as a result of the installation of carp ponds. Rainfall does not exceed 350 mm (14 in) annually, and even that amount is extremely capricious, so that the valley is frequently hit by drought.

Ḥarod Valley. This valley forms the transition between the Bet She'an and Jezreel valleys in climate, as in topography. Toward the west temperatures fall and precipitation increases. Summer breezes rapidly warm up when passing through this narrow corridor. The wall-like escarpment of Mount Gilboa bars winds coming from the southwest. Characteristic of the Ḥarod Valley are climatic differences in accordance with altitude and exposure between sites only a few score yards from each other.

Jezreel Valley. This region is under a stronger maritime influence than are the other interior valleys, yet its climate differs greatly from that of the Coastal Plain. The annual temperature mean increases from 18°C (64°F) in its northwest part to 21°C (70°F) in its southeast corner. Although winter frost is less frequent here than in the Bet She'an Valley, the region is not entirely free of it. Because of the steep Nazareth Chain rising beyond it, the northern part of the Jezreel Valley has a comparatively ample rainfall: 600 mm (24 in) and more, while the south lies, to a certain extent, on the leeside of rain.

Lower Jordan Valley. Meteorological reports of this section of the Rift are less detailed than those of other sections; its description must therefore be more generalized. This region can be regarded as the transition zone between the dry-steppe climate of the Bet She'an Valley and the extreme desert conditions of the Dead Sea. From north to south, barometric pressure, temperatures and evaporation become higher, and rainfall and dew lower. The lowermost flood terrace of the Jordan certainly differs from the higher steps of the valley; in double or triple seclusion from the west, its microclimate, owing to the water of the Jordan and its annual winter inundations, has peak temperatures and a somewhat higher humidity rate than the rest of the region. The eastern bank of the Jordan is more exposed than the western to the hot, dry summer breeze; the broad section where the Yabboq joins the Jordan (Sukkot Valley) has stronger western winds than the narrower passages of the Rift.

Dead Sea Region. The Dead Sea and its surroundings, at the lowest spot on earth and enclosed in high mountain walls to the west and east, is unique in its climatic conditions. The annual mean temperature is highest at the southern end of the Dead Sea: 25.7°C (78°F). In January, a mean of 16.9°C (62.5°F) is registered on the southern, and 14.3°C (57.7°F) on the northern shore, compared to 34.3°C (93.7°F) and 31.9°C (89.4°F) respectively, in August. The highest temperature ever recorded in the region reached 51°C (124°F). The considerable differences between the northern and southern part of the region stem from the structure of the Dead Sea; the wide, deep northern basin functions similarly to the open sea: it sets into motion breezes which mitigate the midday heat, while the shallow southern basin acts thus only to a limited degree. Moreover, the cooling breeze during the hot hours of the day cannot blow over the huge evaporation pans of the Dead Sea Works in the south; being water bodies themselves, they resemble the sea surface in their diurnal pressure regime.

Relative humidity near the Dead Sea, averaging 57%, is among the lowest in the country; the minimum, 45%, is registered for May, and the maximum, 62%, for October. Sharav days, however, are not as dry here as in the Judean Hills. Between 10 and 15 sharav days are counted per year.

The extremely high evaporation rate is used to extract minerals from the Dead Sea waters. High temperatures and strong winds contribute to the evaporation, which would be higher still, if not for the salinity of the Dead Sea waters, the high barometric pressure, and the light mists hovering over the sea on most days. Evaporation is stronger from the northern than from the southern basin and, in the area of the pans, stronger than on the sea shore. It has been calculated that 3.5 m (almost 12 ft) of water would evaporate annually from the surface of the northern basin of the Dead Sea if the water were fresh.

The strong barometric pressure (an average of 800 mm or 32 in) enriches the air above the Dead Sea by 6–8% of oxygen over that above the Mediterranean Sea, a fact which aids fuel combustion in the machines of the Dead Sea Works.

Winds in the Dead Sea Region are remarkably constant. The southern shore has northern winds blowing from the Dead Sea in the morning, and southern winds at night. On the northern shore, wind directions are opposite. As the Rift resembles a narrow corridor in this section, open at its ends but almost hermetically closed on the sides, wind directions other than north and south are rare.

Precipitation amounts in the region are very low. The northern shore of the Dead Sea has an annual mean of 86.3 mm (about $3\frac{1}{2}$ in), but this figure is subject to extreme vacillations. In 1944/45, for instance, 258 mm ($10\frac{1}{3}$ in) were recorded, but only 23.2 mm (less than 1 in) in 1946/47. The southern shore, with an annual average of 54.7 mm (2.2 in), receives less rain than the northern.

The Climate of the Golan and the Ḥermon Shoulder

Detailed observations of the climate in these regions have become feasible only since the Six Day War, although some long-term data are available for two stations, Fiq in the Lower and Qunaītira in the Upper Golan.

As may be expected, sharp contrasts exist between the Lower Golan, where altitudes barely exceed 300 m, and the Upper Golan which not only rises to 1,000 m and more above sea level, but also comes under the climatic influence of the nearby Ḥermon Shoulder. The latter has near-Alpine conditions and constitutes a climatic region unlike any other in the country.

Temperatures. Temperatures of the Golan are generally lower than those of Lower and Upper Galilee, the corresponding regions west of the Jordan, and the annual temperature curve shows sharper differences. As in the rest of the country, January is the coldest, and August the warmest month. While Fiq registers an average minimum of 6.8°C (44.3°F) in January and an average maximum of 33°C (91.4°F) in August, the Qunaītira January minimum attains 3.1°C (37.6°F) and the August maximum only 29.5°C (85.1°F). In the Upper Golan, winter temperatures frequently drop below freezing point, sometimes preserving the snow cover on the ground for weeks on end. On the higher reaches of Mt. Ḥermon, diurnal averages in January and February are mostly below zero.

Humidity and Evaporation. Humidity rates on the Golan Plateau are throughout higher than those of Galilee. While Qunaītira (approximately equaling Mt. Canaan of Upper Galilee in height and latitude) registers a January average of 83%, as against 76% on Mt. Canaan, even Fiq has a January average of 70%. June is the driest month at both stations, with averages at Fiq ranging from 58% at 8.00 hrs, through 32% at 14.00 hrs, to 51% at 20.00 hrs; the corresponding values at Qunaītira read 40.34 and 57%.

Relatively low temperatures and high air humidity cause, particularly in the Upper Golan, low evaporation rates, enabling summer crops to thrive with little or no irrigation, and pastures to provide grazing throughout most or all of the summer.

Precipitation. The annual rainfall at Fiq (455 mm, 18.2 in) is considerably lower than the Nazareth average (639 mm, 25½ in) and only slightly exceeds that of Kinneret (416 mm, 16½ in) which is situated within the Jordan Rift Valley. Qunaītira, on the other hand, receives an annual total of 822 mm (33 in), considerably more than Mt. Canaan (728 mm, 29 in). No exact data are yet available for the Ḥermon Shoulder; precipitation is presumably much higher than at Qunaītira, although not attaining the amounts on the mountain peak and the western slopes of the Ḥermon Massif (in Lebanese territory) which, according to estimates, approach 1,500 mm (60 in) per year.

As elsewhere in the country, January is the rainiest month (219 mm, 8¾ in, at Qunaītira, 110 mm, 4½ in, at Fiq), followed, at Qunaītira, by February and December (157 and 152 mm, 6¼ and 6 in, respectively), while at Fiq the December average (91 mm, 3.6 in) slightly exceeds that of February (88 mm, 3.5 in). Large monthly differences between regions east and west of the Jordan are noticeable in March, when Qunaītira registers precipitation exceeding 134 mm (5.4 in) and Mt. Canaan a mere 72 mm (2.9 in)—a clear indication that late rains increase in importance as one proceeds eastward.

Mt. Ḥermon receives most of its precipitation in the form of snow. Even in the Upper Golan, snowfall is by no means infrequent, a fact which seems to favor the region's water economy and to offer good prospects for certain crops requiring winter cold, e.g., walnut and true pistachio which are being contemplated for the new Upper Golan settlements.

The Climate of Sinai

Our summary of climatic conditions of the Sinai Peninsula is, in most respects, confined to general remarks, as observations have been made at few localities, and only exceptionally were they continued over long periods. Some additional but haphazard information exists for certain other sites, but no data whatsoever are available for the greater part of the peninsula.

The Sinai Peninsula lies between the northern latitudes of 27°30′ and 31°30′N. Accordingly, during the summer, its northern part finds itself in the subtropical high pressure belt, and the south—in the trade winds zone, both markedly arid regions. In winter, Sinai approaches the wet cyclones belt but does not actually enter it, so that chances of rainfall remain slim even in the north of the peninsula.

Local variations from these uniform desert conditions are to be ascribed to the considerable differences in altitude and to the degree of exposure to marine influence. Concerning the latter, however, it must be emphasized that only the Mediterranean Sea has a noticeable effect, whereas the climatic impact of the Gulf of Suez is fairly insignificant, and that of the Gulf of Eilat is practically non-existent.

Temperatures. According to measurements taken in the town of el-'Arīsh in the years 1936–1956, August is the warmest month of the year, with an average temperature of 26.4° C (79.5°F), and January the coolest, with 13.7°C (56.7°F). Although this seasonal span exceeds that of points further north along the Levant coast, it is smaller than that of inland sites and, in fact, of all other parts of the Sinai Peninsula. The daily march of temperature, too, does not show extremes at el-'Arīsh, the diurnal span amounting to 10° C (18° F) in summer, and to somewhat lower values in winter.

Of particular interest is the fact that the el-'Arīsh coast has perceptibly cooler summers than either Tel Aviv, Haifa or Beirut. The curve of monthly average temperatures does not show surprising features, mounting relatively rapidly between April and May (from 18.4 to 21.6°C–65 to 71°F), and descending at a slightly steeper rate between November and December (from 19.7 to 15.4°C—67.5 to 59.7°F).

At even small distances from the Mediterranean shore, diurnal and seasonal temperature curves sharpen considerably, to attain an average August high of 28°C (82.5°F) and a January low of 8°C (46.5°F) at a-Nakhl on the a-Tih Plateau, 150 km south of el-'Arīsh. Here the summer day temperatures often reach 35° C (95° F), but summer nights cool down to 15° C (59° F), this diurnal span of 20° C (36°F) being characteristic of desert conditions.

The high mountains of the south again present a different picture. Averages for the warmest month do not rise above 24°C (75°F), while monthly winter temperatures fall to 8°C (46.4°F). Mountain tops show considerably lower values. American meteorologists who carried out observations on the top of Mt. Catherine during the nineteen-thirties, repeatedly recorded winter minima of −15 and even −20° C (5° and −4° F). The diurnal temperature range, too, is large and, as far as can be ascertained, exceeds that of the a-Tih Plateau.

Along the low, narrow coast of the Suez Gulf and, more so, along the Gulf of Eilat, temperatures are high throughout the year, with August averages of 28–32°C (82–89°F). Three factors combine there to produce this phenomenon: greater proximity to the equator; high mountain walls enclosing the gulfs and preventing inflow of cooling winds; and compression and heating of air masses gliding from the mountain tops toward the shores in calm weather. Suez (Port Taufīq), which lies landlocked at the innermost point of the western gulf, experiences somewhat larger diurnal and seasonal temperature ranges than those at a-Tur situated 220 km further south. Also winter minima are lower at a-Tur than at Suez. Similarly, Sharm a-Sheikh, situated near the southern tip of the peninsula, at the opening of the Eilat Gulf into the Red Sea, registers summer temperatures which are about 2°C (3.6°F) lower than those at Eilat, which lies 150 km further north but is surrounded by mountains.

Winds. Very scanty information is available in this field. Observations made in the north, center and southwest of the peninsula in 1910, and published by J. P. Range in 1924, show that in all three regions the prevailing winds have a western component (64% of all winds of that year at el-'Arīsh on the Mediterranean shore, 79.6% at a-Nakhl on the a-Tih Plateau, and 68.3% at a-Tur on the Suez Gulf coast). Calms were rare everywhere. As one proceeds southward, the importance of northern winds appears to increase. While at el-'Arīsh 26.3% of the winds appears to come from the southwest, and only 6.1% from the north, a-Tur received only 1.4% from the southwest, but 41% from the northwest and 22.4% from the north. The wind regime throughout Sinai seems to be rather uniform.

Precipitation. It is fairly safe to assume that at least 80% of the Sinai Peninsula receives less than 100 mm of rain per year, and that over more than half of its area precipitation does not even attain 50 mm. In addition to the figures of the Israel climatologist D. Ashbel cited below, measurements taken at the beginning of the present century indicate a 35-year average of 83 mm for Port Sa'īd, a ten-year average of 102 mm for el-'Arīsh and a mere 25 mm for a-Nakhl.

The very uneven distribution of rainfall over the winter months as well as over prolonged periods is again characteristic of the desert. Entire years pass without a drop of rain, but sudden downpours of a few hours duration may bring quantities which greatly surpass the local annual average. Thāmed on the a-Tih Plateau, for example, received 164 mm of rain on November 18, 1925, while the annual average recorded there during the 22-year period 1921–1944 amounted to 39.2 mm only. Of these 22 years, 2 were completely rainless, 5 saw less than 10 mm, 4 between 10 and 20 mm, 8 between 20 and 50 mm, one 150 mm and another 313 mm. The November average for a-Tur over the period 1914–1943 is a mere 2.5 mm, but in one of these years 40 mm fell in a single day of this month.

The principal reason for the overall scarcity of precipitation is to be found in the fact that the peninsula is too far removed from the usual path of winterly cyclones wandering over the eastern Mediterranean Basin. Several points on the Mediterranean shore still approach the annual average of 100 mm, but toward the interior rainfall decreases rapidly. In the southwest, along the coastal strip of the Suez Gulf, rainfall amounts to less than 20 mm per annum, and on the Eilat Gulf shore it does not even attain 10 mm. The tops of the high southern mountains, on the other hand, may be assumed to receive an annual precipitation exceeding 150 or even 200 mm. Only a few trial observations have been made there, and it was difficult to make measurements, as most of the precipitation of the region is in the form of snow. The further southward one proceeds in the Sinai Peninsula, the more difficult it becomes to single out typical rain months. Heavy downpours may occur in April or October, while December and January are completely dry. It appears that the sudden rainstorms of the south are caused by local low pressure cells existing for a few hours only, rather than by extensive cyclones wandering over sizeable portions of the earth.

Cloudiness, Relative Humidity and Evaporation. The extremely sparse cloud cover during all seasons and in all parts of the Sinai Peninsula is a further indicator of desert conditions. Even the Mediterranean coast has no month of the year with more than 2/10 of the sky covered by clouds.

The only available data on relative air humidities are those from el-'Arīsh. During the period 1936–1956, an annual average of 72% relative humidity was recorded, a rather high value, with only small monthly deviations, the lowest average reading being 61% for May, and the highest—74% for December. Daily evaporation at el-'Arīsh averaged 4 mm. It is, however, beyond doubt that the above-described conditions at el-'Arīsh differ sharply from those of the rest of the peninsula, and that everywhere else values of cloud cover and air humidity are lower, and of evaporation higher, than on the Mediterranean shore. The highest mountain reaches of the south possibly constitute the sole exception.

The Climate of the Past. The well-developed drainage system of the a-Tih Plateau and of the mountains of the south, the depth to which watercourses have incised their beds, their width, the enormous amounts of coarse debris which were transported by them over large distances and in the process were often rounded to pebbles—all these permit the assumption that the climate of the Sinai Peninsula must have been considerably wetter in the recent geologic past, during the pluvial periods of the Pleistocene, than it is in our own time.

This theory is reinforced by the evidence of vegetation: at a few particularly favorable spots on the peninsula, one encounters relict plant types which normally require much more humidity than is available to them at present. Botanists believe that many species are able to adapt themselves to worsening conditions; such plants would, however, not have taken root at these spots had the latter then been as dry as they are today. In addition, such flora could not have found their way to their presently totally isolated stations, had they not encountered greater humidity in the intermediate space, permitting them to form 'bridges' from their regions of origin.

Flora and Fauna

Vegetation

Three factors determine the composition and density of the plant cover in the country: (a) the position of the country at the crossroads of three continents and two oceans, which has made it a meeting ground for plant species from as widely distant origins as Western Europe, Inner Asia, and North Africa; (b) the Mediterranean climate, along with the 'border of aridity' across the country; vegetation must adapt to prolonged rainless summers, a generally sparse moisture, and frequent drought years which may even become series of years deficient in precipitation; (c) the activity of man, who has lived in this country longer and more continuously than in most parts of the world and has changed the plant cover by unintentional or wilful destruction, by tending certain varieties useful to him and subduing those useless, and by acclimatizing foreign species. Even some of man's positive activities have had negative results, owing to the not infrequent upsetting of the natural equilibrium.

Aridity and Plant Life. Under the local semiarid or arid conditions, plants adjusted to temporary or permanent lack of moisture by cutting down water losses and increasing absorption facility. Plants economize in their water use to various degrees, according to local climate conditions and other environmental factors, by reduction of transpiration. This is done by developing thicker and smaller leaves, by reducing the number of stomata (openings for transpiration), and by acquiring coatings of wax, tiny hairs or thick, cork-like bark. In conditions of extreme aridity, such as in the Central and Southern Negev, leaves are transformed into thorns. Some plants increase water intake through a widespread root system which obtains water from a wider and deeper soil area and by higher osmotic pressure which reinforces water suction. These peculiarities cause the plant cover to be sparser in arid than in wet regions. Many species store water and food in bulbs or tubers, most of which lie dormant through the

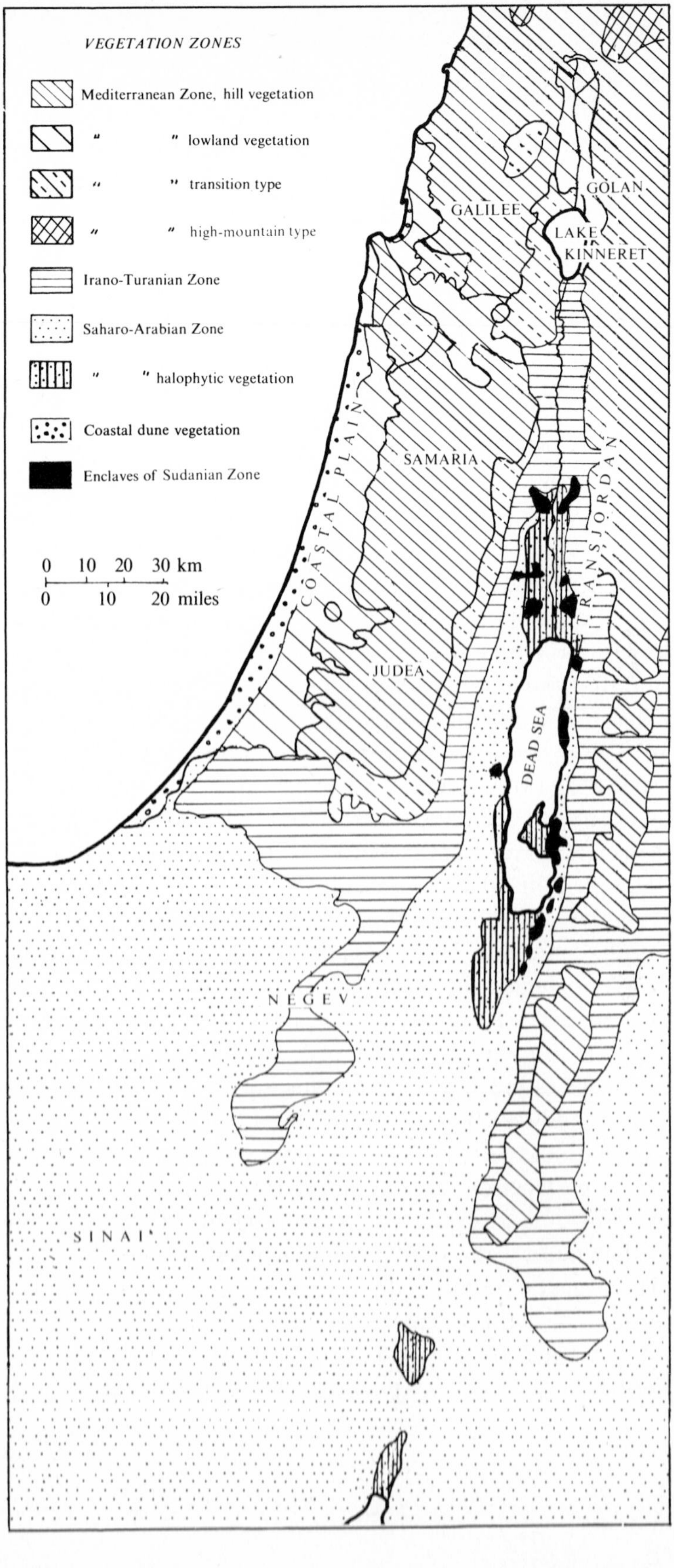

Main phytogeographic regions in the country

dry summer and burst into flower in the rainy season (e.g., *Cyclamen persicur* *Anemone coronaria,* etc.); several, however, bring forth broad leaves in spring b delay flowering until the end of summer (e.g., the squill—*Urginea maritima*

Most of the annual plants adapt their life cycle to the rainy season, whe protection against water losses becomes less vital. The drier the climate, tl shorter the life cycle of such plants becomes. In the Negev or the Judean Deser seeds of annual species may lie years in the soil waiting for a rainy winter, the awake, sprout, grow, flower, and produce new seeds in the course of a few weel before the moisture vanishes. Thorny weeds often exist until midsummer, whi the delicate, broad-leaved annuals normally disappear in April.

A special group are the halophytes (salt lovers), which are prominent in tl playas of the Arava Valley, in the Dead Sea area, and the Lower Jordan Regio Some of these, such as the tamarisk, can eliminate surplus salt dissolved in dro of water they secrete.

Influence of Man. Man's influence upon the plant cover and its composition h been particularly strong in the Middle East, which, during most of the last fi thousand years, has been relatively densely populated. The structure of tl country and the nature of its soils and climate increase the danger of erosio once man's activity has contributed to this process. In the dry summer, fires sprea easily and destroy large expanses of woodland. The first step toward introducir agriculture, thousands of years ago, necessitated clearing the natural forest. Th is excellently described in the Bible; Joshua advised the tribes of Ephraim ar Manasseh, who complained about the lack of arable land in their territories: 'B the mountain shall be thine; for it is a wood, and thou shalt cut it down; and tl outgoings of it shall be thine . . .' (Joshua xvii, 18). Upon the disappearance of tl forest, conditions in the hills quickly deteriorated without the trees to protect tl soil by reducing the onslaught of hard rains, by grasping the soil with their root and by adding organic matter. Naked rock was bared on the hill slopes, ar badland topography developed on many lowland sites. Even worse was tl influence of the herdsman and his flocks. The local black goat, nibbling at your shoots and tree bark, hastened their degeneration into low shrub. The shepher also fells and burns trees systematically to enlarge pasture areas. A third cause forest destruction was the many wars fought in the country and the delibera burning of large expanses to rob the enemy of natural cover.

The natural forests degenerated steadily under the impact of all these factor Three stages are marked in this process: (a) high maquis (in Hebrew—'ḥoresh' where the largest trees still attain 3–5 m (10–16 ft), but most are lowe (b) 'garrigue,' or low maquis, with the original species still present but turned int bushes of 1–2 m (3–7 ft) height, which, developing sideways rather than upward often form an almost impenetrable thicket; (c) dwarf brush (in Hebrew—'batta'), not over 30–60 cm (1–2 ft) high, with many thorny species, the most prominent of which is thorny burnet (*Poterium spinosum*).

Vegetation Zones in the Country

Owing to its geographical position, Israel is the meeting ground for plants of different origin and also constitutes the extreme point of geographical distribution of many species. This explains the large number of plant species represented: up to 2,250, compared to 1,700 in England, 1,500 in Egypt, or 1,300 in Norway—all of these states being much larger in area than this country.

The plants of Israel belong to at least four large phytogeographic regions; (1) the Mediterranean Zone, which comprises most countries bordering on the Mediterranean Sea, as well as a strip of territory along the southern border of Turkey; (2) the Irano-Turanian Zone, dry steppe or desert steppe which stretches from its southwest tip in Israel through Iran, Turkestan and Inner Asia to the Gobi Desert in China; (3) the Saharo-Arabian Zone, pure desert which covers most of the Sahara in Africa, the Arabian Peninsula, and parts of southern Iran; (4) the Sudanese Zone of tropical vegetation which, as its name indicates, is principally represented in central and southern Sudan, and in Israel forms only small enclaves. There are also a few species to be found, mainly in Upper Galilee and the Upper Golan, which are related to the Euro-Siberian Zone.

The Mediterranean Flora. The Mediterranean Zone of vegetation roughly covers, in this country, those areas which receive an annual average precipitation of 350 mm (14 in) or more. It runs from the vicinity of Gaza to the southwest corner of the Judean Hills, turns north in the Arad Region, thence runs 8–12 miles west of the Dead Sea, where it separates the Judean Desert from the Judean Hills proper, continues along the eastern rim of the Hills of Samaria, descends to the Ḥarod Valley near Bet Alfa, traces its border with Bet She'an Valley, and reaches Lake Kinneret near the village of Kinneret. In Transjordan, the Mediterranean Zone includes all the Golan and the Bashan, most of Gilead, the western half of Ammon and Moab, and the northwestern part of Edom.

The Mediterranean vegetation in this country falls into two very different types: that of the Hills and that of the Coastal Plain and interior valleys. The climax vegetation of the Hills, i.e., forest or high maquis, has almost disappeared except on very small areas, e.g., on Mount Meron, in the Naḥal Karkara Gorge of Western Upper Galilee, on several spots on Mount Carmel, etc. In the climax vegetation, different plant associations can be discerned in accordance with local

Aged specimens of the Jerusalem Pine, near Bet Me'ir in the Judean Hills

variations in rainfall, bedrock types and soil depths. These associations are also perpetuated when the forest degenerates into garrigue.

Most sections of the Hills above 300 m (nearly 1,000 ft) are covered by the association grouped around the evergreen Palestinian oak *(Quercus calliprinos)*. This sturdy tree, slow in growth, has small, thick, leathery leaves edged with tiny thorns, and its roots are capable of penetrating the hard limestones and dolomites. Among its associates, the Palestinian terebinth *(Pistacia palaestina)* is the most prominent, recognizable by its dainty, feathered leaves, which in spring have a reddish hue. In northwestern Edom, instead of the terebinth a variety of juniper—*Juniper phoenicea*—appears along with the Palestinian oak. In sections of Upper Galilee and Mount Carmel with particularly high rainfall, the Palestinian oak association is variegated by trees which, with their broader leaves and fresh greenery, indicate the transition to the moist-temperate zone. Among them are the laurel *(Laurus nobilis)*, arbutus *(Arbutus andrachne)*, Judas tree *(Cercis siliquastrum)* with its cordate leaves and purplish-rose flowers, and more rarely, the oriental plane *(Platanus orientalis)* and Syrian maple *(Acer syriacum)*.

In certain portions of Mount Carmel and Galilee having relatively soft limestone, remnants of the association of the Jerusalem pine *(Pinus halepensis)* are preserved.

In the later changes of forest vegetation into low garrigue or batta, bushes

A carob tree, its crown fully developed on the lee side of the wind

become prominent, such as rockrose (*Cistus villosus* and *Cistus salviaefolius*) which bears either rose-colored or white flowers in the late spring. Dominant i the thorny burnet (*Poterium spinosum*), with roots penetrating to a depth of 3 n (10 ft) between the rocks, although its growth above ground hardly exceeds 30 cn (1 ft); this enables the bush to be renewed after it has been burnt or cut. Many o the garrigue bushes have sharp, spicy scents. In spring, both garrigue and batt are rich in gay flowers of all colors and forms.

At lower altitudes, where chalk rocks predominate, the carob tree and it associates often appear alongside the Palestinian oak and its accompanying flora or replace them. The carob (*Ceratonia siliqua*), which is thought to have come to this country only after the Biblical period, is evergreen, dioecious (male and female flowers appearing on separate trees), and belongs to the Leguminosa group. When its growth is not hampered by external factors, it develops a wid crown of dense foliage, with shining dark, thick, leathery leaves, and yields sweet abundant fruit. The carob association also appears on poor kurkar (sandstone ridges in the Coastal Plain, from Netanya northward, and also grows well wher rainfall becomes marginal.

A transitional belt between the Mediterranean and Irano-Turanian zones is to be found on the eastern slopes of Galilee, along the east and southeast rim of the Judean Hills, and in the highest reaches of the Negev Hills (Mount Ramon Mount Loẓ). In the latter region grow isolated specimens of the Atlantic terebinth (*Pistacia atlantica*).

In the central and northern sections of the Coastal Plain, as well as in parts of the interior valleys and on the low Shefar'am Hills in the southwest corner of Lower Galilee, the Tabor oak (*Quercus aegilops var. ithaburensis*) represents the climax vegetation. When fully developed, this is a high, out-branching tree with leaves larger than those of the Palestinian oak. In contrast to the latter, it is deciduous in winter. Its most beautiful specimens are found in the Ḥurshat Tal Nature Park of the Ḥula Valley. *Styrax officinalis* is its associate. As testified to by the map of the British Palestine Exploration Fund of 1871–1878 (the first exact map of the country), a continuous forest of Tabor oak then still covered large stretches of the Sharon. These woodlands were gradually cleared by peasants who came down from their villages in the Samarian Hills, and were finally completely felled by the Turks who needed wood to replace the coal in their railway engines which carried troops and provisions to the Sinai front in World War I. Another tree typical of the Coastal Plain is the sycamore (*Ficus sycomorus*), related to the fig, with thick trunk and broad crown; as it does not reproduce here, it is considered to have been introduced by man. The place of former oak woods is today frequently taken by bushes and grasses such as *Eragrostis bipinnata* and *Centaurea procurrens*.

A giant Tabor oak in the Ḥurshat Tal Park, Ḥula Valley

Ancient sycamores in King George Street, Tel Aviv (the picture was taken in the 1920's)

The Irano-Turanian Zone. In Israel this form of vegetation is principally found in the Beersheba Region, where annual rainfall averages between 200 and 300 mm (8 and 12 in) and where either loess or poor calcareous soils prevail. Characteristic of it are low brush or dwarf bushes. Although at first sight it resembles the batta (the last stage of forest degeneration of the Mediterranean Zone), it is composed of different species. Among these species a strain of wormwood *(Artemisia herbae albae)* is prominent in the Judean Desert and on the lower slopes of the rim of the Transjordan Plateau; the Artemisetum plant association is grouped around it. In the Bet She'an and Lower Jordan valleys, the hardy lotus tree shrub *(Zizyphus loti)* is prominent on marl and basalt soils. After the abandoning of farming in the Middle Ages, it spread, aided by the spring waters which inundated the soil when they were no longer used for crop irrigation; the extremely deep roots of the lotus tree bushes posed great difficulties to the settlers of the Bet She'an Valley in the 1930's and 1940's, who cleared the fields to renew farming.

The Saharo-Arabian Zone. This phytogeographic zone ranks first in area in the country. It includes most of the Negev and the Judean Desert, the Dead Sea Region, the Arava Valley and the southern and eastern parts of Transjordan. This is pure desert vegetation, thriving where rainfall does not exceed 200 mm

Thorny acacias are representative of the Saharo-Arabian vegetation in the southern Arava Valley

(8 in) annually over vast areas. The great majority of plants are low bushes with thickened leaves. Thorns are prominent.

The vegetation cover is very sparse. Over large expanses there is only one plant to the square meter; often, only one to dozens of square meters. Ḥammada slopes frequently remain totally bare, but relatively large concentrations of vegetation are found in wadi beds, where plants utilize the rare floods. These thorny trees and shrubs outline the winding wadi courses and turn them into a salient feature of the desert landscape. Among the low shrubs, the most common are the bean caper *(Zygophyllum dumosi)* and *Anabasis articulata,* both of which assemble around them plant associations of their own. Of the trees, several species of thorny acacias are found which originate in the African savannah. Such trees may remain bare, dry, seemingly dead for months or years, until a flood rushes down the wadi; they then suddenly spring to life and become covered with tiny leaves and blossoms.

Another plant typical of the desert is the broom *(Retama roetam)*, which prefers sand flats to ḥammada slopes. Its leaves are so diminutive as to remain practically invisible; the chlorophyll necessary for its existence is concentrated in its long, tough and elastic stems.

The salt playas around the Dead Sea, in the Arava Valley, and in the Ḥisma Depression of southeastern Edom support a halophytic vegetation, with species such as the juncus rush, the Jordan tamarisk, etc. At the southern end of the Arava (Avrona, Eilat playas), isolated specimens of the 'doom' palm *(Hyphaenea thebaica)* appear, recognizable from afar by their high trunks branching into two or three crowns.

A narrow arm of the Saharo-Arabian Zone extends deeply into the wetter parts of the country; this is the band of sand dunes along the Mediterranean shore. The quick seepage of water into the coarse sand creates conditions for plant growth similar to those of an extreme desert climate. Of the plant species able to live on these sands are some which are found also in the Negev deserts, e.g., the wormwood and the broom; others, such as the white shore lily *(Pancratium maritimum)* and the beach grass *(Ammophila arenaria)*, are restricted in this country exclusively to the Mediterranean coastal dunes.

Doom palms in the Eilat Playa

Papyrus thicket in the former Ḥula Swamps

The Sudanese Vegetation Enclaves. At several oasis spots around the Dead Se (En Gedi, etc.) and in the Arava Valley, as well as in the Lower Jordan Valle (vicinity of Jericho, Sukkot Valley) are to be found about 40 plant specie belonging to this vegetation zone and needing both high temperatures an abundant sweet water. The most prominent of these plants is the lotus tre *(Zizyphus spina Christi).*

Another variety of tropical or subtropical vegetation appears in swamps an shallow lakes. A few remnants of it are found along stream courses in the Coasta Plain (Yarqon, Poleg, Alexander, Tanninim). The largest concentration wa found in the Ḥula Valley, until the completion of the drainage project there in 1958; today these species may be studied only in the Ḥula Nature Reserve an along the drainage canals cutting through the valley. Where lake and swam water is less than 2 m (6 ft) deep, the papyrus reed *(Cyperus papyrus)* reign supreme; it is accompanied by the knotweed *(Polygonum acuminatum).* On th outskirts of lakes and swamps, one finds the purple loosestrife *(Lythrum salicaria)* and oleander bushes, which also grow along stream courses in th intermontane valleys. Here and there, the surface of lake and swamp waters o the Ḥula Preserve supports the floating leaves of the yellow nenuphar and of th rare white water lily *(Nuphar luteum* and *Nymphaea alba).*

Agricultural Crops and Their Associates. Over large areas of the country, th natural vegetation has been replaced by farming crops, some of which originate in the country or in the Mediterranean Region, while others were introduce from afar (all are described in greater detail in the chapter dealing with agriculture, p. 459ff.).

The tending of crops has invariably brought about the spreading of weeds, some closely attached to particular crop varieties, others appearing with most or all crops. Although certain weeds, which appeared only with the introduction of a crop with which they were associated, prefer certain soil and climate conditions and stay within the general limits of vegetation in the country, many are ubiquitous on croplands and are marked by their obstinacy and vitality; a case in point is Bermuda (couch) grass *(Cynodon dactylon).*

Planted Forests and Afforestation. With the beginning of Zionist settlement in the country, the need to plant forest trees was soon recognized. The first species introduced was the eucalyptus, brought from Australia to aid in swamp drainage. It was later found that this fast-growing tree could thrive also in dry regions, and even in the Hills. The most widespread variety in Israel is *Eucalyptus camaldulensis (rostrata); E. gomphocephala* has proved partly successful also in the Foothills and Hills.

After World War I the planting of coniferous forests was accelerated, especially on rocky hill slopes which were too eroded for fruit and other crops. On such terrain the forest tree retains the existing soil and contributes to the forming of new soil, since its roots grind the rock mechanically into meal, dissolve it chemically by secreting carbonic acid, and add organic components. In planted coniferous forests, pines are prominent, particularly the Jerusalem pine *(Pinus halepensis)* which is hardy and modest in its soil and water requirements, but is slow of growth and often develops twisted trunks; the wood is therefore only of limited industrial value. In smaller numbers appear *Pinus brutia,* as well as the stone pine *(Pinus pinea),* the Canary Islands pine, etc. The cypress, second among coniferous trees, is represented by the pyramidal, horizontal and other varieties. Less common are casuarina trees, acacias, robinias, *Celtis australis, Melia azedarach,* poplars, and other species.

Specialized tasks have been allocated to trees in halting moving sand dunes and in protecting fields from wind and water erosion. Sand allows the growth of long-leaved acacias, eucalyptus and tamarisks. In shelterbelts around fields and along roads, eucalyptus is prominent, with tamarisks in second place.

Wildlife

Animal life, like that of plants, is largely determined by geographic conditions. Zoogeographic regions therefore resemble vegetation regions in their extent and borders; to a certain degree, one may speak of animals in this country as belonging to Mediterranean, Irano-Turanian, Saharo-Arabian and Sudanese faunas. Animals, however, differ from plants in being capable of locomotion. They can therefore react, with varying adaptability, to changes in living conditions in a certain place or region, can abandon old and chose new habitats. The blurred and often transient character of zoogeographic borders is strikingly demonstrated in Israel, where, particularly in recent decades, living conditions for animals have thoroughly changed owing to man's activity. Many species of water fowl which were accustomed to nest in the Ḥula Valley or rest there in their passage have disappeared since the swamps were drained; new carp ponds, on the other hand, immediately attract a population of fish-hunting birds, and sparrows appear in a new settlement a few days or weeks after its founding. The opening of the Suez Canal allowed tropical Red Sea fish to reach the Mediterranean, and a great number of species have consequently acclimatized to the lower temperatures and salinity of their new surroundings. On the whole, wildlife is here—as everywhere in the world—becoming progressively impoverished in numbers and variety with the increasing density of human population and technical progress.

Use of pesticides and other chemicals in farming frequently starts a chain reaction, causing the extinction first of lower, and then of higher species which feed on the former. A few species, however, multiply when their natural enemies are decimated.

Development of the Country's Fauna in the Geologic Past. The history of land animals in this country can be traced to the Eocene, when the sea retreated from extensive regions previously covered for over millions of years. The country was then still a part of the Arab-Nubian subcontinent, which stretched south and east and from which the first land animals arrived. When, in the Pliocene, a land connection was created with southeastern Europe, an influx from the Balkan Peninsula followed.

In the Lower Pleistocene, some species had been living in the country for many generations, such as the swine, hippopotamus, rhinoceros, spotted hyena, etc., and others had come later from India, among them wolves, gazelles, wild horses, etc.

Climatic changes during the Middle and Upper Pleistocene and up to the Neolithic Period (7,000 years ago) brought fresh changes in the composition of the local fauna. The animal world of this country has undergone no further profound changes since then, although many species were exterminated through hunting and destruction of forests. The Bible mentions many animals which are no longer found, among them the lion, tiger, bear, deer *(Capreolus pyargus),* Mesopotamian roe buck *(Dama mesopotamica),* wild ox *(Bos primigenus),* and antelope, and even the ostrich and the crocodile. The Biblical list of domesticated animals is also quite long, containing, among others, the horse, donkey, goat, sheep, hen, bee, several kinds of cattle as well as the silkworm; in the sea, in addition to fish the murex snail was caught and the royal purple color extracted from it. The Bible also describes insects, often mentioning plagues of them (fleas, mosquitoes, etc.); it distinguishes between several kinds and developmental stages of locusts, etc.

Marine Animals. The marine fauna on the coasts of this country appears to have been less depleted during human history than land animals. The enormous damage, however, that man is apt to cause in this domain is clearly shown on Israel's Red Sea coast near Eilat, where the construction of the port and the souvenir-hunting by visitors destroyed much of the colorful world of corals and coral fish in a few years.

On the Mediterranean coast, the composition of fauna is determined by the relatively high salinity of the sea (up to 4%). This is reduced in portions of the coastal waters to 3.1% by the Mediterranean Coastal Current, which carries the

Nile waters. Water temperatures vary between 16–29°C (60.5–84°F). These give rise to an Atlantic type of fauna, with the addition of some tropical species. Between the rocks and on the sands near the shore littoral types exist, differing from those of the open sea (pelagic fauna); most of these are autochthones of the eastern Mediterranean Basin. The species of the Labridae and of the Blenniidae fish families are prominent here, along with many crustaceans, mollusks, sea lilies, etc. Cosmopolitan species swim deeper, such as *Mullus barbatus,* known from British coasts, or *Diplodus vulgaris,* which appears in West African and Brazilian waters. Occasionally there are also large brown and green sea turtles, dolphins, and even tooth whales. A total of 300 species of fish have hitherto been identified, but their number in the Mediterranean Sea off Israel's coast is assumed to be much larger.

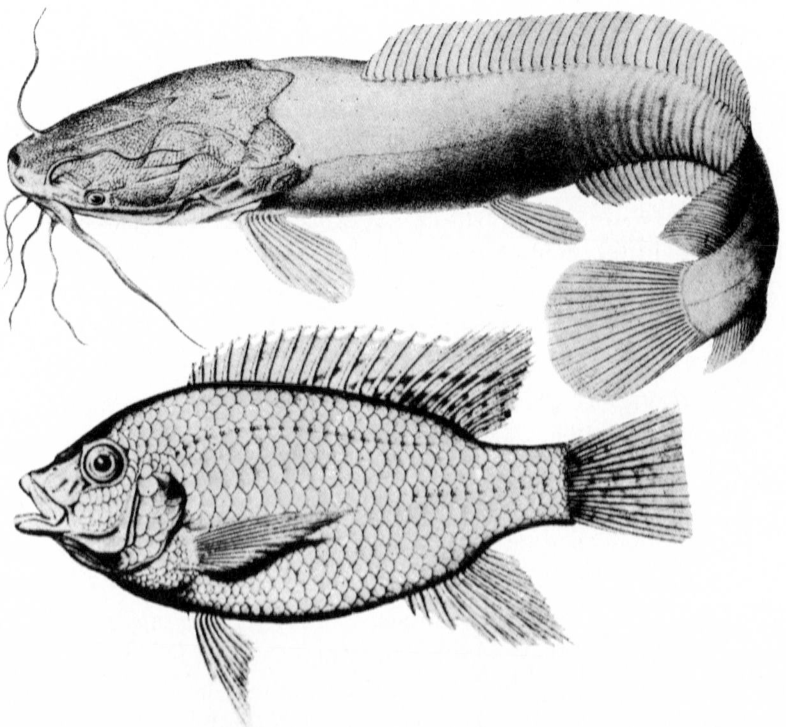

Catfish (above) and St. Peter's fish (below), a mouthbreeder, are to be found in fresh inland waters

The tropical Red Sea fauna on the Eilat Coast stands out by its wealth of strange forms and brilliant colors. The glaringly blue, red, yellow, and green coral fish of the Chaetodontidae, Acanthuridae, Ostraciontidae and other families live among corals of many varieties, together with enormous numbers of shells, crustacea, etc. One of the strangest varieties is the turkey-fish *(Pterois volitans),* which floats with slow movements of nearly transparent fins, and is protected by long back spikes containing poison. Large sharks, hammerfish, sawfish, etc. infest the deeper parts of these waters. Different is the freshwater fauna, today represented mainly in Lake Kinneret. It includes several kinds of carp, six varieties of mouthbreeders of the Cichlidae family, among them St. Peter's fish *(Tilapia galilaea)*, further catfish *(Clarias lazera)*, and others.

Invertebrate Land Animals. Because invertebrates were less decimated by human activity than were the higher classes, they are the best example of the country's position as a meeting ground for creatures of extremely divergent geographic origin. The number of insects, spiders, crustaceans, etc. reaches tens of thousands, and there is an incredible variety of forms and colors. In addition to countrywide species, many are restricted to limited areas. Richest in invertebrate fauna are regions which abound in warmth, water and vegetation, such as the Ḥula Valley, the valleys around Lake Kinneret, and some of the northern parts of the Coastal Plain. The use of insecticides and biological warfare against crop pests or plagues succeeds in reducing the attacked species greatly, but only rarely makes it disappear. The introduction of new farming crops also leads to the appearance of new pests, previously unknown; cotton growing, since the beginning of the 'fifties, caused the spreading of the bollworm *(Earias insulana)*. The introduction of groundnuts brought other species; citrus growers must wage constant war against the Mediterranean fruit fly, etc. Of creatures harmful to man, best known are scorpions, among them the common black and the more dangerous yellow variety *(Nebo hierochunticus* and *Buthus quinquestriatus)*. The bite of a large spider, the black widow *(Latrodectus tredecimiguttatus)*, may cause considerable distress.

Amphibia and Reptiles. The amphibia, whose existence depends on the presence of permanent water bodies, naturally decline in number from the coast inland and from north to south with the increasing aridity in these two directions. They are, however, numerous along the course of the Jordan and those of its tributaries which carry water the year round. Swamp drainage in Israel in recent decades has greatly reduced the number of local amphibia. Most common among them are the triton *(Triton vittatus)*, the fire salamander *(Salamandra maculosa)*, the green toad, and different kinds of frogs.

Reptiles, belonging to the three orders of tortoises, lizards and snakes, are represented by about 80 species. This relatively large number should be ascribed to the generally warm climate and to the long hours of strong, direct insolation over most of the year. The local species include several which are almost extinct in other parts of the world. During hot and wet periods of the Middle Tertiary, many tropical reptiles are assumed to have penetrated into the country. Most of them disappeared when the climate again became drier and cooler, but some were able to adapt themselves to the new conditions. This explains the presence of some reptiles normally found in the jungles of tropical India.

At the beginning of the 20th century, a few specimens of Nile crocodiles were seen in Naḥal Tanninim ('the Crocodile Stream') of the Coastal Plain but have since disappeared entirely. Of the seven local tortoise species, four live in the sea and three on the land.

Of lizards and related species, geckoes are widespread and most spectacular, often penetrating into human dwellings. Interesting, too, is the chameleon, able to change its color according to its surroundings, slow in movement and quick to catch flies by the sudden ejection of its long tongue.

Among the most common nonpoisonous snakes is the sand boa *(Eryx)*. Another is the black snake *(Coluber jugularis)*, up to 2 m (7 ft) long, and a third *(Malpolon)*, somewhat shorter, which is sometimes found even in the built-up area of Tel Aviv. Of the venomous species, one cobra and two kinds of vipers are dangerous, most notably so *Vipera palaestinae*.

Birds. There are about 350 species of birds in the country. About 100 of them are perennial, 50 only summer here, 100 winter, 100 are birds of passage which remain for a few days or weeks, and 50 are but occasional visitors. The distribution of birds has, during recent decades, undergone decisive changes; some species, like the hawk, the vulture *(Gyps fulvus)*, or the eagle owl have been frightened off by man and retreated to lonely gorges hardly touched by civilization, while others, well known from other parts of the world, have been attracted by the newly planted forests and gardens, e.g., the blackbird *(Turdus merula)*, by sown fields (field swallow, crested lark) or by human habitations (Spanish sparrow, house swallow).

The Mediterranean shore harbors gulls and other water birds, but the coast is poor in nesting species. The desert regions, too, have but a sparse population of birds; in the Saharo-Arabian region, the most prominent are the short-tailed raven *(Corvus rhipidurus)*, *Rhodopechys gitaginea*, which prefers an environment of bare rocks, and the courser *(Cursorius cursor)* which is to be found on sand flats. Interesting local varieties are the Dead Sea sparrow *(Passer moabiticus)*, the Judean Desert rockbird *(Oeanthe lugens)*, etc.

Bird passage through the country runs, in spring and before the breeding season, in general from south to north, and in autumn in the opposite direction. Most of the larger birds fly during the daytime, and the smaller ones at night.

There are birds which nest in the country and leave for winter, and others, which nest in Europe, come here to spend the winter, and leave again in April. Of the birds of passage, some species pass through in only one direction and choose a different trail for the return journey. Well-known among the larger birds are the storks which arrive, often in many thousands, in the spring, or the pelicans *(Pelicanus onocrotalus)* which, until the drainage of the Ḥula swamps and lake, spent one or several days there in well-organized fishing. Among the first to arrive in spring is the hoopoe, and in September the water wagtail.

The quail

Mammals. With about 60 species, the variety of mammals is relatively large for the small area of the country, although the number of individuals has greatly decreased, particularly in the present century. Most species here are also known from other parts of the world, but there are also native varieties like the gazelle, the hairy-footed jerboa *(Jaculus jaculus)*, etc.

Many species or varieties have adapted themselves to the semiarid or arid climate of the country and to the sparse food supply. Most of the mammals are nocturnal animals; inactive during the hot hours, they manage with minute quantities of water. On the other hand, there are species requiring abundant water, which live in swampy areas or near lakes, e.g., wild boars *(Sus scrofa)*,

Gazelles

Foxes in captivity

which often cause considerable damage to fruit orchards, fields and vegetable gardens in the Ḥula Valley and around Lake Kinneret. With human settlement becoming ever denser over most of the country, the mammals are first to disappear. Thus the howling of jackals, heard at night in most rural areas, dies down around the sprawling cities.

Vegetation and Wildlife of Sinai

Conditions of vegetation and wildlife in Sinai resemble, to an extent, those of the Negev. The very vastness of the peninsula, however, as well as a number of topographical, climatic and historical features demand that its flora and fauna be described separately from those of the rest of the country.

Aridity as a Determining Factor of Vegetation. As the entire area of the Sinai Peninsula falls within the zone of desert climate, its vegetation cover is accordingly sparse throughout. Moreover, Sinai does not show sharp climatic changes over short distances, a feature so characteristic of the rest of the country.

This explains why by far the greater part of the peninsula belongs to a single vegetation region, namely the Saharo-Arabian Zone of hot and extremely arid conditions. The Irano-Turanian dry-steppe zone forms two enclaves in this wide expanse—the higher reaches of the southern mountains, including also Jebel 'Iqma and the southern outskirts of the a-Tih Plateau, and the vicinity of Rafiaḥ where annual precipitation approaches 150 mm.

Plant Life of Northern Sinai. Near Rafiaḥ, rainfall suffices to sustain a semi-desert flora whose outstanding representative is a strain of wormwood *(Artemisia monosperma).* However, even under these relatively favorable conditions, large expanses are completely devoid of vegetation owing to the presence of moving sands.

To the south and west of this narrow strip, the wormwood is replaced by plants adapted to still more arid conditions, among them *Panicum turgidum* and *Halocnemum strobilaceum.* From the course of Wadi el-'Arīsh westward to the strip running parallel to the Suez Canal, the thick cover of moving sand dunes is an additional factor limiting plant growth. Often, only a few plants are to be found per square kilometer, many of them being species of *Aristida* and of bindweed *(Convolvulus).*

Bushes cause moving sands in Western Sinai to pile up in mounds

Close to the Bardawīl Lagoon, in the coastal stretch between el-'Arīsh and Qantāra, conditions are not uniform. *Arthrocnemum macrostachys* and *Halocnemum strobilaceum* grow on playas covered by a salt crust, and *Nitraria retusa* is one of the characteristic floral elements of their peripheries. Where more water is available, broom and the common reed, which are known from swamps in other parts of the country, make their appearance. The salt swamps southeast of Port Fuād (through which the cease-fire line now runs) have not yet been sufficiently investigated. It appears that the vegetation of this part of Sinai finds support in the relatively high air humidity and rather abundant summer dews.

In the sand dune girdle along the Suez Canal and Suez Gulf, long stretches of terrain are utterly devoid of plant life. Where some moisture is present in the soil, a few tamarisks or bushes of *Hammada salicornica* may thrive, anchoring the moving sand which often almost totally covers them. They are nevertheless able to continue growth above the sand mound, thus causing the sand to pile up even further; in some cases, such heaps rise three meters above their surroundings.

The Vegetation of Central Sinai. This plant region, by far the most extensive in Sinai, encompasses the gravel flats and chalk and limestone hills of the a-Tih Plateau and its environs. Here, the vegetation cover is even sparser than in the areas described above. *Artemisia herbae albae, Anabasis articulata, Zygophyllum dumosum* and *Salsola tetranda* locally replace each other as the dominant species.

The Nubian sandstones on the outer fringe of the crystalline mountain block constitute a separate plant region, characterized by two varieties of caper bush with prominent, thick, fleshy verdant foliage. At a certain stage of its ripening, the caper fruit looses its bitterness and becomes sweet as honey; it is then gathered and eaten by the local bedouin.

The Vegetation of Southern Sinai. In both sections of the al-Qā' Valley running parallel to the Suez Gulf—the northern one stretching between the Qabiliyāt Ridge and the granite massif, and the southern hugging the shore from a-Tur to the southern tip of the peninsula—the vegetation cover is either extremely sparse or totally absent over considerable stretches. The dark sands of this lowland occasionally pile up around bushes of *Nitraria retusa* and *Zygophyllum album.*

The picture gradually changes as one ascends the high crystalline massif. In Wadi Feirān Valley, particularly where the side valleys join it, appear high-grown thorny acacias. In the upper valley sections, above the main Feirān oasis, the manna tamarisk *(Tamarix mannifera)* takes the place of the acacias; the sugar-rich manna itself is secreted by certain grubs living on these tamarisks.

At altitudes exceeding 2,000 m a distinct plant world is encountered, with *Artemisia herbae albae* as the outstanding species. It is interesting to note that

A caper bush in Southern Sinai

Mangroves, mostly of the Avicennia marina bush, seam in the shore of Sinai's southern tip while this plant also appears on Mount Ramon in the Negev at an elevation of 900 m, and in the eastern part of the Beersheba Region even at 400–500 m, in the southern latitudes of Sinai it is restricted to the upper reaches of the mountains. At altitudes exceeding 2,200 m, rare species such as *Ficus pseudo-sycomorus* grow in rock clefts, while at the top of Mount Catherine there occur a number of indigenous plants whose global distribution appears to be limited to this locality. Most plants thriving in the high mountains are notable for their spicy odors.

The Mangroves. Mangroves, typical of many tropical sea shores, stretch from Ras Muḥammad to Nabaq along the Eilat Gulf coast. The mangrove flora contains a number of plant species, the most important being *Avicennia marina.* These plants seem to subsist on more or less fresh groundwater seeping from the land side through the subsoil toward the sea and not mixing with the heavier sea water. Mangrove plants often send out air roots above the water surface to provide their root system with the necessary air.

Wildlife. The most striking feature of the wildlife of this region is the marked contrast between the paucity of fauna on the Sinai Peninsula itself and its abundance in the surrounding sea waters, especially in the two gulfs of the Red Sea. The high temperature of these waters causes corals to thrive, and these in turn support an untold variety of colorful fish, mollusks, etc. The mangroves, along the coast, sustaining a faunal complex of their own, contribute to the variety of marine life. At some distance from the shore, the sea abounds with sharks and other fish which require deeper waters.

The development of land animals, on the other hand, is seriously handicapped by the lack of water and vegetation. In addition, indiscriminate hunting by man, practised from prehistoric times up to the present, has caused further decimation. Since earliest times, the lack of resources in Sinai itself has driven the local inhabitants to rely largely on hunting for provision of their immediate needs, and to eat certain animal species which, elsewhere and under more favorable conditions, are considered inedible. One is struck by the marked difference between the fauna of Sinai and that of the adjoining regions of the Negev. In the latter territory, the wildlife, in particular the gazelles and antelopes, has multiplied under the protection of Israel law, whereas unrestricted hunting in Sinai up to 1967 has all but exterminated these species. Certain animals have completely disappeared, while others appear to be approaching extinction, only a few representatives remaining. A striking example of thoughtless extermination is furnished by the large flocks of quail—recorded in the Bible—which arrive in autumn at the Mediterranean coast of Sinai and are caught en masse by the inhabitants of the el-'Arīsh region, who spread nets on the shore or gather the birds from the beach where they lie exhausted after their long flight over the sea. These birds are not only eaten by the local population but are also exported as a delicacy to Europe or offered to wayfarers along the el'Arīsh-Qantāra road.

Our principal sources of information on Sinai wildlife are to this day the observations made by travellers several decades ago. In view of the changes wrought by man in the interim period, such descriptions do not necessarily fit the present situation, particularly since the authors were not solely reliant on direct observations, but also included tales heard from local bedouin.

Invertebrates. As elsewhere throughout the globe, in Sinai the insects and other invertebrates have suffered less from man's activities than the higher species. In the 1920's and 1930's, over 120 kinds of beetles and about 70 kinds of butterflies were identified there. Frequently, enormous swarms of locusts penetrate into the peninsula from the south. Among the mollusks, the *Helix* land snails merit mentioning; their habitat is in regions of chalk and limestone rocks.

Reptiles. Venomous snakes, e.g., vipers, adders, etc., are represented in Sinai as in the rest of the country, although the peninsula has a few indigenous species not found elsewhere.

Birds. A survey made several decades ago recorded 190 species of birds in Sinai, 76 of which were nesting there. Outstanding among them are birds of prey and carrion hunters, such as ospreys and vultures, and particularly ravens which frequent the vicinity of human dwellings. On the coasts, at least two species of gulls have been identified. Certain of the smaller birds, e.g., *Caprodacus sinaicus Lich.*, are indigenous.

Mammals. As explained above, there is no way of ascertaining whether all mammals mentioned by travellers in the nineteen-thirties are still there today, e.g., hyenas, jackals, foxes, hares, rabbits, antelopes, gazelles, wolves and even panthers. The last-mentioned predators have been reported to have pounced upon sheep and camels although they never attacked humans; the bedouin have attempted to trap them. Wolves, on the other hand, certainly roam the a-Tih Plateau to this day, and the local bedouin are very much afraid of being attacked by hungry packs. Hunting appears to have reduced an indigenous species of ibex *(Ibex sinaitica)* to a last few individuals. Stags (erroneously described as gazelles) mostly frequent relatively flat terrain where plants like nitraria, *haloxylon* and acacias provide them with food.

Part III

Human Geography of the Country

The Archeological and Historical Background

The Land of Israel, sacred to three world faiths, is therefore an intimately known country and one whose prehistory and history have been thoroughly explored. Often scholars doing research into this country's past did not limit themselves to the particular historical problems of their interest. Their curiosity was aroused, for example, by accidentally coming across human bones and prehistoric artifacts during their work here, and they thus became absorbed in a new study. The country was found to present a continuous documentation of nearly all prehistoric periods, from the remotest beginnings up to the present day, although ancient buildings and works of art have generally been preserved less perfectly here than in other areas of the Mediterranean and Middle East.

Our knowledge of this part of the world is greatly enlarged by two additional factors: the Bible, possibly the most comprehensive and reliable document of antiquity, and the art of writing, first invented in this part of the world; inscribed sherds, papyrus scrolls, etc., have thus been found in this country as well as in Egypt, Mesopotamia and other regions, which refer to Palestine itself, to its towns and inhabitants, or to other countries but permit analogies with cultural and political developments in the Land of Israel.

Palestine in Prehistory

The prehistoric periods of the Near and the Middle East should be dated somewhat differently from those relating to Western Europe or America, since here most new cultural developments began earlier than those further north and west. Man is assumed to have first appeared in this country at least half a million years ago, when the Old Stone Age (Paleolithic) began. It ended in our region between 12,000 and 10,000 B.C.E. The Middle Stone Age (Mesolithic) lasted until about 8,000 B.C.E., and the New Stone Age (Neolithic) until about 4,500 B.C.E.; it was followed, in the fourth millennium B.C.E., by the Chalcolithic ('Copper and Stone') Age, which was the transition between prehistory and history.

Paleolithic Period. There are signs that man's habitation in this region has been more continuous than in Europe. This stems from the absence of glacial periods, which, further north, cut him off from nearly all sources of subsistence. The climate of the country, however, has not remained unchanged since the beginning of human population. Fossil plants and animals are evidence that pluvials, i.e., wet periods, paralleled the Ice Ages of Europe in our latitudes. In the Lower and Middle Paleozoic, the climate appears to have been warmer and moister than that of today. Tropical plants and animals abounded, among the latter huge elephants, rhinoceri, hippopotami, etc. Man, living by gathering and hunting, fought these giants for his very life, and depended on them for food and clothing.

At the beginning of the Upper Paleolithic, the climate became more arid; after several more humid intervals, some warmer and some cooler than today, a drier phase followed. The climate has been more or less stable since the end of the Paleolithic.

Many tribes left this country due to the worsening conditions of the climate; those who remained were spurred to greater efforts in improving their tools and in developing new sources of livelihood.

The earliest human traces were discovered in 1962 at a site called 'Ubeydiya, near kibbutz Afiqim in the Jordan Valley. The few human bones found there were identified as belonging to *Australopithecus,* the first erect tool-maker, who preceded even the famous 'Java Man' and 'Peking Man' and was previously known only in South Africa. Tools such as hand axes, ball-like stones and other implements were found, along with bones of giraffes, elephants, zebras, etc.

In the Early Paleolithic the hand axe served as a simple all-purpose tool; the grasping end was rounded, and the other, which struck the worked material, sharpened. At first, stones of all kinds were made into hand axes; later hard flints, 'shelled' painstakingly from the surrounding soft chalk, were preferred. Gradually the art of sharpening edges was perfected, and the flakes splintered off in the process were used as scrapers, arrowheads, etc.

Fire seems to have been taken into man's service at a very early stage; at night fire afforded warmth and security from ferocious animals. The first nuclei of society—the family, the clan, the tribe—were formed around the open fire and the hearth. As the climate became more severe, man was driven from the open field, his exclusive dwelling-place, to seek shelter in the karstic caves of the Hill regions, e.g., in the Naḥal Ammud gorge in Eastern Lower Galilee, Har Qedumim near Nazareth, Mount Carmel, etc. Cults, such as those of the dead and of the hunt, and their resulting crude artistic creations, mark the development of spiritual activity in the Early Paleolithic.

Migrations followed climatic oscillations. Alongside *Palaeoanthropus palaestinensis,* who was related to Neanderthal man, appeared tribes belonging to *Homo sapiens.* The Carmel Caves, with remains of humans of mixed parentage, afford proof that both races belonged to the same human species and were thus able to procreate freely. The Carmel caves reflect progress in the variegation of tools and in their shapes and uses; the dead were buried, and cults became more elaborate. People adorned themselves with shell and stone necklaces, etc., and attempted to sculpture images.

Mesolithic Period. The finds in Wadi Natūf, 10 km (6 miles) east of Ben Shemen in Northern Judea, typify man's achievements in the Mesolithic. The 'Natufian Culture' included fishing hooks, pointed stone arrowheads, sickles of crescent-shaped bones reinforced with toothedged flakes. Wild-wheat grains were gathered and ground in stone mortars, but no agricultural work was done yet.

Flint axe of the Neolithic Period

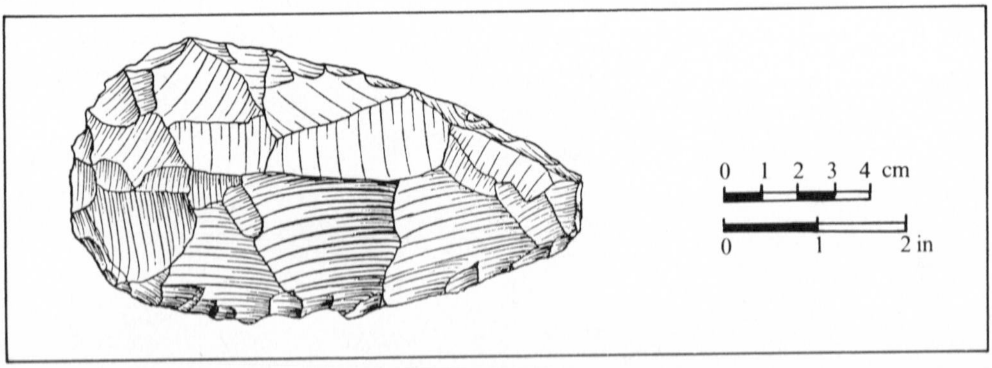

Neolithic Period. The excavations made in kibbutz Sha'ar ha-Golan near the Yarmuk River in the Kinnarot Valley ('Yarmukian Culture') reflect a step above the Mesolithic Culture. This stage marks the beginnings of farming; the soil was dug with primitive hoes or forks, grain was ground in stone mills, and fish caught in nets. The first animals, such as sheep, were domesticated. People settled down and lived in huts. Fertility and ancestor cults ruled spiritual life; this is demonstrated by the 'Venus of Sha'ar ha-Golan,' the shape of a naked woman engraved on a pebble.

The transition from nomadism to a sedentary way of life is most clearly revealed by the excavations at Jericho which may be assumed to be the world's oldest city, dating back to ca. 8000 B.C.E. Its houses were built of brick, and roofed over with clay arches. A thick stone wall, four meters high, surrounded the agglomeration. At the wall's inner margin stands a huge, round stone tower, even today attaining a height of ten meters. Many finds at this level of the Jericho dig point to the beginnings of agriculture. The abundant spring of En Elisha' ('Ein es-Sultan), rising at the foot of the Jericho mound, was used in those early times for irrigation. The most interesting objects discovered at Jericho are nine human skulls, with marly clay replacing flesh and shells representing eyes, which appear to have been devotional objects.

Chalcolithic Period. In this transitional period between prehistory and history, man's progress was accelerated. Farming became the almost exclusive source of

The excavations on the Jericho mound have revealed the remains of what is assumed to be the earth's oldest urban settlement

food. Finds near Ḥadera, in the Northern Sharon, allow the assumption that vegetables were sometimes grown with irrigation. Grain was stored in stone kettles or subterranean storage bins. Artisans specialized, and social and vocational differentiations became pronounced. Permanent settlements were founded in most parts of the country. Objects were dedicated to the fertility goddess (which later, in the language of the Canaanites, assumed the names of 'Ashera' or 'Ashtoret' (= Astarte). Trade developed between distant towns and even between different countries. To commemorate the dead, huge dolmens were erected, or remains were buried in sarcophagi. At Tuleylāt-el-Ghassūl, northeast of the Dead Sea, wall pictures with beautiful geometric patterns in three colors have been discovered ('the Ghassulian Culture'). Near Beersheba a large Chalcolithic settlement was found with artisan shops which produced articles of basalt stone and copper—both raw materials which were transported from Edom or Moab over at least 160–210 km (100–130 miles). Other Chalcolithic settlements which had attained a high level of civilization have been found near the Enot Enan Springs in the Ḥula Valley, and elsewhere in the country. The discovery of beautifully finished copper vessels in a cliff cave of the Judean Desert canyons near En Gedi caused a sensation among archeologists in 1962.

Essential Factors in the Country's History

The geographical position and economic assets of the country create several factors which have fundamentally influenced historical developments during the first 3,000 years (i.e., between 3,000 B.C.E. and the Roman period) and, partly, to this day. These factors can be summed up as follows:

(a) The country is situated midway between the two large river valleys of Egypt and Mesopotamia, which at a very early period became centers of overpowering political might and influential civilizations. These powers met on the soil of this country, mostly in strife, but in some instances they achieved a certain degree of mutual integration. The highways crossing the country, connecting those two centers, assumed great political importance. The desire of both powers to control these roads engendered frequent armed expeditions into this country with the aim of imposing political rule. Palestine therefore passed repeatedly from one empire to its adversary. Political units within the country could be fully independent only when both powers were simultaneously weakened and thus unable to intervene in local government.

(b) Lying on the border between the desert and the sown, the country was witness to the unending struggle between the two. As soon as the control of mighty rulers weakened and the local settlers appeared negligent or helpless, the desert tribes ventured into the cultivated land to plunder it. Eventually, the nomad invaders became farmers in the border region, assimilated and were integrated in the local population. It was then their turn to repel fresh invasions.

(c) According to the geographical origin and character of the changing population and its rulers, the centers of settlement and administration alternated between the Hill regions and the Coastal Plain and interior valleys, and back to the Hills. Peoples coming from the eastern interior, where material civilization was at a relatively low level, preferred the Hills (among these were the ancient Israelites, the Arabs and the Turks); those who came over the western sea, possessing a high degree of technical skill and showing talent and inclination for international trade, moved the center toward the Coastal Plain (Phoenicians, Philistines, Greeks, Romans, Crusaders, Jews of the present time.)

The Bronze Age

Early Bronze Period. The Bronze Age, which lasted about 1,800 years (3100–1200 B.C.E.) in the Middle East, is divided into the Early, Middle and Late Bronze periods; the Early Bronze lasted until 2100 B.C.E.

This first historic period of the country was characterized by attempts to form a more comprehensive social organization and forceful political regime. In the towns public buildings, much larger than the living quarters of the ordinary citizen, were erected. Their construction required a combined effort of all inhabitants. Towns were fortified with strong walls. Ash strata in the ruins of many towns testify to their repeated conquest and sacking by enemies.

In the middle of the third millennium B.C.E., the mighty Accadian empire was founded in Mesopotamia and soon spread its rule over the 'Land of Amurru,' i.e., over the entire region between the Euphrates and the shores of the Mediterranean Sea. The inhabitants of Palestine and Syria then spoke west-Semitic dialects. The Accadian rule introduced cuneiform script everywhere and adapted it to local languages. On the other hand, the Egyptians developed their trade with the cities on the Lebanese coast and tried to secure commanding positions in Palestine. In those centuries the international overland trade used mostly the 'King's Way' in Transjordan, which passed flourishing settlements. Toward the end of this period, the Egyptian grip weakened, and the Palestinians even exerted pressure on the frontiers of Egypt proper. The towns of Transjordan were razed by nomads, and the King's Way had to be abandoned temporarily.

Middle Bronze. At the beginning of the Middle Bronze Period, the Middle Kingdom of Egypt attained new splendor and renewed its rule over Palestine, which was called 'Rthenu.' From then on, the principal thoroughfare between Egypt and Mesopotamia became the Via Maris or 'Sea Road,' which ran in this country along the Coastal Plain, through the Irron Vale, the Jezreel, Bet She'an and Kinnarot valleys, and over the Golan Plateau toward Damascus. The inhabitants of Palestine were then cultivators of grain and fruit and herders of sheep and cattle. An interesting testimony of life and political events in Palestine appears in the so-called 'execration texts,' small clay tablets bearing the names of towns and their rulers who were enemies of Egypt; the smashing of the tablets was to symbolize the downfall of the foe. Jerusalem, Ascalon, Aphek, Sichem and Ḥaẓor are among the Palestinian towns mentioned.

In the eighteenth century B.C.E., a huge wave of migrations swept over Asia Minor and the Middle East; it engulfed Palestine from the north and brought foreign rule to Egypt. The conquerors, in Egypt called 'Hyksos,' i.e., 'foreign rulers,' and who included Semite and Indo-Aryan peoples, overpowered all opponents. Two innovations which they introduced in warfare aided them—horses and chariots. The Hyksos built their capital at Tanis (Ẓo'an) in the east of the Nile Delta and also ruled over Palestine and Syria. The town of Sharuḥen in the Northwestern Negev was their center in this country. Even when they were driven out of Egypt by a powerful local dynasty two hundred years later, their rule over Palestine was maintained for a while. With their final retreat, the Middle Bronze Period came to its end.

The Patriarchs. The advent of the Patriarchs of Israel dates back to the latter part of the Hyksos Period. The description in the Book of Genesis of events and ways of life in this country has been borne out fully by historical and archeological research. Of special interest is the campaign of four Mesopotamian kings, headed by Kedarlaomer of Elam, which is described in Genesis XIV. The expedition took the renewed King's Way in Transjordan, from Damascus through the Gilead to the Land of Moab; the invaders descended to the Dead Sea Region, but did not continue southward to Edom where the highway splits (one branch led to Eilat, and the other descended to Punnon in the Arava Valley, crossed the Negev and reached Egypt through Qadesh Barne'a and the northern Sinai Peninsula).

These events and others also set numerous local and west-Semitic tribes on the move, some of which reached Palestine and Egypt. These tribes were called in contemporary documents 'Hapiru' or 'Habiru,' and many scholars identify them with the Hebrews. 'Abram the Hebrew' and his household were such semi-nomads. Abraham, feeling like a newcomer, wished to acquire the rights of a resident, and therefore paid a large sum for a family tomb site at Hebron; his son Isaac became a wealthy landowner in the Negev where he sowed the fields, intermittently at least; the third generation, Jacob and his sons, regarded themselves as a local tribe fully rooted in the country; the petty war against the town Sichem is typical of the perpetual quarrels between small local kingdoms and tribes in Palestine at that time.

The Patriarchs, being simple herdsmen, seem to have preferred the 'Hill Road,' which ran through regions of relatively sparse population and avoided the more important and sophisticated cities of the Foothills and the coast. The Bible draws a lively picture of these shepherds and their characteristic habits and traditions (hospitality, jealous guarding of heritage rights, etc.); a firm stand was necessary against established and well-fortified towns, whose economy was based mainly on field and garden crops.

Late Bronze. Egypt's new local rulers, not content with expelling the Hyksos from their own land, also attempted to vanquish the foe in Palestine. After a long siege Sharuḥen fell to them. In the middle of the 15th century B.C.E., when the New Kingdom attained the peak of its splendor, Pharaoh Thutmosis III set out on

Lakhish, in the southern Judean Foothills, was an important Canaanite city at least since the second millennium B.C.E. Note glacis and revetment below remnants of wall, surrounded by moat. On top of the hill—the 'Akropolis,' or palace of local king

armed expeditions to the north, took Jaffa by a trick similar to the Trojan horse, besieged Megiddo until it fell, and continued his victorious sweep to the Orontes River in Northern Syria. He set the Egyptian administration over the entire country through governors and army contingents, who supervised the local petty kings and collected the heavy taxes. The country had to send to Egypt great quantities of grain, fruit, wood and minerals, as well as many slaves.

The Egyptian hold over the country weakened in the 14th century B.C.E. Fortified towns were molested and attacked by nomadic tribes, apparently at the instigation of the Hittite Kingdom, which had asserted itself in Asia Minor. Pharaoh Amenhotep IV-Akhnaton, concentrating all efforts in a religious reform in Egypt, thereby neglected his far provinces. Letters on clay tablets in cuneiform script from governors and garrison commanders in Palestine arrived at his newly built capital (the present Tell el 'Amarna), urgently asking for help against the nomads, who were becoming ever more audacious. Some local rulers formed alliances with the Habiru aggressors, became independent of Egypt, and tried to widen their domain by warring against their neighbors. These letters were duly preserved in the royal archives, but apparently no one cared to reply or act for the Egyptian interests. The Tell el 'Amarna letters constitute an invaluable treasure of information on the situation in Palestine at the time. Explicit details are provided about cities such as Ascalon, Gezer, Jerusalem, Sichem, Megiddo, Acre, Ḥaẓor, and others—the occupations of their inhabitants and the unending bickerings of their kings.

In the 13th century B.C.E. another strong dynasty rose in Egypt. Pharaoh Sethi I set out on a punitive campaign against Bet She'an, and commemorated his victory by a stele inscribed in hieroglyphs. Ramses II later fought the Hittites on the Orontes River; after neither side had won a sweeping victory, an agreement was reached fixing the frontier between the two empires along the Yarmuk River. At about the same time (around 1200 B.C.E.), the Tribes of Israel began to occupy the country.

The Iron Age and First Temple Era

The Settlement of the Israelites. The name 'Israel' is first mentioned on an Egyptian stele of Pharaoh Merenptah's time, at the end of the 13th century. The conquest of Transjordan and Cisjordan, described in the Bible (books of Numbers and Joshua) as a single campaign, may in fact have been a process lasting two generations, perhaps even a hundred years. Some believe that the tribes of Asher, Issachar and Zebulon were the first to enter Cisjordan, where they settled in Samaria and expanded their domain to the Jezreel Valley and

Lower Galilee. The conquest of the important town of Sichem is not mentioned in the Bible, possibly because it was in Israelite hands prior to Joshua's battles at Ai, on the outskirts of the Judean Desert, and in the Valley of Ayalon in the Judean Foothills. Rather unclear is the date of the battle 'at the waters of Merom' (this site probably lies in Central Upper Galilee, near Mount Meron), where the Israelites finally routed the Canaanites. Some scholars place this battle after Deborah's great victory over Sisera 'at the waters of Megiddo' in the Jezreel Valley. In any case, the books of Joshua and Judges show clearly that the Israelites contented themselves, of necessity, with the Hill regions (since these had a relatively small and sparse population), while the plains and valleys, particularly the fortified cities, remained undisputed Canaanite property.

The Philistines. A generation or two after the Israelites' migration from the east, the 'Sea Peoples' entered the Coastal Plain from the west; their first moves perhaps even facilitated the Israelite conquest. They began by invading Egypt proper and weakening its power; the Empire could thus not pay proper attention to its northeastern territory. Only after the Sea Peoples were defeated by Pharaoh Ramses III did some of them appear in the Southern Coastal Plain, where they were called 'Philistines' (which may point to a connection with the Pelasgians of the Aegean Sea), and others, called the Sikeles (whose name is possibly related with Sicily), arrived in the Sharon and Carmel Coast. With the Philistines, the Iron Age came to this country, 'because they had chariots of iron' (Judges I,19).

The Days of the Judges, and the First Kings. Triumph and defeat alternated in the struggle of the Israelites for existence in the country. Great victories under the Judges, such as Deborah's, often had very short-lived results because of the isolationism of the tribes, who would unite only in the face of grave danger. The Ammonites, for example, harassed the tribes in Transjordan, the Midianite shepherds invaded the Jezreel Valley to graze their livestock on its fields and meadows, and the Philistines increased pressure in the Judean Foothills on the tribe of Dan. When the situation grew dangerous, first attempts were made to exchange the ancient tribal regime for a stronger, more comprehensive rule, first by Gideon and Abimelech at Sichem, and later by the Benjaminite Saul, who was anointed king by Samuel 'the Seer.' Moving his warriors swiftly between the border regions, Saul forced back Midianites, Ammonites, Amalekites and Philistines. He cleared out the foreign enclaves from the territory of the central tribes and prepared the ground for a strong kingdom, but still was unable to supplant the basically tribal organization of his people. David, who won popular acclaim by slaying the Philistine giant Goliath in the Vale of Terebinths (Ela Valley) and evaded the jealous persecution of Saul, reached this goal. The

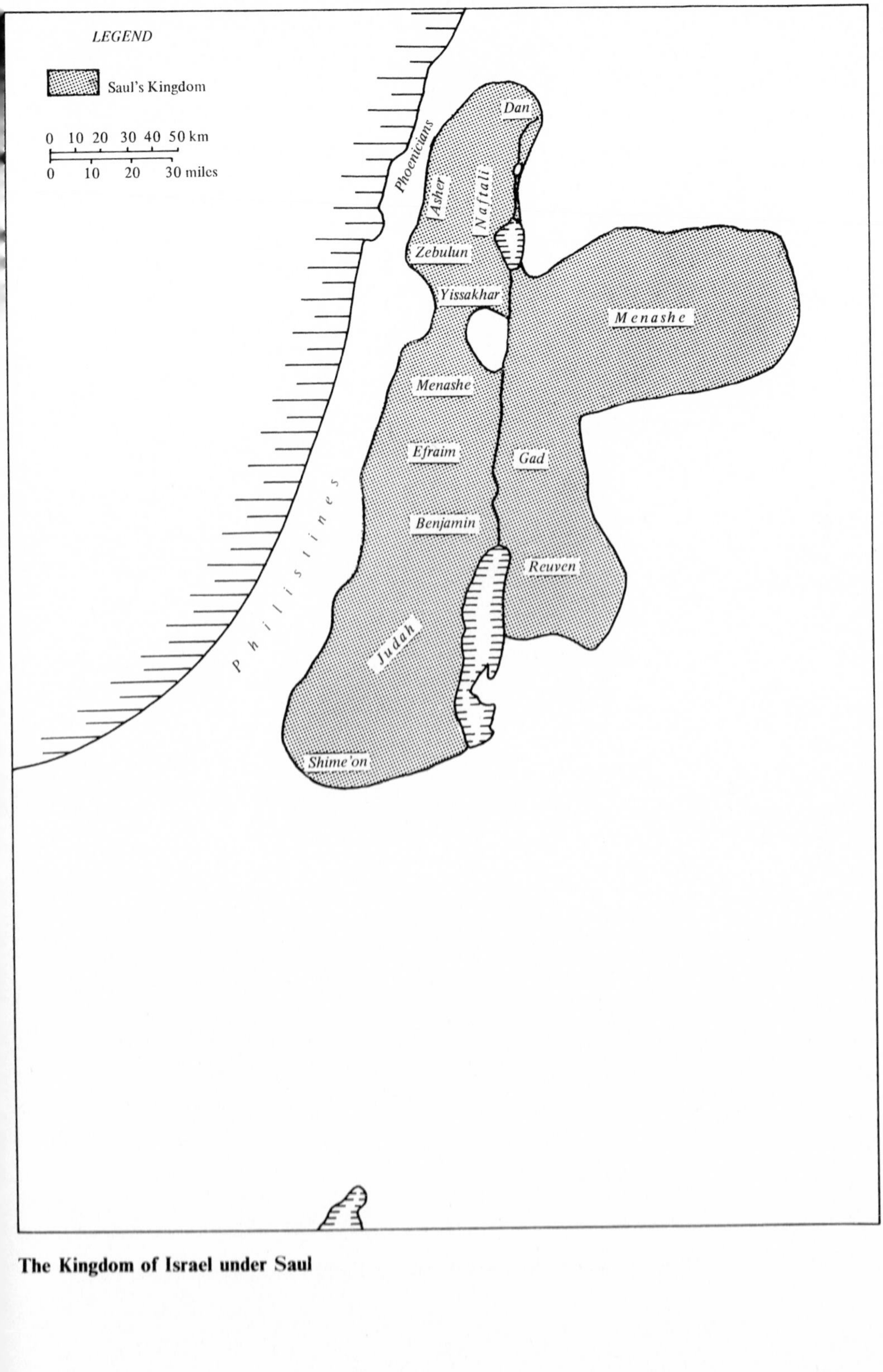

The Kingdom of Israel under Saul

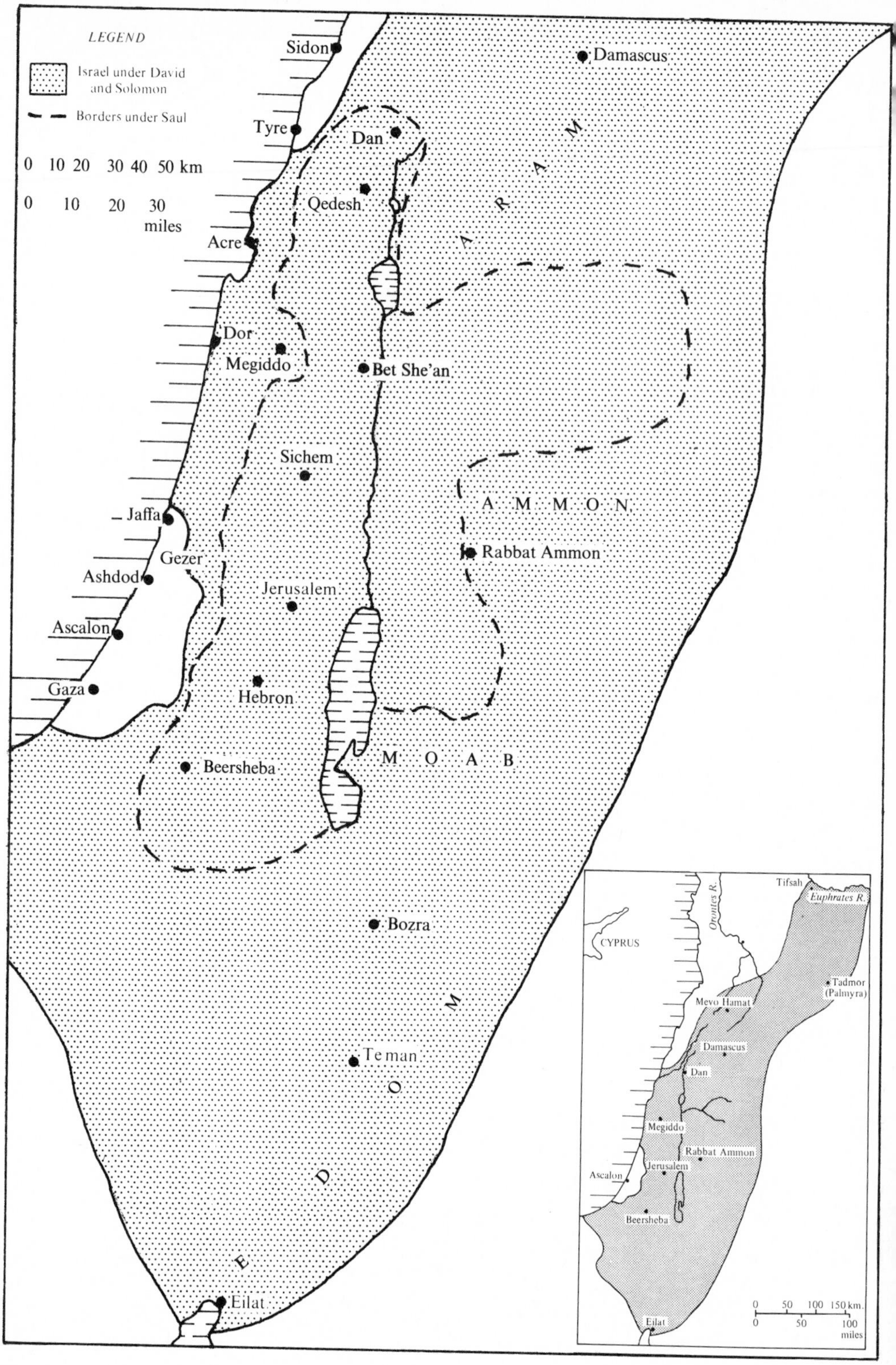

The Kingdom of Israel under David and Solomon (inset: David's territory in its full extent)

Philistines, upon realizing the new rift in the Israelite camp, the rivalry between Saul and David, renewed their pressure. This time based in the Jezreel Valley, they triumphed on Mount Gilboa where Saul and Jonathan met their death. In the meantime, however, David (whom the Philistines regarded as their tool) gathered a band and vanquished the Amalekites in the south. In the eighth year of his rule in Hebron (around 1000 B.C.E.), he cast off Philistine sovereignty, beat their army, which came through the Ela Valley to the Refa'im Vale west of Jerusalem, and took the city—the last Canaanite stronghold in the Judean Hills—'the town of the Jebusite.'

With the transfer of his residence and the home of the Holy Ark to Jerusalem, a city which was considered neutral by the tribes as it did not belong to any of them, David strengthened his position enormously and assured the people's consent for renunciation of tribal loyalties. He established a standing army by mobilizing Israelites and other peoples ('the Crethi and Plethi') and organized a civil administration through a royal cabinet of ministers. At this time Egypt was weaker than ever before; the Hittite Kingdom in the north was shaken by new migrations of peoples; the Assyrians and Babylonians were troubled by the Aramite ascent. All these circumstances finally permitted David to subdue the Philistines, to assimilate all the remaining foreign enclaves, and to establish his rule firmly in the Jezreel Valley and Galilee. He gained victories over the Ammonites, Moabites and Edomites in Transjordan and over their ally, the Kingdom of Aram-Ẓova, conquered all their lands and set the frontier of his empire at Tifsaḥ on the Euphrates River in the north, and at Eilat in the south. Only two narrow coastal strips, that of the Phoenicians from Dor and the Carmel Coast to the north and that of the Philistines from Yavne to the south, seem to have remained outside his domain.

Solomon, David's heir, consolidated his father's achievements through stringent political and economic organization. He built the Temple on Mount Moriya in Jerusalem, divided his monarchy into provinces ruled by governors, erected storage cities and fortresses, imposed heavy taxes and saw to their efficient levying, mined copper at Punnon and Timna and smelted it at Eẓyon Gever, developed foreign trade and signed political and economic treaties with rulers of near and distant countries (e.g., Hiram of Tyre, the Queen of Sheba). Toward the end of his days, dangers loomed when Egypt regained its strength under its energetic new king Shishak, who exploited the indignation of the Israelites about the yoke of taxes and forced labor, lent his support to Jeroboam's revolt, and thus prepared the split of the kingdom.

The Two Kingdoms, and the Fall of the First Temple. The 350 years during which the kingdoms of Israel in the north and Judah in the south existed separately

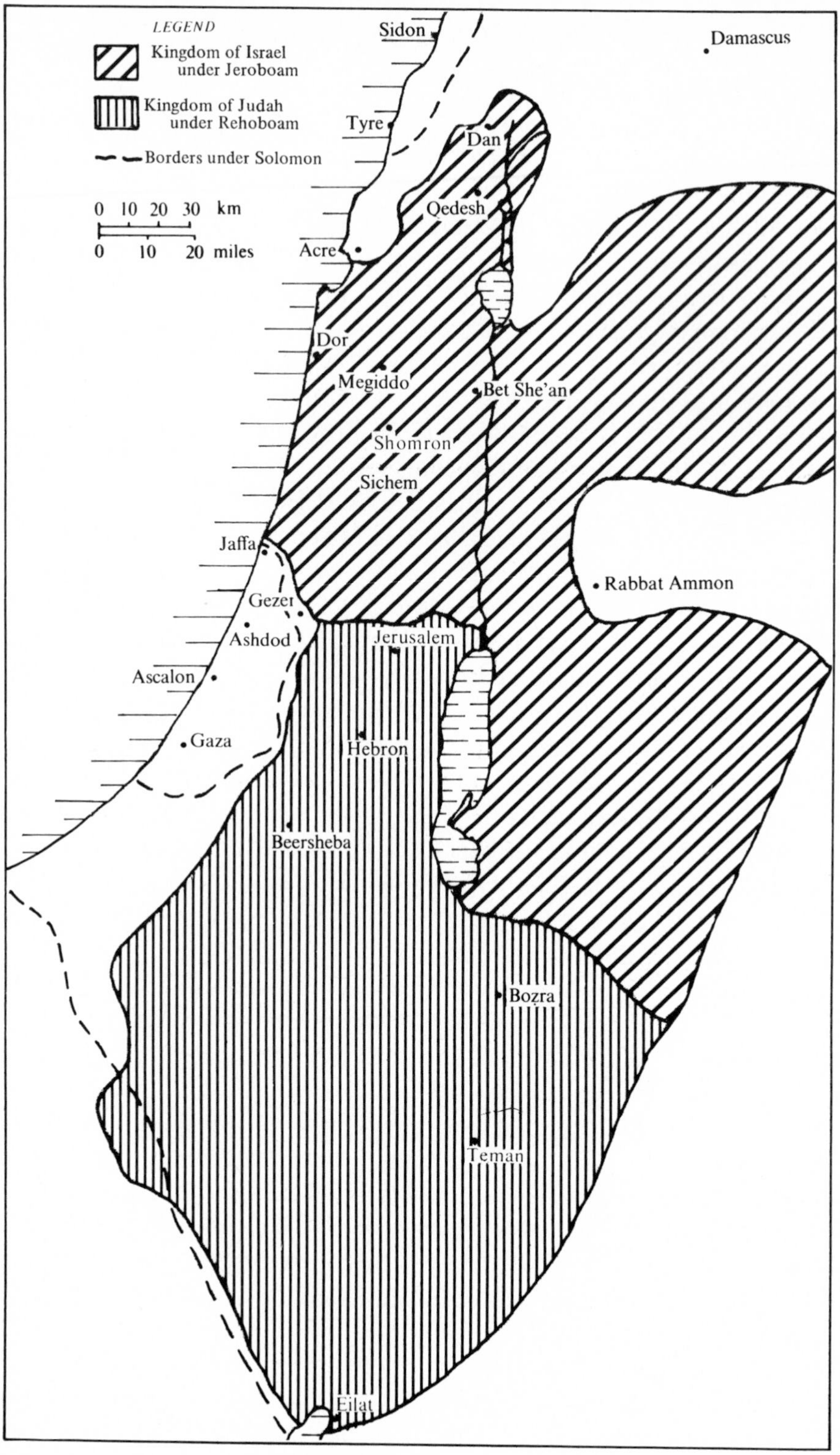

The divided kingdoms of Israel and Judah after Solomon's death

emphasize the extent to which this country's fate depends on the interplay of forces between world powers. Pharaoh Shishak's campaign weakened mainly the Kingdom of Israel, which lost territory in the north and east. The kings of Judah—Rehoboam and Abijam—tried to counteract the growing dangers by building strong defense positions south and west of the Judean Hills—an outer ring of fortresses from Zif (Siph) in the south of the Judean Desert through Adorayim, Lakhish, Azeqa and Ẓor'a to Ayalon, and an inner ring from Bethlehem over Etam, Teqo'a, Bet Ẓur, and Adullam to Sokho. These kings, however, did not reinforce their northern border with the Kingdom of Israel, hoping, perhaps, that the split would be only temporary and that their rule over the whole country would be restored to the limits of Solomon's empire.

In the middle of the 9th century B.C.E., since Egypt was again declining, the two kingdoms, under Jehoshaphath of Judah and Omri of Israel, who had made an alliance, were able to regain some of their former might. This new phase, however, did not last long. Mesha, King of Moab, revolted against Judah and commemorated his success in the 'Mesha stele,' written in ancient Hebrew characters and one of the most important archeological documents of the time. Judah was in dire straits under Jehoshaphath's son Joram, while Israel was shaken by internal unrest culminating in Jehu's uprising against the House of Omri. The northern Aramite Kingdom of Damascus gained strength, repelled the Assyrians, and captured from King Joahaz all of Israel's territory except the capital, Shomron, and its nearest surroundings. An Assyrian return to power gave Israel, under King Joash, and Judah, under Amaziah, another lease on life and a chance to restore their positions. A new peak of political and economic power was reached under Jeroboam II of Israel and Uziah of Judah in the middle of the 8th century B.C.E. The former extended his rule over the Basan, conquered Damascus and again fixed the frontier along the Euphrates River, while the latter assured his mastery of the Negev as well as of Southern Transjordan and Eilat. Uziah aided the development of agriculture and tried to renew copper mining and overseas trade through the Red Sea.

The upsurge of Assyria, however, which had initially aided Israel and Judah by weakening their Aramite enemy led, in 722 B.C.E., only 30 years after the death of Jeroboam II, to the liquidation of the northern Kingdom of Israel. The area of Judah was also reduced. The Assyrians conquered Shomron, led its notables into captivity, captured the fortresses in the Judean Foothills (e.g., Azeqa, Lakhish), and besieged Jerusalem. At that time King Hezekiah enabled his capital to withstand the siege by building the famous tunnel and leading water from the Giḥon Spring to the Shiloaḥ Pool inside the walls of Jerusalem.

The siege was lifted when the Assyrian army was suddenly compelled to return home. But the might of Assyria, which had overcome Egypt, weighed heavily on

Judah during the long rule of King Manasse (699–644 B.C.E.). A last spell of prosperity came under King Josiah, when Babylon replaced Assyria in the Mesopotamian Basin. A spiritual and religious renaissance fired the people of Judah when a volume of the Pentateuch was discovered in the Temple Area and Biblical law was fixed as the fundamental codex of the State. Josiah was even able to extend his borders, briefly, over parts of the former Kingdom of Israel in Samaria and Galilee. Egypt experienced a brief revival as well, and Pharaoh Necho organized a campaign against Babylonia. Josiah, who supported the Babylonians, fell in battle against Necho near Megiddo (609 B.C.E.). Josiah's heirs alternated between Egypt and Babylonia until King Nebuchadnezzar finally resolved to end Judah's existence, destroyed Jerusalem and the Temple, and led the inhabitants into captivity (586 B.C.E.).

The age of the two kingdoms was also that of the great prophets. It began with Elijah and Elisha in the 9th century B.C.E., attained a peak in Isaiah, who was both a preacher and a great statesman, and ended with Jeremiah, who witnessed the destruction of the Temple, and Ezekiel in the Babylonian exile. In their forthright call to the people and the leaders for social justice and against heathen practices, their stern warnings to the kings and the rich in days of apparent well-being, and their compassionate consolation of the people when the dark prophecies had come true, they attained perhaps the greatest heights of the human spirit.

The Second Temple Era

The Persian Period. Babylon's heyday did not last for long. In 539 B.C.E. Cyrus of Persia occupied its territory and a year later issued a decree permitting the exiled Jews to return to their country. Initially, the number of returnees was small, about 40,000 souls. The area of Judea itself had shrunk. The Edomites, driven from their original home by the Nabateans, had settled in the Hebron Hills and the Judean Foothills; the Samaritans or 'Cuthians'—a new people formed by the last inhabitants of the northern Kingdom of Israel and the splinters of other peoples who had been settled there after the Assyrian conquest—occupied parts of Northern Judea, and the Philistines and Phoenicians had grown stronger in the west. The land was desolate, and the local inhabitants scorned the returning Jews. Jerusalem apparently did not become a city again until the time of Darius I in the middle of the fifth century B.C.E., when a second returning group, led by Ezra and Nehemiah, arrived in the country. With Nehemiah's initiative, the Temple and the walls of Jerusalem were reconstructed 'every one with one of his hands wrought in the work, and with the other hand held a weapon' (Nehemiah IV, 17).

Our knowledge of the Persian Period is meager, particularly of the period following the termination of the Books of Ezra and Nehemiah. Archeological evidence in the country testifies to a decrease in population and a material and cultural decline. Toward the end of that period, however, the situation improved. The population grew; farming, handicrafts and trade developed, especially in the coast cities which came under Hellenistic influence, and in the Negev settled by the Nabateans. This people showed great ingenuity in city planning and building, in storing and utilizing their scanty water reserves, and in using the opportunities to trade their farming produce at high prices to the caravans traveling the Negev highways (see below, pp. 218f., 443–444). The Jewish community, which gradually increased in numbers and prosperity, found new ways of national organization with the creation of the Greet Assembly, 'Knesseth ha-Gedola,' which was headed by the High Priest or one of the Scribes.

Hellenistic Period and Hasmonean Kingdom. The swift conquest of the entire Middle East by Alexander the Great (332 B.C.E.)—who was welcomed by the country's Jewish community toward which he showed goodwill—entailed an immediate political change in the country and greatly strengthened the impact of Greek civilization. After his death, however, the political situation reverted to that of the period of the First Temple: the country's fate hinged on the struggle between outside powers. After the division of Alexander's giant empire among the Diadochs, the country alternated between the rule of Egypt's Ptolemies and the Seleucids of Syria and Mesopotamia. In the year 200 B.C.E. Palestine was captured from the Ptolemies by the Seleucid King Antiochus the Great. Both empires were weakened by incessant wars and by internal friction. In the long run, both were overshadowed by Rome, the growing world power in the west. Using this interval between the decadence of the Hellenistic kingdoms and Rome's final triumph in the east, the Jews were able—for a century at least—to regain independence.

Under Ptolemean rule, economic conditions in the country improved. Wheat renowned for its good quality, wine, and olive oil were exported. Sea commerce developed, and with it the increasingly numerous Hellenistic harbor cities. The Nabateans in the Negev thrived on the transit trade of spices and other luxuries between Southern Arabia and the Mediterranean Basin.

The economic prosperity created a new rich class in Judea. The deepening social contrasts soon took on political and cultural aspects. The rich tended to assimilate Hellenism, while the poor remained faithful to their national and religious heritage. When the financial resources of the Seleucid kings were exhausted by the wars, rich Judean families tried to gain political influence by proffering financial aid and were not shy to use community monies for this

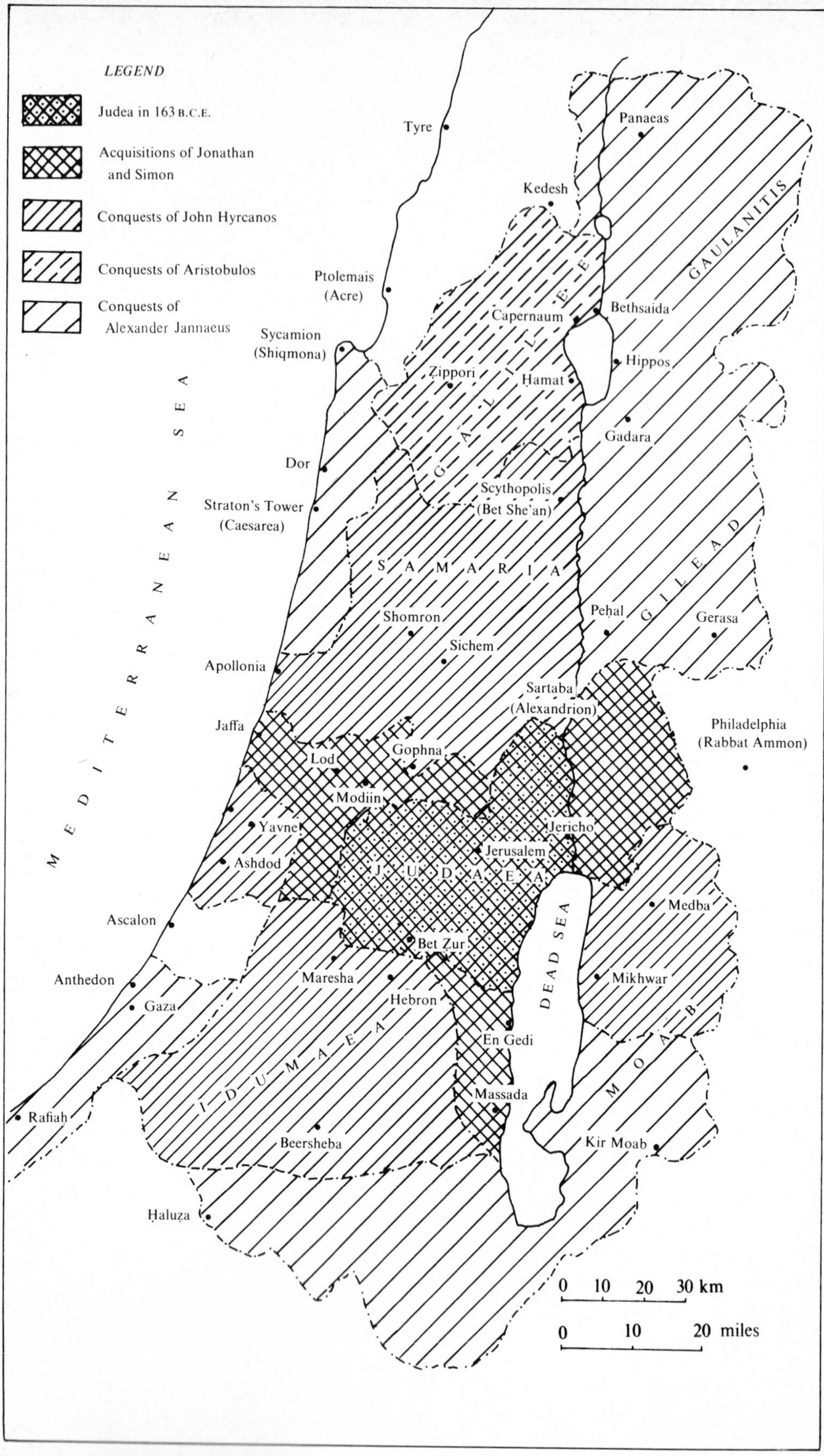

Expansion of the Hasmonean Kingdom, between the days of Judah Maccabee and the reign of Alexander Jannaeus

purpose. This internal competition resulted in the plundering of the Temple's treasure by King Antiochus IV Epiphanes, who, at the same time, took strong measures to force Hellenization upon the Jews. This incited the Maccabean revolt (167 B.C.E.), which at its beginning was only meant to end persecutions and religious suppression. However, when the Hasmoneans succeeded in battle beyond expectations, and were further aided by the growing internal strife in the Seleucid dynasty, their aim became complete liberation and expansion of the free Jewish domain. The first annexations were made by Jonathan, the son of Mattathias, who took Afarayim, Lod and Ḥadid in the northwest and parts of Transjordan; after a brief crisis his brother Simon achieved full independence. He acquired Gezer and Jaffa and thus opened 'a window to the sea' for Judea. A generation later, with John (Yoḥanan) Hyrcanos, the Hasmonean Kingdom grew powerful and expanded at a fast rate. John Hyrcanos annexed the Edomite land of Southern Judea, the Northern Negev, the Coastal Plain between Jaffa and Ashdod, the Cuthian territory in Samaria, the Bet She'an Valley, and the Southern Sharon; Judas Aristobulos added Galilee, and Alexander Jannaeus (Yannai)—the Northern Sharon, Mount Carmel, the Golan, Gilead, Moab, and the Negev Coast up to Rhinokoroura (el-'Arīsh of our days). The subjects thus added were converted to Judaism. Simultaneously, however, the kingdom changed in character, as the Hasmonean dynasty relied on the wealthy classes rather than on the mass of the people. They adopted the ruthless ways of the Hellenistic rulers, and they also seemed to copy the habit of internal rivalry; they thereby promoted their own downfall. After the death of Queen Salome Alexandra, who had restored popular and uncorrupted rule, adopted a prudent foreign policy and allied herself with the Pharisees, the group which cherished Jewish tradition and morals, the Hasmoneans' end was brought about by her two sons, who invited the Roman Pompey to settle their differences.

The Early Roman Period. Pompey occupied Judea in 63 B.C.E. and cut back its borders to their original size. The Hellenistic cities of the seaboard and in Transjordan ('Dekapolis'—the 'Ten City League') had their pagan character restored. The demographic gains by conversion to Judaism in Galilee, Samaria, and the Land of the Edomites, however, remained stable. Julius Caesar allowed Judea a certain degree of political independence and returned its access to the sea through Jaffa. For another short period, under Herod the Great, Judea expanded its borders and regained wealth. The price this time, however, was full political and cultural submission to Rome, as non-Jewish elements in the population were consistently preferred to Jews. During the reign of Herod and his heirs (37 B.C.E.–6 C.E.), in spite of its cruelty and harshness, the population grew, and magnificent buildings and cities were constructed. Typical of this time are

The southwest corner of the Temple Mount, Jerusalem. The massive ashlars of the containing wall are a monument to King Herod, greatest builder in the country's past

expensive imported building materials, e.g., marble and granite, carefully hewn building stones (Western Temple Wall in Jerusalem, Machpela Cave at Hebron, etc.), ingenious port installations, aqueducts, and beautiful statues (Caesarea, Ascalon, etc.), all in the Roman-Hellenistic style.

Since Palestine became a Roman province in 6 C.E., it was at the mercy of procurators and governors who used their office for extortions to enrich themselves as quickly as possible, and thus brought the population to the point of despair. The last flicker of hope was the rule of King Agrippa I, which also gave rise to a spiritual upsurge; Judaism was able, at the time, to spread over wide areas of the Near East. This died out with the king's sudden demise after only three years of rule. Terror and subjugation grew worse, and quarrels with Roman governors and pagan inhabitants led to the Great Jewish War against Rome (63–73 C.E.). Although, again, internal jealousy and rivalry did much to weaken the revolt, Rome, the mightiest of empires, had to pit all its force against the small, stiff-necked people. Many towns in Galilee and the Golan fought obstinately; Yodfat was the last stronghold to defy Vespasian. His son Titus conquered Jerusalem only after a prolonged siege; even when the legions had

Stage of the Roman theater at Bet She'an. In the background is the steep mound bearing 19 strata of the town's earlier past

broken into the city, the defenders still clung to the Temple Area until it was burned to the ground by the Romans (71 C.E.). The defenders of Massada Rock held out for two more years.

Palestine under Roman, Byzantine and Arab Rule

Between 200 B.C.E. and 200 C.E., the inhabitants of Palestine, constantly suffering from wars, persecution and poverty, became deeply absorbed in spiritual matters. Many of the poor sought consolation in upholding and studying ancient Jewish laws and traditions. The first monastic societies appeared; the scrolls discovered in the last two decades bear evidence of their solitary life in the Judean Desert. Besides the Books of the Bible copied by the Qumran monks and the new books they wrote, other fragments were found in the caves of the Ḥever Gorge in 1960, and on Massada Rock since 1963. The same material and spiritual situation drew to one preacher of profound faith, Jesus of

Entrance to one of the many Jewish burial caves at Bet She'arim

Nazareth, the followers who, after his death, formed the nucleus of the new Christian religion.

The Late Roman Period. Untold thousands died in the war against Rome, and further scores of thousands were later led off to Italy as slaves. Roman legionnaires settled in villages near Jerusalem; the Arabic names Qalūniya=Colonia and Qāstel=Castellum are thus derived. The Jewish settlements, however, continued to exist, and only slight changes occurred in the character of the country's population. The spiritual center of the Jewish nation was transferred to Yavne in the Coastal Plain, where Rabbi Yoḥanan ben Zakkay reopened his famous school of the laws, with the consent of Emperor Vespasian. At the same time, Christianity moved away from Judaism and, with the conversion of large numbers of pagans, assumed importance as a separate religious entity in the country. After revolts of Jewish communities in the Diaspora (115–118 C.E.) were suppressed by Emperor Trajan, Roman policy also hardened against the Jews of Palestine. This precipitated another violent revolt against Roman rule, led by Bar Kokhba (132–135 C.E.). The Empire again had to muster all its resources to subdue the Jewish fighters. After the fall of the last fortress, Bethar (southwest of Jerusalem), the Romans took cruel revenge and wiped out entire communities. Many thousands were imprisoned and enslaved; others fled the country. Jerusalem was razed and the pagan city Aelia Capitolina erected in its stead, forbidden to Jews on pain of death.

Although Judea, Samaria, and the Coastal Plain were largely devoid of Jews, the Galilean communities remained mostly intact and even grew with the afflux of refugees. The central School of Laws, with the highest lawgiving authority of the Jews, the Sanhedrin, were transferred from Yavne to Lower Galilee, first to Usha, then to Bet She'arim, later to Ẓippori and finally to Tiberias.

The lot of the Jews was eased under Emperor Septimius Severus and his heirs (193–234 C.E.); Rabbi Yehuda Hanassi became President of the Sanhedrin and was also permitted to carry out administrative functions, such as tax collecting. Agriculture flourished again. Magnificent buildings were erected not only in the non-Jewish cities but also in Galilean villages where beautiful synagogues were built, e.g., in Meron, Kefar Bir'am, Capernaum, etc.; the burial caves of Bet She'arim, with their thousands of graves and finely carved stone coffins, bear witness to the wealth of these Jewish communities and their close links with the Jewish Diaspora.

In the third century C.E. the situation deteriorated again owing to the suffering the Parthian Wars caused all inhabitants of the country, Jews and non-Jews alike. When Christianity became the official religion of Rome, a new chapter in Palestine's history began; the population grew and the economy prospered, but persecution of Jews became more severe. Like other minorities, their lot was alleviated under the brief rule of Emperor Julian 'the Apostate' (360–363 C.E.).

Bas-relief of the Greek goddess Niobe, at Ashqelon, dating from the Hellenistic-Roman period

The Byzantine Period. After the partition of the Roman Empire (379 C.E.), Palestine came under the scepter of the Byzantine rulers. The country prospered, its population increased swiftly, and Christianity gradually became the religion of the majority of the inhabitants while Jews were persecuted and their numbers dwindled through conversions and emigration.

Trade, learning and art flourished in that period. The Byzantine art is represented principally in beautiful mosaic floors of Christian churches and monasteries (Bet She'an, Tabgha), secular buildings (Bet Guvrin, Caesarea, etc.) and of Jewish synagogues (Bet Alfa, Nirim, Tiberias).

The Roman aqueduct leading water from Mount Carmel to Caesarea

The rise in population density entailed the expansion of settlements to semidesert and desert regions. On the bleak Negev Hills and in the Beersheba Region, the Christian descendants of the Nabateans built flourishing cities such as Avdat, Mamshit, Shivta, Niẓẓana, Ḥaluẓa, etc. Town planning and civil administration there aimed principally at saving water. Every inhabitant was required to construct a large cistern of stone bricks and waterproof mortar near his house, while pipes led the rainwater down from the roof. At Shivta, a city where churches, dwelling houses, workshops and streets have been perfectly preserved, the main streets, fitted with narrow, open water conduits, converge on the town center, where three large public cisterns collect rainwater; the cisterns

Apsis of one of Shivta's three churches

were cleaned and well-kept by citizens doing annual turns. Water was ingeniously stored, not only for domestic needs and for maintaining bath houses like the one in Avdat (where the high fees paid by the wayfarers for its use provided the town with an important source of income), but also for farming. The system, used at Avdat and elsewhere in the Negev, has been thoroughly investigated and is being tried out now (see also chapter on soil and water, pp. 443–444).

From the second half of the fifth century, strife between various Christian sects, and the growing Persian danger to the Byzantine Empire helped to alleviate the lot of the Palestinian Jews and of other minorities (Samaritans, Christian minority sects).

The last period of Byzantine splendor in Palestine was that of Emperor Justinian's reign (527–565). He did much to further economic progress, improved municipal water supplies, and built many splendid churches, but he also renewed religious persecution. After his death the Persian shadow loomed ever more ominous over the Byzantine Empire. Between 614 and 629 the Persians occupied Palestine; there are signs that the Jews achieved some autonomy in Jerusalem and renewed the sacrificial service. Although Emperor Heraclius drove the Persians out in 629, he could not long withstand the growing onslaught of the Moslem Arabs. In 630 the Moslems first entered the Negev, in 634 Gaza fell, in 636 the Byzantine army was routed on the Yarmuk River and Tiberias and Galilee were lost; Jerusalem capitulated in 638, and in 640 Islam completed its conquest of Palestine with the occupation of Caesarea.

The Arab Period. The damage caused during the war was soon repaired at the beginning of Arab rule and economic prosperity returned. The Omayyad dynasty with its seat in Damascus was, initially at least, careful to preserve the country's economy; it thus left both Christians and Jews unmolested in their economic positions. Jewish communities flourished at that time both west of the Jordan and in Moab, Edom, Midian and on the shore of the Gulf of Eilat. Tiberias served as a great Judaic spiritual center; there, the Jerusalem Talmud was brought to a conclusion, the vowel system of the Hebrew script invented and many poems as well as legal tracts written. Eventually, however, the high taxes imposed on non-Moslem landowners and peasants caused Jews gradually to abandon farming and turn to commerce and trades, such as weaving and dyeing, gold- and silversmithing, etc.

When, at the end of the 8th and in the 9th century, the Abasside dynasty of Baghdad had replaced the Omayyads, the attitude toward religious minorities hardened, and the country's economy declined. The situation worsened further after the rise of the Fatimide dynasty of Egypt in the 10th century and their conquest of Palestine, when Arab rulers and governors were constantly at war

The White Tower of Ramla, erected by the Mamelukes

with each other. To this were added invasions of Carmathians, an extremist Moslem sect of desert nomads. The resulting confusion encouraged the Byzantines to regain mastery for a few years over the northern part of the country. Their expulsion was followed by fresh bedouin incursions. The nomads even occupied Ramla which at the time served as the country's capital. The Seldjuk Turks had meanwhile set up a strong kingdom in Asia Minor and carried the war to Palestine. They became rulers of Jerusalem in 1071.

These disorders cleared the path for the nomad herdsmen. Wide regions, wrested from the desert under Roman and Byzantine reign, fell back into desolation, and even large parts of the Hills and the Coastal Plain which had been permanently inhabited for thousands of years were now thoroughly devastated. Natural disasters, such as frequent earthquakes, epidemics, etc., completed the ruin. This state facilitated the conquest of the Holy Land by the Crusaders.

Crusaders, Mamelukes and Turks

Crusader Rule. The Crusaders first appeared on the Lebanese shore in 1099; in the same year they landed at Jaffa and took Jerusalem, where their victory was accompanied by a terrible slaughter of Moslems and Jews. The Crusaders' Holy Kingdom of Jerusalem, established by Baldwin I immediately upon the conquest of the city, expanded gradually until the conquest of Ascalon, when it encompassed all of Western Palestine, from the Gulf of Eilat to north of Beirut, as well as large parts of Transjordan and the coast of Syria and Southern Anatolia. When, however, the Seldjuk Turks united Syria and Iraq, Saladdin, a general of Kurdish origin, expanded his rule over Egypt. He dealt the Crusaders recurrent blows until, in 1187, only Tyre remained in their hands. In 1191, they reoccupied Acre and their domain again expanded (although not to its previous extent) until the treaty of 1229 between the German Emperor Friedrich II and the Egyptian sultan. Soon almost all these achievements were lost again as Christian rule was weakened through quarrels between the emperor and his opponents in Europe. After the Mameluke dynasty had risen in Egypt in 1250, its Sultan Beybars set out to destroy the Crusaders' strongholds and reduce their domain. The fall of Acre in 1291 ended Christian rule over the Holy Land; Atlit was the last Crusader fortress to be abandoned.

The Crusaders sought to make up for their weak numbers by constructing a tight network of huge fortresses, the like of which was never seen in the country, before or after. Among them were Beaufort which dominated the knee of the Litani River, Montfort, Jiddīn and Belvoir in Galilee, Atlit, Caesarea, and Arsuf on the coast, Crac du Désert in Moab, and many others. Their numerical

The Crusader fortress Qal'at Nimrud, at the foot of Mount Ḥermon, is only one of the many structures of that period which have preserved their grandeur although they are in ruins today

weakness also compelled the Crusaders, after their initial cruelty, to show greater tolerance toward Moslems and Jews.

The Crusades had far-reaching economic consequences both for Europe which, after hundreds of years, renewed trade with the Arab lands and the Far East, and for Palestine which exported fruit, sugar-cane, olive oil, wine, glass, indigo, etc., to Europe and whose rebuilt harbors served the transit of goods in international trade. Christian and Jewish pilgrims contributed to the country's prosperity.

The Mameluke Reign. The international trade connections were severed abruptly upon the return of Moslem rule. The Mamelukes systematically dismantled every harbor and port and laid waste the entire Coastal Plain in order to bar the way for fresh Christian attempts at conquest. Although the new rulers at first attempted to maintain economic prosperity, at least in the interior of the country, most of the regions soon relapsed into neglect, and the Mameluke Empire became the scene of unending bloody wars between petty potentates. In the second half of the 15th century, local rulers abandoned even the pretext of guarding the inhabitants' security and well-being. The peasants were robbed by governors; bedouin became more unruly than ever and sacked the towns, and many settled places had to be abandoned. Although the Jews perhaps suffered even more than Moslems and Christians, their numbers were swelled, especially after the Catholic Church's introduction of the Inquisition and the Spanish expulsion in 1492, by immigrants who had fled Europe's persecutions.

The Turkish Reign. King Selim of the Ottoman Turks utilized the growing confusion in the Mameluke Empire and captured Syria and Palestine between

The village Peqi'in in central Upper Galilee, whose Jews claim that their families have lived here uninterruptedly since the Second Temple

1512 and 1516. His son, Suleyman the Magnificent, restored order in the country, encouraged trade, rebuilt and fortified villages and towns and, in particular, reconstructed the walls of Jerusalem. Up to the end of the 16th century, the Jewish community progressed, with Safed as its center. The town attracted a great many famous sages; Jewish mysticism developed, and great works of religious literature were written. Jews were active in trades, such as cotton and silk spinning, weaving and dyeing, soap making, etc.

From the end of the 16th century, revolts of the Janissary soldiery shook the Turkish Empire. Greedy local governors often acted, for all practical purposes, independently of Constantinople. In the 17th century, the enlightened Druze governor of Galilee, Fakhr a-Din, attained an important position and, by establishing relations with European powers, tried to shake off Turkish rule altogether and conquer Egypt. He sought to encourage agriculture and trade, and check the bedouin robbers. He was finally defeated by the Turks and beheaded in Constantinople. In the 18th century, the bedouin sheikh Zaher el 'Amr obtained from the Turks 'leasehold rights' over Galilee and, by annexing other regions, ruled over almost the entire country. He was a tyrant who grew rich as a result of bartering the booty of bedouin robbers for that of Christian sea pirates. He organized expeditions against Egypt, entangled himself in war with the Turks, and was finally murdered. After him, Aḥmed el Jazzar ('the Butcher,' thus called because of his cruelty) became governor of the province of Sidon, and transferred his seat to Acre. The city was so built up and efficiently fortified that, with the aid of the British fleet from the sea, it could withstand Napoleon's siege in 1799. This forced him to abandon the campaign which was aimed at occupying Constantinople, cutting off India and, in effect, defeating Britain. The population of the country had by then become abjectly poor and reached its lowest number, not over 250,000–300,000 souls.

Napoleon's campaign, however, renewed the interest of the European powers in the Middle East in general and in Palestine in particular. This was expressed in the aid which the French extended, in the 1820's and 1830's, to the Egyptian ruler Mehemet Ali, who meant to conquer all of the Turkish Empire. His stepson, Ibrahim Pasha, representing him as Governor of Palestine, was a severe master but did introduce some order. Considerable numbers of Egyptian fellahin apparently immigrated to Palestine, where they founded new villages, mainly in the Southern Coastal Plain and in the Ḥula Valley. The Turks finally regained Syria and Palestine, and even a nominal sovereignty over Egypt, with the aid of the British and the Russians, who preferred 'the sick man on the Bosphorus' to the energetic and ambitious Mehemet Ali. Turkey's allies, however, asked for their reward in the form of 'capitulation rights' including jurisdiction over their respective subjects living in Turkey, maintenance of postal agencies in Turkish

The el-Jazzar Mosque in Acre, overlooking Haifa Bay

provinces of the Middle East, special rights in Turkish ports, etc. On the whole, these arrangements contributed to the country's progress since city children attended European schools and villagers received instruction from monasteries in their vicinity. Jews concentrated mainly in the four 'sacred' cities, Jerusalem, Safed, Hebron, and Tiberias and, in smaller numbers, in Gaza, Acre, Haifa, Shefar'am, and Peqi'in. They, too, benefited from the European interest in the country. Wishing to increase its influence, each European power appointed itself guardian of at least one religious minority living within Turkey's border, e.g., the Russians of the Greek-Orthodox, the French of the Catholics, the British and Germans of the Protestants, and the British also of the Druzes and Jews.

In the second half of the 19th century, security conditions gradually improved, nomads were restrained, the hill villagers began to plow fields in the interior valleys and in the Coastal Plain and founded 'dependencies' there which, in the course of time, became villages in their own right. In the cities, Christian pilgrims enlivened trade. On the other hand, wealthy families began to acquire for, at best, nominal payments huge holdings which had formally belonged to the state; like feudal landowners, they leased holdings to landless peasants on sharecropping terms and exploited them by giving credit at usurers' rates.

Such were the conditions in the country on the threshold of Zionist immigration and development.

Safed's Jewish quarter has retained much of its medieval character

Zionist Settlement and the State of Israel

The First Waves of Immigration

Developments within the Jewish Community and on the International Scene. The second half of the 19th century saw new developments within the Jewish community and in those international politics connected with the eastern basin of the Mediterranean Sea. These formed the background against which the Zionist Movement was born and its constructive work in the country begun—an undertaking which culminated in the creation of the State of Israel.

The emancipation of European Jews around 1800 introduced them to modern cultural trends, and enabled them to fill varied posts in the economic, political, and cultural life of their countries. Contrary to expectations, however, they were not readily absorbed and fully assimilated into the life of these countries. In fact, as soon as they began to occupy especially responsible positions in the economy and culture, enmity and jealousy were aroused. This reaction strengthened their national consciousness and finally led them to the idea of the return to their historic homeland and of its reconstruction as a Jewish state. The ideal had always been foremost in Jewish prayer, thought and tradition, but was now translated into a program of political activity and practical work.

In international politics, the importance of the Near East as a communications hub became ever more evident with the introduction of modern means of travel—the railway and the steamship. The plans for the Suez Canal put Palestine in the center of international interest. In the first half of the 19th century, the French aided Egypt and its ruler Mehemet Ali, and wished to enlarge Egyptian territory along the Palestine border at Turkey's expense. Positions changed later when Great Britain became Egypt's protector, and France, with Lebanese and Syrian interests, sided with the Turks. While Turkey attempted to keep its forces as close to the Suez Canal as possible, the British sought to remove them as far as possible from it. The result of this struggle was a demarcation line in 1906, which in effect annexed, at Turkey's and Palestine's expense, the entire Sinai Peninsula to Egypt.

In the 19th century a number of British idealists and statesmen cherished the idea of setting up a Jewish state in Palestine. Some, indeed purely idealistic, sought to right the wrong done to the People of the Book; others regarded this as a tool to sever Palestine from Turkey and bring it under British influence. In any case, the idea of a Jewish state crystallized in the middle of the 19th century in two separate camps—in the minds of Englishmen, such as Sir Lawrence Oliphant, and in the Jewish communities of Eastern Europe, where pious rabbis, such as Z. H. Kalischer and E. Gutmacher, and intellectuals, such as the socialist Moses Hess (author of 'Rome and Jerusalem') and the progressive Leon Pinsker (author of 'Autoemancipation'), advocated the return to Zion. Decisive, however, was Theodor Herzl's activity. At the end of the 19th century, he made the aspirations of the Jewish people a factor of international politics by establishing the World Zionist Organization.

The emancipation and attempts at assimilation did not essentially weaken Jewish solidarity throughout the world. A case in point is that of the Alliance Israélite Universelle, a society founded in France in the middle of the last century to secure equal rights and raise the economic standards of suppressed, backward Jewish communities, particularly in North Africa and the Near East. The French Government, expecting it to enhance French influence in those countries, viewed its work with favor. The Jews of Palestine also enjoyed this aid; Alliance Israélite Universelle eventually became another factor in preparing the conditions for Zionist development of the country.

Interest was also shown by individual Jewish philanthropists, notably Sir Moses Montefiore of England, who promoted the founding of the first Jewish quarters in Jerusalem outside the Old City walls and tried to make the Jewish inhabitants of the country self-supporting by teaching them trades, and even drew them toward agriculture. Montefiore bought land for this purpose near Jaffa and planted a citrus grove (today the Tel Aviv suburb of Shekhunat Montefiore). The Alliance Israélite, working with the same aim, opened the agricultural school Miqwe Israel east of Jaffa, in 1870, to train city Jews to become peasants. A few years later, in 1878, some of the pious Jews who had been leading their traditional life in Jerusalem and Safed showed initiative in founding two villages—Petaḥ Tiqwa on the Yarqon banks in the Coastal Plain, and Ge Oni (later named Rosh Pinna) on the rim of the Ḥula Valley. Both settlements failed; the farmsteads were abandoned after a short time owing to the insurmountable difficulties caused by lack of working capital and farming experience, the choice of malaria-infested sites, and the enmity of Arab neighbors.

The First Immigration. Of the 450,000 inhabitants of Palestine in 1882, about 24,000 were Jews. The first wave of immigration was set into motion by pogroms

Baron Edmond de Rothschild

Theodor Herzl

in Russia, along with that Government's repressive policy against Jews. Hundreds of thousands left Russia in the following decades, most of them for America; a small group of idealists came to Palestine, together with Jews from Rumania and Poland. These immigrants, calling themselves 'Ḥoveve Ẓion' or 'Biluim,' resolved to build their lives in the Homeland and become workers of the soil. Some had formed settlement groups while still abroad and had sent their representatives to buy land for their purposes. They revived Petaḥ Tiqwa and Rosh Pinna, and founded new villages, e.g., Zikhron Yaaqov (on Mount Carmel), Rishon le-Ẓion, Nes Ẓiona and Gedera (all on the Judean Coast). Soon, however, they were in distress. This was caused by the same obstacles which their predecessors had encountered three or four years earlier. On the very brink of despair, they were aided by Baron Edmond de Rothschild's interest in their attempt. He gave each settler's family monthly allowances and developed new settlement and farming plans better adapted to local conditions. Instructors from France arrived to teach settlers the elements of farming, and several more villages were founded (Mazkeret Batya, Bat Shelomo, etc.). Baron Rothschild's administrators, however, showed no understanding for the settlers' idealism, despised their clumsiness in work, tried to class them as charity seekers, and finally broke down their spirit and initiative.

In 1890, following fresh persecutions in Russia, another small wave of immigrants reached the country and additional villages were founded (among these—Reḥovot, Ḥadera, Metulla, Moẓa). All the villages received the Baron' aid which, however, did not bring a decisive change. Some of the newcomers wh settled in the cities (notably, in Jaffa) began to speculate in land instead o adopting productive occupations. They thus hampered Zionist settlement activi ties and drew the attention of the Turkish authorities, who, fearing that th Zionist Movement might become another destructive element within the empire had, from the outset, viewed it suspiciously. Consequently, the authorities sough to bar the entry of Jews to the country and to prevent their acquiring land an establishing new settlements. In 1897, during this period of crisis, Theodor Herz assembled the First Zionist Congress, founded the Zionist Organization, an began feverish work towards obtaining an official Turkish 'charter' for Jewis mass settlement in Palestine.

Bitter criticism of Baron Rothschild's settlement system induced the 'well known benefactor' to transfer the care of the villages to the Jewish Colonizatio Association (ICA), which earlier had already promoted Jewish farming i different parts of the world, particularly in Argentina. ICA founded the trainin farm Sedjera (today Ilaniya) in Lower Galilee and in 1901 began to buy land fo new villages, most of them in Galilee (Yavne'el, Kefar Tavor, etc.).

The Second Immigration. In 1903, fresh pogroms in Russia further emphasize the need to build a 'national home' in Palestine for the Jewish people. Herzl faced with the suspicion of the Turkish sultan, tried to find temporar solutions—a 'night's asylum' in Uganda, or in Northern Sinai, which he calle 'Egyptian Palestine' (see also pp. 377–378).

The Second Immigration had in the meantime begun. It was composed mostl of young people who, influenced by the Socialist ideas in Russia, wished to live a laborers in the Homeland and create a society based on equality and socia justice. They sought to work in the moshavot (Jewish villages), but the vetera settlers preferred the experienced Arab laborers, who were content with lo wages, to these idealists. The newcomers, unable to overcome these obstacles a individuals, set up cooperatives to contract agricultural jobs on a piecework basi and to prepare land for their own settlements. These groups, e.g., 'ha-Ḥoresh' ('the Plowman'), were the first cells of the Histadrut (the Labor Federation) and furnished the beginnings of novel forms of settlement—the communal village ('kibbutz') and the smallholders' village ('moshav'). Another cooperative, 'ha-Shomer' ('the Guardsman'), contracted the guarding of Jewish villages against marauding attacks. The need for Jewish self-defense was largely prompted by the 1908 Young Turks Revolution. The local Turkish administration's enmity toward Zionists and their aspirations increased, and had the unforeseen consequence of strengthening Arab nationalism. 'Ha-Shomer' thus formed the

Arthur Ruppin

Chaim Weizmann

nucleus of 'Hagana,' the comprehensive Jewish defense organization during the British Mandate which eventually became the Israel Defense Army.

In the first decade of the 20th century, the Zionist Organization became an active factor in building the country. Its section for land purchase and development, the Jewish National Fund, first acquired holdings at Ḥulda and Ben Shemen in Judea, at Kefar Ḥittim in Lower Galilee, near Lake Kinneret (Sea of Galilee) and in the Jezreel Valley. In 1908, the Palestine Office of the Zionist Organization was opened under Dr. Arthur Ruppin in Jaffa, and training farms were established for agricultural laborers at the new sites. Dr. Ruppin agreed to let a workers' group take over management of a farm; the first communal settlement, Deganiya, was thus created south of Lake Kinneret. Similarly, the 'ha-Shomer' organization took over the administration of Merḥavya and Tel Adashim in the Jezreel Valley. With its limited means, the Jewish National Fund also promoted urban development, particularly of Tel Aviv, which began as a garden suburb of Jaffa in 1909.

After many crises, the economic situation of the Coastal Plain villages improved with the first success of the citrus groves. There, the industrious Yemenite Jews found employment after they had come to the country in larger numbers since, as Turkish subjects, they did not need immigration permits. They soon became an important element in the economic structure of the moshavot.

Dr. Ruppin's office aided them in establishing their homes on the outskirts of the moshavot, sometimes provided with auxiliary farms. In 1914, the number of Jews in Palestine had increased to 85,000, with 12,000 living in 44 rural communities.

The First World War, the Balfour Declaration

The World War I Period. In World War I the Allies, France, Britain and Russia, opposed Turkey, which had sided with Germany. Each of them strove to secure for itself sizeable portions of the Turkish Empire when the 'sick man on the Bosphorus' would finally expire. Much diplomatic wrangling, therefore, was going on behind the scenes. Each power sought to activate forces within the Turkish Empire which would speed dissolution and later serve as safeguards to its own influence in the Middle East. British diplomats won the consent of Hussein, the Sherif of Mecca, to head the Arab revolt against the Turks by promising him in the 'MacMahon Letters' the rule of the Arab-inhabited parts of Turkey, with the notable exception of Palestine. The British Government simultaneously negotiated with Prof. Chaim Weizmann and other Jewish personalities for the establishment of a Jewish national home in Palestine. French and British representatives, meanwhile, drew up maps delimiting the respective two spheres of influence in the region after the downfall of the Turkish Empire (the 'Sykes-Picot Agreement').

The Turks, well aware of the menace, endeavored to uproot every treasonable factor in Palestine. The Palestinian Jews were viewed with especial suspicion, although the Zionist Organization had, at least officially, adopted strict neutrality in the war. Entire Jewish villages and urban communities were evacuated and their inhabitants exiled; members of the 'Nili' underground organization, working on behalf of the Allies against the Jewish authorities' orders, were captured and executed after torture in Turkish jails. Many Jews managed to flee to Egypt. The inimical Turkish policy reached its peak when all Jews were banned from Jaffa and Tel Aviv in April 1917. The Jews also suffered from the loss of the foreign powers' protection by the annulment of the 'capitulation rights' and from the loss of funds regularly sent to the pious from their European communities. Thousands of Jews in Safed, Hebron, Tiberias and Jerusalem died of hunger and epidemics, and the country's Jews dwindled toward the end of the war to 56,000. However, the hunger also spurred an increased effort for food production on Jewish farms, and ICA (the Jewish Colonization Association) set up new villages for this purpose on its vacant holdings, e.g., Maḥanayim, Ayyelet ha-Shaḥar and Kefar Gil'adi, in the Ḥula Valley. These outlying settlements soon became decisive for inclusion of this northern region in the territory earmarked for the

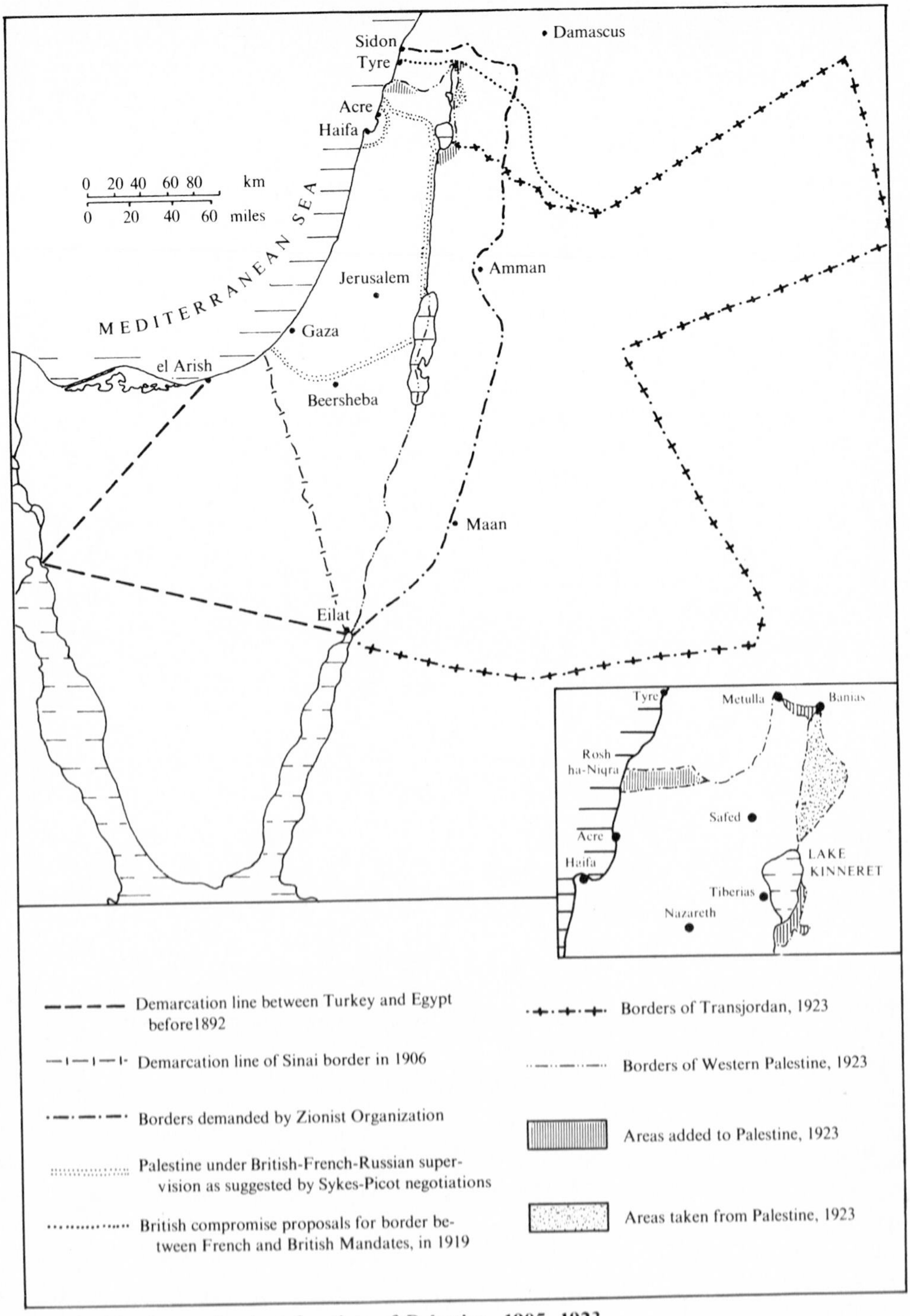

Damascus
Sidon
Tyre
Acre
Haifa
0 20 40 60 80 km
0 20 40 60 miles
MEDITERRANEAN SEA
Amman
Jerusalem
Gaza
el Arish
Beersheba
Maan
Eilat
Tyre
Metulla
Banias
Rosh ha-Niqra
Safed
Acre
Haifa
LAKE KINNERET
Tiberias
Nazareth
Demarcation line between Turkey and Egypt before1892
Demarcation line of Sinai border in 1906
Borders demanded by Zionist Organization
Palestine under British-French-Russian supervision as suggested by Sykes-Picot negotiations
British compromise proposals for border between French and British Mandates, in 1919
Borders of Transjordan, 1923
Borders of Western Palestine, 1923
Areas added to Palestine, 1923
Areas taken from Palestine, 1923

Proposed borders and actual frontiers of Palestine, 1905–1923

Jewish National Home. After the heroic stand of Joseph Trumpeldor and his comrades at Tel Ḥay in 1920, the northern border of the British Mandate was revised in 1923 to include the Ḥula Valley. This was the last stage in the prolonged negotiations following the Sykes-Picot Agreement, by which the Levant countries had been partitioned into a northern French zone of influence and a southern British one. Both parts were to form an Arab state, but one with an international zone in Western Palestine, under the joint supervision of Britain, France and Russia, whose borders were to run, in the south, from Gaza through Hebron to the Dead Sea and, in the north, from Acre to Lake Kinneret.

The Establishment of the British Mandate. In the negotiations with the Zionists, held simultaneously with those of Sykes and Picot, the British were willing to assume exclusive control of the 'international zone' and to enlarge its borders, especially northward. The Zionists proposed that the northern border be drawn between Sidon (es-Saida) and Mt. Hermon, in order to make the waters of the Jordan and the Litani rivers available for the National Home, and the eastern frontier—along the Hedjaz railroad, between Nawa in the Basan and Ma'an in Edom. In the south they requested access to the Red Sea, through the Negev and Edom. These negotiations led to the Balfour Declaration of November 2, 1917, which promised that 'H.M. Government will use their best endeavours to facilitate the establishment of a National Home for the Jewish People in Palestine, providing that nothing shall be done which may prejudice the civil and religious rights of existing non-Jewish communities in Palestine or the rights and political status enjoyed by Jews in any other country.' The British hoped that the Balfour Declaration would not clash with the promises given to the Arabs. King Feisal, Sherif Hussein's son and leader of the Arab national movement, actually met with Weizmann and agreed that Palestine should remain outside the borders of the proposed large Arab state.

The Balfour Declaration became valid in international law at the San Remo Conference in the spring of 1920, where the Principal Allied Powers resolved to name Britain as Mandated Power over Palestine on behalf of the League of Nations which was then to be founded. Definite demarcation of the borders was left for British-French negotiations. In the ensuing deliberations, the British at first demanded the borders proposed by the Zionists, and later compromised upon the inclusion of Safed and the Ḥula Valley in the Mandated Territory. The last border adjustments took place in 1923, when the area between Akhziv and the Ḥanita-Adamit Ridge, as well as a strip of territory east of Lake Kinneret (Sea of Galilee) and the Jordan-Yarmuk Plain were given to Palestine in exchange for a triangle on the Golan slopes, west of Qunaītira, which was included in the French Mandate over Syria.

he British Mandate

Iilitary Rule and the First Years of the Mandate. The Balfour Declaration was ublished at a time when most of Palestine was already under British occupation. fter the Turkish failure to push through to the Suez Canal by way of the Sinai eninsula, General Allenby opened a counteroffensive. In 1917 he took the egev, broke through the Turco-German front near Gaza and drove the Turks om Judea. He entered Jerusalem in parade and installed the military adminis- ation of Palestine there. The Sharon and Samaria fell to the British in 1918, and ialilee in the last stages of the war.

The Jews of the country received the entrance of the British and the Balfour)eclaration jubilantly. It soon became evident, however, that the military dministration was none too enthusiastic about the idea of a national home; ome even openly favored the extremist Arab nationalists' views. The officially ecognized Zionist representatives who arrived in 1920 were cold-shouldered. Iurderous attacks on Jews by incited Arab mobs in Jaffa, Jerusalem, and other laces in 1920 and 1921 were met by little official action towards preventing fresh utbreaks, while Jews who had organized self-defense were severely punished. elations improved only slightly when a civilian administration took over.

The courtyard of Tel Ḥay, in the northwest corner of the Ḥula Valley. The defense of the outpost n 1920, during which Joseph Trumpeldor and seven of his comrades fell, led to the final inclu- sion of this region in the territory of the British Mandate over Palestine

Sir Herbert Samuel, an English Jew and eager Zionist, was named by th British Government as first High Commissioner for Palestine. Confronted wit the unsympathetic attitude of most British officials towards Zionism, he made show of his impartiality in naming one of the most extremist Arabs, Amin al Husseini, as Grand Mufti of Jerusalem, and in giving away state lands in the Be She'an Valley to bedouin, although in the Mandate instructions these lands ha been earmarked for Jewish development projects. Two more fateful steps in th policy of placating the Arabs were taken in 1923: the British Government removing Transjordan from the provisions of the Balfour Declaration, made it a Emirate under British sovereignty and named Hussein's son and Feisal's brothe Abdallah as its ruler. A provision of the same time limited Jewish immigration t Palestine to fit in with the 'absorptive capacity' of the country's economy.

Qiryat Anavim, a communal settlement founded in the Judean Hills west of Jerusalem in 1920

The Third Immigration. Immediately after the World War new immigrants arrived in the country, especially from Eastern Europe where war, revolutions and their aftermath had brought terrible suffering to the Jews. Young people who had prepared for pioneering tasks in the Homeland did not wait for official permits. Upon their arrival, often after an adventurous voyage, hundreds joined the Labor Battalion. This organization had been founded shortly after Joseph Trumpeldor, who had proposed it, fell when heroically defending Tel Ḥay in Upper Galilee. The Labor Battalion took upon itself pioneering work, e.g., roadbuilding in the Jezreel Valley and on the shores of the Sea of Galilee, construction of new suburbs in Jerusalem and elsewhere, etc. One of the groups founded the first settlements of the Ḥarod Valley (En Ḥarod and Tel Yosef), where tracts had just been acquired by the Jewish National Fund. The swamps were dried, and a new form of communal living was shaped—the large kibbutz. In the Western Jezreel Valley, where holdings had also become Jewish national property, Nahalal and Kefar Yehoshua were built as the first smallholders villages. Up to 1926, settlements were added in the Ḥarod, Jezreel and Zebulon valleys, such as Kefar Yeḥezkel, Bet Alfa, Mishmar ha-Emeq, and Kefar Ḥasidim.

In the Southern Sharon two initial clusters of settlements were created with the revival of Kefar Sava (which had been twice destroyed, in the World War battles and, later, in an Arab attack) and with the founding of Herzliya, Ra'ananna and other villages. More villages were founded in the Northern Sharon (Binyamina, etc.) and on the Judean Coast. Urban Jewish communities grew quickly, especially Tel Aviv and Haifa, and the Jewish population in the country increased from 56,000 in 1918 to 108,000 in 1925. On the other hand, the number of Arabs also rose considerably, because of a very high birth rate and a declining mortality rate, and as the result of large-scale free and uncontrolled immigration of Arabs from the neighboring countries who were attracted by the relatively higher standard of living.

The Fourth Immigration. In 1924, Jewish immigration changed in character with the arrival of lower-middle-class elements, mostly small merchants from Poland, severely hit by anti-Semitism and the Polish Government's economic policy. Many of them settled in Tel Aviv and in the other cities, where they attempted to continue in their old occupations. This sudden expansion of small trade was unsuited to the economic needs of the country, and a severe crisis resulted. Many immigrants returned to their countries of origin, having lost much of their modest means. Many others of the 'Fourth Immigration' turned to the villages where, with their investments and labor, they contributed to the sizeable growth of the citrus branch.

In 1925, Lord Plumer, a professional soldier, replaced Sir Herbert Samuel as High Commissioner. The duration of his office was the quietest period of the British Mandate. Although officialdom in general did not revise its fundamentally anti-Zionist attitude, the Jewish national institutions were allowed to continue their work. The Va'ad Le'umi (National Council) was officially recognized as the representative body of Palestinian Jews. The Zionist Organization, trying to mobilize wider Jewish circles in the Diaspora for constructive work in the country, established the Jewish Agency, whose office in the country directed all constructive projects and functioned as representative of the Movement and of world Jewry to the Mandate authorities. Roads were built throughout the country, and the construction of Haifa Port began in 1929.

A turn for the worse came in 1928 when Sir John Chancellor became High Commissioner. His sympathies with the Arab cause soon became evident. The extremists grew active and organized violent attacks in 1929, first at the Wailing Wall in the Old City of Jerusalem and soon in many places inhabited by Jews. The riots were most destructive to the small community of pious Jews in Hebron, who preferred to rely on British police protection rather than accept the aid offered by 'Hagana,' the Jewish self-defense organization. Although Hebron had to be abandoned by those Jewish inhabitants who had escaped the slaughter, attacks elsewhere were repulsed. Some Jewish settlements, such as Be'er Tuvya in the south and En Zetim near Safed, which had suffered badly, were left temporarily but resettled after a short interval. The disturbances spurred the Jews to organize 'Hagana' more efficiently and to increase efforts at rural settlement. Although the Zionist Movement and the Palestinian Jews felt the severe impact of the grave economic crisis throughout the world, new villages were founded in the Coastal Plain in the framework of the 'Thousand Families Settlement Scheme.'

In the wake of the 1929 disturbances, the British Government sent two inquiry commissions to Palestine. Unfortunately, both were biased against the National Home and recommended further limitations of Jewish immigration and land purchase.

The Fifth Immigration, Arab Disturbances

The Fifth Immigration. The Mandatory authorities' attitude toward Zionism softened in 1931, when Sir Arthur Wauchope was named High Commissioner. The limitations recommended by the inquiry commissions were not effected. The rise of Nazism in Germany (January 1933) brought an upsurge of immigration, amounting to over 60,000 in 1935. Besides the Jews of Central Europe—a new element in the country—many thousands came from Poland, Rumania, etc. The Fifth Immigration enriched the country in capital and skills, caused a building boom, quick industrial expansion in the cities, further development of the citrus branch of agriculture, and a general rise in the standard of living of both Jews and Arabs.

The 1936–1939 Disturbances. Confronted with these developments, Arab leaders feared that the National Home might indeed become an irrevocable fact. The might of the British Empire weakened as Nazi Germany and its allies, Italy and Japan, became more aggressive. Consequently, they hoped that armed attacks would break the Zionist endeavor, but would eventually also free them of British rule. They therefore opposed a British proposal to set up a Legislative Council where every national group would be represented proportionately, although this arrangement would have given the Arabs an overwhelming majority and robbed the Jews of the opportunity to participate in deciding the country's future.

In April 1936, the disturbances began with an Arab general strike and murderous attacks on Jews in Jaffa. The raids soon spread over the country, directed against Jewish villages and urban areas. Armed mercenary bands, commanded by the adventurer el-Kaukji, penetrated unhindered into Palestine from all neighboring countries; not always well received by local Arabs, they terrorized the population by killing Arab notables in towns and villages. They also attacked the British who, thus forced into a certain degree of cooperation with the Jews, permitted them to train several thousand men as supernumerary policemen. A lull ensued in October 1936, when the British threatened to take more drastic steps against the rioters. A Royal Commission under Lord Peel was sent to Palestine to inquire into the circumstances of the riots. Its findings surprised the local authorities as well as the British Government: it stated that Jews had a historic right to the country and that the present policy of the authorities contradicted the spirit of the Balfour Declaration. The Commission proposed partition of the country into a Jewish and an Arab State, both under British sovereignty. The Jews were to receive the Coastal Plain north of Gedera, Galilee and parts of the Jezreel Valley, and the Arabs—the rest of Palestine; Jerusalem, Jaffa, with a strip of land connecting the two cities, Bethlehem, the shores of the Sea of Galilee, the Haifa Bay Area and the Eilat coast were to remain under direct British control.

Although most Jewish leaders regarded the proposed narrow borders as a severe handicap, they were prepared to accept the suggestions as a means of rescuing the hundreds of thousands of European Jews whose very lives were gravely menaced by the Nazis. The immediate conclusion of the responsible Jewish circles was that the economic position of the Jewish population in

Palestine had to be strengthened and new regions secured by Jewish settlement in case new borders should be proposed. The Arabs rejected all the Commission's findings, and in September 1937 the disturbances were renewed with increased violence. The British tried to empty the Peel Commission's suggestions of content when the Woodhead Commission reduced the promised independence of Arabs and Jews to local autonomy and left the Jews a single narrow strip of territory along the Coastal Plain. These tendencies were ultimately expressed in the White Paper of May 1939. Upon becoming law, it allowed free purchase of land by Jews in but 5% of the Western Palestine area, and limited immigration to a total of 75,000 souls during the following 5 years; all additional immigration was conditional on the consent of the Arabs.

The Arab disturbances and the authorities' policy were answered by the Jews with intensified efforts to enlarge the settlement network. 'Tower and stockade' villages, erected in a day and prepared to repulse attacks on the first night of their existence, appeared in new regions—in 1936 in the Bet She'an Valley, in 1937 in the Menashe Hills, in 1938 in Western Galilee, and in 1939 in the Ḥula Valley.

Tirat Ẓevi in its first days; the kibbutz was established in 1937, during the Arab disturbances, as a 'tower and stockade' outpost in the south of the Bet She'an Valley

The Second World War and the Struggle for Independence

The White Paper aroused the anger of the Jews. The extremist Irgun Ẓeva'i Le'umi ('Eẓel') urged abandoning the official Zionist policies of restraint, countering Arab assaults by attacks on Arab centers and extending Jewish raids to the British whose cooperation was nonexistent. Although this was a minority view, the entire Jewish camp consented that the so-called 'illegal' immigration must be intensified, so that as many Jews as possible could be rescued from Europe before it became too late. In 1939, tens of thousands of immigrants reached the country in small, battered ships, undeterred by the fact that the British detained them in camps for long periods.

With the outbreak of the World War, the Jews began 'to partake in the British war effort as though there were no White Paper, and to continue the struggle against the White Paper as though there were no war.' Of the 450,000 Palestinian Jews, 150,000 volunteered for military service under the British flag. The British, however, at first took on local citizens for auxiliary units only, in an effort to keep the number of Jewish and Arab soldiers equal; the small number of Arabs who volunteered for service, however, made this principle impracticable. In the 1941 campaign against the Vichy French in Syria, the British accepted Hagana aid. In the later stages of the war, when the front receded from the Middle East and the first shattering news of the Nazi Holocaust and the death of millions of European Jews came through, consent was given for the formation of a Jewish Brigade under the emblem of the Star of David.

The war reduced immigration to a minimum, and entry to the country was barred even to the few who had managed to escape from the Nazi hell. Although the authorities attempted to uphold the land regulations, the Jewish National Fund continued to acquire new holdings. It made special efforts in regions where transfer was possible only by using legal loopholes. New settlements were founded in many parts of the country, among them the first outposts in the Southern Coastal Plain and the Beersheba Region.

Foreign sales of citrus, the country's principal export item, came to a complete standstill with the war. A severe crisis was prevented, however, as Jewish farming and industry were soon integrated in the war effort and geared to provide vital goods to the Allied armies fighting in the Middle East and North Africa.

Hopes at the end of the war for a complete change in British policy as a result of the forming of a Labor Cabinet in Britain were soon dashed. Although hundreds of thousands of the remnants of European Jewry begged to enter the Homeland, certificates were issued only by the hundreds, and extreme measures were taken against the many thousands of illegal immigrants, such as the people arriving on the ship 'Exodus 1947' who were even transported back to Germany.

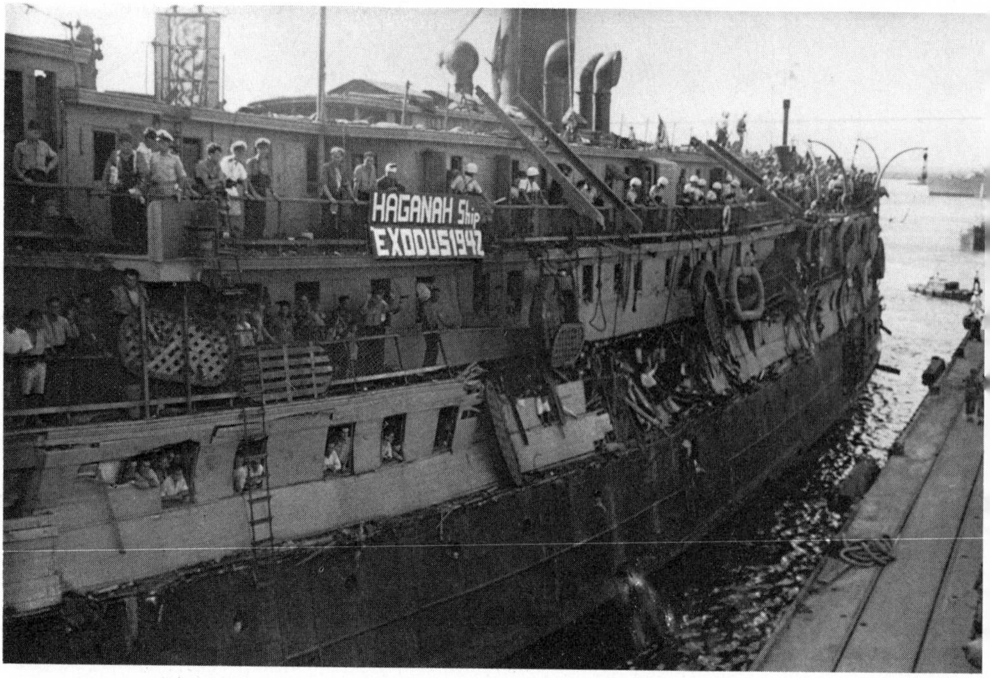

The battered illegal immigrants' ship 'Exodus 1947' in Haifa Port, before being sent back to Europe

The groups of Eẓel and Leḥy (the 'Stern Group,' a most extremist organization) intensified terror attacks against the British, who retaliated with long curfews, arms searches in Jewish villages and towns and, finally, mass arrests of Jewish leaders.

British policy caused growing world indignation. Public pressure in the United States led President Truman to ask that the remnants from the Nazi extermination camps be allowed to immigrate to Palestine. In 1946 an Anglo-American Inquiry Commission proposed to disarm both Jews and Arabs in Palestine, permit the immigration of 100,000 Jews, and restrict British governing powers. When the British agreed only if the Jews would first disarm, world opinion called for a return of the Palestine Mandate to the United Nations: a United Nations Special Commission for Palestine, with only small nations represented, was set up in the spring of 1947. The majority of the Commission voted to partition Palestine into two autonomous states which should maintain close economic ties. The United Nations partition map allocated to the Jewish State Eastern Galilee, the Upper and most of the Middle Jordan Valley, most of the Jezreel Valley, Mt. Carmel, most of the Coastal Plain and the Negev, and to the Arab State—Western and Central Galilee, Samaria, most of Judea, the Lower Jordan Valley and Dead Sea Area, and smaller parts of the Negev. The partition plan was endorsed, on November 29, 1947, by the United Nations Assembly with a vote of 33 to 13, with 10 abstentions.

The War of Independence

In the same United Nations session which voted the partition resolution, the representatives of the Arab states announced their intention to resist the plan, if necessary by force. On November 30, 1947, hostilities were started by Arabs near Lod and in Jerusalem, spread over the entire country, and grew in intensity from day to day. Ambushes and armed assaults of the first days turned soon into systematic sniping against Jewish urban quarters and massed attacks against Jewish villages and whole groups of villages, and culminated, in the spring and summer of 1948, in heavy air and artillery bombardments.

The Arab forces grew with the mass infiltration of organized units from beyond the borders. From the outset, the Arabs enjoyed a vast superiority in arms and ammunition, which became even greater on May 15, 1948, one day after the British left the country and the regular armies of five Arab states—Transjordan, Iraq, Egypt, Syria, and Lebanon—marched into the country, along with volunteers from Saudi Arabia, Libya, and Yemen.

Hagana, the Jewish defense organization, had at the beginning of hostilities 50,000 men and women registered in various stages of training and mobilization, only 3,000 of them in active full-time service. A few thousand more were members of the Eẓel and Leḥy organizations. During the first months of the war, the Jews were armed only with light weapons, which had to be hidden from thorough daily searches by British military police. The situation gradually improved with the manufacture of light arms in the underground factories and with the supply of heavier weapons from abroad, particularly Czechoslovakia. Until the end of the war, however, Jewish forces could in this respect by no means equal their adversaries. If in the end they were victorious, it was thanks to the dedication and intelligence of the individual soldier, to greater mobility of units, to resourcefulness of the high and low command, which exploited every enemy weakness, and to the full cooperation of the fighting forces and Jewish civilian population.

The disconnected battles at the beginning of the war crystallized through the spring months into definite fronts, from the Southern Coastal Plain and Northern Negev to the main cities of Tel Aviv, Jerusalem and Haifa, and to the Upper Jordan course and Upper Galilee. Jerusalem bore the brunt of the battle, with its Jewish quarters under complete siege for months. The siege was only gradually lifted by heavy fighting which opened the 'Jerusalem Corridor' between the capital and the coast .

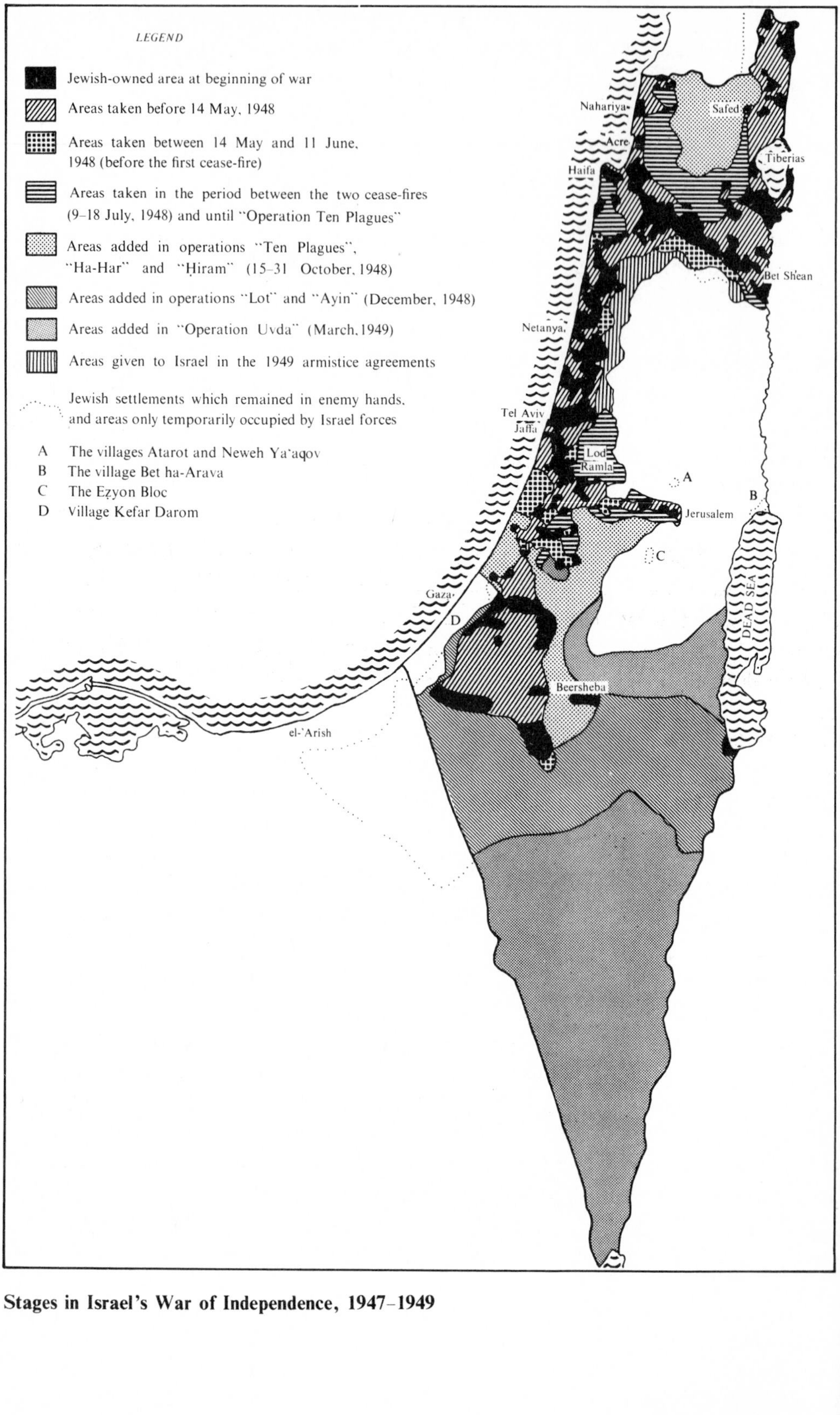

Stages in Israel's War of Independence, 1947–1949

Three main stages are to be discerned in the war: November 30, 1947–May 14, 1948; May 15–June 11, 1948; and July 9, 1948–March 10, 1949. In the first stage, numerous isolated attacks by Arabs on Jewish villages and urban neighborhoods were staved off everywhere, and soon were answered with punitive actions against enemy centers and headquarters. The Arabs turned the village Qāstel in the Judean Hills into a major fortress designed to close the siege around Jewish Jerusalem; Jewish forces attacked this stronghold in a fierce battle, which culminated in its permanent occupation. Similarly, Arab villages in the neighborhood of Mishmar ha-Emeq in the Jezreel Valley fell to the defenders who had routed an 'Arab Liberation Army,' commanded by el-Kaukji, in its bid to take the kibbutz and break through to Haifa. Arab attempts to storm Jewish quarters in towns and cities with a mixed population (Tiberias, Haifa, Jaffa, Safed) or to operate from Arab towns against surrounding Jewish villages (Bet She'an) ended with the unexpected flight of Arab soldiers and civilians from these places.

The second stage opened, one day after the State of Israel was founded, with the invasion of the Arab regular armies; the Egyptian was the largest and strongest in weapons and the Transjordanian Arab Legion the best trained. Front lines became defined; with very few exceptions, Jewish forces prevented villages and quarters from falling into enemy hands, and, in their effort to stem the enemy advance, occupied more places inhabited by Arabs. The mass flight of Arab civilians from predominantly Jewish neighborhoods, on the orders of Arab leaders, took the Jews completely by surprise. This stage ended in the first month-long truce arranged by the United Nations.

In the third stage, which began when fighting was renewed on Arab insistence, the initiative went over completely to Jewish forces, which in the meantime had become the Israel Army. In the 10-day battle until the second truce on July 19, the 'Jerusalem Corridor' between the capital and the coast was finally established. Lod Airport and the towns of Lod and Ramla fell to Israel, as well as parts of Lower Galilee with Shefar'am and Nazareth, and smaller areas in the Southern Coastal Plain. Further Jewish operations were necessitated by the truculence of the invading armies and their breaches of truce terms. 'Operation Ten Plagues' in October 1948 brought the Israelis to Ashqelon, Beersheba, parts of the Northern Negev and Southern Judea; the 48-hour 'Operation Ḥiram' completed Israel's hold on Galilee up to the previous borders of the British Mandate, and 'Operation 'Ayin' removed the Egyptian Army from the Northern and Western Negev, except the 'Gaza Strip.' The concluding operations of the war, largely bloodless, were the occupation of the Eastern and Southern Negev, allocated to Israel in the United Nations partition plan, eastward to Sedom on the Dead Sea, and southward to Eilat on the Red Sea shore.

History of the State of Israel

Founding of the State and Final Establishing of Its Borders. On May 14, 1948 the British Mandate over Palestine ended. The State of Israel was proclaimed by the People's Council, which in that session became the Temporary Council of State. After a few hours the United States of America extended the new State recognition (initially 'de facto'), followed three days later by recognition 'de jure' by the U.S.S.R. Ten more states announced their recognition of Israel during the first month of its existence, and on the first anniversary of its independence the number had risen to 55.

Count Folke Bernadotte of Sweden, appointed Mediator between Israel and the Arab states, succeeded in arranging a first 28-day truce (June 11–July 9, 1948) and, after ten days of fighting, a second one beginning July 19. Bernadotte was killed by extremists in Jerusalem on September 17, 1948. After the last operations resulting from Arab cease-fire violations, the Arabs showed greater willingness to arrive at more permanent arrangements. With the participation of Dr. Ralph Bunche of the U.S.A., Count Bernadotte's successor, armistice talks were held and agreements signed between representatives of Israel, Egypt, Lebanon, Transjordan and Syria, partly in Rhodes and partly at frontier posts between Israel and its neighbors.

The Israeli delegates explained that the borders of the United Nations partition map were drawn assuming that peace and close economic cooperation would exist between Israel and her neighbors; in the new situation existing after Arab aggression, however, these border lines had become untenable. The borders defined in the armistice agreements, therefore, on the whole reflected the front lines at the dates when military operations came to a standstill by cease-fires, and thus coincided with the frontiers of the Palestine Mandate to a larger degree than did those of the United Nations partition map. The Israel-Lebanon and Israel-Syria borders remained unchanged. The border between Israel and Jordan followed the Jordan River from the mouth of the Yarmuk to the southern Bet She'an Valley, ran west, crossed Mount Gilboa, descended to the southern Jezreel Valley, and continued over the Irron Hills to the eastern outskirts of the Sharon Plain. East of Petaḥ Tiqwa, it turned southeast and east to form the Jerusalem Corridor, and south of Israel's capital roughly described three-quarters of an oval which ended near En Gedi at the Dead Sea, and thus left Bethlehem and the Hebron Hills to Jordan. In the Arava Valley and along the Sinai Peninsula, the border again followed that of the Mandate; on the Negev Coast, the Gaza Strip remained outside Israel's territory. The total area of Israel within these borders, which were in force until June 1967, amounted to 20,700 km^2, or 7,993 sq. miles.

Political and Economic Consolidation. As soon as the State came into being, steps were taken toward its political and economic consolidation. Following the population census of November 8, 1948, the elections to the First Knesset, Israel's Parliament, were held on January 25, 1949. On February 16, Dr. Chaim Weizmann was elected as Israel's President; a confidence vote was given to the first Government headed by David Ben-Gurion on March 10. Dr. Weizmann filled his post until his death in November, 1952. He was followed in office by Izchak Ben Zvi, until his demise in April, 1963. Israel's present President is Sh. Zalman Shazar.

One of the first laws passed by the Knesset confirmed the right of every Jew in the world to settle in Israel and become a citizen of the State. Over three years mass immigration doubled the country's population. In 1949, 239,076 immigrants arrived, in 1950—109,405, and in 1951—174,019. This sudden growth caused economic and social problems of the first order.

In contrast to earlier arrivals, these immigrants came penniless, most of them without professional skills. All had to be provided with food and a roof over their head. Hastily, transition camps ('ma'barot') were established, later replaced by semipermanent and permanent housing. All branches of the economy had to be enlarged enormously to absorb the newcomers into the productive cycle. The number of schools had to be tripled, children and adults taught the elements of Hebrew, and courses in all vocations started. To top these off, there was the continual burden of keeping a large force in arms since the Arab states proclaimed their determination to destroy Israel in a 'second round.' The heavy demand of the growing population for consumer goods set in motion an inflation, only little checked by the stringent austerity regime of the first years. Rising prices discouraged exports, and the foreign trade gap widened. Despite the citizens' heavy taxation, the State could hardly have overcome its difficulties without the aid extended by world Jewry. Additional sums came through loans and grants-in-aid from the U.S.A. and other countries and, since 1952, through the reparation payments from Western Germany.

Security and economic considerations alike required that a network of towns and villages be established with great speed over the entire country. The overall figure for Jewish sites of habitation leaped from 330 in 1948 to 795 in 1959, with only minor additions up to the Six Day War. The regional distribution of Jewish settlement underwent substantial changes. The number of villages doubled in the Acre Plain and in Eastern Upper Galilee. Parallel chains of settlements came into being in central Upper Galilee. The Ta'anakh group of 11 villages was established in the south of the Jezreel Valley, and new settlements were founded on the eastern rim of the Sharon. The largest number of villages was set up in Judea—in the Jerusalem Corridor, the Lakhish and Adullam Regions—and in the

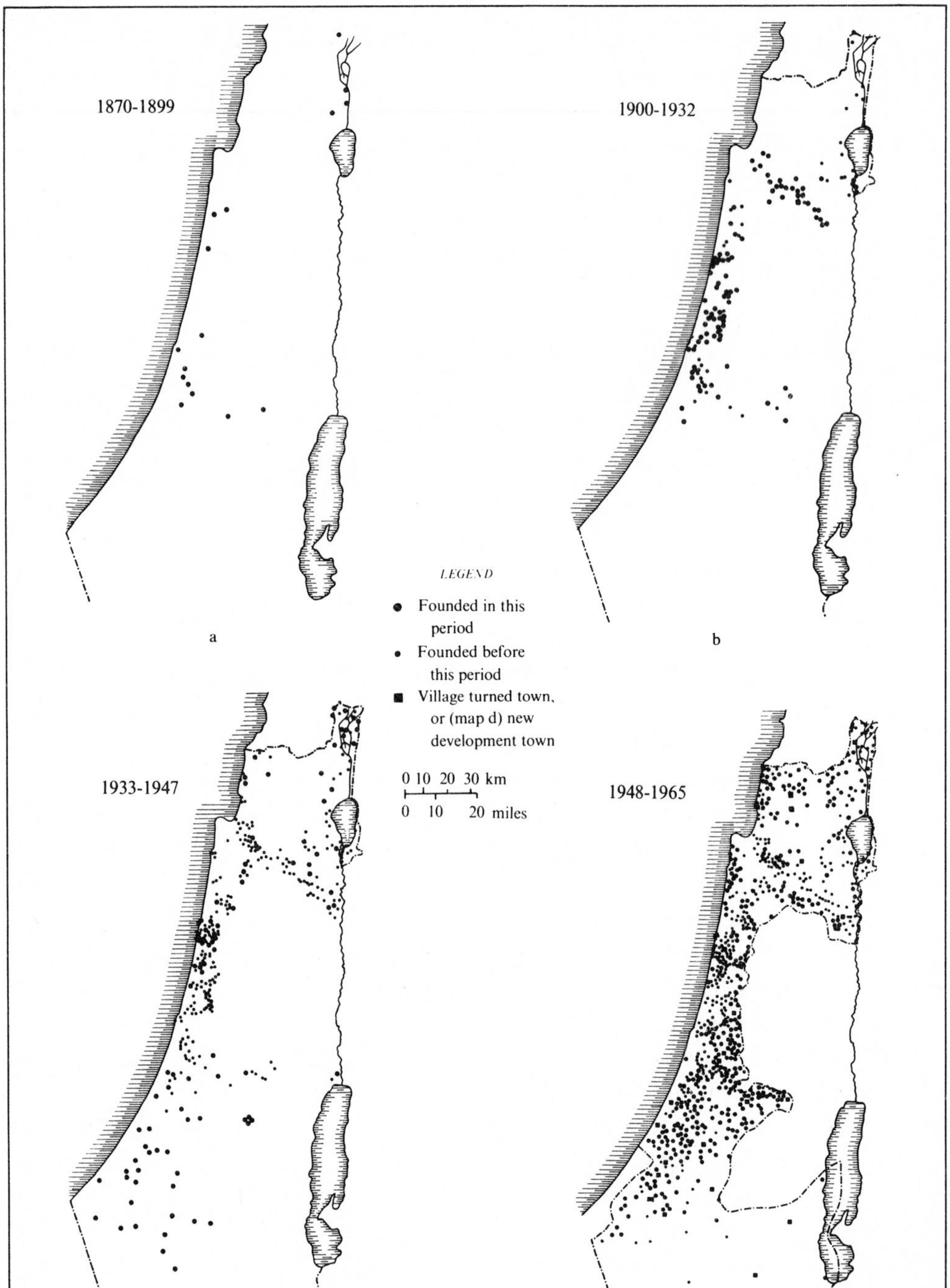

Stages in the spreading of Jewish rural settlement over the country

southern Coastal Plain and the northern Negev. The erection of border outpost settlements made new regions accessible at Korazim north of Lake Kinneret, on Mount Gilboa, and in the Modi'im area of northern Judea. Further beginnings were made in the Irron Hills and in central Galilee. In addition to rural settlements over 20 'development towns' were established, from Qiryat Shemona in the Ḥula Valley to Dimona, Miẓpe Ramon and Eilat in the central and southern Negev. Most of them overcame initial trials, broadened their economic foundations and contributed to draw a denser population to Israel's outlying regions.

Signal progress was registered in creating a solid infrastructure for the economy. Groundwater resources were fully explored and exploited, winter storm waters progressively harnessed, and Jordan waters were led to the country's south through the National Water Carrier which began operating in 1964. Experiments with unconventional methods (artificial rain, desalination of sea and brackish water) hold the promise for future growth of the water potential. The capacity of power plants increased twelvefold between 1948 and 1967, and attained 874,000 kw, with the completion in 1970 of a new 250,000 kw power station in Tel Aviv. Further units in Ashdod and Haifa were, in the same year, in the construction or blueprinting stage.

The road network was continuously extended and improved. Haifa Port was greatly enlarged, and two new shipping ports, Ashdod and Eilat, were opened in 1965. Lod Airport was adapted to cope with up-to-date aircraft and with a steeply mounting traffic.

This activity, together with the population increase quickened by large-scale immigration, resulted in a growth rate of the national product which surpassed that of most other countries, averaging 9% annually. The crop area, after having doubled already in the first four years of Israel's existence, increased further to almost 450,000 hectares in 1967, while the irrigated surface expanded from 30,000 hectares in 1948 to 164,000 in 1967. Agricultural production mounted and was not only able to cover most of the country's food needs but also to yield ever larger quantities of export produce, with citrus heading the list.

The mining branch became important with the renewed and enlarged exploitation of Dead Sea minerals, the drilling of first oil and gas wells, and the growing production of new materials (phosphates, copper, etc.). Israel's industry branched out into new fields and penetrated to primary production. In 1968, over 250,000 persons were employed in manufacturing enterprises, as against 47,000 in 1946; industrial exports of 1968 brought an income of approximately 500 million dollars.

Many financial difficulties arose from the enormous needs of security and of immigrant absorption and from the inflationary trends due to rising consumption and an imbalance between imports and exports. In spite of all these, Israel managed to arrive, in the mid-'sixties, at relative monetary stability. After a devaluation in 1962, and a smaller one following on that of Sterling in 1967, Israel's currency has gained a sound international standing.

Israel was compelled to be constantly on its guard in its relations with the Arab countries of the region. With the murder of King Abdallah in Jordan (1951) and the seizure of power in Egypt by Gamal Abdul Nasser, hopes for a gradual normalization dwindled. The abundant supply of arms by Eastern Bloc countries encouraged Egypt and other Arab states to start a campaign of sabotage against Israel with army-trained infiltrator gangs. As Syria, Jordan and Egypt organized a unified command for their armies and worked out the details of a concerted attack on Israel, the imminent danger was averted by the Sinai Campaign (October 29–November 3, 1956). Israel seized the entire Sinai Peninsula and the Gaza Strip, dismantled all offensive enemy installations and put the Egyptian army out of action. Acceding to a United Nations request, Israel evacuated the territory, completing the withdrawal from the Gaza Strip on March 8, 1957.

The principal achievements of the campaign were almost a decade of relative quiet on the borders and the opening of the vital shipping lane from Eilat to Asia and Africa, when United Nations guards were posted near the Tiran Straits. This led to the laying of the first oil pipeline between Eilat and Haifa and the development of new Negev centers. Trade contacts were established with many new countries in Asia and Africa which, to an increasing degree, enjoyed Israel's technical aid. Foreign investments were attracted by Israel enterprises. The quickened pace of economic progress also brought a new surge in immigration which lasted until the early 1960's. In 1965, however, the slackening of population growth necessitated measures to restrain the inflationary economy and contain the increase in consumption.

The Arabs, fully backed by Soviet policy, stepped up aggression anew, first condemning Israel's peaceful project for the country-wide Water Carrier, although Israel was careful not to infringe on the rights of the two other riverine states, Syria and Jordan, to the Jordan and Yarmuk waters. Their constant threats and preparations for diverting the Jordan headwaters from Israel were followed by ever more frequent terrorist incursions into Israel territory. In May, 1967, Nasser demanded the withdrawal of the United Nations' troops from the Tiran Straits, a request immediately complied with by the evacuation of all UN personnel from the entire Sinai Peninsula and the Gaza Strip. Simultaneously, an Egyptian force of 100,000 was posted in Sinai in proximity to the Israel border, and Nasser declared the Tiran Straits closed to Israel shipping, boasting thereby to having thus reduced Israel to its pre-1956 position and promising to restore the pre-1948 situation, i.e., cessation of Israel's very existence. The Jordanian King signed an agreement on full military cooperation with Egypt. Israel's annihilation was openly proclaimed as the policy of the Arab nations. These developments triggered off the Six Day War (June 5–10, 1967)* which ended in Israel's complete victory and with cease-fire lines fixed along the Suez Canal, the Jordan River and the eastern rim of the Golan Plateau.

Israel's hope for peace was soon dashed and its offer of direct open talks rejected when the Arab summit conference at Khartoum decided on 'no peace, no negotiations and no recognition of Israel.' This stand stymied the moves made within and without the UN framework to promote Middle East peace. The terrorist groups, actively backed by the Arab states, failed in arousing the population of the administered regions to revolt, and their numerous intrusions into Israel, as well as the frequent artillery attacks of Arab regular armies along the cease-fire lines, had much graver consequences for themselves than for Israel.

Israel, on the other hand, entered a new phase of accelerated economic and social progress, with production, exports, tourism, etc., greatly expanding, demand for labor taking the place of unemployment, immigration picking up, and research and cultural activities being intensified. All these contributed to reinforce the country's political and military resilience.

HISTORICAL PERIODS AND EVENTS IN THE LAND OF ISRAEL

Period	*Years (duration)*	*Conditions, cultures and events in the country*
PREHISTORY		
PALEOLITHIC	B.C.E.	
Lower	c. 500,000–100,000	Climate warmer and moister than at present. Primitive man living in the open. Hunting and gathering the sources of livelihood. Rough hand axes and adzes. Fire in man's service.
Middle	c. 100,000–25,000	Climate moister than at present. Man living in caves. Gathering, hunting, Variegation of stone tools, Sling-stones.
Upper	c. 25,000–12,500	Climate drier. Man living in caves. Stone arrowheads, flaked tools, scrapers. Net fishing. Cult of hunting.
MESOLITHIC	c. 12,500–8500	Climate resembling the present. Man living in caves. Gathering, improved hunting techniques. Bow and arrow. Stone saws, sickles. First domestication of animals. First steps in artistic creation.

*Described in detail in the chapters dealing with the Administered Areas, pp. 359–431.

HISTORICAL PERIODS AND EVENTS IN THE LAND OF ISRAEL

Period	*Years (duration)*	*Conditions, cultures and events in the country*
NEOLITHIC	c. 8500–4500	Field crops and gardening. Herding sheep. Grinding stones, digging sticks. First clay tools. Huts, partly subterranean. Fertility cult. Jericho first town.
CHALCOLITHIC	c. 4500–3100	Agriculture. Grain storage in bins and subterranean cavities. Round or quadrangular brick houses. Pottery developed. First use of copper tools. Trade develops. Arts of drawing, painting, sculpturing. Burying of dead in dolmens and sarcophagi.
HISTORY		
BRONZE	3100–1200	
Early	3100–2100	Use of bronze, copper. Fortification of towns. Beginning of writing. Social organization, and developing political regimes. The country called 'Amurru' by the Accadian Empire. West-Semitic seafarers' cities on the coast. The King's Road in Transjordan.
Middle	2100–1546	The Middle Kingdom of Egypt rules over Palestine ('Rthenu'), 2000–1780. Its cities mentioned in the Egyptian 'execration tablets.' Invasions of the Hyksos and their rule over Egypt (1780–1546). The Habiru make inroads into the country. The Hebrew Patriarchs.
Late	1546–1200	The New Kingdom in Egypt, the Hittite Empire in Asia Minor. The el 'Amarna Letters (1387–1366). Continued Habiru invasions of the country. Rule of Pharaoh Sethi I (1318–1299), who campaigns in Palestine and takes Bet She'an. Pharaoh Ramses II (1299–1232) wars in Palestine and Syria, reaches Orontes River.
IRON	1200–586	
Early	1200–930	The tribes of Israel enter the country (1200). Shortly afterward, Philistines and the 'Peoples of the Sea' arrive in the Coastal Plain. Period of the Judges (until 1020). Saul throws off the Philistine yoke, becomes king (1020–1000). Simultaneous decline of the empires of Egypt, Assyria and the Hittites. Reign of David (1000–960). Jerusalem becomes capital of Kingdom of Israel. Reign of Solomon (960–930). Kingdom of Israel at peak of its flower, politically and economically. Toward end of Solomon's reign renewed ascent of Egypt.

HISTORICAL PERIODS AND EVENTS IN THE LAND OF ISRAEL

Period	*Years (duration)*	*Conditions, cultures and events in the country*
Middle and Late	930–586	Partition into Kingdoms of Israel and Judah. The kings Jeroboam of Israel and Rehoboam of Judah (930–881). Dynasty of Omri in Israel. King Ahab (873–853). The Prophet Elijah. Dynasty of Jehu in Israel. Joash King of Judah (836–797). Prosperity of Israel under Jeroboam II (793–752) and of Judah under Uziyah. The Prophet Amos. Toward end of epoch Assyria, strengthened anew, vanquishes the Aramites, takes Galilee from Israel. Fall of Shomron and end of Northern Kingdom (722). The Prophet Isaiah. Last period of flower in Judah under King Josiah. The Pentateuch becomes foundation of the Kingdom's legislature. Fall of Assyria, ascent of Babylon. Increasing Babylonian pressure on Judah. Destruction of First Temple and Babylonian captivity (586).
PERSIAN	586–332	Prophet Ezekiel in Babylon. Persian conquest. King Cyrus' decree and beginning of First Return and construction of Second Temple (538). Second wave of immigrants from Babylonia (457–420). The Scribes, Ezra and Nehemiah. Construction of walls of Jerusalem.
HELLENISTIC	332–63	Conquest of Palestine by Alexander the Great (332). Partition of his empire by the Diadoches (323). Palestine under the Ptolemies (301–200). Frequent wars between Ptolemies and Seleucids. Antiochus the Great conquers Palestine for the Seleucids (200). Oppression of the Jews and their religion under Antiochus Epiphanes. The Maccabean revolt (167). Judah the Maccabee falls in the battle of El'asa (161). Jonathan (161–142) achieves independence for Jewish State. Simon (142–135) takes Jaffa and 'opens a window to the sea.' The Hasmonean Kingdom. John Hyrcanus (135–104) occupies the Edomite lands of Southern Judea, and Samaria. Judah Aristobulos (104–103) completes the conquest of Galilee. Alexander Jannaeus (102–79) adds most of the Coastal Plain and Transjordan, brings kingdom to its peak. Queen Salome Alexandra (Shelomzion, 79–69) makes peace with the Pharisees. Quarrels between her sons

HISTORICAL PERIODS AND EVENTS IN THE LAND OF ISRAEL

Period	*Years (duration)*	*Conditions, cultures and events in the country*
		Hyrcanus and Aristobulos engender the campaign of Pompey and the end of the Kingdom (63).
ROMAN	63–4 B.C.E.	Pompey takes most of Judea's conquests. Hyrcanus becomes 'President of the People,' while Antipater as 'tutor' holds real power. Julius Caesar returns Jaffa to Judea (47). Kingdom of Herod the Great (47–4).
	6–379 C.E.	The Roman Protectorate (6–41). Life of Jesus. King Agrippa I (41–44). The Great Revolt against Rome (63–73). Surrender of Yodefat (67). Destruction of Jerusalem and Second Temple (71). Fall of Massada Fortress (73). The Law School and the Sanhedrin opened by Yoḥanan Ben-Zakkay in Yavneh. The Bar Kokhba revolt (133–135) ends with the fall of Bethar. Spread of Christianity. Persecutions by Emperor Hadrian. Jerusalem becomes Aelia Capitolina. The Sanhedrin transferred to Galilee (140 to Usha and Bet She'arim, 165 to Ẓippori, 230–429 in Tiberias). Respite for Jews under Emperor Septimius Severus (193–235). The Mishna concluded. Renewed reprisals against Jews after Christianity has become state religion in Rome. Short respite under Emperor Julian (360–363).
BYZANTINE	379–640	Prosperity in the country, but Jews persecuted. Persian invasion (614–629) ended by victory of Emperor Heraclius. Moslem conquest of the country (629–640).
ARAB	640–1099	The Omayyad Dynasty (661–807) shows, in the beginning, tolerance toward Christians and Jews and seeks to maintain prosperity, but later oppresses minorities and neglects the country. Under the Abasside Dynasty (807–969) gradual worsening of the situation. Under the Fatimides (969–1091) internal wars, invasions of Mongols, Carmathians. Earthquakes and epidemics.
CRUSADER	1099–1291	Conquest of Jerusalem under King Baldwin I. Crusader rule gathers strength and expands until 1153, but later declines. After Saladdin's victory near the Horns of Ḥittin (1187), only Tyre remains in Crusader hands. From 1192, renewed expansion of Crusader rule over most parts of the country, but from 1244 onward, the

HISTORICAL PERIODS AND EVENTS IN THE LAND OF ISRAEL

Period	*Years (duration)*	*Conditions, cultures and events in the country*
		Mamelukes under Beybars reduce Crusader strongholds. The fall of Acre seals the Crusader epoch.
MAMELUKE	1291–1517	Impoverishment of local population, worsening security situation. Growing immigration of Jews, particularly after expulsion from Spain in 1492.
TURKISH	1517–1918	Selim I (1512–1520) conquers Jerusalem, Suleyman the Magnificent (1520–1566) builds its walls. The Jewish Zhahr el 'Amr fights the Turks (1740). Governor Aḥmed community of Safed attains peak of prosperity. In early 17th century security conditions worsen. The Druze ruler Fakhr e-Din (1650). The Bedouin Governor al-Jazzār (1775–1804) rules most of the country, builds Acre. Napoleon's Near East campaign fails against walls of Acre (1799). Population depleted and impoverished. Mehemet Ali, ruler of Egypt (1831–1840), makes himself master of Palestine; his governor, Ibrahim Pasha, aids the country's progress, settles Egyptian peasants. 'Capitulation rights' of European powers in the country. Founding of Miqwe Israel agricultural school in 1870. Beginning of Zionist development in 1882. Arrival of 'Bilu' immigrants in the country. Aid of Baron E. de Rothschild. After temporary slackening, immigration renewed in 1890. The First Zionist Congress (1897). 1899–1914, the Second Immigration. ICA (Jewish Colonization Association) sets up more villages. The Palestine Office of the Zionist Organization opened in Jaffa (1908). Defence organization 'Hashomer' formed. Yemenite immigration. Tel Aviv (1909) and Deganiya (1910) founded. In 1914, 85,000 Jews in the country, but their number declines to 56,000 in 1918. Balfour Declaration (2 November 1917). Occupation of south and Jerusalem in 1917, center and north in 1918 by British army under Gen. Allenby.
BRITISH MANDATE	1918–1948	1918–1920 military rule of the British. Sir Herbert Samuel first High Commissioner (1920–1925). The Third Immigration. Defense of Tel Ḥay and death of Joseph Trumpeldor (1920). The British Mandate confirmed by League of Nations (1923). The Fourth Immigration (1924–1926). Lord Plumer High Commissioner (1925–1928). Economic crisis

HISTORICAL PERIODS AND EVENTS IN THE LAND OF ISRAEL

Period	*Years (duration)*	*Conditions, cultures and events in the country*
		(1927–1930). Lord Chancellor High Commissioner. Arab disturbances of 1929. Arthur Wauchope becomes High Commissioner (1931). Vigorous development of Jewish community, economic progress. The Fifth Immigration after Hitler's rise to power in Germany (1933). Opening of Haifa Port (1934). The Arab disturbances (1936–1939). Royal Commission under Lord Peel (1936). Beginning of 'illegal' immigration. The White Paper (2 May 1939). The Second World War (1939–1945). The catastrophe of European Jewry entails continuation of 'illegal' immigration, though only on reduced scale. Jews in the country volunteer for Army service. Relations between Jews and Mandate authorities strained after end of war. Vigorous settlement activity in Galilee and Negev. The Anglo-American Inquiry Commission (1946). The United Nations Inquiry Commission (1947). United Nations decision on Palestine partition (29 November 1947). Outbreak of War of Independence.
ISRAEL STATEHOOD	from 1948	Proclamation of State of Israel (14 May 1948). First population census (8 November 1948). Opening of Knesset, Israel's Parliament (February 1949). Occupation of Eilat ends War of Independence (10 March 1949). Armistice Agreements with Egypt, Lebanon, Jordan, Syria. After death of first President of the State, Dr. Chaim Weizmann (1951), Yizchak Ben-Zvi elected President. Economic progress, mass immigration. Terror acts of infiltrators worsen. Arab states' plan of concerted attack on Israel prevented by Sinai Campaign (29 October–5 November 1956). Economic progress resumed. Israel develops ties with African, Asian countries. After demise of President Ben Zvi (1963), Sh. Z. Shazar elected President of Israel. National Water Carrier completed (1964). Ashdod and Eilat ports opened (1965). Evacuation of UN troops from Sinai, closing of Tiran Straits and threats of Israel's annihilation cause outbreak of Six Day War (5–10 June, 1967). Ceasefire lines fixed on Suez Canal, Jordan River and Golan Heights. Renewed and accelerated progress in economy, settlement and cultural activity.

Above—Tabor oaks in the Ḥurshat Tal Park of the Ḥula Valley
Below—view of the Dead Sea and the Moab Plateau

Coral fauna in the Eilat Gulf waters

Installations of the Timna Copper Works

Modern tourist hotel in Tiberias

Ruins of the Crusader fortress Montfort, in the Keziv Gorge of Upper Galilee

Damascus Gate and Christian Quarter of Jerusalem's Old City

Intensive farming of export crops in the Arava Valley

Above—Galilean landscape
Below—view from Rabbi Me'ir Ba'al ha-Nes sanctuary across Lake Kinneret

Demography*

The Population, from Ancient Times to the 19th Century. The Bible tells of repeated attempts to count the population, whether for allocating land to the tribes, taxation, or levying an army. The figures given in the Bible are, however, rough estimates. Scholars try to deduce from such a passage (2 Samuel, XXIV) that the inhabitants of King David's realm toward the end of his reign numbered approximately 5 million, in an area including, besides almost all of Palestine and Transjordan, parts of Syria and the Sinai Peninsula.

The great Jewish historian of antiquity, Josephus Flavius, sets the number of the country's inhabitants at the beginning of the Second Temple period at approximately 3 million.

Between the destruction of the Second Temple and the 19th century, even estimates are unavailable. It may be safely assumed, however, that under Byzantine rule, i.e., between the 4th and 6th century C.E., population density reached the maximum, then decreased gradually until the 17th and 18th century.

A turning point was reached in the early 19th century when, under the short reign of Mehemet Ali's governor, Ibrahim Pasha (1832–1840), the country absorbed many Moslem immigrants from Egypt. However, information about population movement in this country is extremely meager until the very end of Turkish rule.

Population Censuses. The first census ever undertaken, even though on a very limited scale, was that carried out during World War I by the Palestine Office of the Zionist Organization. Relating to the Jewish community only, it aimed principally at following the social and vocational changes since the first Zionist immigration in 1882.

* All tables and most data in this chapter are taken from *Statistical Abstract of Israel*, No. 21, 1970, published by the Central Bureau of Statistics.

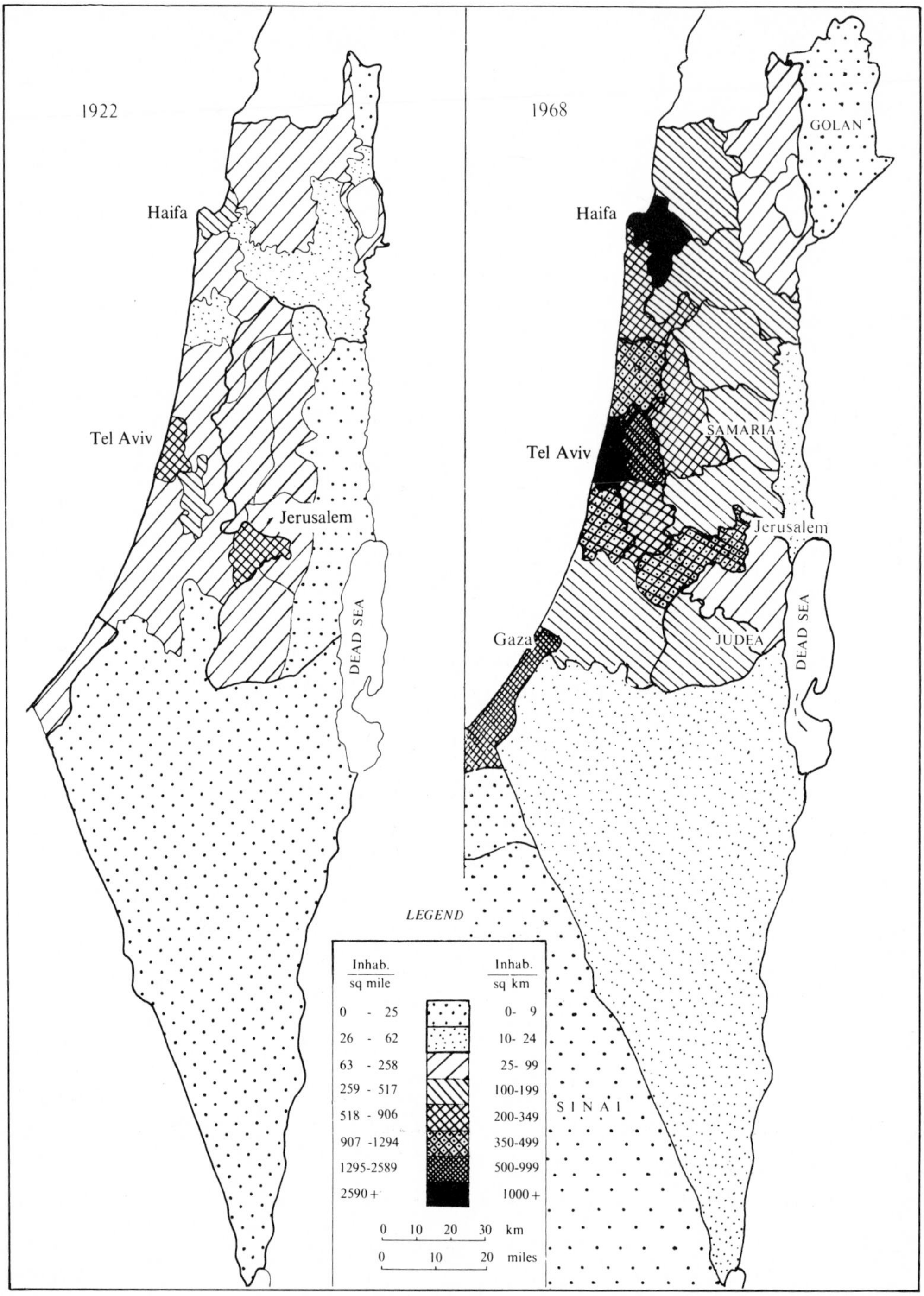

Population density in the country

Under the British Mandate, two censuses were held, in 1922 and in 1931; the first put the total population of Palestine west of the Jordan at 757,182 souls, and the second—at 1,035,821. The estimate for 1946 is 1,876,000. These figures, however, should be regarded with some caution because of the difficulty in obtaining exact data at the time, particularly among the non-Jewish population.

In the State of Israel two censuses were taken, the first in November 1948 and the second in May 1961. The first was actually only a simple population count and its figures were incomplete, particularly with respect to the non-Jewish minorities; theoretically, it comprised all regions then in Israeli hands, i.e., the pre-1967 area of the State except the Southern Negev and those villages on the Samarian border which were ceded to Israel only later in the armistice agreement with Jordan in 1949; in effect, Central Upper Galilee was also not included as the fighting there had ceased only a few days before the census.

The second census, on the other hand, was complete and comprehensive and generally proved the exactitude of the annual calculations made by the Israel Central Bureau of Statistics. This census, of May 22, 1961, established the permanent population of Israel (i.e., excluding temporary residents) at 2,179,500 persons, with 1,932,400 Jews and 247,100 non-Jews, or 88.62 and 11.38% respectively of the total population. At the end of 1969, Israel's population numbered 2,919,200 persons.

The table below shows the increase of population to have been swiftest during the years 1948–1951, approximately 20% annually. From 1952, the growth slowed considerably, to 3% or less per year, owing to the slackening in immigration, but it picked up again to approximately 5% in 1957 and from 1960 onward.

Jewish Population and Immigration. The great majority of the country's Jewish population is composed of immigrants and their offspring who have been coming since the beginning of the Zionist Movement in 1882. From then up to the present, Jewish immigration has continued almost uninterruptedly, although the pace quickened or slowed down owing to changing situations in the country and in world Jewry.

Between 1882 and 1914, absolute immigration figures were still insignificant. Out of approximately 2.5 million Jews who left Eastern and Central Europe in those years, only approximately 55,000–70,000, or 3% came to Palestine. Even of these, many could not overcome difficulties in acclimatization and left the country after a short stay.

In the years of World War I, immigration ceased almost entirely, but was resumed, to a far greater extent, immediately after the end of the war. Under the British Mandate (1919–1948) Jewish immigrants attained an approximate total of half a million. During this period several 'immigration waves' may be discerned,

POPULATION, BY POPULATION GROUPS (ESTIMATES, THOUSANDS) 1948–1969 AT END OF YEAR

Year	*Total population*	*Jews*	*Non-Jews (total)*	*Non-Jews (detailed)*		
				Moslems	*Christians*	*Druze and others*
1948	914.7	758.7	156.0[1]	—	—	—
1949	1,173.9	1,013.9	160.0	111.5	34.0	14.5
1950	1,370.1	1,203.0	167.1	116.1	36.0	15.0
1951	1,577.8	1,404.4	173.4	118.9	39.0	15.5
1952	1,629.5	1,450.2	179.3	122.8	40.4	16.1
1953	1,669.4	1,483.6	185.8	127.6	41.4	16.8
1954	1,717.8	1,526.0	191.8	131.8	42.0	18.0
1955	1,789.1	1,590.5	198.6	136.3	43.3	19.0
1956	1,872.4	1,667.5	204.9	141.4	43.7	19.8
1957	1,976.0	1,762.7	213.1	146.8	45.8	20.5
1958	2,031.7	1,810.1	221.5	152.8	47.3	21.4
1959	2,088.7	1,858.8	229.8	159.2	48.3	22.3
1960	2,150.4	1,911.2	239.2	166.3	49.6	23.3
1961	2,233.6	1,985.5	248.1	173.3	50.5	26.3
1962	2,331.8	2,068.9	262.9[2]	183.0	52.6	27.3
1963	2,430.1	2,155.5	274.6[3]	192.2	53.9	28.5
1964	2,525.6	2,239.2	286.4[3]	202.3	55.5	28.6[4]
1965	2,598.4	2,299.1	299.3	212.4	57.1	29.8
1966	2,657.4	2,344.9	312.5	223.0	58.5	31.0
1967[5]	2,773.9	2,383.6	390.3	286.6	70.6	32.1
1968[5]	2,841.1	2,434.8	406.3	300.8	72.2	33.3
1969[5]	2,919.2	2,496.6	422.7	314.5	73.5	34.6

[1] Estimate for pre-1967 surface area of the State.
[2] Including 1,479 'others.'
[3] Including 1,500 'others.'
[4] In 1964, part of 'others' were transferred to other population groups.
[5] Including population of East Jerusalem.

in accordance with the number of newcomers and their social and cultural background. Periods of relatively large immigrations were the years 1920, 1924–1926, 1933–1936, 1939, and 1946–1948.

Between 1920 and 1936, the urge to leave their countries of birth was particularly strong among Jews in East and East-Central European countries; of the Jews who in those years left Europe, about 15% came to Palestine. Hitler's advent to power in 1933 was the impulse for an immigration wave from Central Europe (Germany, Austria, Czechoslovakia); 63% of the emigrants from these countries at that time were taken up by Palestine.

In the four years 1920–1923, annual immigration figures were constant, with approximately 8,300 persons; they soared to 34,000 in 1925, in which year alone the total number of Jews in the country was increased by 28.5%. Between 1927 and 1931, immigration fell to a yearly 2,000–5,000, and mounted to 37,300 in 1933, 45,300 in 1934 and reached its pre-statehood peak in 1935 with 66,500 persons. Restrictive measures by the authorities caused figures to fall to 30,000 in 1936, 11,000 in 1937 and 15,000 in 1938; the desperate plight of European Jewry, however, drove many thousands to seek entry into the country as 'illegal' immigrants in 1939, when the total again rose to 31,000.

In May 1939, the White Paper drastically reduced immigration, and soon afterwards the Second World War closed the gates for all but a trickle of Jews who managed to save their lives by coming here. The figure for 1940 reads only 11,000, and was lower still in the ensuing years.

Between 1945 and 1948, immigration again assumed larger proportions as most newcomers, remnants of the European holocaust, arrived in devious ways in the ships of 'illegal' immigration, In 1945 and 1946, the number of arrivals amounted to 15,000, in 1946 to 19,000, and in 1947 to 22,000.

With the founding of the State, immigration grew enormously. During the War of Independence in 1948, 119,000 persons arrived; 17,000 in the 4½ months before the State was proclaimed, and 102,000 afterwards. The all-time peak came in 1949 with 240,000 newcomers, who then constituted 26.5% of the total number of Jews in the country. In 1950, 170,000 people arrived, and in 1951, 175,000. Thus, in the first 3½ years of the State, a total of 687,000 immigrants more than doubled its Jewish population. In 1952 a sharp decline began, lowering the number to 24,000 immigrants, and to 11,000 in 1953. From then figures again mounted slowly, reaching 56,000 in 1956, and 71,000 in 1957. Between 1958 and 1960, immigration slackened to an annual of 25,000, but rose again to 48,000 in 1961, 59,500 in 1962, and 62,100 in 1963. The number shrank to 28,500 in 1965, to 13,500 in 1966, and to 12,200 in 1967. With a total of 30,000 in 1968 and nearly 40,000 in 1969, a fresh surge of immigration is in evidence.

In the process of immigration during the years of statehood, entire Jewish communities from certain countries were transplanted to Israel (e.g., Iraq, Libya, Bulgaria, Poland) or at least a considerable part of them (Turkey, Morocco, India, Rumania, Hungary, etc.).

While Jewish population growth was slow until the British Mandate, it was greatly accelerated since then, so that the total was 84,000 at the beginning, and 650,000 at the end of that period. Immigration accounted for 72% of the increase of Jewish population under the Mandate, In the first years of statehood, it rose even more, to 88% between 1948 and 1951, but in the ensuing years (1952–1962) fell to 35%. As shown in the table below, the percentage of Israel-born Jews in the country amounted to 35.4% in 1948, decreased sharply in the following two years of peak immigration, and has since then mounted steadily to 45.05% in 1969.

A basic change took place in the composition of the Jewish population in the years of statehood, with a rise in percentage of those born in Africa and Asia from 9.8% in 1948 to 22.4% in the following year, and 28.7% in 1964; while the percentage of people from Asia was largest in 1952 and has since declined, that of immigrants from Africa rose until 1964. The number of Europeans and Americans in the total Jewish population has gradually declined from over a half to less than a third, although in absolute numbers it has almost doubled.

JEWISH POPULATION, BY CONTINENT OF BIRTH (ABSOLUTE NUMBERS, IN THOUSANDS)

End of year	*Israel*		*Asia**		*Africa*		*Europe, America*		*Total*
	Absolute number	%	*Absolute number*	%	*Absolute number*	%	*Absolute number*	%	*Absolute number*
1948	254	35.4	58	8.1	12	1.7	393	54.8	717
1950	311	25.8	189	15.7	81	6.7	623	51.8	1,203
1952	394	27.1	293	20.2	107	7.4	657	45.3	1,450
1954	471	30.9	293	19.2	121	7.9	641	42.0	1,526
1956	548	32.9	293	17.6	196	11.8	630	37.7	1.667
1958	626	34.6	302	16.7	221	12.2	661	36.5	1,810
1960	708	37.1	303	15.9	228	11.9	671	35.1	1,911
1962	796	38.5	304	14.7	275	13.3	694	33.5	2,069
1964	881	39.4	309	13.8	334	14.9	715	31.9	2,239
1966	976	41.6	312	13.3	341	14.5	717	30.6	2,345
1968	1,071	44.0	312	12.8	350	14.4	702	28.5	2,435
1969	1,125	45.1	315	12.6	355	14.2	702	28.1	2,496

* Except Israel

Jewish Groupings by Descent and Religious Ritual. Sects have never existed in Judaism. Slight differentiations have developed in religious ritual and Hebrew pronunciation in various countries; in no case, however, did they touch upon the meaning and content of the prayers. Jewish groups immigrating to Israel often continue to pray in synagogues of their respective communities. The two main groupings in this connection are: the Ashkenazi rite, including all Jews from Central and Eastern Europe, almost all Western European Jews, and Jews from the Americas, South Africa and Australia; and the Sepharadi and Oriental rites which are followed by communities of the Mediterranean Basin and the Middle and Far East. Hence, two Chief Rabbis traditionally hold office in Israel, one Ashkenazi and one Sepharadi. As the Sepharadi pronunciation of Hebrew—the spoken language of the country— is gradually accepted in all synagogues, religious circles have been striving to abolish the last formal, basically meaningless differences. The aim for the future is to cancel the need of a dual Chief Rabbinate; as a first step, a unified prayer book was introduced in the Israel Army.

In origin and physical features, the Jewish people lacks uniformity. Although, on the one hand, Jews of the Diaspora sometimes differ in their physical traits from the majority population of their host countries, on the other hand, there is hardly any similarity between Jewish groups who have come to Israel from different countries. Little justification is thus seen for the term 'Jewish race.' There are the very dark-skinned Jews from Cochin in Southern India and the 'Falashas' from Abyssinia; blue-eyed and blond Jews from Eastern or Central Europe, some with the prominent Slav cheekbones; dark-haired and long-skulled Mediterranean types from North Africa; thickset types from Kurdistan and Bukhara; lean Yemenites, and many others.

Consciousness of groupings and descent is rapidly being superseded by a national Israeli consciousness, strengthened by a momentous heritage of cultural and religious values; moreover, differences are fast reduced as all young people are educated together in school and frequently intermarry. The last factor, cumulative in effect, will show its full impact in coming generations.

In the 1961 census, the largest among the Jewish groups originating in Asia (besides Israel) is that from Iraq, with 123,000 persons. Actually, this group includes two different elements, the majority, former city dwellers, mainly of Baghdad and Basra, and the rest—villagers from the mountains of Iraqi Kurdistan. Occupying the second place among the Asians with 61,000 persons are Jews from Yemen and Aden, who are distinguished by their colorful traditions and folklore. Third in number are Jews from Turkey, with 44,000 persons; these also fall into two groups, Sepharadim from Istanbul and Izmir who have preserved the Ladino (Judeo-Spanish) language, and oriental communities, mostly from rural areas in southeastern Turkey, e.g., Kurdish and Urfali Jews. Jews from Iran, with 37,000 persons, occupy fourth place. Among the smaller groups from the Asian continent are Indian Jews (who again are sub-divided into the Bene Israel community, mainly from Bombay, the Cochin Jews, and others who went to that country during the last centuries). Furthermore, Israel has several thousand Jews who were born in Syria and Lebanon. Finally, there are the communities who arrived, most of them prior to the nineteen twenties, from the oriental and Asian parts of the Soviet Union, e.g., Georgian Jews, 'Mountain Jews' from Daghestan, Bukharan Jews, etc.

Among the African countries of origin, Morocco, with Tangier, is first in the 1961 census with 112,000 immigrants. Besides the majority from Moroccan cities (Rabat, Casablanca, Fez, etc.), there are the Jews of forgotten villages in the Berber districts on the High Atlas Mountains. Algeria and Tunisia are second,

a

b

c

d

Jewish immigrants: women and children from a) Germany, b) Yemen, c) Morocco, d) Kurdistan

Girl from Poland

Israel-born member of Naḥal Corps

with 40,000 persons, the great majority former French-speaking city dwellers; this group, however, also comprises a small community from the Tunisian island Djerba, where Jews constituted the majority of the population for centuries. In third place are Jews from Egypt, with 36,000 persons (mostly Sepharadim or of other oriental communities, but also some Ashkenazim), and in fourth, those from Libya, with 30,000. Smaller numbers came from South Africa (most originating in Lithuania and other East European countries) after a stay in that country for one or two generations, and a few arrived from Abyssinia.

Among the groups originating in Europe the largest is that of Jews from Poland, with 219,000 persons; about half of these arrived before the Nazi holocaust. Second are Jews from Rumania (147,000) and third, from the Soviet Union (118,000, the majority having immigrated before 1925). All of these are Ashkenazi Jews with Yiddish as their mother tongue. Next come Jews from Germany and Austria (53,000), like most of those from Czechoslovakia (26,000), with German as their original language. Another important group are the Hungarian Jews (29,000). The Sepharadi Jews from Bulgaria (39,000), Greece (11,000) and most of those from Yugoslavia (8,000) constitute a group apart. Immigrants from the Americas and Australia are relatively few in number; they fall into two categories, the predominantly English-speaking immigrants from North America and Australia (who are closely related in their culture and

Iraqi Jew

Sephardi Jew

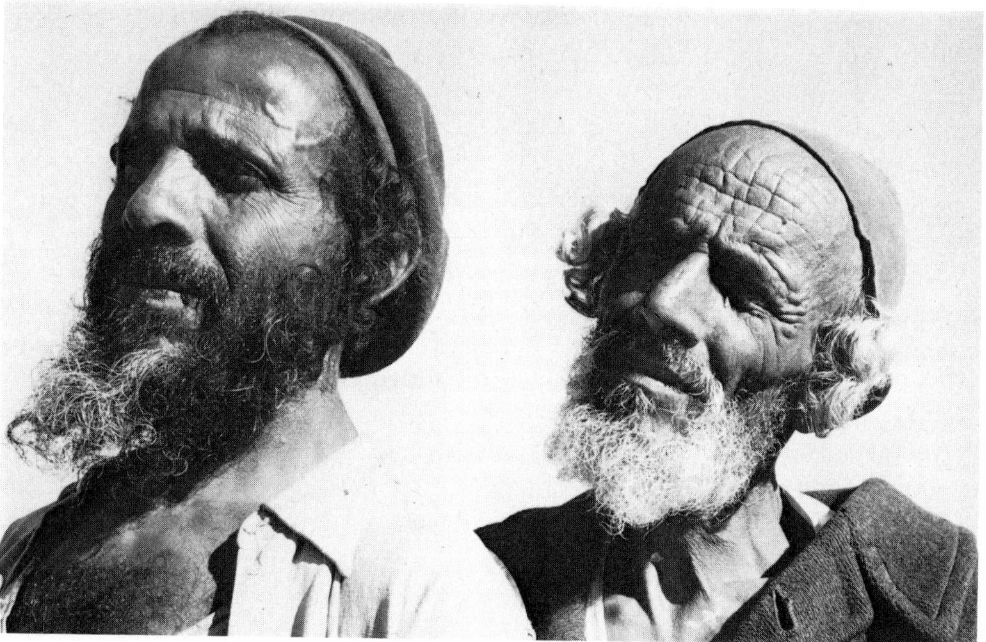

Yemenites

traditions to Jews from England and South Africa), and the Jews from Latin America who, having lived in those countries for, at most, one or two generations, have either Spanish or Yiddish as their mother tongue. In the years after the 1961 census, the pace of immigration of the latter groups has quickened, as has that of Jews from France (in their majority of North African origin).

Population Density and Regional Distribution. The overall population density of Israel amounted, at the end of 1969, to 144.3 persons per square kilometer (373.7 per sq. mile), as compared to 43.1 per sq. km (111.67 per sq. mile) in 1948.

The distribution of population over urban and rural places of settlement has changed profoundly since the beginning of the present century. Around 1900, most of the inhabitants still lived in villages, mostly concentrated in the Hill regions. Today, the picture is the opposite: 82.2% of Israel's inhabitants are urban dwellers (end of 1969), and nearly two-thirds of the total population lives in towns (the other third includes inhabitants of villages and of places of urban character but with no municipal status); the central parts of the Coastal Plain are

POPULATION, BY TYPE OF SETTLEMENT (31 DEC. 1969)

Form of settlement	*No. of settlements*		*Population (thousands)*		*% of total population*	
	Total	*Jews*	*Total*	*Jews*	*Total*	*Jews*
TOTAL POPULATION	877	774	2,919.2	2,496.5	100.0	100.0
URBAN POPULATION	78	74	2,407.7	2,226.1	82.5	89.2
Towns	29	27	1,983.9	1,828.1	68.0	73.2
Urban settlements	49	47	423.8	398.0	14.5	16.0
RURAL POPULATION	799	700	510.9	269.8	17.5	10.8
Large villages	154	56	245.2	43.3	5.8	0.6
Small villages	108	50	74.6	26.9	2.6	1.1
Moshavim (Smallholders' settlements)	346	346	122.5	122.5	4.2	4.9
Moshavim shittufiyim (Cooperative smallholders' settlements)	22	22	5.3	5.3	0.2	0.2
Kibbutzim (Collective settlements)	231	231	84.7	84.7	2.9	3.4
Bedouin tribes	(44)	—	36.8	—	1.3	—
Farms, institutions, schools, etc.	46	45	12.6	12.5	0.4	0.5
Living outside settlements	—	—	3.9	2.2	0.1	0.1

by far the most densely populated, with figures ranging between 250 and 600 persons per sq. km (647.5–1,554 per sq. mile), but 1,190.0 per sq. km (3,082 per sq. mile) in the Haifa subdistrict, and 5,061.7 per sq. km (13,110 per sq. mile) in the Tel Aviv district. The interior valleys are also more closely settled than the Hill regions.

POPULATION, JEWISH AND NON-JEWISH, BY DISTRICT AND SUBDISTRICT (IN THOUSANDS) (31 DECEMBER 1969)

District / *Subdistrict*	*Jews*	*Non-Jews*	*Total*
JERUSALEM*	237.7	76.5	314.2
NORTHERN	244.6	202.7	447.3
Safed	51.4	4.0	55.4
Kinneret	38.1	10.9	48.9
Jezreel	87.7	75.0	162.7
Acre	67.4	112.8	180.2
HAIFA	386.3	68.8	455.1
Haifa	312.0	24.8	336.8
Ḥadera	74.3	44.0	118.3
CENTRAL	482.4	39.1	521.5
Sharon	109.2	24.7	130.9
Petaḥ Tiqwa	171.5	7.3	178.8
Ramla	74.7	6.7	81.4
Reḥovot	130.0	0.5	130.5
TEL AVIV	852.5	8.0	860.5
SOUTHERN	292.6	27.5	320.1
Ashqelon	139.2	0.5	139.7
Beersheba	153.4	27.0	180.4

* Including East Jerusalem

A change in the distribution of the total population over the country's regions was caused in the last decades by the following factors: (a) Jewish immigration, largely concentrated in the three main cities of Tel Aviv-Jaffa, Haifa and Jerusalem, and Jewish settlement, which was at first directed mainly toward the central Coastal Plain, then spread to the interior valleys, and only later penetrated to the South, the Negev and the Hill regions; (b) until 1948, a migration of Arab villagers from the Hill regions to the Coastal Plain, particularly to the vicinity of cities and large Jewish settlements where prospects for employment and sale of farm produce were best. This movement was reinforced by a considerable immigration of Arabs from the neighboring countries which is not recorded in any Turkish or Mandate documents; (c) the abandoning of regions by their Arab inhabitants upon occupation by Jewish forces in the War of Independence. Parts of the Coastal Plain and the Judean Foothills and Hills were then almost entirely evacuated by Arabs, while the majority of non-Jews stayed in Galilee, and about one quarter of the Negev bedouin remained.

The developments in the years of Israel's statehood are illustrated by a comparison of population density between the end of 1951* and the end of 1969 in some of Israel's districts and subdistricts (persons per sq. km); Safed subdistrict, a growth from 38.7 to 82.5; Kinneret s.d.—68.2 to 94.0; Jezreel s.d.—77.7 to 136.0; Acre s.d.—90.4 to 192.6; Ḥadera s.d.—152.7 to 207.3; Sharon s.d.—256.4 to 376.0; Petaḥ Tiqwa s.d.—375.4 to 629.6; Ashqelon s.d.—23.0 to 109.8; Beersheba s.d. (including the entire Negev)—2.7 to 14.1.

Geographical Distribution of the Jewish Population. Zionist settlement and development since the end of the 19th century occurred at a time when a strong worldwide trend toward urbanization was noticeable. Jews, with few exceptions, are city dwellers in the Diaspora. Zionist settlement on the land therefore meant a complete reversal of a global trend. The figure of 280,300 Jews (or 10.8% of a total of 2,383,600 Jewish inhabitants of the country) who, at the end of 1969, were living in rural settlements, must be regarded as a remarkable achievement of the Zionist endeavor.

Planning and development efforts, particularly in the period of statehood, have had a beneficial influence upon distribution of Jews over rural and urban places of habitation and over the various regions of the country. Between 1936 and 1948, 70% of all Palestinian Jews lived in Tel Aviv, Haifa and Jerusalem, compared to 33% in 1968 (the latter figure, however, goes up to approximately 60% when the satellite towns of the Tel Aviv and Haifa conurbations are added). In 1936, 78% of Palestine's Jewish population was concentrated in the central part of the Coastal Plain, between Haifa in the north and Gedera in the south, compared to 12% in Jerusalem and the Judean Hills, 9.6% in Galilee and the interior valleys of the north, and only 0.4% in the Negev. This compares to 69.3% in the Central Coastal Plain,** 9.5% in Jerusalem and the Judean Hills, 10% in Galilee and the valleys, and 11.2% in the South and Negev in 1968. Between 1948 and 1970, a slow but continuous southward displacement of the geographical focal point of Israel's population is noticeable.

The Israeli planning authorities strive to distribute the population more widely over the country's districts: to restrain its growth in the three large cities and their satellites and encourage it in Galilee, in the interior valleys and Hill regions, and

* The figures of 1951 have been chosen, although by that year the maximum immigration had already reached the country; the figures of the 1948 census are inconclusive for a number of subdistricts where most of the non-Jewish population could not be counted.

**This figure is somewhat exaggerated, as the area also includes parts of Mt. Carmel, the Menashe Region and the Jezreel Valley.

particularly in the South and Negev. A forecast which, correctly, set Israel's population at 3 million by 1970 and anticipated the Haifa, Sharon and Tel Aviv regions to yield at least 5% of the total to the rest of the country, must be revised in the light of the changes in the composition of immigration and of the new cease-fire lines resulting from the Six Day War. On the whole, however, the objective (to which the tendency of furthering Jerusalem's speedy growth has now added itself) has even increased in urgency and must be pursued by directing industry and productive services to 'development towns' and underpopulated areas, as well as by founding additional agricultural settlements.

Planners, however, are fully conscious of the fact that the policy of population dispersal has its limitations and will meet with considerable difficulties. The Coastal Plain will continue to exert the strongest attraction, and mechanization of farming will cause the percentage of rural inhabitants to decrease. A long-range forecast for 1980–1982, when Israel's total population is anticipated to attain the four million mark and the overall density 200 per sq. km (518 per sq. mile), must therefore count on a density of 1,000 per sq. km (2,590 per sq. mile) and more in the Coastal Plain between Nahariya and Ashdod—one of the highest rates in the world. Inhabitants of rural areas will then account for far less than 10% of Israel's total population. To cope with such an expansion, great efforts are required in physical planning to safeguard the most efficient use of the limited space available, prevent haphazard development, and clearly define the use of land for residential areas, industry, commerce, farming, recreation, etc.

Age Composition and Natural Increase. Israel's population can, in general, be described as young and its natural increase as relatively large; but as in this respect Jews and non-Jews differ sharply, the two sectors must be described separately.

The country's non-Jews, particularly the Moslems, under the British Mandate attained one of the highest birth rates in the world while their mortality rate declined steeply as a result of improving health conditions. This development has continued unabated in the State of Israel, and has even been accelerated by the fast-rising standard of living. The movement of Arabs from Israeli territory to neighboring countries in the 1948 war did not entail any change in the age structure of the remaining sections of the non-Jewish population since it did not affect particular age groups .

In 1969, nearly half the Moslems of Israel were children under 14 years of age, while in the Jewish section this group constituted less than a third; the figures for the Druze community are close to those of the Moslems, while the Christians stood about halfway between the two extremes. The median age of Jews was 24.6 in 1969 but of non-Jews—only 15.2.

The age pyramid of the Jewish community has been decisively influenced by immigration. In the pre-State days, most Jewish immigrants were younger people; after 1948, however, with the transfer of whole communities of the Diaspora, Israel has often accepted a high percentage of old and infirm among the newcomers. This difference is illustrated by a comparison of the part of the population in the 25–29-year age group (i.e., the one at the peak of its capacity for work and reproduction) before statehood and today: while in 1948 it constituted 8.8% of the total Jewish population, it declined to 7.1% in 1957, and to 5.8% in 1967; immigration after the Six Day War, again being largely composed of young people, contributed to raise the figure to 6.0% in 1969, and even higher—in 1970.

POPULATION, BY POPULATION GROUP AND AGE, 31 DEC. 1967 (PERCENTAGE)

Age	*Jews*	*Moslems*	*Christians*	*Druzes and others*	*Total*
0–14	30.4	52.8	37.8	48.9	33.2
15–29	26.3	23.7	25.5	24.1	25.9
30–44	16.5	12.3	17.8	13.5	16.1
45–64	19.8	7.6	13.0	9.3	18.2
65 +	7.0	3.6	5.9	4.2	6.6

The absolute number of live births of the total population of Israel has increased only slightly in the years of statehood in spite of the steep rise in the number of the country's inhabitants; in 1951, it was 50,547, in 1957—53,940, in 1967*—64,980, and in 1969—73,666. The rate of live births in the Jewish community which was relatively high in the 1920's and the beginning of the 'thirties (35.76 per 1,000 inhabitants for 1923–1925; 30.32 for 1931–1935) declined later (25.74 for 1936–1940), but mounted again in the years between the Second World War and Israel's War of Independence (30.05 in 1947). The immigration of large numbers of Jews from countries with a traditionally high birth rate (Middle East, North Africa) caused the figure to rise even more in the first years of statehood (32.96 in 1950); since then, however, it has declined persistently; it was 21.8 in 1962, rose slightly to 22.6 in 1965 and again fell to 21.5 in 1967; the year 1969 showed another increase, to 23.4.

Among non-Jews, on the other hand, the rate of live births has been rising in recent years. While in 1950 it stood at 43.19, it mounted to 46.65 in 1957, and to 50.58 in 1962, to reach 51.4 in 1964; the figure for 1969 reads 46.4.

* The 1967 data for East Jerusalem are excluded from these and the following figures.

These differences between the communities are accentuated even more when rates of natural increase (i.e., birth minus death rates) are compared. While death and infant mortality rates for the country's Jews are, in the last twenty years, among the lowest in the world, and can hardly be brought down much more (the death-rate was 6.17 per 1,000 inhabitants for 1947 (7.2 in 1969), that for the non-Jews only now equals the average figures for the country (9.48 for 1950, 5.9 for 1969). The result shows in the rates of natural increase which in 1950 stood at 26.48 for Jews and 33.71 for non-Jews, but at 16.2 for Jews and 45.0 for non-Jews in 1964. The 1969 figures read again 16.2 for Jews, and 40.5 for non-Jews.

The Labor Force and Its Distribution in Branches of the Economy. Israel's civilian labor force has grown spectacularly in the years of the State's existence. Even between 1955 and 1969, when immigration had slowed down, it expanded from 631,200 to 990,100. This should be ascribed, to no small degree, to the rising number of working women, which in those years more than doubled, from 142,000 to 293,500. This approaches the rate of gainfully employed women in countries with a progressive economy.

Two outstanding features in the table below showing the distribution of the country's labor force in the various branches of the economy are the high rate of employees in construction and public works and the increasing part of industry, crafts and quarrying in total employment. The first reflects the construction of factories, administrative buildings, roads, etc., necessitated by fast population

EMPLOYED PERSONS, BY ECONOMIC BRANCH AND POPULATION GROUP (PERCENTAGE OF JEWISH AND OF TOTAL LABOR FORCE)

Branch	*1957*		*1960*		*1964*		*1969*	
	Jews	*Total*	*Jews*	*Total*	*Jews*	*Total*	*Jews*	*Total*
Agriculture, forestry, fishing	14.0	16.3	15.0	17.3	10.6	12.9	8.9	10.5
Industry, crafts, quarrying	22.5	22.1	23.8	23.2	26.2	25.3	26.8	26.2
Construction, public works	9.5	9.8	8.9	9.3	9.3	10.2	7.0	8.2
Electricity, water, sanitary services	2.5	2.4	2.3	2.2	2.0	1.9	2.1	1.9
Commerce, banking, insurance	13.5	13.0	12.7	12.3	13.1	12.7	13.2	12.9
Transportation, storage, communication	6.7	6.5	6.4	6.2	7.4	7.2	7.8	7.7
Government, public administration	8.5	8.1	8.3	7.9	8 0	7.6	8.6	8.1
Health, education, welfare, religion, judiciary, etc.	14.8	14.1	14.8	14.1	15.3	14.5	16.9	16.1
Personal services, entertainment	8.0	7.7	7.8	7.5	8.1	7.7	8.7	8.4

growth and the expansion of all branches of the economy. The second figure mirrors Israel's effort to direct a larger part of its labor force toward constructive enterprises, especially toward industry; the percentage of those employed in agriculture decreased, owing to progressive mechanization, although production continues to rise steeply in this branch. The drop in the figures for industry, and particularly for building, in the 1967 statistics is the joint outcome of the preceding economic recession and the Six Day War. This development was reversed in the expansion since the end of 1967.

The figures for Jewish employed persons point to the complete revolution which has taken place in the country. While the professional structure of Diaspora Jewry shows everywhere an 'upside-down pyramid,' with only negligible numbers employed in the primary stages of production (farming, industry), and the greatest part to be found in commerce, services and free professions, the structure of Israeli Jewry has largely been normalized. It resembles that of populations in progressive countries where, as a consequence of mechanization, the percentage of farmers and industrial workers in the total labor force is steadily dropping; the percentage of Jewish agriculturists in Israel is thus, for the time being, higher than that of farmers in the United States, and even in some European countries.

Language, Education and Culture. Hebrew is the first official language of Israel, with Arabic and French second and third; English, however, is even more widely understood than French and is used in communication with tourists and foreign countries; many Government publications, e.g., the *Israel Government Year Book* and the *Statistical Abstract of Israel,* appear in both Hebrew and English.

The Hebrew language, though never as 'dead' as Latin is today, was revived for everyday speech at the beginning of Zionist immigration in the late 19th century. Its foremost champion was Eliezer Ben Yehuda, the linguist who enriched the language by many hundreds of new words essential to modern thought and needs, which he derived from existing Hebrew roots. In 1914, about 40% of the Jews in the country spoke Hebrew as their sole, or at least first, language; Hebrew was then used mainly by people who held Zionist views while the 'old yishuv,' in the country for generations, clung to Yiddish, Arabic or Ladino (Judeo-Spanish); the above figure, however, does not include the Jews of Jerusalem, most of whom then belonged to the latter category.

After the First World War, Hebrew became generally accepted in everyday life and in all Jewish schools, and was constantly enriched by new expressions in science, technical branches, etc. In the 1948 census, 75.1% of all Jews in the country were using Hebrew exclusively or primarily, with the figure for the 2–14-year-old age group at 93.4%. Mass immigration brought these figures temporarily down to 60.0% and 80.3% respectively in 1950. Since then, with 'Ulpanim,' intensive language courses, to aid newcomers in quickly acquiring a good working knowledge of Hebrew, they have climbed anew. In 1961, 75.3% of the Jews aged two years or more spoke Hebrew as their principal language, and 92.8% of the 2–14-year-old group.

The literacy rate of the Jewish population was very high prior to 1948; only 8–10% of people above school age were illiterate. Although school education was not compulsory under the British Mandate and fees had to be paid for elementary school, almost all Jewish children were educated in Jewish schools. Mass immigration from backward countries in the early 1950's caused a temporary decline in the literacy rate, but the introduction of compulsory elementary education, and adult education have since done much to fill the gaps. In the 1961 census, 88.0% of the total population above the age of 14 years was found literate; literacy of males exceeded that of females, 92.9 compared to 83.6%. The highest rate of literacy, 99.0%, was found among Israeli-born males. It is interesting to note that among 1,300,840 Jews above the age of 14 years, 703,430 could read and write Hebrew and other languages, 232,895 only other languages, and 208,030 only Hebrew.

The literacy rate of the non-Jewish population, though still considerably lower than that of the Jews, has risen steeply in the years of statehood. In 1961, 48% of all non-Jews could read and write. Differences between the sexes, however, are very large (68.0% for males and 28.5% for females). The progress made is shown by a comparison between age groups: the younger the group, the higher its literacy rate; while among the 14–19-year-old group it amounted to 83.6% for males and 47.6% for females, it was 30.4% and 12.3% respectively for those above 65 years of age. Literacy of non-Jews was highest among Christians (86.6% for males and 66.1% for females), and lowest among Moslems (60.7 and 14.4%).

The State of Israel has introduced free, compulsory education over nine years—one of kindergarten and eight of elementary school. The rise of the school population mirrors the general population increase in the country. In the school year 1970–71 the overall number of pupils approached 900,000, compared to 140,817 in 1948–49. The number of pupils in Arab education (also included in the above figures) attained 11,129 in 1948–49 and 82,909 in 1967–68.

Great strides have been made in secondary education. While in 1951–52 only 23.4% of Jewish youth aged 14–17 received post-primary education, the percentage doubled to 46.5% in 1961–62, and was higher still (46.9%) in the 1964–65 school year.

Higher education embraces a steadily widening circle, as shown in the chart below. The number of high school students rose from 1,635 to 18,368 between 1948–49 and 1964–65. In the ensuing years, the figures soared even more steeply, as

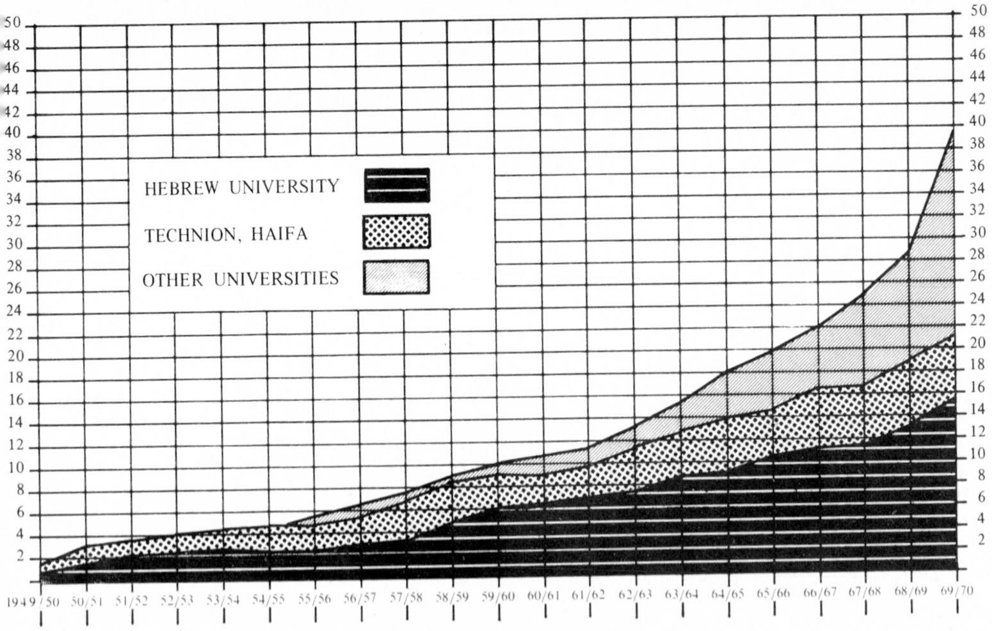

Number of students in Israel's institutes of higher learning

not only veteran institutions (Hebrew University of Jerusalem, Haifa Technion, Weizmann Institute of Science and Volcani Institute of Agriculture at Reḥovot) continued to expand, but younger ones approached them in size, or began to function (Tel Aviv, Haifa, Beersheba universities, Bar Ilan University of Ramat Gan), and as youth arrived from abroad in increasing numbers to study in Israel. In the year 1969/70, the total number of students approached 40,000.

Minorities in Israel*

The number of inhabitants of Israel belonging to religious or national minority groups totalled 422,800 at the end of 1969. They enjoy the same rights and bear the same obligations as all other Israeli citizens although—with the exception of Druzes and Circassians—they are exempt from military service. The State extends its services and facilities, maintains a separate educational network with Arabic as the language of instruction, and aids in upholding their traditions and maintaining their religious institutions. The various religious communities enjoy

* More details are included in the chapters dealing with the areas which came under Israel administration in 1967, see pp. 359–431.

full autonomy. Following the 'millet' system of Turkish and Mandate rule, each recognized community has its own religious courts dealing with certain matters of personal status (marriage, divorce, inheritance, etc.). The State extends special aid to the non-Jewish citizens, to promote their economic and cultural progress. The protection of the Holy Places and free access to them is an obligation the State of Israel took upon itself in the 1948 Proclamation of Independence. After the Six Day War, an additional law was passed providing for special safeguarding of and reverence for these holy sites.

The largest minority group in Israel is that of the Moslems, followed by various Christian denominations, then by Druzes and splinter groups such as Circassians, Bahais and Samaritans.

Moslems. The majority of Israel's Arab-Moslem population may be assumed to be descendants of the country's ancient inhabitants (Canaanites, Samaritans, Jews, Edomites, Helleno-Syrians, etc.), who converted to Islam, most of them in the first centuries after the Islamic conquest, some as late as in the 19th century. The conquerors from the Arabian Peninsula, in contrast, seem to constitute only a fraction in their parentage. Most of the country's Moslems are Sunnites, like the majority of followers of Islam in the world. The inhabitants of some Metuwali villages on Israel's northern border belonged to the Shiite sects, but as these were abandoned in 1948, only few Shiites have remained in the country.

Of Israel's 314,000 Moslems (at the end of 1969), most are concentrated in Lower and Upper Galilee, on the southern outskirts of the Jezreel Valley, in the Irron Hills, and along the eastern border of the Sharon. In the town of Nazareth, Moslems are slightly more numerous than Christians. Relatively large Moslem communities also exist in towns such as Haifa, Jaffa, Acre, Ramla and Lod. In East Jerusalem (whose area, unlike the other new territories under Israel administration, was made part of Israel), more than 50,000 Moslems were registered in 1967. A separate group among the Moslems are the 36,800 bedouin (1969), most of whom live in the Negev; these maintain their tribal organization and ancient customs, but with Government assistance have lately been switching from sheep and goat grazing to agriculture or work in building, industry, etc., and from dwelling in camel- and goat-hair tents to permanent houses. The first semi-urban agglomeration of former bedouin has been established at Basmat Tab'ūn, near Qiryat Tiv'on in Lower Galilee, and similar towns are under construction in the Negev.

The largest mosque in Israel's pre-1967 borders is the Aḥmed Jazzār Mosque of Acre. With the reunification of Jerusalem, two of Islam's most famous shrines, the Dome of the Rock and the el-'Aksa Mosque, have come under Israel's jurisdiction. The Temple Area of Jerusalem, like other Moslem institutions, is

Bedouin children in the northern Negev

administered by Moslem religious authorities. Israel has proclaimed full freedom of worship at these sites, which are open to visits of non-Moslems only outside prayer hours. Moslems from all countries are entitled to visit their Holy Places on their holidays but few from Arab countries avail themselves of this right.

The Christian Communities. Most of Israel's Christians, like the Moslems, originate in the country's ancient inhabitants. Part of them have preserved their faith since the first centuries of the common era, while others were converted during the Crusades. Very few have become Christians in the last centuries. The great majority of them speak Arabic and regard themselves as part of the Arab nation. In 1969, Israel's population included approximately 74,100 Christians, 12,000 of them in East Jerusalem. Another 31,000 were counted in Judea-Samaria, and about 2,000 in the Gaza Strip.

Within the pre-1967 borders, Nazareth and the surrounding area of Lower Galilee, and certain villages in Upper Galilee, were the principal Christian centers. Haifa and Jaffa also have sizeable Christian communities. Prior to the

The Dome of the Rock on Jerusalem's Temple Mount, a beautiful shrine of Islam

Six Day War, city dwellers constituted about two thirds of Israel's Christians; the inclusion of East Jerusalem has further increased this proportion.

Before 1967, Nazareth, Mt. Zion in Jerusalem, the shores of the Sea of Galilee, and, to a lesser degree, Jaffa and other places were Israel's foremost sites holy to Christians throughout the world. With Jerusalem reunited and Judea-Samaria under Israel administration, more of such sites of paramount importance have been added. First among these rank the Church of the Holy Sepulchre and the area of the Mount of Olives in Jerusalem, and the Church and Grotto of the Nativity in Bethlehem. Since the founding of the State, new churches have been erected in towns and villages. The most impressive of these is the Basilica of the Annunciation in Nazareth, built on the foundations of Byzantine and other early churches, which is today the largest church in the Middle East.

Whereas only three high ecclesiastical dignitaries were resident within the pre-1967 frontiers, there are now about 30, among them the Greek-Orthodox, Latin and Armenian-Orthodox Patriarchs, all of whom have their seats in Jerusalem. Their jurisdiction extends over their respective institutions and the faithful of their creeds in the Holy Land, including Transjordan, and, in a number of cases, also over those of other Middle East countries.

The desire of every Christian denomination to be represented near the faith's historical sites explains the large number of communities and church bodies to be found in Jerusalem and Israel. This number has increased from 22 to more than 30 since the Six Day War.

The ancient Mar Saba Monastery in the Qidron Gorge of the Judean Desert

The oldest community in the country is the Greek-Orthodox. In Mandatory Palestine, this was also the most numerous denomination. However, within the 1948 borders of the newly created State of Israel, they held only second place, after the Greek-Catholics. Today their total number in the country approaches 38,000,* over 17,000 of them living within Israel's former borders, principally in Galilee, about 4,000 in East Jerusalem, over 15,000 in Judea-Samaria (with the Bethlehem area and Ramallah as the main centers), and 1,500 in the Gaza Strip. The Greek-Orthodox Patriarch in Jerusalem is independent of any universal church body and assisted by 14 archbishops resident in this country. About 50 churches and monasteries, many of them very ancient, are under his jurisdiction. The laity of this religious group are nearly all Arabs, but the higher clergy are Greek.

Two other Orthodox churches, the Russian and the Armenian, are represented in Israel. The former is divided between the Russian Church in Exile with its center in New York, which exerts authority in East Jerusalem and Judea-Samaria, and the Russian Patriarchate of Moscow which has jurisdiction over its faithful in the rest of Israel.

The Greek-Catholics or 'Melkites' within Israel's pre-war frontiers numbered 23,000 souls, to which have been added another 3,000 persons in the new regions. This is one of the 'Uniate churches' which returned to the pale of Catholicism more than 250 years ago, but retained some of their ritual and their traditional language of prayer which, for the Greek-Catholics in the country, is mainly Arabic. In Israel they are headed by an archbishop whose seat is Haifa, the largest of their communities in Israel. There are Melkite communities in Nazareth and in the villages Mi'ilya and Fassūta in Upper Galilee. In Jerusalem, they maintain a priests' seminary.

Third in number are the Roman Catholics or 'Latins,' with a total of about 22,400 souls, 10,000 in Israel's former borders, 12,000 in East Jerusalem and Judea-Samaria, and 400 in the Gaza Strip. They are headed by the Latin Patriarch whose seat is Jerusalem; prior to 1967, a bishop functioned as Patriarchal Vicar in Israel territory. Various orders and congregations maintain schools, hospices, hospitals, and charitable institutions. The Franciscan Order functions as the 'Custodian of the Holy Land,' and as such is in charge of the principal Holy Places of Catholicism. Most members of this community are Arabs, although there are several thousand Europeans, mainly clerics.

An interesting group are the Maronites, who number over 3,000 in Israel. The members of this ancient community, whose center is Lebanon, regard themselves as descendants of the Phoenicians. Both Syriac (related to Aramaic) and Arabic

* This and the following figures represent the situation in 1967.

Basilica of the Annunciation in Nazareth, largest church building in the Middle East serve as languages of prayer. The Maronites established ties with the Holy See in the 12th century, but, like other Uniates, retained a certain measure of autonomy. In Israel, Maronites live in villages of Upper Galilee, principally at Gush Ḥalav. They are also represented in Jerusalem. Other Uniate churches in the country are the Syrian-, Armenian- and Coptic-Catholics and the Chaldeans.

Protestant groups are comparatively late-comers to the country, having arrived in the 19th and 20th centuries to begin missionary activities, principally among the Greek Orthodox. First among them is the Anglican Church in the Holy Land, headed by an archbishop whose jurisdiction extends over church institutions throughout the Middle East. Second ranks the Lutheran Church. The overall number of Protestants exceeds 5,000, of whom 2,000 live within Israel's pre-1967 frontiers. About half of the country's Protestants are Arabs.

Among the Monophysite churches (which were formed after the first, 'Arianic' schism and, as their name indicates, believe in the 'single nature' of Christ), the Armenian-Orthodox Congregation is the largest in the country. Most of its faithful live in the Armenian Quarter of Jerusalem's Old City. Other such groups are the Coptic-Orthodox, the Syrian-Orthodox, and the Ethiopians.

The Druzes. The Druze faith has its origin in Egypt in the 10th and early 11th century C.E., when it separated from Islam. Suffering frequent persecutions in the Lebanon and Syria, which became their centers, the Druzes developed a tradition of bold warriors but also learned to hide their faith in case of need. This explains the division of the community into a narrow circle of 'initiated,' which also includes women, and a majority who know only the outward customs.

Druzes began to settle in this country in the beginning of the 16th century, under the Druze ruler Fakhr a-Din. In the 1948 war all remained within Israel's borders, and today their position among the non-Jews has been greatly strengthened. Numbering ca. 34,000 persons in 1969, most of them are farmers and live in villages of Western and Central Upper Galilee, in the two villages 'Isfiya and Daliyat al-Karmil on Mt. Carmel, and in Haifa. With the occupation of the northern Golan in 1967, the Druze ranks were swelled by an additional 6,000 who have established close ties with the veteran community.

The Alaouites (Nusairites). Although this creed has its origins in Shiite Islam, it has incorporated many non-Mohammedan elements of faith and has thus become almost a separate religion. The name 'Alaouite' is derived from Ali, Mohammed's son-in-law, who is particularly venerated by the sect. Most of its followers live in the Alaoui (Ansarīya) Mountains of northwestern Syria. After the Six Day War, the Alaouite village Ghājar, on the Lebanese border below Mt. Ḥermon, came under Israel administration.

Druze watchman

The Aḥmedis. This is another sect which has detached itself from Islam. The local community, numbering about 400 persons, living in the small Haifa suburb al-Kababīr, was founded by missionaries from Pakistan in the first half of the Nabatean cities of the Negev (see above, p. 209).

The Bahais. This faith, which has only about 200 members in Israel, nevertheless regards the country as its world center. Bahais live today in far greater numbers in Persia, Iraq, India, the United States of America, and a number of European countries. The faith originated in Persia in the middle of the 19th century when it departed from Shiite Islam. Its forerunner, Mirza Ali Muhammed ('Bab') was executed. His disciple, Mirza Husain Ali ('Baha-Ullah'), acknowledged founder of the Bahai faith, was banned from Persia and spent the remaining years of his life (between 1864 and 1892) as an honored prisoner of the Turks in Acre. Abbas Effendi ('Abdul Baha'), eldest son of the Baha-Ullah, assumed leadership on the death of his father. The Bahai faith has integrated many elements of western philosophy; it lays emphasis less on cult ritual than on the moral relationship between man and his neighbor. The world centers of the Bahai religion are the tomb of the Baha-Ullah near Acre, and the magnificent new temple and library which have been built in the 'Persian Gardens' of Haifa.

The Bahai Shrine in Haifa

The Samaritans. This faith, very close to Judaism, originated during the construction of the Second Temple in the 5th century B.C.E. The creed centers round the Pentateuch and the Book of Joshua and lays emphasis on certain passages pointing to the sanctity of Mt. Gerizim near Sichem (Nablus), instead of Jerusalem. Although it still numbered tens of thousands during the Moslem conquest of the country in the 7th century C.E., the community has shrunken gradually and today numbers no more than 400 souls. Of these, over half live in Nablus, and the rest in the town of Ḥolon.

Since June 1967, close contact between the two parts of the community has become a day-to-day affair, thus contrasting with the previous period when the Israeli Samaritans were permitted to cross the border into Jordan only once a year, to sacrifice the traditional lambs on Mt. Gerizim on their Passover festival.

The Circassians. In contrast to all the groups described above, this is a national, not a religious minority. Sunnite Moslems, the Circassians came to this country (as well as to the Golan and to other parts of Transjordan and Syria) from the Caucasus region when their homeland was occupied by Christian Czarist Russia in the 1870's. In Israel, they live in two villages, Kafr Qāma in Lower, and Reḥanīya in Upper Galilee. Numbering about 2,000 persons, they are eager to preserve their traditions and original language, although they also speak Arabic and, today, even Hebrew. Only very few members of the quite sizeable Circassian community of the Golan remained there after the Six Day War.

Rural Settlement

Arable soil and sources of water are always the first requisites for establishing a village. Wherever peace and order reign, rural settlements tend to develop toward important roads and thoroughfares, and crossroads become commercial centers. In periods of war, however, villages in this country kept their distance from the highways, used by marching armies, who took their provisions and needs from friend and foe alike.

In the history of the Land of Israel, periods of wars and disturbances were incomparably more frequent and prolonged than times of peace and quiet progress. Villages, therefore, mainly tended to keep off the main roads; in choice of sites, conditions of security and defense were almost always decisive. During most of the country's history, the Hills were accessible only with difficulty, and therefore only they were settled, while the Coastal Plain and the Jezreel and Bet She'an valleys, where the international Via Maris thoroughfare ran, were neglected and abandoned. This development was, at times, also aided by a political factor: the Arab, Mameluke and Turkish rulers of the country were always in fear of invasion from the Mediterranean Sea and intended to transform the shore and Coastal Plain into an obstacle to enemy penetration by dismantling ports and laying waste the countryside.

The Arab Village

Hill Villages. Most of the Arab villages are of ancient origin. The continuity of settlement through the ages is shown by the fact that Arabic names of present-day hill villages differ but little from the Hebrew names known from the Bible or the Talmud, e.g., Ḥalḥul, Yatta = Yuta, Dora = Adorayim, Mukhmas = Mikhmash, 'Anata = Anatot, Ti'innik = Ta'anakh, Kafr Manda = Kefar

Mindi, Jish = Gush Ḥalav, Kefar Bir'am, etc. Archeological evidence, too, corroborates the assumption that most Arab villages of the present were preceded by Canaanite, Israelite, Hellenistic and Roman-Byzantine settlements and that they do not differ much from their predecessors in their planning and building style as well as in the mode of life of the inhabitants.

Sites were chosen for best defense against robbers and enemies. Hill tops, or at least upper sections of slopes were preferred although this entailed the discomfort of increased distance to the fields and sources of water. Since buildings were crowded as closely as possible in order to shorten the village's circumference and facilitate its defense by the male inhabitants' limited force, only a few square meters were left for kitchen gardens by each house; as hill tops are normally strongly eroded and are barren rock, the soil for these tiny gardens had sometimes to be laboriously transported up from the valley. Water for the house and for irrigation of the kitchen gardens was carried, often over a long, steep and rocky path, by the women from the well or spring in huge earthenware vessels, delicately balanced on their heads.

Umm al-Faḥm, in the Irron Hills, is typical of Arab hill villages which have expanded considerably during Israel's statehood

Hard Hill limestones, or softer limestones and chalks of the Foothills have served since antiquity as original building material. The hewing and chipping of building stones is a traditional art among the hill peasants. The lack of wood for beams to support a flat roof led to the invention of the arched ceiling, in which every stone supports its neighbor. Since in simple village buildings only narrow arches could be constructed, rooms and houses are small. Upon the domed ceilings or around them, a flat roof is laid to enlarge the family's living space; summer evenings can thus be spent enjoying the cool breeze, and sleep gained on warm summer nights. The roof also serves to store produce, victuals or firewood; fruits and vegetables are dried here, etc.

Where stones abound, the hill villagers build thick, strong walls to isolate the rooms against winter cold and summer heat. Lintels of windows and doors are either held by arches or by single elongated stone ashlars; these systems cause openings to be narrow—windows are often so small that the rooms are only dimly lit even on a bright summer noon.

New trends are noticeable in Arab hill villages during the last 30–40 years, particularly since the founding of the State of Israel. Wealthy farmers leave the crowded original village and build new houses near their fields and gardens. Thus the village nuclei in the hills are often surrounded by loosely built-up areas many times their original size, where houses are strewn rather haphazardly and without comprehensive planning. Although stone continues to serve as the principal material, cement reinforced by iron rods, etc. has also come into use; it makes arches superfluous and permits the construction of large spacious homes.

Villages in the Plain. The Arab village in the plains and valleys differs from that in the Hills, both in shape and history. While villages existed there in antiquity, they were abandoned and fell into decay centuries ago, and their traces were soon obliterated. Only with the improvement of security conditions during the last 100–150 years did new villages appear in the Coastal Plain and the interior valleys. Many of these began as 'branches' of veteran hill villages, with temporary huts and shacks erected by hill peasants who lived in their fields on the Plain only during the sowing and harvesting seasons (such places often bear the Arabic names 'khirbe' = 'ruined, or temporary site,' or 'nazale' = 'descending'). Later, these sites gradually became permanent villages on their own. Other villages were founded by Arab immigrants, particularly from Egypt. In both cases, houses were built of sun-dried mud bricks, the cheapest material available in the plains. Wooden planks, or even twigs, supported the flat roof, also built of mud bricks. This style is a copy of the Egyptian village house, which has been constructed thus over thousands of years, or of the Talmud period house, when in winter Jews said a special prayer for the inhabitants of the plains 'that their houses shall not make their graves,' i.e., the roofs should not cave in under the rain and bury them.

Near the former swamps (e.g., Ḥula Valley, Ḥadera, Naḥal Poleg, etc.), where semi-nomadic tribes camped, the usual dwelling was either a simple hut of papyrus reed mats, or a goat-hair tent. After most of the villages of the plains and valleys were abandoned in the 1948 war, all these structures immediately began to decay, and the villages vanished of themselves in a few years.

The Agrarian System. The layout and mode of life of the Arab village were decisively determined by the agrarian system rooted in the Islamic code. This system was upheld after the country came under the British Mandate, and until 1964 even in the State of Israel. According to it, only very limited areas, mostly urban terrains, are 'mulk' land, i.e., in full private ownership. Two other land categories are 'metruka,' i.e., land in perpetual public ownership for the common good, e.g., grazing lands, woods, roads, market places, etc., and 'mawāt,' 'dead' or abandoned land far from inhabited places, neither cultivated nor claimed by anybody. Most farming land belongs to the 'miri' category, which is theoretically State land but in effect is held by private owners who fulfil their duty as lessees by the payment of a modest land tax. Upon completion of certain formalities, 'miri' lands can be sold or transferred. However, leaving such lands by will to a person of the testator's choice is interdicted, as the Ottoman law prescribes that parents must divide all their holdings among their children. Such division and subdivision of property over the generations often resulted in dwarf lots no longer viable for the individual farmers. This fact was aggravated by the wish of parents to give their sons equal parts; if the holding included both rich and poor soils, each heir

Children and adults in Arab villages enjoy schooling under Government auspices

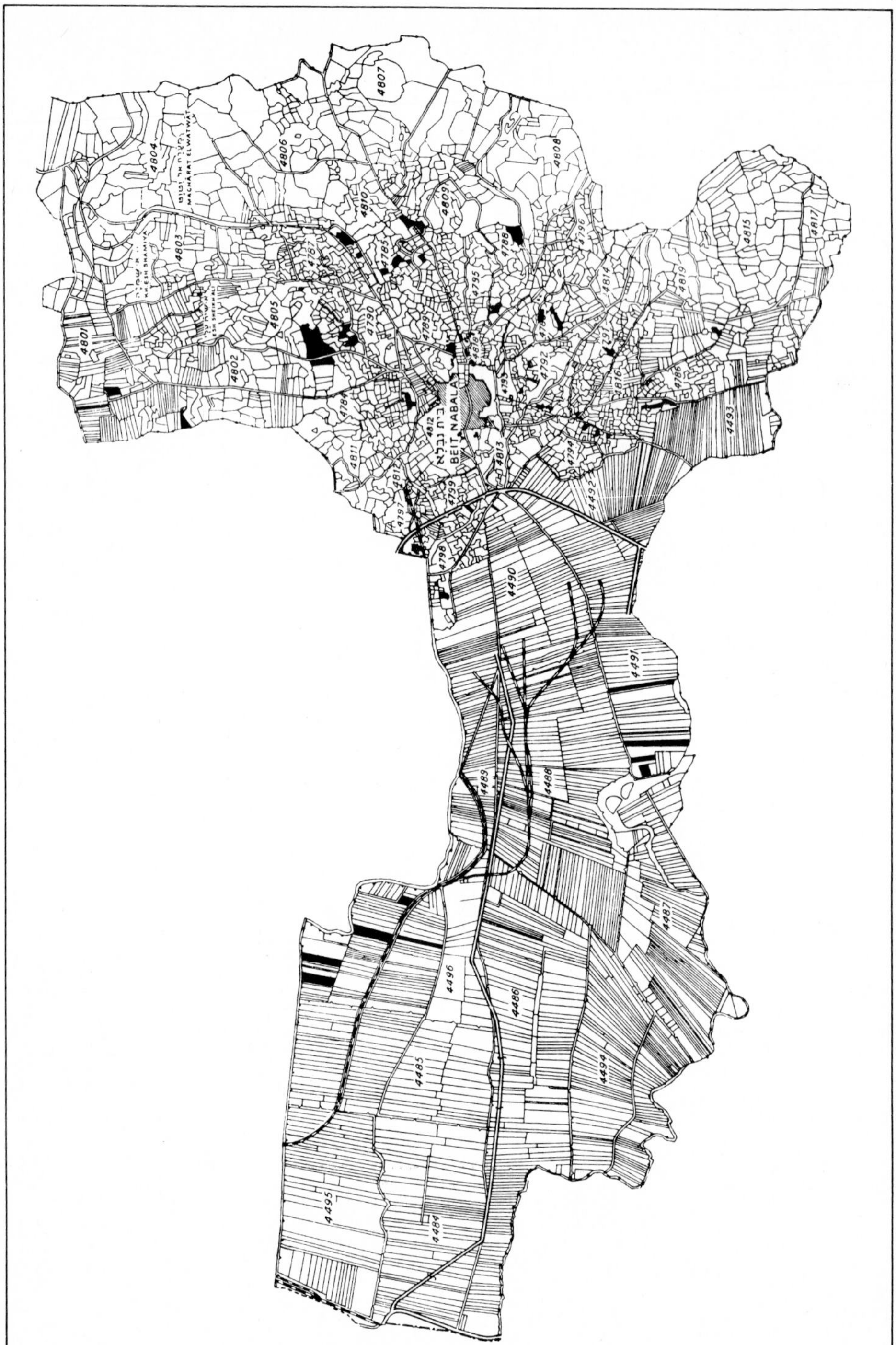

Fragmentation of holdings in Arab village before 1948 (Beit Nabāla) comprising both hilly and flat lands. Note the contrast between strip cultivation in the plain, and irregular dwarf parcels in the hills. The fields in black belong to one holding (from A. Granott, The

received two, three or more parcels of land, ranged according to their quality. The fragmentation of holdings was particularly grave in the hill regions, where the quality of the land often changes over small distances; individual parcels thus sometimes measured no more than a few yards. In the plains and valleys, in contrast, the Arabs used to divide their holdings into long, straight strips, which followed the direction of the plowing; there were sometimes holdings up to two miles long and no more than a few furrows wide.

The last category of land is termed 'waqf,' 'stayed holding.' This is property which has been consecrated by its owners for welfare purposes through religious institutions. Only a small part of this land, however, is 'true waqf' with the fruits actually donated for philanthropic purposes; most is 'popular waqf,' where the donors insert the condition that they and their offspring should enjoy its yields. As waqf land cannot be sequestrated, they were thus frequently freed of debts they had incurred. In 1965, the Knesset thoroughly revised the land code.

The efforts toward justice in the distribution of land property led to the institution of 'mushā'—parcellation of the holdings of a large family, clan, or even a whole village into fields of equal size whose cultivation rights were shifted from one peasant to the next in annual or biennial turns. No individual farmer could thus complain of poorer soil than his neighbor, for the working of poor land in one year was compensated by a better field in the next. This system, however, inevitably led to quick deterioration and exhaustion of the soil, as farmers tended to exploit the land to the maximum and invest a minimum since they knew that the next year it would pass into other hands. No precautions were thus taken against erosion; manure was dried and used as fuel instead of fertilizing the soil.

Economic and Social Development. As holdings became smaller over the generations and the quality of the soil deteriorated, the peasants' situation became ever more precarious. Often fields could be sown only with the aid of loans from wealthy Arabs at exorbitant rates of interest. When, after a short time, they were unable to repay debts, the land passed into the hands of the creditors and the peasants became tenants. A new, hitherto unknown class of wealthy landowners rose during the 19th century.

The fragmentation of holdings would have had even graver consequences, had not new land been brought into the productive cycle. Waste lands, 'mawāt,' belonging to the State were utilized, as peasants could acquire proprietory rights to them if they could show that they had cultivated them over a number of years (usually ten or more) without meeting objections from any side; the holdings could then be inscribed in their name in the land registry under 'miri' conditions. The cultivated area thus steadily increased; but the destruction of natural vegetation, the frequent plowing, and sowing of weak-rooted grains promoted soil erosion since the peasants could not afford costly terracing and other soil conservation measures. Often the terrain was finally abandoned again after several years of cultivation.

Until the present century, the Arab farm was, in general, self-sufficient, with grain as its main crop—wheat and barley in winter, durra (primitive sorghum), sesame, and other species in summer. As grain growing was practiced not only in the plains but also in the hills, it constituted another factor to hasten soil erosion. In both hills and plains grain was complemented by herds of goats and sheep which provided milk, meat, and wool. In the hills, olives were another important branch of farming. Vegetables were grown on a very limited scale near the homes to provide fresh food for the family.

Changes began to be introduced, first under the influence of Christian monasteries lying near Arab villages and, later, of Jewish settlement. Monks, many of them experienced in the Mediterranean type of agriculture, furthered the cultivation of wine grapes and other fruit and instructed the peasants in more efficient farming methods. The first rapid growth of Jewish population and settlement provided gainful employment for Arab peasants and afforded them a more or less fixed source of income. The peasants also learned ways of intensive farming from their employers. They soon copied them on their own holdings and invested the money thus earned. The spreading cities, with their Jewish population, opened a steadily widening market for Arab farm produce. Furthermore, the quest for rural and urban holdings by the Jewish newcomers caused land prices to soar, and many Arab peasants and large landowners grew rich by speculative land sales. This development took place mainly in the neighborhood of the Jewish centers in the Coastal Plain which attracted thousands of Arab villagers from the hills. Arab villages of the Coastal Plain grew rapidly; some of them attained a population of several thousands. They prospered, introduced irrigated crops and planted citrus groves on wide areas. In 1939, half of the 75,000 acres of citrus plantations in the country were in Arab possession.

This economic progress was somewhat retarded by the 1936–39 disturbances, and later by the Second World War. The war of 1948 brought a complete regrouping of the Arab rural population; inside the State of Israel the Arab inhabitants remained in 102 villages, most of them in the Hill regions. The war altered the composition of the non-Jewish population as the percentage of Moslems decreased and that of Christians and Druze rose. It also caused a profound social readjustment. Both the classes of wealthy, often absentee landlords, and of poor, exploited tenant farmers disappeared. Almost all Arab farmers (inside the pre-1967 borders) work their own land today, and discrepancies in the size of holdings are greatly diminished.

The Arab Village in the State of Israel. The events of 1948 brought undoubted suffering not only to those who followed the call of the Arab leaders and became refugees but also, as in every war, to those who stayed in the villages. Since then, however, the non-Jewish rural population has made spectacular progress and the Arab villages have reached a degree of prosperity previously unknown. Marketing conditions for produce are better than ever before, and scientific instruction and experimentation through Government institutions have brought a steep rise in efficiency and crop yields. Most of the Arab hill villages have olive groves and tobacco as their economic backbone and have also introduced intensive branches such as deciduous fruit orchards, vegetable plots, and milch cattle. Government agencies aid in reclaiming and terracing new land, and in replacing those holdings lost by the demarcation of Israel's borders or other causes. Especially important are the economic, health and social services provided by the State (water and electricity supply, building roads to the villages, clinics, schools, etc.). Producers' cooperatives are set up, and there is a beginning of industrial undertakings, especially those linked to farm produce (fruit and vegetable preserves, tobacco processing, etc.). An increasing number of villagers go to the towns and cities to work in the building trade, in industry or services, and most of their earnings are brought back to their homes. Many young villagers receive vocational or scientific training, and the differences in the living standard and mode of life between Arab and Jewish villages steadily grow smaller.

Most of the larger Arab villages have set up local councils and are included in the State budgets for development, education, and other services. The tendency is to organize the other Arab villages in the framework of regional councils along with Jewish settlements and to provide the same services and facilities that are extended to their Jewish neighbors. Local councils of Arab villages are fully assisted in their work by Government experts in municipal matters.

Rural housing schemes have been carried out in a number of Arab villages, and projects are under review for erecting villages or semiurban centers for bedouin, who are becoming settled farmers or work permanently in other occupations.

Jewish Rural Settlement

The development of Jewish agricultural settlement, its special types and social forms were determined by geographical factors (local topography, climate, soils, water, etc.) as well as by the origin of settlers, their ideology, their own financial means and those at the disposal of the settlement institutions, and the skills and principles of planners and settlers.

Geographical Distribution of Jewish Settlement. In Jewish settlement, the first nucleus took form in the Coastal Plain; it was followed by penetration into the valleys of the interior and, only in the later stages, an expansion to parts of the Hills and the Negev.

After two attempts in 1878 had faltered, settlement started with the founding of villages in different regions—Rosh Pinna on the rim of the Ḥula Valley, Zikhron Ya'aqov on the southern spur of Mt. Carmel, Petaḥ-Tiqwa near the Yarqon course, and Rishon le-Zion in the Judean Coastal Plain. Soon, however, the vicinity of Jaffa, the port of entry for all immigrants, became the principal center of Jewish settlement. By 1900, this group of villages had spread south to Be'er Tuvya; a first foothold was gained in the Northern Sharon (Ḥadera), and some 'daughter settlements' were added to the veteran villages of Zikhron Ya'aqov and Rosh Pinna.

Between 1900 and 1914, the first Jewish villages appeared in Eastern Lower Galilee and in the Kinneret Valley, and more settlements were built in the central part of the Coastal Plain. Between 1920 and 1935, the Jezreel and Ḥarod valleys were the heart of Jewish pioneering; in the Sharon, a continuous chain of villages came into being, and the ground was prepared for the comprehensive development of the Haifa Bay area.

During the 1936–39 disturbances, Jewish settlement spread to new regions. 'Tower and Stockade' villages were erected in the Bet She'an and Ḥula valleys, in the Acre Plain, and in hilly Western Upper Galilee. The Jewish population centers of the Sharon and of the Jezreel Valley were linked by a 'settlement bridge' through the Menashe Region, and those of the Jezreel and Kinneret valleys by another 'bridge' through Eastern Lower Galilee.

The most important achievement of settlement policy between the outbreak of the Second World War and the founding of the State was penetration of the Southern Coastal Plain and the Northern Negev.

In the years of statehood, the number of Jewish farming villages has trebled and today approaches 800; they extend over practically all parts of the country within the old borders of the State of Israel except the deserts of the Central and Southern Negev. After the 1967 war, settlement activity has started in the Golan and elsewhere in the new territories and has been stepped up in areas within the pre-June borders (e.g. Arava Valley, Eshkol Region, etc.).

Crystallization of Farm Types. The places of origin of the first settlers and founders of villages and their ideas of farming explain their preference for plains and valleys. Coming from Eastern and East Central Europe, which are mostly flat plains where farming was then almost equated with grain cultivation, they tried to model their new farms in the same fashion. They found fitting soil, outwardly resembling the chernozem of their countries of origin, in the swamp lands of the Coastal Plain and of the interior valleys; these malaria-infested lands were deserted and the prices consequently were not prohibitive.

Baron Edmond de Rothschild took the existing villages under his protection and founded new ones. Two decisive changes were made. Grain crops were replaced by plantations of vines, almonds, etc., with the essentially sound assumption that the farming conditions of this country resembled those of Southern France rather than those of Eastern Europe. Because these fruit species prefer lighter soils, the red sands of the Coastal Plain entered the orbit of Jewish settlement.

A third stage was reached when, in 1899, the ICA society assumed the care of these Jewish villages. Aiming to create a class of real workers of the soil instead of the farm-administrator type which had developed in the plantation villages of the Coastal Plain, ICA saw the solution in farms based on field crops. For this purpose they bought new land, heavy basalt soils in Eastern Lower Galilee (Yavne'el, Kefar Tavor, etc.).

Two types of farming, which characterize Jewish agriculture to this day, took form in the decade preceding the First World War: the citrus farm, and mixed farming based on the dairy herd. Citrus growing was organized efficiently and based on scientific research, efforts in which Y. El'azari-Volcani was prominent. The protagonist of mixed farming was A. Ruppin, who was then head of the Palestine Office of the Zionist Organization at Jaffa. Dr. Ruppin insisted that only the mixed farm ensures a stable economy, where a gain made in one or more successful branches can cover losses incurred simultaneously by another branch.

Both the citrus farm and the mixed farm are most successful in plains and valleys, where water is available for irrigation. For citrus, the red sands of the Coastal Plain are best, while mixed farming can succeed on the intermediate soil types of the Coastal Plain as well as on the heavy soils of the interior valleys.

The outposts established in new regions during the decade before Israel's statehood—the Hills and Foothills, the Northern Negev, etc.—necessitated research and experimentation with additional types of farming to suit conditions in these areas; mass settlement after 1948 increased the urgency of these activities. The requirements of expanding the national economy also called for greater variegation in farming produce. The achievements over the years of statehood can be summed up as follows: a manifold increase of production in almost all branches sufficient to fill the food requirements of the population in all items with few exceptions; large-scale introduction of 'industrial crops' (sugar beet, cotton, groundnuts, etc.), partly for export; adaptation of farm types to conditions of every geographical region, e.g., 'hill farms,' 'foothill farms,' 'plantation farms,' 'field crop farms,' 'grazing farms,' 'Arava Valley farms,' etc.; comprehensive planning of regional settlement networks, where villages are grouped around rural centers, with these, in turn, organically linked to semiurban or urban centers (see below, p. 305ff.); finally, as from the end of the 1960's, furthering of scientifically-grown, highly-intensive export crops (e.g., avocado and other tropical fruit, flowers, out-of-season vegetables and fruits).

Forms of Settlement. Four basic forms of Jewish rural settlement exist in the country—moshava, moshav, kibbutz and moshav shittufi.

The *moshava* (pl. moshavot) is a village of the regular European type, with land, buildings, farming installations, etc., all privately owned. The settler can enlarge his farm by purchasing additional land, may prefer a certain farming branch, and employ as many hired workers as he chooses. The local committee or municipal council limits itself to guarding the public interest against the individual farmer's activity. Moshavot with particularly favorable natural conditions could thus absorb hundreds, sometimes thousands of laborers, start industries, develop trade and become towns and cities of 20,000–70,000 inhabitants (e.g., Petaḥ Tiqwa, Ḥadera, Reḥovot, Rishon le-Zion, Netanya, Herzliya, Kefar Sava, Nahariya) while they maintained agriculture as an important source of livelihood.

The *kibbutz* is a communal settlement. Deganiya in the Kinneret Valley, founded in 1909, was the first small settlement of this kind ('kvutza'), whereas En Ḥarod and Tel Yosef the Ḥarod Valley became the prototype for the 'large kibbutz.' The land of nearly all the kibbutzim is national property (through the Jewish National Fund) or State property. Everything else is collectively owned by the members. The basic principle is 'every member gives to the community to the best of his abilities and receives from it according to his needs.' A new member is accepted after a candidacy of about a year by vote of the general assembly of the kibbutz members without any financial contribution on his part. A member who decides to leave the kibbutz is not entitled to compensation. All needs of the members—food, clothing, education, entertainment, recreation—are fully met by the community. There is therefore no need for the circulation of money within the kibbutz. Government is by the general assembly of members, where most decisions are passed by a simple majority. The assembly elects a management committee as well as a number of special committees to run the farming and service branches. Every member is obliged to accept and fulfil the tasks assigned by the assembly, over and above his regular job.

Each couple in the kibbutz has its own private room or flat. Children are educated in special 'children's houses' and spend several hours a day with their parents. Meals are served in the communal dining hall. Communal laundries, clothing stores, and shoemakers provide for the members' requirements.

Air view of a large kibbutz and its fields in the Ḥarod Valley

Almost all kibbutzim are based on mixed farming, although one branch or another is often more developed in the economy in accordance with the geographic conditions of the kibbutz site. Most kibbutzim have introduced industrial branches, recreation homes, tourist facilities, fishing, etc., to supplement their economies. The only theoretical limitations to the growth of a kibbutz are the land area allocated at the time of its founding or added at a later stage and the quantity of water available within the countrywide or regional planning. Non-agricultural enterprises enable the kibbutz to absorb far more members than the 'family units' of land it was given, and there is thus no obstacle for the development of kibbutzim into 'communal cities' with tens of thousands of inhabitants, as some theoreticians of the kibbutz movement had envisaged and hoped for. In practice, however, the largest kibbutzim have attained a population of 1,500–1,700 which has remained more or less stable for over two decades.

The *moshav* is a smallholders' settlement. The first village of this type was Nahalal, founded in the Jezreel Valley in 1921. Each settler works his separate plot of land, lives in his own household and draws income from his farm's produce. This independence, however, is limited by the four basic principles of moshav life: (a) National ownership of the land—each member receives, usually from the Jewish National Fund, an area no larger than he and his family can

Air view of moshav Nahalal in the Jezreel Valley

Village plan of Nahalal (by courtesy of Dr. Gerald Blake)

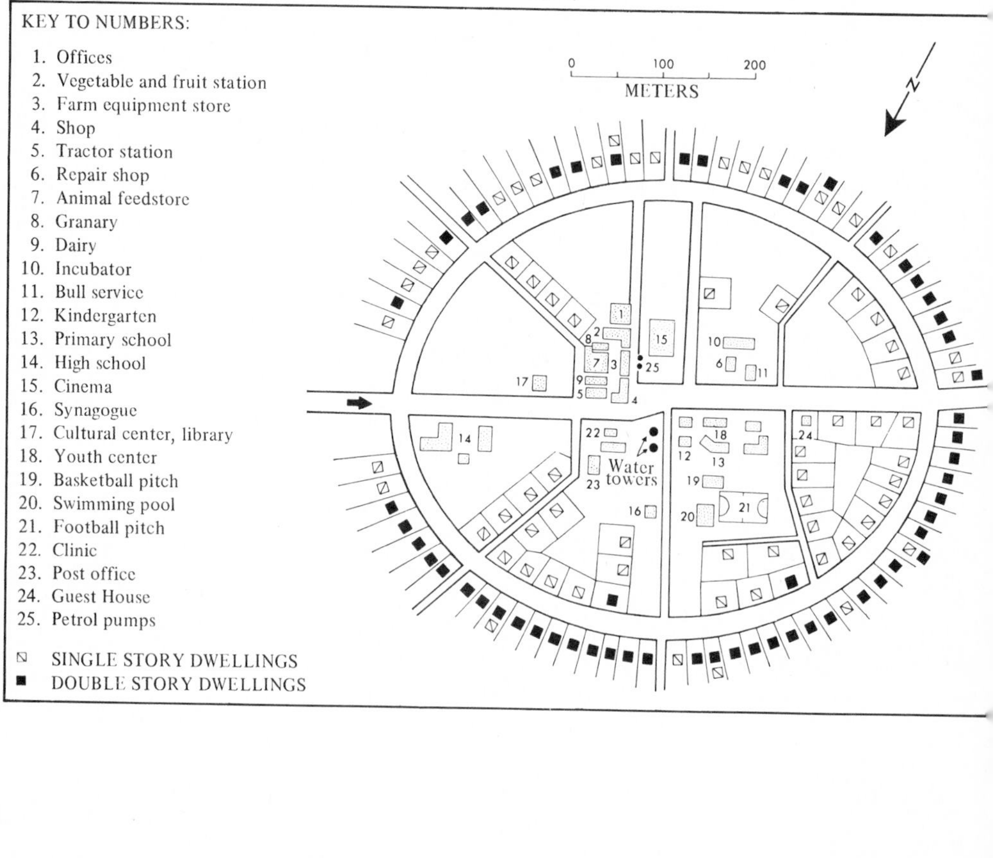

work alone; he may not divide the lot between several heirs nor enlarge it by purchasing additional land; selling the farm to a new settler must have the consent of the moshav and of the national institution which owns the land. (b) Self labor—the settler himself must carry out the work and hire labor only with the consent of the moshav authorities. (c) Mutual aid and responsibility—all members of the moshav are obliged to help in case of illness, conscription, etc.; this insures the smallholder against forces beyond his control and creates a high degree of cooperation between the members. (d) Joint marketing of produce, joint purchasing of farming and even household appliances—with this done by central agencies like those of the Labor Federation ('Tnuva' for marketing and 'Hamashbir' for supply), costs are lowered for the settlers, competition removed, and a certain equality in living standards ensured.

As in the kibbutz, the general assembly of members is the highest authority; it decides, for example, in which cases and how the principle of mutual aid applies, or whether certain farm branches (e.g., citrus, cotton, etc. which need special training and/or machinery) may be taken over as collective enterprises by the entire village or by a cooperative formed by several settlers. A managing committee elected by the assembly carries out its resolutions and takes decisions in matters of secondary importance.

The land allocated for the founding of a moshav is partitioned by the settlement institutions (usually the Settlement Department of the Jewish Agency) into family lots before the village is founded. As the individual settler is entitled to leave his farm to one heir, but not to divide or merge it with other holdings, the number of farmsteads, and consequently the population, are generally stable in a moshav. The years immediately after the founding of the State were exceptional: the availability of land in the vicinity of certain veteran settlements enabled them to absorb substantial numbers of newcomers. The largest moshavim in the country (Nahalal, Kefar Witkin, Be'er Tuvya, etc.) today number between 100 and 120 families (600–900 persons), and the smallest—from 30–40 families (approximately 150 persons).

The *moshav shittufi* is a cooperative smallholders' village, where production is carried out communally, as in the kibbutz, but where family life is self-contained, as in the moshav. The first villages of this type, Kefar Ḥittim in Lower Galilee and Shavey Ẓion in the Acre Plain, were established in 1936 and 1938, respectively. Assignment of work to the members is carried out by the daily 'work sheet,' as in the kibbutz. No gardens or fields are cultivated individually except for flower beds or a few fruit trees near the family house. Each member, both husband and wife, holds a share, the value of which is the comprehensive holding of the community divided by the total number of settlement members: the share value is calculated anew each year in accordance with changes in the total value of the settlement's holdings. By the assembly's resolutions, each family receives monthly household budget adapted to the financial situation of the village Special arrangements are made for the women; they work in the communal enterprises 3–4 hours daily; the rest of their time, as well as Friday, is devoted to the home and children.

As in the case of the kibbutz, there is no theoretical hindrance to the growth of a moshav shittufi into a populous settlement; villages of this type, however, have remained much smaller than the average kibbutz; none exceeds 400 inhabitants.

A variety of the moshav was the *moshav olim*, the immigrant smallholders' village. In the first years of statehood, the vital needs of increasing agricultural production and absorbing masses of unskilled newcomers in productive work were met by seeking a joint solution to both problems in this form of settlement Since there was no time for the immigrants to receive a thorough training beforehand, they had to be given the necessary guidance while they were founding their own farms. They often had to be taught the rudiments of farming as well as elementary rules of organization and social cooperation, even of hygiene, child care, education, etc. A host of instructors were therefore mobilized by Government and Labor Federation bodies, settlement associations, etc.

Every immigrants' settlement was allocated an area sufficient for an auxiliary farm for each settler at the beginning, and a regular-sized farm when he had gained adequate experience to handle it. In the initial stages most branches of agriculture were worked cooperatively; the farms were later divided according to the settlers' wishes. In many cases an intermediate system was devised which contributed to efficiency: large, continuous fields for specified crops (e.g., cotton, sugar beet) were formed from the parcels belonging to different farmers. Mechanized work is carried out for all together, and hand work is done by each farmer. Water installations for irrigation, farm buildings, and equipment are provided for in the budget allotted to each settlement.

Eventually, almost all moshvey olim have become self-reliant economically, adopted the basic principles of moshav life and joined the countrywide moshav movements.

Subvarieties of the moshav olim, transitional in character and adapted to local or regional conditions, were the following: *plantation villages*, which revived abandoned vineyards and groves of olives and other fruit and where settlers worked at first as hired laborers. The groves were later parcelled out and taken over at the settlers' own responsibility. Another type were *grain villages*, set up mainly in the Southern Coastal Plain where fields could at first be cultivated only extensively; the settlers worked either as hired laborers or cooperated with veteran kibbutzim or moshavim. When more water became available, they could introduce intensive farming and their villages could become regular moshavim. A third variety were the *labor villages,* founded mainly in Hill regions where not enough land was suitable for immediate farming, but could be made available through reclamation. In these cases the settlers were employed by the Jewish National Fund in vast afforestation and reclamation programs and were given a small plot of land to begin the rudiments of a farm. As more land was cleared and suited for cultivation, the plots were gradually enlarged to become, finally, full-fledged farms. A last variety are *outpost villages* where settlement is the best way to improve the security situation, but where farming can become profitable only after years of thorough reclamation work. In many of these cases, Naḥal (Pioneer Settler Corps) units of the Israel Army build the villages; soldiers remain, in many instances, after demobilization as permanent settlers.

Blueprints for the Various Settlement Forms. The veteran *moshavot* were planned upon the model of the usual village layout in Eastern or Western Europe. Dwellings were usually built along a broad, straight road, with the farmyard and structures behind it. In accordance with the security situation, buildings were set close together and sometimes connected by an outer protective wall (e.g., Metulla, north of the Ḥula Valley, Miẓpa, Ilaniya in Lower Galilee, etc.). As the moshavot grew, particularly in the Coastal Plain, the original blueprint was overshadowed by new planning, and any uniformity in the building style disappeared. Local authorities dealt only with construction of thoroughfares, administrative buildings, and other public amenities. As moshavot turned into cities, town-planning schemes replaced village blueprints.

Kibbutzim have almost all been built on previously unoccupied sites. This made it possible to prepare blueprints along rational lines, without the impediment of existing structures. Plans for communal settlements were drawn principally by the architect Richard Kauffmann, whose numerous original ideas have since been adopted everywhere. Above all, his schemes considered the functional relationship of structures and groups of buildings, but also suited the basic plan to local topography and to the social and economic conditions and special requirements of each village.

Kauffmann recommended a strict separation between the residential zone and the farmyard. The western section of the area was usually set aside for living quarters. Since in nearly every part of Israel westerly winds prevail, the inhabitants can thus enjoy the fresh sea breeze, while the farmyard smells are removed from the residential zone. The separation between the two areas is often accentuated by planting avenues of trees and lawns along the dividing line.

The communal dining hall with its kitchens is preferably in the center of the residential zone to make it easily accessible to the entire population. A good road should lead to the kitchens to facilitate the approach of the trucks hauling

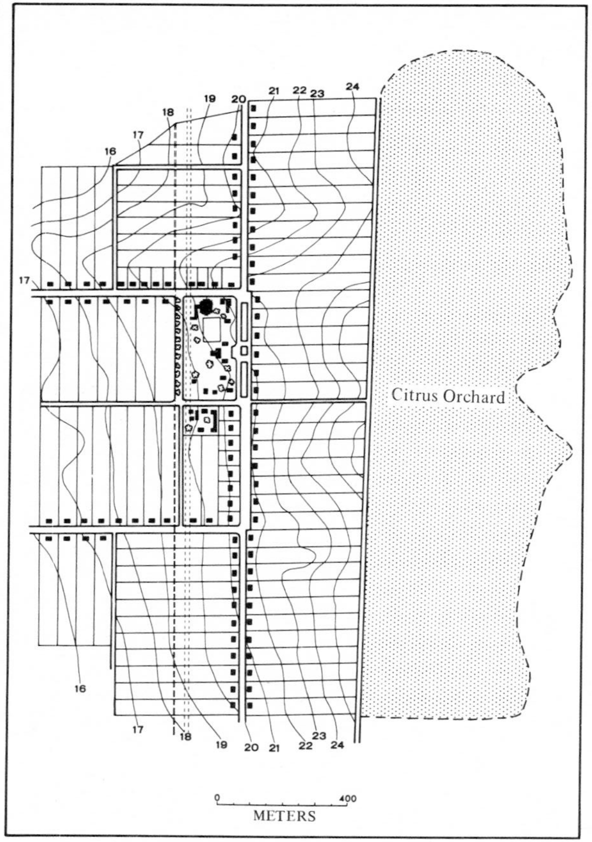

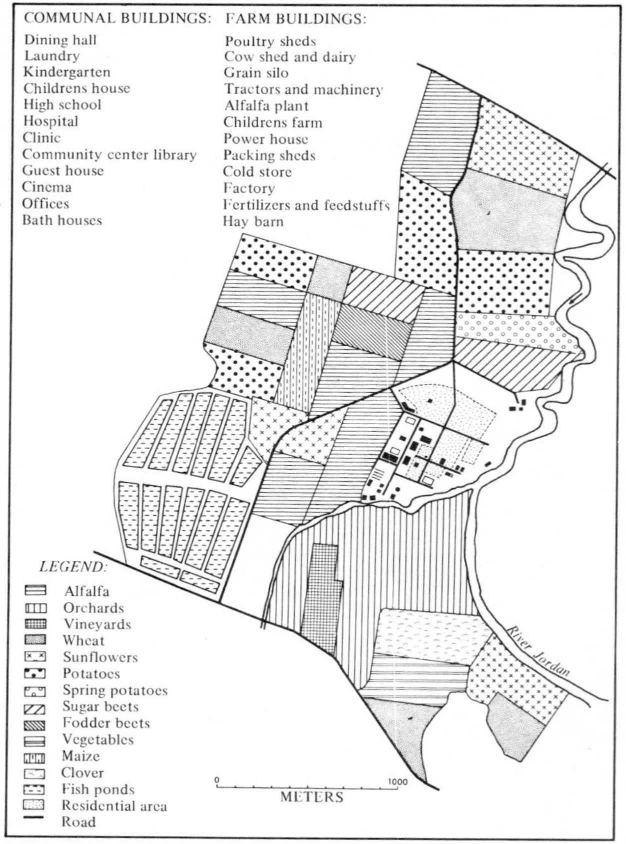

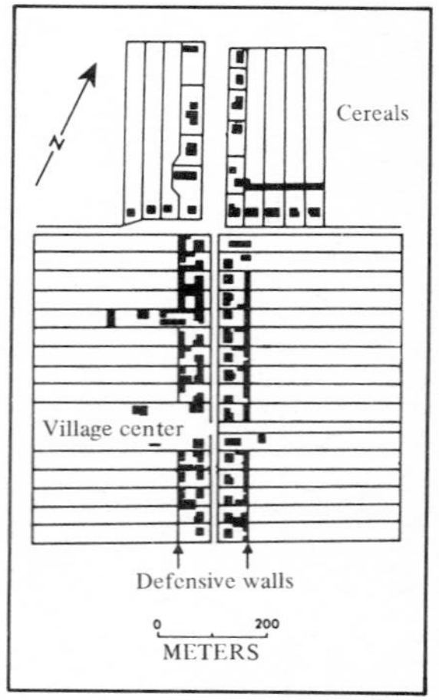

Layout of a moshava (Kefar Tavor) (below), a kibbutz (Kefar Blum) (center) and a new moshav (left) (by courtesy of Dr. Gerald Blake)

provisions. The dining hall, as well as buildings of cultural services (library, theater hall, museum, etc.) are usually surrounded by gardens. On the other hand, clothes depots, laundries, etc. are placed in the residential zone on the border of the farmyard to make for easier connection with the water, power, and steam mains.

In the larger kibbutzim, an entire group of buildings forming a compact entity inside the residential zone serves the children—nurseries, kindergartens, living quarters, school buildings. These are often grouped around a special children's dining hall. Children's quarters are given preference as to climatic conditions and, in case of need, placed on sites least exposed to possible hostile attack.

The family quarters are nearly always one-story buildings. As a rule they are covered with extended red-tile roofs, which give plenty of shade. Local conditions have been taken into account, as in the hot Kinneret and Bet She'an valleys where a shaded porch surrounds each building and windows open to the dominant wind direction with ventilation gaps inserted below them, or on the high ridges of Upper Galilee where roofs are built of reinforced concrete to withstand the raging winter storms. Until recently, most family quarters were elongated buildings with three to eight family rooms all opening onto a common porch. Today, as most couples have their one- or two-room apartments complete with bathroom, etc., two-family houses are preferred, often with entrances on opposite sides of the building to ensure greater privacy.

The residential zone is traversed by driveways, avenues of trees, or pathways which are straight or slightly curving.

In the farmyard, buildings are grouped in accordance with their functional relationship. Cowsheds, for example, often circle the milking shed with its modern milking machines. Cattle sheds, sheep pens and poultry runs are provided with their own barns for straw and fodder. The sheep pens must be at a site whence the flocks can reach their grazing grounds without risk of harming gardens, vegetable plots or crops on the way. Wind direction also plays a part in choosing sites for different farm buildings. Poultry runs thus generally form the last link in the wind direction. Industrial buildings must be placed where they are most easily accessible to the heavy trucks transporting raw materials and finished products.

For the *moshav*, adequate planning is decisive for the smooth functioning of its economic and social life. The blueprints for the first moshavim, like those of the kibbutzim, were designed by R. Kauffmann, who preferred a circular layout. Institutions shared by the community (cultural centers, synagogues, schools, kindergartens, libraries, dairies, storehouses, etc.) are located in the center. The settlers' houses form a wide circle around them; all inhabitants are thus ensured easy access to the village institutions. The farm buildings are located in an outer circle with gardens and fields forming ever wider concentric circles. The principle used is that the more intensively a field is cultivated, the nearer it must be to the farmyard. This arrangement also facilitates water supply and irrigation from the water tower located in the center of the village, on the highest point of the area. This layout, however, is dependent on topographical conditions, and, in fact, only feasible on level land of more or less uniform quality; moreover, it is now regarded as obsolete from the security point of view.

During the first years of statehood, when moshavim had to be set up at top speed, a far simpler layout was generally used. The small houses were built at equal distances along one straight road, or arranged in a T, H or U pattern, so that the immigrant settler could live as close as possible to the land he was to work; the individual holding was planned as a square behind the living quarters. But as the distances between the houses must thus be increased, villages frequently extended over 2–3 km (one to two miles); the walking distance to the moshav's central institutions became unbearably long, and social life suffered.

More recently, preference has been given to settlement blueprints with three or more roads radiating from the center, with 35 meters (38 yards) the maximum distance between houses. This is achieved by limiting the individual field and garden plots to the most intensively cultivated crops; the rest of the holdings remain at greater distances from the built-up area.

The moshav Mesillat Ẓion, on the border between the Judean Hills and Foothills, has been laid out rather compactly

For the *moshav shittufi,* layouts intermediate between those of the kibbutz and moshav are most practicable; the residential area is similar to that of the moshav; the farmyard and field layout, however, are carried out on the lines valid for the kibbutz.

Regional Settlement Schemes. After the War of Independence, settlement of entire regions in the framework of comprehensive planning became feasible in different parts of the country. Such planning permitted best exploitation of the natural features of these regions, facilitated the absorption of the maximum number of settlers in productive employment, and hastened the integration of new immigrants into Israel's life.

The largest region thus developed is the Lakhish Area, in parts of the Southern Coastal Plain and of the southern Judean Foothills. This area is divided into subregions, according to climatic, topographical and soil conditions. Each subregion is assigned special agricultural tasks: the western part specializes in citrus and market gardening; the central one in grain and industrial crops, mostly irrigated; and the eastern in grains, tobacco, grapes, carobs and sheep grazing.

The bulk of settlements in all new regions are smallholders' villages of 40–100 families, arranged in groups of three to six around a 'rural center,' which includes a school, clinic, tractor and machine repair shop, dairy, storehouses, central grocery, cultural institutions, etc., all of which serve the surrounding settlements. This arrangement permits the concentration of immigrants from one country in each village, and thus diminishes danger of friction between different elements. On the other hand, the rural center, where children attend the same school, serves as a common meeting ground and furthers amalgamation of the various elements. Costs for the individual settlement are reduced since all institutions serve 200–400 families simultaneously.

Several rural centers, with their dependent villages, are in turn linked to a semiurban or urban center, which serves up to 10,000 or more families. Here is found the regional administration, factories using raw material produced on the farms of the region, theaters, secondary and vocational schools, hospitals, sport centers, etc.

The Lakhish Region provides a sample of all these arrangements. It receives its water for intensive farming from the National Water Carrier. Its central town is Qiryat Gat which, in 1970, numbered approximately 17,500 inhabitants. Its first factories—for cotton ginning, Scotch tape, ice, bakeries, etc.—were soon followed by larger enterprises, e.g., cotton and wool spinning and weaving mills, a huge sugar factory, etc.

Communication lines link the villages to their respective rural centers and these, in turn, to the central town. Qiryat Gat, for example, is connected not only

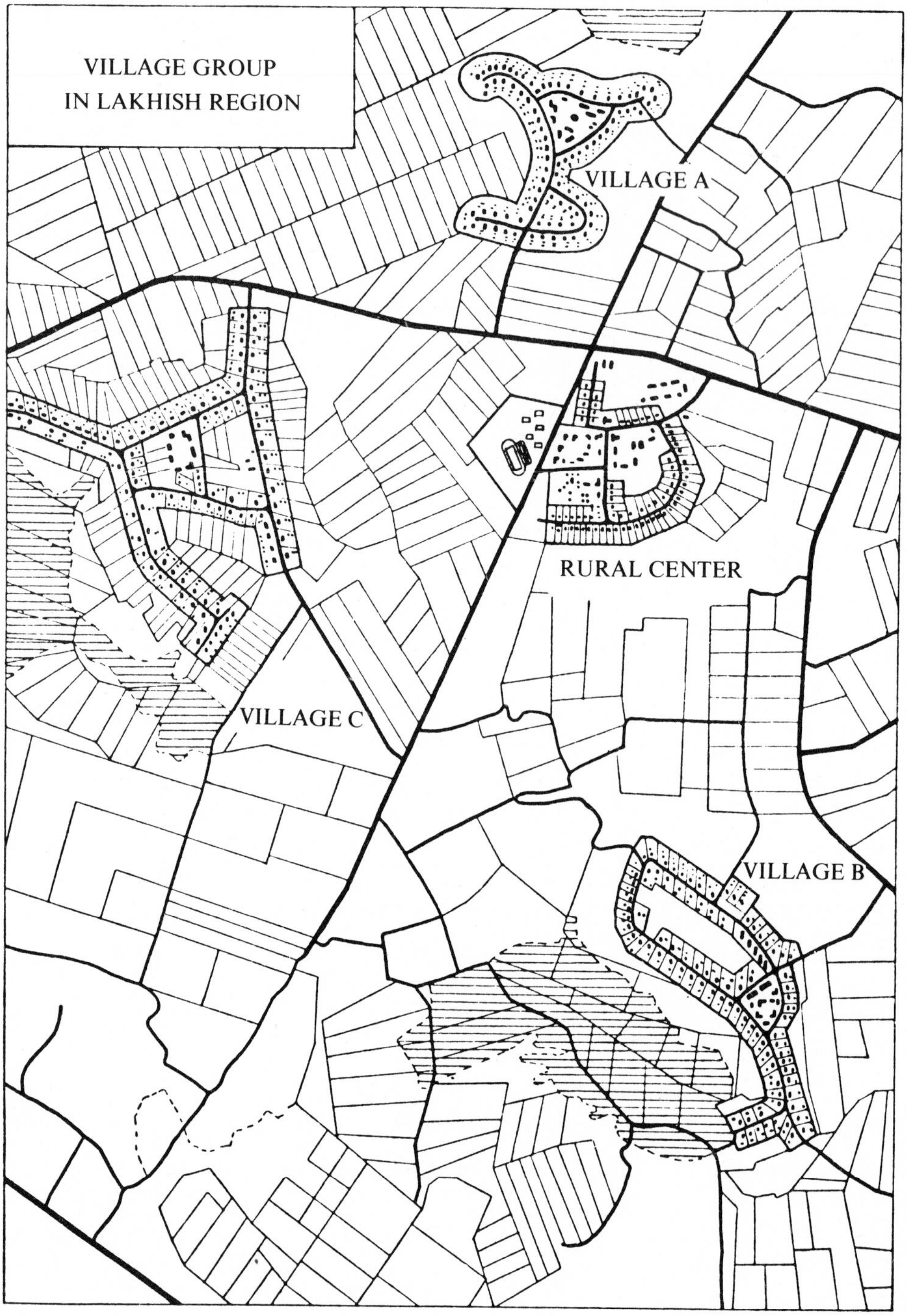
VILLAGE GROUP
IN LAKHISH REGION
VILLAGE A
RURAL CENTER
VILLAGE C
VILLAGE B

by roads to all rural centers and villages of the Lakhish Region but also by first-class highways and a railway line to Tel Aviv, Jerusalem, Beersheba, Ashdod and Ashqelon.

Other areas under comprehensive development include the southern Jezreel Valley ('Ta'anakh Region'), parts of the northwestern Beersheba Region ('Merḥavim' and other regions), and the Adullam Region in the Judean Foothills southwest of Jerusalem, where large-scale soil reclamation had to precede all settlement activity. Some areas are yet in the opening stages of regional development, e.g., those of Adorayim, the southern continuation of the Adullam Region where the sparseness of rainfall adds to the difficulties presented by the poor hill soil, of Mount Gilboa, where most of the terrain is earmarked for afforestation, or of Korazim north of the Sea of Galilee, where, after the removal of the heavy basalt boulders from the slopes, prospects are fair for fruit and out-of-season crops. Special cases of regional planning are met in the Eshkol Region and the Arava Valley, where mild winters favor specialized farm branches, or the wide Arad Region in the northeastern Negev, where settlement is to be based almost exclusively on mining and industry.

A newer project, and one of the largest, is that for the central parts of Upper and Lower Galilee. New farming villages will be based on deciduous fruit and vines, tobacco, and the tending of sheep, poultry, and fur animals. The rural centers are to become more populous than those in other regions, since they are to contain, besides the services to the surrounding villages (to which shall belong existing non-Jewish settlements), small, and perhaps medium industrial undertakings. Larger factories are to be built in at least two towns of Central Galilee.

Lastly, fairly close settlement to be based on both farming and industry is envisaged for the Eshkol Region of the northwestern Negev, which is about to receive water from the National Carrier. Further schemes for the Golan, the Lower Jordan Valley, etc. have been prepared since the Six Day War.

Urban Settlement

Towns and Cities in History

Antiquity of Towns in the Country. The history of most towns and urban centers goes back long before the Arab conquest of the 7th century C.E.; many even date from the second or third millennium B.C.E. If a number of villages ('moshavot') turned towns, and satellite towns of the major cities are disregarded, as well as some of the newest centers founded in Israel after 1948, the only exception is the town of Ramla, which was built in 717 C.E. by the Omayyads to replace nearby Lod as the Arab capital of the country. On the other hand, numerous ancient towns ceased to exist after the Moslem occupation, and urban settlement completely disappeared from whole districts, whether through slow decline and dilapidation as in the Negev, or through deliberate and systematic destruction, as in the Coastal Plain. Even the towns of the hill regions were abandoned or degraded to the rank of villages (e.g., Adorayim in Judea, Gophna and Shomron in Samaria, Ẓippori in Lower Galilee, etc.). Other centers, particularly those sacred to Christianity, lay vacant and neglected through centuries, and revived in the late 18th century after the Turks had conceded Europeans the right to settle there and erect religious institutions (e.g., Nazareth, Bethlehem, Ramallah). In the history of towns, Safed and Tiberias have a special place: Safed was at best an insignificant hamlet until the Crusaders fortified it as one of their strongholds in Galilee. It later flourished as a result of the large Jewish community which concentrated there from the 15th century. Tiberias was founded in Herod's time near the Biblical site of Raqqat (Rakath) and named after the Emperor Tiberius. It served as a spiritual center of Judaism until the early Middle Ages. Later it almost disappeared, but it grew anew in the 16th century when a Jewish community led by Don Joseph Nassi assembled there and briefly hoped to achieve some sort of independence.

Economic Foundations of Ancient Towns. In this part of the world, as everywhere else, trade and commerce formed the principal economic basis for country towns in antiquity. Peasants of the surrounding villages brought their produce to town to barter it against wares of local tradesmen. It appears, however, that during all periods of history farming also constituted an important occupation for city dwellers, whether as a principal or subsidiary source of income (the Bible tells, for instance, of communal threshing floors in front of city gates). This fact was undoubtedly the result of the precarious security situation through most periods of history: many farmers preferred to live within fortified towns without forsaking their holdings, even if this meant dwelling at a considerable distance from their fields and gardens.

In towns near crossroads, trade was lively: local produce was exchanged for wares brought by the caravans, often from great distances, and traders arriving from different directions exchanged goods at these meeting places. At certain spots near the 'border of the desert and the sown' (e.g., Hebron, Beersheba), hill-farming produce was traded for goods of the nomadic shepherds, and sometimes even for luxuries brought from Southern Arabia, East Africa, or India along the important highway linking Eilat to Gaza. Similarly, Bet She'an served as a gateway to the Syrian Desert, to Damascus, and to Mesopotamia.

Services to caravans and travelers (water, food, and other provisions) often provided an important source of income for townspeople, particularly in the Nabatean cities of the Negev (see above, p. 209).

Of a different character were the harbor towns of the Mediterranean and Red Sea shores, where fishing, seafaring, and shipbuilding constituted additional lines of occupation. In some cities, such as Gaza, Ascalon or Eilat, merchants who traveled along continental highways met traders who plied international sea routes, and these contacts livened commerce and formed the basis for specialized trades. In many cases, the principal sea town developed inland, beyond the barren sand dune belt and near the Via Maris (the ancient Sea Road), but it maintained intimate links with the sea trade through 'daughter cities' lying on the shore itself. Distances between the former and the latter sometimes amounted to 3–7 kilometers (2–4 miles). Thus two harbor towns, Maiumas and Anthedon, served ancient Gaza, Ashdod Yam ('Marine Ashdod') was the port for Ashdod, Yavne Yam—for Yavne, and Tyre-on-Sea, built out on its narrow land tongue, had a 'daughter-town,' 'Tyre-on-the-Land.'

Urban Centers Founded by Zionist Settlers. The urban centers founded by Zionist settlers before Israel's statehood had at first been planned as villages but developed into towns and cities because of particularly favorable conditions. Most of these lie in the central section of the Coastal Plain, e.g., Ḥadera, Netanya, Petaḥ Tiqwa, Rishon le-Ẓion, Reḥovot. Since all these 'moshavot' had, in their early days, fairly large areas of cultivable land sufficient for many farmsteads, they soon needed additional hands. Laborers, finding more or less permanent employment in agricultural work, took up residence there. This increase necessitated more economic, social and cultural services. This, in turn, created additional employment and a further population growth. Some of the trade shops in the moshavot eventually grew into small or medium-sized factories and sold their produce to other parts of the country, and even abroad. Some enterprises, however, had been planned from the start to attain a wider scope. The first of these were the large wine cellars built by Baron E. de Rothschild at Rishon le-Ẓion and Zikhron Ya'akov. Reḥovot, where the Agricultural Research Station of the Jewish Agency (now of the State and the Hebrew University) and the Sieff Institute—today the Weizmann Institute—were founded, became an important center of learning and at the same time broadened its economic scope and foundations to absorb additional population.

A separate chapter are the satellite towns and cities of the Tel Aviv conurbation (Ramat Gan, Bene Beraq, Ramat ha-Sharon, etc.) although these, too, began either as farming villages or as garden suburbs. Different from all of these centers, however, is Afula, which is also the only one outside the Coastal Plain, in the Jezreel Valley: although planned to become the urban center for its region, for a long time it did not fulfil this hope. Until 1948 it numbered hardly 3,000 inhabitants since the farmer settlers of the Valley preferred Haifa, still at a convenient distance for them; only now, as a result of industrialization and development, has Afula grown to about 17,000 inhabitants.

New Towns and Cities. Since the State of Israel was created, more moshavot in the Coastal Plain have attained town status (Nahariya, Herzliya, Kefar Sava) or at least assumed an urban or semiurban character (Zikhron Ya'aqov, Ra'ananna, Nes Ẓiona, Gedera). Country towns formerly inhabited by Arabs exclusively (Ramla, Medjdal=Ashqelon, Beersheba, Bet She'an) or partly (Safed, Tiberias) were in 1948 abandoned by all or many of their inhabitants and later repopulated by Jewish immigrants. This necessitated the creation of entirely new economic foundations for such towns and often a remodeling of their town-planning blueprints.

In a third group are those towns laid out in the period of statehood to serve as centers of regional settlement projects or to fulfil special economic tasks. Thus, Eilat was built as Israel's gateway to the Red Sea and Indian Ocean; from the start it was also envisaged to become a first-rate tourist center. Dimona was initially intended to serve as a residential quarter for laborers of the Dead Sea Works and the Oron phosphate mines, and after a short time it was provided with large textile factories and other industries to form a broad basis for its economy. Arad was established to house further employees of the Dead Sea Works, and

LEGEND

Founded	Town, City	Urban Settlement
Before 1917	●	●
1918-1931	■	■
1932-1947	▲	▲
1948-1954	□	□
1955-1965	○	○
In administered areas	×	

0 10 20 30 km
0   10   20 miles

Qiryat Shemona

Nahariya
Acre   Maalot
Karmiel   Safed
Haifa
Tiberias
Nazareth
Afula
Bet She'an
Hadera   Jennin
Netanya   Tul Karm
Nablus
Herzliya   Kefar Sava
Petaḥ Tiqwa
Tel Aviv-Jaffa
Bat Yam
Rishon le-Zion   Lod
Ramla   Ramallah
Rehovot
Jericho
Ashdod
Bet Shemesh   Jerusalem
Ashqelon   Bethlehem
Gaza
Qiryat Gat
Sederot   Hebron
Deir el-Balah   Netivot
Raḥah
Ofaqim
el-'Arish
Beersheba   Arad
Dimona
Yeroḥam

Miẓpeh Ramon

–·–·– Border, armistice lines
        existing since 1949

······· Border, armistice lines
         before June, 1967

------ Cease-fire lines,
        since June, 1967

Eilat

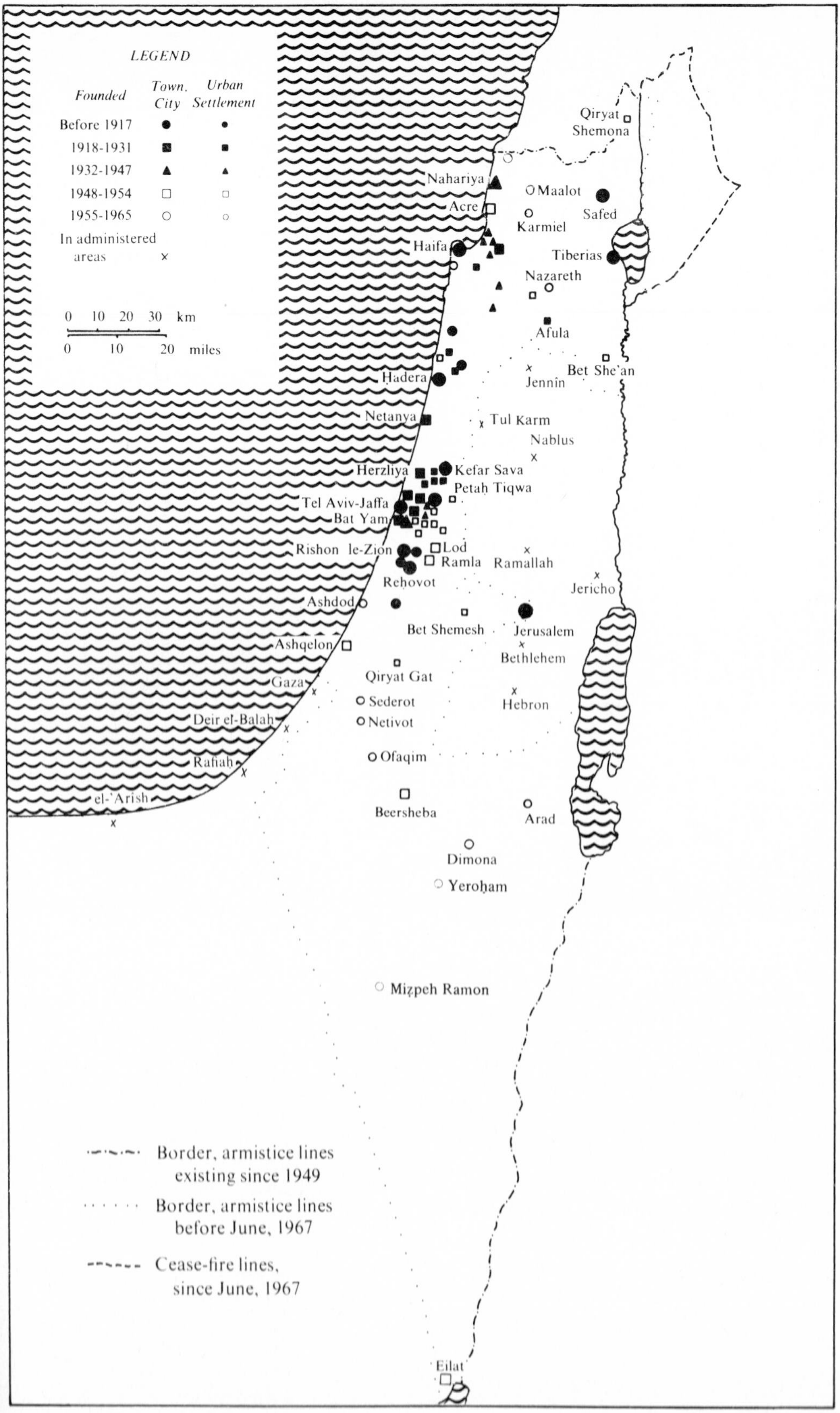

Urban settlements in the country

AGGLOMERATIONS OF 10,000 INHABITANTS AND MORE IN ISRAEL

Name	*8.11.1948*	*31.12.1969*	*1982 forecast*[2]	*Townplanning outline scheme*
Acre[1]	4,016	33,500	52,000	65,000
Afula	2,504	16,700	32,000	50,000
Ashdod	—	35,600	75,000	140,000
Ashqelon[1]	—	39,200	60,000	80,000
Bat Yam[1]	2,325	76,600	80,000	110,000
Beersheba[1]	—	74,500	100,000	140,000
Bene Beraq[1]	9,305	69,700	80,000	100,000
Bet She'an[1]	—	12,200	16,000	20,000
Bet Shemesh	—	10,100	. .	. .
Dimona	—	21,600	32,000	50,000
Eilat[1]	—	13,200	32,000	50,000
Giv'atayim[1]	9,632	44,400	50,000	60,000
Ḥadera[1]	11,811	30,500	45,000	60,000
Haifa[1]	98,618	214,500	300,000	350,000
Herzliya[1]	5,287	37,300	45,000	55,000
Hod ha-Sharon	3,514	12,600	18,000	20,000
Ḥolon[1]	9,561	84,700	125,000	175,000
Jerusalem[1]	83,984	283,100[6]	250,000[7]	320,000[7]
Kefar Sava[1]	5,516	23,700	35,000	40,000
Lod[1]	1,056	28,000	36,000	45,000
Nahariya[1]	1,722	21,100	30,000	35,000
Nazareth[1]	18,500[3]	32,900[4]	50,000[5]	60,000[5]
Nes Ẓiona	2,355	12,000	15,000	18,000
Netanya[1]	11,589	62,500	90,000	130,000
Or Yehuda	—	12,000	. .	12,000
Pardes Ḥanna-Karkur	. .	13,300	. .	. .
Petaḥ Tiqwa[1]	21,879	80,000	90,000	110,000
Qiryat Atta	3,229	25,000	38,000	60,000
Qiryat Bialik	2,107	13,900		
Qiryat Motzkin	3,483	14,500	60,000	90,000
Qiryat Yam	910	16,500		
Qiryat Gat	—	17,400	38,000	50,000
Qiryat Ono	—	14,200	. .	. .
Qiryat Shemona	—	15,400	30,000	40,000
Qiryat Tiv'on	. .	10,000	14,000	16,000
Ra'ananna	5,912	12,300	16,000	20,000
Ramat Gan[1]	17,162	112,600	110,000	130,000
Ramat ha-Sharon	1,107	16,600	. .	. .
Ramla[1]	1,547	29,900	45,000	55,000
Rehovot[1]	12,522	35,600	45,000	55,000
Rishon le-Ẓion[1]	10,433	44,100	70,000	120,000

AGGLOMERATIONS OF 10,000 INHABITANTS AND MORE IN ISRAEL

Name	*8.11.1948*	*31.12.1969*	*1982 forecast*[2]	*Townplanning outline scheme*
Rosh ha-Ayin	—	11,100	16,000	25,000
Safed[1]	2,317	13,100	20,000	25,000
Shefar'am	. .	10,500	. .	. .
Tayyibe	. .	10,900	. .	. .
Tel Aviv-Jaffa[1]	248,459	382,900	500,000	550,000
Tiberias[1]	5,555	23,600	35,000	45,000
Tirat Karmel	—	13,200	. .	14,000
Umm al-Faḥm	. .	11,500	. .	. .
Upper Nazareth	—	13,200	5	5

[1] Status of township.
[2] For this date a total population of 4 million is anticipated.
[3] Figure of 31.12.1949.
[4] Without Upper Nazareth.
[5] Together with Nazareth.
[6] Including East Jerusalem.
[7] Excluding East Jerusalem.

thereupon to become a large center of chemical and other industries. Ashqelon was founded as a site of industry, recreation, and tourism in the Southern Coastal Plain; Ashdod as Israel's second-largest port on the Mediterranean seaboard; Qiryat Mal'akhi as a semiurban center in closely settled rural surroundings of the Southern Coastal Plain; Qiryat Gat as the urban center of the Lakhish Region. Bet Shemesh was built to absorb greater numbers of settlers in the Jerusalem Corridor area, particularly on an industrial basis. In the north, new urban and semiurban centers include Migdal ha-Emeq and Yoqne'am on the circumference of the Jezreel Valley, Qiryat Naẓrat in Lower Galilee, Karmi'el on the border of Lower and Upper Galilee, Ma'alot in Western Upper Galilee, and Qiryat Shemona and Ḥaẓor in and near the Ḥula Valley. All these settlements are planned to draw industry and productive services to hitherto underpopulated regions and to create a closely interlocked rural and urban economy and a more balanced distribution of population over all parts of Israel.

The growth of exaggerated population concentrations in one or several huge centers is a complicated problem today in many countries; in Israel, this is aggravated by the small size of the country and by its special security situation. Some countries have been aided in this respect, to a certain degree, by a difference in wage levels between regions of dense and sparse population which attracts enterprises to the latter. In Israel, however, this factor is absent; on the contrary, commodities are often more expensive at outlying places like Eilat, so that workers there must be paid certain premiums. To attract investors and settlers to new towns and cities, other means must be used, such as cheap building land and housing, loans, subsidies and tax exemptions. Such a policy is successful, particularly where enterprises also find geographical advantages such as markets and raw materials close at hand to even out high transport costs and other overheads. This explains, in part, why larger enterprises often show greater readiness to go to 'development towns' than do small undertakings. Proximity of raw materials, for instance, has been decisive in attracting to Beersheba industries of ceramics, insecticides and other chemicals; to Qiryat Gat, Qiryat Shemona and Bet She'an—cotton gins and spinning mills; to Afula and Qiryat Gat—sugar factories, to Ramla and Bet Shemesh—cement plants, etc. The Sharon, the Southern Coastal Plain and the Jezreel, Kinneret and Ḥula valleys are seen as the natural location of food-processing and preserve plants. Markets explain placing of garages and machine shops for farming equipment in centers of developing agricultural regions, e.g., Qiryat Gat, Beersheba, Qiryat Shemona, etc.

Industries which can be drawn with relative ease toward development regions are those of comparatively low transport costs; a case in point are diamond-cutting and polishing plants now found in many new towns, from Eilat in the south to Qiryat Shemona in the north.

Tourism and recreation have greatly aided the progress of veteran towns, and of villages which have become towns or cities during the period of statehood (Tiberias, Safed, Nahariya, Zikhron Yaaqov, Netanya, Herzliya) as well as of new centers, e.g., Eilat, Ashqelon, Caesarea.

In the early years of statehood, housing was a decisive criterion in settling new immigrants in towns abandoned in the War of Independence as well as in new development centers, even if the immigrants could not be given immediate employment. In the first stages of development, public works and investment (such as construction of houses and roads, land reclamation, etc.) provided the livelihood for most of the newcomers. Incidentally, these activities in most cases constitute the necessary groundwork for industrialization of a new center. When factories are opened in development towns, a growing percentage of the local labor force gains permanent employment in partly skilled or skilled work.

Planning and Building in Ancient Cities. Urban settlements existed in this country at least since the Early Bronze Period (third millennium B.C.E.) and perhaps since the preceding Chalcolithic Era.* The typical remnant of an ancient city here, as in many parts of the Middle East, is a flat-topped, very steep-sided and often rectangular hill or hillock, called 'tel' or 'tell' in both Hebrew and Arabic. What

* Jericho, assumed to be the world's oldest city, dates back to the Neolithic Era (see p. 196).

today most strikes the spectator is the extremely small area of towns built on such mounds—several thousands lived crowded on 5 acres or less; the most important and populous cities (Ḥaẓor, Jerusalem) covered barely more than 6–7 ha (15–17 acres). As in the case of ancient villages, this crowding stems from the need to build a strong wall and to defend it with the relatively small resources and manpower of the city. To save space, lanes between rows of houses were just wide enough to permit the passage of a beast of burden, and often houses were built against the city wall itself (see Joshua, II, 15: 'For her house was upon the town wall, and she dwelt upon the wall').

Usually, cities had only one gate, which was reinforced by all technical means available. Open spaces on both sides of the gate served the public need as assembly square, market place, threshing floor, court of judgment, etc. In those times of peril and frequent warfare, cities sought to perfect their fortification techniques; thus revetments, steep, slippery glacis and deep moats in front of city walls came into use in the Hyksos epoch (1750–1550 B.C.E.). As seen in Lakhish and many other sites, the gate of the inner wall was frequently placed at some distance from the outer one. The enemy, having forced the outer gate, had to pass through the narrow corridor between the two walls still held by the defenders, who then rolled heavy rocks or poured boiling water or oil upon the invader. The casemate system divided the space between the two walls by partitions into chambers used for food and weapon storage; at Lakhish, an archive of inscribed sherds was discovered in a casemate chamber near the gate.

The palace of the local king or ruler was in the center of many Canaanite towns and at their highest point. Another wall often surrounded such an 'akropolis' which, with its structures and courtyards, sometimes occupied half or more of the city area.

Upon enemy conquest, the town was first burned down and its buildings razed. A new town was later built on the rubble. The usual mound therefore contains strata of different cities, sometimes ten, fifteen or (as at Ḥaẓor) even more than twenty, each new one built upon the foundations of its predecessor. Thin layers of ashes mark the seams between the strata and testify to the destruction that preceded each new city. To stand firm, a new wall had to be set back from the outer rim of its predecessor, so that the city area shrank gradually with repeated conquests and reconstructions, and the typical shape of the 'tel' resulted.

The influence of Hellenistic civilization and the improved security situation under Roman rule brought about a decisive change in town planning. The Hellenistic cities on the Mediterranean seaboard as well as towns of the interior (Shomron, Ẓippori, etc.) and the cities of the Dekapolis in Transjordan had much larger areas than earlier urban agglomerations. The new cities boasted magnificent edifices—pagan temples, theaters, hippodromes, palaces of governors, etc., besides spacious, ornate buildings erected by well-to-do citizens. Columns adorned house entrances and also surrounded public squares. Houses were provided with stone pipes leading water even to the upper stories and a good sewage system was installed. Late Roman and Byzantine art added beautiful mosaic floors to these achievements.

In the Middle Ages, the country's cities declined in number, and those which continued to exist shrank in area and took on a drab appearance. With the worsening security situation, protective walls had to be built again, but only very little has been preserved of those structures. An exception, again, is Ramla, where a few remnants provide fine examples of Omayyad architecture. The Crusaders built grand castles and fortresses to keep their hold over the countryside, but of the main cities, only Acre has impressive remains of some Crusader structures. The Mameluke conquest entailed further decline, and the Turks did very little to improve the appearance of urban agglomerations. A decisive change took place only since the end of the 19th century.

Towns began to expand beyond their former limits. Where Christians were influential (Nazareth, Bethlehem, Ramallah, Ramla), towns soon took on better shape than purely Moslem ones. Hill towns such as Safed, Nazareth, Ramallah, Bethlehem or Hebron, where hewn stone constituted the principal building material, had a better appearance than agglomerations of the plains and valleys (e.g., Bet She'an, Jericho, Lod, Gaza), where mainly mud bricks were used for building. Small towns along the rims of the hill areas, like Shefar'am, Jennīn and Tul Karm, resemble the hill towns rather than those of the plains. The use of black basalt as a building stone gave Tiberias its particular character.

Two Arab towns, Beersheba and Nablus, were newly built in the first decades of the 20th century. Beersheba was set up by the Turks as an administrative center to restrain the unruly bedouin. The town planning was done by German engineers, who laid out ruler-straight roads intersecting at right angles and constructed a few government edifices of solid stone and covered with red tile roofs reminiscent of the style then in vogue in Central Europe. But within this modern setting, Arab inhabitants were allowed to erect mud-brick hovels, and due to the dry climate and shortage of water there was hardly a trace of greenery in the town.

Those veteran moshavot which gradually assumed urban character were aided in their development by the original layout along one or several broad roads. Besides the old, modest, one-family houses began to appear structures of two or more stories, built of concrete, flat-roofed and fashioned along straight, clear lines accentuating the horizontal. In these towns, a strange contrast is frequently still noticeable between the remaining structures of rural character and those erected at later stages.

Narrow lane in the Old City of Acre

Until 1948, the built-up area of veteran moshavot did not always expand rationally. Private owners could sell farming land for building purposes, so that orange groves were frequently uprooted and gardens and fields given up for building, while nearby sand dunes or rocky slopes remained unused. Not always were provisions made to separate residential, commercial and industrial areas. Only toward the end of the 1930's did municipalities begin to set aside appropriate plots for industrial areas, which they provided with installations for water, electricity, sewage, etc., to attract new enterprises and create employment facilities for the growing population. At about the same time, municipal authorities of former moshavot began to plant public gardens and generally improve the outer appearance.

Immediately upon cessation of hostilities in the War of Independence, Israel was confronted with the double task of absorbing mass immigration and resettling abandoned urban agglomerations. Empty structures were put under the authority of the Custodian of Abandoned Property to be rented to the newcomers housed in them. The first immigration wave after statehood occupied vacant dwellings in towns near the main cities, such as Ramla, Lod, Yavne, etc.; these agglomerations were for a while almost as crowded and derelict as when they had been inhabited by Arabs, since little could be done to repair and improve the existing structures. When a few months later all usable flats in these towns were occupied, newcomers were sent to towns in other parts of the country, e.g., Ashqelon, Bet She'an, Tiberias, Safed, Beersheba.

In the middle of 1950, all these existing dwellings had already been distributed; modern long-range planning of urban development was then started, and its guiding principles began to crystallize. A forecast and outline scheme for each town's future growth, which took into account geographical and economic assets and limitations, was prepared.

At first, one- or two-story single-row houses were the rule, with space allotted between them for gardens or auxiliary farms; this was done so as to give the newcomer a settler's feeling and to create a tie to his place of residence. Later, however, denser building and higher houses were preferred since land became scarcer and it was felt that spreading over too large an area would impair the social and economic life of an urban agglomeration. For the larger new towns the principle of self-contained neighborhood units was adopted: each quarter was provided with its own services (e.g., shopping center, clinics, schools, etc.) to save time in the citizens' daily chores; all units, however, are linked by adequate communication lines. In addition to residential units, quarters are often designed for specialized use (commerce, industry, tourism and recreation, etc.) and are then fitted out for their respective purpose.

The outline scheme for *Beersheba,* for example, the principal center of the

The city of Dimona, provided with lawns and gardens, has introduced a novel element into the desert scenery of the Negev Hills

Negev, which was only a small town numbering 3,000 to 5,000 inhabitants before 1948, envisages a total population of 140,000 and groups six neighborhood units (with 3–4 more to be added later) around a new civic and commercial center. There is also a large industrial area on the southeast and east side of the city, close to the railway line and easily approached by the interurban road system.

Similarly, the outline scheme for *Ashqelon* in the Southern Coastal Plain, worked out for a town of 80,000 inhabitants, is based on four self-contained units: furthest inland the original town (former Medjdal), at a considerable distance from it to the southwest, the Afridar quarter with its bathing beach and hotels, north of the latter the Barne'a quarter, and southeast of it the Southern Hills quarter. The nature preserve park with its spectacular antiquities gives Ashqelon its special character and tourist interest.

The greatest efforts of recent years in urban planning and development (besides those for the three main cities) were devoted to *Ashdod* in the Southern Coastal Plain. It is the country's second large port on the Mediterranean Sea, serving parts of central and all of southern Israel, including the Tel Aviv area; the city's site has been chosen to attract great numbers of settlers to the South, to shorten transport routes for imports and exports of the southern half of the

The new city of Ashdod, rapidly expanding over the sand dunes of the southern Coastal Plain

country, to utilize the wide expanse of barren sand dunes for urban development and to build an additional small inland port at the mouth of the Lakhish stream. Since the erection of the power station in 1958, which today supplies current to most of southern Israel, the new city has been growing rapidly. The outline scheme plans for a population of 140,000, with scope for further enlargement. At a swift rate, apartment houses were built and medium-sized and large factories established. The construction of the port was started in 1961; by 1965 its first stage was completed, and the harbor was opened to shipping. A second construction stage was begun in 1968. In the same year, the country's longest bridge, connecting Ashdod Port with the city, was opened to traffic. In its final form, the port will have a main breakwater 2,900 m (9,515 ft) long; its harbor basin will measure 150 ha (370 acres), and its terrestrial area 100 ha (247 acres), 20 ha (50 acres) of which are being won from the sea. The port is linked to the railway net by a trunk line, and roads radiate from Ashdod to the north, east and south. In 1970–71, construction of another huge power plant and of an oil refinery was started.

A particularly interesting blueprint is that for *Arad*, in the northeast Negev bordering on the Judean Desert. The site on the watershed, 640 m (over 1,900 ft) above sea level, was chosen to obtain the maximum cooling effect of the strong westerly winds. The town, planned for 50,000 inhabitants, will spread over a limited area to reduce internal distances and, even more, to relieve the feeling of isolation in the vast surrounding desert. Part of the buildings have balconies arranged so as to shade sidewalks at all hours of the day. Buildings are grouped around patio courtyards where gardens and small parks may thrive protected from the desert. A separate, compact, industrial quarter has been planned; however, the largest enterprise, a chemical combine under construction in 1969 and geared initially to produce phosphoric acid from Negev phosphates and waste products from the Dead Sea, lies halfway between Arad and Dimona. Finally, the eastern extremity of the town planning area, with its grand view over the Judean Desert, Dead Sea and Moab Plateau, is earmarked for luxury hotels.

Jerusalem

Geographical Background. Jerusalem, Israel's capital, today lacks most geographical assets which normally determine the growth and development of urban centers. The city lies on the hill crest, and the approach to it is not easy. Between 1948 and 1967 the Israel portion of Jerusalem was hemmed in by the frontier on three sides and could be reached only from the west. It has no agricultural hinterland of value; food and industrial products, electricity, and even water must be brought from afar. The hilly topography renders planning difficult, and the hard bedrock makes the preparation of building ground expensive. The roots of Jerusalem's existence are therefore in the conditions of antiquity, when this site was chosen because of its easy fortification and proximity to important crossroads. Jerusalem eventually became one of the most important spiritual centers of the world; this significance forms the basis for its life today, in spite of all geographical, economic and political drawbacks.

In the second millennium B.C.E., Jerusalem lay near the junction of the Hill Road (which ran from the Jezreel Valley over Sichem, Bethel, Bethlehem and Hebron to Beersheba and the Negev) with the west-east road from the coast to Transjordan. The town was built on a narrow ridge which drops abruptly to the upper Qidron Valley in the east and to the Ben Hinnom Gorge in the west and south; in antiquity, there was another narrow gorge dividing the ridge lengthwise into a broader western and very narrow eastern portion; the latter was the original Mount Zion or Mount Moriya (today, the name Mount Zion is used for the western part). Small springs at the eastern side of the ridge, notably Giḥon and En Rogel, were additional assets.

Ancient Jerusalem. At the lower, southern tip of the eastern ridge lies the Ophel ('Fortress'), the most ancient part of the city. Steep slopes secured it on three

Partial view of Jerusalem's Old City. In the foreground are Jaffa Gate and the Citadel with David's Tower (bottom, right). In the middle ground is the Christian Quarter with the cupolaed Church of the Holy Sepulcher. Further back appears part of the Temple Mount and, on the horizon, Mount Scopus

sides, and only in the north was a low wall needed for protection. As the city grew, this wall was shifted further north. After David had conquered the 'City of the Jebusite,' he included in it the broader central section of the Moriya ridge and widened the narrow passage leading to it from the Ophel by building the Millo ('Filling'). David erected his palace in the new part of the city, and Solomon constructed there the First Temple. Scholars have discussed whether, under the later kings of Judah, the city walls already included the broader western portion beyond the narrow gorge (called 'Tyropoion' by Josephus Flavius), or whether only country houses stood there, whose inhabitants found refuge within the walls in times of siege; new light was shed on this problem in 1970 when excavations in the Jewish Quarter west of the Western Wall bared a section of the Broad Wall of the First Temple Period which had been reconstructed by Nehemiah. In any case, the city spread over both hills and expanded northward before the first century B.C.E., until its destruction after the Bar Kokhba uprising in the second century C.E. Present-day walls of the Old City, built in 1536 under the Turkish Sultan Suleyman the Magnificent, cover a smaller area. The location of certain of its seven gates (Herod's, Damascus and New gates in the north, Jaffa Gate in the west, Zion and Dung gates in the south, and St. Stephen's (Lions') Gate in the east) is thought to be identical to that of the gates of antiquity.

Inside the walls, where all the city's inhabitants lived until the middle of the 19th century, four quarters are distinguished: in the northwest corner, the Christian Quarter grouped around the Church of the Holy Sepulcher, in the southwest, the Armenian Quarter, and in the center and northeast, the Moslem Quarter. From St. Stephen's Gate westward to the Holy Sepulcher runs the Via Dolorosa which passes through the Moslem Quarter and is flanked by several churches, monasteries, and Christian charitable institutions. The artificially flattened ground on Mt. Moriya, where both the First and the Second Temple stood (since King Herod's time supported by the pillars and vaults of the vast subterranean "Solomon's Stables") today bears two of the holiest shrines of Islam—the Dome of the Rock (Omar Mosque) and the el-'Aksa Mosque. The Temple Area is surrounded by the colossal Herodian enclosure wall, preserved in the east, south and west; a larger section of the Western Wall, the most venerated site in Jewish tradition, was bared to view after 1967, and archeological excavations further south, north and west have added to our knowledge of the city's layout in the Second Temple period and of historical events of those and later times. Between the Western Wall and the Armenian Quarter lies the Jewish Quarter, which had to surrender in the 1948 fighting. Under Jordanian rule, this quarter deteriorated, and all its synagogues were systematically destroyed. Following the Six Day War, reconstruction was started there in order to restore some of its previous character (see below).

Water Supply, Ancient and Modern. As long as inhabitants were few, the rainwater stored in stone cisterns, together with that of the Giḥon and En Rogel springs, covered all needs. King Hezekiah built the 'Niqba,' the winding tunnel beneath the Ophel ridge through which the water of the Giḥon Spring was led west to the Shiloaḥ Pool, where it was safer from enemy attack. From this pool the 'King's Gardens' in the Ben Hinnom Gorge could be irrigated. During the Second Temple period, two stone pipes adducted the water of strong springs south of Bethlehem, stored there in the so-called Solomon's Pools. Since then up to the British Mandate, no improvement of Jerusalem's water supply was carried out. At that time, two pipelines were laid to bring water to the capital—from the Ein Farī'a spring in the northeast and, later, from the Rosh ha-'Ayin springs in the west. The latter line was 50 km (over 30 miles) long and required pumping from 45 m (150 ft) to 800 m (2,500 ft) above sea level. After this line was blocked by the Arabs in the 1948 war, the Israel Government built two new pipelines to carry water to Jerusalem, at first from the vicinity of Reḥovot, and later from the Kefar Uriya wells in the Judean Foothills. Immediately after the city's reunification, the municipality greatly increased the supply to East Jerusalem, making available water pumped to the city from the west. In 1969, the first deep well drilled within the municipal limits yielded 350 m^3 of water per hour. Additional drilling operations are now under way, in the hope of discovering new sources which will ease the problem of the steeply mounting demand.

The New City. As a result of the gradual population rise, space between the walls of the Old City became ever more crowded, particularly in the narrow Jewish Quarter. Jews were therefore the first to found new quarters outside the walls; in 1858 Mishkenot Sha'anannim was built west of the Old City, soon followed by Yemin Moshe and by Naḥlat Shiv'a in the northwest. At about the same time, churches began to establish hostels and other institutions outside the walls for the benefit of the growing flow of Christian pilgrims; the 'Russian Compound' is notable among these.

The New City spread mainly toward the northwest along the road leading to Jaffa, which was then the only port in the country. From this direction most goods were brought and pilgrims, both Jewish and Christian, arrived from overseas and enlivened trade in the city. The first Jewish quarters were crowded together in a narrow space primarily for security reasons. The Yemin Moshe quarter was even surrounded by a wall and its gates closed every evening. Those first quarters which the inhabitants built exclusively with their own means (e.g., Naḥlat Shiv'a) were shabby in appearance and lacked uniformity in style and layout. Others, where construction was partly or wholly financed by philanthro-

On the Giv'at Ram campus of the Hebrew University, Jerusalem

ists (like Yemin Moshe, which was aided by Sir Moses Montefiore and bears his name), were better planned, generally with row houses of one or two stories. The Mea She'arim quarter took on particular importance. Founded in 1875 north of Jaffa Road by pious Jews from the Old City, it has, to this day, remained a stronghold of Jewish orthodoxy. Although these quarters are today among the poorest and most crowded in Jerusalem, they were, at the time, an important step forward from the conditions of the Old City.

At the end of the 19th century, first garden suburbs made their appearance; those of non-Jews (e.g., German Colony and Greek Colony, Katamon, etc.) preceded modern Jewish quarters (Reḥavya, Bet ha-Kerem, Talpiyot, etc.). In all these it was attempted to lend beauty to the individual house and surrounding garden, and to plan streets, water, sewage and electricity networks along rational lines while details were kept within the framework of the urban outline scheme.

The British Mandate authorities aimed to preserve Jerusalem's beauty and historical treasures. All outer walls had to be built of the fine local stone, which is both durable and in harmony with the landscape. Rules limiting the height of structures and floor space percentage covering the ground were issued, and care was taken to retain open spaces and preserve the skyline, particularly of sites of natural beauty and historical interest. An effort was made to fit the main roads to

The Hadassah Hospital, at Jerusalem's western outskirts

traffic densities, and a 'ring road' was planned to connect the outer suburbs with each other. On the other hand, the authorities rejected industrialization as not befitting Jerusalem's character, and they did not encourage a rapid population growth.

Planning Jerusalem up to the Six Day War. In the first years of statehood, the most pressing tasks were repair of the enormous damage caused in the War of Independence battles, absorption of thousands of new immigrants, and preparation of a new outline scheme fitting in with the border which then divided the city between Israel and Jordan; at a later stage came zoning into residential, commerical, administrative, cultural and industrial units. With the Hebrew University campus and the National Museums as pivotal points, a large center of Government institutions, of local administration, and cultural and commercial institutions was laid out. The whole area was well-integrated in the general blueprint of the capital. Care was taken to conserve and restore sites of rcheological and historical interest, to maintain open spaces and develop green belts, and to plan the layout in advance, so as to permit organic amalgamation vith those parts of Jerusalem which at the time were closed off by the border. After 1967, this provision facilitated reunification of the city.

Jerusalem's hilly topography was taken into account: the ridges and upper lopes, which are well-drained in winter and cool and agreeable in summer, were eserved for building, while valleys were earmarked for parks, gardens and fruit orchards.

The frontier which surrounded Israeli Jerusalem left the west as the only direction for the city's expansion. It was therefore decided to let the outline scheme hinge on the huge 'Buildings of the Nation' (Binyeney ha-Umma) at Romema, the dominant height of the Jerusalem urban area which lies astride the main western entrance of the city. Accordingly, the existing commercial center was planned to expand northwestward to Romema. The buildings of the Government ministries and the new Knesset edifice, surrounded by lawns and gardens, adjoin this area to the south. Still further south lie the impressive campus of the University and the National Library, the National Museums, and related institutions. This whole complex is thus situated between the older quarters in the east and the expansion belt of residential suburbs (Qiryat Moshe, Bet ha-Kerem, Bayit we-Gan, Qiryat Yovel, etc.) in the west and southwest. The huge Hadassah Hospital is today the extreme point of westward expansion.

Contrary to the view of the Mandate authorities, industry is now regarded as an element indispensable to Jerusalem's economy. Owing to the city's geographical position, light industries are easiest to develop here. In addition to the enlarged existing industrial area at Tel Arza in the northwest, a second, at Giv'at Sha'ul in the west, is developing rapidly.

Owing to economic and security considerations, the planning authorities regard the road system linking the capital to the rest of the State as particularly important. After the War of Independence, a single highway to Tel Aviv in the northwest was open; the railway line became usable again after border corrections in the Israel-Jordan armistice of 1949. Since then, additional roads, which converge on the city from the west and southwest, were constructed.

As elsewhere in the country, the large new suburbs in the west and southwest (Gonen, Qiryat Yovel, etc.) were laid out as self-contained neighborhood units. Prior to 1967, they had to absorb many newcomers settling in Jerusalem and aid in thinning out the overpopulated older quarters further east, some of which have been earmarked for replanning and reconstruction.

In an outer circle around these suburbs spreads a green belt of parks, forests and playgrounds. Landscaping and planting of parks and lawns accentuate sites of historical interest all over the city. Although the law prescribing the facing of

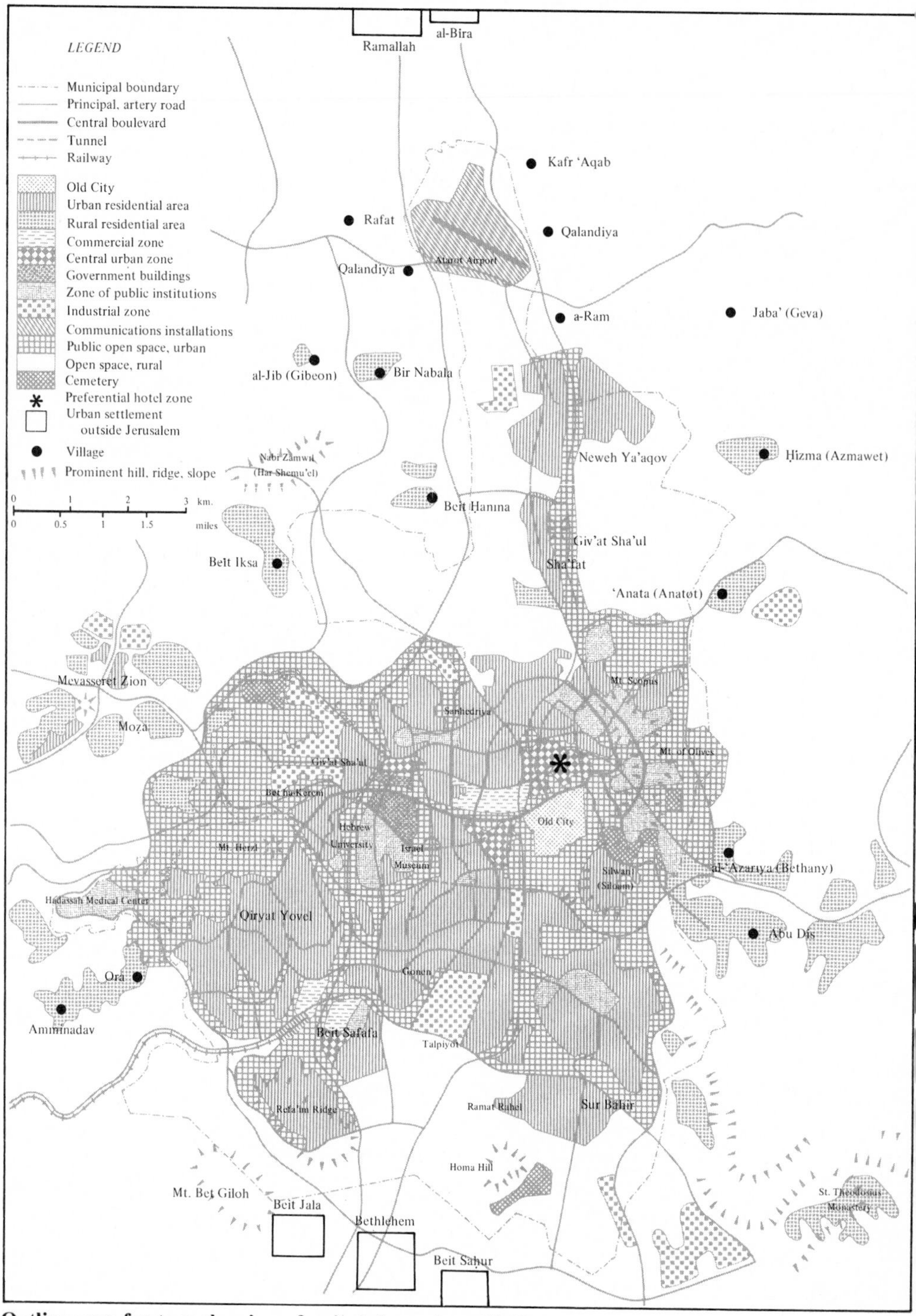

Outline map for townplanning of united Jerusalem (1968)

buildings with natural stone has been relaxed in parts of the city to prevent unnecessary rises in the cost of popular housing, it has been retained for all respresentative sections of the city.

Growth and Planning since Reunification. Immediately after the Six Day War, all military installations, fences and shell-proof concrete walls which had separated the two parts of the city were removed, and the connecting streets and roads paved and opened. Next, unseemly structures obstructing the view of the Old City wall were torn down, the wall itself and its gates painstakingly repaired, and the first gardens of a planned green peripheral belt planted in front of it. Inside the Old City, hovels were demolished close to the Western Wall. Two additional rows of its ashlars, hidden in the rubble, were uncovered and a wide square in front cleared, paved and readied for prayers. The reconstruction of the Jewish Quarter and its historic synagogues was begun, and institutions of religious study moved in, their pupils forming the nucleus of the Old City's renewed Jewish community. South of the Temple Mount, archeological excavations were started early in 1968. The slight damage caused to Christian churches and institutions during the fighting was repaired at Government expense, and church building and renovation work (e.g., on the Holy Sepulcher), which had been in progress prior to June 1967, were resumed.

Jerusalem boundaries were redrawn, giving the capital a municipal area exceeding 100 sq. km, the largest in the country. The eastern city limits, encompassing Mount Scopus and the Mount of Olives, touch on the upper rim of the Judean Desert without, however, including the rural villages al-'Azarīya (Bethany) and Abu Dis; they continue along the Qidron Gorge and incorporate into the capital's area the semiurban agglomeration of Sur Bahīr. In the south, the boundary runs close to the town of Bethlehem, and in the west it includes the Hadassah Medical Center as well as part of the ridge north of the Arazim Vale. In the north, a spur of the municipal area stretches beyond the suburb Sha'fāt, extending for a distance of 12 km from the city center to approach the town of Ramallah and bring the Atarot Airfield under the city's jurisdiction.

Within the new city limits, the Jerusalem population numbered, at the end of 1969, 283,100 inhabitants, thereof some 74,000 non-Jews (Arab Moslems and Christians, Armenians, European Christians, etc.). The capital's reunification led to an immediate and rapid population growth, as many Israelis and new immigrants decided to take up domicile there.

One of the main problems of the Jerusalem master plan lies in reconciling the quest for a continuous built-up area with the necessity to preserve and enhance numerous historical sites, sacred to three world religions. These sites comprise, inter alia, the entire Old City, the Qidron and Ben Hinnom gorges, the 'City of

David' to the south, Mount Scopus and the Mount of Olives, and many more Both inside and outside the Old City walls, gardens have either been laid out or are blueprinted, while other areas to the east and south have been earmarked as public open spaces or sites for preservation and reconstruction. Overcrowding in the Old City could possibly be remedied by resettling some of the inhabitants elsewhere in the city. However, the Old City is not to be viewed as a museum piece, but should continue to serve as a residential and, to an extent, commercial area, with the additional development of tourist facilities.

Another difficult task, which since June 1967 has assumed great urgency, lies in securing efficient traffic arteries leading through and around Jerusalem. The existent main thoroughfares have become totally inadequate, particularly Jaffa Road which carries the bulk of both urban and interurban traffic. A network of new broad roads has been blueprinted in order to provide alternative approach routes from all directions, enabling vehicular traffic to cross the municipal area to destinations beyond it (e.g., from Bethlehem directly to Ramallah) without clogging Jerusalem's main arteries. Adequate parking facilities must also be provided throughout the city. The numerous protected historical sites and edifices and, primarily, Jerusalem's hilly terrain, render this program highly expensive, as entire complexes of nonessential buildings will have to be demolished. In addition, earth-moving work, on a very large scale, must be carried out and long road tunnels will have to be excavated in the ridges.

In order to arrive at an acceptable joint solution to the traffic, social and economic problems, planners prefer not to concentrate industry, commerce, administration, tourism, etc., each in a separate area, but rather to distribute them evenly throughout the city, thus shortening the distances between residential quarters and sites of employment and more evenly spreading traffic flow during rush hours. For example, a group of science-based industries to be located at Meqor Ḥayyim in the south is to be linked by a direct highway to the Giv'at Ram university campus.

Jerusalem planners must take into account the prominence given by the events of 1967 to the four pillars of the city's economy—country-wide administration, institutes of higher education, tourism, and industry. As more and more Government ministries and other central offices move to the capital, an increasing need is felt to depart from the original plan of concentrating all Government buildings in the area of the Knesset, and to distribute them over other sectors, including East Jerusalem.

The Hebrew University has seen the return of its original campus atop Mount Scopus, where, beginning with the Harry S Truman Research Institute, an intensive restoration and building program was launched in 1968, comprising lecture halls and dormitories for thousands of students. Other institutes of learning, e.g., eshivot, Christian theological seminaries, etc., are in the construction or lanning stage in various parts of the city.

In view of the growing need for tourist accomodation and services in erusalem, large sums of public and private capital are being invested in hotel uilding, and suitable sites have been earmarked for these purposes throughout he city, with an area in the south, on a ridge northwest of former Government Iouse, planned as the principal hotel center.

The capital is attracting increasing numbers of industrial enterprises, particu-arly of the electronics and other science-intensive branches, for which new areas ave been set aside in the south and northeast.

While the pre-1967 blueprint called for expansion of the commercial area only westward, under the new conditions the first logical step is seen as the linking ogether of the two existing centers of West and East Jerusalem (Jaffa and Ben Yehuda Streets, and the area north of Damascus Gate, respectively). At a later date, secondary commercial centers will be developed in most suburbs.

New housing developments call for the largest share of both space and investments. While the southwest (Qiryat Yovel, etc.) continues to serve as the sector of intensive apartment building, and vacant lots elsewhere are increasingly being used for new constructions, a concentrated effort is now being directed toward the favorable terrain in the northeast, beyond the former armistice line. New residential quarters, under construction since 1968, promise to provide accomodation for tens of thousands of citizens, both Jews and non-Jews, and to link western Jerusalem with Mount Scopus in the east and Sha'fāt in the north.

The advisability of a large conurbation centered on Jerusalem is a debatable point. Most experts hold that such a development should not be encouraged, so as not to spoil the landscape on the approaches to the city, of singular beauty and great spiritual significance to mankind. In the long run, however, it may prove difficult to prevent an at least partial amalgamation of satellite towns like Bethlehem or Ramallah with the capital city on which their economy is largely dependent. The solution appears to lie in detailed planning and landscaping, protecting skylines and open spaces wherever necessary, locating new suburbs where they least interfere with the scenic vistas, and reducing buildings to a height tolerable from the esthetic point of view.

Tel Aviv-Jaffa

The Geographical Setting. There is archeological evidence of Jaffa's uninterrupted inhabitation at least since the Neolithic Period, i.e., for 7,000–10,000 years.It seems that the geological setting made the site particularly suited for human settlement: an underground fault line is assumed to run from the shore to the southeast; its uplifted southern side created Jaffa Hill, which slightly juts into the sea. Settlers were attracted to this site with its sea breeze and easy defensibility The hill forms two shallow bays, a larger one in the north and a smaller one in the south. Alternately protected from the waves with the changing wind direction these served ancient seafarers as double anchorage. Together with the hill's uplift kurkar reefs were also elevated from the sea bottom (one, in Greek legend, the rock to which Andromeda was tied and later freed by Perseus); normally, these reefs served as breakwaters and only in heavy storms constituted a menace to shipping. The hill also checks the landward penetration of sand dunes consequently, fertile soil lies east of it, while further south the sand-dune belt attains almost 8 km (5 miles) width. In the north, where a number of kurkar ridges mostly covered by loose sand are close to each other, the dune belt is only between 300–600 m (1,000–2,000 ft) wide. Small springs and wells at small depth may also originate in the underground fault. Jaffa Hill, in any case, blocks the course of Naḥal Ayalon to the sea and causes it today to turn sharply north and join the Yarqon stream near its mouth (in prehistoric times the former stream seems to have had its outlet south of the hill, but this was blocked by accumulating sands thrown up by the sea); at the bend of Naḥal Ayalon, spreading swamps used to bar access to Jaffa Hill; at certain times they may have been regarded as another security asset.

The Yarqon's mouth served as a second anchorage for the flat-bottomed ships of antiquity; this explains the existence of another fortress town there on Tel Qāsila; the stream bed secured this hillock from the south and seems to have repeatedly constituted a border line between tribes or small kingdoms.

Jaffa's History. Prehistoric hunters and fishermen settled on Jaffa Hill and at other sites south of the Yarqon. In the Chalcolithic Period, farmers tilled the fertile soil at the hill's foot. During the Early Bronze, Phoenician seafarers not only exploited the double anchorage as one of their stations along the Levant coast but also seem to have fortified the hill against attacks from the land. At least since the beginning of the second millennium B.C.E., Jaffa was also an important market place along the Via Maris (Sea Road).

Under King Solomon, the Bible reports, cedar wood for the construction of the Temple was brought to Jaffa by King Hiram of Tyre, and thence transported to Jerusalem. The Tel Qāsila excavations allow the assumption that the town there was Israelite, while in Jaffa itself Phoenician and Philistine elements still prevailed.

In spite of the frequent changes in Jaffa's fortunes, population and culture, it remained at all times the principal port in the country. Toward the end of the

First Temple period, it was described as a 'Cuthian,' i.e., pagan, city; later, it accepted Hellenistic civilization. Because of its proximity to and relative ease of communication with Jerusalem, however, a strong Jewish community also found its place in Jaffa, long before Simon the Hasmonean made the city 'the gateway to the islands of the sea' (Maccabees I, 14, 5). The Hasmonean kings aided and developed Jaffa, but they systematically suppressed all other Hellenistic cities on the seaboard. After Pompey's occupation in 63 B.C.E., Jaffa resumed its Hellenistic character, but its economy underwent little change. The city continued to thrive also under Byzantine rule and under the early Arab caliphates. The Crusaders used Jaffa as a port in their campaign to conquer Jerusalem. The city declined after the Crusades—under the Mamelukes and Turks—but renewed its growth in the 18th century, when links between Palestine and Europe became closer and Christians were permitted to make pilgrimages to the Holy Land. Jaffa began to spread to the low ground east of the hill. First orange groves were planted, and fruit gardening became one of the occupations of its citizens. Since the end of the 19th century, Zionist immigrants settled in Jaffa, at the side of the 'old yishuv' of Jews, and soon Jaffa was regarded as the Zionist center of the country. In 1908, the Palestine Office of the Zionist Organization was opened in Jaffa under Arthur Ruppin. In 1909, the progressive Jewish inhabitants provided the initiative for founding a comfortable, modern garden suburb, which became Tel Aviv.

Tel Aviv's Geography. Only thirty years after its founding, Tel Aviv was the largest city in the country, although modern conditions deprive it of most of the advantages which had made Jaffa thrive in antiquity. Tel Aviv's phenomenal growth, like the continued importance of Jerusalem, is therefore explained by historical circumstances rather than by geographical assets. The straight, shallow shore of Tel Aviv does not favor construction of a modern port. The climate is less agreeable than that of most other places in the country since the kurkar hills bar the cooling sea breeze, and high humidity makes summers sultry. Neither sand dunes nor kurkar are particularly suited as foundations for modern buildings, and sections of the city are easily flooded by winter rains. On the other hand, Tel Aviv's position in the central part of the Coastal Plain is today a positive factor; the highway issuing from here to Jerusalem also retains its importance.

The Beginnings of Tel Aviv. In 1909, two societies set up by Jaffa Jews, 'Aḥuzat Bayit' and 'Naḥlat Binyamin,' chose the barren sand dunes north of Jaffa for the suburb they planned to build, simply because plots there were offered at a reasonable price. The founders, it appears, did not dream that their garden suburb

First multistory buildings stand out on the Tel Aviv skyline. Domed structure left of center is the Tel Aviv Central Synagogue

would become the pivot of a conurbation numbering a million inhabitants; had they planned things thus beforehand, they would certainly have preferred the wide dune area south of Jaffa to the narrow northern strip. Characteristically, the dominating building of early Tel Aviv was the Herzliya Gymnasium, situated at the north end of Herzl Street, the first Hebrew secondary school in the country.

Trends in Tel Aviv's Expansion. With its swift growth in the 1920's and 1930's, Tel Aviv expanded from the Jaffa border northward along the band of sand dunes and sandstone ('kurkar') ridges, and around 1935 it reached the south bank of the Yarqon. To the east, its growth was constricted by the German colony Sarona and by some Arab villages. The Arab farmers enjoyed a mounting prosperity because of the expanding market in the nearby city, and they saw no reason to sell their land even at speculative prices. The distance between the southern and

Tel Aviv's sea front. Jaffa Hill, jutting out into the sea, is seen in the background

northern end of the city increased and soon exceeded 5 kilometers (3 miles) while the width between the shore and the easternmost houses measured only a few hundred meters. This fact made services (such as communications, water, electricity, etc.) expensive for the northern part of the city. The shortage of building ground engendered land speculation, so that North Tel Aviv became the domain of the relatively well-to-do who could afford high rents for their apartments.

Under these conditions, medium and large industrial enterprises in need of adequate building space preferred the smaller agglomerations which had meanwhile come into being on Tel Aviv's circumference (Ramat Gan, Bene Beraq, Ḥolon, etc.); these, in turn, grew into small or medium-sized cities. Until the 1930's, Tel Aviv itself had many small enterprises which could sometimes be run in one room of the owner's private flat. Only on the southeast rim of Tel Aviv and near the border of Jaffa did somewhat larger factories of the metal, food and other branches concentrate; none, however, employed over 20 laborers. The bulk of the city's economy was based on commerce, on cultural activities (the city served as the seat of all Hebrew dailies and theaters, of most publishing houses, etc.) and on its being the administrative center of the Jewish population of the country (seat of the Labor Federation, the political parties, etc.). All of these institutions concentrated in the south of Tel Aviv, along Herzl Street, Allenby Road, and their side streets.

Developments since the Second World War. With the outbreak of the Second World War, conditions changed gradually since the German inhabitants of Sarona were interned in the village and later transferred from the country; the area was then purchased by Jews, and in 1948 it became the transitional seat of the Israel Government institutions. The municipal area expanded eastward when new residential quarters began to be built also north of Sarona. This development quickened after 1948, when the villages there were abandoned. On April 24, 1950, Jaffa was united with Tel Aviv and the municipal area thus enlarged to 4,242.5 ha (over 10,000 acres). Although the incorporation of Jaffa, with its destitute quarters, dilapidated structures and winding lanes, demanded great efforts in reconstruction, the new areas thus added to Tel Aviv opened vistas in rational planning. Since statehood, the city's residential and commercial quarters have tended to expand principally northeastward. Building quality has improved perceptibly since the 1950's; since the early 1960's, multistoried structures began to go up, particularly in the center of the city. The focus of social and commercial life, too, has shifted northeast, from Allenby Road to Dizengoff Square and Dizengoff Road. Tel Aviv's waterfront (ha-Yarqon Street) has, with its large hotels, become the primary center of tourism in the country. The quarter on Jaffa Hill, a problematic poverty area still partly in ruins in the 1950's, has in the 1960's been transformed into an attractive center for artists and entertainment, where the romantic beauty of the ancient buildings has been fully preserved. The former inhabitants of the quarter were provided with accomodation in new suburbs of the city.

A comprehensive reconstruction scheme has been drawn up for a modern banking and commercial center to extend, mainly along the shore or at a small distance from it, from Jaffa's Jerusalem Boulevard to Tel Aviv's Ben Yehuda Street in the north and to King George Street up to Malkhei Israel Square in the northeast. This plan for urban renewal will include the former Jaffa slum quarter of Manshiye. The entire 13-km shore-front between Herzliya and Bat Yam is also slated for redevelopment, with certain areas to be won from the sea.

The Conurbation. Tel Aviv's border today, contiguous with satellite towns almost in its entire length, merges with them into a solid built-up area for 12 km (7 miles) to the east, and even larger distances from north to south. In the east, the satellite

Migdal Shalom Tower, Israel's tallest building, dwarfs business structures of Herzl Street, Tel Aviv's oldest thoroughfare

chain stretches through Giv'atayim and Ramat Gan to Bene Beraq and touches upon Petaḥ Tiqwa. In the south, the cities of Bat Yam and Ḥolon link up with Jaffa. In the southeast, only the fields of the veteran farming school of Miqwe Israel form a curtain of green between Jaffa and the small industrial or semi-industrial centers of Azor, Bet Dagan, etc. In the northeast, Ramat ha-Sharon forms the continuation of Tel Aviv's new suburbs and connects them with the town of Herzliya. The communities of Ra'ananna, Hod ha-Sharon, Kefar Sava, Petaḥ Tiqwa, Yehud, Lod, Ramla, Rishon-le-Zion, Nes Ẓiona and Reḥovot form an outer ring. The inhabitants of the conurbation proper numbered in 1970 over 800,000, and together with the outer ring well over one million, i.e., 30 or 40% respectively of the total population of the State of Israel (within its pre-1967 borders), while the conurbation occupies only 0.8%, and together with the outer ring 3%, of the country's area.

Similar to developments in other world conurbations, a migration has been noticeable, since the early 1960's, from Tel Aviv proper to the satellite towns, particularly to the south, where Bat Yam has increased its population by an annual 7.0%, and Ḥolon by 6.2%. While the growth of the eastern satellites has been more modest (Bene Beraq 4.1%, Giv'atayim 3.6%, Ramat Gan 2.2% annually), Tel Aviv's population has dropped over the last decade by more than 10,000 to number 382,900 (thereof 6,900 non-Jews) at the end of 1969. The city fathers, however, expect this trend to be reversed in the future, and predict for Tel Aviv (in its present boundaries) 650,000 inhabitants by the year 2000. Experts in country-wide planning are more conservative in their forecasts, assuming this figure to be closer to 475,000, and definitely not exceeding 550,000.

The economic and social future of the whole country requires particular efforts in planning and directing the development of such a huge concentration. The scarce reserves of Israel's good farming land must be preserved, the efficient functioning of all the economic branches safeguarded, and security aspects taken into consideration. Planning for the conurbation, however, meets with special difficulties, among them the fact that most land in the region is privately owned and its prices are rising steeply. This causes a 'creeping' of industries, housing, and other projects to the outer fringe with its cheaper holdings; unused waste stretches inside the conurbation constitute a problem for planning.

The planners' guiding principle is, on the one hand, to integrate fully the agglomerations of the conurbation. On the other hand, they want to allow the communities of the outer ring to base their economy separately, so that their inhabitants should not have to commute to work, shopping, and entertainment over long distances.

Planners attempt to direct further building primarily to the waste stretches inside the conurbation, and later to the broad sand-dune belt south of Jaffa and

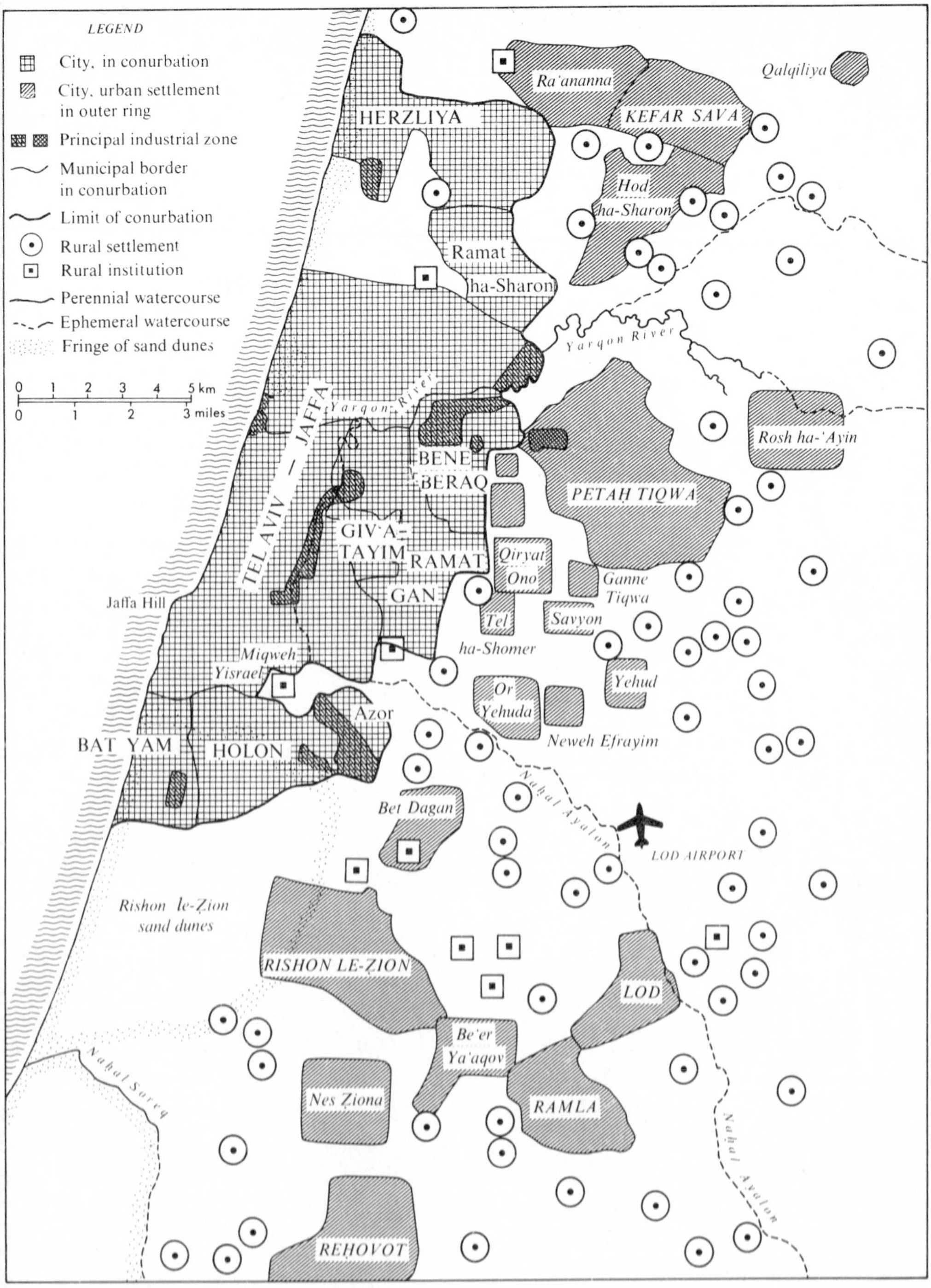

The Tel Aviv conurbation and its outer ring

west of Rishon le-Ẓion. Finally, in the northern Judean Foothills, the city of Makkabit is planned. On the other hand, efforts are made to retain the highly valuable farm lands in the Herzliya-Kefar Sava-Petaḥ Tiqwa areas, around Lod and Ramla, and between Bet Dagan, Rishon le-Ẓion and Reḥovot. In addition, stretches of agricultural land and parks are to be guarded within the conurbation as a green belt. Additional zones for industry must be laid out mainly in the outer parts of the conurbation, since the existing ones, like Giv'atayim-Ramat Gan-Bene Beraq, Ḥolon-Azor, etc., are already largely occupied. Public installations serving the whole conurbation (e.g., hospitals, high schools, etc.) or the whole country (e.g., Lod Airport) must be located in or near the outer fringe.

One of the most difficult planning tasks consists in laying out an efficient network of urban and interurban lines of communication. Highways from the south of the country to the north are, as far as possible, re-routed to bypass the crowded conurbation centers, and other roads are adapted to cope with the ever-increasing volume of traffic. An urban and suburban communication network by trains, partly subways, is under review.

Haifa, Acre and the Bay

The Natural Setting. Apparently, the Haifa Bay is the most convenient for shipping and development of port facilities of all sections on Israel's Mediterranean coast. This is particularly true today of the southern part of the bay, where Mount Carmel protects the shore from the prevailing southwesterly winds and the water is deep enough for ships to drop anchor close to the shore. Easy lines of communication open in different directions—through the Jezreel and Dothan valleys to the Hills of Samaria, through the Jezreel, Ḥarod and Bet She'an valleys and the Yarmuk Gorge to Transjordan and Damascus, over the Shefar'am Hills to Lower Galilee, through the Bet ha-Kerem Valley to Central Upper Galilee, through the Carmel Coast to the Sharon and the southern sections of the Coastal Plain, and through the Acre and Tyre valleys (between which the Rosh ha-Niqra Cape presents only a minor obstacle) to the northern parts of the Levant Coast. The Haifa Bay lands are rich in freshwater sources. Although a belt of sand dunes exists (they widen in the central part of the bay's shore and until recently were paralleled in the east by stretches of partly brackish swamps, particularly along the Qishon and Na'aman streams), even in antiquity easily cultivable soils could be found at the foot of Mount Carmel, on the eastern outskirts of the Zebulon Valley, and near Acre. The bay waters were rich in fish and in murex shells, from which the precious purple dye was extracted; the fine sand at the mouth of the Na'aman served as a raw material for glassmaking.

In spite of all these obvious advantages, however, Acre in history surpassed Jaffa in importance for short intervals only, and it could hardly compete with the port cities further north (Tyre, Sidon, Beirut, etc.). Haifa seems to have begun its existence only in the Second Temple period and, except for the last fifty years, was at best a small town ranking a poor second to Acre.

. The reason for this incongruity is in the incomplete protection of the Acre port and the security difficulties of Haifa's site. True, Acre lies on a land tongue jutting into the sea which can be protected from the land side by a relatively short wall. Since this tongue, however, is directed south and not west, it creates only one shallow bay on its eastern side, and this is protected only when the wind blows from the northwest. Steep Mount Carmel rising behind Haifa was no security asset, but, on the contrary, a menace, for enemies or robbers could hide in the dense brush of its slope to pounce suddenly on the town beneath. The blunt Carmel Cape is insufficient protection from storms, and the deep shore water was a drawback in antiquity rather than an advantage. It made construction of jetties well-nigh impossible, while for the flat-bottomed ships a depth of $\frac{1}{2}$–1 m (2–3 ft) was sufficient. The twin towns of Haifa and Shiqmona therefore built their harbors not at the modern port's site, but in the shallow waters in front of the Carmel Cape.

The land tongue of Acre, seen from the east. Walls surround the Old City both from the land and sea side. Waters of the bay appear at lower left, open sea—at the upper rim of the picture

Acre's History. Acre is first mentioned in the Egyptian 'execration texts' of the 18th century B.C.E., but it may be assumed to have existed a long time before that date, perhaps even since prehistoric times. On the mound of ancient Acre, lying inland at a distance of over one mile from the sea (Napoleon's Hill), potsherds of the Early Bronze Age have been found. In present-day Acre clear archeological evidence of an urban settlement exists only for the 4th century B.C.E. and later; continuous inhabitation since then, however, may have obliterated earlier traces. In the Hellenistic and Roman periods, the twin cities Acre-on-Sea and Acre-on-Land existed side by side. Later, Acre-on-Sea grew in importance while the city on the land dwindled into 'Acre Village' and then disappeared. Alexander Jannaeus, the greatest Hasmonean king, failed to conquer the city, which had meanwhile taken on the character of a Hellenistic 'polis' and changed its name to Ptolemais. In the Great Jewish War, Vespasian used the city as a base for his Galilean campaign. A large Jewish community is later reported, which buried its dead outside the city limits. Prosperous Acre was conquered by the Crusaders in 1104, made their principal port, and thoroughly fortified. The massive walls and pillars of an ancient crypt or refectorium, one of the earliest Gothic structures existent, bear witness to the city's importance. Acre remained the capital of the Holy Kingdom of Jerusalem even after Jerusalem itself was lost. Acre's fall in 1291 marked the end of the Crusades.

Acre regained prominence in the late 17th and in the 18th centuries, especially when it was the seat of the governors Zaher el'Amr and Aḥmed el Jazzạr who rebuilt and fortified it magnificently in medieval-oriental fashion with building materials plundered from ancient Caesarea—Roman marble, granite and porphyry columns, etc. Jazzār, striving to make the city a major trading center, constructed a number of 'khāns' or caravan inns, rectangular courtyards with a cistern or well to water the camels, surrounded by two-story buildings with the upper story borne on columns. The fortifications, two thick walls with a deep moat in between and provided with openings for cannon muzzles, surrounded Acre on land and sea and successfully withstood Napoleon's siege in 1799.

In the 19th century, Acre stagnated, and in the 20th century it even declined while Haifa developed rapidly. Since the Turks lifted the prohibition on building beyond the walls in the first decade of the present century, the 'New City' was created on the north side, and laid out with straight, and sometimes broad roads. Another new suburb has been developing since 1949 in the east, between the walled city and Napoleon's Hill, while further south, nearer the shore, the industrial area centering on Acre Steel City is taking shape.

Haifa's History. The oldest settlement identified within Haifa's present municipal boundary is near the southeast corner of the bay; pottery found there belongs to the Late Bronze Period. In Roman times, a relay station called Calamon may have stood at the same site, but this was never a town and had no fortifications.

The name Haifa, together with the neighboring town of Shiqmona (Sycamion), is first mentioned under Roman rule. The Romans erected a fortress uphill, Castrum Samaritanorum, where they posted Samaritans (known for their enmity toward Jews and therefore dependable in guarding them in the twin-cities below). In 1100, Venetian Crusaders took the town after an obstinate defense by its Moslem and Jewish citizens. Haifa fell to Saladdin in 1187, returned briefly to Crusader rule under Louis IX of France between 1250 and 1265, and was destroyed by the Mamelukes. A squalid fishing hamlet near the Carmel Cape in the 18th century, it was razed by Governor Zaher el 'Amr. He immediately rebuilt it further east, but even then, however, he hardly improved its economic position. Only in the middle of the 19th century did it begin to grow slowly, numbering 2,000 inhabitants in 1854, among them Jews, most of whom originated from Morocco. The founding of the German Templar colony on the Mount Carmel slope in 1868 aided its development.

Since the beginning of the present century, the construction of railways (Haifa-Damascus in 1905, Haifa-Lod-Egypt, completed in 1919) and of roads made Haifa an important traffic hub. The advantages of Haifa's deep-water anchorage were recognized and led to the construction of the large, modern port completed in 1934. The Kirkuk-Haifa oil pipeline was laid and the Haifa Oil Refineries were installed between 1936 and 1939.

Haifa's vast potentialities had been recognized by Theodor Herzl, who made the town, still insignificant when he visited it in 1899, the focus of his visionary novel 'Old-New Land.' Before World War I Jews began to acquire land on the Carmel slope, particularly on the broad level step 40–60 m (180–200 ft) above the sea, where a site was prepared for the Technion (Israel Institute of Technology) and where in 1920 the modern Jewish quarter Hadar ha-Karmel was founded. In 1925, the Technion opened its gates to students. The early 1930's saw the forming of the nuclei for the garden suburbs atop Mount Carmel—the French Carmel at its northwest extremity, the Central Carmel, and Aḥuza further to the southeast. With the construction of the port and dredging of its bottom, a strip of land was added to downtown Haifa. Room was thus provided for the port installations as well as the broad King's Way thoroughfare. The area became a center of banking, wholesale trade, and enterprises connected with the port's activities.

Greater Haifa Town Planning. The first step toward comprehensive town planning for Haifa was taken in 1928. At that time the Jewish National Fund's acquisition of the flat strip of land adjoining the bay shore almost up to Acre gave scope for allocating areas to different functional tasks. The southern section, near

View from Mount Carmel over Haifa's Hadar ha-Karmel quarter, the port and the bay

the mouth of the Qishon Stream, was earmarked for small, medium and large industry, as it is nearest to the city and to the port (which was then about to be built) and could be most easily linked by branch lines to the railway. The oil harbor was built there in the years before the Second World War. Between 1952 and 1956 the Qishon harbor was built to serve Israel's high-sea fishing fleet. It also contains a floating dock for ship repairs, and ship construction wharfs. Inside the industrial zone, most factories giving off obnoxious fumes (Oil Refineries, Chemicals and Phosphates, Nesher Cement Works, etc.) were placed furthest from the city to the east, where they were last in the chain of dominant wind direction.

North of the industrial zone and separated from it by an avenue of trees, the 'Qerayot' (garden cities) were laid out, at first with small, one- or two-family

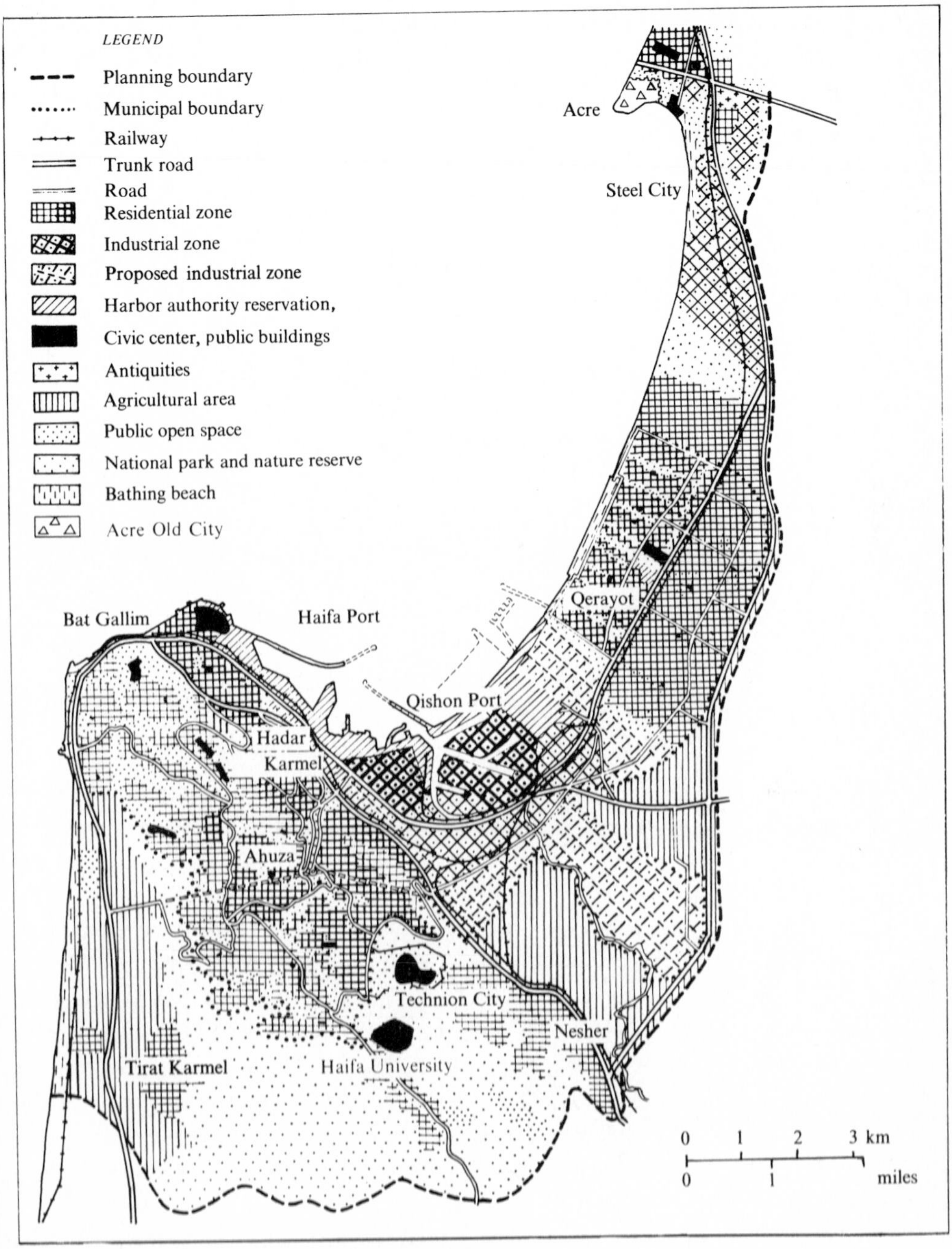

Outline map for townplanning of the Haifa-Acre area

homes, and later superseded (particularly in the last decade) by large apartment houses. The Qerayot (Qiryat Ḥayyim, Q. Motzkin, Q. Bialik, Q. Yam, etc.), originally meant to house workers of the industrial zone, soon took up other strata, among them many people employed in Haifa City or within the Qerayot.

The northern section was originally designated for farming, and between 1937 and 1939 three kibbutz settlements were set up there. A fourth zone crystallized around the Ata textile works further east, near the foot of the Shefar'am Hills; it includes industry, residential quarters (some of them with auxiliary farms), and farming villages.

In the years of statehood, several changes have been introduced into this basic blueprint. Haifa and Acre are now conceived as the main supports of the comprehensive regional scheme for urban development, and the opportunities provided by the great variety in landscape forms are utilized. West of the former agricultural zone and south of Acre, more and more industrial enterprises take up the dune strip, while to the east, residential quarters are pushing north, leaving to farming only the heavy soils further inland. Simultaneously, growing parts of Mount Carmel are included in the town planning scheme. The residential quarter of Hadar ha-Karmel climbs the slope and links up with the zone of apartment houses, villas and hotels on the mountain crest. Sections of Mount Carmel further east are included in Haifa with the spread of residential areas such as Neve Sha'anan and Qiryat Remez and with the construction of the large campus of the Technion ('the Technion City'). On the mountain top southeast of Aḥuza, the Haifa University campus, designed by world-famous architect Oscar Niemeyer, is taking shape. In the hilly parts of the city, the principles applied resemble those of the Jerusalem blueprint: since the hill crest is cut by deep gorges into narrow spurs running west and east, the spine of Mount Carmel, the spurs, and part of the upper slopes are reserved for building while parks and orchards occupy the gorges. Sections of Mount Carmel, with their abundant and variegated vegetation, have been set aside as nature preserves.

Downtown Haifa spreads west; modern residential quarters occupy the level space between the port area, the Carmel Cape, and the Carmel slope. The city also expands beyond the cape and spills over into the narrow Carmel Coast. Here, an arrangement resembling that of Haifa Bay becomes noticeable—a manufacturing zone occupies the low area west of the Haifa-Tel Aviv railway and highway, and the houses climb the slope of Mount Carmel. About $1\frac{1}{2}$ km (1 mile) south of the Carmel Cape, a strip of farming land still remains, wedged in between the industrial and residential zones. Planners wish to restrain further expansion in this direction.

An outer ring of satellites includes places of habitation of partly rural or semirural character. Outstanding among them is Qiryat Tiv'on in the Tiv'on Hills in the southeast, which also has recreation facilities. Tirat Karmel south of Haifa, in the Carmel Coast region, Nesher, Kibbutz Yagur, and Rekhasim in the southeast, and Qiryat Ata and its neighbors in the east also form part of the ring.

Haifa numbered, at the end of 1969, 214,500 inhabitants within its municipal boundaries, while the Haifa-Acre conurbation exceeded 300,000. The port, whose capacity is steadily expanding, the docks and expanding shipbuilding trade, and notably heavy industry, for which Haifa is becoming the primary center of the country, together with the region's assets for tourism, which are not yet fully exploited, warrant a further rapid population growth. Estimates of 500,000 inhabitants in the region in the next decade therefore do not seem exaggerated.

The Road System

Roads in History. At a very early stage, a difference became apparent between the international highways and routes, and local communication lines. The latter served for herdsmen to drive their flocks, or for lone tradesmen and peddlers to travel between inhabited places with their few wares or tools. The former bore large, rich merchant caravans, their numerous carriers heavily laden, or armies with their weapons, chariots and provisions. The wayfarers of the local roads, traveling on foot, did not require road paving and could overcome topographical difficulties such as steep, rocky slopes or deep, dry wadi beds. However, they needed wayside hostels for a safe night's rest and inhabited places with water and markets for food and other commodities. The travelers on the international highways, on the other hand, who were provisioned with drinking water and food, and often tents for the night's camp, were largely independent of the local population, but their vehicles and animals needed a well-prepared roadway along the topographically easiest path.

It is often hard to decide whether an existing place of habitation attracted travelers and caused the road to turn toward it, or whether an existing road contributed to the founding and growth of a town at its side. In general, towns seem to have profited from local roads, while they feared the armies marching on the international highways who took all they needed from the inhabitants, frequently by use of force. Distant rulers often used those towns which were situated along the road as fortresses to secure the way for their expeditionary armies.

The country's topography, in general, does not favor traffic. The hill ridges, running mostly from north to south, bar the way inland from the coast, especially in Judea. For south-north travel, four lanes were then open: through the Coastal Plain, along the main hill crests, through the Jordan Rift, and over the Transjordan Plateau. The Coastal Plain and Transjordan Plateau thoroughfares, relatively the easiest, became two of the main highways of antiquity, the Via Maris (Sea Road) and the King's Way.

The *Via Maris* was perhaps the most important highway of the ancient world. Coming from Egypt, it ran through Rhinokoroura (present-day el-'Arīsh), near the mouth of Wadi el-'Arīsh on the Sinai coast, and reached the sown land at Rafiaḥ. It thence ran north, along the inland rim of the barren sand-dune belt. After crossing the bed of Naḥal Soreq, it forked out into an eastern branch, which reached the border of the Foothills at Lod, and a western branch, which, after touching on Jaffa, led eastward again along the Yarqon stream; the branches reunited at Aphek (Antipatris). The Via Maris, continuing north along the border between the Sharon Plain and the Samarian Hills, avoided the brush and swamps of the plain with its dangers of robbers and malaria. From the northeastern corner of the Sharon, the highway crossed the Samarian Hills through the Irron Valley, and reached the Jezreel Valley at Megiddo. Here it split again: its northern route ran over the plateaus of Eastern Lower Galilee to the northwest shore of the Sea of Galilee, and thence over the Rosh Pinna Sill to the Benot Ya'aqov Bridge on the Jordan south of the Ḥula Valley, and reached Damascus through the Upper Golan; the southern route descended through the Ḥarod Valley to Bet She'an, there turned north, passed the fortress town of Bet Yeraḥ at the southern end of the Sea of Galilee and the town Aphek of the Lower Golan, and ascended through the Upper Golan to Nāwa in the Bashan, and from there straight north, also to Damascus. The desert track between Damascus and Mesopotamia constituted the continuation of the Via Maris.

The *King's Way* of Transjordan led from the Eilat shore through Edom, Qir Moav (Kerak), Dibbon, Ḥeshbon, Rabbat Ammon and Ashtarot to Damascus. In Edom, it had to traverse several profound canyons of the streams running down to the Arava Valley and cross the precipices in sharp turns instead of making the wide circuit to the desert in the east; this track seems to have been chosen to adhere to the water sources and the food supply of the sown land. An important side branch of the King's Way descended from Petra to the copper site of Punnon in the Arava Valley, and crossed the Negev and the Sinai Peninsula into Egypt.

Of the local thoroughfares, the longest was the *Hill Road,* which, after crossing the Sinai Peninsula, entered the country at the Qadesh Barne'a oasis, ran through Beersheba, climbed through the valley of Naḥal Ḥevron to the comfortably flat hill crest where it proceeded over Hebron, Bethlehem and Jerusalem to Bethel. The interior rift valleys of Samaria rendered its northern section more circuitous, as it had to descend steeply into the Levona Vale, pass through the Mikhmetat and Nablus (Sichem) vales, then wind its way near the town of Shomron and issue through the Dotan Vale into the Jezreel Valley. The tilted blocks of Galilee barred the way straight north, so that the road turned northwest, where it reached the sea at Acre, by way of Ta'anakh, Megiddo, Yoqne'am, and 'Geva of the Equestrians.'

Least continuous was the road through the *Rift Valley*. The Dead Sea, into whose waters precipitous cliffs drop on west and east shores, separated it into a southern section, along the Arava Valley, and a northern paralleling the Jordan River. In the Lower Jordan Valley, where the eroded lissan marl, the hot climate and the lack of water present serious obstacles, the existence of a road can be verified only from the Second Temple period.

Most of the west-east roads were of local importance. They connected major centers of habitation with the principal north-south roads. Following the structural features of the country, they were more numerous in Samaria and Galilee than in Judea and the Negev.

Principal road junctions in the Coastal Plain were Gaza in the south and Acre in the north; at a later stage, also Jaffa and Caesarea became traffic centers. In the interior, political changes entailed repeated displacements of road junctions. In the Northern Negev, for example, the town Ḥaluẓa replaced Beersheba as communications hub in the Roman and Byzantine periods. In Judea, Jerusalem became a major crossroads only under King David, when it replaced Gibeon. While Jerusalem served as capital of the country during the Second Temple period, roads radiated out in all directions, despite topographical difficulties: to the north to Samaria and Galilee, to the south to Hebron and Beersheba, to the northwest over the steep Bet Ḥoron Ascent, to the southwest through both the Naḥal Soreq Gorge and the Ela Valley, to Jericho in the east over the steps of the Judean Desert (one of them being Ma'ale Adummim, 'Edomite Ascent'), and to the southeast the arduous 'Road of the Edomites,' which crossed the broken terrain of the central Judean Desert and the northernmost section of the Arava Valley; for a short time, a branch of the latter road crossed the Dead Sea at its narrowest point, south of En Gedi, and it is assumed that beasts of burden waded through shallow water to the Lissan Peninsula and climbed to Qir Moav (Kerak).

In Samaria, Sichem and Shomron rivaled for supremacy as traffic centers. In the Jezreel Valley, the strategic site of Megiddo constituted the most important crossroads until its decline under Roman rule.

In Transjordan, west-east roads were most numerous in the Lower Gilead and Lower Golan, where conditions are easiest, both topographically and climatically. In the Hellenistic and Roman periods, these roads linked the cities of the Dekapolis—Gadara, Gamala, Dion, Hippos, etc.

By far the best of all ancient roads were those built by the Romans, who regarded them as a decisively important aid for maintaining their hold over the scattered provinces of the empire. Roman engineers calculated the tracks to

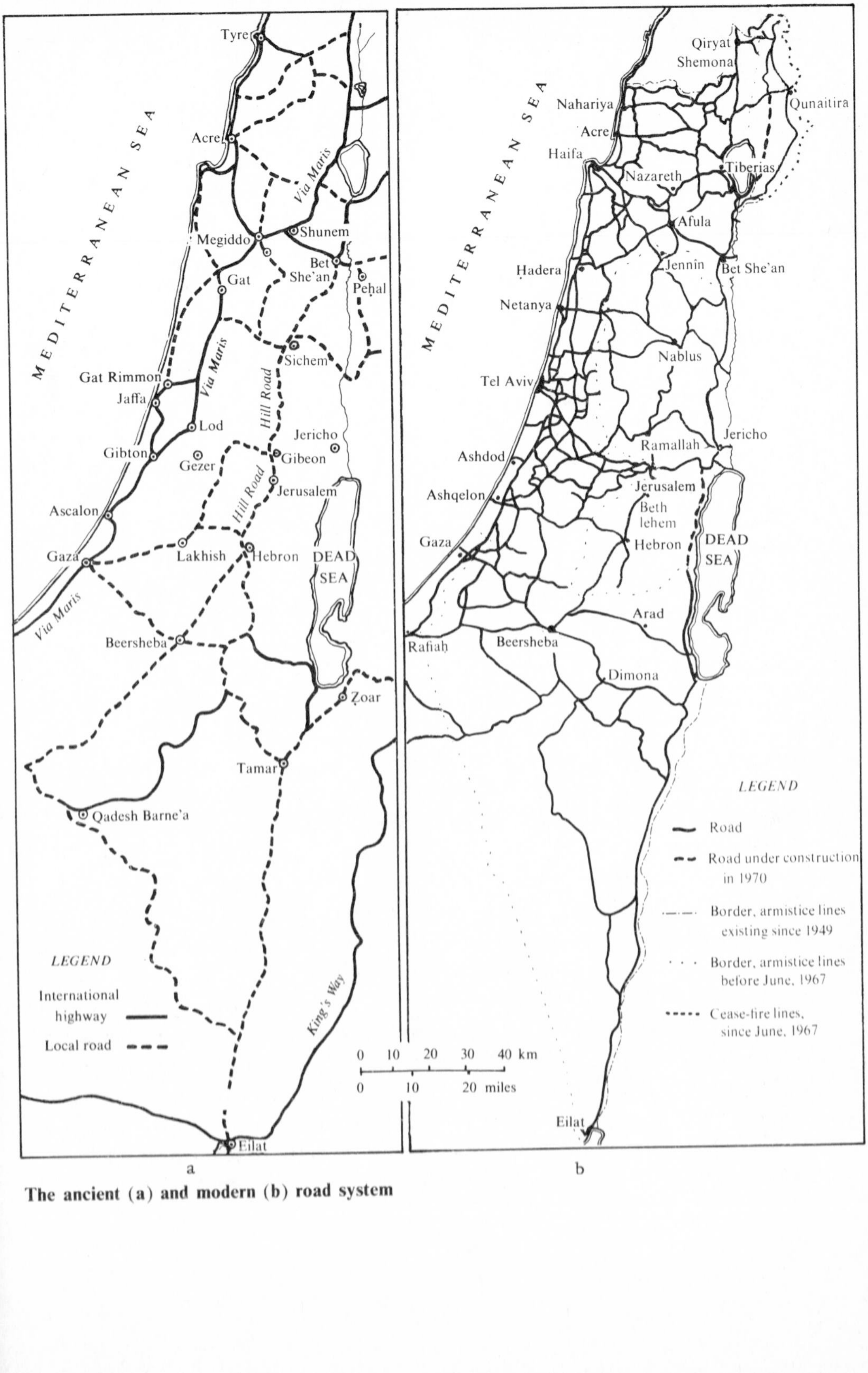

a b

The ancient (a) and modern (b) road system

choose; the roads were smoothly paved, and bridged over the wadi courses. Among the outstanding Roman-built highways in the country are the routes Caesarea-Antipatris-Jerusalem, Gaza-Jerusalem, Jerusalem-Jericho-Philadelphia (Rabbat Ammon)-Gerasa, Jerusalem-Legio (Megiddo), and Acre-Tiberias.

With the end of Roman rule, roads fell into disrepair. The Crusaders tried to improve some of the highways but never attained the standards of Roman times. Until the end of the 19th century, there were no paved roads, goods were transported on camels or donkeys, and travel was either by foot or on horses and camels. Although lines of communication followed the general tracks of Roman roads, they had degenerated into tortuous paths; care was taken only of crossings over dry wadi beds and stream fords.

The enlivenment of seafaring in the Mediterranean Sea and the growing stream of pilgrims to the Holy Land at the end of the 19th century made a thorough improvement of the road system inevitable. The existing tracks were partly adapted to the passage of caravans and coaches ('diligences'). Prime attention was given to the roads leading to sacred sites, e.g., the links between Jaffa and Jerusalem, Haifa and Nazareth, or the lengthwise route of Hebron-Bethlehem-Jerusalem-Nablus-Nazareth. These tracks were paved and provided with bridges and culverts, so that they became all-weather roads. Before the First World War, they totaled 450 km (280 miles) in length.

The first years of the British Mandate saw much repair, improvement, widening and asphalting of roads to fit them for motorized traffic. In 1932, the road network reached a length of 950 km (590 miles). Until then, however, least care was taken of roads in the Coastal Plain, since the authorities did not wish to create a serious competition to the railway there.

The increase in immigration and citrus exports of the 1930's necessitated a further expansion of the road network, and the mounting prosperity in the country provided the means to finance it. In 1936, the first highway running the whole length of the Sharon was finally built between Tel Aviv and Haifa: a road link was also established between the port-city of Haifa and the flourishing farming region of the Jezreel Valley.

Efforts to complete the road system were redoubled during the Second World War, when the country was the hinterland of the Allied front in the Libyan Desert and of the operation to free Syria and Lebanon from the Vichy French. In the south, and even more in the north, new roads were laid out. Among these was the Megiddo-Afula road in the Jezreel Valley, which created a direct link between the Coastal Plain and the Sea of Galilee. The country's road system was connected with Transjordan and Syria to the east and north as well as with Egypt through the Sinai Peninsula. On the eve of Israel's statehood, Palestine had 2,660 km (1,650 miles) of motor roads.

From the late 19th century, several railway lines were installed to supplement the road system. The first line, for the benefit of pilgrims, was built by a French company between Jaffa and Jerusalem. Second came the line Rafiaḥ-Gaza-Lod-Tul Karm-Haifa; this was later, between the two world wars, linked to al-Qantāra in Egypt and to Beirut in Lebanon. Two narrow-track lines were added: from Haifa through Afula to Bet She'an and Ẓemaḥ at the southern shore of the Sea of Galilee where it linked up with the Hedjaz Railway through the Yarmuk Valley; and from Afula south to Nablus and then west to Tul Karm. The War of Independence paralyzed all rail traffic, and later only the Jaffa (Tel Aviv)-Jerusalem line and that section of the coastal railway running from Ashqelon through Lod and Haifa to Nahariya were renewed.

The Present Road System. The road network still mirrors, to some extent, the country's morphological structure although today's technical means enable builders to overcome most topographical difficulties; some highways still follow ancient road tracks. The borders existent between Israel and her neighbors between 1949 and 1967 put many roads out of use completely or in part, lent increased importance to other roads, and necessitated the construction of new highways to replace those cut by the frontiers. The latter is illustrated, for example, by that section of the Jerusalem-Tel Aviv highway built by Israel immediately after the cessation of hostilities in 1948, between Sha'ar ha-Gay and Ramla (the 'Road of Courage') to circumvent Latrun, then in Jordanian territory, or the Jordanian route reconnecting the City of Jerusalem with Bethlehem, which ran east of the Israel border. Furthermore, new economic requirements, expansion of old and construction of new urban centers, as well as regional settlement projects necessitate investment of large means and efforts in roadbuilding. To cope with the ever-increasing traffic, all major interurban highways continually have to be widened.

Israel's principal traffic arteries connect the three main cities of Tel Aviv, Jerusalem, and Haifa; lead from Tel Aviv and Jerusalem south to the Negev and Eilat; and from Tel Aviv and Haifa north and east, to Galilee and to the Central and Upper Jordan Valley. The Tel Aviv-Haifa highway bears by far the heaviest traffic; constructed in the early 1950's, it runs along the shore from Tel Aviv through Herzliya and Netanya up to Ḥadera, where it continues west of the former Ḥadera-Haifa road, since 1970 in its entire length a modern four-lane, and partly six-lane highway. The older road, paralleling the new one in the east between Petaḥ Tiqwa, Ḥadera and Atlit, today connects (together with the Ramla-Lod-Petaḥ Tiqwa highway) Jerusalem with Haifa.

Extremely important is the connection between Ḥadera in the Coastal Plain through the Irron Valley to Afula in the Jezreel Valley and thence to Tiberias;

The six-lane Tel Aviv-Jerusalem highway near Qāstel Mount. The Capital's outskirts are seen on the horizon

this follows the track of the ancient Via Maris. Another heavy-duty road, which has been widened into a four-lane highway, links Tel Aviv with Lod Airport.

In the Southern Coastal Plain, three highways today run parallel to each other; nearest to the shore is the road which passes from Tel Aviv through Yavne and Ashdod to Ashqelon up to the northern end of the Gaza Strip near Yad Mordekhay and thence southeast where it joins the parallel eastern road near the new urban center of Sederot; this will soon function as a regional road only, and a toll highway will run over the sand-dune areas further west to connect Tel Aviv with Ashdod. A second highway runs from the Bet Dagan junction through the veteran centers of Rishon le-Zion, Reḥovot and Gedera and splits near the development town of Qiryat Mal'akhi; its western fork links up with the Gaza-Beersheba road near the kibbutz Sa'ad, while the eastern one passes Qiryat Gat and reaches the Beersheba highway near Eshel ha-Nasi. The third road branches off the Tel Aviv-Jerusalem highway at the Naḥshon Junction, runs west to join the former road for a short stretch between the Re'im and Aḥim junctions, and then turns south and southeast to lead directly to Beersheba.

Great strides in roadbuilding have been made in the Negev, and further highways are under construction or projected for the near future. A highway built in 1957 links Beersheba through Dimona and Miẓpe Ramon with Eilat, and another, 127 km (79 miles) long, descends from Dimona to Sedom. The new Arad development region is crossed by a road from Beersheba to Arad and the Dead Sea shore north of Sedom and is planned to be directly connected with Ashdod. The En Gedi-Sedom-Eilat highway runs a straight course along the Dead Sea and the Arava Valley, and is paralleled in the northwest by a link connecting the Arad-Sedom and Beersheba-Dimona-Sedom highways (passing the Ẓefa-Ef'e phosphate field and chemicals plant). Another road is planned through the Besor development region in the northwestern Negev.

The main highways of the central and northern valleys and of Galilee are the following: Haifa-Acre-northern border; Acre-Safed; Haifa-Nazareth-Tiberias; Haifa-Afula-Bet She'an; and Bet She'an-Tiberias-Rosh Pinna-Qiryat Shemona-Metulla. Numerous secondary roads in these regions already form a dense network; more are under construction or in the planning stage.

New Railways. Although Israel's railways are secondary to the roads, which carry the bulk of traffic, several highly important lines have been added since statehood, and more are in the offing. The busiest line is the Tel Aviv-Ḥadera one, along the shore (constructed in the first years of statehood), which joins the old line to Haifa near Pardes Ḥanna. The veteran Lod-Pardes Ḥanna line along the eastern border of the Sharon communicates between Jerusalem and Haifa. Second in importance is the Tel Aviv-Qiryat Gat-Beersheba railway, operating since the mid-'fifties, to which a branch line to Ashdod has been added; the continuation to Dimona was completed in 1965, and those to the Oron and Ẓefa-Ef'e phosphate mines were completed in 1970. Projected is the Beersheba-Eilat line, and a Sedom-Eilat line is under consideration.

Roads in the Administered Areas. In Judea-Samaria, the Jordanian authorities saw to the maintenance of existing roads from the Mandate era. They devoted special attention to thoroughfares leading from the West Bank to Transjordan: the Jerusalem-Allenby Bridge-'Amman road was transformed into a broad and comfortable modern highway; the Nablus-Dāmiya Bridge road running through the Farī'a Valley was made passable for vehicles of all kinds, and a new road was built through the northern Judean Desert to to connect Ramallah with Jericho. In addition, metalled, albeit narrow-track roads were constructed to give access to practically all villages of the region. Railroad traffic, on the other hand, was not renewed. Since the Six Day War, Israel has done much to improve existing roads, widening particularly the main south-north thoroughfare (Beersheba-Hebron-Bethlehem-Jerusalem-Ramallah-Nablus-Jennīn). Immediately after the war, the Ayalon Valley (Latrun) road was repaired and re-opened to vehicles not exceeding 4 tons, thus shortening by 9 km the journey between Jerusalem and Tel Aviv. A particularly important new road, built in extremely different terrain, is the En Gedi-Ein Feshkha link which connects Eilat and Sedom with Jerusalem, Bet She'an and Eastern Galilee.

In the Golan, Syrian-built roads principally served military requirements. These have now undergone thorough repair, and in addition to the three existing links with veteran Israel territory (the Banias-Mas'ada, Gesher Benot Ya'aqov-Qunaītira and Ḥammat Gader-Fiq roads), a fourth highway is under construction. A venture of special interest are new roads blazed to a 2,200 m-high peak of Mount Ḥermon and on the mountain's western slopes.

In Sinai, roads existing before 1967 have been repaired, and new connecting links have been added.* Israel is constructing a new broad highway from Eilat south to Mifraẓ Shelomo (Sharm a-Sheikh).

* For further details on Sinai roads, see pp. 367–371.

Part IV
The Administered Areas

The Sinai Peninsula

Soil, Water and Farming

Natural conditions for farming are extremely difficult in Sinai. Only a few thousand hectares are at present under cultivation there, less than one tenth of one percent of the total surface. It is difficult to envisage that this area could have been much larger in the historic past. In general, farming is limited to a few oases, and even there the fields are tilled only intermittently and haphazardly. Grazing grounds are also sparse. Thorough planning may make possible a certain expansion of the area under cultivation even if no water is brought to Sinai from the outside in large quantities. However, should novel methods make water available in adequate amounts and at a reasonable price, a revolutionary change may be brought about, both in agriculture and in settlement conditions.

Soil and Water. The largest concentration of land suitable for cultivation, principally loess and loess-sand soils, is to be found along the lower course of Wadi el-'Arīsh, south of the town of same name. Smaller parcels of similar soils are located near the Negev border in the east, between 'Aẓmon (el-Quẓeīma) and Kuntīlla. In the Pelusian Plain south of the Bardawīl Lagoon, between el-'Arīsh and Rumāni, date palms cover stretches of land between the sea shore and the salt playas, wherever only a thin cover of moving dunes hides the underlying more fertile soil. In the eastern section of the coastal region, between el-'Arīsh and Rafiaḥ, conditions are more problematic, as the dune cover is thicker there.

Relatively ample reserves of groundwater exist in the northwestern part of the coastal region, but even here the water is decidedly brackish, and a chloride content of 700–1,000 milligrams per liter is regarded as still acceptable (in most parts of Israel, 350 mg/liter is considered as the upper limit for irrigation). The high salt content is explained by the fact that the groundwater migrates over considerable distances before arriving at the wells or small springs, dissolving en route salts from the rocks or sands through which it seeps. Moreover, a large

Water is drawn from a 30-ft deep well in the Wadi Feirān marl stratum. A primitive leather container and a winch serve the purpose percentage of the water is lost by evaporation as soon as it reaches the surface, leaving behind a more concentrated solution of salts.

The oases in the valleys of the crystalline massif of the south, and particularly those of Wadi Feirān, owe their existence to strata of marl deposited in sections of these valleys by streams or lakes of the geologic past. These relatively porous marls hold the water of sudden rain storms, which rushes down the impervious granite walls of the mountain sides.

In 1926, the British Governor of Sinai, C. S. Jarvis, took the initiative in restoring ancient water-storage dams and building new ones in the Qadesh Barne'a oasis of northeastern Sinai. The installations then built have since lost much of their value, as the local inhabitants neglected their proper maintenance. The larger storage dam of a-Ruweīsa, built in the 1930's in the lower course of Wadi el-'Arīsh to hold 12 million m^3 of flash floodwaters annually for the irrigation of plantations on the side of this watercourse and the watering of flocks, has in the meantime silted up and is today practically unusable.

Agricultural Crops. By virtue of its tolerance of high soil and water salinity, the date palm produces the most important agricultural crop of the peninsula. Date palm plantations cover expanses of the coastal region between el-'Arīsh and Rumāni and in the area of 'Aẓmon and Qadesh Barne'a. In the oases of western and southwestern Sinai (e.g., 'Uyūn Mūsa, Wadi Tāyyibe near Abu Rudeīs, Sayyidna Mūsa near a-Tur, in the Wadi Feirān valley, etc.), they constitute the principal, and often the only branch of agriculture. In sandy areas, date palms are often planted in deep pits, in order to bring their roots closer to the underlying fertile soil and the groundwater table.

Near the Mediterranean coast, between el-'Arīsh and Rafiaḥ, and to some extent also in other areas, rhicinus bushes have been planted in recent years. These are able to thrive on poor sandy soils and subsist on minute quantities of water. Thanks to the introduction of hybrid seeds and progressive cultivation methods developed by Israel experts, yields have risen steeply since 1968. The demand for castor oil on world markets has increased greatly of late, as it has been found to be of superior quality for the maintenance of aircraft engines and other sensitive machinery, and is also used in the plastics industry. El-'Arīsh has a factory for the production of castor oil.

In the oases, vegetables, tobacco, grain, etc., are often grown, normally as intercultures between the date palms. Lemon, apple and mango trees are also to be found at several localities. In some oases and in vicinity of el-'Arīsh, there are groves of pomegranates, olives and almonds. The upper Wadi Feirān oases with their relatively cool climate have isolated grapevines and deciduous fruit trees, and the St. Catherine Monastery tends a few age-old vines and olives trees.

Ancient date palms in the ’Uyūn Mūsa oasis of western Sinai

In the experimental farm south of el-'Arīsh, at present the site of the settlement of Naḥal Sinai, attempts are being made to grow olives, citrus and other fruit trees, as well as fodder, cotton and other fields crops. At Naḥal Yam further west, out-of-season crops are grown on a small scale, partly under plastic covers.

Mineral Resources

The peoples of antiquity possessed knowledge of the presence of mineral resources in Sinai, and the peninsula is possibly one of those regions which saw the first attempts at quarrying or mining such treasures. At Sarābit al-Khadm in southwestern Sinai, for example, not far from the present-day manganese mines of Umm Būghma, traces of turquoise (and perhaps also copper) mines have been discovered, which were operated by Egyptian pharaohs of the third or second millennium B.C.E. In view of the harsh conditions of this desert country and its very sparse population throughout the historic past, such periods of mineral exploitation were invariably of brief duration. Slaves or prisoners-of-war generally constituted the labor force of such mines and appear to have lived under the most abject conditions.

During the last decades, the Egyptian Government made efforts to develop the exploitation of a number of mineral resources in Sinai (e.g., manganese, gypsum, ceramic clays, lignite, etc.). Even in our own century, however, mining methods were largely reliant on cheap labor and remained rather primitive. It appears that future mining activities will have to be rationalized and mechanized, and transport and sales organization streamlined, in order to become integrated within the framework of a progressive economy. Exceptions to this rule are the oil wells in the Suez Gulf and on its shores, which are operated in cooperation with international petroleum companies, with a production securing adequate returns.

Manganese. In the crystalline rocks, the Nubian sandstone series and its mostly Paleozoic marine intercalations which outcrop over a vast area in southern Sinai, the quarrying of manganese ore has attained economic proportions. Egypt has supplied this ore to a number of industrial nations in recent years.

The mining site, Umm Būghma, lies about 30 km to the east of the Suez Gulf port of Abu Zuneīma, at an altitude of 500–600 m. The unpaved road leading up to the mines winds through a narrow gorge between precipitous rock walls. At Umm Būghma, manganese is found over a surface area of about 10 km^2. It occurs in layers 10–60 cm thick to which its concentrates lend a sooty black color. The overall thickness of the stratum containing the ore is between 1 and 4 m; this bed

The manganese mines in the Nubian sandstone belt of Umm Būghma overlies the Nubian sandstone and is located at the base of a Carboniferous sequence of dolomites and shales. The ore contains, in various combinations, up to 18–20% manganese and 25–35% iron. Reserves are estimated at between 2 and 4 million tons.

The manganese deposits were discovered in 1898, and regular mining operations began in 1918. Since 1956, the working of this ore has been in the hands of an Egyptian government corporation. In 1960, production reached a peak of 284,000 tons of ore containing manganese and iron (this figure includes a few thousand tons of manganese mined elsewhere in Egypt). During recent years, annual production averaged 180,000 tons. The ore was transported by cable cars from the mines to the foot of the mountains, and thence by a narrow-gauge railway to Abu Zuneīma harbor. Egypt exported crude ore only, but a modern plant for smelting and beneficiation of the ore, capable of producing a concentrate of 90% manganese and iron, was under construction and about to be run in at the outbreak of the Six Day War.

The existence of additional manganese deposits near Sharm a-Sheikh, not far from the southern tip of the peninsula, has been reported, but no survey has been made there to the best of our knowledge, nor were any other steps taken to exploit this ore.

Copper. Copper ores are present both in the Nubian sandstone series and in the crystalline rocks of southern Sinai. A number of sites have been indicated on maps, e.g., in the vicinity of Umm Būghma and to the southeast, in the regions of the high mountains (e.g., near Jebel Mūsa), and near Sharm a-Sheikh, about 25 km north of Ras Nasrāni. The Egyptians started investigations near Umm Būghma, at sites where slag and other remains point to the mining of the ore in antiquity, both for purposes or ornamentation and for smelting of the metal. Probes were also made further to the southeast, but no exploitation was yet under way at any of these localities.

Iron and Other Metals. Iron occurs, together with manganese, at Umm Būghma, and it may safely be assumed to be present over fairly large expanses of southern Sinai. Until now, however, no ores are known with a ferrous content sufficiently high to justify mining expenses under the difficult conditions of Sinai, where transport costs in particular are exceedingly high because of the large distances and difficult terrain.

The possibility exists that the rocks of southern Sinai contain additional metals, e.g., lead, tin, zinc, gold, etc. However, there is no information available on concentrations of such metals which might have attracted miners of antiquity or could justify attempts at present-day exploitation.

Clays, Glass Sands. From Umm Būghma northward, in the direction of Jebel a-Tih, deposits of high-quality kaolinite clays have been discovered in a stratum overlying the manganiferous rock. Parts of these deposits were quarried intensively by the Egyptians during recent years. At Abu Zuneīma, heaps of mined kaolinite were found, ready for shipping overseas. Deposits of bentonite also appear to have been worked, this clay mineral being used for drilling mud in the oil fields along the Suez Gulf shores. Additional clay deposits are thought to exist elsewhere in southern Sinai. Glass sands, virtually free of iron impurities, occur quite extensively in the Nubian sandstones series of southern Sinai. However, it is not known whether the Egyptians had quarried this material or were considering such operations prior to June 1967.

Gypsum. An extensive area of gypsum deposits has been located on the low ground near the Suez Gulf shore, stretching from Ras Matārma in the north to Abu Zuneīma in the south. Certain quantities were quarried in the last years.

Coal. Considerable deposits of lignite were discovered in Middle Jurassic rocks of Jebel Maghāra in northwestern Sinai during the last decade. Commercial reserves are estimated at 35 million tons. Mines were opened in two measures, one 135 cm thick, and the other 70 cm. Annual production of 150,000 tons of lignite was planned for the first stage, to be stepped up to 300,000 tons around 1970. Here, too, mining operations were based on cheap labor, as approximately 1,000 men appear to have been engaged in working underground galleries prior to the Six Day War. Various European countries provided knowhow and machinery. Most of the lignite was destined for the Egyptian iron smelters at Heluan, where it was to be used together with imported high-grade coal in the ratio of 3 : 1.

Oil. There is no doubt that the oil buried in the rocks of the Sinai Peninsula and in the shallow parts of the shelf off the coast is far more valuable than all other mineral deposits taken together. Oil was first discovered in 1946 on the Suez Gulf shore. Since then it has been ascertained that the entire Suez Gulf, together with the adjoining coastal belts, constitutes a fairly important oil province. Production mounted from year to year. The first wells were sunk on land near the northern end of the gulf (Ras Sūdar, Āsal, Abu Rudeīs, etc.). Although the reserves in these early wells are now dwindling, the southward extension of these oil fields has been established. On the Sinai side of the gulf they stretch at least as far as Ras Gārra which is no more than 60 km from the southern tip of the peninsula.

The marine rock strata which contain the oil belong mostly to the Pliocene. Wells drilled in the sea bottom are usually found to be more productive than those on the land. Thus, on the western side of the gulf (which remained in

Egyptian hands after the Six Day War), the marine fields 'al-Morgan' and '23 July' are the most productive. On the Sinai side, the two Beleīm fields are the richest. 'Terrestrial Beleīm' had, at the beginning of 1967, 71 productive wells, and 'Marine Beleīm'—16; the marine field, however, equaled the yield of the terrestrial one, and was superior to the latter in that in all of its wells the oil reached the well mouth under free flow, while on the land pumping was necessary in 41 wells.

In 1966, Egypt obtained 6.5 million tons of oil from its own sources, out of 7 million tons required by its economy. Of this quantity, 4.5 million tons came from the wells on the Sinai shore which are at present in Israel's hands. It is estimated that the production of the existing Sinai oil fields can be increased, without great difficulty, to 10 million tons per annum. In addition, there are good prospects of finding oil also in northern Sinai, along the Mediterranean coast of the peninsula.

Roads

By virtue of its geographic position, the Sinai Peninsula constitutes a land bridge between Africa and Asia on the one hand, and between the Mediterranean and the Red Sea on the other. This explains the prime importance of roads traversing the peninsula, particularly those running in a west-east direction. Among the latter, we find three ancient international arteries: the Sea Road or Via Maris, connecting the Nile Valley with Mesopotamia, whose westernmost section follows the Mediterranean coast of Sinai; the Way of Shur, crossing Sinai between Isma'īliya and Niẓẓana and continuing westward to the central Nile Delta and eastward to Beersheba, where it links up with the Hill Road ascending to Hebron, Bethlehem, Jerusalem, Ramallah and Nablus; the Pilgrims' Road which, coming from Cairo and running across Sinai, connects Suez with Eilat, and then continues along the west coast of the Arabian Peninsula to the Islamic centers of Mecca and Medina. Control of these roads was the sole motivation of the various powers who sought possession of the Sinai Peninsula, and thus the role of Sinai in world history and politics has been determined almost exclusively by these traffic arteries.

The Sea Road. The path traced by the Via Maris, which does not seem to have changed much from antiquity to the present day, was largely dictated by topography. Today, a railroad parallels the highway. The Sea Road follows, wherever possible, the narrow strip of ground between the salt swamps to the north and the moving sand dunes to the south, affording easy passage. In many

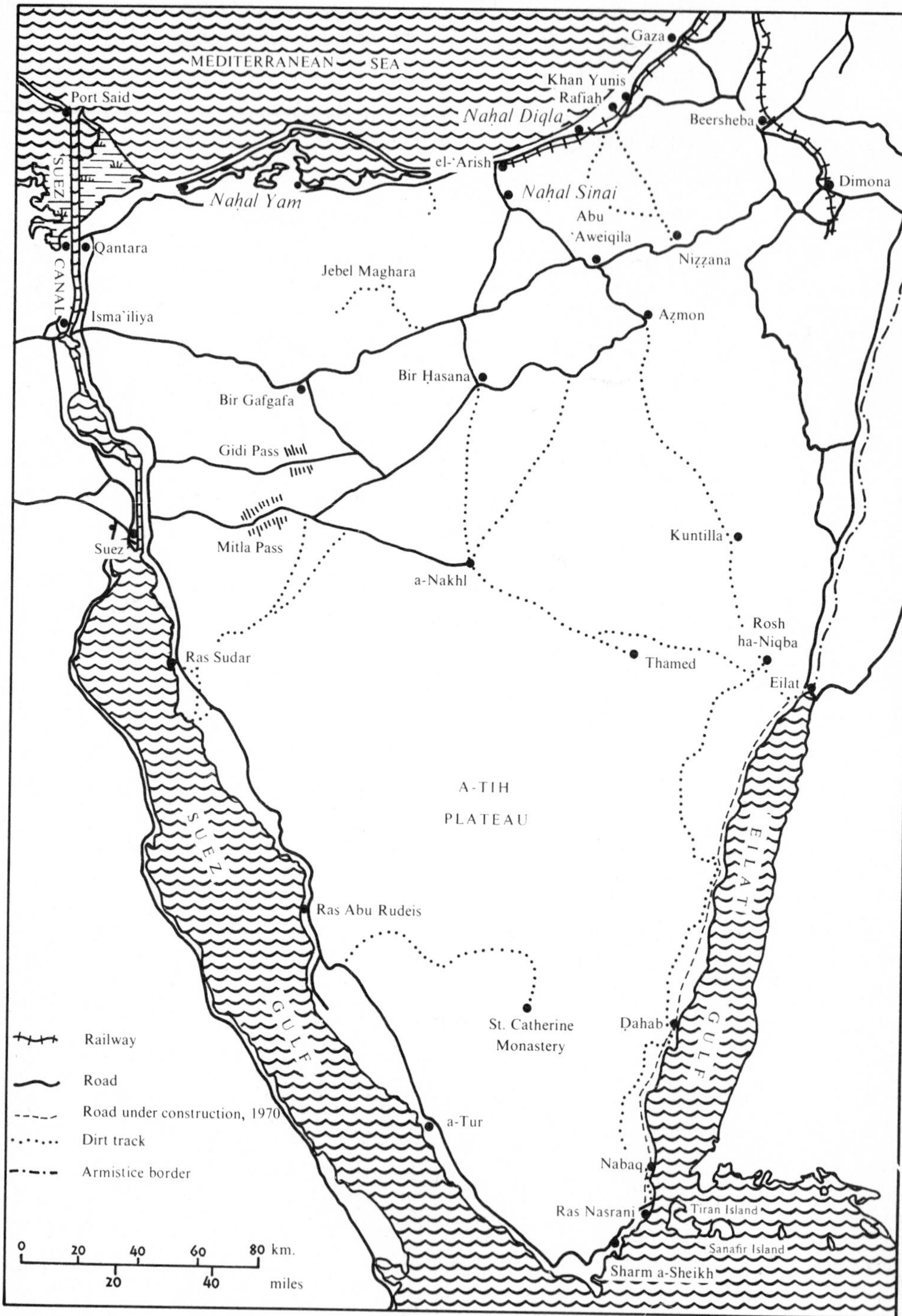

Roads and centers in Sinai

places it passes close to sites with water cisterns, wells or oases which may serve as resting places for wayfarers. The Via Maris enters Sinai from the west at al-Qantāra, near the southern extremity of the salt marshes which stretch from Port Sa'īd southward between the al-Mānzala Lagoon of Egypt and the a-Tīna Bay west of the Bardawīl Lagoon (which is called, in ancient Jewish literature, the 'Sirbonian Sea'). The road runs northeastward along the rim of the swamps, approaches the western tip of the Bardawīl Lagoon near Rumāni, and thence continues to el-'Arīsh where it crosses Wadi el-'Arīsh near its mouth. At Rafiaḥ the road enters the 'sown land' of Israel—the former western border of the Gaza Strip. The Sinai stretch of the Sea Road is approximately 200 km long.

The Way of Shur. The route of this ancient road is assumed to be almost identical to the present Isma'īliya-Niẓẓana highway. The road encounters more topographical obstacles than the Sea Road, and waterholes are less frequent along its course. It crosses flat North Sinai, running between the hill groups of Jebel Yi'allaq and Jebel Ḥallāl to the south, and Jebel Maghāra and Jebel Lībni to the north. Bir Gāfgafa in the west, and Abu 'Aweīqila in the east, desert stations along its course, were of strategic importance in both the 1956 and 1967 campaigns. It is considered probable that the Patriarchs descended to Egypt along the Way of Shur and that the Children of Israel, in their exodus from Egypt, again passed along certain sections of this road. The distance between Isma'īliya and Niẓẓana along this highway exceeds 240 km.

The Pilgrims' Road. Of the three west-east thoroughfares, the Pilgrims' Road, called Dharb el-Ḥaj in Arabic, is the most difficult to traverse. While the aforementioned two roads have been metaled and today provide for the ready passage of motorized traffic along their entire length, the Pilgrims' Road is surfaced only in its western section, between the Mītla Pass and a-Nakhl. The Mītla Pass winds between the hills of the uplifted outer rim of the a-Tih Plateau. The road descends to the plateau center of Qāla'at a-Nakhl (the name means 'Date Palm Fortress,' although today no such trees grow there), where it crosses the upper course of Wadi el-'Arīsh. Here, the Pilgrims' Road takes a more southeasterly turn, to pass Thāmed and the Rosh ha-Niqba Pass, whence it descends to Eilat. This highway was already in existence several hundred years before the advent of Islam and appears to have served both nomads wandering between Arabia and Egypt, and Roman and Nabatean merchants. It was also used for military expeditions, e.g., during a Turkish attempt to break through to the Suez Canal in World War I, and by an Israel column in the 1956 Sinai Campaign. In 1967, in the period preceding the Six Day War, the Egyptians were preparing to advance along this line with the aim of severing Eilat from the rest of

Israel. The length of the Pilgrims' Road in Sinai, like that of the Way of Shur, is about 240 km.

North-South Roads. Two major north-south roads cross Sinai, the eastern one passing close to the Negev border, and the western route running along the Suez Canal and the Suez Gulf shore. While the eastern thoroughfare was important in antiquity, the western road rose to prominence only during the last decades. Forming the eastern highway, two roads meet at the 'Aẓmon (al-Quẓeīma) junction: one comes from Rafiaḥ via Niẓẓana, and the other from el-'Arīsh through Bir Laḥfān and Abu 'Aweīqila. From 'Aẓmon onward the road follows a south-southeasterly course, paralleling the former Israel-Sinai border. Its principal stations are Kuntīlla and Rosh ha-Niqba. The terrain crossed by this track, though by no means easy, is nevertheless far smoother than that along the Beersheba-Miẓpe Ramon-Eilat highway because, in contrast to the latter, the former circumvents the Negev Highlands block in the west instead of ascending it and crossing its ravines and craters. Traffic along the road was brisk in the days of the Nabateans, who carried goods to and from the Mediterranean ports and continued their way from Eilat to their capital Petra in the mountain region of Edom.

The western highway is paralleled by a railroad between Port Fu'ād (opposite Port Sa'īd) and Port Taufīq (opposite Suez). Being suitable for vehicular traffic over most of its length, it provides an access to Sinai's most important mining sites (oil wells, manganese mines, gypsum and kaolin quarries). The road approaches the southern end of the peninsula and then turns to the northeast, terminating at Ras Nasrāni near the Tirān Straits.

Connecting Roads. Road sections connecting the main highways have been developed chiefly in north Sinai, where the Egyptians made efforts to build and maintain them, principally for military purposes. In central and southern Sinai, by way of contrast, only few such roads are to be found.

An important thoroughfare issues from el-'Arīsh to the south. From Bir Laḥfān it takes a turn to the southwest, to meet the Way of Shur west of Jebel Lībni, and then continues southward to Bir al-Ḥāsana where it again follows a southwesterly course, finally joining the Pilgrims' Road at a site called Sidr al-Ḥeitān in front of the Mītla Pass. More desert tracks issue from the Bir al-Ḥāsana crossroads, one running south to a-Nakhl, and another northeast to the vicinity of 'Aẓmon. The a-Nakhl junction, too, is linked with 'Aẓmon by a dirt track. The newly metaled roads include the thoroughfare connecting the two former military camps, Bir a-Thamāde on the Pilgrims' Road and Bir Gāfgafa on the Way of Shur, and the road leading from Bir a-Thamāde, over the Gidi Pass (north of the Mītla Pass), to the Small Bitter Lake. A side road branching off the Way of Shur climbs Jebel Maghāra and provides access to its lignite mines.

In the west and southwest, several short roads have been built, leading from the main highway to the oil fields near the coast. Also of importance are several second-class roads, one of which leads to the Umm Būghma manganese mines, while another, apparently very old, reaches the St.Catherine monastery via the Feirān oasis.

The Suez Canal

The Suez Canal undoubtedly represents one of the most profound man-made changes on the physical map of the globe. The Canal connects the Mediterranean with the Red Sea, and through them—the Atlantic with the Indian Ocean. The waterway has not only shortened lines of maritime communications and greatly influenced world commerce, but has also had a certain impact on natural conditions, enabling, for instance, marine fauna to pass from the Red Sea to the Mediterranean, where it acclimatizes to its new surroundings.

History of the Canal. The idea of linking the Mediterranean with the Red Sea was conceived long before our times. Ancient authors such as Aristotle and the geographer Strabo report that a canal was dug between an eastern arm of the Nile Delta (no longer in existence) and the Suez Gulf. Herodotus tells of Pharaoh Necho's attempt to excavate a canal which, according to the historian, took toll of the lives of 120,000 workers. A stone tablet found at Isma'īliya bears an inscription relating the conquest of Egypt by the Persian King Cyrus and of the digging of a canal at his behest. Under the Roman Emperor Trajan, a similar canal was in use and remained so until the first period of Islamic occupation in the 8th century. In the 15th and 16th centuries, Venetian merchants thought of reviving Mediterranean commerce, which had suffered since the discovery of a sea route to India via the Cape of Good Hope, by opening anew the sea lane to the Red Sea. Napoleon, during his Middle Eastern campaign of 1798–99, considered a similar enterprise, but his engineers hesitated as they erroneously assumed the Red Sea level to be 10 m higher than that of the Mediterranean.

In the middle of the nineteenth century, Ferdinand de Lesseps, a retired French diplomat living in Egypt, won for this project the support of the Khedive Ismail, then ruler over Egypt on behalf of the Turkish Empire, and also succeeded in mobilizing capital in France for the construction of the Canal. Work began in 1859, first carried out by 20,000 Egyptian forced laborers who were later replaced by 4,000 workers brought over from Europe. The capital investment amounted to £ 18 million. On 19 November, 1869, the Canal was opened at an impressive ceremony to which numerous Heads of State from all parts of the world were invited.

Following the initiative of the British Prime Minister Benjamin Disraeli, Great Britain secured for herself the greater part of the Suez Canal Company stocks, paying for them the sum of £4 million. The Canal thus became the lifeline of the British Empire.

In 1888, an international conference endorsed the Constantinople Convention, which stipulates that the Canal has to remain open for the ships of all nations without exception, in times of war as in times of peace. Egypt infringed on this principal clause by closing the Canal to Israel shipping after the 1948 War, also ignoring a decision by the UN Security Council, in September 1951, ordering her to permit the passage of Israel ships.

In July 1956, Egypt unilaterally nationalized the Canal Company, prompting the Security Council to call, once again, for free and unhampered maritime passage through that waterway—a call which, once again, went unheeded. At the end of October, France and Great Britain occupied parts of the Canal Zone, at the time of the Sinai Campaign, which in turn caused Egypt to close the Canal for a couple of months. After the Six Day War of 1967, Egypt sealed off the Canal anew, while Israel forces were posted on the eastern bank of the Canal.

Length of the Canal and of Its Sections. The Suez Canal measures 164 km in length from its northern entrance, between the twin cities of Port Sa'īd and Port Fu'ād, to the southern inlet, where the three cities of Suez, Port Ibrahīm and Port Taufīq are situated. The general direction of the Canal is north-south. The presence along its course of three natural water bodies, Lake Timsaḥ and the Small and Great Bitter lakes, facilitated excavation work. In its northernmost section, over a stretch of 53 km between Port Sa'īd and al-Qantāra, the Canal runs through the shallow al-Mānzala Lagoon and the mud flats to the south which are periodically flooded by sea water. The second section, from al-Qantāra to the entrance of Lake Timsaḥ near Isma'īliya, is 29 km long. Here, near al-Balāḥ, the Canal bifurcates, permitting simultaneous passage of shipping in opposite directions; such two-way traffic is impossible along other sections of the Canal. South of the point where the two arms meet again, is the revolving bridge of Firdān, providing for road and rail traffic between Egypt and Sinai. The section between the northern entrance of Lake Timsaḥ and that of the Great Bitter Lake measures $17\frac{3}{4}$ km and that inside the two Bitter Lakes—35 km. The southernmost section ending at Port Taufīq is $28\frac{3}{4}$ km long.

Upon completion of the Canal in 1869, it was already evident that its dimensions (depth—$7\frac{1}{2}$ m, surface width—57 m, bottom width—24 m) were

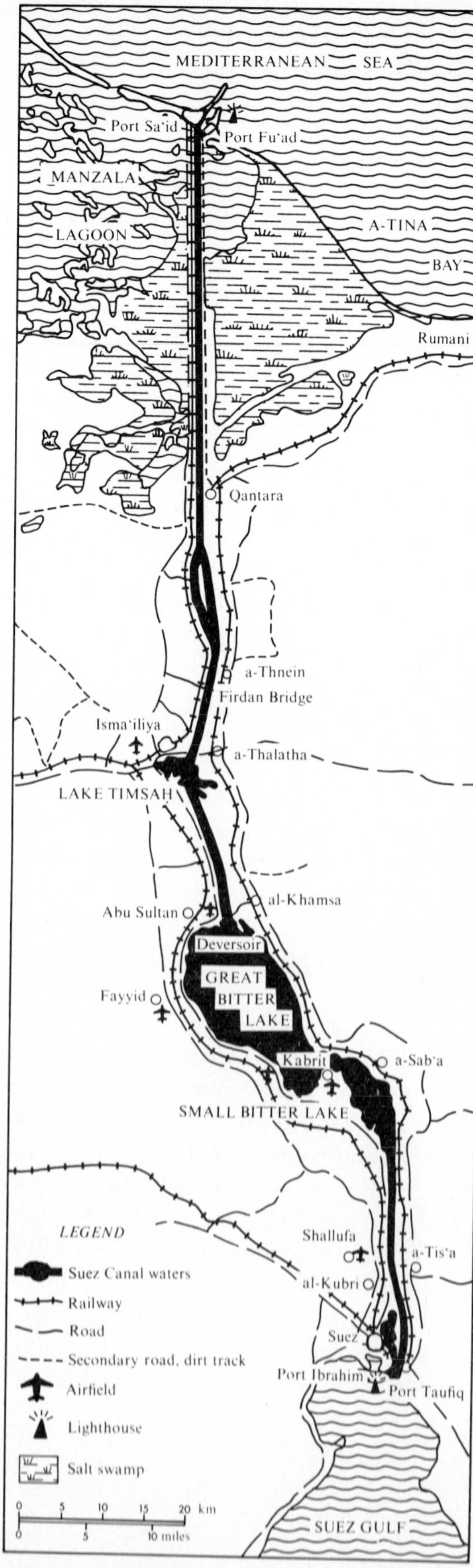
MEDITERRANEAN SEA
Port Sa'id
Port Fu'ad
MANZALA
LAGOON
A-TINA
BAY
Rumani
Qantara
a-Thnein
Firdan Bridge
Isma'iliya
a-Thalatha
LAKE TIMSAH
al-Khamsa
Abu Sultan
Deversoir
GREAT
BITTER
LAKE
Fayyid
Kabrit
a-Sab'a
SMALL BITTER LAKE
LEGEND
Suez Canal waters
Railway
Road
Secondary road, dirt track
Airfield
Lighthouse
Salt swamp
0 5 10 15 20 km
0 5 10 miles
Shallufa
a-Tis'a
al-Kubri
Suez
Port Ibrahim
Port Taufiq
SUEZ GULF

The Suez Canal

inadequate to permit passage of the larger motor vessels then in use. It was therefore enlarged immediately, this stage of the work reaching completion in 1875. Subsequently, the Canal has undergone several widenings and deepenings. Its present minimum surface width is 100 m, increasing to 164 m along certain sections, and the bottom width is 65 m. Ships of a maximum draft of $11\frac{1}{2}$ m can pass through the Canal.

Maintenance and Navigation Problems. The huge quantities of sand incessantly introduced by the frequent desert dust storms on both sides of the Canal cause large-scale silting of this waterway. Continuous dredging is therefore imperative to prevent blockage of the Canal within a brief span of time. In the ninety-year interval between the Canal's completion and its closure in 1967, the quantity of earth dredged from it was six times greater than that excavated during its actual construction. In 1957, when Egypt resolved to re-open the Canal after the Sinai Campaign, several months of intensive dredging work were necessary before ships could pass through. In view of the fact that all work on the Canal has been suspended for a considerably longer period after the Six Day War, experts doubt whether the huge expenditure involved in clearing this waterway would be warranted, even should a political settlement make provision for its re-opening.

To these difficulties of maintenance must be added the damage constantly caused to the Canal bottom and walls by ships passing through, and by waves and currents they set in motion. Ships' keels throw waves obliquely toward the Canal sides from where they are forcefully turned back to swirl in a strong vortex in the ships' wake. This not only causes extensive erosion damage to the Canal itself but also makes navigation extremely hazardous. The captains of all ships seeking passage are therefore required to enlist the services of a pilot of the Canal Company who is intimately acquainted with local conditions.

Past Use and Profitability Prospects. Sea lanes were decisively shortened by the Suez Canal. The distance between Marseilles and Bombay, for example, measures only 9,000 km via the Canal, as compared to 19,000 km along the Cape route. Since the Second World War, traffic through the Suez Canal has increased by leaps and bounds. While in 1946 the total tonnage passing through amounted to 21 million, it attained 107 million in 1955, and close to 250 million in 1966. It should be noted that the proportion of crude oil transported through the Canal has increased steadily, amounting to 75% of the total tonnage in recent years. This explains the great disparity in loads traveling in different directions, with about 80% of the total tonnage moving from south to north. The number of passengers passing through the Canal reached 500,000 in peak years, but has decreased rapidly over the last decades, with air travel replacing passenger ships.

Even should the Canal be opened anew in the future, its prospects do not seem as promising as might be inferred from the figures cited above. The reason for this lies in the increasing use of supertankers of 100,000 tons and more load capacity; passage in the Canal is restricted to ships of 45,000–65,000 tons. The route distance becomes a less important factor in transport costs as the load of the individual ship increases. A preferable solution to the oil transportation problem is seen by many in the plan to lay pipelines between two ports open to giant ships, e.g., the 42-inch line operating since 1969 between Eilat and Ashqelon, or the one planned to link Suez with Alexandria. Such pipelines may, in the long run, totally supplant the Suez Canal.

Sinai in Modern History

The Problem of Political Borders. Only toward the end of the nineteenth century was serious consideration given to the drawing of exactly defined political borders for Sinai. The peninsula had never constituted an independent political unit. Whoever controlled the highways crossing Sinai was inherently held to be its ruler. In most periods of the historic past, both Sinai and Palestine came under the same power, e.g., the Persian Empire, the realm of Alexander the Great, the Roman and Byzantine empires, the early Arab caliphates, the rule of the Mamelukes and Turks. All these felt little need to give formal expression to their ownership of Sinai, and were, in general, content with safeguarding for themselves the peninsula's vital thoroughfares, occasionally also attempting exploitation of some of its mineral wealth.

The situation began to change gradually after Napoleon's campaign to Egypt and Palestine (1797–1799) brought the eastern Mediterranean basin into the orbit of European power politics. This development was accelerated when the idea of building the Suez Canal was mooted.

Since the sixteenth century, Palestine and Egypt were included within the borders of the Ottoman Empire. Turkish rule was interrupted for but a brief ten-year spell between 1831 and 1840, when the Egyptian Governor Mehemet Ali revolted against the Sultan and extended his rule over Palestine, appointing Ibrahim Pasha as his governor in the latter province. By the treaty of 1841 Palestine was returned to direct Turkish rule; Egypt retained certain autonomy but the Sultan became the Egyptian Khedive's suzerain. Even at that juncture no need was yet felt for a clear delimitation of the frontiers between Turkey and Egypt. In 1882, however, the British occupied Egypt and in fact took over its administration. The Khedive was permitted to remain in his post and his formal allegiance to the Turkish throne was not questioned. As master of the Suez

The small Almogim (Jezirat Far'un) Island south of Eilat, crowned by the ruins of a large fortress the Crusaders erected to serve their campaign aimed at the conquest of Mecca

Canal, Great Britain from now on saw her interest in removing the Turks as far as possible from the Empire's lifeline. Turkey countered by claiming most of Sinai for herself in 1892. The triangle el-'Arīsh-Suez-Eilat was then considered to form part of Turkey's Palestinian provinces, while South Sinai was held to be a separate Turkish region. Anglo-Egyptian interests were respected, to some extent, on the east bank of the Suez Canal and in the Pelusian Plain.

British pressure grew over the years. In 1906, Britain demanded a frontier running from el-'Arīsh to Eilat, and British troops actually occupied an area close to the latter site. Turkey came up with a compromise proposal to partition Sinai by a line running straight from el-'Arīsh to Ras Muḥammad, thus giving Egypt exclusive control over the Gulf of Suez, and leaving Turkey in control of the Gulf of Eilat. Britain replied with a sharp ultimatum to the Sublime Porte. The Sultan backed down and gave his consent to a boundary securing for Egypt not only the regions Britain had demanded but also the area of Turkish Palestine between el-'Arīsh and Rafiaḥ, which had never been discussed previously. This new border line became, after the First World War, the frontier of the British Mandate over Palestine and, in the 1949 Armistice Agreement with Egypt, along most of its length, also that of the State of Israel. After the Sinai Campaign of 1956 had temporarily removed the border, it was again given validity in 1957, but ceased to exist after the Six Day War of 1967.

Attempts at Jewish Settlement in Sinai. The idea of Jewish settlement in Sinai, first raised at the beginning of the twentieth century, was soon caught up in the struggle over delineating political borders there. In 1899, Davis Trietsch, a delegate to the Zionist Congress, presented a program for comprehensive Jewish settlement in Eretz Israel, which was to include also its marginal areas. It contained proposals for 'Egyptian Palestine,' i.e., Sinai, and particularly the Pelusian Plain west of el-'Arīsh. Trietsch outlined plans for the construction of 'garden cities' where trade and industry were to be developed alongside agriculture, in order to absorb a maximum number of immigrants. The idea was taken up with interest and enthusiasm by Theodor Herzl, who in those days was meeting with mounting difficulties in his efforts to obtain from the Turkish Government a 'charter' officially endorsing large-scale Jewish settlement in Palestine. In 1902, Herzl contacted the British Government headed by Joseph Chamberlain, with Lord Lansdowne as Foreign Minister. He requested a concession for a Jewish national region in Sinai to be developed under Egyptian control. The British initially favored Herzl's scheme, seeing in it a means, in the first phase, of establishing a buffer zone between Turkey and the Suez Canal and, later, eventually of pushing Turkey out of Palestine proper. Herzl won over to the idea the British Lord Nathaniel Rothschild and, through him, other wealthy Jews who promised support for the venture once its execution became feasible.

Chamberlain asked the British Governor of Egypt, Lord Cromer, to examine with good will the details of Herzl's project. It appears, however, that Lord Cromer feared that an autonomous Jewish community would, in the long run, upset British Middle East policy more than promote it, He probably also disliked the urgency of Herzl's pleas, which sprang from his desire to alleviate the rapidly deteriorating situation of Russian and Rumanian Jewry in those days. Lord Cromer stipulated that a fact-finding expedition should first go to Sinai and report on conditions there before he could form an opinion.

The members of this expedition were three Englishmen representing the Egyptian Government, and four Jews—the British Colonel Avigdor Goldsmid who was well acquainted with the relevant problems, having directed Baron Hirsch's Jewish settlement enterprise in Argentina; the Viennese architect O. Marmorek, one of Herzl's close associates in the Zionist Movement; two Palestinians, the doctor Hillel Jaffe, and the agronomist Dr. Zelig Soskin. The expedition toured Sinai, principally its northern parts, in the months of February and March, 1903. In its report it did not in any way question the feasibility of the project, but discussed practical steps to be taken for its execution. Among its suggestions were the construction of dams to retain flash floods coming down through Wadi el-'Arīsh and its tributaries, the development of the Pelusian Plain with the aid of Nile water which was to be led to Sinai instead of flowing unused into the sea, rinsing of salts from the soil with sweet water prior to its intensive cultivation, construction of a port at or near el-'Arīsh, founding of factories, exploiting fishing grounds in the Bardawīl Lagoon and in the Mediterranean Sea, etc. The expedition also recommended the setting up and running of experimental farms for a certain period before the launching of large-scale settlement in Sinai. This last proposal embittered Herzl who awaited the expedition's return in Cairo, as he saw in this a delay endangering the speedy rescue of East European Jewry. The entire project, however, met with the resolute opposition of Lord Cromer, based on the contention that no surplus Nile waters were available for Sinai. In reaching his decision he was possibly influenced by the wish to retain such waters for irrigation in the Sudan, a country in whose development British policy was interested at the time. Herzl tried to save at least part of the scheme by abandoning the claim to Nile waters and restricting his request to the el-'Arīsh area. However, even these concessions failed to gain him the British Governor's consent.

The failure of Herzl's plan did not yet spell the end of Zionist attempts at settlement in Sinai. Between the years 1905 and 1913, efforts were repeatedly made to acquire land holdings between Rafiaḥ and el-'Arīsh, an area lying close to Turkish Palestine yet outside Turkish jurisdiction. Such projects were initiated both by Palestinian Jews, by Zionist groups of Eastern Europe and by a society set up for this purpose by Zionists in Germany. Several missions set out for Gaza, Rafiaḥ and Cairo, to survey land plots, collect data on ownership of the tracts in question, on legal conditions, etc. The principal difficulty arose from the fact that most of the bedouin offering land for sale could not verify their ownership, as the holdings were not entered in the land registry. Efforts in this direction ceased with the outbreak of the First World War and the drawing of the British Mandate borders.

Sinai Battles in Israel's War of Independence. Toward the end of 1948, the military initiative was gradually gained by the Israel Army. In 'Operation Ḥorev' (also called 'Operation Ayin'), Israel soldiers crossed the Sinai frontier at Niẓẓana, advanced along the 'Way of Shur' to the Abu 'Aweīqila fortifications, and thence turned northwestward to take up positions at the southern entrances of el-'Arīsh. Near Rafiaḥ, they also reached the Sea Road leading to el-'Arīsh, and approached the town of Gaza. The operation came to a halt when Britain warned that her troops stationed near the Suez Canal might intervene on behalf of Egypt. In the ensuing Armistice Agreement with Egypt, the former Sinai frontier was reestablished and the Gaza Strip was placed temporarily under Egyptian administration.

The Sinai Campaign. In 1956, the ever-increasing infiltration of terror gangs sent from Egypt to carry out murder missions against Israel's civilian population, and the concerted plan of Arab states to wage a war of extinction against Israel in the spring of the following year, made the Sinai Campaign inevitable. On October 29, the Israel Army launched a three-pronged attack; from Niẓẓana toward 'Aẓmon and Abu'Aweīqila; from the Paran Plateau toward Kuntīlla; and from Eilat over the Rosh ha-Niqba Pass toward Thāmed. On the first day of fighting, paratroopers were dropped over the Mītla Pass where they dug in while fighting a fierce battle.

On the following day, Israel forces gained control over the road between Rosh ha-Niqba and Mītla Pass, together with the strongholds of Thāmed and a-Nakhl. Other units took up positions round Abu 'Aweīqila. On October 31, this fortress fell, as did the strategic crossroads west of Jebel Lībni. Simultaneously, forces advanced along the Rafiaḥ–el-'Arīsh axis. Most phases of the operation were concluded on November 2, when Israel colums, complying with the demand of the British and French, halted their advance at a distance of 10 miles from the Suez Canal, after another column had reached Ras Nasrāni and the Tirān Straits over hazardous routes from Rosh ha-Niqba, along or near the Eilat Gulf coast. By November 3, Israel forces had occupied the entire peninsula, and all Egyptian resistance had ceased.

Complying with UN demands and relying on promises that its shipping rights would henceforth be safeguarded and the peace on the Egyptian border be kept by a UN force, Israel carried out, between January and March 1957, its gradual withdrawal from Sinai and the Gaza Strip, at the same time reserving the right to renewed action should Egypt again try to interfere with shipping in the Tirān Straits.

The Six Day War. Egypt did not adhere to the understanding reached in the United Nations, and the Suez Canal remained closed to Israel vessels. The Arabs never ceased to proclaim their intention of wiping Israel off the map. In the spring of 1967, Egypt took the initiative in challenging Israel, after the Soviet Union had deliberately supplied her with false information on alleged Israel troop concentrations along the Syrian border. Beginning from May 15, Egypt assembled an aggressive force in Sinai near the Israel border, comprising at least 100,000 soldiers and 900–1,000 tanks. Requesting and obtaining the immediate evacuation of the UN Emergency Force, Egypt sent troops to take up positions at Ras Nasrāni. The Egyptian President declared the Tirān Straits closed to Israel shipping, adding that should Israel interpret this as an act of war, such a development would be welcomed by Egypt. Nasser gave further emphasis to these threats by declaring his full support for the al-Fataḥ terror organization and stepping up the shelling of Israel border villages.

Moved by the need to secure her very existence, Israel responded on the morning of June 5, 1967, opening with an air strike against enemy airforce bases that destroyed on the ground most of the military aircraft of Egypt and the other belligerent Arab countries. Four Egyptian airfields in Sinai were among those put out of action. On the same day, three Israel columns swept into Sinai. The northernmost column forced its way through enemy formations between Khan Yūnis and Rafiaḥ in the Gaza Strip and advanced, after hard-won battles, along the Sea Road toward el-'Arīsh, at whose outskirts it arrived in the evening; another force had pushed forward and reached the approaches of the airfield south of the town. The central column grouped itself around Abu 'Aweīqila and blocked the el-'Arīsh–Abu 'Aweīqila road near Bir Laḥfān.

On the morning of June 6, Abu 'Aweīqila fell and the occupation of el-'Arīsh was completed. At noon, Israeli troops entered Gaza. That evening, the northern forces stood at Rumāni northeast of al-Qantāra. In the center, the crossroads west of Jebel Lībni fell into Israel hands, while the southern force reached the Pilgrims' Road at Thāmed. On June 7, the northern arm posted itself along the Canal bank at al-Qantāra and occupied the vast camp of Bir Gāfgafa, while the central force advanced rapidly over Bir Ḥāsana and Bir a-Thamāde to the Mītla Pass, thereby cutting off the enemy's main line of retreat. When, on the same day, Israel forces borne by ship and helicopter arrived at Ras Nasrāni near the Tirān Straits, they found it deserted. On June 8, all seven Egyptian divisions were utterly routed, and disorganized enemy troops attempted to reach the Canal and swim across. On June 9, Israel completed the occupation of the peninsula; in the evening Egypt accepted a cease-fire. Since that date, Sinai has been under Israel administration. The menace to Israel by an Egyptian military build-up has been removed by at least 250 kilometers. A final decision on Sinai's future must be included in a formal and binding peace treaty to be concluded between Israel and Egypt.

Population and Settlements

Throughout its history, Sinai has been a very thinly populated region. During most periods, the majority of its inhabitants were nomads or semi-nomads who derived their modest livelihood from local sources—the poor pasture lands and a few oases where date palms, and occasionally certain other crops, can be grown. In addition, there were semi-nomads living from fishing, principally in the Bardawīl Lagoon, and to a smaller extent, from shell fishing and pearl diving on the Suez and Eilat Gulf coasts. The minority were people settled in Sinai by outside factors in order to fulfil two main tasks—to secure and maintain the important highways which cross the peninsula, and to exploit mineral resources. Whereas most of the nomads can trace the continued presence of their tribes in Sinai through many generations, the above-mentioned minority group is characterized by mobility and a lack of roots in the region. A third population unit, set apart from the others, is constituted by Greek-Orthodox monks, mainly at the St. Catherine Monastery, and by the Jabalīya tribe supplying services to this monastery.

Population Figures. Numerically, Sinai's population appears to have undergone frequent and extreme fluctuations. This is illustrated by data of the last fifty years: an estimate in 1917—which may be incomplete—gave a total of 5,430 persons for the entire peninsula. Shortly before the Six Day War of 1967, the Egyptian authorities put the figure of Sinai's population at approximately 130,000: 100,000 in the north of the peninsula, and the rest spread throughout its other parts. In the census carried out by Israel in the fall of 1967, 33,441 persons were counted in northern Sinai, the estimate for the other regions not exceeding a few additional thousands. This indicates that the Egyptian figures of early 1967 had been obviously exaggerated—even allowing for the demographic dislocation caused by the war. Up to the summer of 1968, former inhabitants of Sinai were permitted to return in exchange for repatriation of Egyptian citizens, but these movements do not seem to have substantially influenced the population total. Certain changes may occur in the future, following, for example, the opportunity given to inhabitants of the Gaza Strip to move to other regions under Israel's administration, or the establishment of *Naḥal* (Pioneer Settler Corps) villages in Sinai.

The Nomads. Ancient inhabitants of Sinai, presumably nomad hunters, left testimony of their presence in the form of rock paintings and, later, in the second millennium B.C.E., also of inscriptions (the 'proto-Sinaitic' signs constituting the oldest alphabetic script hitherto known). Such graffiti are most frequently

Nomads with their camels resting in a rock gorge of southern Sinai

encountered in the south, e.g., in Wadi Mukāttab ('Inscription Valley') northwest of the St. Catherine Monastery.*

Two main groups are usually distinguished among the present-day bedouin inhabitants: those of the a-Tih Plateau and northern Sinai. Among the latter are members of three large tribes known also in the Negev before 1948: the Tiyāha (whose name, 'Wanderers,' is identical with that of the a-Tih Plateau); the Trabīn of northwestern Sinai (their name, derived from the Arabic 'trab' = 'soil,' points to their semi-nomadic existence, as they have apparently always sown fields in addition to herding flocks); and the Aḥyawāt of eastern Sinai bordering on Eilat.

* A far larger number of inscriptions there, mostly in Greek, dates from Nabatean times (first century C.E.).

The St. Catherine Monastery is laid out as a rectangular fortress. At the side of the magnificent church of Byzantine age, a mosque was built so as to discourage Moslem attacks

Many of the Sinai bedouin have adopted a more or less sedentary life in or near oases, particularly in northwestern Sinai between el-'Arīsh and al-Qantāra. They have, however, retained their tribal organization and bedouin lore and customs. The largest of the oases is al-Quẓeīma (presumably Biblical 'Aẓmon), about 20 km south of Niẓẓana in eastern Sinai, near the Biblical site and springs of Qadesh Barne'a. An archeological survey made there after the 1956 Sinai War revealed remnants of the Late Bronze and Iron ages (the latter corresponding to the period of the Judges and the Kings), as well as of Roman, Nabatean and Byzantine occupation. Other oases are to be found in southwestern Sinai, e.g., 'Uyūn Mūsa southeast of Suez, Wadi Tāyyibe near Abu Zuneīma, and Sayyīdna Mūsa near a-Ṭur.

The bedouin of southern Sinai are known under the collective name of Ṭawarāt, which is supposedly connected with the town of a-Ṭur, for a number of centuries the only permanently inhabited site in this part of the peninsula. Their principal tribe is the Sawālḥa, most members of which live in the coastal strip near the Suez Gulf.

A group apart from the rest of the Sinai inhabitants are the Jabalīya ('Mountain People'). These were originally Christians whom Emperor Justinian sent to Sinai from Egypt and Dacia (present-day Rumania) to attend as lay servants the monks of the St. Catherine Monastery that was founded, at his behest, circa 550 C.E. In the course of time, the Jabalīya appear to have absorbed other elements, among them perhaps also Negro slaves. Most of the Jabalīya were converted to Islam as early as the first centuries after the Mohammedan conquest (640 C.E.); the last Christian among them, an old woman, is reported to have died around 1750. In spite of their common faith, the other Sinai inhabitants refrain from contacts with the Jabalīya and regard them as inferior. Following ancient custom, the monastery rewards the bedouin for their services with monthly flour rations and other naturalia. After June, 1967, the Israel Government has undertaken provision of the monastery with flour for this purpose. Most of the Jabalīya live at the large Feirān oasis (which tradition tends to identify with Biblical Rephidim), while a smaller number dwell in the immediate vicinity of the monastery.

The Non-Nomads. The vast majority of the St. Catherine monks have invariably been of Greek origin, the Greek-Orthodox authorities selecting candidates. In the past, as many as 300 are reported to have dwelt there at one time. Their number dropped to about thirty in the last century, and at present there are only nine monks resident at the monastery.

The earliest of the fortresses guarding roads in Sinai are thought to be those built along the Via Maris. One of the oldest of these appears to have stood at the present site of el-'Arīsh. As this name means 'Hut' in Arabic, some scholars propose identifying this locality with the exodus camp of Sukkoth (the Hebrew word for 'huts'). The Greeks called the town 'Rhinokoroura' which may be translated as 'City of Cut Noses' and alludes to the tale that here an Egyptian ruler kept prisoners maimed in this cruel way. Alexander Jannaeus, the Hasmonean king, conquered Rhinokoroura, presumably intending to seal the marine trade outlet of his Nabatean enemies. Even in later centuries, el-'Arīsh maintained its importance, and Napoleon, on his Palestinian campaign (1799), was surprised to encounter a strong fortress here, the resistance of which caused a fatal delay in his march to the north.

Qāla'at a-Nakhl, situated at a crossroad in the interior, rose to significance with the increase of Moslem pilgrimage to Mecca via the Dharb al-Ḥaj. Its importance waned, however, when Egyptian pilgrims began, in the last century, to show preference for the sea voyage to Jedda. This development gave prominence to a-Ṭur and its anchorage; more than 30,000 pilgrims were kept

The anchorage of a-Ṭur, the pilgrims' town of southwestern Sinai

Scene from the outpost settlement Naḥal Yam, established in 1967, whose principal occupation is fishing in the Bardawīl Lagoon

there annually in quarantine on their return voyage from Arabia. Thus, a staff of Turkish (and later, Egyptian) and foreign doctors, medical orderlies, customs officers, etc., was added to the local population of fishermen and pearl divers.

The Sinai mining sites have undergone rapid development during the last two decades. First in importance were the oil fields along the Suez Gulf shore (Ras Sūdar, Abu Rudeīs, Beleīm, Abu Dūrba, Ras Gārra), the manganese mine site of Umm Būghma and the manganese harbor at Abu Zuneīma. A laborers' camp was under construction in 1967 near the lignite mines on Jebel Maghāra. None of these localities was inhabited by a truly permanent population of any size, and they were characterized by the sharp contrast between the adequate housing provided for experts and the miserable hovels serving native and Egyptian workers.

Since the construction of the Suez Canal, a few settlements developed also on its eastern bank, although these were, as a rule, no more than suburbs of far larger centers on the western side. The latter receive fresh water from the Nile and hence enjoy green fields and gardens, while on the Sinai side but little was done to alleviate the starkness of the desert. Opposite Port Sa'īd, at the northern entrance of the Canal, stands Port Fu'ād (outside the area under Israel control); opposite al-Qantāra lies Eastern Qantāra; Isma'īliya has a small suburb on the east bank. The small station of a-Shatt confronts the triple city of Suez-Port Ibrahīm-Port Taufiq near the southern outlet of the Suez Canal.

In the Six Day War, all mining sites were abandoned, but the population remained in el-'Arīsh where approximately 30,000 inhabitants were registered in the census of August, 1967. Over 1,000 residents stayed in Eastern Qantāra (until continuous Egyptian shelling necessitated evacuating them, for their own safety, to el-'Arīsh), and smaller numbers at other places along the Canal and at a-Ṭur.

A new chapter in populating Sinai was opened in 1968 with the establishment of the first three outpost settlements, Naḥal Yam whose principal occupation is fishing in the Bardawīl Lagoon, Naḥal Sinai which is developing a large farm south of el-'Arīsh, and Naḥal Diqla on the Mediterranean shore further east.

The Gaza Strip

'The Gaza Strip'—A Political Entity

The term 'Gaza Strip' dates from the last stages of Israel's War of Independence; it received political validity in the 1949 Armistice Agreement between Israel and Egypt, when it was recognized as a separate entity, albeit temporarily under Egyptian supervision. This discrete political existence of the Strip was terminated by the Six Day War, which brought it under Israel military administration; the final decision about its future awaits the signing of peace treaties between Israel and its neighbors.

The Gaza Strip, although constituting a demographic entity sharply differing from the bordering regions, possesses no distinct geographical characteristics. It belongs to Israel's Coastal Plain: the area to the southwest of Naḥal Besor forms a part of the Negev Coast, while north of this watercourse stretches the Philistian Plain. Climatically, the Gaza Strip comes under the moderating influence of the Mediterranean Sea. Although its area is small, rainfall is unevenly distributed; while the annual average remains below 150 mm at Rafiaḥ, at the southwestern extremity of the Strip, the area lying north of the city of Gaza receives approximately 400 mm per year.

The Gaza Strip came into being when the invading Egyptian Army chose, in May 1948, to advance northward along the coastal road, through a region settled almost exclusively by Arabs. At that stage, the Egyptians occupied a far larger area, but in the ensuing operations 'Ten Plagues' and 'Ayin,' the region under their control was whittled down to a narrow strip between Rafiaḥ and Gaza. According to the Armistice Agreement, the Strip remained outside Israel; two small stretches of land already occupied by Israel forces—the surroundings of the village Beit Ḥanūn (northeast of Gaza), and the area of 'Abasān east of Rafiaḥ—were added to it. The length of the Gaza Strip, from Rafiaḥ to Beit Ḥanūn, thus measures 45 km, and its width 5–7 km in the northern section, attaining a maximum of 12 km at the southern end. The area of the Gaza Strip totals 362 km^2.

The Population of the Gaza Strip. With the emergence of the Gaza Strip as a political entity, its population underwent profound changes. To the existing 50,000–60,000 inhabitants (end of 1947) were added large numbers of Arabs who had, as a result of the war, abandoned their villages, towns and bedouin encampments in the Southern Coastal Plain and the Negev. The refugees swelled the population figure to an estimated 180,000–200,000, practically all of them Arabs and, in their overwhelming majority, of the Moslem faith. The only Jewish village in the Strip, the small kibbutz of Kefar Darom, after having displayed obstinate resistance for over a month against the overwhelming odds of the Egyptian Army, left its site at the order of the Israel Command in June, 1948.

A population census was held by the Israel authorities in the Gaza Strip between the 10th and 14th September, 1967. The figures obtained in this census can be regarded as reliable, in contrast to those of the Mandatory authorities who accepted the information given by heads of families, although it must have been clear that these were inclined to gross exaggeration, be it to boast of the number of their offspring or to obtain advantages in rations, social aid, tax relief, etc. When the Gaza Strip came under Egyptian administration, the authorities themselves became the principal factor in deliberately inflating census figures, particularly those of refugees whom they regarded as an important weapon in their anti-Israel propaganda campaign. Food rations were distributed by UNWRA to refugee families in accordance with the number of their members. In order to obtain more rations, non-existent persons were added to the lists and the deaths of family members were never reported. This explains the discrepancy of 22% between the Egyptian 1966 estimate of 454,960 inhabitants for the Gaza Strip, and the 354,000 souls actually registered by the Israel census. Together with northern Sinai, the figure attained 390,000. Between the Six Day War and the date of the census there was no emigration worth speaking of which could account for this huge difference. By the end of 1968, the population of the Gaza Strip and northern Sinai had decreased to 356,000, the cause for this development being seen in emigration, principally to Jordan.

Even after the true figures have been established, however, the fact remains that the Gaza Strip is one of the most densely populated areas of the world, averaging 973.2 inhabitants per km^2 in the 1967 census.

Population Groups. The Gaza Strip population differs from that of any other world region in that refugees make up an absolute majority there. The 1967 census revealed that families whose heads were born in areas held by Israel since 1949 numbered 207,250 souls, i.e., 58.9% of the total population. Of these, however, only 149,396 lived in refugee camps, while the rest had established their homes in villages and towns. On the other hand, there were about 23,000 non-refugees dwelling in the camps, bringing the total camp population to 172,521. The latter figure makes up only 58% of that appearing on the UNWRA rolls, i.e., 316,776 camp inhabitants.

Another feature singling out the Gaza Strip from all other Arab regions is the extremely high percentage of urban population. In the census, urban settlement accounted for 282,803 inhabitants, or 79.4% of the overall population of the Gaza Strip. Even when the camps are excluded from the calculation, there are 149,489 town dwellers, as against 31,368 villagers. Another 1,105 were described as nomads, while 1,778 lived beyond the confines of villages or towns.

Age and Sex. Although the 1967 census, being the first registration of the population, cannot establish the annual birth rate, data can be deduced from the age composition. It was found that this rate is very high, with the 0–14 years group constituting over half (50.6%) of the Gaza Strip population. This figure, although somewhat inferior to that for Moslems inside Israel's former borders (53.1%), is incomparably higher than that for Israel's Jewish population (31.6%). The youngest age group, of 0–4 years, makes up nearly 20% of the total. It emerges that the number of births must be very large in the Gaza Strip. The small difference between this figure and that for Israel's Moslems is to be ascribed to the superior medical care and sanitary conditions in Israel.

Creeds. Out of 398,702 souls registered in the 1967 census, 385,644, or 99%, were Moslems, while only 2,543 were Christians, and 1,515 either belonged to other religions, professed no religion or did not give clear answers. At the time of the census, the Gaza Strip had no Jewish inhabitants. Most of the Christians lived in the city of Gaza (1,649 souls), The age-group composition of the Christian community was much closer to that of Israel Jews, with approximately 37% in the 0–14 years group.

Occupations. Although most of the Gaza Strip population resides in urban areas, farming provides the principal source of income. Not only villagers but also urban dwellers work variously sized parcels of land. Many inhabitants of refugee camps have found permanent or temporary employment in agriculture.

Fishing is another occupation of importance. Although the haul, averaging an annual 1,000 tons, is small in relation to the number of people working in this branch, it contributes substantially to the local food supply. Of late, a considerable portion of the Gaza fish catch finds it way to Israel markets.

Prior to 1967, the Gaza Strip had practically no serious industrial enterprises employing up-to-date working methods. On the other hand, there were numerous small workshops, particularly in traditional crafts such as pottery, weaving, food

Fishermen with their boats and nets on the Gaza beach

processing, etc. In 1968, the first industrial plants, primarily based on local farm produce, were set up by Israelis and Israel authorities. During the following year the site for an industrial zone at the northern end of the Strip was prepared; here factories are to be established, several of which will be run cooperatively by local and Israel enterprises. In addition, thousands of laborers from the region have found employment in construction work, farming, industry and development projects in various parts of Israel, thus largely solving the Gaza Strip's ingrained problem of unemployment.

Commerce, mostly small retail shops and peddling, provide employment for a considerable number of people, especially in urban communities. However,

Gaza potters find, since 1967, an improved market for their painted ware

occupational groups are not clearly delimited, because farmers and tradesmen frequently sell their own produce or that of their neighbors on the markets, and shopowners and peddlers occasionally hire themselves out for work of all kinds or keep small auxiliary farms near their homes.

Agricultural Branches. As a result of the great population density, the strain on existing soil and water resources is enormous. Every stretch of land fit for cultivation is exploited. This is true even of dunes, wherever more fertile soil is hidden at small depth beneath the sand. Out of the 362 km^2 of the Gaza Strip, 26' were under cultivation in 1967.

Although the groundwater reserves are large in relation to the amounts of loca rainfall, overpumping constitutes a serious hazard, and most wells are in acut danger of becoming saline if exploitation at the present rate is continued for a few more years. The area has 1,200 wells, yielding 65 million cubic meters of water annually. Experts advise reducing pumping to half this volume, with particular attention to be paid to the southern half of the Strip where the danger of salination is most imminent and where the irrigated area may have to be reduced.

In 1967, irrigated crops covered 13,700 hectares, citrus groves heading the list with 9,200 ha. This branch of agriculture, which expanded in the Gaza Strip mainly during the last two decades, produces the principal export item of the area, amounting to 2–4 million standard cases of fruit annually. Until recently, East European countries were the main customers for Gaza citrus fruit. Under Israel administration, government institutions and citrus growers' associations extend all possible aid to Gaza citrus farmers, improving cultivation and pest control methods, marketing and export organization, etc.

Of the remaining area under irrigation, ca. 1,000 ha are planted with olives, vines and deciduous fruit, while 3,500 ha produce vegetables and field crops. Often, two to three different crops are raised simultaneously on the same plots, with rows of vines planted between date palms and narrow vegetable beds occupying the remaining space. Among the important annual species are melons and watermelons, which thrive unwatered or require auxiliary irrigation only.

The most important unirrigated plantations are those of date palms, centering on the town of Deir al-Bālaḥ, while rhicinus bushes are prominent in the southernmost part of the Gaza Strip. Wheat is the principal field crop.

The City of Gaza. From the very earliest times Gaza has constituted one of the principal centers in the south of the country. Situated on the Via Maris, it served, in the second millennium B.C.E., as an administrative city, the residence of the Egyptian governor of the Land of Canaan. In the 13th century B.C.E., the Philistines (or Caphtorites=Cretans) annihilated the Avite inhabitants of Gaza and made the city the southernmost, and probably the largest, of their five centers. The Bible reports that Gaza was taken by the tribe of Judah, but also includes the city among those places lying 'in the remaining country,' i.e., not occupied by the Israelites. In the 8th century B.C.E., the Assyrians captured Gaza, and in the 7th, Pharaoh Necho conquered the city while on his campaign against the Babylonians. Later, however, it again came under Babylonian rule, to be occupied, in the 6th century, by the Persian king Cambyses. In the 5th century Gaza fell to Alexander the Great, after whose death it repeatedly changed hands between the Ptolemaic and Seleucid kingdoms. In the 2nd century, Simon the Maccabee took the town and settled Jews in it. After the Hasmoneans lost it temporarily, Alexander Jannaeus reconquered it. In the 1st century B.C.E., Pompey made Gaza a free 'polis' and restored its Hellenistic character. In their revolt against Rome, the Jews attacked Gaza and partly destroyed it, but the cit was rapidly rebuilt. Under Byzantine rule, Gaza's Jewish community flourishe anew, side-by-side with Samaritan and Karaite communities. The Jewis presence is attested to by the beautiful mosaic floor of a 6th century C.E synagogue, discovered on the Gaza sea shore in 1967. The city came under Ara rule after the Moslem conquest in 643 C.E. Under the Arab caliphates, the city' Jewish community prospered, but its numbers dwindled during the Crusades an under Mameluke and Turkish rule. In the 17th century, Gaza was the scene o Shabbetai Zvi's pseudo-messianic movement. During Napoleon's conquest i 1799, the town came under heavy bombardment, and was again partly destroye in the year-long battle raging in its vicinity between Allied and Turco-Germa forces during the First World War (1917). The last Jewish inhabitants left Gaz during the 1929 riots.

Shortly before the War of Independence, the population of Gaza stood at approximately 20,000 inhabitants. This number was rapidly swelled by the refugee influx; in the 1967 census, 118,272 souls were registered in Gaza, 30,479 of them living in camps within the municipal boundary. Gaza is thus the largest city in the regions administered by Israel, and occupies fourth place among the country's cities (after Tel Aviv-Jaffa, Jerusalem and Haifa).

It appears that in its historic past, Gaza's built-up area has alternately expanded and contracted. Most of its ancient remnants have been discovered on the mound which today is the city center, with narrow, winding lanes. However, antiquities are also found three kilometers further west, near the sea shore, at a location marking the site of the twin towns Maiumas and Anthedon (or a single town bearing both names) which provided Gaza with harbor facilities. During the period of Gaza's prosperity under Roman and Byzantine rule, the stretch between the shore and the city center was probably a residential area. For many centuries thereafter, however, this expanse remained empty, until the British Mandatory authorities allocated land, almost free of charge, to anyone prepared to build a house on these dunes within five years of signing a contract.

Today, Gaza's principal east-west artery runs through this area, leading to the sea shore. While along the road's western section are located government buildings and homes of relatively well-to-do citizens, the houses in the city center and in the refugee quarters are rather shabby. During the last two decades, the city also expanded its limits eastward to the Ashqelon-Rafiaḥ highway and beyond it to the kurkar ridge on which is located the important strategic position of Sheikh 'Ali al-Muntār. In the northwest, Gaza gradually links up with the agglomerations of Jabālya and Nāzala. Within the municipal boundaries, however, are found numerous open areas, partly used for orchards, field crops and kitchen gardens.

View of Gaza's principal east-west thoroughfare

No functional arrangement or elements of town planning are recognizable in the distribution of housing, industry, commercial quarters, etc., the sole possible exception being the stretch along the east-west artery, which has in sections been provided with flower beds and avenues of trees.

During the 19th and early part of the 20th century, the Gaza shore anchorage possessed a certain importance, serving two purposes—export of Negev barley, mainly to British breweries, and as a harbor for local fishing boats. While the settlement of Ashqelon fishermen in Gaza after the War of Independence led to the expansion of the latter branch, the export of malt barley had already declined prior to the First World War, and today has stopped altogether. In the years 1948–1967, the Gaza harbor was used both for mercantile transport of goods between the Gaza Strip and Egypt, and as the port of exit for certain quantities of local citrus sent abroad. Since the Six Day War, Gaza citrus fruit is dispatched to Europe mostly through Ashdod port. To relieve the pressure on Ashdod, however, the reactivation of Gaza Port for citrus exports is being examined.

Khān Yūnis. Until the War of Independence, this was, apart from Gaza itself, the only population center of the Strip possessing at least a semi-urban character.

The impressive gate of the Khan Yūnis 'khan'

Some scholars identify the town with a spot mentioned in the 5th century B.C.E. by Herodotus under the name of Ienisos. Clear evidence of its existence is at hand only beginning with the 14th century C.E. when Yūnis, the governor of a Mameluke sultan, set up here a wayfarers' inn ('khan'), thereby creating a commercial center. The population of Khan Yūnis increased from 11,220 in 1944 to 52,997 in 1967 (of whom 23,475 lived in camps). Khan Yūnis, though maintaining its second place among the agglomerations of the Gaza Strip, is being challenged by Rafiaḥ which has expanded at a much faster rate. The economy of the town is founded almost exclusively on farming.

Rafiaḥ. The name of Rafiaḥ is mentioned for the first time in Egyptian documents of the second millennium B.C.E. During the periods of the First and Second Temple, it saw battles between Egyptian and Mesopotamian hosts, and between the armies of the Ptolemies and Seleucids. Alexander Jannaeus annexed the town to his kingdom. Its prosperity as a Hellenistic city dates mainly from the 1st century B.C.E., when Gabinius rebuilt it. Jewish and Samaritan communities lived here under Byzantine and Arab rule. During the Crusades this town ceased to exist and only saw rebirth when the British Mandatory authorities set up army camps at its site, thereby drawing a considerable number of people to Rafiaḥ. Most of them settled on the Palestinian side of the frontier then running through it, and a minority on the Egyptian side. After the War of Independence, refugees were housed in the abandoned army camps. The population of Rafiaḥ thus increased from 1,400 in 1931 and 2,500 in 1945 to 49,812 in 1967, whereof 39,000 were refugees.

Although the meager soil and water resources are exploited as far as possible for agriculture, and space for construction is ample, particularly on the west side of the former border, the difficult local conditions are reflected in poverty and unemployment which are move evident here than anywhere else in the Gaza Strip.

Deir al-Bālaḥ. This center lies 14 km from Gaza. It seems to have existed since the Byzantine period, when it bore the Hebrew name 'Darom' ('South') or 'Kefar Darom' and had Jews among its inhabitants. During the early days of the Arab caliphates, a fortress stood here. Toward the end of the Middle Ages, its name was changed to 'Deir' ('Monastery') and the word 'al-Bālaḥ' ('of Date Palms') was added to it. In fact, verdant date palm groves are a conspicuous feature of the landscape to this day, but there are also citrus orchards and plantations of almonds, pomegranates, vines, etc. The town grew from 1,600 inhabitants in 1945 to 18,118 in 1967; of the latter figure, 11,103 were refugees. The original name of this spot was revived with the establishment of Kibbutz Kefar Darom at the eastern outskirts of Deir al-Bālaḥ in 1946; this settlement was abandoned during the War of Independence and rebuilt in 1970.

Judea and Samaria

'Judea-Samaria' as a Political and Administrative Unit

The term 'Judea-Samaria' was chosen in the fall of 1967 to describe a political and administrative unit composed of those regions of Western Palestine which had been invaded by Transjordan in 1948 and had thus come under Jordanian rule between the Armistice Agreement of 1949 and the Six Day War, and which since 1967 have been under Israel military government. This term supplants the name 'West Bank,' used by the Jordanians up to 1967 to designate those parts of their kingdom west of the Jordan River. Actually, the area includes not only the larger part of the two geographical provinces of Judea and Samaria, but also the western half of the Lower Jordan Valley.

The course of the River Jordan and the Dead Sea coast clearly delimit the eastern border of Judea-Samaria. The old armistice line tracing the boundaries in the north, west and south reflects, along most of its length, the deployment of forces when the battles of the War of Independence were brought to a sudden halt by the 1948 cease-fire arrangements. Only minor adjustments were later made to this line, as an outcome of the armistice negotiations, and by subsequent agreements within the framework of the Mixed Armistice Commission, e.g., areas ceded to Israel in the Irron Vale and Irron Hills, on the eastern fringe of the Sharon and on the northwestern margin of the Judean Hills; areas ceded to Jordan northeast of Kibbutz Lahav and near the villages Wadi Fukīn and Beit Īksa in Judea; a strip of land giving Israel control of the Tel Aviv-Jerusalem railway line along its entire length; and stretches of 'no-man's land' and 'demilitarized zones' in Judea, along the Būdrus-Modi'im-Beit Tul border section and within the municipal limits of Jerusalem.

In the fall of 1967, after all of Western Palestine had come under Israel's control, the municipal boundary of reunited Jerusalem was redrawn, and its area was finally incorporated into Israel and separated from Judea-Samaria which remained under military government. After this border correction, the area of Judea-Samaria totals 5,505 km^2.

Jewish Villages in Judea-Samaria Abandoned in 1948. Until the year 1948, seven Jewish villages existed in the area of Judea-Samaria but had to be abandoned in the Independence War. Four of them (Kefar Eẓyon, Massu'ot Yiẓḥaq, En Ẓurim, Revadim) constituted the Eẓyon Bloc in the Hebron Hills, which fell in a bitter battle on the eve of the founding of the State of Israel (12–13 May, 1948). Two villages north of Jerusalem, Neweh Ya'aqov and 'Atarot, were evacuated on the order of the Israel military command on May 17, 1948. A similar fate befell the kibbutz Bet ha-'Arava, the Rabbat Ashlag potash works and the Kallia Hotel at the north end of the Dead Sea, whose inhabitants and defenders reached Sedom in the south by boat, on May 19, 1948. There were also other tracts of land under Jewish ownership, both of the Jewish National Fund and private individuals, particularly north of Jerusalem; these had not yet been brought under cultivation at the time and were taken over by Arab neighbors or the Jordanian authorities.

The Population

Development of the Population. According to the census carried out by the Israel authorities in the fall of 1967, the number of inhabitants of Judea-Samaria totaled 598,637. The Jordanian Government had made two population counts on the West Bank, the first in 1952, arriving at the figure of 667,000 inhabitants, and the second in 1961, indicating a total of 730,000 souls. Comparing these two figures on the assumption that they are more or less correct and do not contain deliberate exaggerations, it emerges that the population of Judea-Samaria grew in the course of a decade by 63,000 persons only, i.e., at an annual rate of 0.9%, as against a natural increase of 4.5% per year for Israeli Arabs during the same period. The reason for these differences lies in emigration, which was particularly high during the years 1948–1952 but continued until the Six Day War. In the 1967 census, about one third of the families in Judea-Samaria stated that they had relatives abroad, 90% of them in Arab countries.

Geographical Distribution. The overall population density in 1967 amounted to 109 inhabitants per km^2. The population distribution over Judea-Samaria is, however, extremely uneven, as the area comprises two totally different regions—the fields and orchard lands of the Hills and the intermontane valleys, and the empty waste area, comprising the Lower Jordan Valley, the eastern slopes of Samaria and the Judean Desert.

Judea-Samaria contained, in 1967, eight administrative districts. In 1968, their number was reduced to seven and their borders were redrawn by the Israel administration, enlarging the Tul Karm and Jennīn districts at the expense of that of Nablus, partitioning the rural parts of the Jordanian Jerusalem District between those of Bethlehem and Ramallah, and including in the Jericho-Jordan Valley District the entire geographical region of the Lower Jordan Valley. As, however, the 1967 census figures still refer to the former district borders, the latter have to serve as a guideline for analyzing the population distribution. The largest was the Nablus (Shekhem) District with 1,587 km^2, followed by the Hebron District with 1,056 km^2. The other districts were considerably smaller, Ramallah extending over 770 km^2, Jennīn—572 km^2, Bethlehem—565 km^2, Jericho—338 km^2, Tul Karm—332 km^2, and Jerusalem—without the section now reunited with the rest of the city—284 km^2. The Tul Karm District lay entirely within the fertile zone, and that of Jericho entirely in the desert. About two thirds of the Jennīn and Ramallah districts belonged to the fertile area, as did over half of the Hebron and Nablus districts; on the other hand, over half of the Jerusalem District and the greater part of the Bethlehem District fell within the desert. This explains the regional population density which was relatively high in the Tul Karm District (218 inhabitants per km^2 in the 1967 census), average in the districts of Jennīn (137), Ramallah (115) and Hebron (112), below average in Nablus (96) and Bethlehem (88), and very low in the Jericho District (27).

After the Israel occupation, nearly all inhabitants remained in their towns and villages, with the exception of the population of the refugee camps near Jericho, who crossed the Jordan together with a number of the citizens of the town of Jericho. With these movements, the situation in the Lower Jordan Valley returned approximately to what it was before 1948, prior to the establishment of the camps whose occupants were never actually permitted to gain a true economic foothold in the region.

Sex and Age. In contrast with the world average which shows males and females to be approximately equal in number (slightly more males being born, but females having a greater life expectancy), the 1967 census figures for Judea-Samaria revealed 985 males (in the Gaza Strip only 940) for every 1,000 females. This discrepancy is apparently the outcome of considerable emigration of young men to Transjordan and other Arab countries, particularly the oil principalities on the Persian Gulf coast. This assumption is corroborated by the figures for the different age groups: while in the 0–14 years group there were 1,123 males for every 1,000 females, the figure for the 15–29 years group is 839, and for the 30–44 years group—745 only. On the other hand, the sex ratio of the advanced age group (65 years and above) also differs from the world picture, as males slightly predominate in Judea-Samaria (1,109). This phenomenon may perhaps be explained by the life pattern of women in the traditional rural society, who age prematurely due to numerous childbirths and hard physical labor.

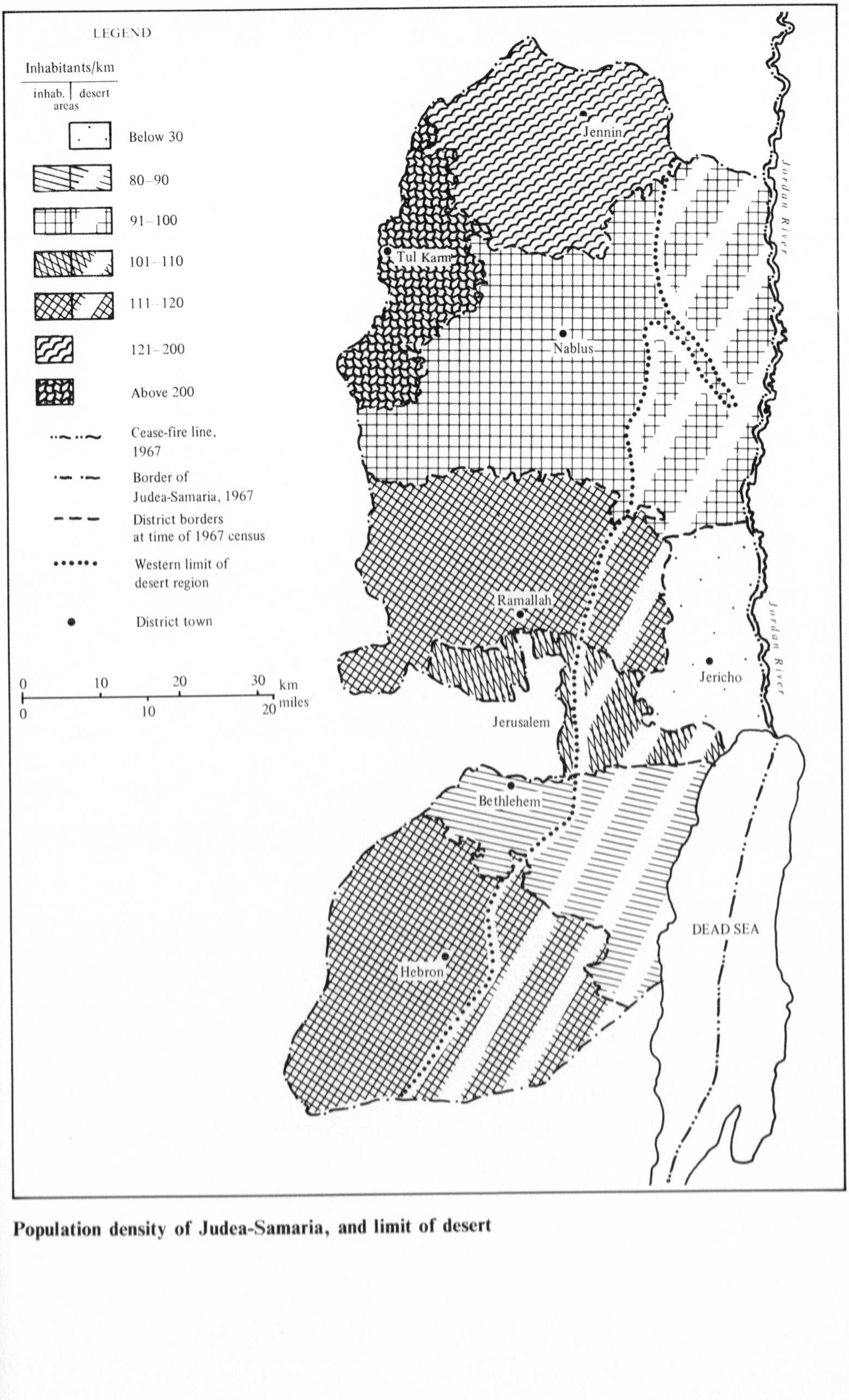

Population density of Judea-Samaria, and limit of desert

The population distribution over the various age groups testifies to a steep natural increase, although this is still somewhat inferior to that of Israel's non-Jews. Of the entire population, 48.4% belonged to the 0–14 years age group, as against 53.1% of Israel Moslems, but only 31.6 of Israel Jews. For the Christian community of Judea-Samaria, children up to 14 years constitute 38% of the total.

Religious Communities. About 94.5% of the population of Judea-Samaria are of the Mohammedan faith, the rest being mostly Christian. The districts of Hebron, Nablus, Tul Karm and Jerusalem are almost exclusively Moslem. Also in the Jennīn District, the number of Christians is negligible, with the exception of a single village, Zabābida, which has a Christian majority. In the Ramallah District, Christians are more prominent, not only in Ramallah town where they constitute a little over half of the population, but also in the villages of Jīfna, Bir Zeit and Tāyyiba where they are in the majority, and in 'Abūd where they approach 50%. While only few Christians live in the villages of the Bethlehem District, they constitute about two thirds of the residents of the towns of Beit Jāla and Beit Saḥūr, and nearly half the population of Bethlehem proper.

As in the rest of the country, the overwhelming majority of the Moslems in Judea-Samaria are Sunnites. Although the holiest Islamic shrines of the country—the Dome of the Rock and the 'Aksa Mosque—are in Jerusalem, Judea-Samaria has a number of important sites of worship, the Double Mosque over the Makhpela Cave in Hebron (Māsjid el-Khalīl) heading the list. Many beautiful mosques, both old and modern, are to be found in Nablus and the other urban communities and also in most villages. Religious bodies such as the 'Waqf' maintain schools, hospitals and other social and religious institutions. These, and likewise the religious Moslem Sharī'a courts, continue to function without interference under Israel administration.

Of the 29,644 Christians counted in the 1967 census, approximately half belong to the Greek-Orthodox Church, and about a quarter to the Catholic (locally called 'Latin') Church, while 10% are followers of the Greek-Catholic Uniate Church, and the rest members of other denominations and sects. The Church of the Nativity in Bethlehem and the Church of the Holy Sepulcher in Jerusalem rank among Christendom's most holy places. There are other Christian sacred sites in Judea-Samaria, among them the place of Jesus' baptism by John on the Jordan near Jericho. Villages having a sizeable Christian population can easily be recognized by the prominent church buildings. Although East Jerusalem itself has been administratively separated from Judea-Samaria, the Christian communities of the region continue to be under the control of their central institutions in the capital and to maintain with them close organizational and personal ties, as in the past.

Over half of the adherents to the Samaritan faith in the world, about 250 persons, live in Nablus. Since the Six Day War, contacts between the Samaritans of Nablus and their brethren living in Ḥolon, near Tel Aviv, have become much closer.

Labor Force and Occupations. The labor force in Judea-Samaria was, under Jordanian rule, particularly small in relation to the total population, amounting to only 22%. This can be partly explained by the exceptionally high percentage of the 0–14 years age group, and by the large number of people who over the years found employment abroad. The actual percent of gainfully employed people, however, was somewhat higher, because women working on their husbands' farms were not included in the statistics.

Unemployment, high under Jordanian rule and in the first months of Israel administration, has been on the decline since the beginning of 1968 and practically disappeared in 1970, thanks to development projects undertaken in Judea-Samaria (road-building, etc.), to employment of laborers from the region in building, farm work, etc. in veteran parts of Israel and to intensification of farming and industrialization in the region proper. Simultaneously, a sizeable increase in wages has caused a rapid improvement in the living standards of the working class and augurs well for the narrowing of social differences in Judea-Samaria.

According to a Jordanian census of 1961, 37.1% of employed males worked in agriculture, 11.6% in industry, crafts, mining and quarrying, 10.4% in building, 8.2% in commerce, 2.9% in electricity, water and transport services, 14.6% in other services, and 15.2% were described as 'unspecified.' As these statistics include East Jerusalem, it must be assumed that in the regions today comprising Judea-Samaria, the services and commerce sections are less strongly represented than in the figures cited above.

In general, a picture of an underdeveloped economy emerges from these facts. Industry was only in its infancy. Before 1967, 14,000 persons were reported to be employed in industry, but there were only two enterprises in Judea-Samaria employing over 100 workers, while the average for the great majority of plants was 3–4 workers only. Most enterprises were small, labor-intensive workshops, singly or jointly owned, with branches like garment making, shoe manufacture, carpentry, small handicrafts and arts preponderant. Working methods were generally primitive and quality of products was often low. Under Israel administration, the local manufacturers began to adopt a new approach. Existing factories have, between 1967 and 1970, enlarged their premises, acquired new machinery, and doubled or tripled their production as well as the number of their employees. New enterprises were opened in the textiles, plastics, food products and other branches. This entailed an increase in the number of industrial laborers from 1,500 in 1967 to 7,000 at the beginning of 1970. Factories started to take on contract jobs from Israel enterprises or export products over the Jordan bridges to Arab countries.

Tourism was on the rise in Jordan during the 1960's. In 1966, 616,832 visitors were counted, as against 162,058 in 1961. Of these, the great majority came to the West Bank, particularly to Jerusalem. The increase is impressive, even when persons coming from European and American countries alone are taken into account: 75,568 persons in 1961, and 175,024 in 1966. The first months after the Six Day War understandably saw a slump in foreign tourism which, however, was more than compensated for by the vast numbers of Israeli sightseers visiting Judea-Samaria. Larger numbers of foreigners toured the areas in 1968–1970, as Judea-Samaria partook in the great rise of Israel tourism. It must be emphasized, however, that at present, as in the past, Jerusalem and Bethlehem are the main beneficiaries of overseas tourism.

Rural Settlement and Agriculture

Number of Villages and Their Inhabitants. The inhabitants of villages constitute 71% of the overall population of Judea-Samaria. The rural component has always been preponderant in the area's social and economic fabric. It has now increased still further owing to the separation of East Jerusalem from the region. The above figure does not, however, provide a full reflection of the region's rural character, as numerous inhabitants of the refugee camps, even of those situated within the boundaries of urban communities, work in agriculture, mainly as hired laborers, and many of the townspeople themselves practice farming, either as a principal or auxiliary occupation.

There are 380 villages in Judea-Samaria, 45 of them with populations exceeding 2,000. The average village is, therefore, larger than most Jewish rural settlements, but somewhat smaller than Arab villages inside Israel's 1949 borders, the latter having grown during the twenty years of statehood at the unusual rate of 5% annually. Most villages in Judea-Samaria have absorbed refugees from the areas which became part of Israel, but only in rare cases does their number exceed 20% of the local population. Generally speaking, the villages of Nablus District have a smaller refugee population than those of the rest of Judea-Samaria, and refugees are more strongly represented in villages near the former border than in the interior.

Most of these villages have been in existence for hundreds and even thousands of years. A number of them have preserved both their site and their original name since the time of the First or Second Temple. In the Hills of Samaria, eight refugee camps have been added to the existing villages during the last two decades, three of them in or around Nablus, one near Jennīn, another near Tul Karm, but only three in a truly rural setting, one of them being no longer occupied. Of the nine camps in the Judean Hills, five are located in the rural area.

In the Hills of Samaria and in Northern Judea, only few new villages have made their appearance in the last twenty years. Most of these were former 'akhrāb,' i.e., daughter settlements of larger villages, which have now become independent rural communities. A number of small villages were established in the Farī'a Valley, where the irrigated farming area has greatly increased. The most striking change has occurred in Southern Judea—east and south of Bethlehem and west, south and east of Hebron—where nomads, peasants from other villages or refugees have been settled. This has brought about a further shift of the 'border between desert and the sown,' the oscillations of which have, for thousands of years, invariably been dictated by political, economic or demographic circumstances.

The Village Layout. In contrast with the Arab villages included in Israel since 1949, those which came under Jordanian rule have extended but little beyond their narrow, congested confines of antiquity. Some hill villages are perched on hilltops (e.g. Ḥalḥul near Hebron, Jib = Gibeon in the Jerusalem Hills, Silwād in the southern part of the Samarian Hills, etc.), but most are located on the upper reaches of the slopes.

Economic Foundations. In almost all villages of Judea-Samaria, farming provides the sole source of livelihood, and hardly any manufacturing or service branches have developed there. The transition from subsistence farming to the raising of commercial crops, slow in the preceding period, has been greatly accelerated under Israel administration.

Water and Irrigation. Water consumption in Judea-Samaria averaged, until 1967, over 80 million cubic meters annually, whereof approximately 75 million m^3 were used for agriculture, and the rest for domestic and municipal consumption. The irrigated area attained 7,000 ha, much thereof, however, only receiving auxiliary watering. Since 1968, new wells have been sunk, mainly in Samaria, with the aid of Israel geologists and engineers, and irrigation is expanding.

The water potential of Judea-Samaria is estimated at close to 400 million m^3, whereof 160 million may be derived from groundwater sources (of these about 50 million brackish water), 40 million from surface runoff, and 190 million from rivers, mainly the Jordan and its tributaries.

Farming Methods. But few innovations in farming methods were introduced in th recent past. To the present day, the sickle often serves for reaping grain. Use o chemical fertilizers is still infrequent, and tractors and mechanized farmin equipment are seldom encountered. Few efforts have been made to improve see varieties and introduce new crops. All this results in low yields. The grape an olive harvests of the local farmers amount to half the Israel average for the crops, while the local wheat yields were only a quarter or less of those obtaine on established Israeli farms.

Since the setting up of Israel administration, however, a thoroughgoing chang has become noticeable. Field days are arranged for local farmers, with practic demonstrations of agricultural equipment and new methods, selected seeds a provided on easy terms, and peasants from Judea-Samaria are given th opportunity to visit Israel farms and acquire knowledge of modern systems o work and organization. The plan is to centralize professional guidance in a autonomous local institution, and agronomists, graduates of Arab universitie receive in Israel supplementary training so as to direct later farm developme programs on their own. The Ministry of Agriculture budgets ever larger sums fo all these purposes (IL 2 million in 1967/68, IL 10 million in 1969/70, and IL 1 million in 1970/71).

There appear to be fair chances for progress, as the peasants are assiduous an eager to learn. Many villages, particularly in the Hebron Hills, have during th last decades extended their cultivated lands by building new terraces and othe reclamation measures. A considerable part of the acreage thus won has bee planted with vines. The area under cultivation has expanded since the beginnin of the 'fifties, and is now approaching the limit of the cultivable acreag estimated at less than one third of the overall area, i.e., 180,000 out of 560,00 hectares. Over half of this land is under plantations, which in most cases are no irrigated. The figures for 1967 are as follows: olive groves, 60,000 ha; vineyard about 17,000 ha; other fruit trees (mainly figs and almonds), 17,000 ha.

Irrigated farming is, on the whole, restricted to the Wadi Farī'a and Sukko valleys, and to the Jericho oasis. Less than 15,000 ha were under regular irrigatio in 1967.

In the *Hebron Hills,* viticulture is prominent, producing sweet, late-ripenin grapes. Olives, almonds, and, on a modest scale, other deciduous fruit are als grown. Wheat is sown even on narrow hill terraces. Sheep and goat herding i important, particularly in villages near the desert border.

In the *Jerusalem Hills,* no particular branch has prominence. A developme characteristic of the last few years is the inclusion in the agricultural cycle o marginal lands on the desert border, especially east of Bethlehem, despite th scant rainfall and its extreme seasonal variations which often lead to crop failure

In the *Bethel* and *southern Samaria Hills,* olives cover wide areas on the slopes and constitute the principal farming branch. In the *central and northern Samaria Hills* with their broader valleys (Levona, Mikhmetat, Sokher, Sanūr, Dotan, etc.), field crops are important. Not only winter grain and legumes are sown there without irrigation (wheat, barley, lentils, peas, etc.), but also certain summer crops, e.g., maize, durra, sesame, etc. In northern Samaria, tobacco of satisfactory quality is grown. While in Judea vegetables are in general restricted to small kitchen gardens, this branch is fairly well developed in North Samaria. Vegetables, unwatered or only under auxiliary irrigation, are sold in large quantities to Transjordan. About 20% of the truck farm output was made up in 1967 and 1968 of tomatoes, and another 20% of watermelons. In the valleys of the north, particularly the Dotan Valley, small citrus groves have lately been planted. Citrus plantations are important on the Sharon border, around Qalqīliya and Tul Karm. New crops promising a more secure income, like cotton, are being introduced, to replace perishable produce which encounters marketing difficulties.

It is in the *Jericho oasis* and the *Farī'a and Sukkot valleys* that farming takes on a unique character. In the Farī'a Valley appear, side by side with grain crops, vegetables, grapes and deciduous fruit, and also citrus and banana plantations. In the environs of Jericho, one encounters, in addition to the above-enumerated crops, also date palm and pomegranate groves and plantations of tropical fruit, e.g., mango, guava, etc.

A few experimental farms have contributed to the progress of agriculture in Judea-Samaria. Those meriting mention are 'Ein 'Arrūb south of Kefar Eẓyon in the Hebron Hills, formerly under the supervision of the Jordanian Ministry of Agriculture, and the private farm of the former politician Musa el-'Alami near Jericho, where methods of rinsing the soil of salt with fresh water, developed by the kibbutz Bet ha-'Arava which had existed nearby up to 1948, were employed.

Of the gainfully employed in Judea-Samaria, 37.1% worked in agriculture in 1961.* In actual fact, the percentage was far higher, as women and children engaged in seasonal work in the fields are not accounted for in the labor force figures. Prior to the Six Day War, approximately half of Jordan's agricultural produce came from the West Bank. A considerable part of the yields was sold east of the Jordan River, whence vegetables and fruit were also exported to Saudi Arabia, Kuwait and other Arab countries. In 1966, the total value of the West Bank's farm produce reached ca. 4 million dinars (equaling 35 million IL). These

* This figure includes East Jerusalem which today is separated from Judea-Samaria. In the Hebron District, the percentage amounted to 44.0, and in the Nablus District—to 46.4.

markets have been largely preserved for the farmers of Judea-Samaria, thanks t Israel's 'open bridges' policy. It is estimated that during the first year of Isra administration, 40 million IL worth of farm produce was marketed in Transjo dan; the 1969 figure was considerably higher. Further quantities were sold local or permitted to be brought to Israel, mainly for the canning industry.

The Urban Population

Urban Settlements and Their Geographical Distribution. The population of th eleven urban settlements of Judea-Samaria numbered, in the 1967 census, 174,45 inhabitants, or 29% of the total. Actually, only eight urban centers exist i Judea-Samaria, as the two townships of Ramallah and Bīra, and the three c Bethlehem, Beit Saḥūr and Beit Jāla, constitute continuous urban areas. Of thes 8 centers, 7 serve as district capitals (Nablus, Jennīn, Tul Karm, Ramallah Bethlehem, Hebron and Jericho); Qalqīliya alone does not have this functior Four of the eight centers are situated in the Hill region proper (Nablus Bethlehem, Ramallah and Hebron), while three (Jennīn, Tul Karm and Qalqīliya lie on its northern and western outskirts, and one (Jericho) is located in the Lowe Jordan Valley.

All four hill towns lie on the ancient Hill Road, at points where this arter meets other thoroughfares. All of them are at least 4,000 years old. Nablu (Shekhem, Sichem) and Hebron were reckoned among the country's princip cities and ruled over fairly large areas in their vicinity. In most periods of history they were well fortified and bore a pronouncedly urban character. Bethlehem wa only able to attain a similar status for shorter periods, while Ramallah inherite the role of ancient Bethel, identical with the present village of Beitīn, about 5 kr to the northeast.

In contrast, the towns on the fringe of the Hill region are younger, at leas when considered as urban communities; in fact, Jennīn and Tul Karm bea semirural characteristics to this day, while Qalqīliya is hardly more than a larg village. Jericho differs from all other centers in that it lies beyond the Hill region being a typical oasis town in the Jordan Valley.

Some former towns of Judea-Samaria, important either in the Canaanit period, in the times of the First and Second Temple, or in the Roman an Byzantine periods, have today dwindled into small villages or ceased to exis altogether. Among these are to be included Gibeon in Judea and Tirẓa in th Samarian Hills which flourished more than three thousand years ago, an Gophna, Aqraba and others which only later rose to significance. The mos magnificent ancient city is Shomron north of Nablus, whose present Arabi

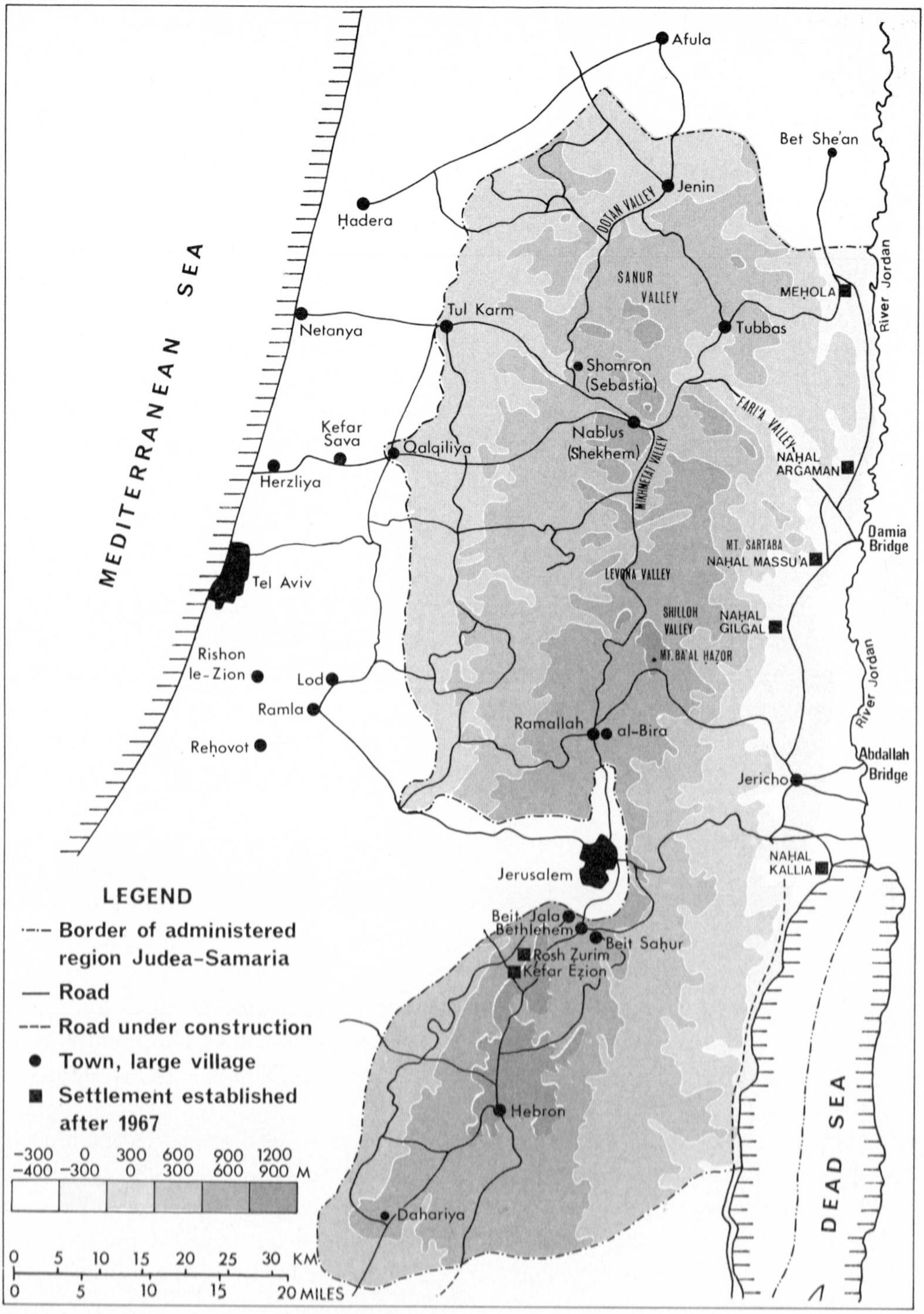

Judea-Samaria—altitudes, towns, new settlements

name, Sebastiye, perpetuates Emperor Augustus' Greek appellation 'Sebaste' ('The Illustrious'), given it by King Herod who erected numerous grandiose buildings there.

Hebron. In the 1967 census, this city numbered 38,348 inhabitants, nearly all them (38,073) Moslems. Although Hebron has almost doubled its population since 1948, no more than 8% of the present residents hail from regions which in 1948–1949 became Israel.

Hebron, although lying at approximately 930 m above sea level, is situated in a narrow valley surrounded by hills which rise 50–100 m above it. Its site can scarcely be described as a crossroad, as the access roads reaching it from the west and east do not precisely meet and have never been easy for traffic. On the other hand, Hebron lies near the 'border between the desert and the sown' and has therefore served, since ancient times, as a meeting place where the sedentary peasant and the nomad herdsman exchanged their goods.

Hebron occupies an important place in Israel's tradition and in Jewish history and lore. It features prominently in the Patriarchs' tales, and is the object of one of Joshua's great conquests. Here, David originally set up his kingdom, and even after the transfer of the capital to Jerusalem seven years later, Hebron remained a national and religious center. From its second name referred to in the Bible, 'Qiryat Arba' ('City of Four'), historians conclude that four villages or quarters were amalgamated into it. Sherds and other remnants from the Late Bronze period (i.e., the times of the Patriarchs and of the ensuing Canaanite and Hittite settlement) have been found on the hills hemming in present-day Hebron from the north and south.

Jews returning from Babylon in the 6th and 5th century B.C.E. settled in Hebron, but soon thereafter the city was taken by the Edomites, who in turn were conquered by the Hasmonean kings. King Herod erected beautiful buildings in and around the city, the mighty ashlars of the Makhpela Mosque providing a striking example. Under Byzantine rule, Hebron shrank to village size but renewed its growth after the Mohammedan conquest, when the church above the Makhpela Cave was converted into a Moslem sanctuary named Ḥarām al-Khalīl, 'Sanctuary of (God's) Friend,' alluding to Abraham. Al-Khalīl is today Hebron's Arabic name.

A small Jewish community had lived in Hebron at all times up to the bloody Arab riots of 1929, when many of its Jewish residents, including women, children and the aged, were murdered. A few months later, some Jews came back to Hebron, but were forced to leave it finally with the outbreak of the 1936–39 disturbances. After the Six Day War, young Jews took the initiative in reestablishing this community.

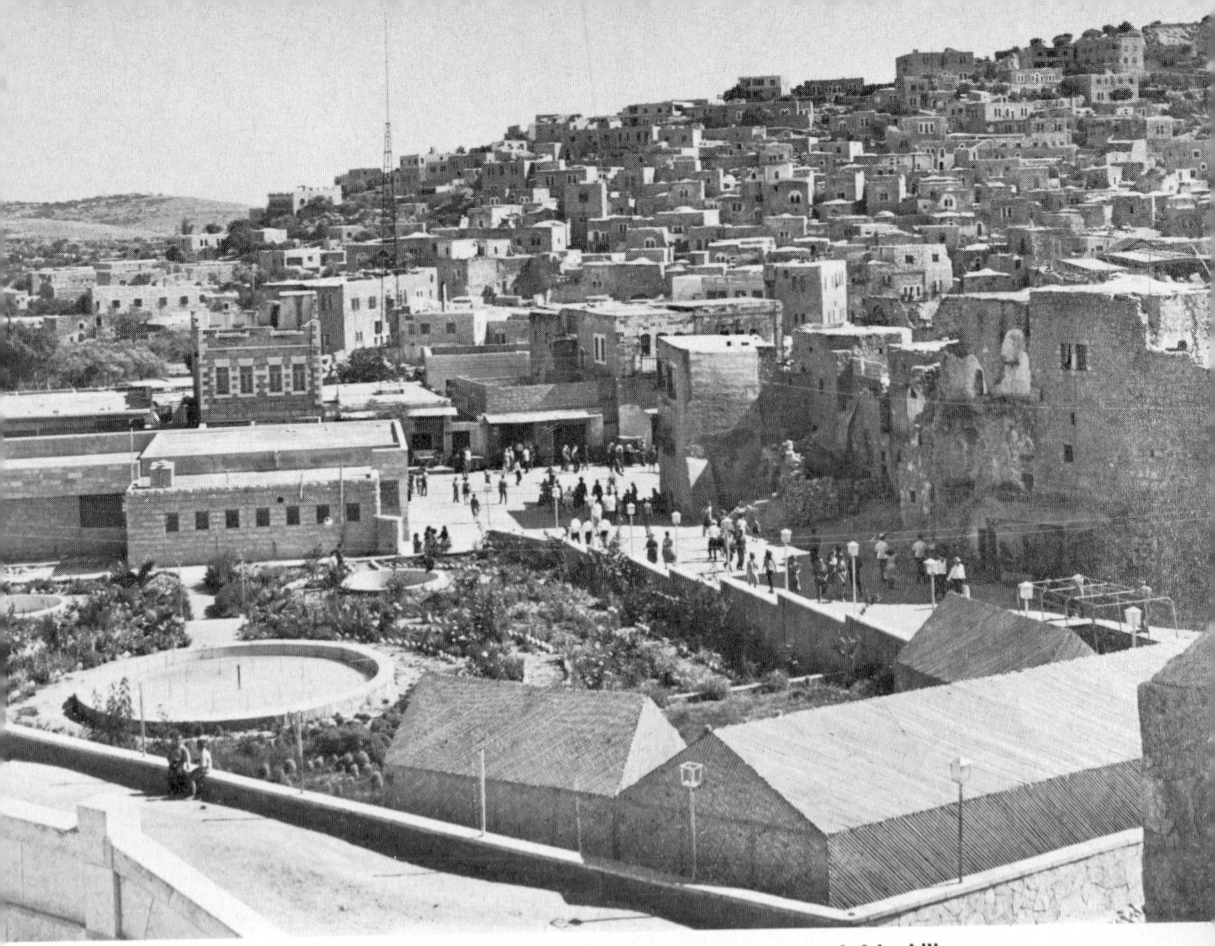

Part of Hebron, viewed from the Makhpela Mosque. The town center is surrounded by hills

To this day, Hebron's economy is based on retail trade and handicrafts, e.g., pottery, glass-blowing, tanning, etc. Farming constitutes an auxiliary branch within the city limits but is the principal occupation of citizens dwelling on the town outskirts. Of late, tourism has become a new source of income, particularly since the establishment of Israel administration.

Hebron's built-up area has expanded since 1948, mainly northward along the road leading to Bethlehem and Jerusalem, and today approaches the large village of Ḥalḥūl. Even before the Israel occupation, some of the overcrowded interior quarters around the Makhpela Double Mosque were razed as a first step toward landscaping and development.

Bethlehem. The 1967 census registered 16,313 inhabitants for this town; if one disregards those dwelling in the refugee camp in its confines, the figure drops to 14,439. Together with the adjacent towns of Beit Saḥūr (5,380 inhabitants) and Beit Jāla (6,041), Bethlehem today forms a social and economic unit which, moreover, maintains close ties with nearby Jerusalem, being about to link up with the latter's built-up area.

Bethlehem—partial view

The proximity of Jerusalem doubtlessly had a decisive influence on Bethle hem's development even at a very early stage, when this town served as a bastior guarding the southern approaches to the larger city. Before David conquerec heathen Jebus, Bethlehem protected the area allotted to the tribe of Judah from th foreign enclave to the north. Conversely, King Rehoboam later fortified the towr as the principal link in his inner ring of forts guarding the capital from the south.

As in the case of Hebron, the Edomites took Bethlehem from the Jew returning from Babylon but lost it to the Hasmonean king John Hyrcanus. Its importance to the Christian world as the birthplace of Jesus contributed to the city's progress in the late Roman and Byzantine periods. Constantine erected the Church of the Nativity which was destroyed in the 6th century by Samaritans, but soon rebuilt by Emperor Justinian. To the present day, Christian pilgrimage decisively contributes to Bethlehem's economy, giving rise, inter alia, to the local industry of mother-of-pearl and olive wood souvenirs. The Israel authorities aid Bethlehem in promoting its tourist trade and industries and enabled the town, through loans, to carry out development projects such as the building of a large commercial center.

The triple town Bethlehem-Beit Jāla-Beit Saḥūr, taken as a whole, has a Christian majority of 55% (14,400 out of a total population of 27,000), while in Bethlehem proper, Moslems slightly outnumber Christians.

Ramallah and Bīra. These two townships today virtually constitute a single urban complex, although the administrative division is being upheld. Ramallah has a

60% Christian majority (6,966 out of 12,134 inhabitants in the 1967 census), in contrast to the almost purely Moslem Bīra with its 13,037 inhabitants.

Bīra is assumed to occupy the site of the Biblical town of Be'erot, while some scholars identify Ramallah with Ramatayim-Ẓofim. The vicinity is rich in Biblical sites (e.g., Rama, Giv'a, Bethel, Ai, Gibeon, etc.), and excavations at a number of them (Ai, Gibeon, Tel a-Nasba=Miẓpe Shemuel, etc.) confirm the Bible's description of these places and of events which took place there. Ramallah, lying at an altitude of 870 m, dominates the northern part of the Judean Hills. Its position readily explains its selection by the Mandatory Government as the site for the country's broadcasting station, and its development as an important summer resort. Wealthy Arab citizens built their villas in the town, and foreign tourists, principally from the Arab countries, spent shorter or longer vacations there. This branch of the local economy has suffered somewhat as the outcome of the Six Day War.

Jericho. Among the urban agglomerations of Judea-Samaria, Jericho stands out by virtue of its great age and unique character as a desert oasis, and also on account of the extreme fluctuations in its population figures over the last century. In 1840, the troops of the Egyptian governor Ibrahim Pasha razed the town before they withdrew from the country. Jericho was again destroyed in the conflagration of 1871. Since the turn of the century the population has increased, to number about 3,000 in the nineteen-forties. After the War of Independence it grew apace, when refugee camps were set up in the vicinity. During the last two decades, winter tourism was encouraged, and many hotels and restaurants gave Jericho a new character. While the Jordanian authorities estimated the population of Jericho and its environs at 80,000 souls shortly before the June 1967 war, only 6,931 were counted in Jericho and the nearby camp in the Israel 1967 census, with approximately another 2,000 in the surrounding area.

Historians and archeologists are almost unanimous in proclaiming Jericho to be the first settlement in the world to have assumed an urban character. Man was drawn to this site by the presence of the nearby Elisha Spring ('Ein a-Sultān). A protective wall and a tall, round tower were built in the Neolithic period, 10,000 years ago. The early inhabitants practiced agriculture and made clay figurines, but had not yet mastered the art of producing fire-hardened pottery. Jericho flourished throughout the Chalcolithic and Bronze periods, and declined only after its conquest by Joshua. King Herod, who died in Jericho, adorned the city with numerous large edifices. From the time of the Mohammedan conquest in the seventh century C.E., however, Jericho was no more than a small village although the splendid 'Umar Hishām palace was built north of it; only for a brief period, during the Crusades, did Jericho regain some of its former importance. This

Looking over the Jericho oasis east toward the Moab Plateau wall

tropical oasis, endowed with an abundant water supply at all times, always produced crops which were rare elsewhere in the country.

Nablus. Numbering 44,000 inhabitants, Nablus is today the largest town of Judea-Samaria; if one incorporates in this reckoning the refugee camps within the municipal boundaries and the adjacent villages which are gradually taking on suburban status, this figure swells to 70,000.

It appears that the town's economy was from the outset based on rich resources of water, a good farming hinterland and a convenient position in the country's communications network, where the north-south Hill Road is met by several good east-west roads coming from northeastern Samaria, from Gilead and the Sukkot Valley in the southeast, from the central Sharon (Netanya, Tul Karm) in the west, and from the southern Sharon (Kefar Sava, Qalqīliya) in the southwest. Up to 1948, a narrow-gauge railway line connected Nablus with Jennīn and Afula in the north and with Tul Karm in the west.

The name Shechem or Sichem appears in the Tell el 'Amarna letters of the 14th century B.C.E., where its king is accused of cooperating with the Ḥabiru intruders against the Egyptian overlords. Joshua assembled the Children of Israel in Sichem to address them with his last words. It was at Sichem that Abimelech, son of Gideon the Judge, made a first attempt at establishing a monarchy over the Israelites. Solomon's son Rehoboam was anointed king at Sichem, and it was here that the northern tribes revolted against him and set up their separate kingdom under Jeroboam. Although Jeroboam's successor, Baasha, transferred the Northern Kingdom's capital to Tirẓa in northeastern Samaria, Sichem continued to retain much of its importance. The Assyrian conquerors in the eighth century B.C.E. here settled fragments of peoples from various parts of their realm, who, together with the remnants of the Israelites, formed a new people—the Samaritans—whose sanctuary became Mount Gerizim near Sichem; John Hyrcanus destroyed the Samaritan temple. After Vespasian had razed the city in the Jewish War of the 1st century C.E., it was rebuilt further west, between Mount Gerizim and Mount Ebal, and assumed the Roman name Flavia Neapolis, later Arabicized into Nablus.

It appears that up to the time of the town's destruction by the Crusaders, the Samaritan community constituted the major element of the population; their numbers began to shrink rapidly after Nablus' reconstruction by the Arabs in the 13th century. Throughout most periods of history, a small Jewish community existed in Nablus, increasing somewhat in the 19th century to 120 souls but quitting the town at the beginning of the 20th century when it became a focal point of intransigent nationalism and religious intolerance. In 1967, 98.5% of Nablus' residents were Arab-Moslems, while Christians numbered 370, and Samaritans 250 souls.

The fact that the town has been inhabited uninterruptedly for most of its historic past explains the relative poverty of archeological finds on its mound, Balata, at the eastern outlet of the Nablus vale, where it widens into the Sokher Valley. Most of the buildings in the town are new, because earthquakes destroyed Nablus in 1838, and again in 1927. Narrow, winding oriental streets are therefore few in number. Spacious markets and roads were laid out when Nablus was built anew, and even the center of the town has to this day vegetable and fruit gardens and some ornamental flower beds. Wealthy citizens have built their villas on the slopes of Mt. Gerizim and Mt. Ebal. The Samaritan quarter lies at the foot of Mt. Gerizim. A few small factories, mainly for soap-making which is the town's traditional industry, based on the large olive plantations of the region, lie at the western extremity of the city, while at the eastern end the beginnings of a modern industrial quarter are visible.

Tul Karm. This town lies at one of the more accessible gateways from the Sharon Plain to the Samaria Hills. It is located at the intersection of the north-south arteries of the Haifa-Lod railroad and motor road, both running along the western edge of the Hills (a section of the ancient Via Maris), with the west-east highway leading from the coast to Nablus. The rich farmlands of the surrounding area have contributed toward its development.

Archeological finds reveal that an agglomeration has existed here at least since the Roman period. Tul Karm's name has its roots in the Aramaic 'Tur Karma' ('Vineyard Hill'), which was used by the Samaritan inhabitants of the Middle Ages and by the Crusaders. In the past few hundred years, Tul Karm assumed the form of a small village, but expanded anew as from the beginning of the 20th century with increase in traffic passing through. This development came to a halt in the nineteen-thirties, with the construction of the Petaḥ Tiqwa-Ḥadera highway which bypasses the town in the west. Despite the fact that the Israel-Jordan armistice border of 1949 encircled Tul Karm on the southwest, west and northwest, the town increased its population considerably, becoming an administrative center while farming in its surroundings was intensified. The town has an agricultural school established by the Mandatory Government with a monetary contribution by the Jewish philanthropist J. S. Kadoorie. In the 1967 census, Tul Karm numbered 15,275 inhabitants, nearly all of them Moslems, one third living in a refugee camp.

Jennīn. In 1967, this town had 13,365 inhabitants, the vast majority being Moslems. Jennīn is usually identified with the Biblical En Gannim. In historical documents, it is named 'Kan' by the ancient Egyptians, 'Ginat,' 'Ginai,' etc., during later periods, and 'le Grand Guérin' by the Crusaders. During the Second Temple period it was populated by Samaritans.

Jennīn lies at the south corner of the Jezreel Valley, where roads radiate northwestwards to Haifa, northwards to Afula and Nazareth, and southwards through the Dotan Valley to Nablus. Thus its situation, together with the abundant water supply and fertile soil in the vicinity, provides this town with an economic basis. During the last decades, Jennīn lay at the apex of the aggressive 'Arab triangle' of Samaria, which explains why battles were fought around it in the 1936–1939 disturbances, in the Independence War and in the Six Day War.

East Jerusalem and Judea-Samaria in the Six Day War

5 June 1967. When war broke out on the morning of this day on the Sinai front, it was still assumed that the Jordanians would refrain from attacking Israel or, at most, content themselves with a few token salvoes. The Israel Army, therefore, prepared to reply to localized Jordanian fire. As from the late morning hours, owever, the Jordanians set up a barrage of shells along the entire length of the order with Israel, particularly concentrating on West Jerusalem, on the Kefar Sava vicinity and even the Tel Aviv area. At 13.00 hrs, Arab Legion troops forced heir way into Government House (which served as the headquarters on the UN Truce Supervision Organization) in Jerusalem, seizing it from the UN personnel tationed there, and immediately prepared for further advance into Israel erritory. This compelled the Israel Army to re-define its strategic objectives, albeit still on a limited scale, including occupation of the ridge dominating from he north the Qastel-Jerusalem section of the main highway leading to the capital; liquidation of enemy positions around Qalqīliya from which the Tel Aviv area had been hit; and dislodging of the Jordanians from the Irron Hills, within shelling range of the Ramat David airfield in the Jezreel Valley. However, when the Jordanian Army, in the course of the day and the ensuing night, brought up its armor to forward positions in Judea and Samaria, with an Iraqi division following in the rear, it became evident that there was no alternative to extending the sphere of Israel's military involvement to the entire area west of the Jordan. Throughout the war, Jerusalem constituted the focus of fighting.

A Jerusalem brigade cleared the enemy from Government House two hours after the latter had entered it, and thence advanced eastwards, taking Ṣur Bāhir and thereby severing the Jerusalem-Bethlehem road. An armored unit arriving in the Jerusalem Corridor from the Coastal Plain began at midnight to pierce enemy defences opposite Ma'ale ha-Ḥamisha and Qāstel, took the villages of Biddu and Nābi Ṣamwīl, and thrust forward to appear on the next morning at the Jerusalem-Ramallah road in front of Tell al-Ful, the site of the Biblical Giv'at Sha'ul. The Latrun enclave was taken on the first evening, and from there a column advanced toward Ramallah over the Bet Ḥoron ascent.

6 June. In the north, forces crossed the border in the noon hours of June 6. One column advanced from the southern Jezreel Valley in the direction of the Kafr Dan and Yamūn villages, while a second, setting off from the Irron Hills, marched against the village of Yā'bed. That night saw the fall of the village Birqīn, on the outskirts of the Dotan Valley, and on the next morning the force was posted at the road connecting Jennīn with central Samaria, there to turn northeastwards against Jennīn itself.

On the Jerusalem front, a paratrooper unit entered the battle at 02.00 hrs. and attacked the heavily fortified Police School and Ammunition Hill. In a cruel encounter, this force also broke through the Naḥlat Shim'on quarter to Sheikh Jarrāḥ, attaining its objectives around 10.00 hrs. The paratroopers then battled their way through the American Colony quarter southeastwards to the Rockefeller Museum, where they confronted the Old City wall opposite Herod's Gate, and reestablished the link with the isolated Israel position on Mount Scopus. Furth north, the strongly fortified Giv'at ha-Mivtar and French Hill were taken by t armored brigade, whereupon the large suburb Sha'fāt fell. In the evening hou Israel forces entered the town of Ramallah. That afternoon the Jerusale Brigade had taken the Abu Tor quarter in hand-to-hand combat. During t evening, the paratroopers began their ascent of Mount Scopus and the Mount Olives.

Meanwhile, an infantry column had marched against the town of Qalqīliya the Sharon, occupied it, and advanced eastwards to the village of 'Azzūn.

On the Jennīn front, Israel forces threw back a counterattack of Jordani tanks and took the town of Jennīn, overcoming massive opposition whi centered mainly on the huge police fortress at the town's western entrance. In t morning, the village Yā'bed southwest of Jennīn was taken. From this point, t Israel column reached the highway leading to Nablus and advanced along i breaking through a formidable road block of Jordanian tanks. An armore brigade joined the battle, crossing the border on Mount Gilboa and advancir through the villages of Deir Abu Dha'īf, Jalqamūs and Tilfīt, to reach the ro leading to Tubbās and proceed in that direction.

7 June. On this day, Jerusalem was re-united with the conquest of the Old City b Israel forces. In the morning hours, the Augusta Victoria building, the Jordan ans' last stronghold on Mount Scopus, came under intensive fire from the groun and air and was then assaulted and taken from the side of the Hebrew Universit compound in the northwest. Immediately, the Israel forces turned west t descend into the Qidron Valley opposite St. Stephen's Gate, where they joine other forces which had advanced from the Rockefeller Museum, circling th northeast corner of the Old City wall. After the gate itself had been burst open b a tank shell, the Old City was entered by three units who mopped up the las pockets of resistance, ascended the Temple Mount and reached the Western Wa at 10.00 hrs.

While the paratroopers fought inside the Old City, the Jerusalem Brigad advanced along its southern wall. In the afternoon, enemy resistance on th strongly fortified hill near Mar Elias monastery was broken, and therewith th way was opened for the conquest of Bethlehem and Hebron. After the latter tow had fallen, the Israeli advance split into two columns, one heading toward Dhaharīya on the road leading to Beersheba, and the other taking the paralle road in the east to Samu'a (Eshtemo'a). On that day, an armored brigad advanced northward from Ramallah in the direction of Nablus, where it joine other Israel forces who where approaching the city from the northeast afte having overcome, during the night, the resistance of strong Jordanian armore ɪnits in the Kufeīr-'Aqāba area and then taking Tubbās without encountering urther opposition. An Israel tank column which entered Nablus was at first ;iven a friendly reception by the local inhabitants who mistook it for Iraqi einforcements, and was thus able to gain control of the city with relative ease. Two other columns pressed forward at the same time toward Nablus, one from Azzūn in the west, and another from the Jennīn area in the north, after having viped out at dawn a Jordanian force of 25 tanks at the Qabatīya road fork, in the outh of the Dotan Valley.

Other Israel columns moved eastwards through the Judean Desert to Jericho, eached the Jordan River and its mouth in the Dead Sea, and blew up the bridges here. After the fall of Nablus, a force descended through the Farī'a Valley to the Damīya Bridge. The occupation of the entire West Bank was thus completed in he course of three days.

The Golan

The Golan as a New Administrative Unit

The Golan, westernmost of the three parts of the Bashan, stretches from tl Upper Jordan Rift and Lake Kinneret eastward to the course of Naḥal Ruqqā Practically all of its territory was occupied by the Israel Army in the last two da of the June 1967 War, as were also certain areas belonging to other geographic units—the 'Ḥermon Shoulder' in the southeast corner of this mountain massi the Nukheīla area which constitutes the northern end of the Ḥula Valle stretching from Dan and Dafna northward to the Lebanese frontier; and tl Bethsaida (Buteīḥa) Valley which forms part of the Kinneret depression. Tl Golan as an administrative unit under Israel government comprises 1,250 km The district borders on Lebanon over a length of 20 km, on Syria—80 km, and c Jordan—20 km. The cease-fire line in existence since the June 1967 battles begi at the Lebanese border 5 km north of Mājdal Shams, whence it runs east-soutl east, with an indentation to the southwest, passing about 4 km east of the Berekh Ram lake and 3 km east of Qunaītira. From there it continues southward at distance of a few kilometers east of the Qunaītira-Butmīya road; the latter site the easternmost point under Israel's control, and there the line turns southwes touching the bank of Naḥal Ruqqād and following it to the mouth of this strea in the Yarmuk River, where it joins the Jordanian border. A strip of no-man land, ranging from a few hundred meters to 2.5 km in width, parallels tl cease-fire line in the east.

Population of the Golan. In contrast to the other regions which came unde Israel's control as a result of the Six Day War, the Golan was almost totall abandoned by its inhabitants. It appears that a large number of the forme residents, whose livelihood stemmed from services extended to the Syrian Army took flight together with the soldiers. Thus, nearly all Moslem-Sunnite Arabs lef as did most of the Moslem Circassians. Even among the Christians—whos numbers had been very small prior to the war—only few remained, making up no more than 1% of the total population registered in the Golan in the census of autumn, 1967. The Druzes were the only community to stay in their five villages (Mājdal Shams, Mās'ada, Bāq'ata, 'Ein Qūniya, Siḥīta), and they thus came to constitute over 90% of the population of the region, about 5,800 souls out of the total of 6,400.

An exception to the above general picture is encountered in the village Ghājar at the Lebanese border, on the east bank of Naḥal Senir; its inhabitants, who belong to the Nusairi (Alaouite) faith, did not leave their homes. Two other villages of the same community, al-Fit and Za'ūra, lying southeast of Banias, were abandoned during the fighting.

Only the six villages mentioned above remained inhabited, while all others were found deserted when Israel troops entered them. In the district capital, Qunaītira, 206 persons were counted in the census, mostly Circassians; however, a considerable number of them left at a later date. At present, nearly half the total Golan population lives at the village Mājdal Shams which, in the 1967 census, had 2,929 inhabitants.

Druzes and Alaouites. Immediately after the Israel occupation, the Golan Druzes expressed their wish to become citizens of Israel and established close ties with the members of their faith living in Galilee and on Mount Carmel. Their economy was in no way impaired by the war and its consequences, and firm economic links have already been forged between their villages and Israel enterprises, both for the marketing of their farming produce and for providing them with employment in Israel development projects and factories. The Government extends to them aid in setting up public institutions, e.g., schools and clinics, improving education facilities, etc. In the summer of 1968, local autonomy was accorded to the Golan Druzes and village councils were set up in their localities. The sole Nusairi village, Ghājar, northwest of Dan, has a domed prayer hall resembling a mosque.

Sex and Age. In analyzing these statistical data, it is advisable to overlook those minority groups which are today represented in the Golan by but a few individuals and whose composition is in consequence purely accidental; only the Druze community is therefore treated here. As in the case of other minority groups in Israel and in the rest of the new regions, this population is young and has a very low median age, the 0–14 years group making up 46.5% of all Golan Druzes. Although somewhat lower than the average for Israel Arabs, this figure permits the conclusion that the birth rate is equally high. The average household in the Druze village in 1967 numbered 5.5 persons.

In composition of sexes, the Druze community is very close to the averag world picture; in the 1967 census, males (2,929) nearly equaled females (2,946).

Agriculture. In farming practice, the outskirts of Mount Ḥermon with the Druze villages contrast sharply with the Golan Plateau, abandoned by its forme inhabitants. Near Mount Ḥermon, limestone, dolomite and chalk form th parent rock, and soils are of the terra rossa and rendzina types. Here, deciduou fruit—apples, plums, peaches, apricots, almonds, and cherries— have pride c place, but vines and olives are also grown. Although the region enjoys ampl precipitation, the peasants use spring and stream waters for at least auxiliar irrigation of their plantations and vegetable plots. Cattle, sheep and poultry ar kept in limited numbers, complementing the structure of farmsteads.

On the basaltic Golan Plateau, in contrast, wheat-growing and herding c cattle and sheep were in the recent past exclusive farming branches. Cultivatio methods were primitive and yields poor. During the last two decades, many field were excluded from the agricultural cycle as the Syrian Army laid mines there c seized them for other military purposes. The peasants of the Upper Golan ha made only minor efforts to free their fields from the boulders covering then Stones were only collected to set up narrow fences indicating ownership right.

Springs are relatively rare on the Golan Plateau, as most rainwater seeps int the soil, drains off underground toward the Jordan Rift or flows in surfac streams in the same direction.

The Circassian villages, most of which lay south of Qunaītira, were superior i living standards, housing and farming methods to the rest of the Golan villages Unlike the latter, for instance, they planted fruit and ornamental trees near thei homesteads and invested greater efforts in the preparation of their fields fo crops, sometimes clearing stones and often using less primitive farming tools

The Bethsaida Valley, enjoying a warm climate, an abundance of water an deep, heavy soils, constitutes a farming region on its own. Until fairly recently however, these assets were hardly exploited, and neglect led to the formation c malaria-infested swamps. The blame for this situation falls largely on the feuda system of land ownership, as most of the valley belonged to a single family. Th poor tenants raised mainly grain crops and some vegetables. Large expanses wer used solely for grazing or left fallow. In the years immediately preceding 1967 some small groves of bananas and citrus were planted on the strip next to th bank of Lake Kinneret.

The Town Qunaītira. Although a few remnants of the Byzantine period have bee found at Qunaītira, until the middle of the 19th century this locality was know only as a khan or wayfarers' inn. It was only then that Circassians, who ha

Druze farmers of Mājdal Shams, at the foot of Mt. Ḥermon, working on the village's threshing floor

found refuge in several provinces of the Turkish Empire, were settled here by th Turkish Government. Broad roads were laid out in the town, and brick or basa stone houses were built. The population increased gradually, from 1,500 at th turn of the century to 15,000 shortly before the Six Day War. Its economy wa basd on trade, small workshops and farming, as well as on administration, a Qunaītira served as a district center. During the 1960's, when most Syrian uni were concentrated in this region next to the Israel frontier, the services extende to the army gained in importance. On the other hand, the town lacked industry c any kind.

Attempts at Jewish Settlement in the Golan

In the early phases of Zionist settlement, the Golan was the object of speci interest, both on account of the low land prices prevailing there and because of i soil and climate conditions which gave promise for the development of farmin similar to that in eastern Europe, the region of origin of most of the settle candidates.

Rumthanīya. The first attempt was made by Jews of the 'old yishuv' of Safe Fifty-two families founded a society named 'Bene Yehuda' which negotiated fo the acquisition of a large tract of 15,000 dunams at Rumthanīya, in the Uppe Golan, about 15 km south of Qunaītira. Some of its numbers went there in 188 and sowed winter grain. With the advent of the following summer, they prepare to build houses, terrace fields and carry out other development programs, bu were compelled to leave when the Turkish governor of Damascus refused t append his signature to the transfer of the land to Jewish ownership.

Bene Yehuda. Approximately 20 member families of the 'Bene Yehuda' Societ did not despair of settling in the Golan even after the attempt at Rumthanīya ha failed. They sent an emissary to Europe and America who succeeded in raisin some funds for the purchase of a part of the lands of Bir Sheqūm village, 5 km northeast of the present-day kibbutz En Gev. In 1898, 10 families arrived at th site which, in honor of the society, they named 'Bene Yehuda.' They met wit untold difficulties, e.g., the lack of even the most basic necessities, the Turkis authorities' prohibition on construction of houses, crop failures, etc. Despit their preparedness for a most frugal life, most of them were not able to hold ou for long. Nevertheless, six families struggled on until 1912, but by the followin year only one remained, which abandoned the site in 1920, when one of its son was killed by Arabs while working his lands.

Bethsaida Valley. In 1904, a group of Jews who had been peasants in their native Crimea accepted the proposal of the Kurdish-Moslem proprietor of lands in the Bethsaida Valley to settle there, initially as his tenants, with the prospects of purchasing the holdings for themselves at a later stage. A number of them took up this offer, and yields of the first season were promising. However, the housing provided was primitive and they suffered severely from malaria, as they had chosen to settle within the swamp area. In the hour of their distress, local quarrels broke out as a further disrupting force, and the last of this group left the valley in the following summer.

Baron Rothschild's Lands in the Bashan. The boldest attempt at settlement ever undertaken in the region was that in the Bashan east of Naḥal Ruqqād, on both banks of the 'Allān stream, i.e., beyond the limits of the area which came under Israel control in 1967. Zionist associations of Russia and Rumania took the initiative in acquiring land there. Baron Edmond de Rothschild consented to participate in the venture and contributed a substantial sum of money. Between 1894 and 1896, the purchase was finalized, notwithstanding the numerous obstacles the Turkish-Syrian administration placed in the way of registering the land in the name of the company Baron Rothschild had founded for this purpose. Theoretically, an area measuring between 100,000 and 120,000 dunams had been bought, but a survey showed that in actual fact it amounted to no more than 75,000 dunams. A farm was set up at Jilīn, as well as a colony which was named Tif'eret Binyamin, and two additional settlement points. The number of families living there amounted to 16 or 17. The authorities, however, claimed that these people had no right settling there as they were not Turkish citizens, and at the end of 1897 sent soldiers to expel them. A second attempt, this time to bring in Syrian-Jewish settlers, similarly met with failure. Baron Rothschild transferred the lands to the ICA Society which maintained its administration under a Jewish director who resided first at Jilīn and later at Sakhm al-Jolān. His duties were to keep watch over the property and raise the leasehold fees from the Arab lessees. After the First World War, a Jewish administrator returned there on behalf of PICA (which had taken over ICA holdings in Palestine). This official was a farmer from Kefar Tavor who up to 1940 spent several months each year in the Golan. In that year the rule over Syria passed into the hands of the Vichy-French allies of the Nazis.

Throughout the days of the Second and Third Aliya, attempts at renewing Jewish settlement in the Bashan never ceased. Expeditions to the area were organized by the Labor Battalion and by the Ha-Po'el ha-Ẓa'ir Movement. Leaders of the Jewish community in the country and the Zionist Movement energetically supported the idea. However, the hope that the French Mandate authorities would adopt a more favorable attitude toward Jewish settleme plans than their Turkish predecessors faded in the 1930's.

Conquest of the Golan in the Six Day War

Since the establishment of the State of Israel, the Syrians surpassed her oth neighbors in aggressiveness. In the 1960's Syria became the principal base c Arab terrorist gangs seeking to infiltrate into Israel, and it was the steadil heightening tension along the 77 km stretch of the Syrian armistice lines whic ultimately led to the Six Day War. The Syrians invested enormous efforts i building military installations along this border, fully exploiting the topograph cal features which were all in their favor: the slopes of Mount Ḥermon dominat the Ḥula Valley from the north, while east of this valley the Golan Plateau rises a an abrupt wall, which is particularly steep south of Kefar Szold. High and almos vertical escarpments fringe the east shore of Lake Kinneret. From the upper rir of these escarpments the terrain rises further but more gently toward the eas This not only made access from the Israel side extremely difficult, but als enabled the Syrians to develop a highly efficient system of fortifications simultaneously defensive and offensive. On the escarpment rims, they poste artillery and tanks which could readily strike at any object in the Israel village down in the valley. Behind these were located several strings of fortifications an dugouts, with artillery emplacements, able to fire at targets in Israel territory ove the heads of their own forward positions. All trenches and dugouts were so wel protected by reinforced concrete and earth roofs that they were practicall invulnerable to shelling and aerial bombardment.

5–8 June. Documents found in military camps in the Golan show that the Syrian were preparing to penetrate into Israel at two points—opposite Ayyelet ha-Sha ḥar and near Lake Kinneret—and to reach the line Gush Ḥalav-Safed in Uppe Galilee in the course of one day, with the final aim of taking all of northern Israel including Haifa. June 5, 1967, was set as D-Day for their attack. However, wher fighting broke out on the morning of the same day on the Sinai front, the Syrian were content with heavy, continuous shelling of Jewish settlements along the entire length of the border. On 6 June they attempted to invade Israel at Tel Dan. Ashmura and She'ar Yashuv, but were soon driven back. The shelling caused very heavy damage, but the Israel artillery retaliated with increasing strength.

9 June. On that day, Israel columns moved against the Golan in the hours befor noon, when the battles on the other fronts had been won and the air force was free to concentrate its full efforts here. At 11.30 hrs., units crossed the border north of Kefar Szold where the ascent is somewhat less steep than in the other sections. With heavy artillery support, the column advanced and took the Syrian position of Na'amūsh. At that point it split up into two parts, one heading southeast to reach Qāla'a, while the other moved northeastward to Za'ūra, taking the positions above that village in a fierce battle at 16.30 hrs. Simultaneously, other columns advanced further north and south. In gruelling fighting, the position of Tel al-Fakhr was taken, whereupon the strongest of the Syrian forward fortifications, Tel 'Aziziyāt, could be attacked from the rear. The southern column captured the village of Rawīya situated above Kibbutz Gonen. All other Syrian strongpoints along the border north of the Benot Ya'aqov Bridge also came under attack, thus bringing about the foundering of the entire Syrian defense system by that evening.

10 June. On this second and last day of fighting on the Syrian front, Israel forces advanced with great speed. In the north, they closed in on Banias and took the village, and then turned westward to occupy the Nukheīla pocket between the Israel and Lebanon borders. After doubling back eastward, they ascended over Za'ūra to Mās'ada, where the Syrians fled, leaving behind them large quantities of equipment without even attempting to destroy them. Further south, the column which had entered Qāla'a proceeded over Mansūra to Qunaītira. The town was reached at 14.00 hrs, and was entered almost without resistance. Other units arrived at Qunaītira from the south. After having overcome the last desperate Syrian resistance at Rawīya, they had first advanced southward to Kafr Naffākh and then continued along the main road leading from the Benot Ya'aqov Bridge to Damascus. The last enemy positions down at the bridge were also cleared.

At the same time, an attack was launched on the Lower Golan from the south, the main effort being directed against the Tawafīq-Kafr Ḥārib ridge above the kibbutzim of Tel Qaẓir and Ha-On. At 15.30 hrs, Tawafīq was stormed by paratroopers. After this battle, the advancing columns encountered only limited resistance. They reached el-'Al, which had already been taken by an airborne unit, and then the Butmīya road fork, where they met other columns which had come from Qunaītira in the north and from Darbashīya in the west. Finally, a helicopter-borne unit occupied positions on the Ḥermon Shoulder. Therewith, an easily defensible line, running along the highest points of the Upper Golan in the north, and along the Ruqqād course in the south, was established when the cease-fire came into force in the evening.

Construction of dwellings for the kibbutz En Ziwwan, situated south of the volcanic cone Tel Avital

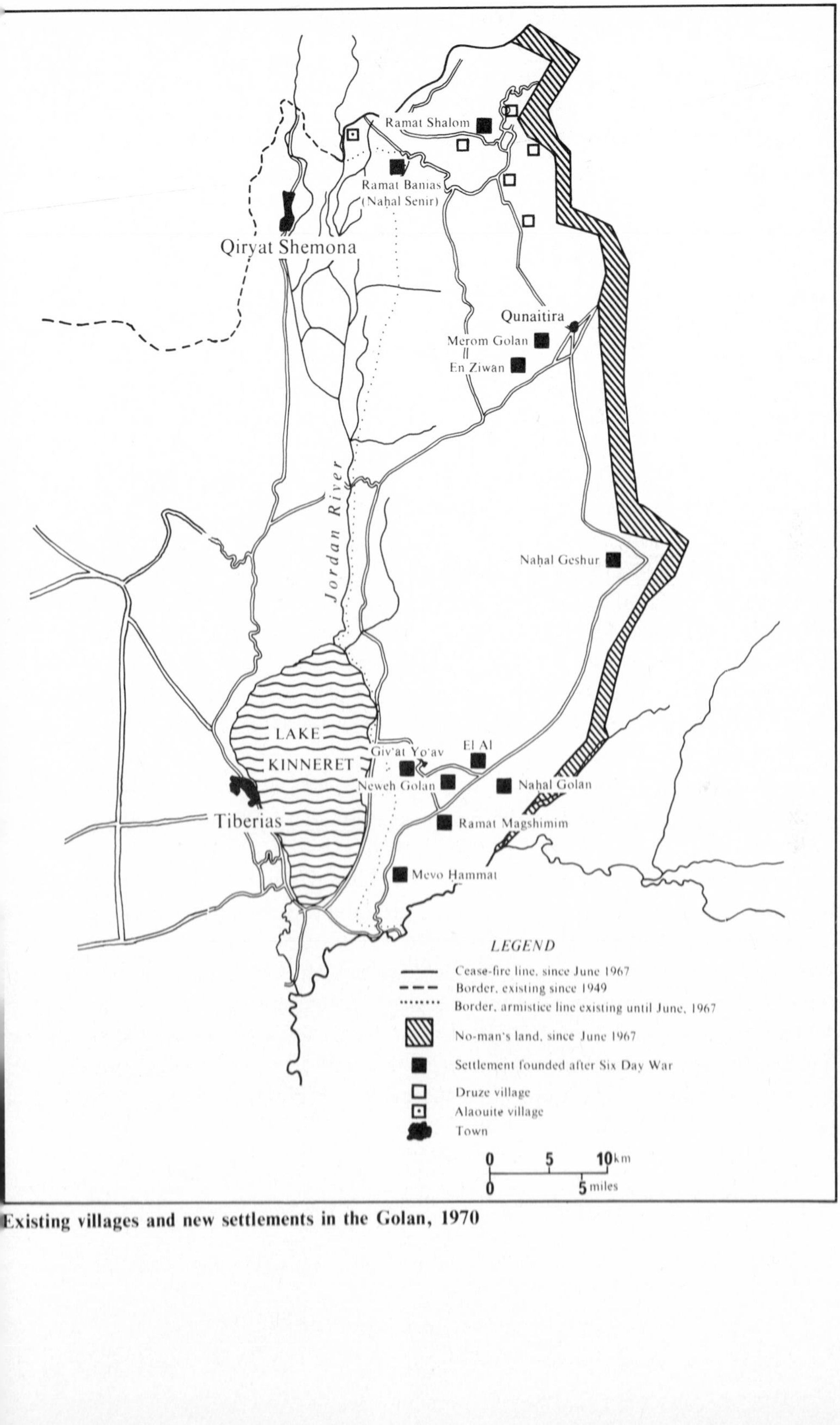

Existing villages and new settlements in the Golan, 1970

Settlement Activity After the Six Day War

After the Six Day war, the entire Golan, except the northern corner with its Druze villages, was found to be deserted by the former occupants. The establishment of Jewish farming settlements in this virtually empty area therefore constituted an urgent necessity, both from the security and the economic points of view. In the course of the first two years of Israel administration, ten farming villages were established, partly as military and partly as civilian outposts, consisting of six kibbutzim and four moshavim.

In the northern part of the region, Merom Golan, founded as the first settlement on 16 June, 1967, chose as its site the western entrance to the town Qunaītira. It was followed by En Ziwwan, situated south of the mountain Tel Avital. In addition, Ramat Banias was set up on land that had always been Israel territory but access to which had previously been barred by Syrian military positions.

In the central sections of the plateau, Naḥal Geshur constitutes the easternmost settlement of the country. The largest number of villages was founded in the southern Golan, where the deeper soil is more conducive to agriculture. There, Mevo Ḥammat and Giv'at Yo'av were established near the western plateau rim, El Al, Ne'ot Golan and Ramat Magshimim, in the center, and Naḥal Golan close to the cease-fire line. The area under cultivation amounted, in the second season, to 5,000 ha, with field crops (mainly wheat) and vegetables as principal branches. In addition, grazing areas were developed for beef cattle and sheep; the former are being brought, in the first development stage, to 10,000 head, and the latter to 5,000.

The settlement authorities envisage increasing the number of farming villages in the Golan to 22 at a second development stage, with a combined population of 12,500 and a cultivated area of 17,000 ha. Soil reclamation work and construction of water storage dams and access roads has been carried out since 1967 and is to be continued in the future. The region's principal north-south highway is to run further west than the present road.

In addition to the projects concerned with farming villages, roads were constructed, thereof two on Mount Ḥermon, reaching the 2,224 m-high top in Israel's hands. In 1969 and 1970, further roads were paved on the mountain. There are plans for setting up a new urban center for the Golan and developing the branches of the Bethsaida Valley for farming, fishing and recreation.

Part V
The Economy and Its Foundations

Soil and Water

Soils, Conservation and Reclamation

Soil Types in Israel. Two factors, the parent rock and the climate, determine soil physiognomy. Even Israel's pre-1967 borders, including a great variety of both rocks and climatic conditions, consequently displayed a wide range of soil types. Most similar to the parent rock in composition is young soil; in mature or old soils, climatic and other environmental factors are decisive while the origin of the rock meal is hardly identifiable. Soils mature most rapidly in a tropical-humid climate. Israel's central and northern parts, with relatively high temperatures and only winter rains, are intermediate in this respect and engender special Mediterranean soil types; in the Negev, desert soils prevail.

Highly important for farming is the ratio between the formation of new soil and its disappearance by erosion. Particularly in the hill regions, the topsoil is washed off faster than new soil can form from the bedrock beneath. The young soil usually has no chance to mature and grow old; therefore, most soils in the country are classed as young.

As Israel's soil types have been described in greater detail in the chapters of the book dealing with the geology and morphology of the country's regions, a brief recounting of their geographical distribution and properties will suffice here.

In the *Negev,* besides the dead rock meal, the reg and hammada types of the desert proper, the fine-grained, semiheavy, yellowish brown loess of the Beersheba Region is found. Loess, potentially fertile because of its inclusion of minerals needed by plants, is, however, liable to crumble into dust when dry, and it is then transported by winds over small or large distances. Under the winter rains, conversely, it forms a hard, impenetrable crust. This causes surface waters to collect in flash floods, which, in turn, create a badland topography. In the southwestern part of the Beersheba Region, shifting sand dunes are prominent, often underlain by loess. In the Arava Valley, a number of oases and brackish playas are found where soils are heavy and mostly saline.

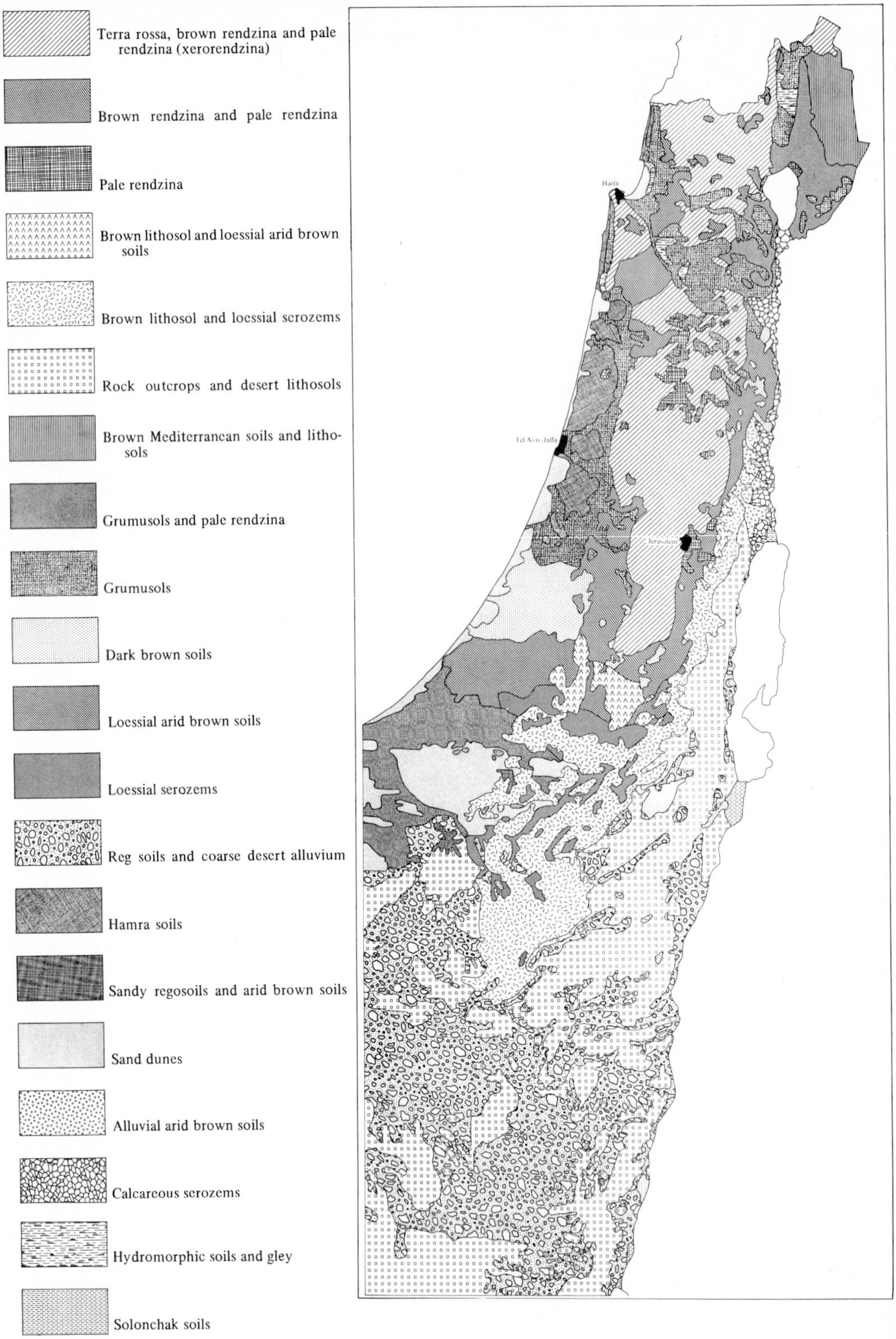
Terra rossa, brown rendzina and pale rendzina (xerorendzina)
Brown rendzina and pale rendzina
Pale rendzina
Brown lithosol and loessial arid brown soils
Brown lithosol and loessial serozems
Rock outcrops and desert lithosols
Brown Mediterranean soils and lithosols
Grumusols and pale rendzina
Grumusols
Dark brown soils
Loessial arid brown soils
Loessial serozems
Reg soils and coarse desert alluvium
Hamra soils
Sandy regosoils and arid brown soils
Sand dunes
Alluvial arid brown soils
Calcareous serozems
Hydromorphic soils and gley
Solonchak soils
Haifa
Tel Aviv-Jaffa
Jerusalem

Soil associations in the country (by courtesy of Prof. D. H. Yaalon)

Most typical of the *Coastal Plain,* besides the barren dune belt along the shore, are the coarse-grained 'red sands' (ḥamra soils), which are adaptable to farming because of the fine-textured cover of minerals on each grain. The eastern parts of the Coastal Plain and terrains adjoining watercourses are characterized by heavy terra rossa and alluvial soils, partly blackened by swamps which covered them, either in the geologic past or until a few decades ago. Most sand-loess, red sand-loess and red sand-loess-terra rossa types are suitable for farming but are gravely threatened by gullying.

In the *Foothills* and *Hills,* light gray to grayish brown soil is characteristic of terrains of Senonian and Eocene chalks, and terra rossa of Cenomanian and Turonian limestones and dolomites. Rendzina is basic in reaction and high in calcium content and, when occurring in desert or semidesert areas, is also high in sodium and potassium. It is not inherently very rich but has the advantage of being easy to till. Terra rossa is reddish brown, moderately heavy and well-suited to many crops. Eastern Galilee and the Golan have dark basalt soils resembling terra rossa in their properties.

The *Interior Valleys* and the northern sectors of the *Jordan Rift* (Jezreel, Ḥarod, Ḥula valleys, etc.) are characterized by black, alluvial swamp soils, rich in organic components and very heavy. They hold water well but tend to become a clinging mud in the winter rains and form hard clods separated by deep cracks in summer. After the drainage of the Ḥula Lake and Swamps, fertile peat soil was uncovered. In the Central and Lower Jordan Valley, lissan marls are prominent. These are deposits of an inland lake which covered these sections of the Rift, partly until the Upper Pleistocene. Such marl soils are whitish, light gray or yellowish and not particularly fertile but they may be enriched by manure and chemical fertilizers, and are usually easy to plow. From the Bet She'an Valley southward, lissan marls become increasingly saline.

Soil Conservation and Reclamation Methods. On the *loess* and *loess-sand* soils of the Beersheba Region, conservation and reclamation methods must remedy the gullying caused by runoff and prevent the damage of wind erosion. With the rolling topography prevalent in most of the region, exact contour plowing is required, so that each furrow, instead of promoting runoff, aids in absorbing the rainwater. Where slopes are steeper, broad earth terraces are constructed, sometimes reinforced along the edges by the planting of deep-rooted perennial grasses or by rows of trees. Flat ditches are dug in contour lines beneath the terrace rims to catch surplus rainwater.

Farmers are advised to break the hard crust formed on the loess after each rain by frequent harrowing or disc-plowing. This diminishes the danger of flash floods forming on the surface and aids absorption of rainwater.

Heavy soil of a brackish playa in the southern Arava Valley cracks when drying; the hard polygonal clods curl up along the edges

Severe gullying and badland formation near Be'eri in the western Beersheba Region. Fields in background have been won by leveling and closing of gullies, and are now protected by shelter-belts planted between them

Where gullying has been severe and formed a badland topography (along Naḥal Besor, near Be'eri, in the vicinity of Dorot and Ruḥama, etc.), bulldozers are employed to level off hummocks and fill most of the zigzagging gullies. Only a few wadi beds are left, after their courses have been straightened and their banks strengthened by planting eucalyptus and other fast-growing and sturdy species, to prevent flash floods from bursting out and cutting new gullies through the fields.

A recent feature in Negev reclamation is the deep, two-directional plowing of land subject to severe gullying; small quadrangles up to 60 cm (2 ft) high are thus created where fruit trees can be planted and other crops grown. Forest and fruit trees are frequently set on earth ridges 60 cm–1 m (2–3 ft) high, which run in contour lines; it has been found that more moisture is absorbed and is better retained in the loose soil of these ridges where plant roots can easily mesh out and trees grow twice as fast as in the customary low-lying planting holes.

Novel research on ancient Nabatean cultivation methods is being carried out at the Avdat experimental farm, directed by Prof. M. Even-Ari of the Hebrew University. Slopes are cleared of stones to make their surface smooth and promote runoff toward low-lying wadis. Cleared stones are sometimes piled up in geometrically arranged heaps to direct the water to canals which lead it to the fields laid out inside the neatly leveled and terraced wadi courses. The crops then receive the rainwater falling on a manifold larger surface. Similarly, orchards are planted experimentally in wadi beds near Be'erotayim on the Sinai border and irrigated almost exclusively by infrequent and short-lived flash floods, whose flow is regulated by protective dikes.

Negev dust storms are countered by planting shelterbelts around crop fields. These consist of 2–4 parallel rows of trees which decelerate the wind force, restrain wind erosion, and cut down the evaporation of water from the upper soil stratum caused by hot summer gusts striking over the surface. Measurements show that the wind slackens to 60% of its original speed to windward of the shelterbelts and to 50% on their lee side. The area protected by the trees exceeds their own height by far, tenfold on the windward, thirtyfold on the lee side.

In the loess area of the South, tamarisks are planted on earth ridges to serve as shelterbelts

Shelterbelts, mainly of eucalyptus and tamarisk, are placed at intervals of 350–750 m (1,200–2,500 ft). Here, too, trees are set on earth ridges which enable them to subsist on an annual rainfall of 200 mm (8 in) and less, without any irrigation even in their first year of life.

Drifting *sand dunes* which threaten neighboring fields, roads or installations, can best be checked by tree planting. Tamarisk, eucalyptus and long-leaved acacia have been found capable of rooting themselves in barren sand. Planting along the fringe of dune areas is often sufficient to protect neighboring crop fields; planting the entire surface with trees harnesses the dunes and, by adding organic material, may slowly transform them into tillable soil.

Novel use has been made of sandy tracts, particularly along the Mediterranean coast, for growing certain species of fodder grasses. Another experiment, hitherto conducted on a very limited scale by the late Dr. H. Boyko, consists in growing crops on coarse sand and irrigating them with large amounts of salt water; most of the water immediately percolates to a great depth and returns to the sea. A small part of it, however, evaporates, is recondensed on the sand grains as fresh water, and is retained there colloidally for absorption by plants.

In the *Hills* and *Foothills*, the age-old art of terracing is paramount in the conservation of terra rossa and rendzina soils. Its two main stages—clearing of rocks which hinder the plow, and construction of terrace walls—are interdependent, since the stones cleared are used for building the walls along the terrace edges. The alternating layers of hard limestone or dolomite and of soft marl in the Cenomanian and Turonian formations, which give slopes a steplike appearance, are conducive to this method and explain why this country was among the first to practice terracing.

In recent years, several phases of hill reclamation have been mechanized. Terraces are laid out to be as broad as possible (depending on the slope angle). The first phase, generally, is the examination of the terrain to show whether the depth of the soil warrants the investment. This is normally done by a rooter drawing a furrow at the depth of about 60 cm (2 ft). A novel method of geophysical subsoil photography is now being tested which, it is hoped, will be less expensive and reveal the subsoil structure in greater depth. The second step is deep plowing by bulldozers, which uproot boulders and shove many of them to the terrace edge. Where compact bedrock outcrops, dynamiting is sometimes necessary. The remaining surface stones are piled and carried on tractor-drawn sledges to the terrace edge, where the dry stone walls are built by hand. Today, two low parallel walls are preferred; the surplus rocks and stones fill the space in-between. All terraces are set out in exact contour lines, sinuous on the hill slopes, which are repeated by the rows of vines or fruit trees planted there. In Galilee, particularly, the garrigue or maquis brush must also be rooted out when

In hill slope terracing, huge bulldozer-rooters are employed—scene from western Upper Galilee

terraces are prepared for farming. The investment is generally heavier in terra rossa zones than in rendzina.

In *alluvial soils* of the Coastal Plain, the interior valleys, and even in small intermontane vales, 'agricultural drainage' is frequently necessary to lower a high groundwater table. This entails, in most cases, cutting deep, narrow ditches to convey the surplus water to the nearest watercourse. Sometimes, clay pipes must be laid instead.

Soil conservation and reclamation work in Israel with few exceptions is carried out by the Jewish National Fund.

Water and Water Development

Water constitutes the critical factor of Israel's economy. It is decisive for the country's agricultural potential, as one ha of irrigated land has a crop value of 3 ha and more of nonirrigated soil. Moreover, wide areas of relatively fertile soil, such as those in the Northern Negev, are cultivable only when irrigation is possible, since the annual rainfall in these regions is insufficient for the success of any crop. Water is needed in ever larger quantities for industry and for the home use of Israel's fast-growing population.

Measured against these requirements, Israel freshwater sources are extremely limited; even when fully exploited, irrigation water can be brought, at most, to only 0.20 million ha (500,000 acres) of a maximum of 0.55 million ha (1,360,000 acres) of irrigable land. Israel had the highest world percentage of exploitation of available water sources (90%), even before the National Water Carrier was put into full use.

Water Sources. An estimated average annual total of 6,000 million m^3 of rainwater falls on Israel's pre-1967 area; with the addition of the water draining toward it from outside the old borders, the annual amount comes to 10,000 million m^3. Of this, 60–70% evaporates immediately or shortly after falling, or is lost through evapo-transpiration by the vegetation. Another 5% or more becomes surface runoff to the Mediterranean Sea, the Dead Sea and the Red Sea. Even of the remaining quarter which percolates into the subsoil, much is lost through underground drainage into the sea.

These figures are liable to vacillate strongly from one year to the next, since the usable portion depends on the total amount of rainfall and on other climatic circumstances. Higher temperatures cause immediate evaporation of more rainwater. A fine drizzle will have a higher percentage of evaporation than a heavy shower; violent downpours, on the other hand, increase surface runoff. In most cases, the ground absorbs water and allows its percolation toward the end of the rainy season more readily than at its beginning.

The geological structure of the country can be regarded as generally favorable to water absorption into groundwater horizons. The Cenomanian and Turonian limestones and dolomites on the surface of the rainier portions of the Hills are rendered highly permeable by karst processes while the thinner intercalations of impervious marl prevent the water from percolating too deeply. Small quantities of this water appear on the natural steps of the hill slopes as small springs, which usually flow only ephemerally. Larger springs are fed by the groundwater flow which divides along the main subterranean watershed in the Hills (not identical with the surface watershed) and then runs west and east. They are situated on the outcroppings of the permeable rock strata, on the border of the Coastal Plain and the interior valleys, as well as on fault lines. In addition to springs in such contact zones (e.g. the Kabri, Na'aman and Rosh ha-Ayin springs in the west, Enot Enan, En Ḥarod, the Bet She'an Valley springs or En Gedi in the interior), water is also derived from many wells drilled there. The considerable groundwater quantities stored deeply beneath the Coastal Plain are equally supplied by subterranean flow from the Hills.

Most of the surface runoff in this country is ephemeral. In the Negev and the South, wadis fill for no more than a few hours after each rain; one watercourse may carry a flash flood while its neighbor remains dry. In the southern sections of the Coastal Plain and in the Judean Hills, the flow of streams sometimes lasts for several days, and in the northern parts of the country, the flow of some is sustained for a few weeks or months. A few streams are perennial (e.g. Yarqon, Naḥal Ḥadera, Keziv, Ga'aton, etc.), although in summer their flow is usually reduced to a trickle. The Jordan, with some of its tributaries, has the only more or less constant flow, and it can be described as a small river.

Estimates of the total freshwater quantity annually available in Israel are between 1,500 and 1,940 million m³, although the optimistic figure of 3,000

Nabatean dams in a wadi course at Mamshit in the Negev Hills hold floodwaters to this day. The lowermost dam has been added under the British Mandate

million m^3 has also been mentioned; if the higher of the two first figures (1,940 million m^3) is used as a basis, about 1,100 million m^3 can be supplied by smaller springs and by wells from the groundwater horizons, 215 million from the Yarqon and its springs, close to 400 million from the Jordan, and 200 million by interception and storage of seasonal surface flow and flash floods and by reclamation of waste waters. In 1968, Israel's water consumption exceeded the volume of 1,400 million m^3, whereof 1,150 million m^3 were used by agriculture, and ca. 300 million m^3 by industry and domestic consumption.

The uneven distribution of water sources and of arable land is to be taken into consideration: while the regions north of the Yarqon comprise slightly less than 50% of Israel's cultivable soil, they contain over 85% of available water resources.

Water Use in the Ancient and Recent Past. In the early history of the country, efforts were directed mainly toward assuring drinking water for towns and villages by building stone cisterns for rainwater storage, capturing spring water, etc. Outstanding in this respect were the ingenious methods employed by the

'Solomon's Pools,' south of Bethlehem, provided water to Jerusalem already in the Second Temple period

Nabateans in the Negev (see pp. 209, 218ff.) and the water installations of ancient Jerusalem (see p. 324). Irrigation techniques, developed mainly in the Roman and Byzantine periods, were later almost entirely forgotten. Hill villages continued to use cisterns for storage of drinking water. In the 18th century the governors of Acre built a spectacular aqueduct to the city from the Kabri springs. In the 19th century shallow wells, which began to be dug in the Coastal Plain, touched the 'nazaz' water horizon. Lighter soils which require large amounts of irrigation water were still impracticable for farming at that time.

A basic change began in the early 20th century, when deeper wells began to be sunk and water was pumped from greater depths and conducted through pipes over larger distances, all as a result of the introduction of mechanical equipment. In the 1920's and 1930's, geological surveying began to probe subsoil conditions for drilling in many parts of the country. In 1936, the national Mekoroth Water Company was set up; its first job was the drilling of wells in Haifa Bay and in the Jezreel Valley and the distribution of the water found, to Haifa and the agricultural settlements in these regions. The Mandate administration laid the pipeline between Rosh ha-Ayin and Jerusalem and provided it with several boosters. Water was pumped from the Sea of Galilee and diverted from the Jordan and Yarmuk courses to the fields of the Jordan-Yarmuk Plain. In the 1940's, water was derived in increasing quantities from the main aquifers of the Coastal Plain (Saqiye formation, and the deeper rock strata), and regional distribution of spring and well water was undertaken in the Ḥarod and Bet She'an valleys. In 1947, a few weeks before the outbreak of the War of Independence, the two small pipelines from the Gevar'am and Nir Am wells in the Southern Coastal Plain reached the outpost settlements in the Northern Negev, with an annual transport capacity of 1 million m^3.

Water Administration. In the first years of statehood a new body, 'Tahal' ('Water Planning for Israel'), was set up to direct all planning and research in line with a national water scheme encompassing all parts of Israel and all forms of water supply and distribution. The Government holds 52% of the Tahal shares: Tahal also carries out water research, planning and similar operations in foreign countries. Administrative control of water matters is held by a Water Commissioner whose staff includes divisions for hydrological service, engineering control, water utilization, and water rights. A Water Law enacted by the Knesset stipulates that all water within the borders of Israel is State property and regulates its exploitation and allocation.

Groundwater Use and Regional Projects. Since the first years of statehood, more groundwater has been brought into the national economy cycle. New areas where

The aqueduct built through the Acre Plain in the 18th century

numerous wells have been drilled include the Carmel Coast, the eastern reaches of the Sharon, the Southern Coastal Plain, the Judean Foothills, and the vicinity of Beersheba.

Great progress has been made in regional water schemes. In the early 1950's new pipelines with a yearly capacity of 15 million m^3 replaced the two primitive pipelines from Nir Am to the Northern Negev. In 1955, more water reached the South and Negev with the completion of the first stage of the Yarqon-Negev project. The Rosh ha-Ayin springs supply about 100 million m^3 through 107 km (66 miles) of prestressed concrete pipelines 165 cm (66 in) in diameter; this line made the settlement of the Lakhish Region feasible. A second line, 180 cm (70 in) in diameter, was laid in the early 1960's from Rosh ha-Ayin to the south. It parallels the former in the west and supplies 45 million m^3 per year to the Tel Aviv conurbation. Instead of being supplied by water pumped from Rosh ha-Ayin, Jerusalem receives water from two parallel lines, which led water first from the vicinity of Reḥovot and later from Kefar Uriya in the Judean Foothills.

An undertaking comparable in size to the Yarqon-Negev system is the Western Galilee-Qishon project, begun in the 1950's with the installation of an artificial storage lake near Kefar Barukh in the center of the Jezreel Valley. At first, the lake served to intercept the winter flow of Naḥal Qishon and other local streams; later, a pipeline, of 76–122 cm (30–48 in) diameter, was laid from the abundant springs and wells of Western Upper Galilee and of the Acre and Zebulon valleys into the Jezreel Valley. The somewhat saline water of the Na'aman spring is thereby diluted by the fresh water coming from Galilee. The Kefar Barukh Lake, enlarged to hold a volume of 7 million m^3, permits an annual increase in capacity of the project from the initial 60 million m^3 to 180 million m^3.

Another regional project of special interest is that of the Jordan-Yarmuk Plain and the Bet She'an Valley. Since many of the strong springs emerging at the foot of Mount Gilboa and in the Bet She'an Valley are too saline for irrigation, installations were prepared to render as much water as possible usable for farming branches: the flow from the springs is concentrated and led through three parallel open concrete canals with high, intermediate and low salinity respectively; the first is diverted and used for fishponds, while the water of the second and third is diluted by mixing and thus becomes available for irrigation. The Kinneret-Bet She'an line takes water from the Sea of Galilee and joins the Bet She'an blending plant. Part of it is distributed on the way to the Jordan-Yarmuk Plain settlements, where it replaces the water of the Yarmuk River (partly harnessed for the Jordanian East Ghor Project) while the rest reaches the Bet She'an Valley and is integrated there into the local distribution scheme.

Of smaller scale than the above-mentioned are regional projects such as those of the Ḥula Valley, and of Central and Upper Galilee. The water of the latter is

The Bet She'an blending plant of fresh and saline waters

supplied partly from local springs and wells and partly from the Enot Enan springs in the Ḥula Valley; from that point it is pumped up over a height of almost 700 m (2,300 ft). Another scheme is that in the Judean Foothills, which exploits groundwater and distributes it to the Adullam Region and adjoining areas; yet another is the pipeline bringing water from Yotvata and other Arava Valley wells to Eilat.

The National Water Carrier. The idea of comprehensive development and exploitation of all potential water resources was expounded in the 1930's by Walter Clay Lowdermilk in his book 'Palestine: Land of Promise.' The project was worked out by the American engineer James B. Hays and put forward in his report 'T. V. A. on the Jordan,' modeled on the Tennessee Valley Authority. It proposed to exploit all opportunities for water development for the benefit of Palestine as well as her neighbors. It included points such as maximum use of groundwater sources and interception of ephemeral storm water, drainage of the Ḥula Lake and Swamps, and irrigation of the Lower Jordan Valley. All headstreams of the Jordan were to be collected by a countrywide carrier and diverted close to their sources so that the water should flow down freely without

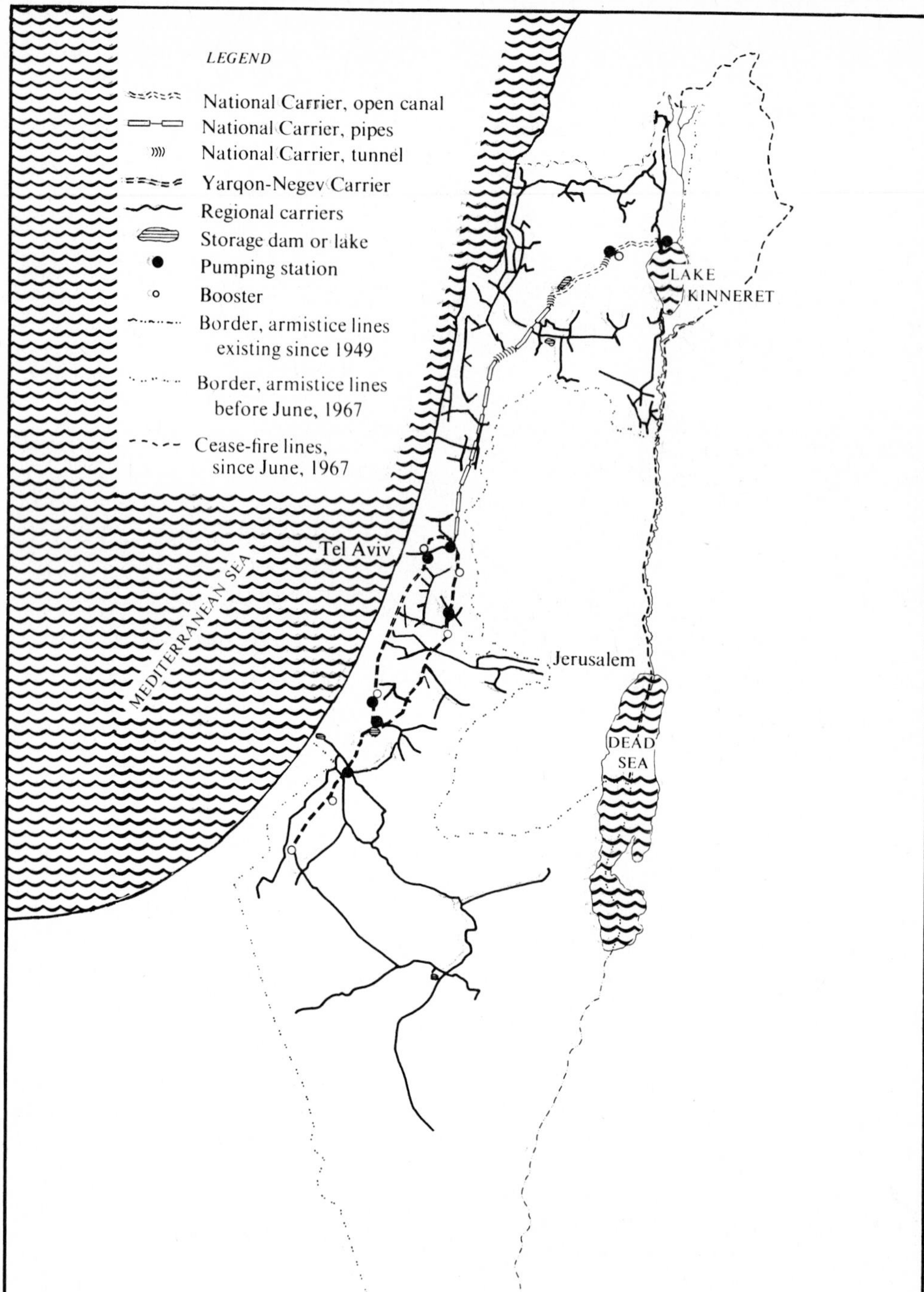

The National Water Carrier and regional projects

need of much pumping; water from the Litani River was to be led down from Lebanese territory into the Ḥula Valley. The cheap electricity thereby produced was to be at Lebanon's disposal, and the water at Palestine's. The Yarmuk River was to be diverted to the Sea of Galilee to replace the Jordan waters. Most important, a seawater canal was to be dug from the Haifa Bay to the Dead Sea to replace the Jordan's flow of fresh water and to use the level difference of 395 m (over 1,300 ft) between the Mediterranean and the Dead Sea for electricity production on a vast scale.

Arab opposition caused a gradual reduction of this visionary project, although Israel's neighbors, too, were thus relinquishing the chance for marked advantages. Even the more modest Jordan Valley Development Plan, promised financial backing from the United States and worked out by the representative of the American President, Ambassador Eric Johnston, although at first endorsed by the technical experts and governments of the Arab states and Israel alike, was later, out of political considerations, rejected by the Arab League Council in 1955. The Israel National Water Project has been devised in a manner permitting it to be integrated into an overall regional scheme if future political developments make such implementation feasible. Simultaneously with Israel's work on its National Carrier, the Kingdom of Jordan, with American aid, built the first stage of its East Ghor Project, diverting into the eastern part of the Jordan Valley, to a point north of the Yabboq, water from the Yarmuk River which, at its junction with the Jordan on Israel's border, carries a quantity of water approximately equaling that of the latter river.

The main conduit of the Israel carrier, in the shape finally adopted and completed in its first stage in the mid-'sixties, falls into the following sections: Lake Kinneret—the Sea of Galilee—whose area amounts to 165 km^2 (64 sq. miles) and whose capacity is estimated at 3 billion m^3 water, serves as principal reservoir and issuing point of the carrier. From the northwest corner of the Sea of Galilee, the water is pumped through pressure pipes to 256 m (797 ft) above the lake level ('Eshed Kinnarot'), and then runs in an open canal over a distance of about 16 km (10 miles) to the Ẓalmon pumping station and reservoir (20 ha area, 800,000 m^3 volume). On its way it passes the deeply incised gorges of Naḥal Ammud and Naḥal Ẓalmon by siphons. A second pumping station raises it to 147 m (492 ft) above sea level. It then enters, through pressure pipes, into the Bet Netofa Valley by way of a 800 m ($\frac{1}{2}$ mile)-long tunnel under the narrow ridge near Eilabūn village. Here, an open canal leads to the southwest end of the Bet Netofa Valley, passes through a reservoir (40 ha area, 1.5 million m^3 volume) where the water is kept 48 hours and leaves the valley through the mile-long Shimron Tunnel. From there onward, the line runs exclusively through 270 cm (108 in) prestressed pressure pipes. It crosses the Jezreel Valley in its western part. Between

Giant pipes of the National Carrier are laid in the Coastal Plain

Ha-Zore'a and Mishmar ha-Emeq the line enters the 7 km (4 miles)-long Menashe Tunnel, composed of two sections, and emerges near the northeastern corner of the Sharon. It then runs due south through the Coastal Plain, and is connected at Rosh ha-Ayin with the Yarqon-Negev line which proceeds to the Zohar Reservoir in the Lakhish Region and to the Northern Negev west of Beersheba. The total length of the main conduit amounts to 142.5 km (88.5 miles). The carrier supplied 180 million m^3 of water annually in the first stage; in 1968, the quantity was raised to 356 million m^3, and to a somewhat larger amount in 1970–1971.

Technical and other reasons led to the choice of the Sea of Galilee as the central storage reservoir. The Bet Netofa Valley, originally envisaged for the purpose because it is about 360 m (1,200 ft) higher than the Sea of Galilee, turned out to be unsuitable because of the high porosity of the limestone formations in the surrounding hill ridges. Secondly, the Sea of Galilee, one of the most outstanding landscape features in the country and sacred both to Christian and Jewish tradition, would have shrunk greatly if the Jordan waters had no longer reached it, while the Yarmuk was not available to run through the lake.

Israeli water planning, therefore, had to put up with two disadvantages—the low level of the Sea of Galilee which necessitated a large capital outlay for water pumping, and the high salinity of the lake water caused by mineral springs on the lake bottom and on its banks. The salt content of the lake shows seasonal vacillations. The increase in fresh water entering the Sea of Galilee from the Jordan and other streams in winter lowers the salinity of the lake; as the lake level mounts, its water weighs heavier on the spring sources at the bottom and reduces the flow of at least a number of them. At the end of 1963, for example, after five consecutive drought years, salinity in the lake rose to over 400 milligrams per liter, but dropped by 50 mg/liter after 4 months of ample rains. In the winter of 1968–69, salinity decreased to below 250 mg/liter. In that peak-rain winter, the Kinneret water level rose to a maximum, flooding installations and fields on the lake banks and necessitating the opening of the sluices at the Jordan outlet. Hundreds of millions m^3 were thus allowed to flow unused to the Dead Sea. This experience lent greater urgency to a project of constructing a concrete containing wall along the lake's circumference to permit the raising of the constant water level by 1 m and more. This will increase the water quantities at the disposal of the National Carrier and reduce the outflow of the saline springs at the lake bottom. It is also hoped to reduce the salt content of the Sea of Galilee waters permanently by half, by diverting the saline springs on the shore and by plugging most outlets of the saline springs on the lake bottom, so that their water concentrates at a few spots and can be sucked into diversion pipes and thus be removed from the lake.

The Bet Netofa Reservoir of the National Carrier

These efforts are aided by intensive research to determine the salinity ceiling of irrigation water permissible for each soil type, and each crop. Scientists are conscious of the fact that such experiments require time and caution, as salinity may accumulate in soils and become noxious, and 'fatigue' may be noticeable on perennial crops after several years of irrigation with brackish water. To make saltier water usable in farming, crops little affected by salinity are tried out in the more arid regions of the country.

Storm-Water Interception and Recharge of Underground Horizons. Holding up the ephemeral flow of streams and wadis and storing these waters from winter to summer, or from a rainy year to a dry one, meets with several grave problems in this country. The quantity of water to be won does not always warrant the large outlay necessary for impounding dams and artificial lakes and reservoirs. A large percentage of the water thus stored is lost through evaporation from the reservoir surface during the long, dry summer. At most of the sites chosen for experimental storage installations (e.g., En Kerem Dam near Jerusalem, Bet Netofa Storage), the bedrock was soon found to be highly porous; the stored water soon disappeared through cracks and fissures, and the cost of grouting (injection of concrete into the cracks) was prohibitive. In some instances, as in the Ayalon Valley Dam, the silt brought down with the floods makes the bedrock more impervious. But even where this is not the case, the failure may turn out as a blessing in disguise: the water from the reservoirs percolates to the depths, joins the groundwater, is protected from evaporation losses, and can be drawn up again in wells in the vicinity. Consequently, the next step was to direct stored storm-water to the subsoil, intentionally. The pilot installation here is the Shiqma Storage Dam, on the coarse, pervious sand dunes of the Southern Coastal Plain at Karmiya near the Gaza Strip border. The first years of water storage in the Shiqma Reservoir have been successful. To prevent a reduction of the basin bottom's perviousness by the silt brought down with the flash floods, the water is first kept for a few days in a transit basin where the silt is allowed to settle. Toward the end of the 1960's, a second, larger project was executed with the interception of floodwaters of a number of streams running down from the

Interface sweet groundwater is captured near the sea shore in northeastern Sinai; the system of leaving the water unprotected from evaporation is, however, hardly advisable

Menashe Hills to the northern Sharon. Similar enterprises of this kind are blueprinted for most major stream courses in the Coastal Plain.

A considerable part of the supplementary water won in various ways is to be used for recharging water horizons, principally in the Coastal Plain. This practice has become routine since the late 1960's. In the decade before the National Carrier was put into operation, planners took the calculated risk of overpumping, with a view to 'repaying the debt' as soon as surplus water became available. Overpumping lowers groundwater horizons so that infiltration of sea water is imminent; when the reserve of underground flow sinks below 30%, the interface (dividing line between fresh and sea water) is drawn upward and causes salination of wells. A novel experiment, however, has been undertaken, in which groundwater is tapped at the very edge of the sea, where it is of surprisingly low mineral content; this is not expected to affect the interface equilibrium and is hoped to add an annual 40 million m^3 of fresh water to the economy.

Part of the water brought with the National Carrier is also allowed to percolate to the groundwater horizons of the Coastal Plain. Of the 276 million m^3 of supplementary water to be won from various sources under Tahal development plans until 1971, 70 million are earmarked for recharge of underground horizons, over and above those quantities of water from the National Carrier which are channeled underground via Coastal Plain wells.

An idea proposed recently is 'runoff inducement' on areas which hold no promise for farming and cannot be put to any other economic use, particularly in hill and desert areas where adduction over large distances makes water expensive. A similar method, albeit more primitive, was used in the Negev by the Israelites and Nabateans of antiquity (see pp. 218f.). For this purpose, it is proposed to treat soil surfaces both mechanically (by smoothing, compaction, etc.) and chemically (with crusting and binding substances) to make them waterproof and thus harvest 80–90% of the rainfall which they receive. The runoff would be caught in cisterns, ponds and storage dams, or used for groundwater recharge.

Water Saving and Reclamation of Wastewater. Prevention of water waste is essential in a country with such limited resources. Notable progress has been recorded, and more efforts are being made to cut down consumption per capita in households and per produce units in factories. Even more important is the research into the optimal irrigation rate for each crop and each climate and soil type; in some instances, water consumption can thus be halved and yields improved at the same time. The novel system of growing crops under plastic covers also entails considerable savings in irrigation water. Further water economy is in the offing with the spreading of the 'trickle irrigation' system, invented in Israel, which equally promises a simultaneous increase in yields. In ndustry, efforts are being made to promote recirculation of cooling water, or use of sea water instead of fresh water wherever equipment is not endangered by corrosion.

Hopes are attached to experiments with films spread over open water surfaces undertaken in different countries. These must spread very thinly over a wide area, be cohesive and elastic and remain intact when the water surface is curled by waves, and be selectively pervious, i.e., permit oxygen from the air to penetrate into the water while they prevent water vapor from rising into the air.

The reclamation of sewage water for irrigation after treatment and purification is of equally great importance. An estimated 90 million m^3 can thus be annually reclaimed in the principal cities alone, 5% of the country's water potential. Such schemes entail considerable cost, as urban sewage systems must be altered, concentrated, and directed to treatment plants, and the purified water must often be channeled through special pipes to separate it from drinking water. Several additional results can be obtained by sewage reclamation: beach pollution of the seaside cities can be stopped when the sewers no longer issue into the sea, and compost plants can win highly valuable organic fertilizers from sewage. A larger wastewater treatment plant has been installed in the Haifa area; the Jerusalem and Beersheba plants, although operating on a smaller scale, enable experts to watch the effect of such water on soils like terra rossa or loess.

The most comprehensive project of this kind was begun in 1968 on the Rishon le-Ẓion dunes, to reclaim, in the first stage, 15 million m^3 of sewage water from the Tel Aviv conurbation, through sunlight radiation, algae and filtration in the sands. Ultimately, an annual quantity of 112 million m^3 is anticipated to run there through 20 oxidation ponds. A sharp controversy, however, arose between the town of Rishon le-Ẓion and other neighboring communities and the water planning authorities, as the project was feared to be a potential source of inconvenience and a health hazard to the inhabitants.

Unconventional Methods. All steps undertaken or planned for maximum utilization of existent water resources are of vital importance, even for the country's immediate needs. This is particularly true of the National Water Carrier, which promises the largest addition of water to the quantities utilized. Planners are aware, however, that the development of further resources is imperative for Israel's future and that this must be done by unconventional methods.

Artificial Rain, and Groundwater Exploration at Depth. First experiments in inducing rain clouds to yield a larger part of their water content by seeding them with a mixture of silver iodide and acetone were made in Israel in 1960. For that purpose, a 'random date seeding' schedule, developed in Australia, was adapted to local conditions. The seeding is done both from planes which meet incoming clouds 5–10 miles out at sea, and from burners on the ground sending a mixture of acetone and silver iodide particles up into the clouds. The results of eight seasons showed precipitation to be increased by an average 15%, and in some instances up to 25%, yields which are superior to those of other experimenting countries. In 1968–69, it was therefore decided to introduce cloud seeding as a routine operation on a national scale, with an anticipated yield, at a relatively low price, of an annual 180–200 million m³ of supplementary rainwater. After runoff and evaporation, about 60 million m³ of this quantity would remain for the national economy's water balance.

More cautious hopes are attached to the exploitation of deep groundwater reserves which are probably extant beneath desert areas. Three categories are to be distinguished here: in the Ḥaẓeva region of the Arava Valley, considerable reserves are mooted to be stored in porous limestone strata beneath the Ḥaẓeva Series, which in wells may rise to the surface as artesian waters and which are possibly replenished from rainfall in the Hebron Hills further northwest. At greater depth, Nubian sandstone strata, similar to these below the Sahara Desert, are thought to store water which is considered to date from the last pluvial periods, i.e., preserved for at least 30,000 years. An attempt was also made to discover juvenile water (formed by chemical processes from magma) beneath the Eilat Hills, but this search has not yet met with success.

Water Desalination. In the long run, desalination of brackish spring and sea water is to be regarded as the decisive step towards solving the water problems of this country. Technically, separation of water from its mineral content presents no problem, but ways must be found to perform such operations on an economically feasible basis.

As far as brackish spring and well water is concerned, membrane systems use either the electrodialysis method which seems to have justified itself from the economic viewpoint, or 'reverse osmosis.' After the first electrodialysis plant had been run on a laboratory scale for over a decade at the Negev Research Institute of Beersheba, a larger experimental station with 5,000,000 m³ annual production was set up at Ẓe'elim in the northwestern Negev. An installation capable of processing more than double this quantity was in 1969 under construction at Mash'abe Sadeh, south of Beersheba.

For desalination of seawater, the salt content of which is up to ten times greater, freezing and distillation are the principal methods. Eilat has a distillation plant the daily capacity of which, after improvements, was stepped up to exceed the original target by 10%, attaining over 4,000 m³; a second plant, with a 3,000

The desalination plant of Eilat, employing the distillation method

m^3 daily capacity, was set up there in 1970. This town also possesses an intermittently operated, smaller freezing plant, applying a system perfected by Israeli scientist A. Zarchin. The invention of a novel device capable of separating ice crystals from other particles and applicable to freezing as well as to other desalination methods, was published by Haifa Technion scientists in 1970. Modifications in the distillation process have been introduced according to suggestions of another Israeli expert, Eng. A. Osdor, bringing about 'flash distillation' at low pressure (i.e., in a partial vacuum) and at relatively low temperatures, at the same time using a novel type of heat exchanger to cut down energy requirements. One further step is the 'direct contact method' proposed by Professor Abraham Kogan of the Haifa Technion: a cold stream of desalted water is brought into contact with a stream of hot brine, taking up condensing water vapor flashed off by the latter. In the process, the cold stream gains heat which it returns to the system in a 'heat recovery unit.' Bundles of copper tubing and partition sheets thus become redundant, capital investments can be greatly reduced, while the heat transfer becomes much more efficient and the need for an outside supply of energy is reduced. As the water won in all these forms is virtually salt-free, it can dilute more brackish water and thus further increase usable quantities.

In 1964, the United States of America agreed in principle to cooperate with Israel in this field, and make this country a pilot plant for the solution of this problem of world-wide importance. President Johnson, as one of his last acts in office, presented to Congress a bill for a grant-in-aid to Israel amounting to 40 million dollars, and a further loan of 18 million for this purpose. Israel is to decide whether to operate the installation with conventional fuel or with atomic power. In all events, the proposed plant is to be a double- or triple-purpose installation, combining the production of electric power with desalination and, eventually as a by-product, also winning chemicals from the seawater. Although the original blueprint of the plant capable of producing 100 million m^3 of desalted water was, for technical reasons, reduced to a capacity of 50 million, it will certainly be, for some time to come, the largest installation of its kind, and provide experts from all interested nations with the opportunity to investigate this sphere.

Agriculture

General Conditions

Among the factors determining the character of farming in Israel are the dearth of principal resources—soil and water—and the great variety in climatic and other conditions. The latter are conducive to a wide range of branches, cultivation systems and crops, all in an extremely limited area. About 4,500 km^2 (1,112,000 acres) of the pre-1967 surface of Israel are estimated as capable of yielding crops without irrigation, with another 1,000–1,500 km^2 (247,000–371,000 acres) capable only when water is brought from afar. An additional 2,000–3,000 km^2 (494,000–741,000 acres) are, to some extent, usable for pasture or afforestation.*

It is therefore clear that Israel's agriculture must strive for maximum intensivity and efficiency. As labor for Israel farming is neither cheap nor abundant, mechanization is stressed. This tendency often leads to problems, in view of the small size of most farming units. The collective or cooperative form of farming, however, aids full utilization of heavy equipment, as one set can serve a village or even a group of villages. Each of the rural centers, established in the framework of regional planning, is provided with large tractor garages and repair shops. Local industry, especially factories located in kibbutzim, have brought onto the market smaller types of agricultural machinery or tools specifically adapted to local conditions, such as mountain plows, small tractors, etc. Increasing mechanization reduces the amount of labor in relation to yield. Another trend is towards farm specialization in one or a few particular branches, most of them capital- and labor-intensive and export-oriented. Countrywide and regional planning and allocation of production quotes for each crop have largely

* The agriculture of the areas under Israel's administration since 1967 and its branches are described in the relevant chapters, i.e., Sinai, pp. 359–363; Gaza Strip, pp. 392–393; Judea-Samaria, pp. 404–408; Golan, p. 422.

solved the problem of surpluses. Research institutes extend to the farmers continuous guidance in soil treatment, pest control, etc.

The Character of Mediterranean Farming. 'Mediterranean agriculture' took shape thousands of years ago. It is noted for its variety of products and its ability to provide basic food requirements. Mediterranean farming comprises three principal branches—field crops, with wheat foremost; fruit, with the olive and the grape most important; and flocks of sheep and goats, which utilize marginal lands, and in turn, provide milk, meat and raw material for cloth. The small irrigated kitchen garden of vegetables may be added; it has been tended in this area at least since the Chalcolithic period.

Three main agricultural regions can be distinguished within Israel's narrow area: the Coastal Plain and the valleys of the interior, the Hill regions, and sections of the Jordan Rift with a near-tropical climate. This fact brought about the crystallization of different farm types early in history, with trading in products of various regions following soon after.

The country's location at the crossroads of three continents, although the cause of frequent devastation by warfare, brought it into contact with distant lands and their produce, and aided the introduction and acclimatization of new crops. Several of these innovations, e.g., citrus and cotton, still occupy an important place in Israel's farming. These two seem to have been known in the Roman period or earlier, but disappeared for a thousand years and were returned to cultivation only during the last century. Other species, such as bananas, groundnuts, and sugar beet, were introduced in the present century. This country constitutes the fringe of the global distribution zones for several species, which have here attained standards of yield and quality far superior to those in their regions of origin.

Farming Branches

Cereals. Grain and fodder farming is important on heavy or semiheavy soils, such as the eastern and southern parts of the Coastal Plain, and the Jezreel and Ḥarod valleys, the Beersheba region, etc. While fluctuations in annual rainfall had previously caused field crops alternately to expand and contract in the South, the increasing use of auxiliary irrigation there is stabilizing the overall area of field crops with an average of 275,000–280,000 ha (679,600–702,000 acres). In 1967–68, 54,000 ha field crops were under irrigation.

Among the *winter cereals,* wheat occupies first place in value in Israel, as in most Mediterranean countries. However, Israel cannot yet meet the local demand from its own wheat production. In the Hills, on the other hand, wheat-growing in the tradition of the Arab peasants is not being encouraged, for it is less profitable where modern machinery cannot be employed, while it accelerates soil erosion on the slopes. Introduction of choice pest-resistant seed strains (e.g., dwarf wheat), better fertilizing and improved agrotechnical methods have tripled average yields from 800 kg/ha of in 1948 to 2,400 in 1965. Top yields, up to 7,000 kg/ha, have been reaped in 1970 on certain farms. During the 1960's, the increase in production reduced the need for importing this commodity from 85% to an average 50% of local consumption. In 1968, auxiliary irrigation of 8,500 ha of wheat reduced drought losses. In the record year 1967, 220,000 tons of wheat were harvested, but only 165,000 tons in 1968, during which year Israel's wheat consumption amounted to 320,000 tons. Planning aims at obtaining the latter quantity exclusively from local production by 1975, when ca. 10,000 ha of wheat will receive auxiliary irrigation. The total wheat area scheduled for the 1970/71 season was 100,000 ha.

Barley, grown mainly as cattle and poultry fodder, is second in value, and generally first in area. Its soil and water requirements are modest, making it suitable for dry regions such as the Northern Negev or Bet She'an Valley. It

Wheat harvesting in the Northern Negev

ripens early and thus sometimes permits a summer crop on the same field. The barley-sown area in 1963–64 totaled 73,145 ha (180,740 acres), but shrank in the ensuing years, owing to the expansion of wheat, to cover only 43,337 ha (106,068 acres) in 1966–67. The two remaining winter grains are limited in importance: *oats* constitutes a sideline, and *rye* is grown rarely.

Summer cereals show a wider variety, but two crops are of prime importance—maize and sorghum. *Maize* gives satisfactory yields even when grown without watering, and exceptional yields under irrigation—up to four tons of maize have been harvested from one acre. Maize is cut mainly while green and fed either fresh or after silage to animals; its grains also provide raw material for various kinds of food and industrial products (cornstarch, glucose, starch, etc.). In *sorghum* cultivation, Israel farmers have succeeded in growing hybrid varieties which give excellent yields. Sorghum is principally a fodder crop.

Pulses, Fodder Crops. Among *fodder crops* other than cereals the accent is on *pulses* and other legumes, which, in addition to their great nutritive value, enrich the soil nitrate content. Cereals and legumes are frequently grown in mixed seed, harvested green, then dried and stored to be fed to the animals over the whole year. *Clover* and *alfalfa* give excellent green fodder; alfalfa meal is prepared in special factories and sometimes even exported. *Fodder beet, fodder melons, horse beans,* and other species are also important.

Industrial Field Crops. Much aid is being given to so-called *'industrial crops,'* where the return per area exceeds that of other field plants. The important species are those providing oil, fibers and sugar. Of the oil-containing crops, *groundnuts* have been successful; originally planned to supply the raw material for margarine production, they were soon found to be of such excellent quality for direct consumption that they are in demand on the local market and also appear on the country's export list. Their irrigated area averages 3,000–5,000 ha (7,500–12,500 acres). Other oleaginous plants are *sunflower* and *safflower (Carthamus).*

A number of plants yield both oil and fiber, with *cotton* first. Cotton growing, only introduced on a commercial scale in 1953, on the whole suffices for Israel's highly developed textile industry, and export of long-staple cotton has begun. Cotton is usually grown in Israel under irrigation; in limited areas in the north it can thrive on rainfall alone. As it can adapt to various soil types, it is found in most parts of the country, with the exception of pronouncedly hilly regions. First tried in the Bet She'an Valley, it has spread north to the Ḥula Valley, west through the Jezreel Valley to all parts of the Coastal Plain, and south and east again to the Judean Foothills and the Northern Negev. Its area in 1964 was 12,135 ha (under 30,000 acres), to which an unirrigated area of 690 ha (1,700 acres) has to be added.

Cotton growing and picking has been mechanized. Israel's yields per area unit are among the world's highest

In 1967, the cotton area increased to 24,769 ha (61,204 acres), (whereof 4,639 ha—11,463 acres—were unirrigated) and, in 1968, to 26,500 ha (65,482 acres).

Sugar beet grows well on heavier soil, even in the Northern Negev. When sown in winter and harvested in early summer, it needs only little irrigation. The principal sugar beet regions are the Jezreel Valley and the Southern Coastal Plain. About one-third of Israel's sugar requirements are covered by local production, although imported sugar is often considerably cheaper. The branch is therefore not envisaged to grow considerably beyond its present size.

Tobacco is cultivated mainly in Arab villages, particularly those in the Hill regions. Macedonian varieties, cross-bred with other oriental strains, have improved in quality. Hit by plant disease, tobacco cultivation was considerably reduced in the beginning of the 1960's, but recovered toward the end of the decade. However, the future of this branch, which requires cheap labor, in Israel's progressive agriculture is doubtful. Irrigated Virginia tobacco is being grown on an experimental scale.

Fruit and Vegetables: *Citrus* is first in Israel's fruit growing, as well as in its agricultural exports. Citrus orchards first appeared as an important branch just before World War I. They spread quickly in the 1920's and 1930's, and reached an extent of 30,000 ha (75,000 acres) by 1938–39. That year also marked a record achievement of exports, 15 million cases, mainly of the Shamouti variety of oranges. However, during World War II and afterwards, when the country was first cut off from the world market and later troubled by the internal disturbances which culminated in the War of Independence, the citrus-planted area shrank in 1948 to 12,000 ha (30,000 acres) and exports to 3 million cases. Great efforts have been made since then to reestablish this important export branch. In the 1967–68 season, the citrus area reached 44,700 ha (110,500 acres). Citrus export tonnage

Picking oranges

rose to 507,000 in 1963 (40 cases roughly equal to one ton). After a drop to 450,000 tons in 1964 owing to a bad harvest, the export figures have shown a constant rise, attaining 559,000 tons in 1965, 567,000 tons in 1966, and 678,000 tons in 1967. In the following years, quantities further increased, but returns, which amounted to 75 million dollars in 1966 and to more than 85 million in 1967, have in later years failed to keep apace with the export volume. This is mainly to be ascribed to the fact that prices tend to decline as other producers as well as Israel step up exports, a development which began to make itself felt in the late 1960's. Among the citrus exporters, Israel has earned a name for the excellent quality of her fruit and at the same time attains record yields per area unit.

Most oranges grow on the red sands of the Coastal Plain; in the 1950's, the area expanded, particularly to the Southern Coastal Plain, and reached the northern outskirts of the Beersheba Region. Citrus groves are planned to constitute one of the main branches in the new Besor Development Region of the northwestern Negev. Grapefruit thrives on the heavier interior soils no less than in the Coastal Plain. It has been grown for decades in the Ḥarod and Kinneret valleys, later entering the lower reaches of the Judean Foothills. Lemons, tangerines, mandarins, citrons, etc., constitute smaller items in the country's citrus production and exports.

The *vine* is of ancient Israeli tradition, but due to the law forbidding Moslem believers to drink wine, vineyards almost entirely disappeared up to the last century. The vine is best adapted to conditions of the Hills and Foothills, but it also thrives well in areas of coarse sand in the Coastal Plain and on heavy soils of the interior valleys. Its deep roots enable it to subsist on a comparatively small amount of water. Jewish farmers grow vines with irrigation, mainly for table grapes. Efforts are being made to foster again the cultivation of wine grapes, as home consumption of local wines and liquors increases and progress is recorded in exports of wines and spirits. Vineyards covered 10,700 ha (26,440 acres) in 1967–68, of which 5,600 ha (13,840 acres) were wine grapes.

The *olive,* like the vine, has occupied a central place in the farming of this country since antiquity. Needing no irrigation, it thrives very well in the Hills. For centuries, olive oil was Palestine's only export item; it also maintained the country's foremost industry of that time—soap production. Vast olive groves still characterize villages in mountainous Galilee, and their total area in Israel amounts to about 30,000 acres. Yields are apt to vary greatly from one year to the next. It is difficult to fit this branch into a modern rural economy because of the seasonal oscillations in labor requirements: over most of the year olives need little care, while picking demands a large number of hands. The Arab peasants, with their large families, can manage harvests easier than is possible on the modern Jewish farm. Attempts are being made to tackle the problem by grafting new varieties with higher yields and larger individual fruit on existing trees, by keeping the tree crowns low and thus within easy reach, etc. On an experimental scale, olive groves have been planted in the desert hills of the central Negev.

Deciduous fruits, especially plums, peaches, apples and pears, are expanding in area; they covered 11,100 ha (26,935 acres) in 1964–65. As they must be irrigated, their cultivation is more expensive in Israel than in Europe; they are grown primarily to cover local demand, and only small quantities can, because of early ripening, find a market abroad as out-of-season fruit. Deciduous fruit thrives well in the Hills and in the Ḥula Valley, where winter cold is welcome to this branch. To prevent overproduction, planners seek to limit new plantations to hill villages which have only a small range of other crops on which to base their economy. *Almonds,* modest in their water requirements, were planted in the Negev in the 1960's.

Additional fruit species to be found in Israel include the *pomegranate,* which thrives even on slightly saline soils; it is principally grown in the Bet She'an Valley. Much more important are tropical varieties, such as *bananas* which were first introduced into the hot Kinneret Valley, but have later spread also to the Coastal Plain with its mild climate; sites protected from strong winds, such as the Carmel Coast, are preferred for these plantations. Bananas have become a popular local food as well as an important element in Israel exports.

The *date palm* also belongs to the group of tropical fruits. It can tolerate slightly brackish water and soil, is therefore grown in the Kinneret and Bet She'an valleys, and has recently been introduced into the desert playas of the Arava Valley. Finally, there are tropical newcomers to the country such as the *guava,* the *mango,* and especially the *avocado;* the latter now finds good export markets in Europe.

Garden crops in Israel are extremely varied and provide the market with fresh *vegetables* in all seasons. Almost all European vegetables grow in Israel, and in addition, some subtropical and tropical species (eggplants, etc.). *Potatoes* and several *pulses* for market consumption (green peas, string beans, lentils, etc.) in this country belong to the garden, and not to field crops, as they do in parts of Europe and America. *Strawberries* also constitute an important item on the list of garden crops. All require irrigation, and most can be harvested several times a year, even in the middle of winter. Vegetable production amply supplies local demand. Intensive horticulture under glass or plastic covers, including both out-of-season vegetables and certain fruit and flowers, greatly expanded in the 1960's. In 1968, an area of 1,800 ha was under cultivation, and was extended in the following two years. Closely linked with research and aided by an efficiently organized transport system and sales and advertising apparatus, this branch is making rapid progress in exports and promises to play an important role in the

Out-of-season vegetables, fruit and flowers are often grown under plastic covers. This method, both reducing water needs and hastening ripening, has priority in Arava Valley settlements.

country's foreign trade. The overall area under vegetable culture amounted to 19,614 ha (48,466 acres) in 1966–67, whereof 4,325 ha (10,687 acres) were occupied by potatoes.

Seed-growing has met with success in Israel, and numerous new varieties have been cultivated and adapted to local conditions, mainly in specialized seed farms. *Medicinal plants,* spices and plants providing perfumes and etheric oils are being tried out. *Flowers* and flower bulbs are grown in different parts of the country, in the Coastal Plain, the Ḥula and Arava valleys, etc. Gladioli, roses, anemones, etc., are airfreighted abroad in steeply mounting quantities. Israel also supplies bulbs, shoots, etc., to foreign gardeners.

Fruit and vegetables are directed to export both fresh, and processed in various forms—canned, dried, frozen, etc. Planners expect agricultural exports to attain $250 million in value by 1975/76, thereof $70 million processed crops.

Livestock and Poultry. Until the recent past, *sheep and goats* represented the principal form of livestock in this country, as in most of the Mediterranean region. Jewish farmers, on the other hand, made endeavors to rear milch cattle and laying hens to secure a supply of milk and eggs for a Jewish population mainly accustomed to a European diet. Moreover, it was soon recognized that the local black goat is the principal culprit for the degeneration of wild plant growth in the country and, consequently, for the grave erosion damage of the last centuries. This branch was therefore restricted. At present, it is progressing gradually in keeping with the improvement of natural pasture. Israel's herdsmen have succeeded in crossbreeding a race of white milch goats of abundant yields. The local fat-tailed sheep mainly produces milk for cheese production, and it also yields some meat; its wool is of the coarse type principally suited for carpet making. Merino wool sheep of Australian origin have been introduced and are tended in increasing numbers.

Poultry raising in Israel is run on American lines in a highly mechanized manner, with meat and egg production complementing each other. There exist a number of ultramodern poultry slaughterhouses which sell the hens ready for cooking, packed in plastic bags. Valuable poultry preserves, such as goose liver and paste, are being exported on a small scale. Geese, it has been found, can be helpful in orange groves, where they consume couch grass and other weeds. Another asset lies in the fact that modern poultry runs can be maintained where the soil basis for fodder growing is restricted or absent. This also suits the branch

Israel's poultry branch has become almost an industrial enterprise

to hill farming where choice of crops is naturally limited; hill villages are lately given preference in planning quotas for poultry runs. Turkey raising is a speciality of settlements in different regions.

Eggs and poultry today fully meet local demand. However, a large percentage of fodder needs (and especially fodder concentrates) must be imported. This makes the products so expensive that only Government subsidies can make them readily available to the public. The branch has utilized the country's climate, where hens continue to lay eggs in midwinter almost at the same rate as in summer, and thus eggs have been exported to Europe in the winter over a number of years. Since competition in this field, however, is stiffening and prices are low, exports can hardly cover the foreign currency layout of the branch. Planning authorities therefore seek to adapt output to local demand, with the exception of specialized export commodities (turkeys, goose liver, etc.). The number of laying hens is therefore likely to remain stable at around 7 million over a number of years, even if a certain widening of the local market occurs.

Dairy cattle present even more complicated problems. Some economists, faced with the water problem, advise a reduction of the area of irrigated fodder in favor of crops more rewarding to the national economy, especially 'industrial crops,' but the branch has to be maintained sufficiently so as to fully cover local consumption of milk and milk products. Attempts are being made to replace at least part of the imported fodder concentrate by local products (e.g., carobs, molasses). Milch cows on Jewish farms give record average milk yields, and Israel has started exporting pedigree cows.

Cattle distribution over the country's regions has recently been determined by geographical factors. Thus the branch is closer to those areas where plain land, heavier soils, and not too expensive water make fodder crops rewarding. Herds of *beef cattle,* dependent almost exclusively on natural pasture, are kept by some Arab villages in the moister parts of Galilee as well as by a few settlements in the Judean Foothills and (still experimental) in the Arava Valley where they feed on the vegetation of salt playas and swamps (Ne'ot ha-Kikkar, Yotvata). In 1967, over 221,000 head of cattle were counted in Israel, including 56,950 head of beef cattle on Jewish farms; beef cattle on Arab farms are not included in these figures. For the 1970's, an annual increase of 2,500 head of beef cattle is envisaged.

Other Farming Branches. Carp breeding in ponds and *bee keeping* merit mention. The latter, only a sideline in Israeli farming, can be linked to citrus cultivation and to afforestation projects. Fish can replace meat as a source of animal protein. Israel's farmers have acquired outstanding skill in this branch and are frequently invited abroad as instructors in fish breeding. On the other hand,

Hilly areas, like the Adorayim Region in southern Judea, which hold little promise for more intensive farming, are increasingly used for pasturing of beef cattle

the scarcity of water impedes further expansion of fish ponds. It is planned to concentrate fish breeding either in reservoir lakes which have in any case to be constructed in the framework of national water planning (e.g. Bet Netofa, Qishon Reservoirs), or to use mainly water which is too saline for irrigation of crops (as in the Bet She'an Valley). New projects are aimed at adding variety to the carp pond population by the introduction of other fish, e.g., Brazilian 'pejare,' and restocking Lake Kinneret and other water bodies. Experiments are also conducted with the breeding of *minks, chinchillas* and other fur animals, in connection with Israel's developed fur industry. This branch is also seen as a means to support hill settlement. Its feasibility depends on world market prices no less than on the success in breeding such animals here.

AGRICULTURAL AREA, PRODUCTION, EXPORTS

Item, branch	*Unit*	*1949 (1948/49)*	*1955 (1954/55)*	*1960 (1959/60)*	*1965 (1964/65)*	*1969 (1968/69)*
Total cultivated area	km^2	1,650	3,590	4,075	4,128	4,132
Field crops, area	km^2	1,094	2,607	2,856	2,732	2,674
Wheat, area	km^2	303	473	593	720	1,127
Wheat, production volume	'000t	21.2	36.0	41.3	150.1	155.8
Irrigated area	km^2	300	890	1,305	1,508	1,662
Cotton, area	km^2	—	23	105	174	327
Cotton fibers, prod. volume	'000t	—	2.2	10.7	21.5	39.2
Cotton seed, prod. volume	'000t	—	4.0	16.9	35.4	61.0
Vegetables, potatoes, melons, pumpkins, area	km^2	66	209	208	224	263
Vegetables, potatoes, melons, pumpkins, prod. volume	'000t	119.0	329.0	430.0	517.1	677.5
Fruit plantations, area	km^2	355	515	722	835	853
Citrus, area	km^2	125	195	328	410	420
Citrus, production volume	'000t	272.2	392.0	609.6	878.3	1,178.1
Citrus, exports, return	million $	18.0	31.6	46.6	71.2	91.5
Table grapes, area	km^2	36	65	74	64	47
Wine grapes, area	km^2	12	35	41	52	58
Olives, area	km^2	137	133	123	114	106
Olives, production volume	'000t	10.7	2.8	6.8	10.5	21.1
Pome & stone fruit, area	km^2	23	38	70	89	93
Nuts, almonds, area	km^2	2	3	17	28	39
Bananas, area	km^2	5	14	21	23	20
Tropical fruit, area	km^2	1	4	8	15	28
Fish ponds, area	km^2	15	37	49	61	54
Fish, prod. volume*	'000t	3.5	11.0	13.9	19.3	21.9
Meat, production volume	'000t	7.5	27.0	81.4	116.7	143.0
Poultry meat, prod. volume	'000t	5.0	16.3	45.7	74.0	93.5
Milk, production volume	million liters	86.0	192.1	317.8	367.4	456.0
Eggs, prod. volume	million units	242.5	503.5	1,114.0	1,296.0	1,218.8
Afforested area**	km^2	53	195	299	417	522
Total agricultural exports, return	million $	18.1	34.2	63.1	86.5	118.0

* Including yields of ponds, lake and sea fisheries.

** To these figures, an area of natural forests covering 350 km^2 and partly under restoration is to be added.

Structure of Farms and Countrywide Planning

In the early stages of Jewish settlement, villages were determined to specialize in certain branches, e.g., vines, almonds or grain farming. Failure of one branch often led to the reorientation of entire villages to a new crop. Realizing the impracticality of such a system, leading figures in Jewish settlement adopted the idea of mixed farming. Foremost among them was Arthur Ruppin (see also p. 231f.). In his view, agricultural and financial equilibrium are reached in a mixed farm composed of many branches: farm land can be used most rationally when every crop is allocated the field best suited to its needs. Until recently, all collective and most smallholders' villages were based on this principle.

Scarcity of soil and water, however, has brought about a review of this conception. Also the fact that farming is becoming increasingly mechanized and science-based, with each branch demanding specialized knowledge, makes multiple-activity farming units obsolete. It is sufficient for the country's agriculture to represent a thoroughly planned and well-balanced 'mixed farm' on a national scale. Within this wide frame, every region should specialize in branches best fitted to local conditions and most rationally used (the farms in the 'red sands' belt of the Coastal Plain, for example, in citrus). The State can further the expansion of branches which are most vital for the national economy and check others which are in danger of overproduction or marketing difficulties. The individual farmer can be protected by the State through a flexible system of taxes and subsidies. Farming circles lately favor specialization of each individual farm unit in one or two branches only, even if the village as a whole has a greater variety of crops.

Export-oriented intensive horticulture, producing flowers, out-of-season crops and tropical species, is seen to hold great promise for the country's future economic development. New villages established or planned in the Arava Valley, the Eshkol Region of the western Negev, the Lower Jordan Valley, etc., are to be based primarily on this branch.

The success of Israel's agriculture is to be ascribed, in no small measure, to the farmers' general readiness to cooperate both with scientific bodies and national authorities coordinating production, marketing, etc.

Mining, Industry, Services, Foreign Trade

Mining

Mining Conditions in Israel. Mining assets are not especially bountiful in Israel. Plutonic, metamorphic, and terrestrial sedimentary rocks, which almost exclusively are apt to hold metals, occupy only a small part of the country's area. Coal is absent, and oil and gas reserves could hitherto be ascertained in limited quantities only. Marine rocks, on the other hand, particularly in the Negev, have been recently found to hold more nonmetals than anticipated, while the Dead Sea constitutes a treasure trove of valuable chemicals.

Transport expenses are the most decisive factor in the cost of minerals; in Israel, those are relatively high, in spite of the small size of the country. This is due to the elongated shape of the country and to the circumstance that the sites of most minerals are in outlying regions (Central and Southern Negev, Dead Sea) where the topography also makes construction of roads and railroads difficult. Moreover, the hot climate and lack of water at these sites create further mining difficulties and add further expenses. Israel does have relatively long coast lines facilitating sea trade and transport, but this advantage is at present largely offset by the closure of the Suez Canal to Israel shipping. This prevents inexpensive sea transport of raw material from the Eilat coast to processing plants in the center of the country and to the most important customers abroad, and necessitates the use of costly land routes. For mineral exports Israel must thus maintain a double inland transportation system, directed to the Mediterranean shore for Europe, America and West Africa, and to the Eilat Gulf—for East Africa, South and East Asia, and Australia.

History of Mining and Quarrying. Quarrying of building stone is a form of mining which always constituted an important branch of the country's economy. Table salt was also extracted on the Dead Sea shore and elsewhere (the Medba Map of the Byzantine Period shows, on the Dead Sea, a salt-laden boat going north). The only metal mined in the past was copper and that, too, only during relatively short periods beginning, it seems, in the Chalcolithic; it later gained importance under the reign of King Solomon and in the days of the Nabateans. The exploitation of other minerals (e.g., asphalt on the Dead Sea shore, or saltpeter near Bet Guvrin for primitive manufacture of gunpowder) was, at best, ephemeral and only locally important.

In modern times, the idea of extracting minerals from the Dead Sea was expounded by different authors at the beginning of this century, among them Theodor Herzl. With the rapid rise in the importance of chemicals in world industry during and after the First World War, prospects for nonmetallic minerals found in adequate quantity and quality improved. The British Mandate administration, however, was none too eager to promote exploitation, perhaps fearing that knowledge of mineral treasures in the country might draw the attention of outside political factors and thus further complicate its political situation. When the Palestine Potash Company wished to begin operations, it was given the concession with some reluctance; only in the Second World War could it fully develop its activities as its products were then of strategic importance. The Mandate authorities had some knowledge of the presence of minerals in the Negev but decided not to publish these facts. Only a small sulfur mine was exploited by the British near Be'eri, south of Gaza in the Negev Coastal Plain, but at least near the surface it was found exhausted when the State of Israel took over in 1948.

Under Israeli statehood, systematic survey and exploration of mineral resources began. The results allow the conclusion that although the country is not among the mineral-rich regions of the world, exploitation of a number of mineral deposits is worthwhile; those of the Dead Sea hold first place.

Minerals of Crystalline Rocks. This rock series is represented within Israel only in the Eilat Hills. There, briefly and on a small scale, *granite* found close to the town of Eilat was quarried, cut, polished, and exported as ornamental building stone; technical and economic difficulties have meanwhile caused production to be discontinued.

Most other minerals of this series occur in dikes crisscrossing the plutonic rocks; there is *orthoclase,* which can be used for the glazing of ceramic wares, *mica* of the muscovite and biotite varieties serving among other purposes as isolating material for electrical appliances, and *baryte* needed in chemical industries. The mining of all three has not yet been attempted.

Nubian Sandstone Series. These terrestrial sediments appear in Israel, with marine intercalations of the Paleozoic and Mesozoic, in the Eilat Hills and on the bottom

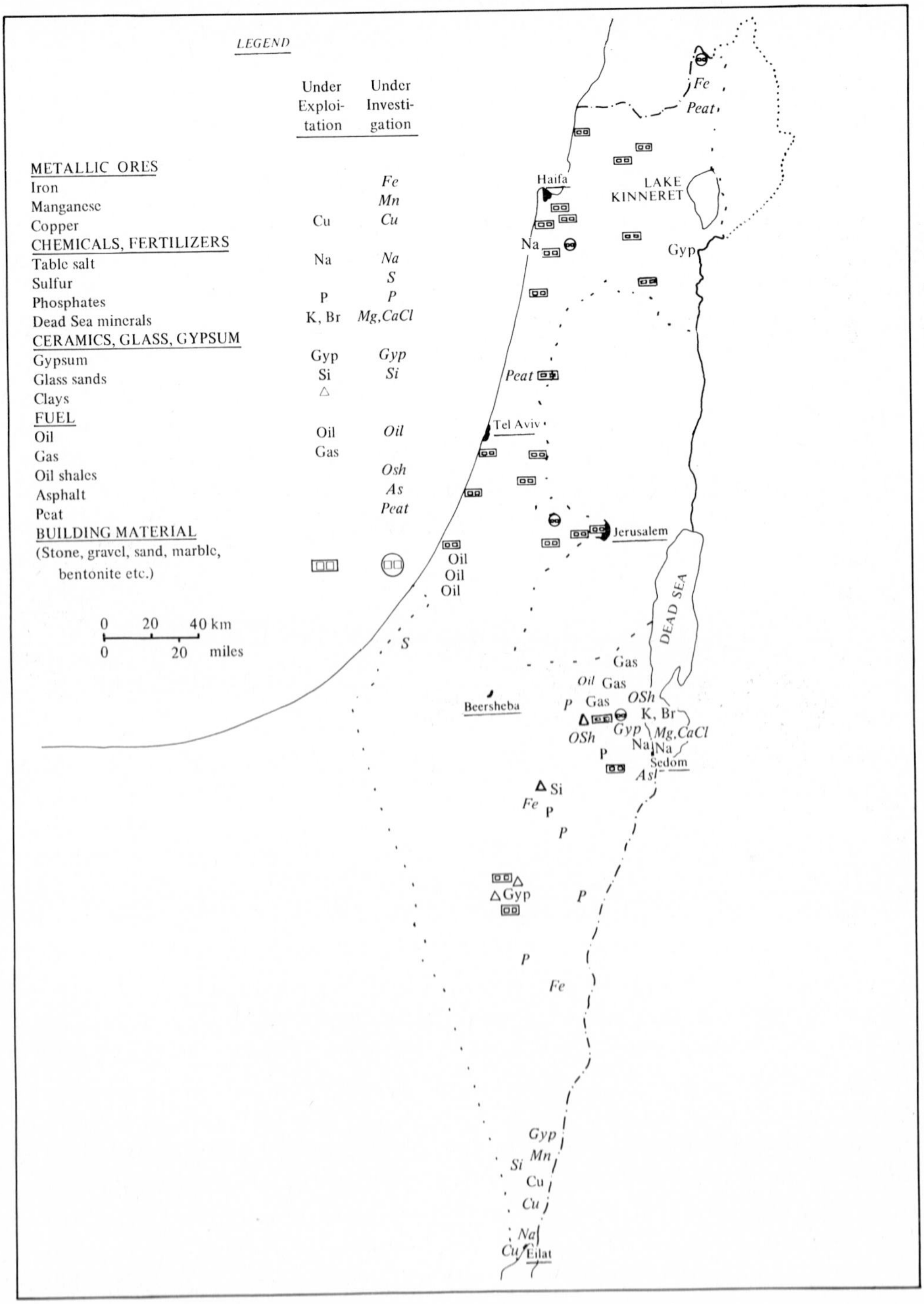

Mineral resources in Israel

Partial view of the Timna Copper Works. Hills in background contain both plutonic rocks and Nubian sandstone

of the three cirques (Small, Large and Ramon) in the Central Negev. They have been found to hold three metals—copper, manganese and iron, and three nonmetals—glass sand, gypsum and ceramic clays.

Of metal ores, only *copper* has hitherto been found exploitable. It occurs at Timna, 25 km (15 miles) north of Eilat, mostly as chrysocolla ($CuSiO_3 \cdot 2H_2O$) and bluish-green malachite ($CuCO_3 \cdot Cu(OH)_2$); concentrates of this ore, of great beauty, are used for jewelry, today as in antiquity ('Eilat stone'). The copper content of the ore is, at 1–3%, not high but still deserves mining efforts. Proved reserves amount, according to latest data, to 22 million tons of crude ore, but potential reserves are thought to be considerably larger. This copper has its origin in the crystalline rocks of the vicinity, where it was eroded by streams and then deposited in shallow bays. Some geologists have mooted the presence of richer copper ores in the depth of the crystalline rocks themselves.

In 1957, the Timna Copper Works were built, and were run in in 1958. The ore is mostly mined in open pit. The Timna Works produce copper cement of approximately 80% metallic content, which is exported. Production processes include crushing of the ore, flotation in water, and treatment with sulfuric acid and iron slags. In 1967 and 1968, copper production averaged 9,000 tons. In 1969, work was begun at Timna II, 2 km from the initial site, where ore with a copper content of 1.6% is won in open-cast and shaft mining, bringing the annual output to 15,000 tons. The construction of electrolytic copper refineries at Timna is under study.

Manganese appears at Timna near the copper ores, some of it of a fair metal content, but irregularly deposited and thus difficult to mine. Manganese prices have, therefore, for the time being, not been regarded as justifying the investments necessary.

Only a small part of the *iron* deposits in this country belong to the Nubian sandstone series. A hematite-limonite type of good quality has been located near the spot where Naḥal Paran issues into the Arava Valley, but the total quantity hitherto known there is negligible. Limonite crusts have been found on Jurassic limestones in the Large Cirque, but are indifferent both in quantity and quality. Limonite ores occur in outcrops of Lower Cretaceous chalks in Galilee, particularly on the Menara slope of the Naftali Hills above Qiryat Shemona. Since they are of the type of the Lorraine 'mint' where beneficiation is easy by mechanical treatment, and they are situated relatively near the Acre Steel Mills, their exploitation may become feasible in the future.

The nonmetals of the Nubian sandstone series hold greater promise. *Gypsum* of good quality occurs on the surface of an area of a few square miles, and to a depth of 150 cm (500 ft), in Triassic strata on the bottom of the Ramon Cirque, in Cretaceous rocks in many spots of the Southern Negev, and in Pliocene deposits near Gesher and Menaḥemya, where the Hills of Lower Galilee border on the Jordan-Yarmuk Plain. Principally needed for cement production, gypsum has since been quarried at Gesher to cover the needs of the Nesher cement factory near Haifa, and the Ramon Cirque gypsum has been mined since the 1950's and sent to the Ramla and Bet Shemesh cement factories in Judea.

Ball clays and *fire clays* are worked on the bottom of the three craters in the Negev, particularly in the Ramon Cirque. The ball clays on the whole cover the needs of the local ceramics and building materials industry. Two varieties found in the cirques are flint clay, known for its refractory quality, and bentonite clay, used as an additive to animal feed. With the discovery of a beneficiation process for low-grade material, the prospects for overseas marketing of locally calcinated Israel fire clays have decreased, despite their satisfactory quality.

Glass sands, practically free of traces of iron and therefore of satisfactory quality, have been discovered on the bottom of the Large and Ramon cirques and have been quarried there since 1953. Further deposits have been located near

Eilat. Supplying the basic raw material for the developed local glass industry at Haifa and Yeroḥam, they aid to cut down imports of this commodity.

Minerals of Marine Rocks. Marine rocks, which cover most of Israel's surface, are relatively poor in minerals. Besides building stones and other building materials quarried all over the country, phosphates, oil and natural gas are of importance here.

Phosphates, of calcium phosphate and apatite types similar to those found in Morocco and other North African and Middle Eastern countries, have been located in Senonian chalks in the Negev, notably at Oron, southeast of the Large Cirque, near the Ẓefa and Ef'e wadi courses in the Arad Region east of Dimona, southeast of the Small Cirque (Makhtesh Qatan) in the Meshar Basin in the Central Negev Hills and near En Yahav in the Arava Valley. In addition, phosphates containing stronger—and perhaps exploitable—traces of uranium than those found at the other sites have been located in the Ḥatrurim Region southeast of Arad.

Phosphate mining was begun in 1951 at Oron (the name of the site, meaning 'light,' refers to the phosphorescence of the mineral). Production rose from 17,000 tons in 1952 to 210,000 in 1959 and to 300,000 in 1963; of the latter quantity, 175,000 tons were exported. Although relatively poor with 23–27% of active phosphorus content, the ore is being upgraded mechanically by crushing and sieving to 29–30%. In 1963–64, a giant calcination kiln was set up at Oron, raising the phosphorous content to 33–35%. As mining was simultaneously begun on the Ẓefa-Ef'e field (with a content of 28–33% phosphoric oxide, one of the world's richest phosphate deposits), output increased rapidly, totaling 1 million tons in 1968 and expected to increase further to 1.5 million tons, boosted by production from the Makhtesh Qatan field since 1966. Phosphate sales were IL 21 million in 1967, and IL 35 million in 1968. The Ẓefa-Ef'e ore is to serve the nearby phosphoric acid plant, to be run in in 1971, as a principal raw material.

Oil and Gas. Israel, with the other countries on the Levant coast and those portions of Egypt adjoining the Red Sea, is in an oil province separate from that of the Persian Gulf countries. While the shores of the Suez Gulf have shown themselves to be rich in petroleum (see p. 366f.), oil prospects in Israel proper seem to be more modest. Some exploratory drillings were started by the authorities in the last years of the British Mandate and were renewed soon after the State of Israel came into being. In 1955, the first oil in commercial quantity was discovered at Ḥeleẓ in the Southern Coastal Plain, in a subsoil anticlinal structure of Lower Cretaceous rocks, most of them sandstones. Up to 1969, no reserves of fluid oil could be located in other parts of the country, but the Ḥeleẓ field was widened by oil finds in the field of Beror to the south, and of Kokhav to the north. In 1968, Ḥeleẓ had 37 producing wells, and proven reserves were reported as amounting to 2.75 million tons. Since 1964, annual production has remained more or less stationary, averaging 200–250 million liters.

Experts consider the oil-bearing structure of Ḥeleẓ to extend along most of the Coastal Plain, from Nahariya in the north to Ḥaluẓa in the Western Negev. Beginnings have been made to search for oil in the marine shelf off Israel's Mediterranean shore where prospects are considered to be relatively favorable. The overall petroleum reserves in Israel's pre-1967 frontiers were estimated in 1968 to be 300 million tons (natural gas included).

Drillings in the anticlinal structures of Rosh Zohar, Mt. Kiddod and Mt. Kanna'im in the Arad Region, where the main crest of the Judean Hills meets those of the Negev Hills, have since the mid-fifties yielded substantial quantities of methane gas. The gas is piped to the installations of the Dead Sea Works, to the Oron calcination kiln and to the Ẓefa-Ef'e phosphoric acid plant. As the former two installations began to function in 1964, production of natural gas jumped in that year to 29.5 million m^3, compared to 9.8 million in 1963. Proven gas reserves of Rosh Zohar were given in 1968 as the equivalent of 1.25 million tons of liquid oil. *Bitumen* and *asphalt*, pointing to an impregnation of chalks or limestones with oil, appear in the southern part of the Judean Desert and on the western shore of the Dead Sea. They have not yet been exploited commercially.

Quarries for sand, lime, etc., as well as limestone and alluvial soil for cement production, exist in most parts of the country, and fully cover the needs. Good limestone resembling whitish or yellowish marble (although not true, i.e., crystalline, marble) is quarried at sites like Segev in Lower Galilee, Ḥefẓi-Bah on the slope of Mt. Gilboa, etc. In the Arad Region, reddish and black marble-like limestones have been found; the same region also has bentonite from which white cement can be produced. The quarrying of coarse building sand (locally called 'zifzif') on the sea shore was prohibited by law in 1964, as the depletion of sand destroys the beaches and increases the erosive power of incoming waves.

Minerals of the Dead Sea. Of the minerals contained in the waters of the Dead Sea, potash (potassium chloride) and bromides are being won in industrial processes, and table salt is produced as a sideline. In future, magnesium and calcium chloride may be added to the list.

The licence for exploiting Dead Sea resources was obtained in 1929, and production was started in 1931 by the Palestine Potash Company, founded by British and Jewish-Palestinian partners, which set up its factory at Kallia at the northern end of the Dead Sea. In 1937 the company added auxiliary installations at Sedom at the southern end of the Dead Sea, where more space was available

One of the Dead Sea Works installations, Sedom

for evaporation pans. In the 1948 War of Independence the Kallia Works were utterly destroyed by the Arab Legion and remained in Jordanian territory while a small crew of laborers held out at Sedom and preserved the site for Israel. In order to revive operations at Sedom, the Beersheba-Sedom road had to be constructed; it was completed in 1952. The machines and installations which had largely become useless through corrosion had to be replaced before production could begin. In 1955, the Bromide Company was founded and built its factory near the Sedom Potash Works; soon after, both enterprises were integrated into the Dead Sea Works.

The first stage in extraction of salts from the Dead Sea waters consists in accelerating the natural process of accumulation of dissolved salts in the water up to saturation, i.e., where precipitation and deposition begin. The water is therefore led into shallow evaporation pans where common salt (sodium chloride) and gypsum (calcium sulfate) precipitate and sink to the pan bottom; the remaining brine is transferred to a second set of pans where the water is allowed to evaporate completely; it leaves behind carnallite, whose principal constituents are magnesium chloride and potassium chloride. The latter is separated in further industrial processes. Bromine is won after the potash has been extracted from the carnallite. Chloric acid is added to combine with the magnesium and displace and isolate the bromine; this is finally purified when led through glass pipes where it is exposed to cold air streams. The bottling plant for fluid bromine for export is at Beersheba.

Decisive for the extent of production is the area available for evaporation pans. From the existing pans, south and southeast of Sedom, about 135,000 tons of potash were produced in 1960–61, 143,000 in 1961–62, 151,000 in 1962–63, and 188,000 in 1963–64. In 1963, work began on the installation of new pans within the southern basin of the Dead Sea proper, an undertaking financed with the aid of a World Bank loan. The area of evaporation pans covered 100 km^2 (about 40 sq miles) in 1969. Many kilometers of dams, and 40 km (25 miles) of large dikes were built to protect the pans and separate them from the open parts of the Dead Sea. Following these operations, *potash* output attained 320,000 tons in 1964–65, and approached 1 million tons in 1970, when a new plant employing the hot leaching process came into operation. A further increase, to 1.2 million tons of potash, is envisaged. High quality table salt and industrial salts are thereby won as by-products. Bromine production rose from 5,120 tons in 1964–65 to 7,626 tons in the following year, and approached 10,000 tons in 1967; a further doubling of output is anticipated.

The production of metallic *magnesium*, requiring vast amounts of cheap electric power, has been postponed to a later date. A plant for the production of magnesite to furnish steel ovens had been planned, but was later shelved because changes in the technology of steel production have reduced world demand for this material; it is anticipated that novel uses for the Dead Sea magnesium will be found. *Calcium chloride,* which serves as a detergent in the chemical industry and a source of *chloric acid,* is put to use in the Arad phosphoric acid plant.

Additional table salt is won from the Mediterranean Sea in the evaporation pans at Atlit on the Carmel Coast, and is also quarried as rock salt from Mount Sedom.

Industry

Israel's industry and its growth are conditioned by three facts: relative poverty in raw materials; absence of historical continuity, of a gradual transition from local artisanship to large-scale industrial activity; the particular skills of Jewish immigrants, who had concentrated abroad on the finishing stages of manufacture or on commerce, especially in the textile branch. Industry, therefore, had to develop here from the final stages toward the basic ones. Before and shortly after the First World War, industrial activity began with repackaging and adaptation of imported goods for local sale, soon took over finishing, then secondary processes, finally 'deepened' to reach primary production. Industry had also to broaden its initial framework of small, often one-man workshops, to attain mass production and proceed from manufacture for restricted local markets—often following specifications of single customers—to cover the needs of an entire country and to divert an increasing portion of its produce to exports.

History of Industrial Development. Until the end of the 19th century, the only branches in this country which could, to any degree, be described as industries were soap production, practiced principally at Nablus and based on the olive crop of the region, and printing, mainly in Hebrew characters. With the beginning of Zionist settlement, Baron Edmond de Rothschild took the initiative in introducing reforms in farming and industrial development. He established the large Rishon le-Zion and Zikhron Ya'aqov wine cellars, aided in the founding of flour mills and attempted to establish additional industries, such as glass production at Dor (Tantura) on the Carmel Coast.

Among the early enterprises were the salt factory at Atlit and the Shemen factory for soaps, edible oils, etc., in the Haifa Bay area. In the 1920's and early 'thirties, immigrant craftsmen opened small enterprises in the cities, particularly in Tel Aviv. More often than not these were small workshops based almost exclusively on the labor, initiative, management and skill of the proprietors. Some of these expanded gradually, took on more laborers, and introduced machinery. A new phase opened in 1934–35 with the arrival of immigrants from Central Europe who came with some capital and with experience in industrial management. Some of the enterprises then founded ventured into secondary production stages. Between the two world wars, individual Jewish investors from the country and from abroad took the initiative for, and participated in, the erection of novel industrial branches and enabled the founding of several enterprises which became decisive for the country's economy (electricity, the Potash Company, etc.).

A propelling force for industrial development were workers' cooperatives, and especially the Histadrut (Labor Federation), which was founded in 1920. Going far beyond the normal activity of labor organizations throughout the world, the Histadrut set up large enterprises under its own auspices, and particularly endeavored to penetrate to basic production and 'conquer' heavy industry. In addition, communal settlements began, since the mid-'thirties, to add industrial branches to their rural economies.

This development was not viewed very favorably by the Mandate authorities. Since industrialization constituted the most efficient means for a quick expansion of the absorptive capacity of the country's economy, they did little to encourage it, so as not to justify larger immigration quotas and upset what they considered the desirable demographic and political equilibrium in Palestine. Local production was thus not protected by tariffs; foreign goods were freely imported from the Commonwealth as well as from all other countries, without any stipulation of reciprocal trade. When the Arabs here and abroad proclaimed in the mid-'thirties a boycott of Jewish industry in Palestine, imports from neighboring countries were even enlarged. The boycott, however, did not greatly affect the fledgling industry, as its products were anyhow scarcely directed toward Arab markets.

Industrial expansion quickened in the Second World War when this country served as a hinterland for the Allied armies fighting in North Africa and the Mediterranean basin and was required to supply vital strategic goods. This growth was due, however, to Jewish initiative only and was financed mainly by local capital. Incidentally, industrial products of Palestine then began to find outlets in Middle East countries which, owing to war conditions, were no longer reached by supplies from Europe and America. The number of industrial undertakings grew from 1,550 in 1937 to 2,500 in 1946, and that of persons employed in industry—from 21,000 to 47,000. The gross value of production mounted from 8 to 44 million £P, and electricity consumption by industry—from 20.3 to 74.5 million kwhr.

In the first years of statehood, many new enterprises were opened by immigrants, as well as by veterans who before had worked as foremen in existing factories. The branches of metals, textiles and food made up the bulk of industrial growth in those years. Most of these new undertakings began with very limited means, were very small, and reduced the average figure of persons employed per enterprise from 21.4 in 1948 to 11.5 in 1954. In the same period, the total of persons employed in industry rose from 50,000 to 90,000, and the consumption of electricity jumped from 80 million kwhr in 1948 to 270 million kwhr in 1954, i.e., from 1,600 to 2,800 kwhr per worker.

The Government of Israel, striving both to widen employment facilities and to further basic industries and branches contributing to exports or obviating imports, planned its import quota and tariff policy to protect local manufacture. It also aided industry by extending loans, credits, and direct subsidies, by preferential allocation of import licenses for raw materials, and by other measures. Undertakings considered to contribute sizeably to the country's economic progress have been classed as 'approved enterprises,' which enjoy benefits with regard to income tax, depreciation, import duties, property taxes and credits from the Development Budget. The Government itself functions in a number of vital basic industries, either as an active or a silent partner; its declared policy, however, is to transfer its part to other sectors, public or private, as soon as such enterprises are able to attract ordinary investment.

Present Trends and Development Plans. Following the increase of investments—private, cooperative, public or State—both the total volume of industry and the average size of enterprises have been rising since the middle 1950's. In 1965–66, the number employed in enterprises engaging 5 or more persons had risen to 184,200 (owners and self-employed workers excluded). In the recession year 1966–67, the number dropped to 172,400, but mounted steeply after the Six Day War, attaining 202,600 in 1968–69. Industrial exports amounted to $262,489,000 in 1963, and to $554,000,000 in 1969. The number of industrial plants with over 100 employees grew from 163 in 1958 to 403 in 1968/69, and the average number of employees per enterprise (employing 5 or more persons) from 23.8 to 31.2.

As the next table shows, enterprises in the main cities tend to be smaller than those in their outer rings or in rural districts; the greatest disparity between the percentages of establishments and those of persons engaged is shown in the Northern, Southern and Haifa districts where it points to relatively large plants. In Tel Aviv, on the other hand, city enterprises tend to be small.

Between 1955 and 1966, Israel's industry also saw a spectacular advance in mechanization and output per worker. Industrial consumption of electricity amounted in 1969 to 1,660.5 million kwhr, compared to 270 million kwhr in 1954. The progress in productivity is indicated by a comparison of the indices of the number of employees which rose by 62.3% between 1958 and 1966, to those of production value which mounted by 145.1% in the same period. The changeover

REGIONAL DISTRIBUTION OF ESTABLISHMENTS ENGAGING 5 EMPLOYED PERSONS AND MORE*

1967/68

District	*Establishments*		*Persons employed*	
	Absolute numbers	*Percentage*	*Absolute numbers*	*Percentage*
Jerusalem	368	6.2	9,200	5.1
Northern	356	5.9	16,500	9.2
Haifa	819	13.7	32,800	18.3
Thereof: Haifa City	653	10.9	22,300	12.4
Central	916	15.3	32,600	18.2
Tel Aviv	3,290	54.9	72,300	40.3
Thereof: Tel Aviv City	2,385	39.8	45,800	25.5
Southern	237	4.0	16,000	8.9
Total	5,986	100.0	179,400	100.0

* From *Statistical Abstract of Israel,* 1970, No. 21.

from individual workshops to managerial factories is also apparent in the increasing emphasis laid on vocational training and technical specialization, foremen and key-workers, on production streamlining and efficiency, and on scientific research in industry.

A decision taken in 1965 to restrain for a time the economy's growth rate in order to prevent inflation caused a temporary decrease in the number of persons engaged in industry, thereby, however, only little affecting the volume of production and of industrial exports. Manufacturing benefited from this policy by a sizeable improvement in the produce-per-worker ratio and the elimination of certain unprofitable enterprises.

The Six Day War opened a new chapter of rapid industrial growth. It was recognized that in its military supplies Israel must become increasingly independent of outside sources; this necessity was brought home by a French embargo on aircraft and armaments unilaterally applied to Israel. Production for defense, in fact, became the decisive factor in Israel's industrial progress since 1967. This explains why metals and, foremost, electronics, together with other science-based industries, head the list of expanding branches. Simultaneously, great strides were made in gearing manufacturing to exports. In the spring of 1968, an Economic Conference took place in Israel, attended by prominent economic leaders and experts from many countries. The participants resolved to set up an Investment Company to aid sound and profitable enterprises, take an active share in management, develop markets for Israel products abroad, seek subcontracts for Israeli component manufacturers, train Israeli personnel, etc.

By mid-1968, industrial output had already risen 29% above the pre-recession peak. During 1968, industrial performance improved by 14%, and industrial exports of the same year totalled 526 million dollars, an 18% increase over 1967. In the two years 1968–1969 alone, industrial output rose by more than 50% and attained the value of IL 10,700 million in the latter year. In 1968/69, exports of electrical and electronics equipment went up by 97% and of metal products—by 149%.

A ten-year industrial development program, formulated late in 1968, set the target of tripling industrial production (from 9,000 to 25,000 million IL) and of quadrupling industrial exports, which are to attain 2,000 million dollars, by 1980. This would entail an annual 10% increase in output. In addition to metals, electronics and other science-based industries, greatest emphasis is laid on the chemicals branch.The industrial labor force, which grew considerably after the Six Day War, is planned to increase further during the 1970's, although at a slower rate than output and exports, as new establishments are mostly capital-intensive and automation is being progressively introduced.

The plan seeks to give further impetus to the trend of dispersal of industrial undertakings over all parts of the country, as dictated by demographic, political and security needs. The disadvantage of greater transport distances can, in certain cases, be overcome by placing enterprises close to sources of raw materials or to factories handling other stages in the same production line. A case in point is the Arad Chemical Industries, which has been erected at Ẓefa in proximity to the Arad gas wells, the Dead Sea Works and the Ẓefa-Ef'e and Oron phosphates. For science-based enterprises, Reḥovot, Haifa and Jerusalem are becoming principal centers, as the Weizmann Institute, the Technion and the Hebrew University, respectively, guide them and actively take part in their development.

Industrial Branches. In relation to the size of the country and of the total of industry, Israel's manufacture, which comprises almost all principal branches and most stages of production, is highly diversified. This is an asset which minimizes the dangers of isolation for a short emergency period and allows wider scope for the exploitation of local physical and human resources. On the other hand, concentration on fewer branches and on mass production would, perhaps, increase efficiency and improve the country's standing as a competitor on world markets. Economists feel that although most branches should continue to exist and new ones be added, emphasis should be laid on those affording a chance of superior performance and promising to become a support to the national economy and to exports.

A motor car factory in Haifa. The trend is to go over from assembly of imported parts to their production in the country

In the geographical distribution of industrial branches, no clear tendencies are recognizable in Israel. During the last decades, industry the world over has emancipated itself to a mounting degree from dependence on local conditions (e.g., the textiles branch, earlier preferring sites with high air humidity, can now, as a result of air conditioning systems, choose locations as it sees fit). Naturally, enterprises using bulky raw materials, or producing wares expensive to transport, seek, even more than others, proximity of ports and principal markets. For all branches, the main cities are preferable because of easier availability of labor, machinery, spare parts, etc. The neighborhood of mining sites, or of farm produce (e.g., cotton, sugar beet) carries decisive weight only in a few instances. No wonder, therefore, that in 1963–64 56.8% of all enterprises and 43.1% of all persons employed in industry were concentrated in Tel Aviv and its district. When Haifa, its district and the Central District are added, the figures mount to 84.7% and 79.4%, respectively.

A comparison with 1967/68 data (which only relate to establishments employing 5 or more persons) reveals a certain success of the policy aiming at a better geographical distribution of industry, and, in its wake, of population. Tel Aviv City and District account for 54.9% of enterprises and for 40.3% of employees. Together with Haifa City and District and the Central District, the figures read 83.9 and 76.8%, respectively.

The *metal* branch, employing the relatively largest number of workers, shows greatest variety, both in the thousands of items produced, and in the size of enterprises, from the largest factories in the country to one-man workshops. Basic production stages are concentrated in the Haifa Bay area—the Acre Steel City, large foundries, and other plants. Emphasis is laid on rolling and casting processes rather than on smelting.

All subdivisions of the metal branch are represented in the country, including machine building, toolmaking, production of household goods and building parts, electrical appliances, electronics, etc. Especially important are those goods which are to cover typical needs of Israel households (e.g., refrigerators) or of local farming (e.g., irrigation pipes and sprinklers); the latter category often is produced in kibbutz plants. Important are armament plants, which strive to supply the bulk of Israel's security requirements and to recover—through exports—at least part of the foreign exchange needed for arms acquisition abroad. Progress is also being made in the local automobile industry, which began with the assembly of imported parts but is gradually proceeding to their production on its own. A similar basic trend is aimed at in the Israel Aircraft Industries near Lod Airport—with over 13,000 employees (in 1970) Israel's biggest single enterprise—as well as in the shipbuilding yards of Haifa Bay, in the new Bet Shemesh Turbomeca turbine and jet engine plant, etc.

Building materials are a veteran branch of Israel's industry; among the first large plants opened in the country were a factory for silicate bricks near Tel Aviv and one for roof tiles at Moẓa near Jerusalem. The most important plants at present are the three cement factories at Nesher in the Haifa Bay area, at Ramla, and at Bet Shemesh in the Judean Foothills; they cover the vast needs of local construction and in certain years produce sizeable quantities for export. Specialized plants manufacture prefabricated building parts, asbestos plates, etc.

Ceramics and *glass* industries have also existed in Israel for several decades. To a rising degree, they are based on locally mined raw materials. This enables the industry, to some extent, to follow the policy of geographical dispersal; in addition to the main center in Haifa Bay and plants manufacturing scientific glass instruments which are linked to the Hebrew University in Jerusalem and to the Weizmann Institute at Reḥovot, a large ceramics plant operates at Beersheba, and a glass factory at Yeroḥam in the Central Negev.

In *diamond polishing,* Israel is among the foremost world producers. The industry is based exclusively on the superior skill of experts who immigrated from Belgium and Holland shortly before and during World War II. As all raw diamonds are purchased abroad, the added value of the produce is relatively low; Israel polishers are specialized in jewelry gems. Exports therefore depend on the markedly fluctuating foreign markets. All this does not detract from the importance of the branch which tops the list of Israel's exports, bringing in an income of 215.9 million dollars in 1969. The first diamond polishing plants were opened at Netanya in the Sharon; today, the largest number is concentrated in the Tel Aviv conurbation. The virtual absence of transport cost differences, however, facilitates the dispersal of the industry; it has now penetrated to some centers in the hill regions and is found in development towns throughout the country.

The *chemical* industry already plays a decisive role in Israel's economic life, and is expected to expand even more rapidly in the near future. In 1968, steps were undertaken to coordinate the work of the main enterprises in this field (Dead Sea Works, Haifa Refineries, Chemicals and Phosphates, Israel Petrochemicals, Haifa Chemicals, Arad Chemical Industries, etc.), aiming at the annual export total of 500 million dollars within ten years, as against $79.2 million in 1969. Accenting heavy chemicals, Israel produces the three basic fertilizers (nitrates, potash, phosphates). Israel has begun to manufacture highly concentrated combinations with minimum dead weight, such as potassium nitrate and potassium metaphosphate, or specialties like di-calcium phosphate which is an important fodder additive; such new lines and many others open excellent export prospects. Preparations were made in 1969 for setting up a magnesium plant near the Arad Chemicals Factory. Strides are being made in the electrochemical and petrochemical branches, with production of such fundamental

Diamond polishing is one of Israel's foremost industrial branches

requirements as hydrochloric and sulfuric acid, caustic soda, soda ash, etc. Beginnings have also been made in producing basic raw materials for the plastics and rubber industries (e.g., ethylene, polyethylene, carbon black, etc.). A Haifa firm produces citric acid. Additional enterprises, in various stages of planning and construction, promise further variety in chemical production.

Alongside the large plants for basic chemicals, in Haifa Bay, the Arad phosphoric acid complex, etc., there are pharmaceutical works, some of which also produce antibiotics. Several of these are among the veteran industries in the country. They are situated in the Tel Aviv and Haifa areas, in Jerusalem, etc. Others produce detergents, pesticides (Beersheba), colors and paints, soaps, matches and other goods.

In the *rubber* branch, two tire factories, at Ḥadera and at Petaḥ Tiqwa, occupy an important place among the country's exporters. A third one has been founded in Upper Nazareth. Israel's *plastics* industry has, in recent years, been characterized by progressive diversification and by production of basic materials. The veteran small plants have been joined by medium-sized and large enterprises.

The *wood* and *paper* industry is almost wholly dependent on imported raw materials. The veterans in the branch are small furniture workshops, which keep close to their markets in the cities and smaller urban centers. Many kibbutzim also have carpentry shops. A few enterprises have recently gone into specialized serial production of quality furniture and are successful in exporting on a modest scale. Skill has put three plywood plants (at Afiqim, near Pardes Ḥanna and at Ashqelon) among the country's top exporters. Relatively young is paper production (at Ḥadera). Printing, on the other hand, is among the few branches with an age-old tradition in the country; as early as the 16th century, a Hebrew printing press was in operation at Safed, and the first steps in Zionist settlement and the revival of Hebrew as a spoken language were accompanied by the opening of printing presses in Jerusalem, Jaffa, and elsewhere. Today, Israel ranks high, internationally, in per capita production of books and newsprint. Although printing is now one of Jerusalem's important industries, Tel Aviv serves as the principal center of the branch.

Textiles is a field in which Jews have a long-standing tradition in many countries of the world. The capital and skill brought by immigrants helped found the industry in the 1920's, mainly in the Tel Aviv region and in the Haifa Bay area (Qiryat Ata). This branch also began its development in the country in the last production stages—manufacture of apparel and finishing and dyeing of cloth, and only later reached the basic phases of weaving and spinning. Until the introduction of cotton growing in the first years of statehood, the industry had to rely exclusively on imported raw materials (the wool of the local sheep being fit for carpet weaving only). Cotton gins developed along with cotton growing. Rayon and artificial fibers are also being produced in the country.

A recent feature is the introduction of large textile plants into development towns (Qiryat Gat, Yeroḥam, Dimona, Ofaqim, Ashdod, Afula, Qiryat Naẓrat, Bet She'an, Qiryat Shemona, etc.) where they often constitute the principal basis for employment. The industry, with its highly variegated produce, supplies most local requirements. The fashion industry, with its main center in Tel Aviv, has recently expanded to new towns such as Or Aqiva, Karmiel, Ḥaẓor, etc., and is directing an increasing proportion of its produce to exports.

The *leather* and *fur* branches are somewhat similar to textiles in their structure and their traditional place as occupations of Jews abroad. Both must rely almost completely on imported raw materials, and both predominantly run plants of small or intermediate size. The leather branch supplies the local market, although firms specializing in leather apparel can point to spectacular achievements in export markets. Also Israel's furriers work principally for exports, both in the form of dispatch of products abroad and of sales to foreign tourists in Israel.

The *food* branch is highly diversified in the size and nature of its enterprises. It is also the most widely dispersed over the country's regions and settlement types, since the manufacture of many products is closely tied to local markets or is naturally located in rural surroundings. Besides standard plants fulfilling daily requirements (e.g. bakeries, dairies, flour mills, slaughter houses, etc.), others are typical of the country's special farm produce and work largely for exports (e.g., citrus preserves, olive oil, canned groundnuts, etc.). Still others exist thanks to special local food customs, to requirements caused by the local climate (e.g., the large number of factories for soft beverages), or to the treatment of bulk imports of food (e.g., the huge 'Dagon' grain silos in Haifa Port). Besides factories preparing local foodstuffs for export or local sale (e.g., canned and dehydrated vegetables and fruit, meat and fish preserves, beer, wines and liquors, etc.), others have made a name for themselves in quality products made from imported raw materials (e.g., chocolate, sweets, instant coffee, etc.). More recent is sugar production from sugar beet in which plants at Qiryat Gat and Afula are engaged.

Tobacco and cigarette factories produce almost exclusively for the local market. They usually blend local tobacco with imported leaf.

Productive Services, Capital Inflow and Foreign Trade

Transport and Communications. The smooth functioning of these two interrelated services is a vital condition of production in agriculture and industry; their efficient performance is a prerequisite to the economic future of a country. This axiom is perhaps even truer of Israel than of other countries, as the elongated borders lengthen interior communication lines and the closure of all land frontiers makes Israel's world trade dependent on well-developed sea and air links. In addition, these services themselves become productive branches when passengers or goods are transported outside the country; they then appear on the payment balance as invisible imports or exports, as the case may be. Two large projects, one in the construction stage in 1969 and the other under detailed examination, promise to give Israel considerable advantages in this field—the Eilat-Ashdod large-diameter oil pipeline, and the Mediterranean-Red Sea 'land bridge.' They offer prospects of replacing, to a degree, the functions of the Suez Canal, out of use since 1967. The 42-in pipeline, completed in 1969, will later be brought to its full annual load capacity of 60 million tons of oil. Israel expects to gain not only the transport fees, but also to refine a sizeable part of the crude oil for export. While the Haifa Refineries have enlarged their production capacity to beyond 6 million tons annually, the construction of a second refinery, with an annual capacity of 3 million tons, was started at Ashdod in 1970; the enterprise is expected to go into production in 1973. The 'land bridge' utilizing the Eilat-Ashdod highway and, partly, the Dimona-Ashdod railway, is planned principally for the transport of packaged goods.

Road transport takes precedence over rail transport, for the reasons explained in the chapter dealing with roads. The number of vehicles in Israel in 1969 was 239,480, nearly more than fivefold the figure for 1960; most of this growth, however, is attributed to the rapid rise in the number of private cars (which increased fourfold in this period, from 24,000 to 131,312) and motorcycles, which do not enter the category of economic services. Still, trucking freight on Israel's roads has doubled in volume every ten years. The bold program for widening and improvement of existing highways, affording higher speed and cutting down accident rates, and for shortening of transport distances by building new roads (e.g., the Ashdod–Arad–Sedom–Eilat road) is decisive for making Israel's farming, mining and industrial products more competitive on export markets.

The improvement in urban and interurban bus services (which carry most of Israel's passenger traffic) also has a palpable impact on the country's economy. The increase in the number of buses (from 1,432 to 3,982) and tripling of their seating capacity (from 47,000 to 148,000) between 1951 and 1969, has led to a reduction in the time and energy expended on travel to and from work.

Rail communications are also rapidly improving as the stock of engines, freight, and passenger cars is being thoroughly renewed, and timetables, as well as the whole railway network, are better adapted to transport needs. Railways are especially important for bulk transport—imported grains from Haifa Port to all parts of the country; citrus fruit for export to Haifa and Ashdod; Negev and

Scene from Ashdod Port

Dead Sea minerals to the centers of the chemical industry and to the ports, etc.

Since *shipping* is decisive for Israel's links with the outside world, greatest efforts are being devoted to the rapid enlargement of the Haifa Port capacity and to the continued construction of the two new ports—Ashdod and Eilat. The need for further expansion is demonstrated by the figures for the total tonnage handled in the ports, which increased from 4,775,000 in 1966–67 to ca. 7,000,000 in 1969.

At the time the State was founded, Israel's fleet consisted of a small number of tiny, aged and rundown ships which had brought illegal immigrants to the country during the last years of the British Mandate. German reparations, among other factors, contributed in making Israel a minor maritime power, which has perhaps one of the most modern fleets in the world. In 1970 it numbered 115 ocean-going vessels (cargo ships, bulk carriers, tankers, containers, and a few passenger liners)—with a load capacity of approximately 2 million tons, compared to 52 ships of about 500,000 tons in 1960–61, and 94 ships of 872,000 tons in 1964. New ships ordered promise to bring Israel's merchant fleet to a tonnage of ca. 3 million by 1971. In 1968, 4,500 sailors served on Israel merchant vessels. The difficulties in hiring more Israel personnel lead to efforts in maximum automation of new ships. The principal Israel shipping company is Zim, founded in 1945 by the Jewish Agency, the Histadrut, and the Israel Maritime League; other companies, both publicly and privately owned, operate at its side. A shipping bank aids the growth of maritime assets. Israel has a naval academy and seafarers' schools.

Almost all Israel ships have been ordered in foreign yards. A beginning in shipbuilding has, however, been made with the Israel Shipyards Company

Scene at Lod Airport

founded in 1961, which initially produced 3,000-ton vessels and later started to build ships of larger capacity. Israel passenger liners sometimes run between foreign ports, particularly during off-seasons (e.g., between North America and the West Indies), and Israel freighters, by working on tramp service, thus earn additional foreign currency. Israel shippers have also assisted developing countries (e.g. Ghana, Burma) in building up their own merchant navies.

Aviation development became equally vital upon establishment of the State. In November 1948, the national El Al Israel Airlines was registered. Soon the company was responsible, besides keeping contact with European and other overseas airports, for carrying mass immigration from certain Middle East countries (the 'Magic Carpet' operation bringing Jews from Yemen, and the mass transport of Iraqi Jewry). To make up for the relatively small number of aircraft the company can operate, it tries to keep its fleet as modern and efficient as possible. It was among the first to introduce turbo-prop engines in the late 'fifties and replaced them with jets a few years later. In 1968, the company for the first time flew over one million passengers between Asia, Europe, America and Africa (compared with 400,000 in 1964); it carried 430,000 tourists to and from Israel, handling about half the total air traffic of the country. By 1975, El Al expects to carry 2 million passengers and to increase its airfreight volume (important for export branches, such as flowers, out-of-season fruit, diamonds, etc.) to 25,000 tons as against 8,000 tons in 1968.

Internal air traffic, mainly operated by the Arkia Company, is of secondary importance, but has been boosted somewhat in the period after the Six Day War, when Jerusalem's 'Atarot Airfield and flights over Sinai were included in its network. The most important air connection continues to be that between Eilat and the center and north of the country.

The expansion of *postal services* keeps pace with the growing needs of the economy. Very spectacular is the growth of the telephone service: the number of telephones per 100 inhabitants has risen from 2.4 in 1949 to 14.4 in 1969. The service is fully automated, with direct dialing between all parts of the country. After June, 1967, East Jerusalem and the administered territories were integrated into the national network.

Tourism. Catering to foreign tourists, although technically it belongs to the services category, is one of the prominent productive branches in Israel's economy. In terms of foreign currency, it has doubled its earning capacity from $45 million in 1963 to $90 million in 1968 (these figures exclude the foreign currency incomes of the national carriers Zim and El Al). The number of incoming tourists has climbed from 30,000 in 1949 to an average 40,000 between 1954 and 1956, to 160,000 in 1961, 252,000 in 1964, and 432,000 in 1968. Even this, however, is thought to be much below the country's potentialities; Israel can attract even more visitors because of its landscape, antiquities, historical and spiritual significance and the social and economic innovations created in a rapid development process.

The vast tourism potential requires fast expansion of hotel accomodation, transport and entertainment facilities, etc. In preparing these services, several trends lately noticeable in tourism to Israel have to be taken into account: instead of being preponderantly composed of Jews, as in the past, it takes on a more international character; in addition to middle-class tourists, visitors from lower income groups are being increasingly attracted. The reunification of Jerusalem and access to Judea-Samaria have opened new vistas especially for Christian pilgrimage to the Holy Land.

Capital Receipts, Imports and Exports. The capital inflow into the country has been high throughout, even during the British Mandate period, when it was primarily supplied by Jewish contributions and by the means brought by the immigrants, particularly in the 1930's. In the first years of statehood, the financial participation of World Jewry in Israel's development tasks increased manifold, but it was still insufficient to finance mass immigration—this time arriving penniless—and its absorption. In this period, grants-in-aid, surplus food, and other assistance from the United States and elsewhere played a considerable role in aiding the economy's survival in spite of this enormous strain. Since 1953, German reparations to the State of Israel and personal restitution to Israeli citizens became a powerful factor for economic progress. Voluntary financial participation of World Jewry in Israel's development reached an unprecedented level in the Emergency Campaign immediately after and since the Six Day War.

Besides direct contributions, Jews, and to some extent non-Jews, have participated in Israel's economic tasks since the early 1950's through buying Israel Development Bonds. This has been followed, in the late 'fifties and particularly since the devaluation of the Israel Pound in 1962, by increasing private investment from abroad under strict business terms. This latter development points to a growing confidence in the resilience of the country's economy. Simultaneously, direct aid from the United States had declined to only 2% of the total capital import in 1962. Income from Western Germany, too, has dropped relatively since 1962, when it constituted 40% of all capital coming in from abroad. Economists point to the need to direct capital inflow to rigorously selected purposes in order to stimulate productivity without increasing the purchasing power of the population; such a rise would reinforce inflationary tendencies which, in turn, would add to the pressure on imported goods, discourage exports, and slow the country's progress toward economic independence.

The necessities of building an economy from its very foundations, of absorbing an immigration which has increased the country's population more than fourfold in the first 20 years of statehood, and of preserving the State's security in the face of a relentless military menace—all these explain the difficulty in matching imports fully with exports. The enormous growth of Israel's economy as well as its principal problems are illustrated by the following figures (all in IL, at 1969 prices): the Gross National Product went up from 4,337 million in 1950 to 24,096 million in 1969; the per capita GNP from 2,135 to 5,512; imports—from 1,781 to 7,956 million; exports—from 164 to 3,687 million. The trade deficit grew in the same period from 1,617 to 3,687 million.

As shown in the table, exports have almost doubled every four years in the period of statehood, to cover, in 1967, over two thirds of Israel's imports. 1968 was a very successful export year, with sales exceeding those of 1967 by at least 20%. Simultaneously, however, imports have increased at an even greater pace, mainly owing to defence purchases, causing the trade gap to widen anew. Whereas planners predicted, for 1971, total imports (including invisibles) to amount to $2,000 million, and total exports—$1,525 million, it became clear by 1970 that defense requirements demand much greater expenditure than anticipated , so that the target of narrowing the trade gap will not be achieved in the near future. This fact calls for efforts in increasing efficiency in production of export goods, in packaging, promotion, etc. Preference must be given to those lines which promise a high added value, and Israel must strive to attain a more favorable balance of trade with other countries. The signing in 1970 of a trade pact with the Common Market is of crucial importance in this respect. Economic advisers advocate stepping up the growth of services earning foreign currency, with the hope that they will eventually account for over half of Israel's total exports.

BALANCE OF FOREIGN TRADE

Year	*Net imports* ('000$)	*Net exports* ('000$)	*Excess of imports over exports* ('000$)	*Exports as % of imports*
1949	251,906	28,495	223,411	11.3
1951	381,682	44,754	336,928	11.7
1953	279,929	57,636	222,293	20.6
1955	334,453	89,056	245,397	26.6
1957	432,829	140,127	292,702	32.4
1959	427,291	176,383	250,908	41.3
1961	583,912	239,082	344,830	40.9
1963	661,987	338,285	323,752	51.1
1965	810,956	406,095	404,861	50.1
1967*	754,111	517,245	236,866	68.6
1968*	1,087,549	602,105	485,444	55.4
1969*	1,290,974	683,236	607,738	52.9
1969**	1,304,317	750,665	553,652	57.6

* Excluding trade with administered territories.
** Including trade with administered territories.
From *Statistical Abstract of Israel,* 1970, No. 21.

*Main Import and Export Commodities.** Outstanding among *food imports* are those basic commodities which local farming either cannot produce at all, or not in the required quantities. This list is headed by the cereals, both for human consumption and animal fodder, accounting for $53.4 million in 1967; wheat alone was bought for $21 million in 1966, but after the excellent local yields of 1967, expenditure on this commodity dropped to $8.4 million. Other important items are meat and livestock ($13.3 million in 1967), sugar ($5.8 million) and coffee ($5.2 million).

* Figures given here and in the following paragraphs—most of them cited from *Statistical Abstract of Israel, 1968*—serve only to illustrate the relative importance of various import and export items. Naturally, major changes may occur from year to year.

The Diamond Bourse, Ramat Gan

Fuel is an item requiring a large outlay of foreign currency, particularly mineral oil and oil products which accounted for$55.6 million in 1967. With the oil-refining capacity, fuels and other oil products have begun to appear both on Israel's import and export list. In 1967, $52.5 million was spent on the import of chemicals (including raw materials for therapeutics and finished products). Oil seeds, accounting for $32.6 million in 1967, serve for the production both of food stuffs and industrial goods. Relatively large amounts also go to the import of *rubber,* which is the principal basis for tire exports. Similarly, imports of *timber,* amounting to $24.5 million in 1967, include raw materials for several of Israel's top exports (e.g., citrus crates, plywood, etc.). This is even more true of rough *diamonds,* which were bought in 1967 for $137 million and totally re-exported after cutting and polishing. Raw textile fibers to the sum of $15.8 million were imported in 1967; the decrease in raw cotton imports, from $9.8 million in 1964 to $4.7 million in 1967, mirrors the increasing use by Israel's industry of locally grown cotton. *Metal* ores, ingots and parts to the value of $63.2 million were imported in 1967. This outlay is likely to increase further with the expansion of the local metal branch. One of the largest items in imports is *machinery* of all kinds, which totaled $99.1 million in 1967; *motor vehicles* and their accessories accounted for $26 million. The expenditure for *ships* and *aircraft,* of course, varies largely from year to year; thus, $58.3 million were spent for ships in 1964, $12.7 million in 1966, and $28.2 million in 1967, while the outlay for aircraft rose from $4.4 million in 1965 to $13.5 million in 1966, decreasing again to $9.7 million in 1967.

Among Israel's *agricultural exports, citrus* holds first place. The principal varieties included in this category are Jaffa oranges (Shamouti type), Jaffa late oranges (Valencia type), grapefruit and lemons. The dollar income from this branch, being dependent on the markedly vacillating prices on foreign markets, can hardly be predicted from one year to the next even if a forecast of the quantity of fruit in coming years is possible. Thus, the sale of fresh fruit brought $74.8 million in 1966, and $85.3 million in 1967. Also important among farming exports are *eggs* (eating and hatching), which brought $5 million in 1965, $3.9 million in 1966, and $6 million in 1967. Other noteworthy items are cotton, groundnuts, hard wheat, avocados, bananas, guava, mango, strawberries, grapes, melons and out-of-season vegetables, as well as goose liver. Flower exports (gladioli, roses, anemones, etc.) have shown a sharp rise.

Industrial exports have increased continuously and steeply thoughout the period of statehood, totaling $55 million in 1955, $153.5 million in 1960, $480 million in 1967, and $605.8 million in 1969. Among these, *diamonds* are first ($20.2 million in 1955, $60.9 million in 1960, $193 million in 1967, and $253.5 million in

Citrus loading in Eilat Port

1969). Even the relatively low added value of this export does not detract from its importance.

In the line of *food products,* citrus juices and preserves, olive oil, other fruit preserves, chocolate and sweets, instant coffee, and alcoholic beverages are represented in exports. New lines are dried and frozen vegetables.

Minerals and mineral products have become prominent on Israel's export list since the mid-1960's, yielding an income of $7.4 million in 1964, and $19.2 million in 1966. After a certain drop in 1967, potash exports increased to 600,000

IMPORTS OF FOREIGN GOODS, EXPORTS OF ISRAEL GOODS AND TRADE BALANCE, BY COUNTRIES OF PURCHASE AND DESTINATION (1967–1969) (BY CONTINENTS AND SELECTED COUNTRIES) ('000$)

Country	*Imports*		*Exports*		*Trade Balance*	
	1969	*1967*	*1969*	*1967*	*1969*	*1967*
ALL COUNTRIES	1,319,091	768,486	723,769	554,931	−595,322	−213,555
EUROPE	805,211	421,879	389,352	334,589	−415,859	− 87,290
EUROPEAN ECON. COMMUNITY	397,256	183,822	188,542	160,554	−208,714	− 23,268
France	51,245	32,659	37,126	18,938	− 14,719	− 13,721
Italy	70,203	26,697	11,124	7,529	− 59,079	− 19,168
Belgium and Luxembourg	48,138	26,634	45,205	36,402	− 2,933	− 9,768
W. Germany	155,360	62,282	64,061	59,257	− 91,299	− 3,025
Netherlands	71,710	35,550	31,026	30,959	− 40,684	− 4,591
EUROPEAN FREE TRADE AREA	362,619	203,227	144,283	127,620	−218,336	− 75,607
United Kingdom	245,594	146,244	74,850	70,503	−170,744	− 75,741
Sweden	31,687	10,207	11,401	9,545	− 20,286	− 662
Switzerland	49,735	27,280	34,030	27,168	− 15,705	− 112
OTHER COUNTRIES OF EUROPE	45,336	34,830	56,527	46,415	+ 11,191	+ 11,585
ASIA	33,687	27,333	106,423	71,892	+ 72,736	+ 44,559
AFRICA	31,216	27,394	34,267	24,438	+ 3,051	− 2,958
AMERICA	345,578	215,053	162,467	104,824	−183,111	−110,229
North America	319,785	200,920	153,683	99,107	−166,102	−101,813
United States	309,326	197,079	135,713	89,925	−173,613	−107,154
Central America	548	325	2,973	2,126	+ 2,425	+ 1,801
South America	25,245	13,808	5,811	3,591	− 19,434	− 10,217
OCEANIA	4,003	3,497	5,460	2,880	+ 1,457	− 617
UNCLASSIFIED COUNTRIES	99,396	73,330	25,800	16,310	− 73,596	− 57,020

tons in 1968, to exceed those of the preceding year by 50%, and attained 800,000 tons in 1969. Falling potash prices on the world market temporarily reduced cash return on this item, but the situation improved anew at the end of 1969. Shipments of phosphates reached 800,000 tons in 1968 and were scheduled to exceed 1 million tons in 1970, while copper and cement exports remained rather stable in the late 1960's. Magnesium, it is hoped, will be added to the list in the 1970's. Export incomes will in future be raised through production of high-grade compounds. *Drugs,* including antibiotics, also rank on the export list.

Textiles and *clothing* are constantly on the increase ($3 million in 1955, $18.2 million in 1960, $39.4 million in 1964, and $80.6 million in 1969); specialized products, such as Orlon yarns and rayon for tires, show a particularly steep rise. Wearing apparel and panty-hose, more or less stable over a number of years, showed a marked export rise after 1967.

Two highly important items, based on local skill, are *automobile tires* and *plywood*. *Paper* products, books, artistic handicrafts and religious articles are products characteristic of Israel, but their export figures fluctuate and do not carry great weight in the total balance.

The *metal* branch developed rapidly in the 1960's when new products, among them arms, were added to other typical export commodities such as refrigerators, cars and car parts, steel pipes, textile machinery, transformers, radios, electric motors, etc.

Israel Trade Relations. As shown in the table above, the United States of America heads the list of exporters to Israel. It is followed by Great Britain, and the German Federal Republic. From these three countries alone, Israel has, in recent years, purchased over half of its imports. Europe as a whole accounted in 1965 for 57% of Israel's imports, and for approximately 60% in 1967. Imports from America constituted almost 35% of the total in 1965, but later remained stable at an average of 25–27%. Asia, Africa and Oceania sold to Israel 10% or less of her import goods.

In Europe, outside the two economic blocs of the West, (the Common Market and EFTA), Yugoslavia was an important supplier to Israel. Trade with countries associated with COMECON has come to a virtual standstill, a notable exception being Rumania which has even considerably increased her trade with Israel.

Among buyers of Israeli *exports*, the United States, the United Kingdom and West Germany occupy the first places, usually in that order; France, however, lags behind Switzerland, Holland and Belgium. In general, it appears that the larger the total volume of Israel's trade with a particular country, the larger is the trade gap between Israel's imports and exports. In addition to efforts for further diversification of Israel's trade relations throughout the world, the State is interested in reducing the disparity of the trade balance, particularly with those countries for whom it constitutes an important customer.

Bibliography

GENERAL

ABEL, F. M., *Géographie de la Palestine,* I–II, Paris, 1933–1938.

Atlas Geografi-Histori shel Ereẓ Yisrael (Geographical-Historical Atlas of the Land of Israel), edited by M. Avi-Yonah, Israel Army General Staff, Chief Education Officer. [Hebrew].

Atlas Israel (Atlas of Israel). Cartography, Physical Geography, History, Demography, Economics, Education, Dept. of Surveys, Ministry of Labor and Bialik Institute, 1956–1964. [Hebrew].

AVI-YONAH, M., *The Madaba Mosaic Map,* Jerusalem, 1954.

AVI-YONAH, M., *Map of Roman Palestine,* 2nd ed., Oxford, 1940.

BENTOR, Y. K. and VROMAN, A., 'A Structural Contour Map of Israel,' *BRCI,* 4, pp. 125–135, 1954.

BENTWICH, N., *Palestine,* London, 302 pp., 1934.

BONNE, A., *Palästina, Land und Wirtschaft,* Berlin, 333 pp., 1935.

BRAWER, A. Y., *Ereẓ Yisrael* (The Land of Israel), Bialik Institute-Dvir, 531 pp., 1954. [Hebrew].

BRAWER, M. and KARMON, Y., *Atlas ha-Mizraḥ ha-Tikhon* (Atlas of the Middle East), Yavneh, Tel Aviv, 1964. [Hebrew].

BUCKINGHAM, I. S., *Travels in Palestine,* London, 1821.

BURCKHARDT, J. L., *Travels in Syria and the Holy Land,* London, 1822.

CONDER, C. R. and KITCHENER, H. H., *Map of Western Palestine, in 26 sheets,* London, 1880.

CONDER, C. R. and KITCHENER, H. H., *The Survey of Western Palestine, Memoirs of the Topography, Orography, Hydrography and Archaeology,* 3 vols., London, 1881–1883.

CRESSEY, G. B., *Asia's Lands and People,* McGraw-Hill, New York, pp. 388–398, 1951.

EFRAT, E. and MESSING, H., *Millon le-Geografiya we-Lidi'at ha-Arez* (Dictionary of General and Israel Geography), Massada, Tel Aviv, 309 pp., 1960. [Hebrew].

Enẓiqlopediya Ivrit (Hebrew Encyclopedia), Vol. VI: *Erez Yisrael* (The Land of Israel), Massada, Tel Aviv, 1,172 pp., 1957. [Hebrew].

Enẓiqlopediya Miqra'it (Biblical Encyclopedia), 5 vols., Mosad Bialik, Jerusalem, 1955–1968. [Hebrew].

Ereẓ Yisrael. Annual Volumes. Archeological, Historical and Geographical Studies, I–X, Israel Exploration Society ed., Jerusalem, 1951–1970. [Hebrew].

FISHER, W. B., *The Middle East,* Methuen and Co. Ltd., London, 514 pp., 1950.

GUÉRIN, N. V., *Description de la Palestine,* I–III, Paris, 1868–1880.

GUTHE, H., *Bibelatlas,* 2nd ed., Leipzig, 1925.

HAREL, M. and NIR, D., *Geografiya Shel Ereẓ Yisrael* (Geography of the Land of Israel), Am Oved, Tel Aviv, 1969. [Hebrew].

HUNTINGTON, E., *Palestine and Its Transformation,* London, 1911.

Facts about Israel. Annual Volumes, Ministry for Foreign Affairs, 1950–1970.

Lexikon Miqra'i (Biblical Lexicon) (eds. Soli'eli and M. Barkuz), 2 vols., Dvir, Tel Aviv, 1965. [Hebrew].

MARMARDJI, A. S., *Textes géographiques arabes sur la Palestine,* Paris, 1951.

MUNK, S., *Palestine, Description géographique, historique et archéologique,* Firmin Didot Frères, Paris, 704 pp. et env. 100 gravures, 1845.

NEUBAUER, A., La Géographie du Talmud, Paris, 1868.

ORNI, E., *Moladtenu* (Our Homeland), R. Mass, Jerusalem, 200 pp., 1957. [Hebrew].

ORNI, E., *This is Israel.* A Guidebook, Achiasaf, Jerusalem, 336 pp., 1962.

PALMER, P. and GUTHE, H., *Die Mosaikkarte von Madeba,* I, Leipzig, 1906.

PAPORISH, Y., *Yedi'at ha-Areẓ, Geografiya Fizit we-Yishuvit* (Israel's Geography, Physical and Human), Czaczyk, Tel Aviv, 1960. [Hebrew].

PRESS, Y., *Enẓiqlopediya shel Ereẓ Yisrael* (Encyclopaedia of Palestine), 4 vols., R. Mass, Jerusalem, 1948–1955. [Hebrew].

REIFENBERG, A. A., *The Struggle between the Desert and the Sown,* Bialik Institute, Jerusalem, 1950.

Research Council of Israel. *Desert Research, Proceedings of International Symposium,* Sponsored by the Research Council and UNESCO, 643 pp., 1952.

RITTER, C., *Die Erdkunde von Asien,* Bd. 8, Abt. 2, Berlin, 1848–1854.

RITTER, C., *Vergleichende Erdkunde der Sinai-Halbinsel, Palästina und Syrien,* Berlin, 1850.

ROBINSON, E., *Physical Geography of the Holy Land,* London, 1865.

SCHATTNER, I., *Mapat Ereẓ Yisrael we-Toldoteha* (The Map of the Land of Israel and Its History), Bialik Institute, Jerusalem, 204 pp., 1951. [Hebrew].

Statistical Abstract of Israel, Israel Bureau of Statistics, No. 21, Jerusalem, 1970. [Hebrew and English].

The Survey of Western Palestine, Vols. I–III, 1881–1889; *The Survey of Eastern Palestine,* Vols. I–II, Palestine Exploration Fund, London, 1889.

TAVENER, L. E., *The Revival of Israel,* Hodder and Stoughton, London, 128 pp., 1961.

TRIETSCH, D., *Palästina-Handbuch,* Berlin, 1912.

VILNAI, Z., *Israel Guide,* Jerusalem, 1970.

VILNAI, Z., *Ha-Mapa ha-Ivrit shel Ereẓ Yisrael* (The Hebrew Map of Palestine), The Jewish Palestine Exploration Society, 1944. [Hebrew].

VOLNEY, C. F., *Voyage en Egypte et en Syrie, 1783–1785,* Paris, 1825.

THE COUNTRY, ITS STRUCTURE AND GEOLOGICAL HISTORY

AMIRAN, D. H. K., 'Qawey Yesod be-Mivne ha-Areẓ mi-Ẓafon le-Viq'at Be'ersheva' (Fundamental Traits in the Structure of the Country North of the Beersheba Depression), *Ereẓ Yisrael, Annual of the Israel Exploration Society,* Vol. 4, pp. 9–23, 1956. [Hebrew].

AVNIMELECH, M., *Ẓefunot Sal'ey Arẓenu* (The Secrets of Our Rocks). Sketches on Palestine's Geology and Paleontology, Sifriat ha-Po'alim, 324 pp., 1948. [Hebrew].

BLANCKENHORN, M., *Syrien, Arabien und Mesopotamien. Handbuch für regionale Geologie,* Bd. V, Heidelberg, 1914.

LARTET, L., 'Essai sur la géologie de la Palestine,' *Ann. Sci. Géol. I,* 1, Paris, 1869.

PICARD, L., *Structure and Evolution of Palestine,* Geological Department, Hebrew University, Jerusalem, 134 pp., 1943.

THE NEGEV

BENTOR, Y. and VROMAN, A., *Ha-Mapa ha-Geologit shel ha-Negev* (The Geological Map of the Negev), Israel Army ed., 1951. [Hebrew].

BITAN (Buttenwieser), A., *Meḥqar Topo-Aqlimi be-Ḥevel ha-Besor* (Topo-Climatic Survey of the Besor Region), Jewish Agency Settlement Dept., 315 pp., 1967. [Hebrew].

BRASLAVI (Braslavsky), Y., *Hayada'ta et ha-Areẓ* (Know Thy Country), Vol. II, *Ereẓ ha-Negev* (The Land of the Negev), 506 pp. 1947; Vol. IV, *El Elat we-el Yam Suf* (Toward Eilat and The Red Sea), 532 pp., Ha-Kibbutz ha-Me'uḥad ed. [Hebrew].

DEBUCHY, V., *Le Néguev, ou la conquête de l'impossible,* Ecole Pratique des Hautes Etudes, Paris. 364+33 pp., 1968.

EFRAT, E. and GABRIELI, E., *Physical Master Plan of the Northern Negev,* Ministry of the Interior, Planning Dept., 1967. [Hebrew and English].

GLUECK, N., *Rivers in the Desert—the Exploration of the Negev,* Weidenfeld and Nicolson, London, 302 pp., 1959.

KALLNER-AMIRAN, D. H., 'Geormorphology of the Central Negev Highlands,' *IEJ,* I, pp. 107–120, 1950/51.

LAWRENCE, T. E. and WOOLLEY, C. L., 'The Wilderness of Zion,' *Palestine Exploration Fund Annual,* III, London, 1914/15.

LOEHNBERG, E., *Ha-Negev ha-Raḥoq* (The Far Negev), Am Oved, Tel Aviv, 192 pp., 1954. [Hebrew].

MESTRAS, J., 'Israel Contre le Désert: la mise en valeur du Néguev,' *C.O.M.,* 9, pp. 181–201, 1956.

PICARD, L., 'Geomorphology of Israel, Part I: The Negev,' *BRCI,* I, 1–2, 1951.

PICARD, L. and SOLMONICA, P., *On the Geology of the Gaza-Beersheba District,* Jerusalem, 1936.

THE COASTAL PLAIN

AVITZUR, SH., *Naḥal ha-Yarqon* (The Yarqon River), Ha-Kibbutz ha-Me'uḥad ed., 231 pp., 1948. [Hebrew].

AVNIMELECH, M., 'The Geological History of the Yarqon Valley and the Influence on Ancient Settlements,' *IEJ,* I, pp. 77–83, 1950/51.

AVNIMELECH, M., 'Late Quaternary Sediments of the Coastal Plain of Israel,' *BRCI,* 2, pp. 51–57, 1952.

BEN ARIEH, Y., NASHIV, Y. and REICHMAN, S., 'Ḥof ha-Karmel ha-Deromi—Seqira Geografit' (The Southern Carmel Coast—a Geographical Survey), *Yedi'ot ha-Ḥevra la-Ḥaqirat ha-Areẓ,* 26, pp. 3–14, 1962. [Hebrew].

BEN ARIEH, Y., NASHIV, Y. and REICHMAN, S., 'Ha-Shimmush ha-Ḥaqla'i be-Qarqa ha-Ḥof shel ha-Karmel ha-Deromi' (Agricultural Use of the South Carmel Coast Lands), *Yedi'ot*, 26, pp. 48–70, 1962. [Hebrew].

EFRAT, E. and GABRIELI, E., *Physical Master Plan of the Coastal Strip*, Ministry of the Interior, Planning Dept., Jerusalem, 22 pp. and 17 maps, 1966. [English Abstract].

EFRAT, E., *Physical Master Plan of the Jerusalem-Ashdod Region*, Ministry of the Interior, Planning Dept., 1967. [English Abstract].

EMERY, K. O. and BENTOR, Y. K., 'The Continental Shelf of Israel,' *Sea Fisheries Research Station Bull. 28*, Jerusalem, pp. 25–41, 1960.

GHALLAB, E.S., 'Constant and Variable Factors in the Interrelations between the Judean Plateau and the Maritime Plain of Palestine,' *BRSGE*, 24, pp. 201–225, 1951.

GRADER, P. Z. and REISS, Z., *On the Lower Cretaceous of the Ḥeleẓ Area*, Bull. 16, Geologic Survey of Israel, 11 pp., 1958.

LOEHNBERG, A. E., 'The Buried Structure of Rosh ha-Ayin in the Central Coastal Plain of Israel,' *IEJ*, II, pp. 145–152, 1952.

KARMON, Y., 'Geographical Aspects in the History of the Coastal Plain of Israel,' *IEJ*, VI, pp. 33–50, 1956.

NIR, D., 'Artificial Outlets of the Mount Carmel Valleys through the Coastal "Kurkar" Ridge,' *IEJ*, IX, pp. 46–54, 1959.

NIR, D., 'Etude sur la morphologie littorale d'Israël,' *AdG*, 68, pp. 424–436, 1959.

PICARD, L. and AVNIMELECH, M., *On the Geology of the Central Coastal Plain*, Jerusalem, 1937.

RANGE, P., *Die Küstenebene Palästinas*, Berlin, 1922.

RIM, M., 'Sand and Soil in the Coastal Plain of Israel,' *IEJ*, I, pp. 33–48, 1950/51.

SHALEM, N., 'Considerazioni sull'origine delle sabbie Palestinense da Ras en-Nakura al confino Egiziano,' *Società dei Naturalisti e Matematici di Modena*, 6A, Vol. III, pp. 47–52, 1928.

THE HILL REGIONS

AMIRAN, D. H. K., NIR, D. and SCHICK, A. P., 'The "Lake" of Dalton: Agam Dalton,' *IEJ*, a, pp. 246–259, 1959.

AVNIMELECH, M., *Etude géologiques dans la région de la Shéphéla en Palestine*, Grenoble, 1936.

BRASLAVI (Braslavsky), Y., *Hayada'ta et ha-Areẓ* (Know Thy Country), Vol. I., *Ha-Galil we-Imqey ha-Ẓafon* (Galilee and the Valleys of the North), 1956; Vol. V, *Beyn Tavor we-Ḥermon* (Between Tabor and Hermon), 1960. [Hebrew].

FLEXER, A., 'The Geology of Mount Gilboa,' *BRCI*, 7, 1OG, pp. 64–67, 1961.

HAREL, M., 'Reduced Aridity in Eastern Lower Galilee,' *IEJ*, VII, pp. 256–262, 1957.

NIR, D., 'Les marges méridionales du phénomène karstique en Israël,' *Revue Geogr. Alpine*, 52, pp. 533–541, 1964.

OPPENHEIM, M., 'The Geology of the Southeastern Galilee Lava Fields,' *BRCI*, 11 G, pp. 58–84, 1962.

PICARD, L., *Geological Researches in the Judean Desert*, Jerusalem, 1931.

PRAUSNITZ, M. W., 'The First Agricultural Settlements in Galilee,' *IEJ*, IX, pp. 166–174, 1959.

SCHICK, A. P., *Geomorfologiya shel Ḥevel Menashe* (Geomorphology of the Menashe Region), Hebrew University, Jerusalem, 272 pp., 1963. [Hebrew].

SCHWOEBEL, V., 'Das westpalästinische Mittelland,' *ZdPV*, 53, 1930.

SCHWOEBEL, V., 'Die Verkehrswege und Ansiedlungen Galiläas in ihrer Abhängigkeit von den natürlichen Bedingungen,' *ZdPV*, 27, pp. 1–151, 1904.

SCHWOEBEL, V., 'Die geographischen Verhältnisse des Menschen in der Wüste Juda; *Palästinajahrbuch des deutsch-evangelischen Instituts*, III, Jerusalem, 1907.

SHIFTAN, Z. L., 'The Geo-Hydrology of the Safad Region,' *BRCI*, Vol. I, 4, 1952.

YEDAYA, M. and GIL, E. (eds.), *Ma'aravo shel ha-Galil* (The West of Galilee), Sullam Ẓor—Ga'aton Regional Study Circle for Knowledge of the Country, 292 pp., 1961. [Hebrew].

Yehuda Wirushalayim (Judea and Jerusalem), Volume of the 12th Convention of the Israel Exploration Society, 208 pp., 1957. [Hebrew].

Ẓefat we-ha-Galil (Safed and Galilee), Volume of the Israel Exploration Society, 1959. [Hebrew].

THE JORDAN RIFT AND ITS BRANCHES

ALMOG, Y. and ESHEL, B. Z., *Ezor Yam ha-Melaḥ* (The Dead Sea Region), Am Oved, Tel Aviv. 583 pp., 1956. [Hebrew].

AVNIMELECH, M., 'On the Geology and Morphology of the Megiddo Area,' *JPOS*, 19, pp. 18–37, 1939.

BEN-ARIEH, Y., 'Some Remarks on the Last Stages of the Formation of Lake Tiberias,' *Israel Journal of Earth Sciences*, 13, 2, pp. 53–62, 1964.

BEN-ARIEH, Y., 'Tentative Water Balance of the Lisan Lake,' *Israel Journal of Earth Sciences*, 13, 1, pp. 42–47, 1964.

BEN-ARIEH, Y., *The Changing Landscape of the Central Jordan Valley*, Magnes Press, Jerusalem, 131 pp. and maps, plates, 1968.

BLANCKENHORN, M., *Naturwissenschaftliche Studien am Toten Meer und im Jordantale*, Berlin, 1912.

BRASLAVI (Braslavsky), Y., *Hayada'ta et ha-Areẓ* (Know Thy Country), Volume III: *Yam ha-Melaḥ Saviv Saviv* (The Dead Sea and Its Surroundings), Ha-Kibbutz ha-Me'uḥad ed., 508 pp., 1956. [Hebrew].

DELEEUW, A., *Some Information on Lake Tiberias*, Israel Ministry of Agriculture, Water Dept. Report No. 1, 1950.

GLUECK, N., *The Jordan*, Westminster Press, Philadelphia, 1946.

IONIDES, M. G., 'The Jordan Valley,' *RCAJ*, 38, pp. 217–225, 1951.

KARMON, Y., *Emeq ha-Ḥula ha-Ẓefoni* (The Northern Ḥula Valley), Hebrew University, Y. L. Magnes ed., 108 pp., 1956. [Hebrew].

KARMON, Y., 'The Drainage of the Huleh Swamps,' *G.R.*, 50, pp. 169–193, 1960.

KARMON, Y., 'The Settlement of the Huleh Valley since 1838,' *IEJ*, 3, pp. 4–25, 1953.

KLEIN, C., *On the Fluctuations of the Level of the Dead Sea since the Beginning of the 19th Century*, Israel Ministry of Agriculture, Water Commission, Hydrological Service, Hydr. Paper No. 7, Jerusalem, 1960.

LAMBERTY, M. A., 'Fluctuations in the Level of the Dead Sea,' *G.R.*, 52, pp. 602–603, 1962.

LYNCH, W. F., *Narrative of the United States Expedition to the River Jordan and the Dead Sea*, 2nd ed., London, 1850.

MOLYNEUX, A., 'Expedition to the Jordan and the Dead Sea,' *Journ.Royal Geogr. Soc.*, 18, pp. 104–130, 1848.

NEUMANN, J., 'On the Water Balance of Lake Tiberias,' *IEJ*, 4, pp. 246–249, 1953.

NEUMANN, J., 'Energy and Evaporation from Sweet Water Lakes of the Jordan Rift,' *BRCI*, 2, pp. 337–357, 1953.

NEUMANN, J., 'On the Water Balance of the Lake Huleh Swamps 1942/43–1946/47,' *IEJ*, 5, pp. 49–58, 1955.

NIR, D., *Ezor Bet She'an* (The Bet She'an Region), Ha-Kibbutz ha-Me'uḥad ed., 200 pp., 1960. [Hebrew].

NIR, D., *La Vallée de Beth Cheane—la mise en valeur d'une région à la lisière du désert*, A. Colin, Paris, 182 pp., 1968.

NOVOMEYSKY, M., *The Dead Sea*, Transactions of the Institute of Chemical Engineers, Vol. 14, 1936.

OREN, O. H., 'Physical and Chemical Characteristic of Lake Tiberias,' *BRCI*, 11g, pp. 1–33, 1962.

ORNI, E., *Huleh, Background and Development*, Jewish National Fund, Jerusalem, 54 pp., 1952.

PICARD, L., 'Zur Geologie der Besan-Ebene,' *ZdPV*, Bd. 52, 1929.

PICARD, L., *Zur Geologie der Kischon-Ebene*, Liepzig, 1928.

PICARD, L., 'Zur Geologie des mittleren Jordantals,' *ZdPV*, Bd. 55, 1932.

PICARD, L., *The Pleistocene Peat of Lake Hula;* BENTOR, Y., *Air Photographs and Geological Mapping in the Negev*, Geological Institute, Jerusalem, 22 pp. and plates, 1952.

QUENNELL, A. M., 'The Structural and Geomorphic Evolution of the Dead Sea Rift,' *Quarterly Journ., Geol. Society of London*, 114, pp. 1–24, 1958.

SCHATTNER, I., *The Lower Jordan Valley—A Study of Fluviomorphology of an Arid Zone*, Jerusalem, 1961.

SCHULMANN, N., 'The Geology of the Central Jordan Valley,' *BRCI*, 8, pp. 2–3; 36–90, 1959.

SCHWOEBEL, V., *Der Jordangraben*, Breslau, 1921.

SHALEM, N., *The Valley of the Hule*, Tel Aviv, 1937.

SHIFTAN, Z. L., 'An Artesian Aquifer of the Southern Dead Sea Basin,' *BRCI*, 76, pp. 27–52, 1958.

SHIFTAN, Z. L., 'New Data on the Artesian Aquifers of the Southern Dead Sea Basin and Their Geological Evolution,' *BRCI*, II, 2, pp. 121–128, 1952.

The Huleh and the Upper Jordan Region, Volume ed. by Youth and Hechalutz Dept. of World Zionist Organization and Jewish National Fund, Jerusalem, 253 pp., 1954.

YARON, F., 'The Springs of Lake Kinneret and Their Relationship to the Dead Sea,' *BRCI*, II, 2, pp. 121–128, 1952.

YARON, F. and HEITNER, M., 'The Chloride-Bromide Ratio of the Water Sources of the Eastern Emek Yesreel and of the Beisan Valley,' *BRCI*, II, 2, pp. 121–128, 1952.

YEVIN, SH. and HIRSCHBERG, Z. (eds.), *Erez Kinarot* (The Land of Kinarot), Sifriyat Kav le-Kav, Tel Aviv, 166 pp. and plates, 1950. [Hebrew].

TRANSJORDAN

BRUENNOW, R. E. and DOMASZEWSKI, A., *Die Provincia Arabia*, 3 vols., Strassburg, 1904–1909.

CONDER, C. R., *The Survey of Eastern Palestine, I: The Adwan Country*, London, 1889.

Ha-Golan, Leqet Ma'amarim (The Golan, Collected Articles), Internal Publication of the Israel Exploration Circles of the Kibbutz Movement, 382 pp., 1970. [Hebrew].

IONIDES, M. G. and BLAKE, G. S., *Report on the Water Resources of Transjordan and Their Development*, 1939.

KONIKOFF, A., *Transjordan, an Economic Survey*, Economic Research Institute of the Jewish Agency, 120 pp., 1946.

MUSIL, A., *Arabia Petraea*, Vol. II: *Edom*, Wien, 1907–1908.

NEISTATT, M., *Ha-Golan* (The Golan), Ma'arakhot (Israel Army), 213 pp., 1968. [Hebrew].

SCHUMACHER, G. and STEUERNAGEL, C., 'Der Adschlun,' *ZdPV*, Bd. 47, 1924.

SCHUMACHER, G., 'Der Dscholan,' *ZdPV*, Bd. 9, 1886; 'Der Südliche Basan,' *ZdPV*, Bd. 20, 1897.

THE CLIMATE

AMIRAN, D. H. K. and GILEAD, M., 'Early Excessive Rainfall and Soil Erosion,' *IEJ*, IV, pp. 286–295, 1954.

ASHBEL, D., *Bio-Climatic Atlas of Israel*, Meteorology Dept. of the Hebrew University, Jerusalem, 151 pp., 1951. [Hebrew and English].

ASHBEL, D., *Die Niederschlagsverhältnisse im südlichen Libanon, Palästina und im nördlichen Sinai*, Berlin, 1930.

ASHBEL, D., 'Frequency and Distribution of Dew in Palestine,' *G.R.*, 39, pp. 291–297, 1949.

ASHBEL, D., *Regional Climatology of Israel*, ed. Meteorology Dept. of the Hebrew University, Jerusalem, 244 + 17 pp. [Hebrew and English].

BIEL, E. R., *Climatology of the Mediterranean Area*, Chicago, 1944.

BITAN-BUTTENWIESER, A., 'A Comparison of Sixty Years' Rainfall between Jerusalem and Tel Aviv,' *IEJ*, 13, pp. 242–246, 1963.

FEIGE, R. and ROSENAU, E., *Rainfall Atlas of Palestine*, Jerusalem, 1940.

FEIGE, R. and ROSENAU, E., *Rainfall in Palestine and Transjordan*. Appendix: *Geology and Water Resources of Palestine*, by G.S. BLAKE and M. G. GOLDSCHMIDT, Jerusalem, 1947.

GILEAD, M. and ROSENAN, N., 'Ten Years of Dew Observation in Israel,' *IEJ*, IV, pp. 120–123, 1954.

NEUMANN, J., 'Evaporation from the Red Sea,' *IEJ*, II, pp. 153–162, 1952.

NEUMANN, J., 'On the Incidence of Dry and Wet Years,' *IEJ*, VI, pp. 58–63, 1956.

ROSENAN, N., 'One Hundred Years of Rainfall in Jerusalem—A Homotopic Series of Annual Amounts,' *IEJ*, V, pp. 137–153, 1955.

SHALEM, N., 'Stabilité du climat en Palestine,' *Revue Biblique*, 58, pp. 54–74, 1951.

FLORA AND FAUNA

BODENHEIMER, F. S., *Animal Life in Palestine*, Jerusalem, 1935.

BODENHEIMER, F. S., *Prodromus Faunae Palaestinae*, Cairo, 1937.

BODENHEIMER, SH., *Ha-Ḥay be-Arẓot ha-Miqra* (Wildlife in Lands of the Bible), Bialik Institute, Jerusalem, 350 pp., 1950. [Hebrew].

EIG, A., 'A Contribution to the Knowledge of the Flora in Palestine,' *Inst. Agr. and Nat. Hist., Agr. Exp. Sta. Bull.*, 4, pp. 1–72, 1926.

EIG, A., *Les éléments et les groupes phytogéographiques auxiliaires dans la flore palestinienne*, I, II, Beih. Rep. spec. nov. veg., 63, 1931–1932.

EVENARI, M., 'Ecological Investigations in Palestine on the Vegetation of Kurkar Hills,' *BRCI*, I, 1–2, pp. 48–58, 1952.

FEINBRUN, N. and ZOHARY, M., 'A Geobotanical Survey of Transjordan,' *Pal. Journ. Bot.*, 6, 1955.

GINDEL, Y., *Ha-Ya'ar we-ha-Ye'ur be-Yisrael* (Forest and Afforestation in Israel), Forestry Research Laboratory, 344 pp., 1952. [Hebrew].

ORNI, E., *Afforestation in Israel* (2nd ed.), Jewish National Fund, Jerusalem, 78 pp., 1969.

POST, G. E. and DINSMORE, J. E., *Flora of Syria, Palestine and Sinai* (2nd ed.), 2 vols., Amer. Univ. Publ. Fac. Arts and Sci. Ser., 1, Beirut, pp. 1–639; 1–928, 1931–1932.

ZOHARY, M., *Mavo la-Geobotaniqa shel Ereẓ Yisra'el* (Introduction to the Geobotany of the Land of Israel), Hashomer Hatzair ed., 278 pp., maps, 1944. [Hebrew].

ZOHARY, M., 'A Geobotanical Soil Map of Western Palestine,' *Pal. Journ. Bot.*, 4, pp. 24–35, 1947.

ZOHARY, M. and FEINBRUN, N., 'Outline of Vegetation of the Northern Negev,' *Pal. Journ. Bot.*, 5, pp. 96–114, 1951.

ZOHARY, M. and ORSHANSKY, G., 'The Vegetation of the Huleh Plain,' *Pal. Journ. Bot.*, 4, pp. 90–105, 1947.

ZOHARY, M. and ORSHANSKY, G. 'Structure and Ecology of the Vegetation in the Dead Sea Region of Palestine,' *Pal. Journ. Bot.*, 4, pp. 178–206, 1949.

THE ARCHEOLOGICAL AND HISTORICAL BACKGROUND

AHARONI, Y., 'The Negev of Judah,' *IEJ*, VIII, pp. 26–38, 1958.

AHARONI, Y. and ROTENBERG, B., *Be-Iqvot Melakhim u-Mordim be-Midbar Yehuda* (Tracing Kings and Rebels in the Judean Desert), Massadah, Tel Aviv, 162 pp., 1960. [Hebrew].

ALBRIGHT, W. F., *The Archaeology of Palestine*, Penguin Books, 271 pp., 1949.

ALT, A., *Kleine Schriften zur Geschichte des Volkes Israel*, 3 vols., München, 1953.

APPLEBAUM, SH., *Archaeology in Israel*, Israel Today Series, No. 10, Israel Digest, 32 pp., 1962.

AVI-YONAH, M., *Bimey Roma u-Vizantion* (In the Days of Rome and Byzantium), Bialik Institute, Jerusalem, 274 pp., 1962. [Hebrew].

AVI-YONAH, M., *Historiya Geografit shel Ereẓ Yisra'el* (Historical Geography of the Land of Israel, from the End of the Babylonian Exile up to the Arab Conquest), Bialik Institute, Jerusalem, 231 pp., 1962. [Hebrew].

AVI-YONAH, M. and YEVIN, SH., *Qadmoniyot Arẓenu* (The Antiquities of Israel), Ha-Kibbutz ha-Me'uḥad ed., 344 pp., 1955. [Hebrew].

BEIN, A., *The Return to the Soil—a History of Jewish Settlement in Israel*, Youth and Hechalutz Dept. of the Zionist Organization, 576 pp., 1952.

BEN ZVI, I., *Ereẓ Yisra'el we-Yishuvah taḥat ha-Shilton ha-Otomani* (The Land of Israel under Ottoman Rule: Four Centuries of History), Bialik Institute, Jerusalem, 478 pp., 1962. [Hebrew].

BRASLAVI (Braslavsky), Y., *Le-Ḥeqer Arẓenu* (The Research of Our Country, The Past and Its Remnants), Ha-Kibbutz ha-Me'uhad ed., 390 pp., 1954. [Hebrew].

CARMEL, M., *Ma'arakhot Ẓafon* (Battles of the North), Ha-Kibbutz ha-Me'uḥad ed., 286 pp., 1949. [Hebrew].

CONDER, C. R., *The Latin Kingdom of Jerusalem*, London, 1897.

DALMAN, G., *Orte und Wege Jesu*, 3 Aufl., Gütersloh, 1924.

DOTHAN, T., *Ha-Pelishtim we-Tarbutam he-Ḥomrit* (The Philistines and Their Material Culture), Bialik Institute, Jerusalem, 1967. [Hebrew].

DUBNOV, S., *Weltgeschichte des jüdischen Volkes*, 10 Bde., Jüdischer Verlag, Berlin, 1924.

GARROD, D. A. E. and BATE, D. M. A., *The Stone Age of Mount Carmel, Excavations at the Wadi el-Mughara*, Vol. I, Oxford, 1937.

GARSTANG, J., *Joshua-Judges*, London, 1931.

GRAETZ, H., *History of the Jews*, 6 vols., the Jewish Publication Society of America, Philadelphia, 1945.

GROUSSET, R., *Histoire des croisades*, 3 vols., Paris, 1935.

HABAS, B., *Migdal we-Ḥoma* (Tower and Stockade), Labor Fed. ed., 202 pp., 1939. [Hebrew].

KENYON, K. M., *Archaeology in the Holy Land*, 2nd ed., Methuen, London, 328 pp., 1965.

KLEIN, SH., *Ereẓ Yehuda* (The Land of Judah), Dvir, Tel Aviv, 289 pp., 1939. [Hebrew].

LAMB, Y., 'Crusader Lands Re-Visited,' *NGM*, 106, pp. 815–852, 1954.

LESTRANGE, G., *Palestine under the Moslems*, London, 1890.

NEUVILLE, R., *Le paléolithique et mésolithique du désert de Judée*, Archive de l'Institute de Paléontologie Humaine, Mémoire 24, Paris, 1951.

NOTH, M., *Geschichte Israels*, 3 Aufl., Göttingen, 1956.

PRAWER, J., *Toldot Mamlekhet ha-Ẓalbanim be-Ereẓ Yisra'el* (A History of the Latin Kingdom of Jerusalem), 3 vols., 561, 544 pp., separate index 105 pp., 1962. [Hebrew].

ROBINSON, E., *Biblical Researches in Palestine, Mount Sinai and Arabia Petraea*, 3 vols., London, 1841.

RÖHRICHT, R., *Geschichte des Königreichs Jerusalem*, Innsbruck, 1893.

ROTH, C., *Short History of the Jewish People*, East and West Library.

SCHÜRER, E., *Geschichte des jüdischen Volkes im Zeitalter Jesu Christi*, 4 Aufl., Leipzig, 1907.

SHOR, F., 'Conquest of the Holy City,' *NGM*, 124, pp. 838–857, 1963.

SHOR, F., 'Crusader Road to Jerusalem,' *NGM*, 124, pp. 797–837, 1963.

SMITH, G. A., *The Historical Geography of the Holy Land*, Following the 25th ed., 1931, re-edited by Fontana Library, London, 512 pp., 1966.

STEKELIS, M., *Les monuments mégalithiques de Palestine*, Archives de l'Institut de Paléontologie Humaine, Mémoire 15, Paris, 1935.

TADMOR, N. H. et al., *The Ancient Desert Agriculture of the Negev*, 2 vols., Israel Ministry of Agriculture, 1957–1958.

WEITZ, Y., *Hitnaḥalutenu bi-Tqufat ha-Sa'ar* (Our Settlement in Stormy Times), Sifriyat ha-Po'alim, Tel Aviv, 202 pp., 1947. [Hebrew].

YADIN, Y. (ed.), *Megillat Beney Or bi-Vney Ḥoshekh* (The Scroll of the War of the Sons of Light against the Sons of Darkness), Bialik Institute, Jerusalem, 397+vi pp., 1955. [Hebrew and English summary].

YADIN, Y., *Ha-Mimẓa'im Mimey Bar-Kokhba bi-M'arot ha-Iggarot* (Judean Desert Studies—The Finds from the Bar-Kokhba Period in the 'Cave of Letters'), Israel Exploration Society and Bialik Institute, Jerusalem, 292 pp. and 108 plates, 1963. [Hebrew].

YADIN, Y., *Torat ha-Milḥama be-Arẓot ha-Miqra* (The Art of War in the Lands of the Bible), International Publishing Co., Ramat Gan, 416 pp. and plates, 1963. [Hebrew].

YEVIN, SH., *Milḥemet Bar Kokhba* (Bar Kokhba's War), Bialik Institute, Jerusalem, 264 pp., 1952. [Hebrew].

DEMOGRAPHY

AMIRAN, D. H. K. and BEN-ARIEH, Y., 'Sedentarization of Beduin in Israel,' *IEJ*, 13, 1963.

AVIDOR, M., *Education for a Growing Nation*, Israel Today Series, No. 1, Israel Digest, 24 pp., 1961.

BEAUJEU-GARNIER, J., 'L'Immigration dans l'Etat d'Israël,' *AdG*, pp. 57–61, 1952.

BEN ZVI, I., 'The Druze Community in Israel,' *IEJ*, IV, pp. 65–76, 1954.

BIANDRINI, M., 'La distribuzione attuale della popolazione in Israele,' *Bol. Soc. Geogr. Italiana*, 7, pp. 368–399, 1954.

ELATH, E., 'Population Problems in Israel,' *RCAJ*, 60, pp. 47–56, 1952.

GRUSHKA, T. (ed.), *Health Services in Israel, 1948–1958*, Ministry of Health, Jerusalem, 1959.

GUREVITCH, D. and GERTZ, A., *Statistical Handbook of Jewish Palestine*, Jerusalem, 1947.

MARK, E., *The Bedouin of the Negev*, Manchester University Press, 15 + 260 pp., 1968.

MILLS, E., *Census of Palestine, I–II, 1931*, Alexandria, 1933.

MÜHSAM, H. V., 'Enumerating the Beduins of Palestine,' *Scripta Hierosolymitana*, Vol. III, pp. 265–280, 1955.

RABIN, CH., *The Revival of Hebrew*, Israel Today Series, No. 18, Israel Digest, 20 pp., 1958.

SHIMONI, Y., *Arvey Ereẓ Yisra'el* (The Arabs of Palestine), Am Oved, Tel Aviv, 476 pp., 1947. [Hebrew].

SMITH, C. G., 'The Boundaries and Population Problems of Israel,' *Geography*, 37, pp. 152–165, 1952.

SUPER, A., *Absorption of Immigrants*, Israel Today Series, No. 18, Israel Digest, 32 pp., 1961.

TAMSMA, R., 'Changes in the Jewish Population Pattern of Israel, 1948–1957: Some Human-Geographical Causes and Consequences,' *TESG*, pp. 170–182, 1959.

VILNAY, Z., *Mi'utim be-Yisra'el*, Reuben Mass, Jerusalem, 268 pp. [Hebrew].

RURAL SETTLEMENT

Agricultural Settlement Dept., Jewish Agency (ed.), *The Composite Rural Structure—a Settlement Pattern in Israel*, Jerusalem, 45 pp., 1960.

AMIRAN, D. H. K., 'The Pattern of Settlement in Palestine,' *IEJ*, III, pp. 65–78; 192–260, 1953.

AMIRAN, D. H. K., 'Two Types of Border of Aridity in Palestine,' *XVIIIe Congrès International de Géographie*, Rio de Janeiro, pp. 461–465, 1956.

AMIRAN, D. H. K., *The Expansion of Settled Land in Israel*, Abstracts of Papers of the 18th Geogr. Congress, Rio de Janeiro, 1956.

ASSAF, A., *Moshvey Ovdim be-Yisra'el* (Moshav Ovdim in Israel), Ayanot, Tel Aviv, 304 pp., 1954. [Hebrew].

Atlas of Settlement in Israel, Population and Housing Census, 1961, Publication No. 14, Central Bureau of Statistics, Jerusalem, 1963.

BARATZ, J., *A Village by the Jordan*, Tel Aviv, 1960.

BEN DAVID, J. (ed.), *Agricultural Planning and Village Community in Israel*, UNESCO, Paris, 159 pp., 1964.

BIENHEIM, K. L., *Physical Planning of Collective Settlement in Israel*, FAO Congress, Israel, Tel Aviv, 1956.

BLAKE, G. H., 'The Origins and Evolution of Israel's Moshav,' *Kulturgeografi Århus*, 109, 1969.

COHEN, R., *Yesodot ha-Mesheq ha-Qibbutzi* (Foundations of the Kibbutz Economy), Ha-Kibbutz ha-Me'uḥad ed., 278 pp., 1956. [Hebrew].

DARIN-DRABKIN, H., *Der Kibbutz*, Stuttgart, 1964.

DESROCHE, H., *Au Pays du Kibboutz*, Union des Coops. des Consommations, Bâle.

ELAZARI-VOLCANI, I., *The Fellah's Farm*, Agr. Exp. Sta., Reḥovot, 128 pp., 1930.

ERES, A., 'Die landwirtschaftliche Planung in Israel,' *Ztschr. f. ausl. Landwirtschaft*, 6. Jg., Frankfurt a/M., pp. 64–73, März 1967.

GRANOTT, A., *The Land System of Palestine: History and Structure*, Eyre & Spottiswoode, London, 359 pp., 1952.

GRANOTT, A., *Agrarian Reform and the Record of Israel*, Eyre & Spottiswoode, London, 301 pp., 1956.

HARMAN, A., *Agricultural Settlement*, Israel Today Series, No. 2, Israel Digest, 36 pp., 1969.

Hebrew University (ed.), *Le-Herkevo ha-Ḥevrati shel ha-Kefar ha-Ivri be-Ereẓ Yisra'el* (The Social Configuration of the Jewish Village in Palestine), Massada, Tel Aviv, 239 pp., 1945. [Hebrew].

ILLERIS, S., 'Recent Changes in the Settlement Geography of Israel,' *Særtryk af Geografisk Tidsskrift*, København, 63 Bd., pp. 43–63, 1964.

Jewish Agency, Land Settlement Dept., and Israel Ministry of Housing: *Rural Planning in Israel*, Tel Aviv, 1964; *Land Settlement in Israel*, Jerusalem, 51 pp., 1970.

KADAR, G., *The Moshav—the Economic Aspect*, International Farmers' Convention 1959, 1960.

KAPLAN, B., *The Lakhish Settlement Project*, State of Israel Study Group on Problems of Individual and Group Settlement, Tel Aviv, 1956.

KEREM, M., *The Kibbutz*, Israel Today Series, No. 27, Israel Digest, 36 pp., 1963.

KORN, Y., *Darkah shel Tenu'at ha-Moshavim*, (The Path of the Moshav Movement), Labor Fed. ed., 29 pp., 1958. [Hebrew].

LADOR, Y., *Hityashvutenu ba-Areẓ 1870–1954* (Our Settlement in the Country, 1870–1954), Ofek, Tel Aviv, 300 pp., 1955. [Hebrew].

MEISTER, A., *Principes et Tendances de la Planification Rurale en Israël*, Ed. de Minuit, Paris.

MEYER, E., *Der Moshav*, List-Gesellschaft, Basel-Tübingen, 123 pp., 1967.

NAWRATZKI, C., *Die jüdische Kolonisation Palästinas*, München, 1914.

ORNI, E., *Forms of Settlement* (5th ed.), Youth and Hechalutz Dept. of Zionist Organization and Jewish National Fund, 178 pp., 1963.

ORNI, E., *L'Agriculture en Israël, formes de la vie rurale*, Centre israélien de Documentation, Paris, 30 pp., 1963.

PARAN, U., 'Kibbutzim in Israel: Their Development and Distribution,' *Jerusalem Studies in Geography*, 1, pp. 1–36, 1970.

Publications on Problems of Regional Development: (1) *Regional Cooperation in Israel,* 148 pp.; (2) *Survey of Regional Cooperation in Three Regions of Collective Settlement* (Cohen, E. and Leshem, E.), 89 pp.; (3) *Development Trends of Spatial Rural Cooperation in Israel* (Weitz, R. and Prion, I.), 108 pp.; (4) *Urban Zones of Influence in the Southern Coastal Plain of Israel* (Cohen, Y.), 112 pp.; (5) *Inhabited Rural Centers in Israel* (Shapiro, O.), 161 pp., National and University Inst. of Agriculture, Rehovot, 1968–1969.

ROSENFELD, H., *Social Changes in Arab Villages,* Israel Ministry of Agriculture, 1963.

RUPPIN, A., *The Agricultural Colonization of the Zionist Organization in Palestine,* M. Hopkinson, London, 209 pp., 1926.

SAMUEL, E., Handbook of the Jewish Communal Villages in Palestine, Jerusalem, 1945.

SHAMIR, Y., *Ha-Ba'ya ha-Agrarit we-ha-Yishuv ha-Kibbutzi* (The Agrarian Problem and Collective Settlement), Sifriyat ha-Po'alim, Tel Aviv, 301 pp., 1953. [Hebrew].

SHARON, A., 'Collective Settlement in Israel,' *Town Planning Review,* 23, pp. 255–270, 1955.

SHATIL, J., *The Way of Life in a Collective Settlement,* FAO Congress in Israel, Tel Aviv, 1956.

SHATIL, J., *L'Economie collective du Kibbouts israélien,* Editions de Minuit.

TABENKIN, Y., *Ha-Ḥevra ha-Qibbuẓit* (The Kibbutz Society), Ha-Kibbutz ha-Meuḥad ed., 59 pp., 1954. [Hebrew].

URI, Y., *Bintiv Moshav Ovdim* (The Way of the Moshav Ovdim), Youth and Hechalutz Dept. of Zionist Organization, 84 pp., 1950. [Hebrew].

URBAN SETTLEMENT

ABBADY, I. (ed.), *Jerusalem Economy,* Collective Volume, Jerusalem Chamber of Commerce, 1950.

AMIRAN, D. H. K. and SHAHAR, A., 'Estimates of the Urban Population of Palestine in the Second Half of the Nineteenth Century,' *IEJ,* X, pp. 181–183, 1960.

AMIRAN, D. H. K. and SHAHAR, A., 'The Towns of Israel, Principles of Their Urban Geography,' *G.R.,* 51, pp. 348–369, 1961.

BENSHEMESH, SH., *Seminar on the Supply and Allocation of Land for Housing and Related Purposes (Israel),* Paris, 1965.

BEN SIRA, Y., BERLER, A., MERTENS, H. and TAMIR, J., *Housing Policy in Regions of Rapid Population Growth in Israel,* Israel Ministry of Housing, 43 pp., 1964.

BRUTZKUS, E., *Physical Planning in Israel,* Jerusalem, 85 pp., 1964.

BRUTZKUS, E., 'Tikhnun Kalkali u-Fizzur Ukhlusim' (Economic Planning and Population Dispersion), *Economic Quarterly,* VI, pp. 321–336, 1959. [Hebrew].

DALMAN, G. H., *Jerusalem und sein Gelände,* Gütersloh, 1930.

DASH, J. and Efrat, E., *The Israel Physical Master Plan,* Israel Ministry of Interior, Planning Dept., 91 pp. and 35 maps, 1964.

DASH, J., DOUDAI, A., EFRAT, E., GLIKSON, A. and KAHANE, A., *National Planning for the Redistribution of Population and the Establishment of New Towns in Israel,* Israel Ministry of Interior, Planning Dept., 38 pp., 1964.

EFRAT, E., *Aspeqtim Geografiyim ba-Tikhnun ha-Fizi shel Ezor Yerushalayim* (Geographical Aspects in the Physical Planning of the Jerusalem Region [Abstract]), Israel Ministry of Interior, Planning Dept., 20 pp., 1963. [Hebrew 189 pp. and English summary].

EFRAT, E., 'The Hinterland of Jerusalem and Its Economic Significance,' *E.G.*, Vol. 40, No. 3, pp. 254–260, 1964.

ELIASH, Y., 'Temurot be-Ir Midbar' (Changes in a Desert Town), *Ha-Mizraḥ ha-Tikhon,* 8, pp. 19–25, 1957. [Hebrew].

HAEZRAHI, Y., *Yerushalayim asher Baḥarti* (The Jerusalem I Have Chosen), Carta, Jerusalem, 310 pp., 1970. [Hebrew].

ISAAC, F., 'A Deteriorating Urban Core, Ideology and Economics in the Landscape of Tel Aviv,' *TESG,* 54, 52 pp., 1961.

KAHANE, A., 'Aufgaben und Einfluss der räumlichen Planung bei der wirtschaftlichen und sozialen Entwicklung Israels,' *Raumforschung und Raumordnung,* 21. Jg.

KAPLAN, Y., *Ha-Arkheologiya we-ha-Historiya shel Tel Aviv-Jafo* (Archeology and History of Tel Aviv-Jaffa), Massada, Tel Aviv, 107 pp., 1959. [Hebrew].

KARMON, Y., 'Eilat—Israel's Red Sea Port,' *TESG,* 54, pp. 117–126, 1953.

KENDALL, H., *Jerusalem, the City Plan, 1918–1948,* His Majesty's Stationery Office, London, 123 pp., maps, plates, 1948.

MELJON, Z. (ed.), *Towns and Villages in Israel,* Union of Local Authorities in Israel, Tel Aviv, 384 pp., 1966.

ORNI, E., 'Städtische Siedlungen Israels,' *Geographische Rundschau,* 5/1970, pp. 165–174.

REIFENBERG, A., 'Caesarea, a Study in the Decline of a Town,' *IEJ,* I, pp. 20–32, 1950/51.

SCHATTNER, I., 'Haifa: a Study in the Relation of City and Coast,' *IEJ,* IV, pp. 26–46, 1954.

SCOFIELD, J., 'Jerusalem, the Divided City,' *NGM,* 115, pp. 492–531, 1959.

SHAHAR, A., *Megamot Hitpatḥut be-Tel Aviv* (Development Trends in Tel Aviv), Tel Aviv Municipality, 36 pp., 1964. [Hebrew].

SHAHAR, A., *Urban Renewal—an Interdisciplinary Symposium,* Inst. for Planning and Development, Tel Aviv, 259 pp., 1968.

SHARON, A., *Tikhnun Fisi be-Yisra'el* (Physical Planning in Israel), Israel Government Printer, 80 pp., plates, maps, 1952. [Hebrew and English].

SPIEGEL, A., *New Towns in Israel, Urban Planning and Regional Development,* List Gesellschaft Publications, K. Kramer Verlag, Stuttgart, 192 pp., plates, maps, 1966. [German and English].

THE ROAD SYSTEM

GOTTMANN, J., 'La route et l'eau en Asie sud-occidentale,' *AdG,* 47, pp. 575–601, 1938.

HAREL, M., 'The Roman Road at Ma'aleh ha-Aqrabim (Scorpion's Ascent),' *IEJ,* IX, pp. 175–199, 1959.

ORION, M., 'Eser Shenot Hitpatḥut ha-Taḥbura' (Ten Years of Transportation Development), *Economic Quarterly,* V, pp. 336–346, 1958. [Hebrew].

SOIL AND WATER

AVITZUR, SH., *Le-Toldot Niẓẓul Koaḥ ha-Mayim be-Ereẓ Yisra'el* (The History of Exploitation of Water Power in the Land of Israel), Avshalom Institute for Homeland Studies, Tel Aviv, 110 pp., 38 pp. plates, 1960. [Hebrew].

AVITZUR, SH., 'On the History of the Exploitation of Water in Ereẓ Israel,' *IEJ,* 10, pp. 37–45, 1960. *Ba'yot ha-Mayim shel Yisra'el* (Israel's Water Problems), Hebrew University, Geography Dept., Jerusalem, 97 pp., 1955. [Hebrew].

BLAKE, G. S. and GOLDSCHMIDT, M. J., *Geology and Water Resources of Palestine,* Jerusalem, 1947.

Chemical Analyses of Water from Rivers, Springs, Wadis, and Wells, Government of Palestine, Dept. of Land Settlement and Water Commissioner, Jerusalem, 1948.

DAN, J., KOYUMDJISKY, H. and YAALON, D. M., 'Principles of a Proposed Classification for the Soils of Israel,' International Soil Conference, New Zealand, 1962.

DE LEEUW, A., 'Decade of Water Development in Israel,' *Technion Yearbook,* New York, 1958.

GIL, N. and ROSENSAFT, Z., *Soils of Israel and Their Land Use Capabilities,* Part I, Israel Ministry for Foreign Affairs, 12 pp. and maps, 1962.

GOLDSCHMIDT, M. J. and JACOBS, M., *Precipitation over and Replenishment of the Yarqon and the Naḥal ha-Tanninim Catchments,* Hydrological Service, Jerusalem, 1959.

GOTTMANN, J., 'L'Irrigation en Palestine,' *AdG,* 44, pp. 143–161, 1935.

Government Tourist Corporation, *Ha-Mayim be-Yisra'el* (Water in Israel), Jerusalem, 35 pp., illustr., 1965. [Hebrew].

KARIV, Z., *Water Development and Water Costs in Israel,* Israel Nat. Comm. for the International Committee on Irrigation and Drainage, Tel Aviv, 1960.

LOWDERMILK, W. C., 'An Inventory of the Land of Israel: Land Classification for Use with Soil Conservation,' *IEJ,* III, pp. 162–177, 1953.

Mekorot Water Co., *Ha-Movil ha-Arẓi* (The National Carrier), Tel Aviv, 1965. [Hebrew].

ORNI, E. and YAALON, D. M., *Conservation and Reclamation of the Soil,* Israel Today Series, No. 26, Israel Digest, 46 pp., 1971.

ORNI, E., 'Wassernutzung in Israel und ihre Probleme,' *Geographische Zeitschrift,* 57, Jg. 3, pp. 198–204, 1969.

PELED, A., 'Operation of the Freeze Desalination Plants,' *1st Internat. Symposium on Water Desalination,* Vol. III, pp. 1–10, 1965.

PRUSHANSKY, Y., *Water Development,* Israel Today Series, No. 11, Israel Digest, 32 pp., 1961.

RAVIKOVITCH, S., *Soils of Israel, Their Nature and Agricultural Value,* Internat. Farmers' Convention 1959, Jerusalem, 1960.

SHIFTAN, Z. L., 'The Application of Hydrology in the Development of Israel's Water Resources,' *Lecture before the 13th Meeting of the Executive Committee,* Internat. Comm. on Irrigation and Drainage, Jerusalem, 14 pp., 1962.

SHMUELI, E., *Irrigation and Irrigation Research in a Semi-Arid Country,* The National and University Institute of Agriculture, Rehovot, 1964.

Water Measurements, Govt. of Palestine, Dept. of Land Settlement and Water Commissioner, Jerusalem, 1947.

WIENER, A., *Israel's Water Development Policy: The Israel National Water Plan,* Israel Ministry for Foreign Affairs, 12 pp. and maps, 1962.

YAALON, D. H., 'Classification and Nomenclature of Soils in Israel,' *BRCI,* 8, 2–3, pp. 91–117.

YAALON, D. H., 'On the Origin and Accumulation of Salts in Groundwater and Soils of Israel,' *BRCI,* 11G, 3, pp. 105–131.

YAALON, D. H., 'Saline Irrigation Water in Calcareous Soils,' *BRCI,* 5B, pp. 83–97, 1955.

AGRICULTURE

Ben Arieh, Y., 'A Comparison of Agricultural Land Use in a Semi-Arid Region: Ashqelon—Bet Guvrin Area,' *Jerusalem Studies in Geography,* 1, pp. 107–128, 1970.

Cohen, S. B., 'Israel's Fishing Industry,' *G.R.*, pp. 66–85, 1957.

El-Zur, A., Magnes, J. and Samueloff, S., *Les recherches sur les zones arides en Israël,* Centre Israélien de documentation sur les pays de langue française, Paris, 16 pp., 1963.

Halperin, H., *Changing Patterns in Israel Agriculture,* Routledge & Co., London, 290 pp., 1960.

Halperin, H., *Agrindus (Integration of Agriculture and Industries),* London, 1963.

Horin, Y., *Development of Agriculture in Israel,* International Farmers' Convention, Jerusalem, 1959 ed., 1960.

Kedar, Y., 'Water and Soil from the Negev—Some Ancient Agricultural Achievements in the Central Negev,' *G.J.*, 123, pp. 179–187, 1957.

Levie, E. L., *The Economics of Citrus Growing in Israel,* Wageningen, 1962.

Lowdermilk, W. C., 'A New Agriculture in an Old Land,' *The Atlantic Monthly,* 1961.

Luz, K., *Agriculture in Israel,* Jerusalem, 1959.

Nuttonson, M. Y., 'Agroclimatology and Crop Ecologies in the United States,' *G.R.*, 37, pp. 136–456, 1947.

Ophen, J.D., 'The Citrus Industry in Israel,' *MEA*, 5, pp. 51–58, 1954.

Rokach, A., *History of the Citrus Industry in Israel,* International Farmers Convention, Jerusalem 1959, 1960.

Weitz, R., *Darkenu ba-Ḥaqla'ut uwa-Hityashvut* (Our Ways in Agriculture and Settlement), Am Oved, Tel Aviv, 339 pp., 1959. [Hebrew].

Weitz, R. and Rokach, A., *Agriculture and Rural Development in Israel—Projection and Planning,* Division of Publications, Rehovot, and Settlement Dept. of Jewish Agency, 140+XL pp., 1963.

Zeligman, N., Rosensaft, Z., Tadmor, N., Katznelson, Y. and Naveh, Z., *Ha-Mir'e ha-Tiv'i be-Yisra'el* (Natural Pasture in Israel), Sifriyat ha-Po'alim, Tel Aviv, 379 pp., 1959. [Hebrew].

Zohary, D., 'Notes on Ancient Agriculture in the Central Negev,' *IEJ,* IV, pp. 17–25, 1954.

MINING, INDUSTRY, SERVICES AND FOREIGN TRADE

Amiran, D. H. K. and Karmon, Y., 'The Expansion of the Dead Sea Works,' *TESG,* pp. 210–223, 1964.

Ball, M. W. and Ball, D., 'Oil Prospects in Israel,' *Bull. Amer. Assoc. Petrol. Geol.*, 37, 1953.

Blake, G. S., *The Mineral Resources of Palestine and Transjordan,* Jerusalem, 1930.

Blake, G. S., *The Stratigraphy of Palestine and Its Building Stones,* Jerusalem, 1936.

Fischler, G., *Energiewirtschaft in Israel,* Veröffentlichg. d. List-Gesellschaft, Bd. 42, Basel/Tübingen, 1965.

Horowitz, D., 'Fundamental Trends in Israel's Economy,' *MEA,* III, pp. 139–149, 1953.

Hovne, A., *The Economy of Israel,* Israel Today Series, No. 23, Israel Digest, 36 pp., 1963.

ISSAWY, CH. (ed.), *The Economic History of the Middle East, 1800–1914,* University of Chicago Press, 543 pp., 1966.

KARMON, Y., 'Zur Wirtschaftsgeographie Israels', *Ztschr. f. Wirtschaftsgeographie,* Hagen, 1960.

KRIVINE, D., *Transport and Communications,* Israel Today Series, No. 28, Israel Digest, 40 pp., 1964.

MARCUS, A., *Mivne ha-Ta'asiya be-Yisra'el,* (The Structure of Israel's Industry), Am Oved, Tel Aviv, 136 pp., 1954. [Hebrew].

MARCUS, A., *Industry in Israel,* Israel Today Series, No. 8, Israel Digest, 40 pp., 1959.

MEIR, Z., *The Labor Movement,* Israel Today Series, No. 20, Israel Digest, 44 pp., 1961.

NATHAN, R., GASS, O. and CREAMER, D., *Palestine: Problem and Promise,* Washington, 1946.

PICARD, L., 'History of Mineral Research in Israel,' *Isr. Econ. Forum,* IX, No. 3, 1947.

SINAI

ADAMS, W. H., *Mount Sinai, Petra and the Desert,* Nelson, Edinburgh, 1879.

ALBRIGHT, W. F., 'Exploring in Sinai with the University of California African Expedition, 1948,' *BASOR,* 109, pp. 5–20.

AWAD, H., 'La Péninsule du Sinaï, problèmes morphologiques,' *Bull. Ass. Géogr. Français,* pp. 42–47, 1941.

AWAD, H., 'Présentation d'une carte morphologique du Sinaï,' *Bull. Inst. Désert. Egypte,* Vol. 2, No. 1, pp. 132–138, 1952.

AWAD, H., *La Montagne du Sinaï Central, étude morphologique,* Le Caire, 1951.

BALL, J., *The Geography and Geology of the Southeastern Desert,* Egypt. Survey Dept., Cairo, 1916.

BAR DEROMA, H. Y., *Ha-Negev* (The Negev—mostly devoted to Sinai), Jerusalem, 16+641 pp., 1935. [Hebrew].

BEADNELL, H. J. L., *The Wilderness of Sinai,* Arnold Co., London, 1927.

BÜDEL, J., *Sinai, "die Wüste der Gesetzesbildung," als Beispiel fur allgemeine klimatische Wüstenmorphologie.*

DAVEY, J. C., 'Report on Southern Sinai,' *Mining Magazine,* Vol. 78, Nos. 1–4, pp. 9–20; 76–87; 144–152; 212–214, 1948.

DEMANGEOT, J., 'Les Régions morphologiques de la presqu'île sinaïtique,' *Rev. Géogr. Lyon,* Vol. 28, No. 2, pp. 135–141, 1953.

EL GABALY, M. M., 'The Soil, Water Supply and Agriculture in Northeastern Sinai,' *Bull. Inst. Désert. Egypt.,* Vol. 4, No. 1, pp. 125–153, 1954.

EL SHAZLY, E. M., 'Classification of Egyptian Mineral Deposits,' *Egypt. Journal of Geology,* pp. 1–20, 1957.

HAREL, M., *Massa'ey Sinai* (Sinai Journeys), Am Oved, Tel Aviv, 318 pp., 1968. [Hebrew].

JARVIS, C. S., *Yesterday and Today in Sinai,* Blackwood & Sons, London, 280 pp., 1938.

JARVIS, C. S., *Three Deserts,* London, 313 pp., 1936.

KADDAH, M. T., *Soil Survey of the Northwest Sinai Project,* Inst. Désert. Egypt., Publ. No. 6, 109 pp., 1956.

KADER, A., *Die Sinaiwüste,* Mitt. d. Thür. Naturforsch.-Ges., 106 pp., 12 plates, maps, 1922.

KLAER, W., *Untersuchungen zur klimagenetischen Morphologie in den Hochgebirgen Vorderasiens,* Keyser, Heidelberg-München, 1962.

MARTONNE, E., 'Une Reconnaissance géographique du Sinai,' *Ann. Géogr.,* Paris, Vol. 28, No. 2, pp. 135–141, 1953.

MOON, F. W. and SADEK, H., 'Topography and Geology of Northern Sinai,' *Petrol Research Bull.,* No. 10, Cairo, pp. 1–154.

SA'ID, R., *The Geology of Egypt,* Elsevier, New York, 1962.

SCHAMP, H., 'Das Hochgebirge des südlichen Sinai und die Frage seiner diluvialen Vereisung,' *Die Erde,* Berlin, Jg., pp. 18–25, 1952.

SCHICK, A. P., 'Tiran, the Straits, the Island and Its Terraces,' *IEJ,* VIII, pp. 120–130; 189–196, 1958.

SHAFEI, A., 'Historical Notes on the Pelusian Branch, the Red Sea Canal and the Route of the Exodus,' *Bull. Soc. Géogr. Egypt.,* Vol. 21, pp. 231–287.

SHATA, A., 'Oil Possibilities of Northern Sinai,' *Bull. Inst. Désert. Egypt.,* Vol. 2, No. 2, pp. 111–116, 1952.

List of Abbreviations

AdG	Annales de Géographie
Ann. Sci. Geol.	Annales des Sciences Géologiques
BASOR	Bulletin of the American School of Oriental Research
BRCI	Bulletin of the Research Council of Israel
BSRGE	Bulletin de la Société Royale de Géographie d'Egypte
COM	Cahiers d'Outre-Mer
E.G.	Economic Geography
G.J.	Geographical Journal
G.R.	Geographical Review
IEJ	Israel Exploration Journal
JPOS	Journal of the Paleontologic Oriental Society
MEA	Middle East Affairs
NGM	National Geographic Magazine
RCAJ	Royal Central Asian Journal
TESG	Tijdschrift voor Ekonomische en Sociale Geografie
ZdPV	Zeitschrift des Deutschen Palästina-Vereins

Index

Bir Laḥfān, army camp 370, 380